This book is for Papa.

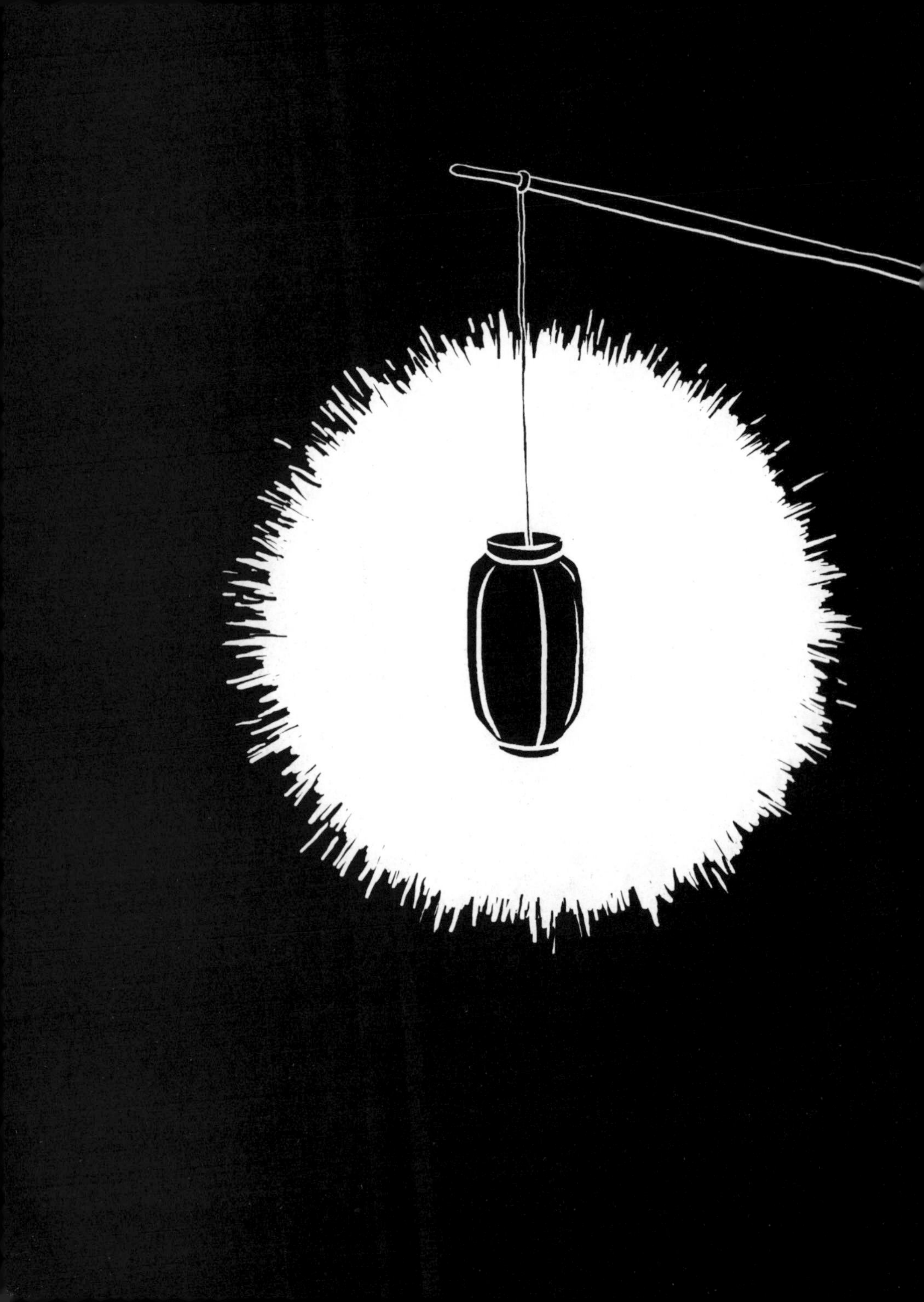

AUGUST MOON

Diana Thung

Top Shelf Productions
Atlanta / Portland

August Moon
© 2012 Diana Thung

ISBN: 978-1-60309-069-8

Published by Top Shelf Productions
PO Box 1282, Marietta, GA 30061-1282, USA
Visit our online catalog at www.topshelfcomix.com

Publishers: Brett Warnock and Chris Staros
Cover and Layout Design: Chris Ross

First Printing, October 2012.
Printed in Canada

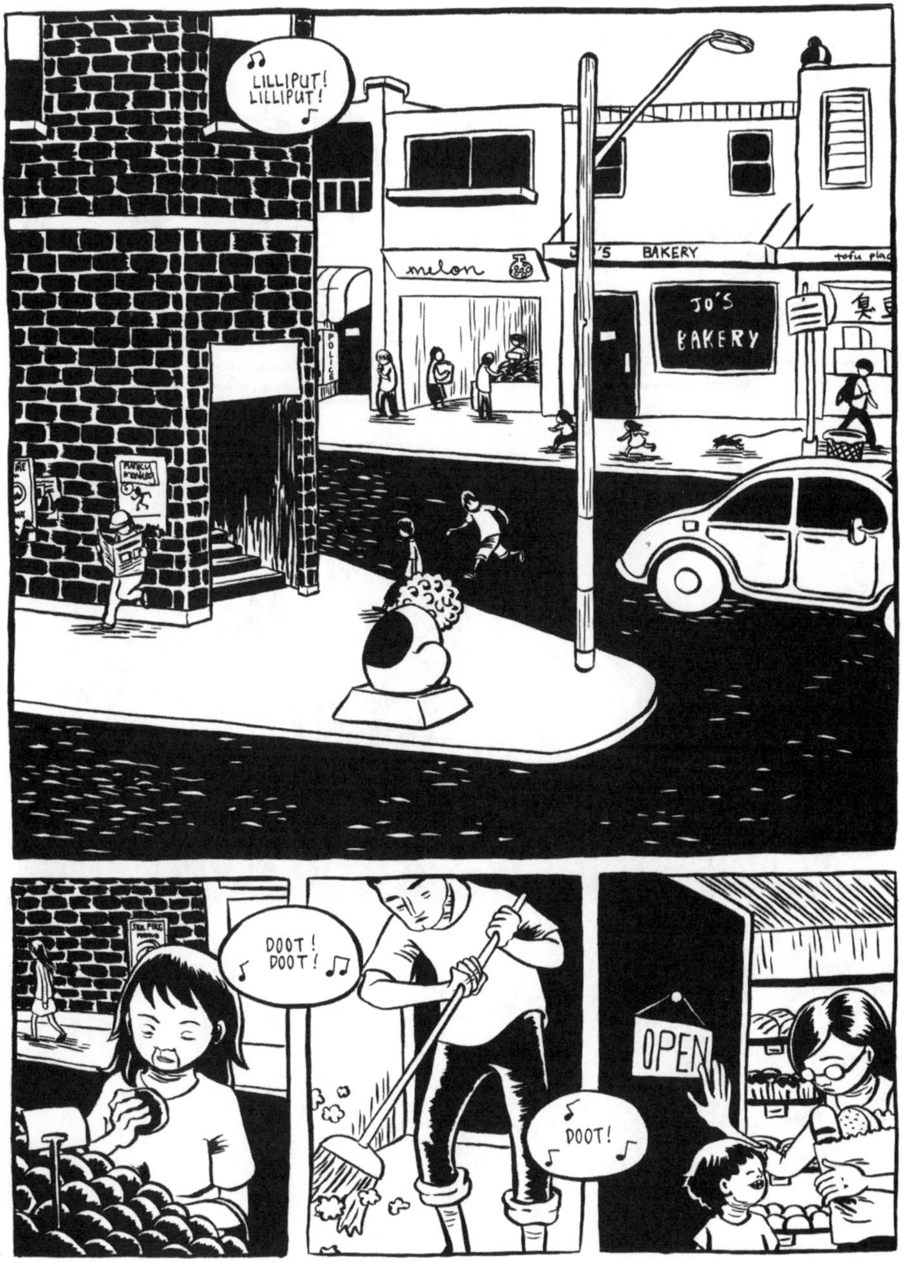
LILLIPUT! LILLIPUT!
melon
POLICE
JO'S BAKERY
DOOT! DOOT!
OPEN
DOOT!

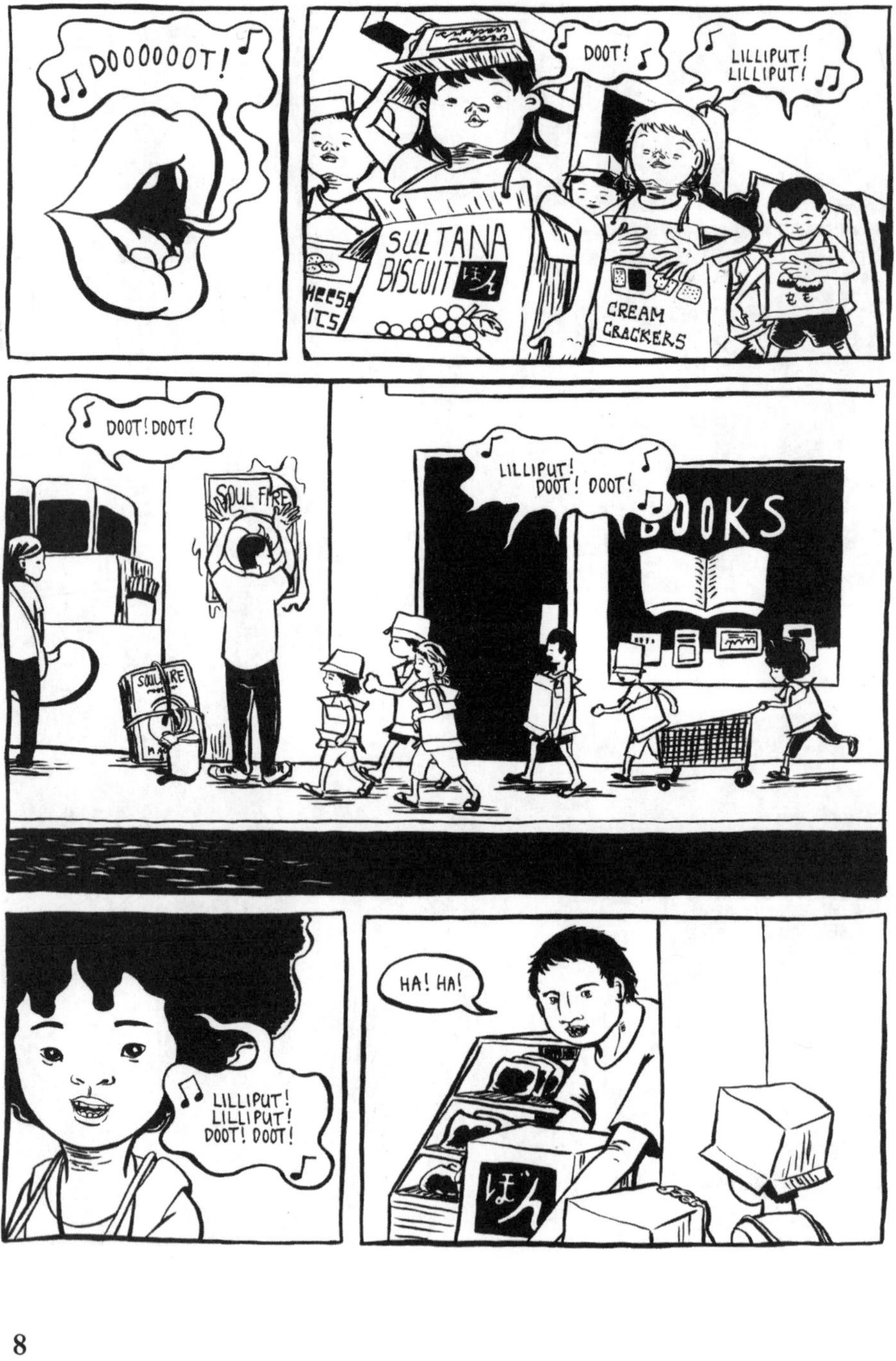
DOOOOOOT!
SULTANA BISCUIT ぼん
CREAM CRACKERS
もも
DOOT!
LILLIPUT! LILLIPUT!
DOOT! DOOT!
SOUL FIRE
LILLIPUT! DOOT! DOOT!
BOOKS
LILLIPUT! LILLIPUT! DOOT! DOOT!
HA! HA!
ぼん

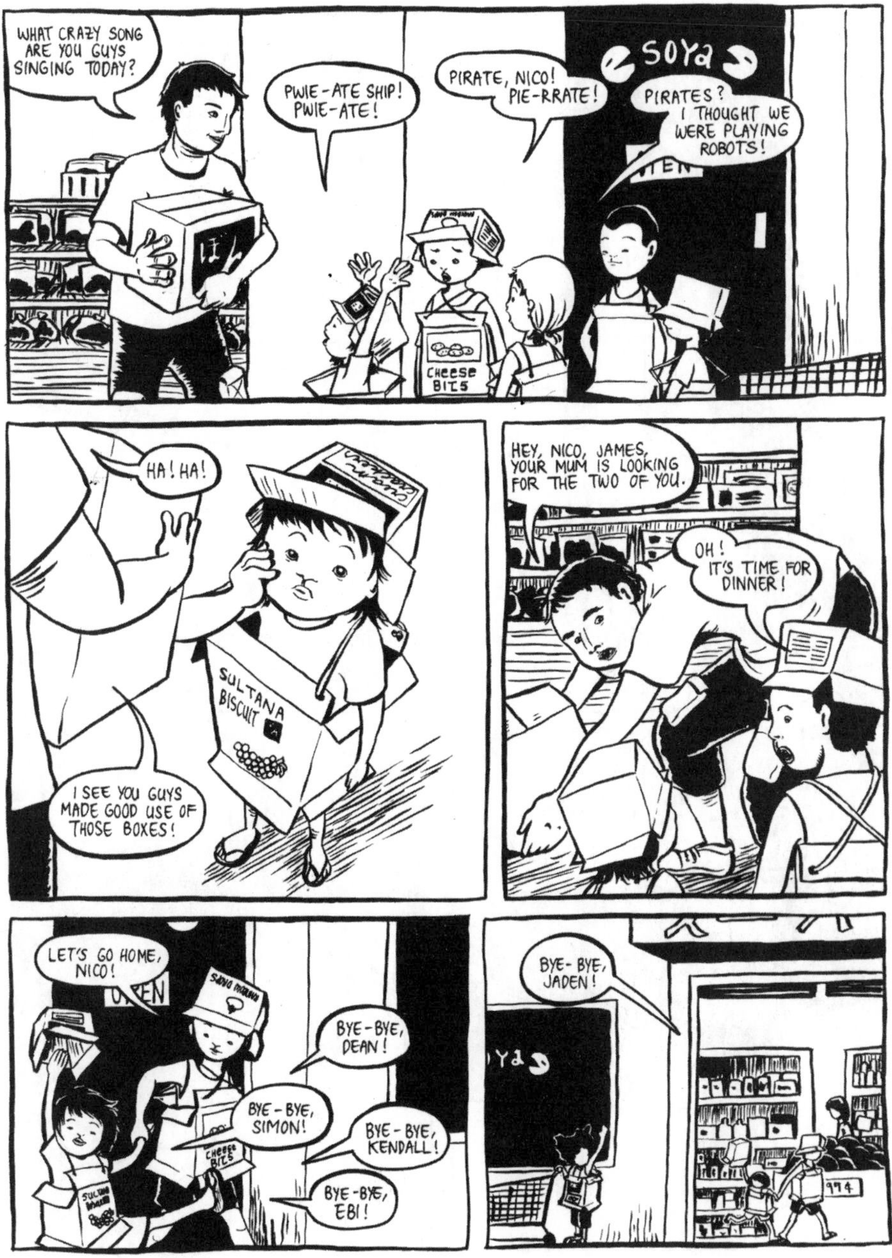
WHAT CRAZY SONG ARE YOU GUYS SINGING TODAY?
PWIE-ATE SHIP! PWIE-ATE!
PIRATE, NICO! PIE-RRATE!
SOYa
PIRATES? I THOUGHT WE WERE PLAYING ROBOTS!
CHEESE BITS
HA! HA!
SULTANA BISCUIT
I SEE YOU GUYS MADE GOOD USE OF THOSE BOXES!
HEY, NICO, JAMES, YOUR MUM IS LOOKING FOR THE TWO OF YOU.
OH! IT'S TIME FOR DINNER!
LET'S GO HOME, NICO!
BYE-BYE, DEAN!
BYE-BYE, SIMON!
BYE-BYE, KENDALL!
BYE-BYE, EBI!
BYE-BYE, JADEN!

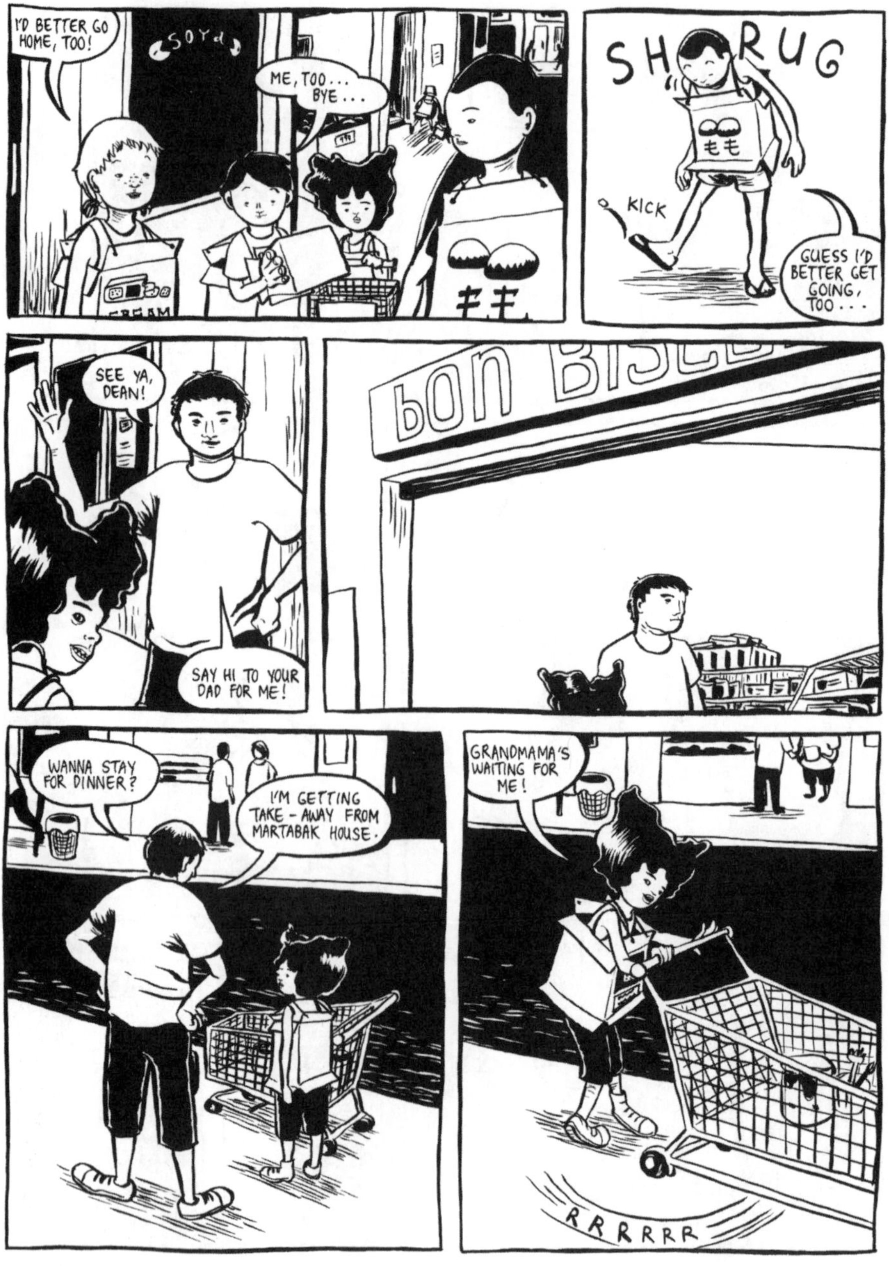

I'D BETTER GO HOME, TOO!
SOYA
ME, TOO... BYE...
CREAM
もも
SHRUG
KICK
GUESS I'D BETTER GET GOING, TOO...
SEE YA, DEAN!
SAY HI TO YOUR DAD FOR ME!
BON BISC
WANNA STAY FOR DINNER?
I'M GETTING TAKE-AWAY FROM MARTABAK HOUSE.
GRANDMAMA'S WAITING FOR ME!
RRRRRR

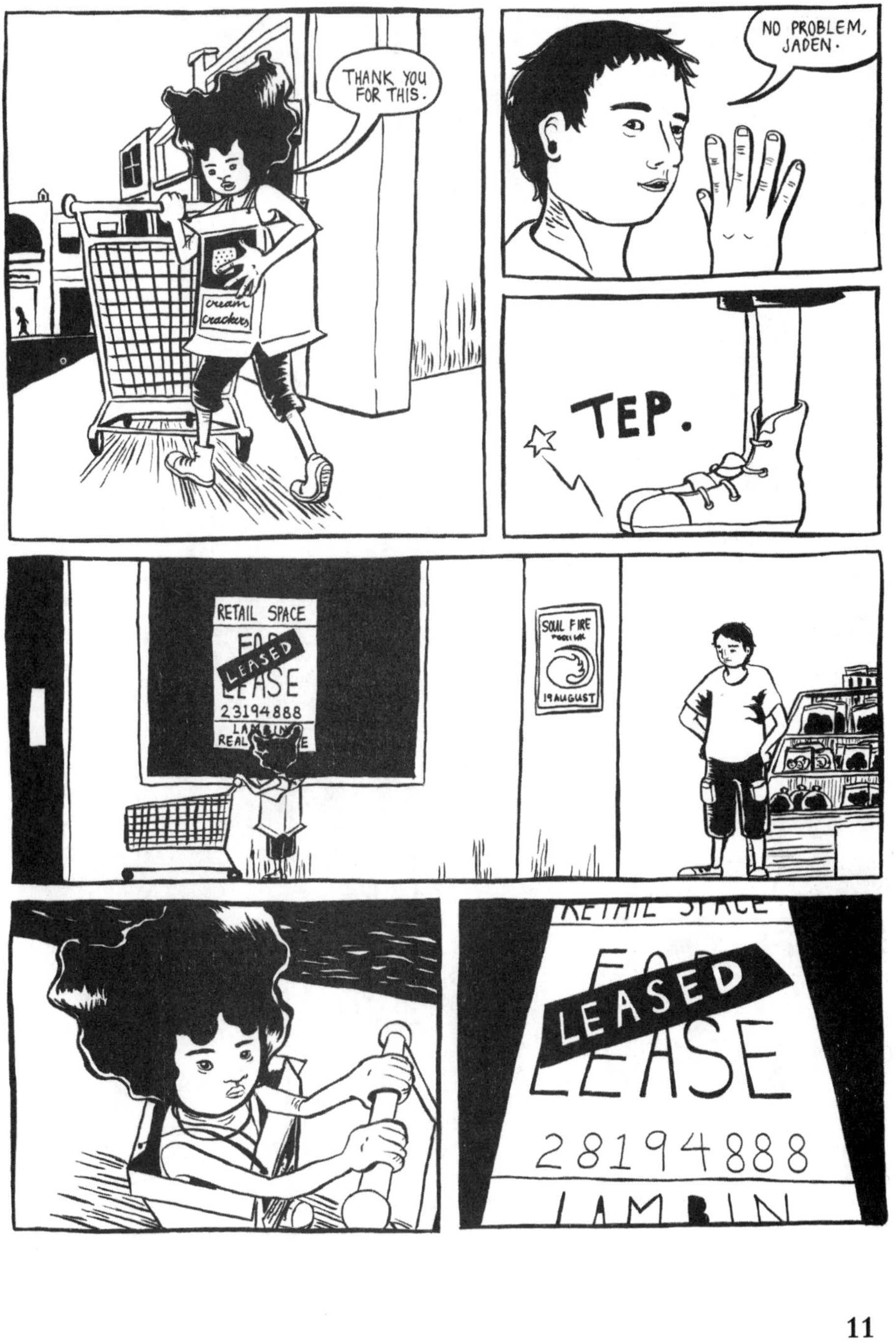
THANK YOU FOR THIS.
cream crackers
NO PROBLEM, JADEN.
TEP.
RETAIL SPACE
LEASED
LEASE
23194888
SOUL FIRE
19 AUGUST
LEASED
LEASE
28194888

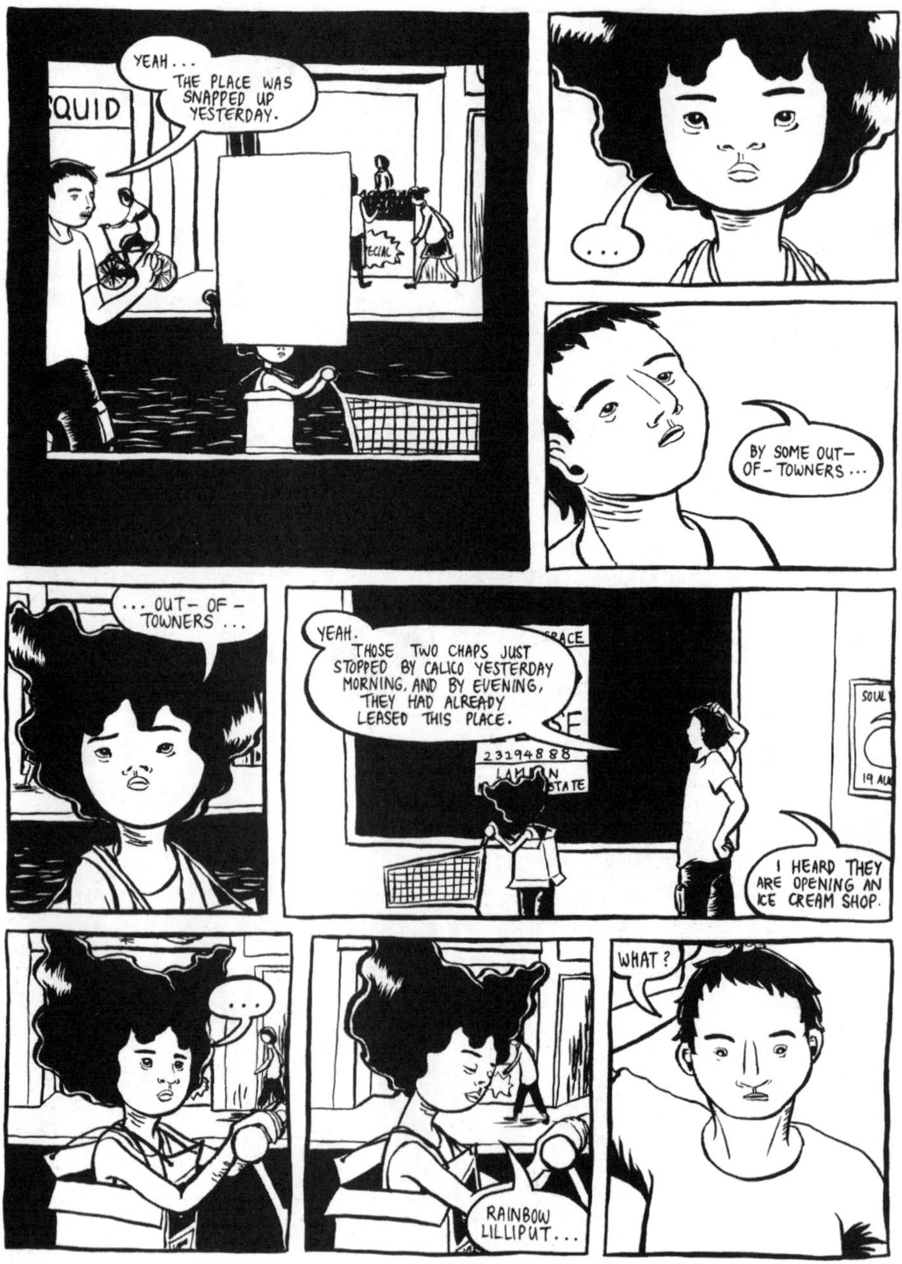
YEAH... THE PLACE WAS SNAPPED UP YESTERDAY.
SQUID
...
BY SOME OUT-OF-TOWNERS...
...OUT-OF-TOWNERS...
YEAH. THOSE TWO CHAPS JUST STOPPED BY CALICO YESTERDAY MORNING, AND BY EVENING, THEY HAD ALREADY LEASED THIS PLACE.
23194888
I HEARD THEY ARE OPENING AN ICE CREAM SHOP.
...
RAINBOW LILLIPUT...
WHAT?

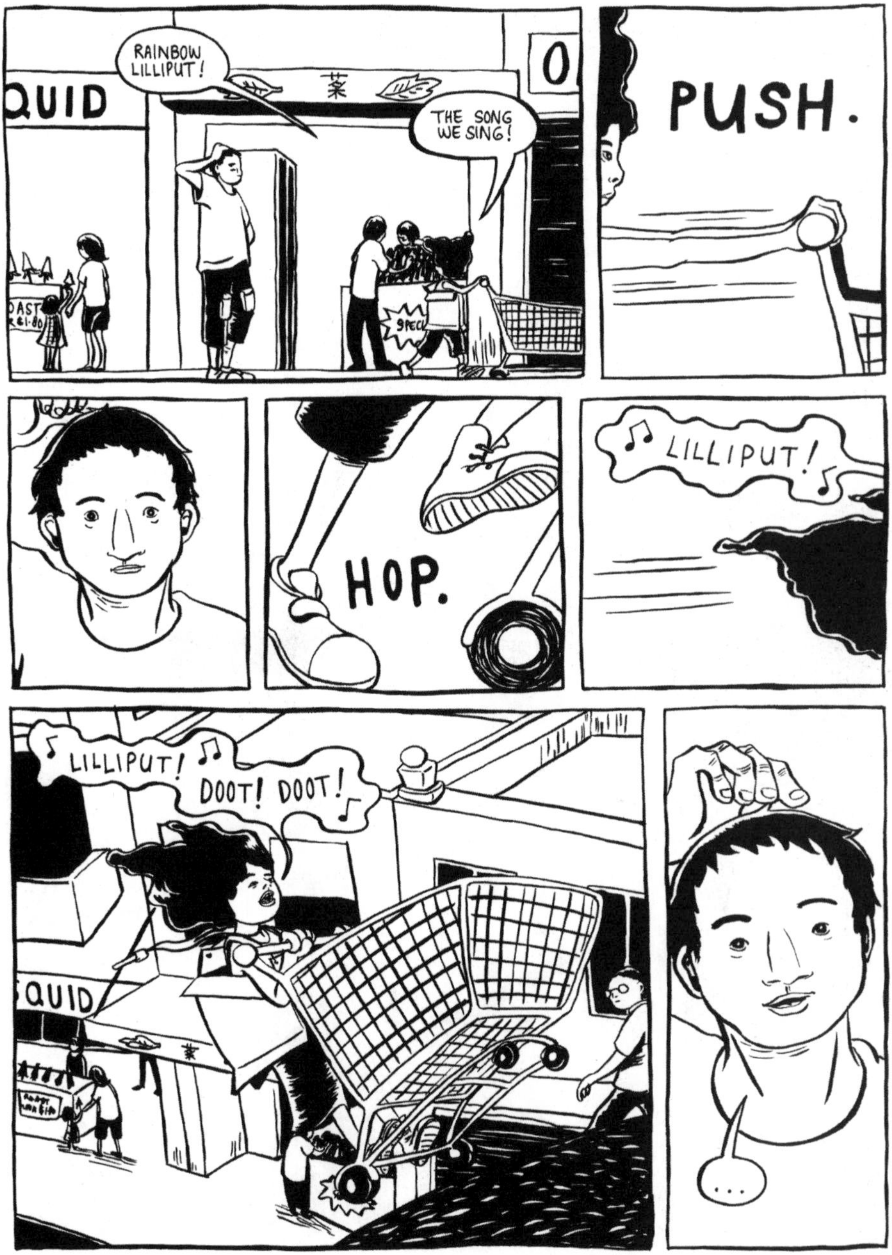
QUID
RAINBOW LILLIPUT!
THE SONG WE SING!
PUSH.
HOP.
LILLIPUT!
LILLIPUT!
DOOT! DOOT!
QUID
...

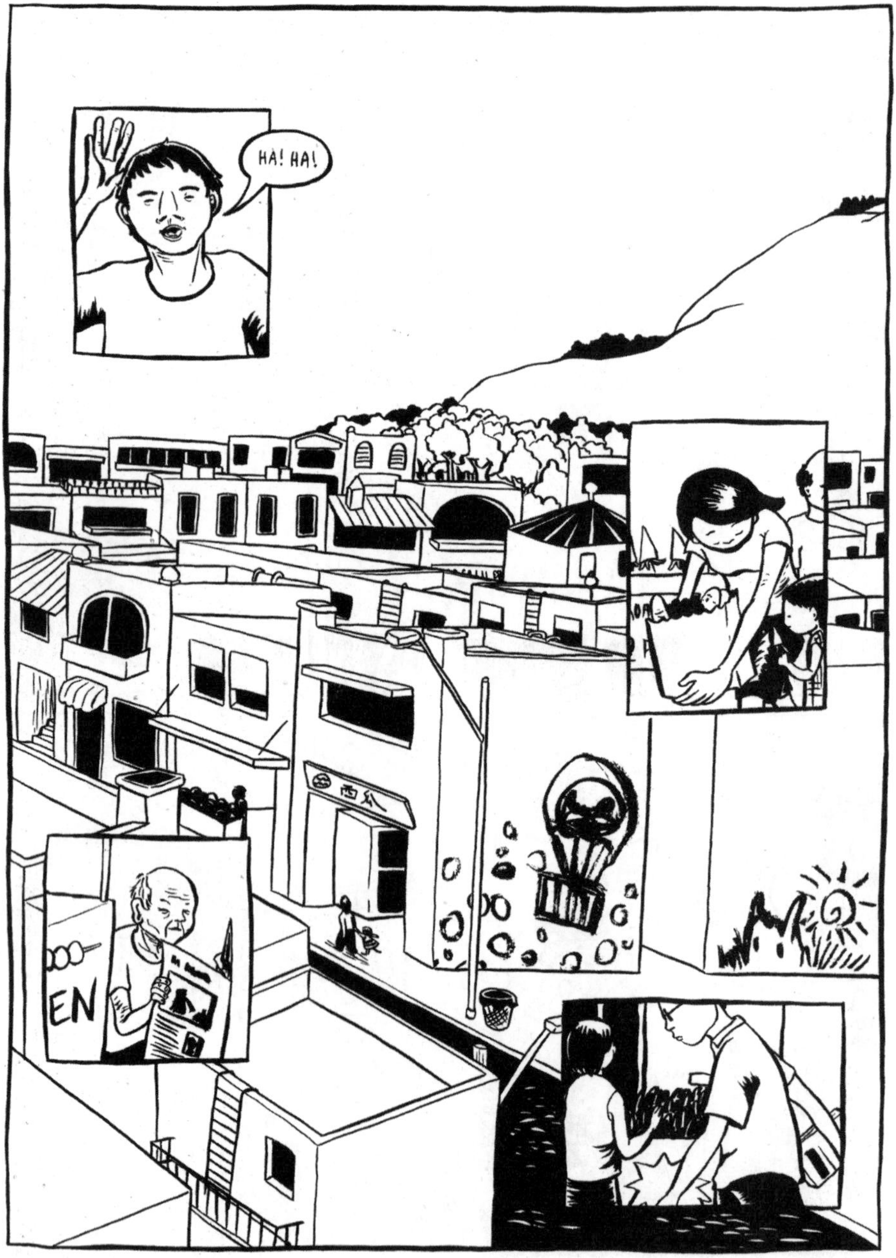
HA! HA!
EN

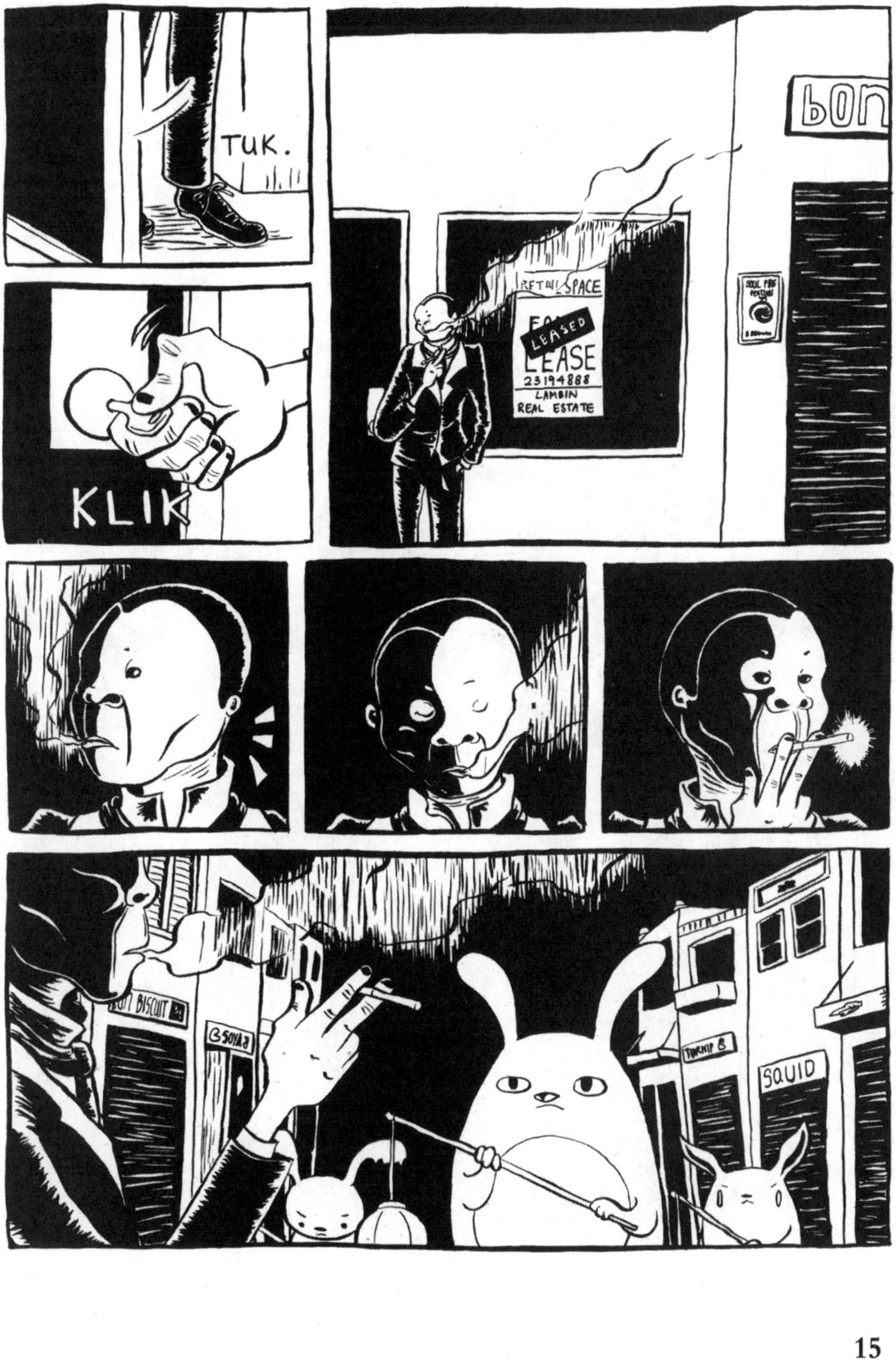
TUK.
KLIK
bon
SPACE
LEASED
LEASE
23194888
LAMBIN
REAL ESTATE
BISCUIT
TURNIP 8
SQUID

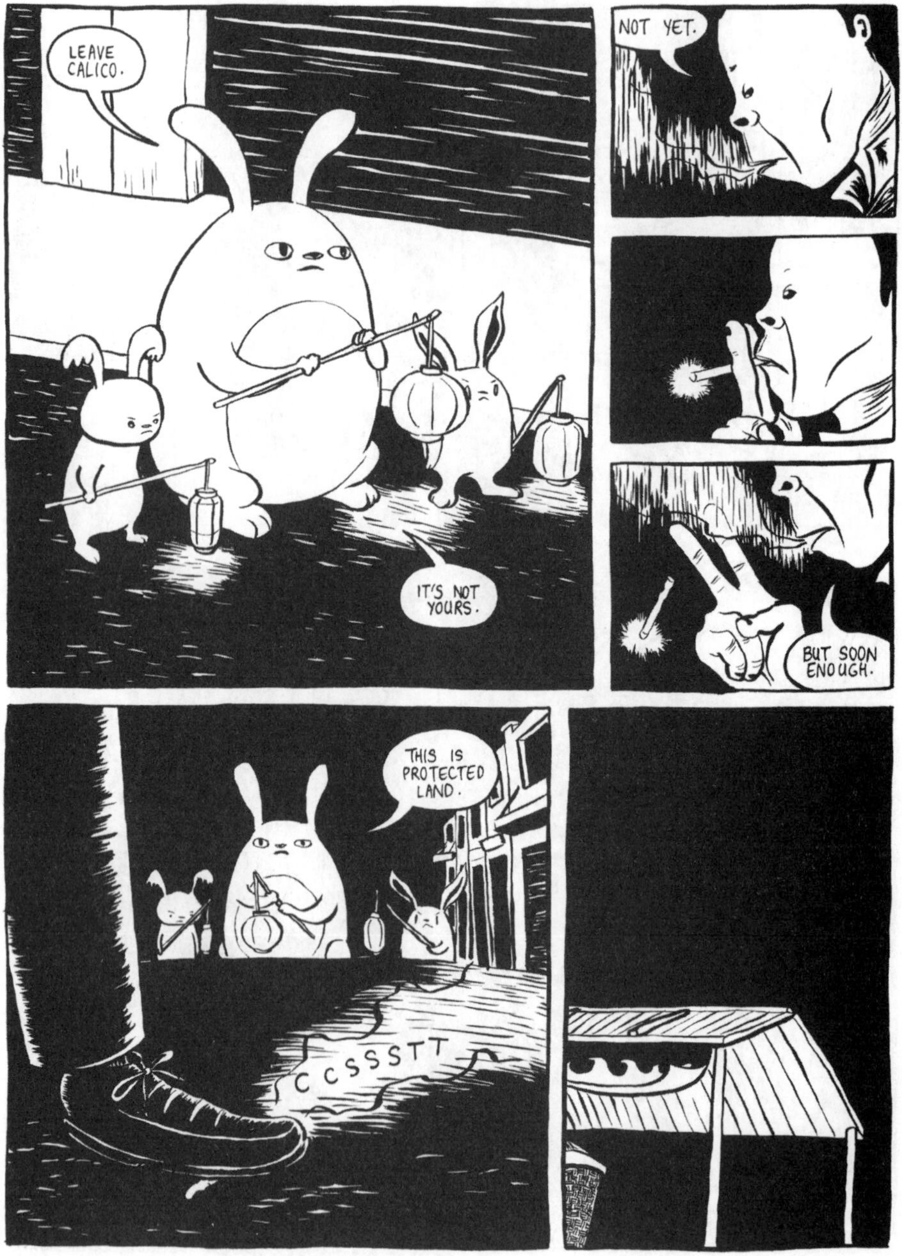
LEAVE CALICO.
IT'S NOT YOURS.
NOT YET.
BUT SOON ENOUGH.
THIS IS PROTECTED LAND.
CCSSSTT

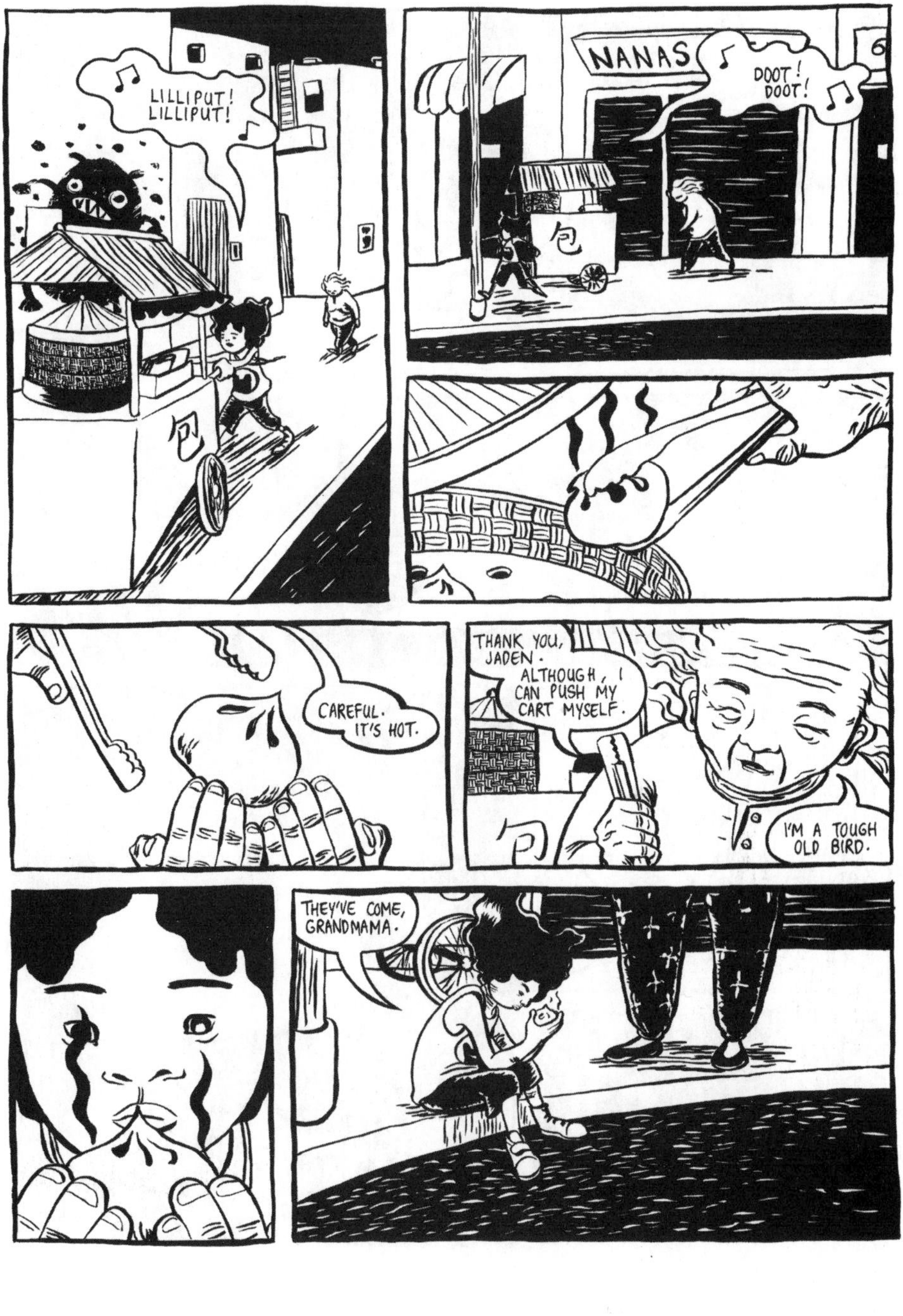
LILLIPUT! LILLIPUT!
NANAS
DOOT! DOOT!
包
CAREFUL. IT'S HOT.
THANK YOU, JADEN.
ALTHOUGH, I CAN PUSH MY CART MYSELF.
I'M A TOUGH OLD BIRD.
THEY'VE COME, GRANDMAMA.

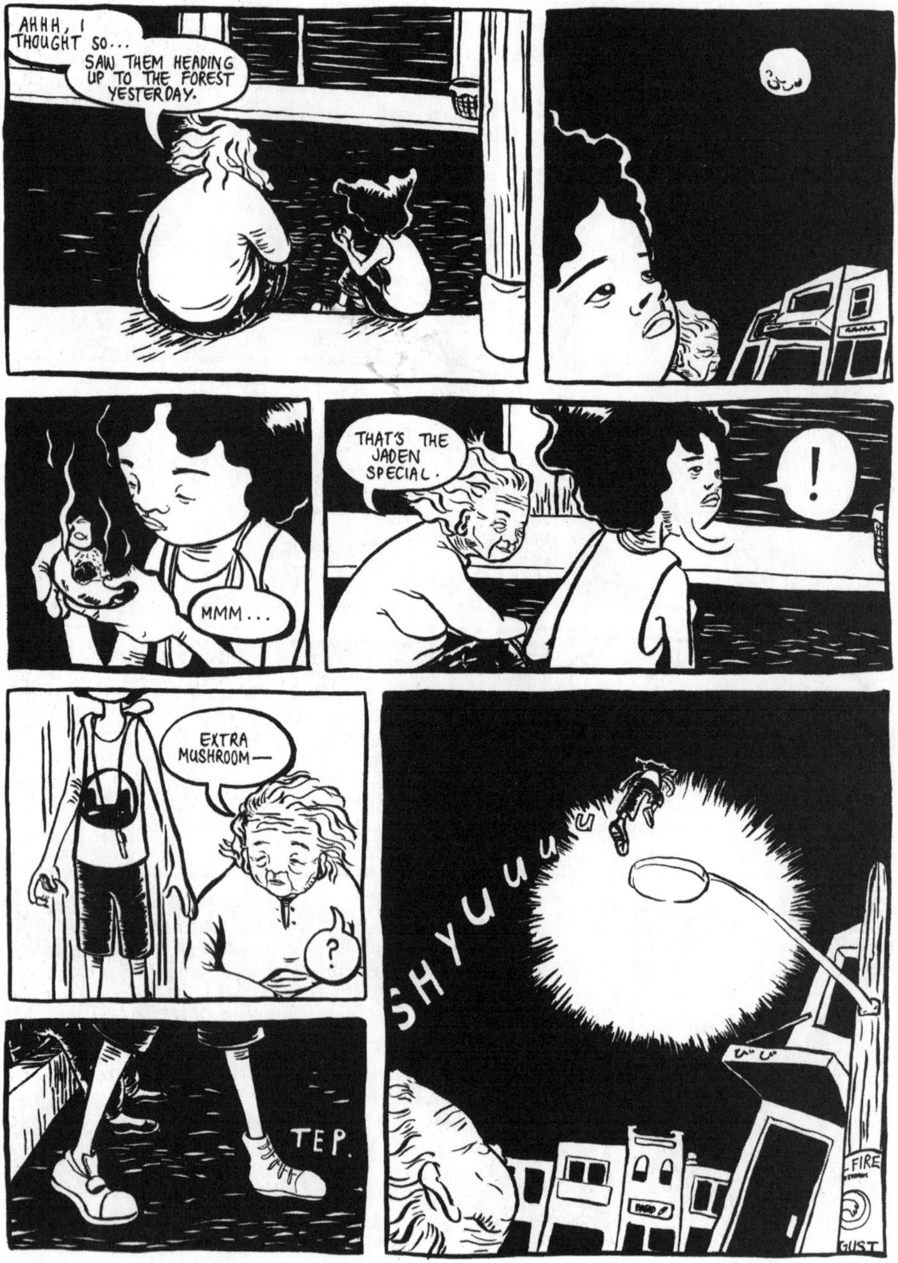
AHHH, I THOUGHT SO...
SAW THEM HEADING UP TO THE FOREST YESTERDAY.
MMM...
THAT'S THE JADEN SPECIAL.
!
EXTRA MUSHROOM—
?
TEP.
SHYUuuuu
FIRE
GUST

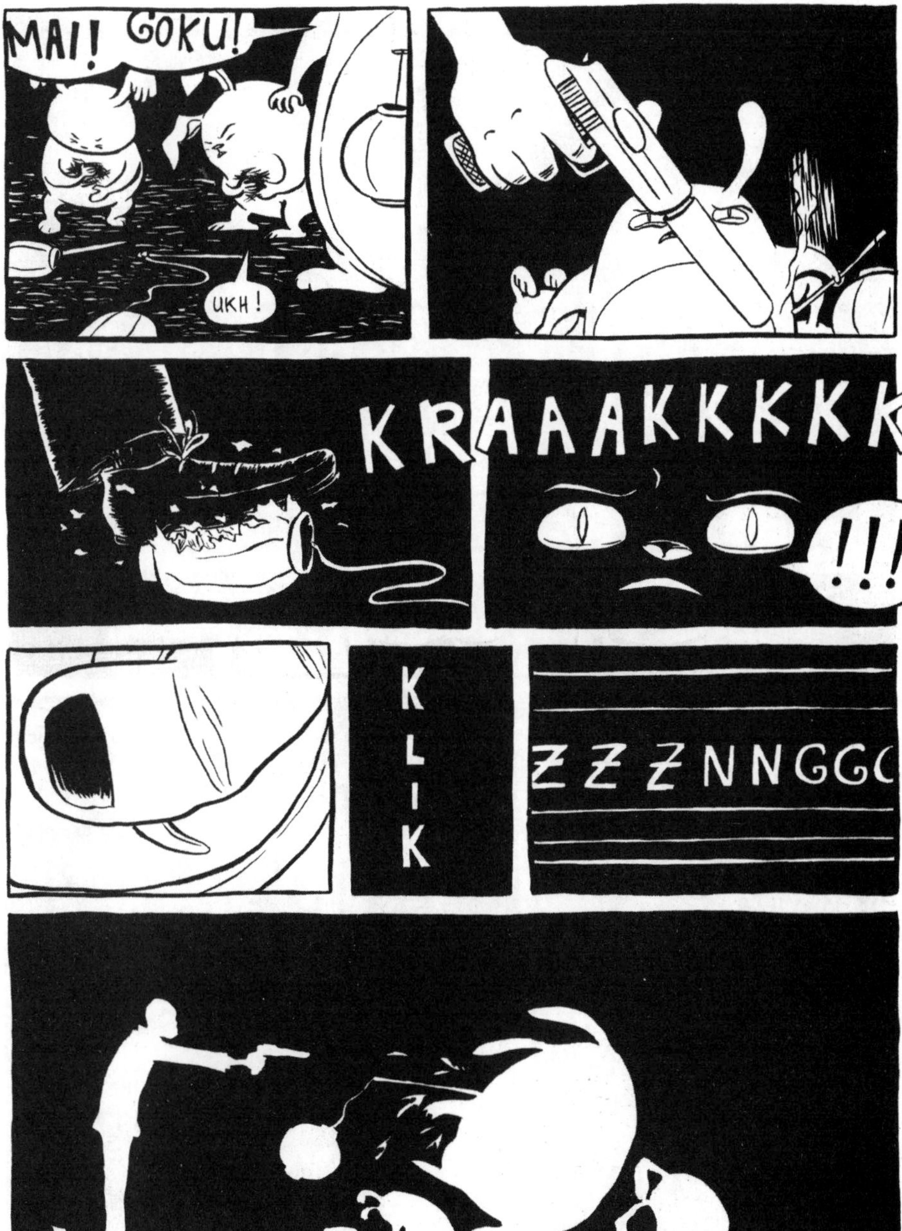
MAI! GOKU!
UKH!
KRAAAKKKKK
!!!
KLIK
ZZZNNGGC

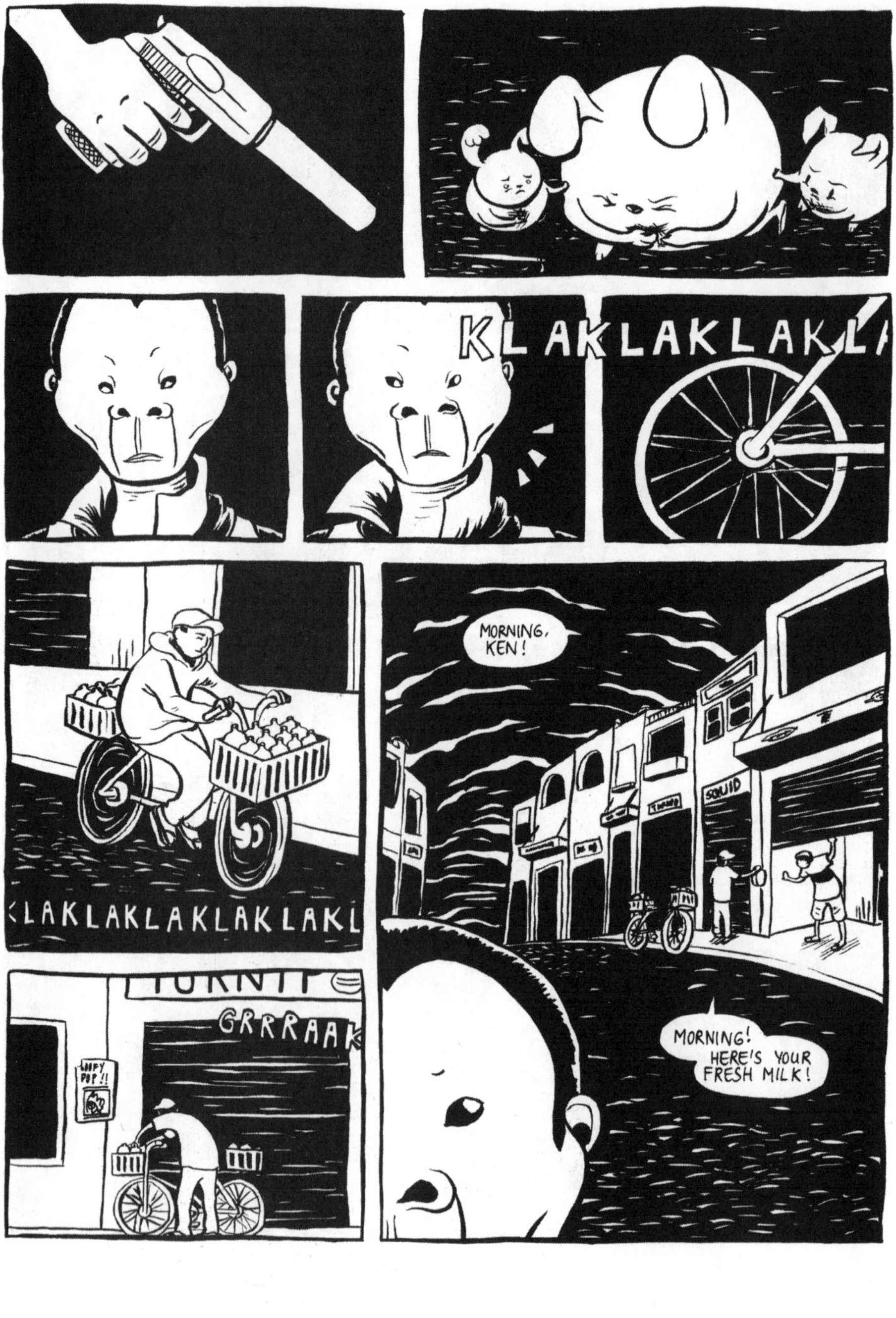
KLAKLAKLAKL
LAKLAKLAKLAKLAKL
MORNING, KEN!
GRRRAAK
MORNING! HERE'S YOUR FRESH MILK!

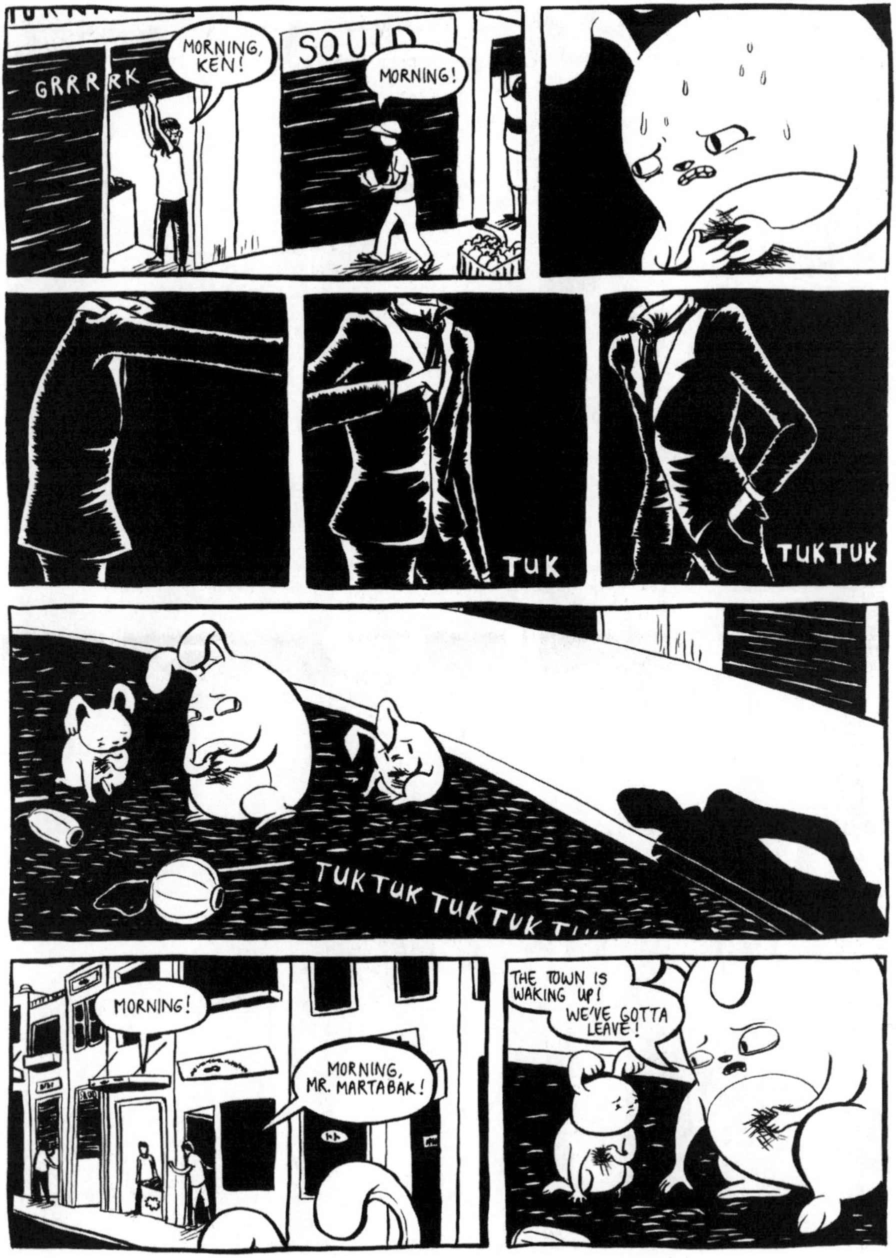
GRRRRRK
MORNING, KEN!
SQUID
MORNING!
TUK
TUK TUK
TUK TUK TUK TUK
MORNING!
MORNING, MR. MARTABAK!
THE TOWN IS WAKING UP!
WE'VE GOTTA LEAVE!

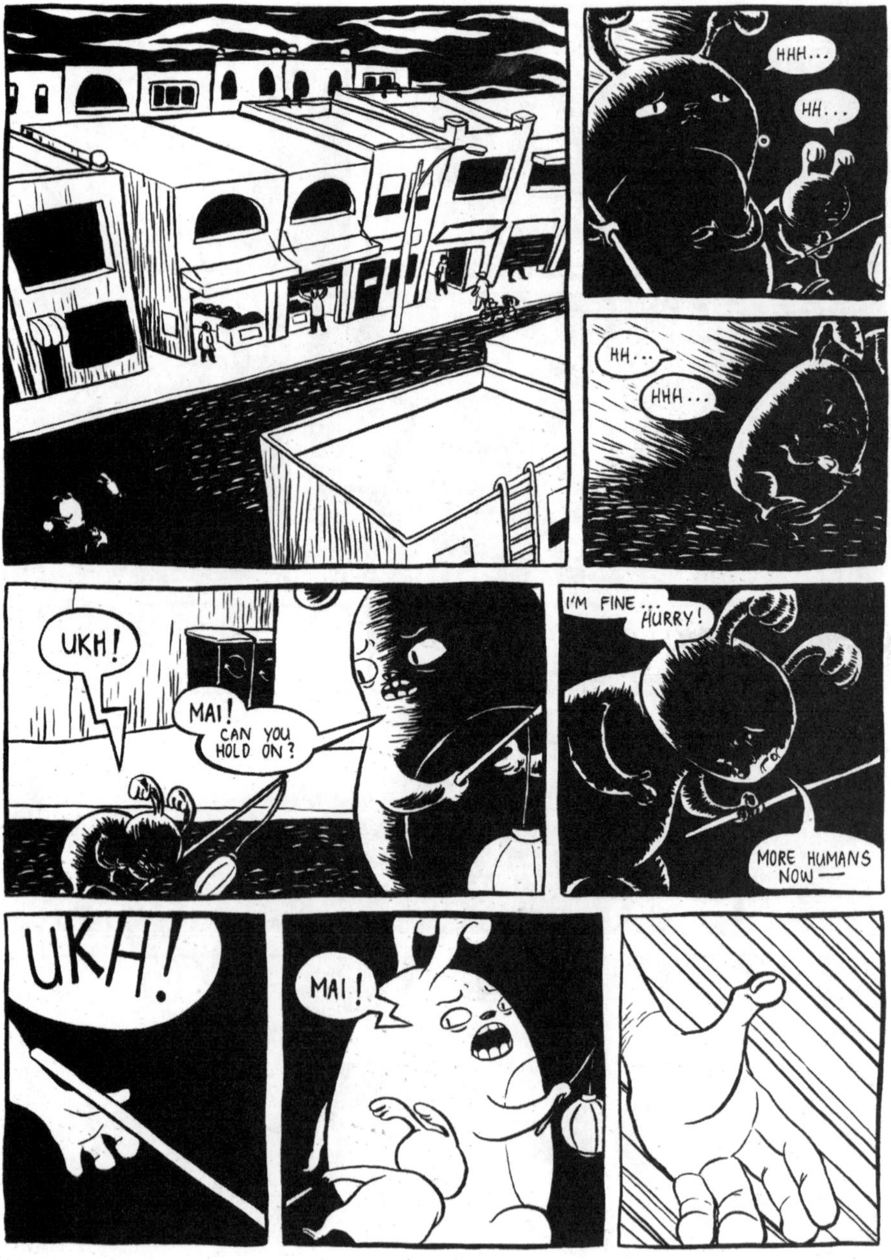
HHH...
HH...
HH...
HHH...
UKH!
MAI! CAN YOU HOLD ON?
I'M FINE... HURRY!
MORE HUMANS NOW—
UKH!
MAI!

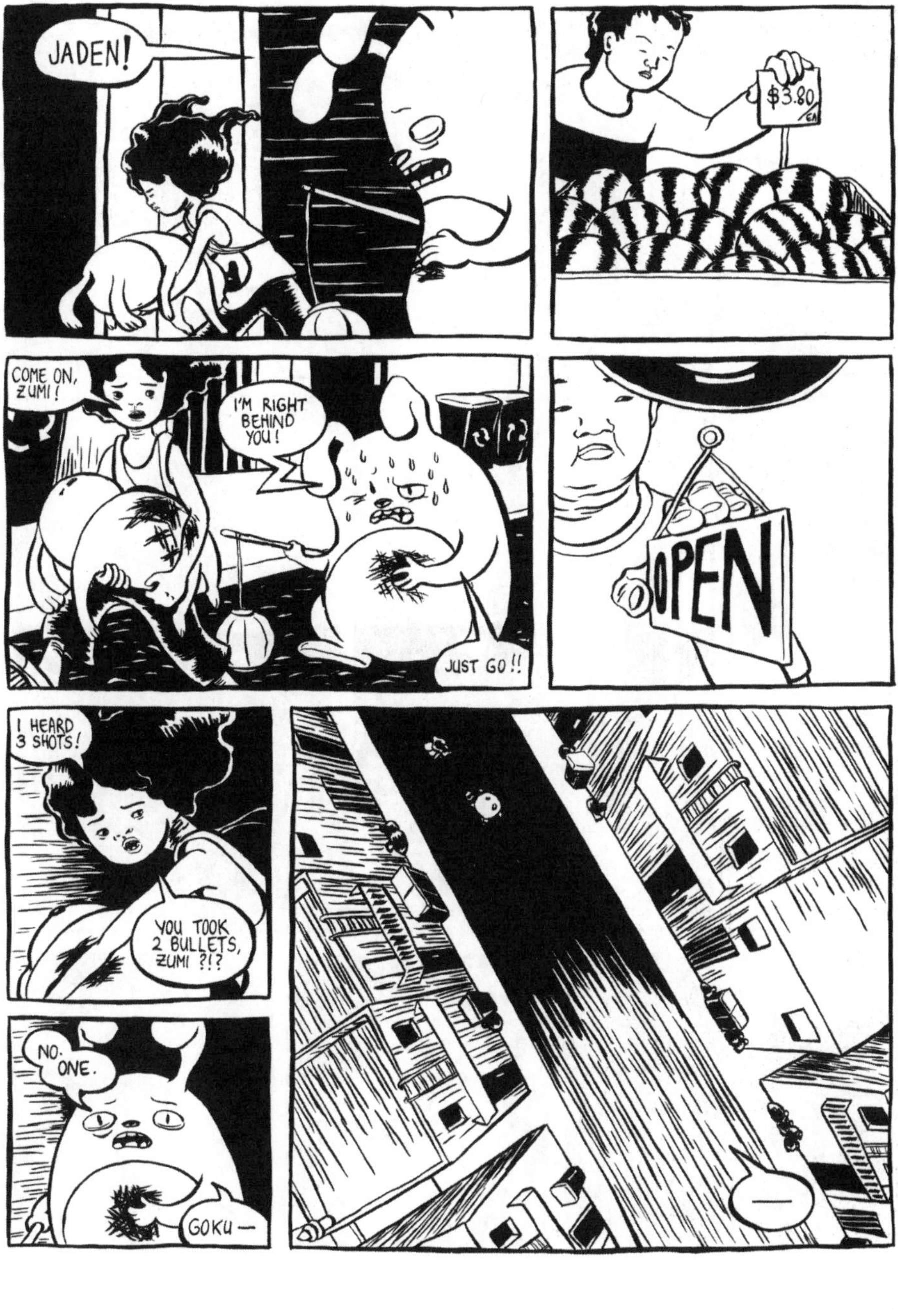
JADEN!
$3.80
EA
COME ON, ZUMI!
I'M RIGHT BEHIND YOU!
JUST GO!!
OPEN
I HEARD 3 SHOTS!
YOU TOOK 2 BULLETS, ZUMI ?!?
NO. ONE.
GOKU—
—

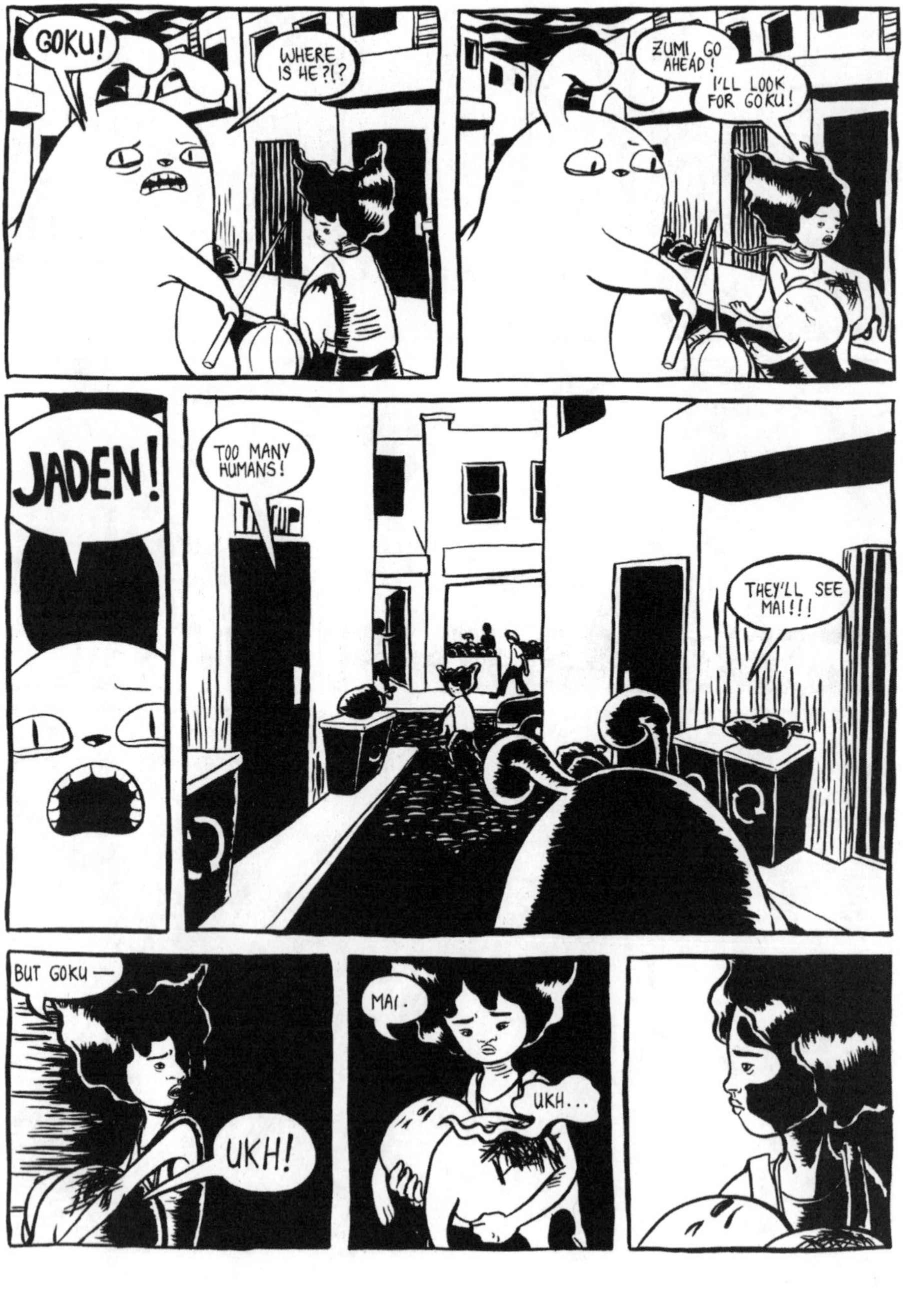
GOKU!
WHERE IS HE?!?
ZUMI, GO AHEAD!
I'LL LOOK FOR GOKU!
JADEN!
TOO MANY HUMANS!
THEY'LL SEE MAI!!!
BUT GOKU —
UKH!
MAI.
UKH...

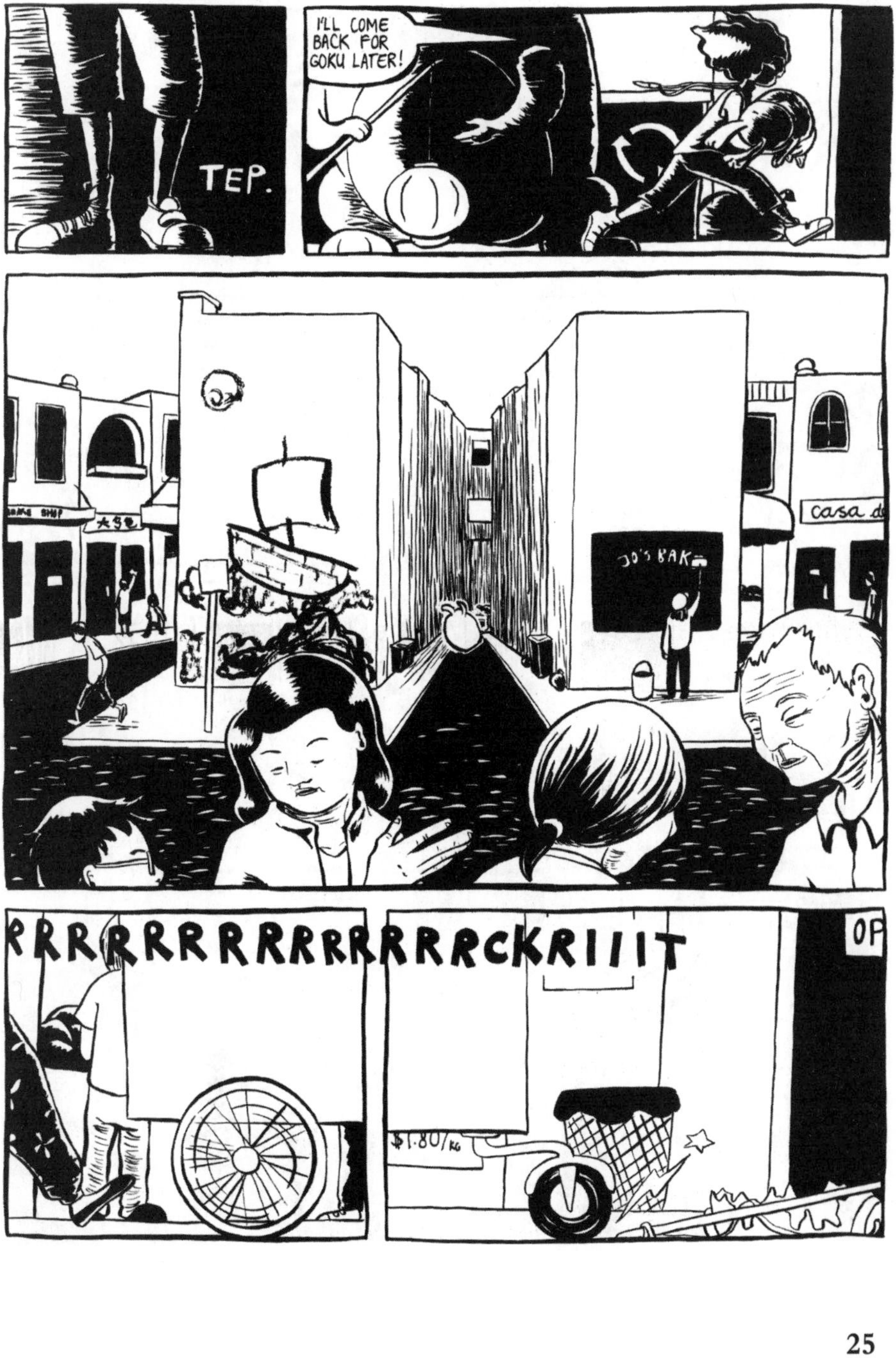
TEP.
I'LL COME BACK FOR GOKU LATER!
casa d
JO'S BAK
RRRRRRRRRRRRRCKRIIIT
OP
$1.80/KG

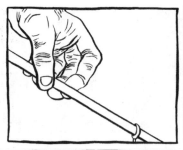

KKR RRRSSSSSHHHH

19 AUGUST

. . .

GOOD MORNING, GRANDMAMA! YOU'RE AS EARLY AS ALWAYS!

OH, MORNING, JOHN. WHAT ARE YOU DOING UP SO EARLY?

SCHOOL'S OUT FOR THE YEAR, ISN'T IT?

TEACHERS STILL GO TO SCHOOL DURING THE SCHOOL HOLIDAYS, GRANDMAMA.

SOUL FIR
FESTIVAL

19 AUGUS

. . .

WELL...

SEE YOU AROUND, GRANDMAMA. I HAVE GARBAGE TO DISPOSE OF.

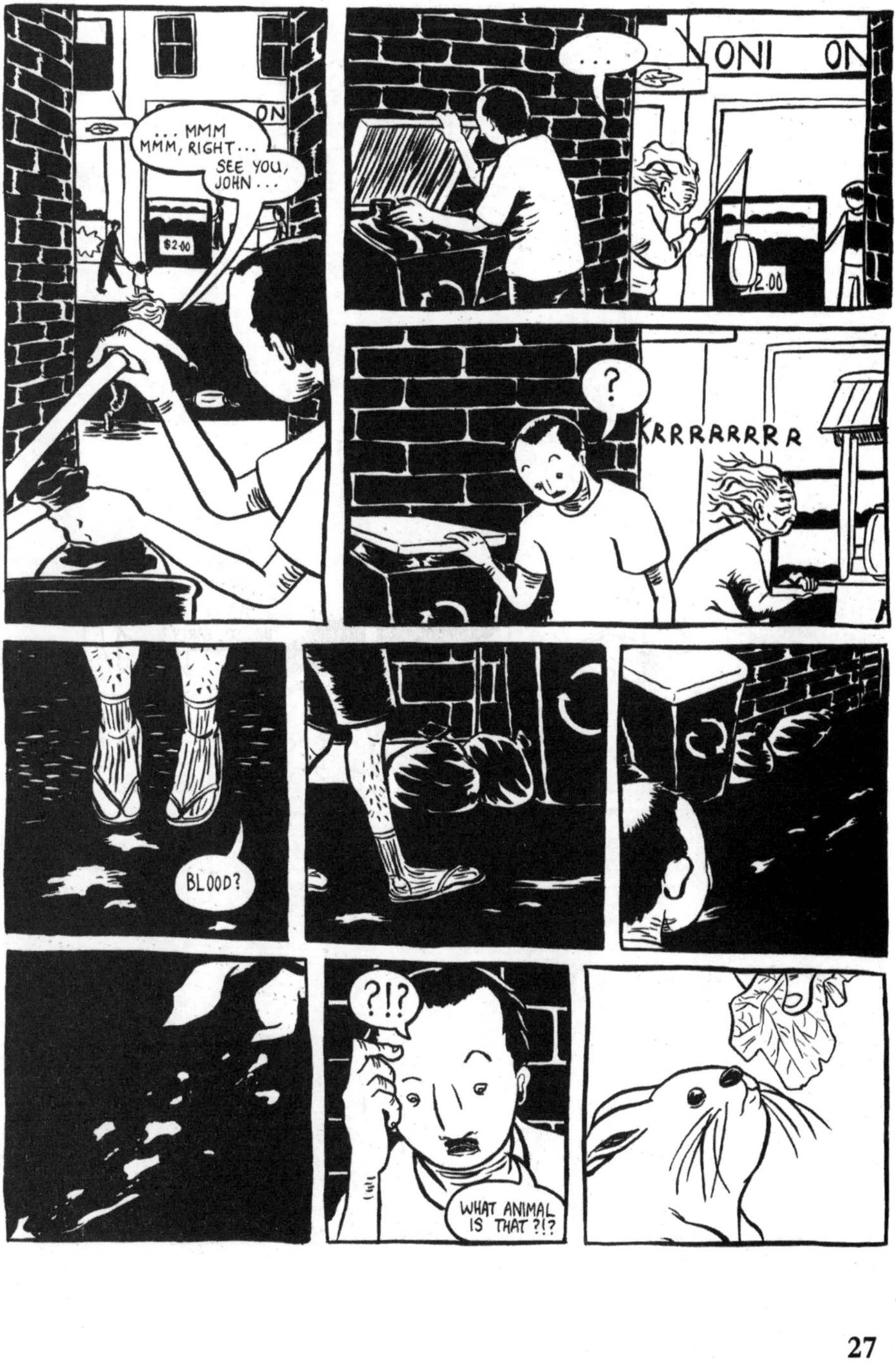
... MMM
MMM, RIGHT...
SEE YOU,
JOHN...
$2.00
ON
...
ONI ON
2.00
?
KRRRRRRRR
BLOOD?
?!?
WHAT ANIMAL
IS THAT ?!?

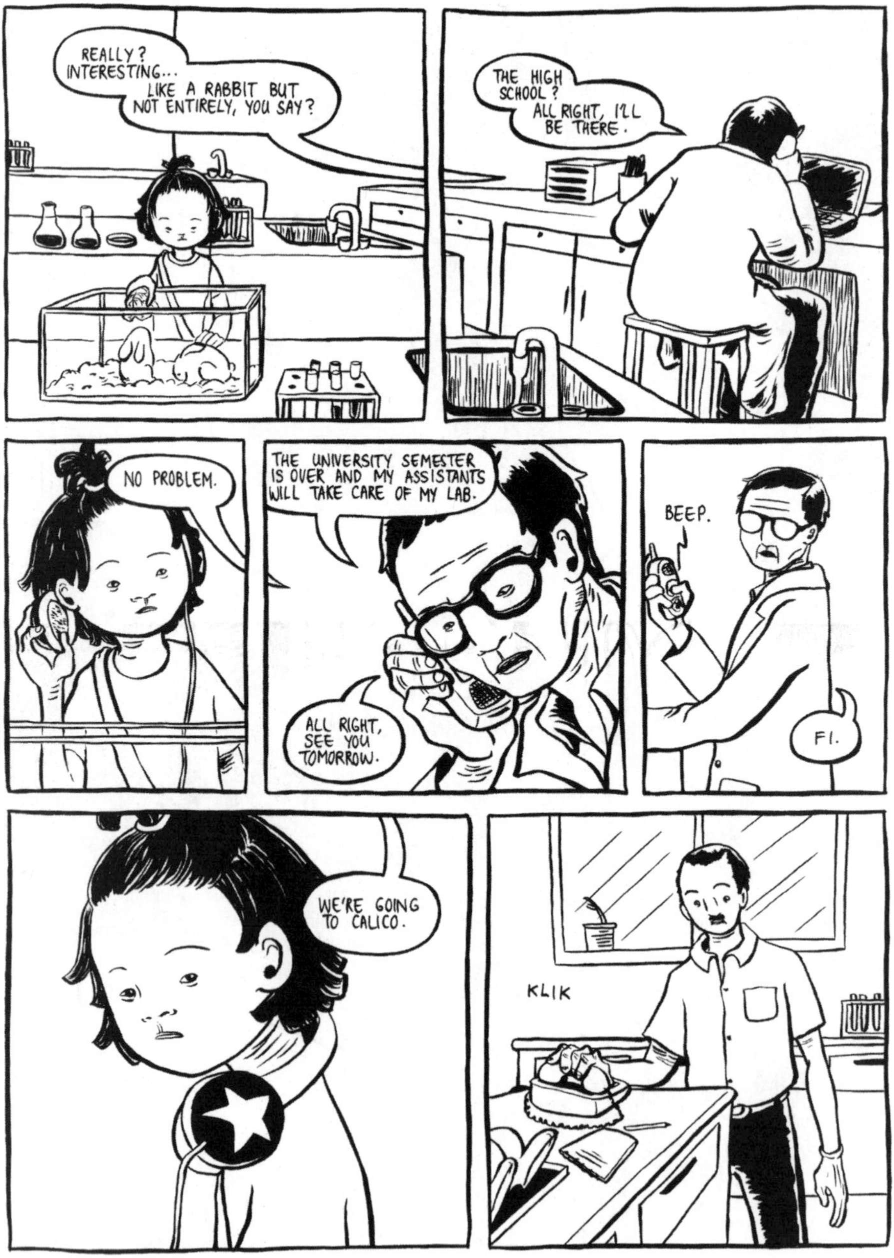

REALLY? INTERESTING... LIKE A RABBIT BUT NOT ENTIRELY, YOU SAY?
THE HIGH SCHOOL? ALL RIGHT, I'LL BE THERE.
NO PROBLEM.
THE UNIVERSITY SEMESTER IS OVER AND MY ASSISTANTS WILL TAKE CARE OF MY LAB.
ALL RIGHT, SEE YOU TOMORROW.
BEEP.
FI.
WE'RE GOING TO CALICO.
KLIK

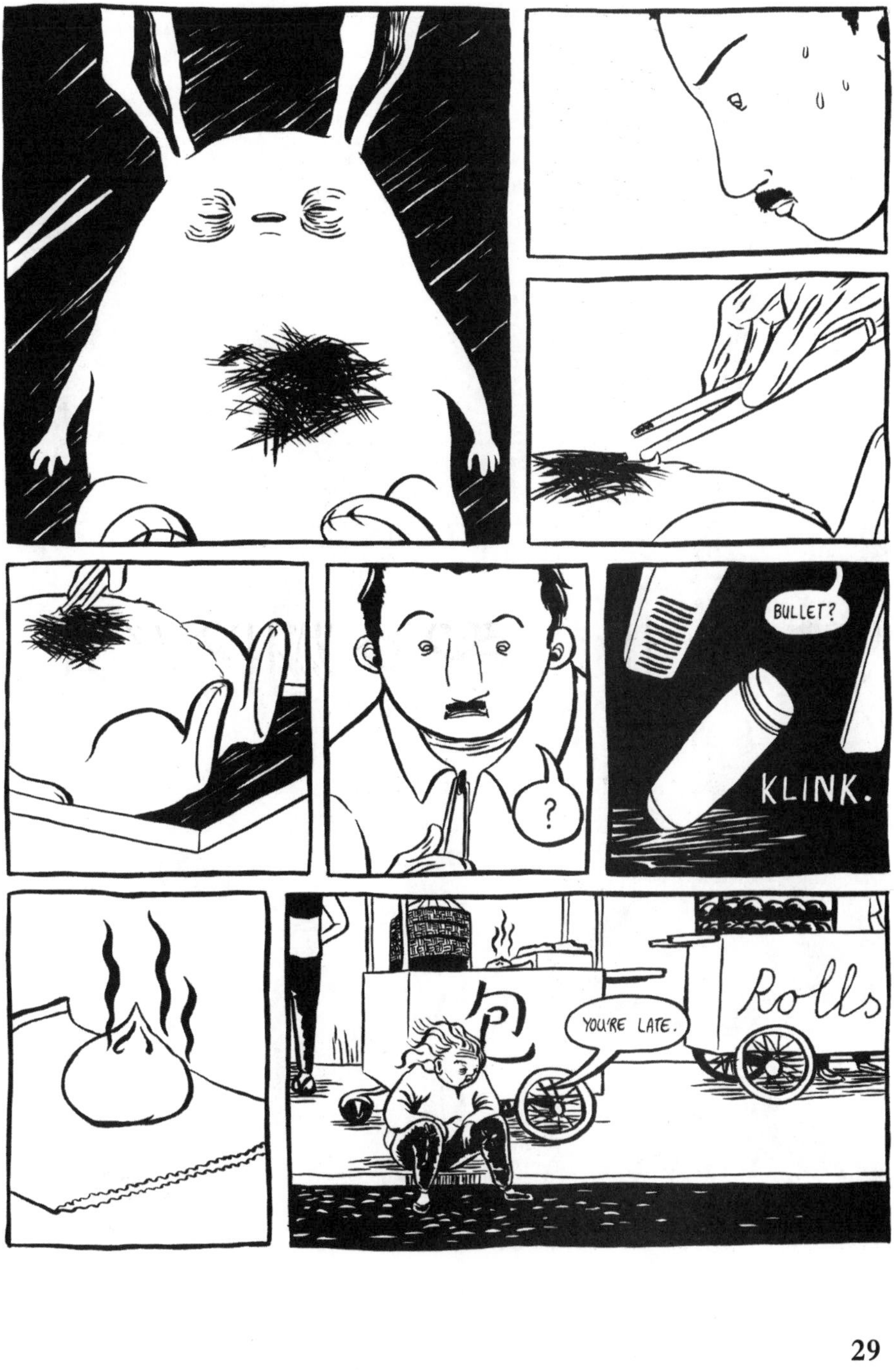
?
BULLET?
KLINK.
Rolls
YOU'RE LATE.

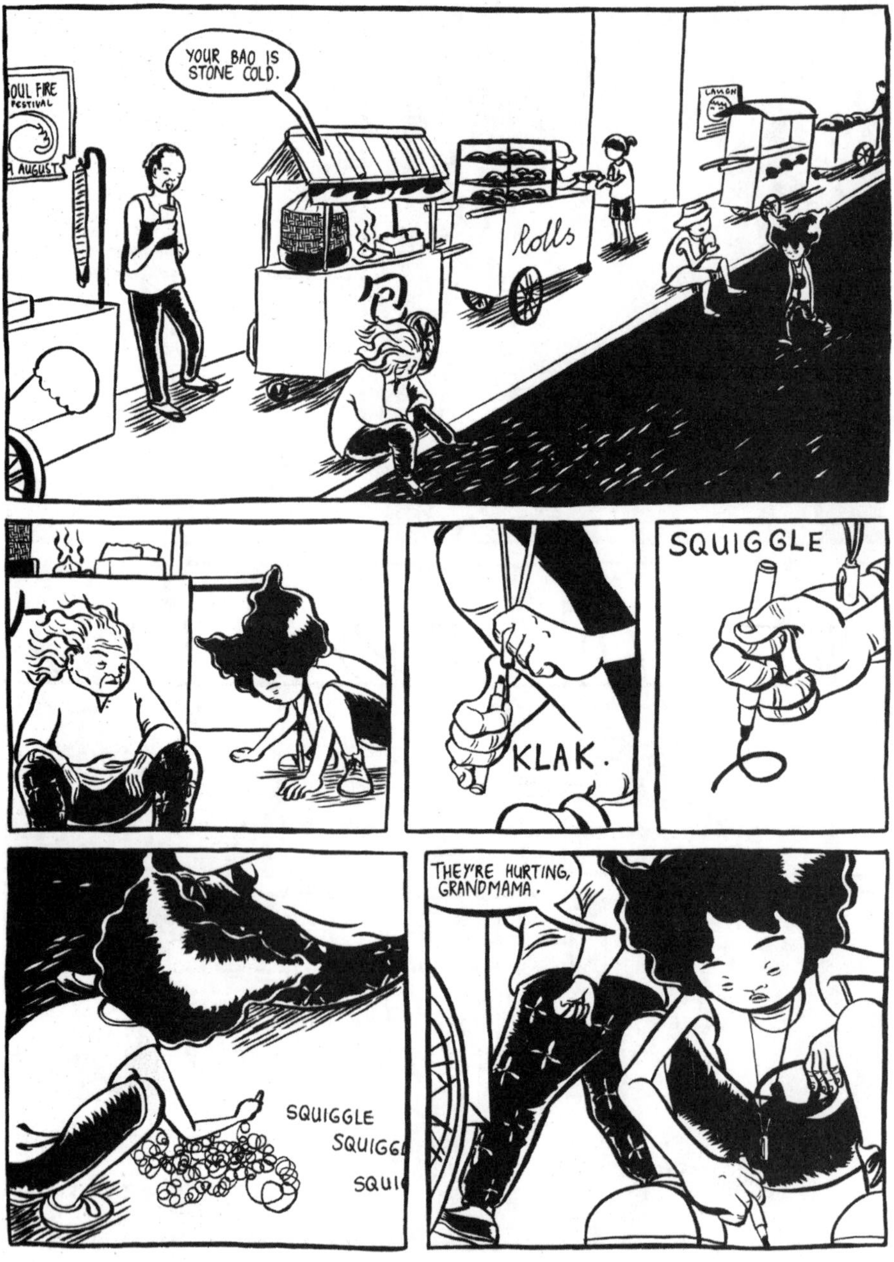
SOUL FIRE
FESTIVAL
AUGUST
YOUR BAO IS STONE COLD.
Rolls
包
KLAK.
SQUIGGLE
SQUIGGLE
THEY'RE HURTING, GRANDMAMA.

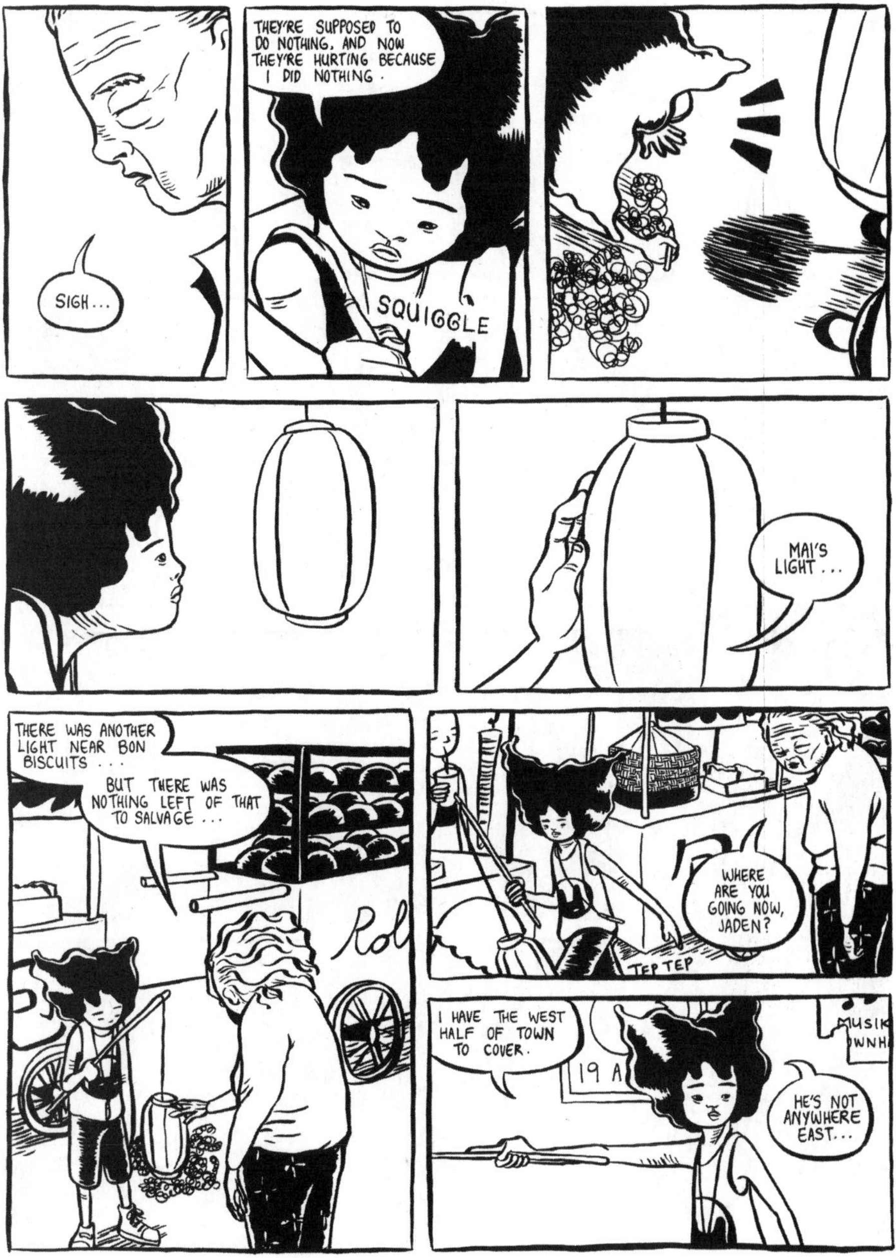
SIGH...
THEY'RE SUPPOSED TO DO NOTHING, AND NOW THEY'RE HURTING BECAUSE I DID NOTHING.
SQUIGGLE
MAI'S LIGHT...
THERE WAS ANOTHER LIGHT NEAR BON BISCUITS...
BUT THERE WAS NOTHING LEFT OF THAT TO SALVAGE...
WHERE ARE YOU GOING NOW, JADEN?
TEP TEP
I HAVE THE WEST HALF OF TOWN TO COVER.
HE'S NOT ANYWHERE EAST...

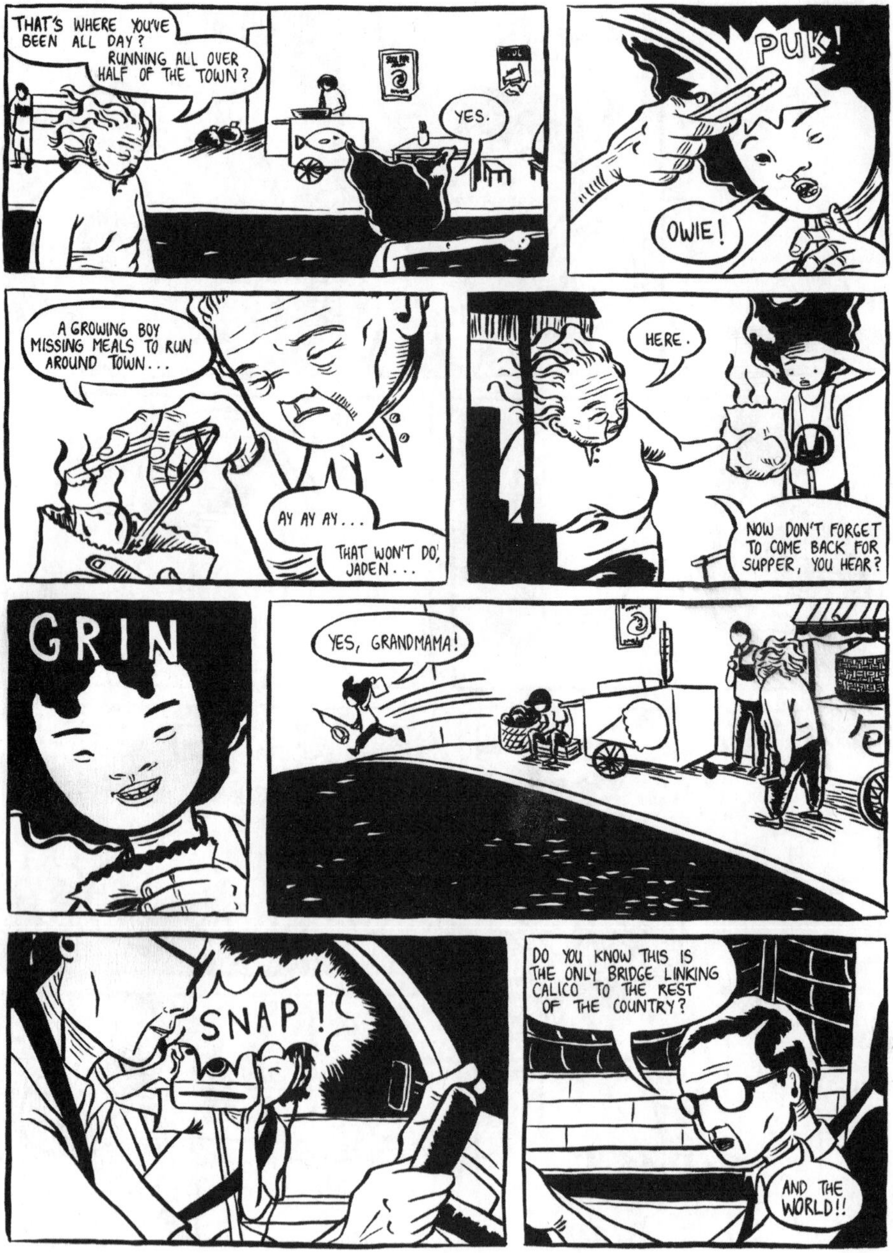
THAT'S WHERE YOU'VE BEEN ALL DAY?
RUNNING ALL OVER HALF OF THE TOWN?
YES.
PUK!
OWIE!
A GROWING BOY MISSING MEALS TO RUN AROUND TOWN...
AY AY AY...
THAT WON'T DO, JADEN...
HERE.
NOW DON'T FORGET TO COME BACK FOR SUPPER, YOU HEAR?
GRIN
YES, GRANDMAMA!
SNAP!
DO YOU KNOW THIS IS THE ONLY BRIDGE LINKING CALICO TO THE REST OF THE COUNTRY?
AND THE WORLD!!

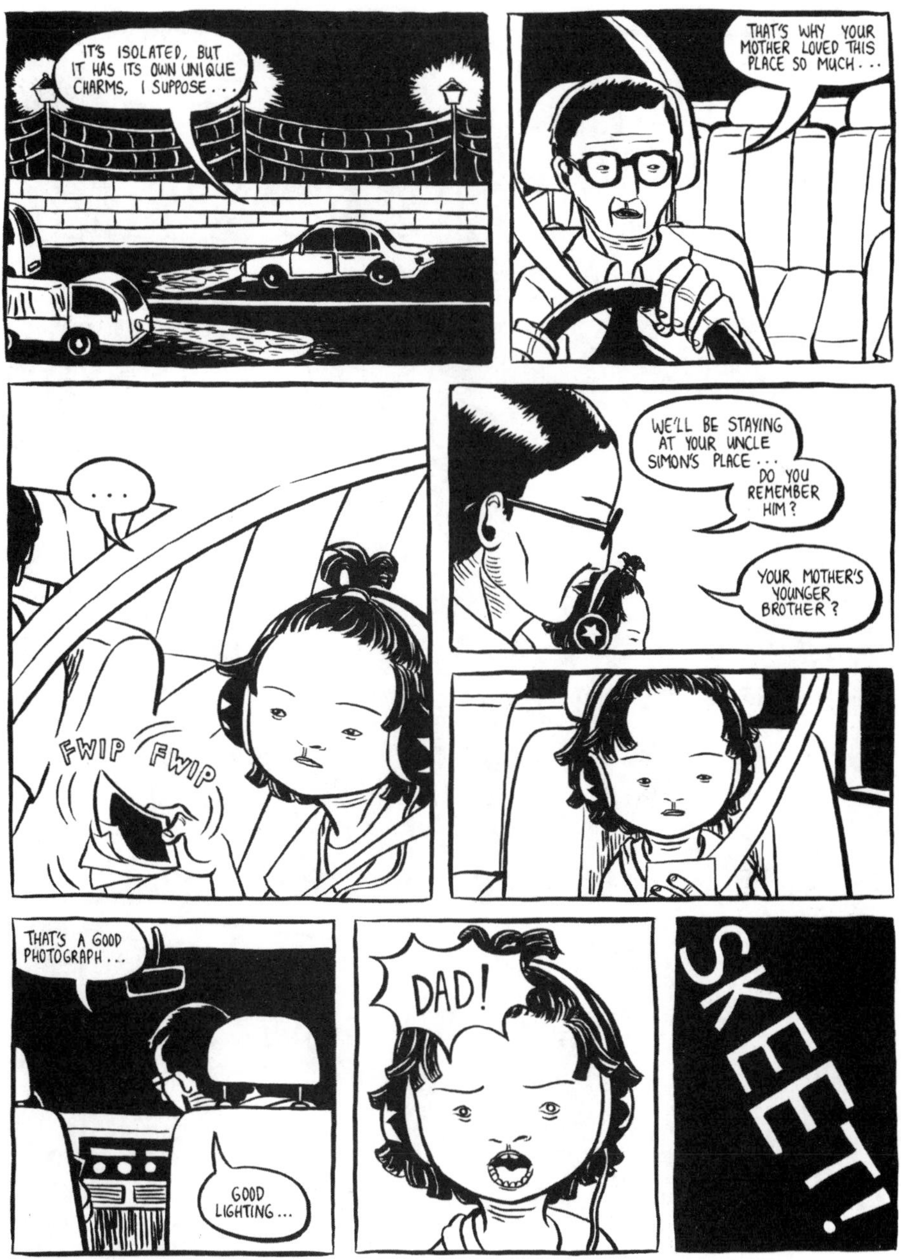

IT'S ISOLATED, BUT IT HAS ITS OWN UNIQUE CHARMS, I SUPPOSE . . .
THAT'S WHY YOUR MOTHER LOVED THIS PLACE SO MUCH . . .
. . .
FWIP FWIP
WE'LL BE STAYING AT YOUR UNCLE SIMON'S PLACE . . .
DO YOU REMEMBER HIM?
YOUR MOTHER'S YOUNGER BROTHER?
THAT'S A GOOD PHOTOGRAPH . . .
GOOD LIGHTING . . .
DAD!
SKEET!

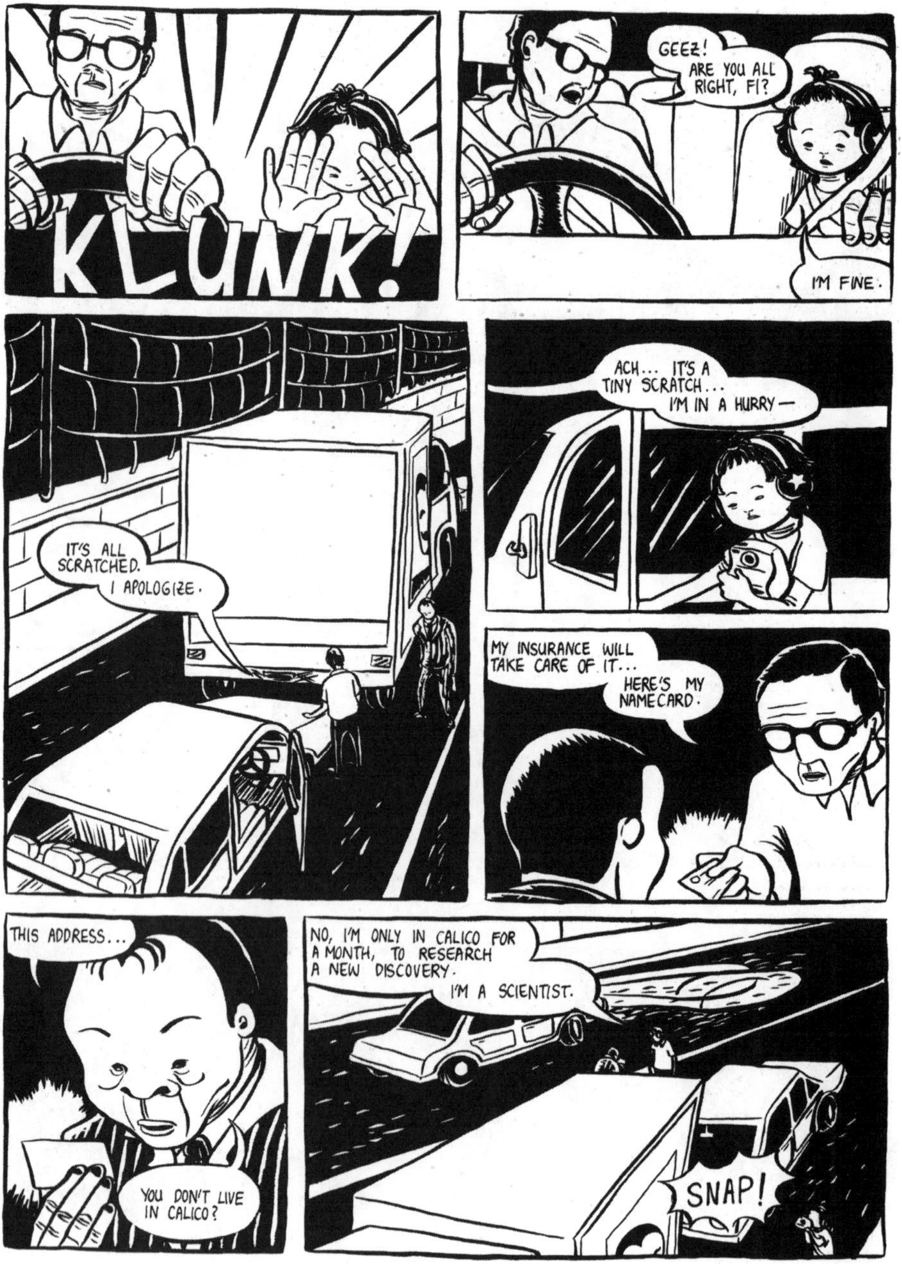
KLUNK!
GEEZ!
ARE YOU ALL RIGHT, FI?
I'M FINE.
IT'S ALL SCRATCHED.
I APOLOGIZE.
ACH... IT'S A TINY SCRATCH...
I'M IN A HURRY—
MY INSURANCE WILL TAKE CARE OF IT...
HERE'S MY NAMECARD.
THIS ADDRESS...
YOU DON'T LIVE IN CALICO?
NO, I'M ONLY IN CALICO FOR A MONTH, TO RESEARCH A NEW DISCOVERY.
I'M A SCIENTIST.
SNAP!

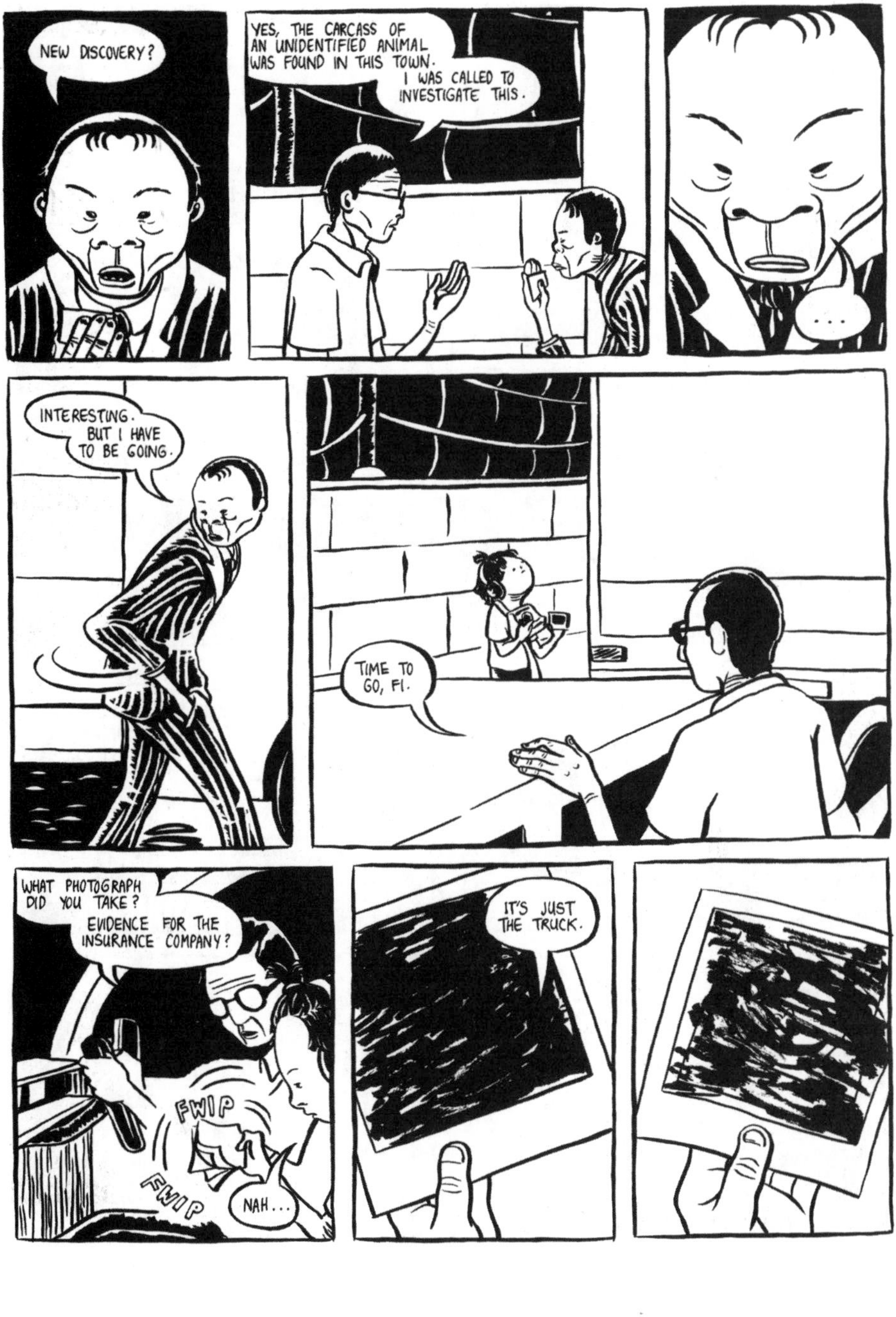
NEW DISCOVERY?
YES, THE CARCASS OF AN UNIDENTIFIED ANIMAL WAS FOUND IN THIS TOWN.
I WAS CALLED TO INVESTIGATE THIS.
...
INTERESTING. BUT I HAVE TO BE GOING.
TIME TO GO, FI.
WHAT PHOTOGRAPH DID YOU TAKE?
EVIDENCE FOR THE INSURANCE COMPANY?
FWIP
FWIP
NAH...
IT'S JUST THE TRUCK.

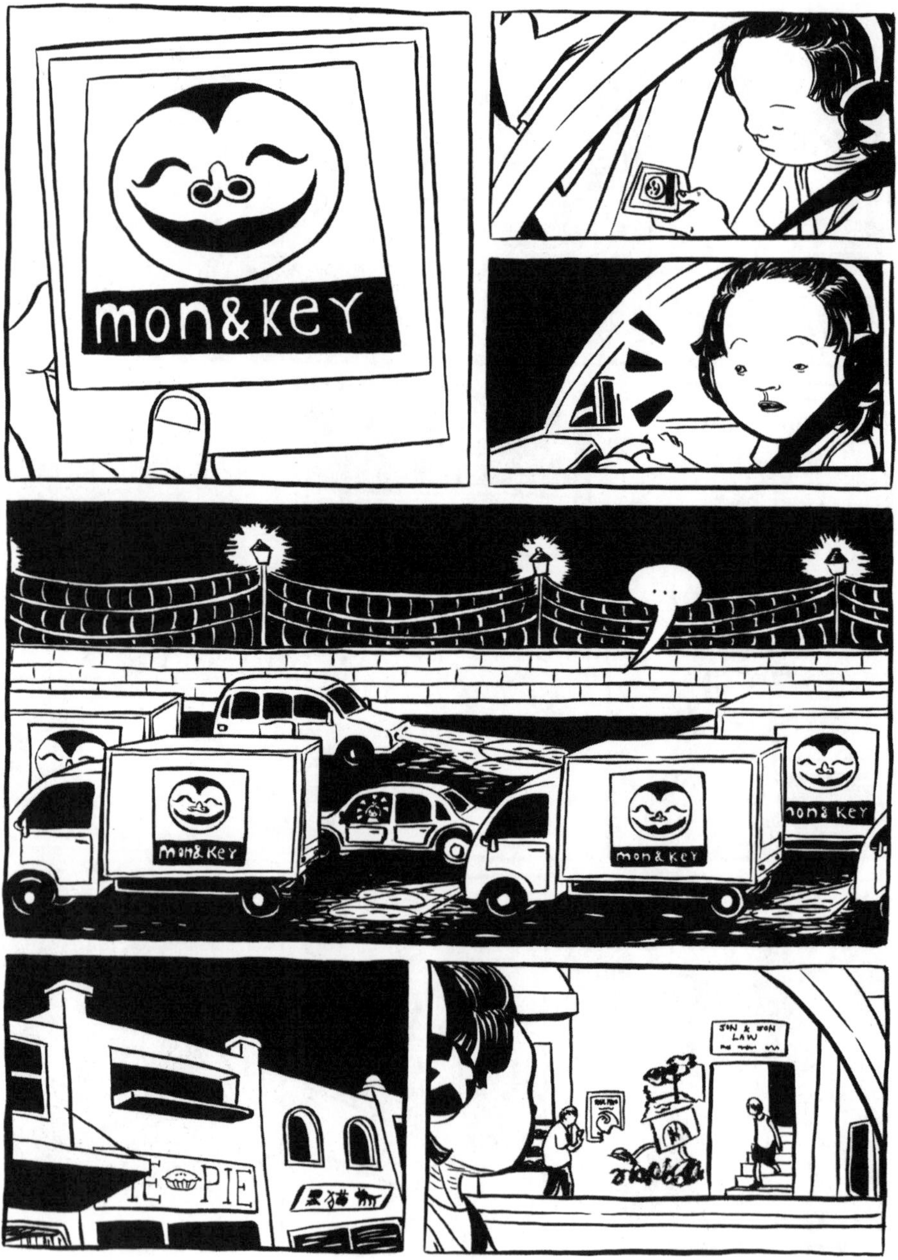
mon&KEY
...
mon& KEY
mon& KEY
JON & WON LAW
PIE

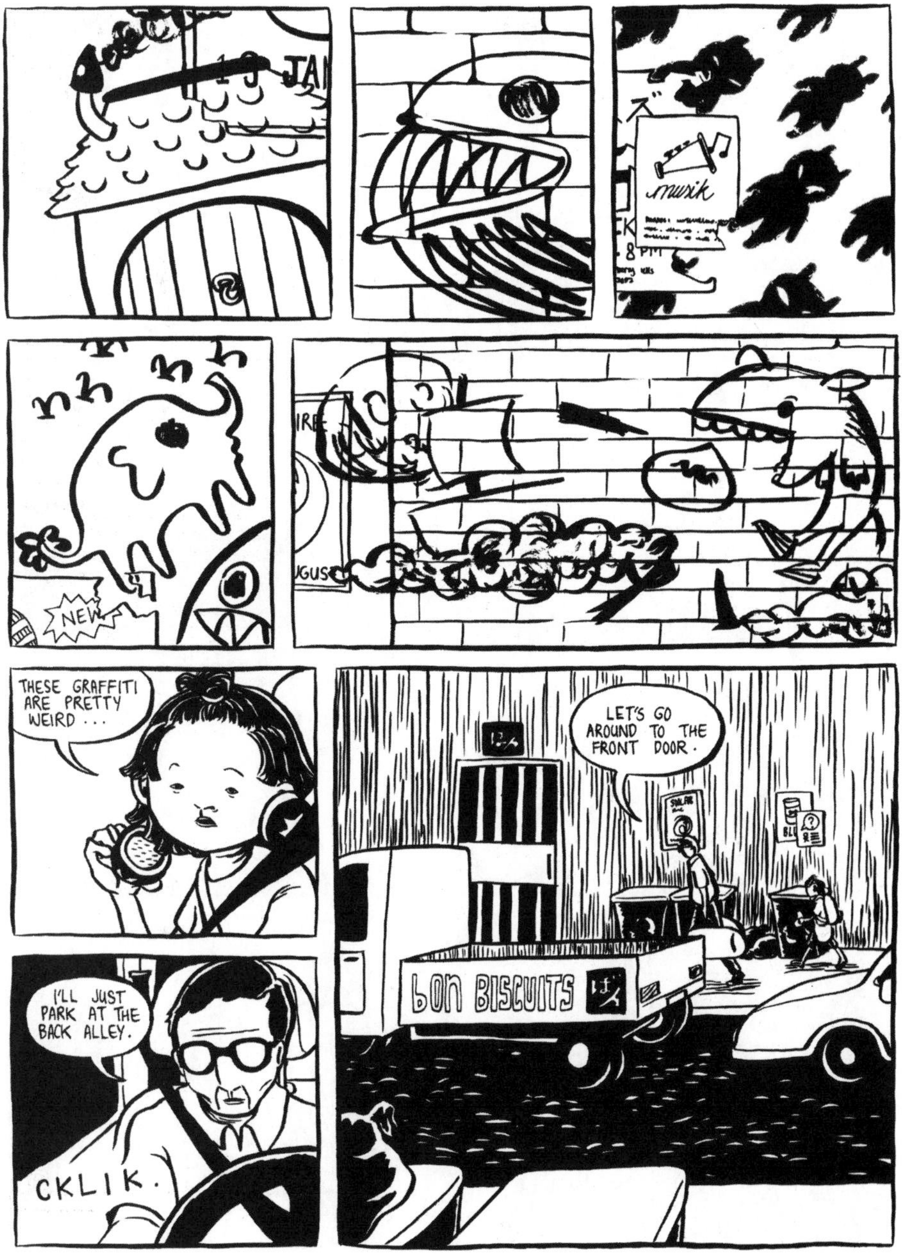
musik
NEW
THESE GRAFFITI ARE PRETTY WEIRD...
I'LL JUST PARK AT THE BACK ALLEY.
CKLIK.
LET'S GO AROUND TO THE FRONT DOOR.
bon BISCUITS

20% OFF
Sweet cup
SNAP!
?
SNAP!
FEE - FI -
FO - FUM!

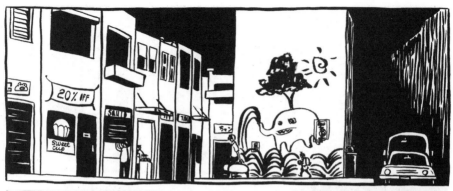

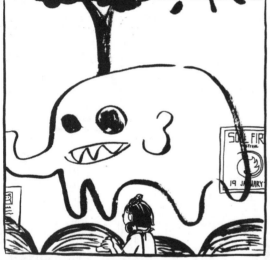

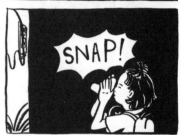

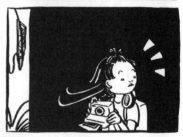

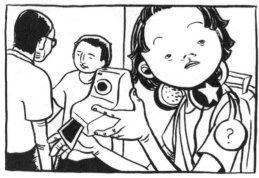

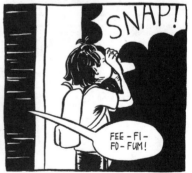

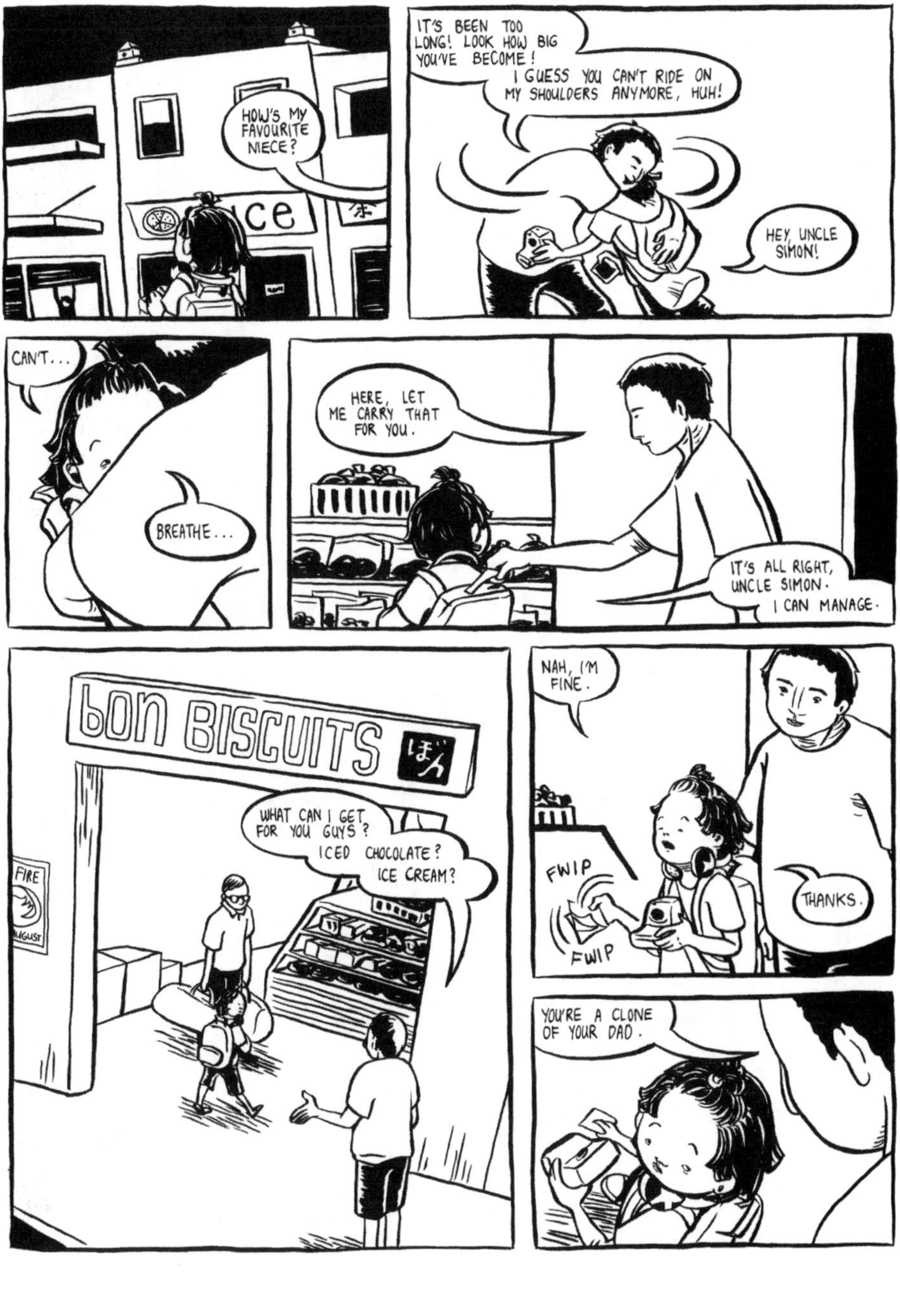
HOW'S MY FAVOURITE NIECE?
ice
IT'S BEEN TOO LONG! LOOK HOW BIG YOU'VE BECOME!
I GUESS YOU CAN'T RIDE ON MY SHOULDERS ANYMORE, HUH!
HEY, UNCLE SIMON!
CAN'T...
BREATHE...
HERE, LET ME CARRY THAT FOR YOU.
IT'S ALL RIGHT, UNCLE SIMON.
I CAN MANAGE.
bon BISCUITS ぼん
WHAT CAN I GET FOR YOU GUYS?
ICED CHOCOLATE?
ICE CREAM?
FIRE
NAH, I'M FINE.
FWIP
FWIP
THANKS.
YOU'RE A CLONE OF YOUR DAD.

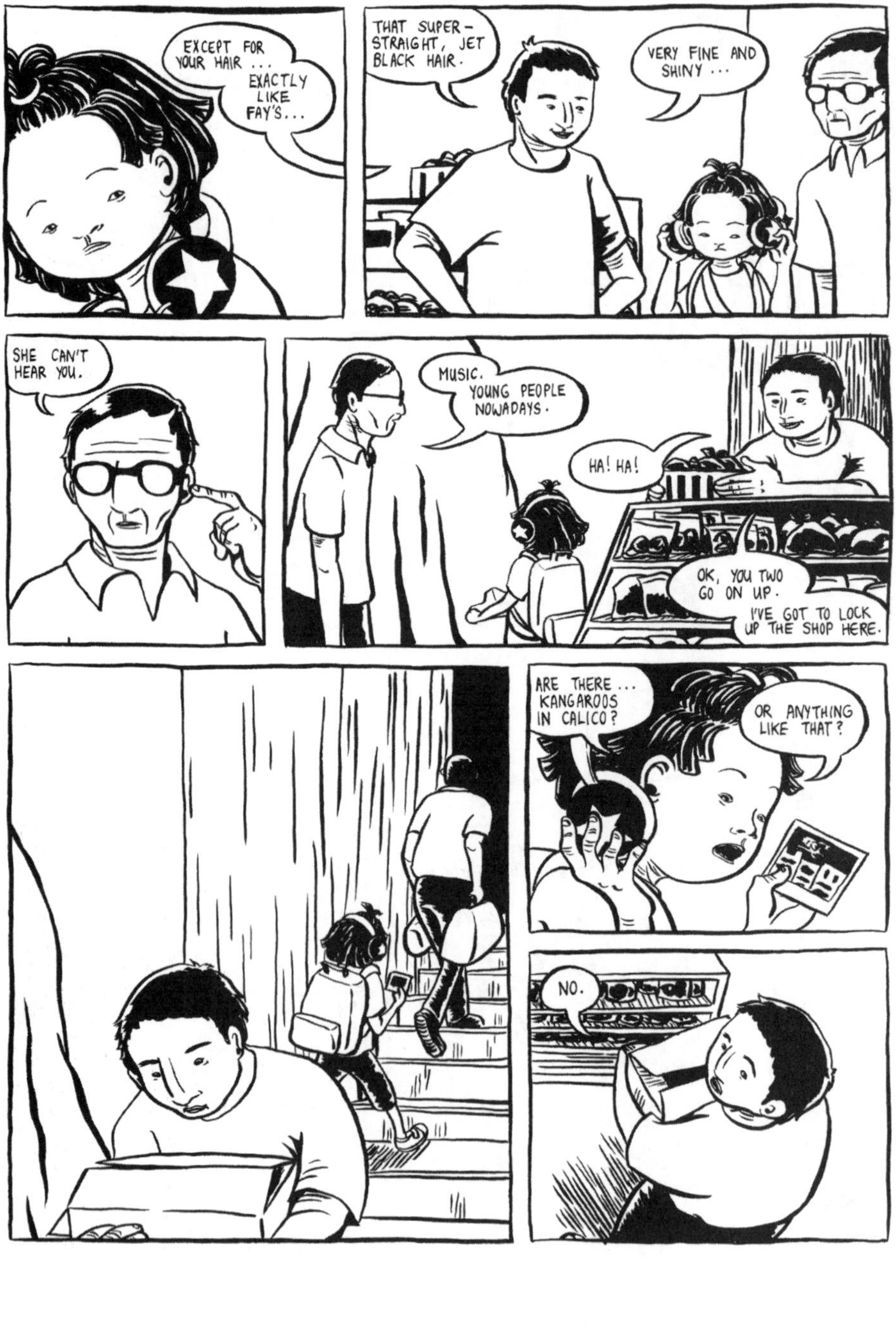
EXCEPT FOR YOUR HAIR ...
EXACTLY LIKE FAY'S...
THAT SUPER-STRAIGHT, JET BLACK HAIR.
VERY FINE AND SHINY ...
SHE CAN'T HEAR YOU.
MUSIC. YOUNG PEOPLE NOWADAYS.
HA! HA!
OK, YOU TWO GO ON UP.
I'VE GOT TO LOCK UP THE SHOP HERE.
ARE THERE ... KANGAROOS IN CALICO?
OR ANYTHING LIKE THAT?
NO.

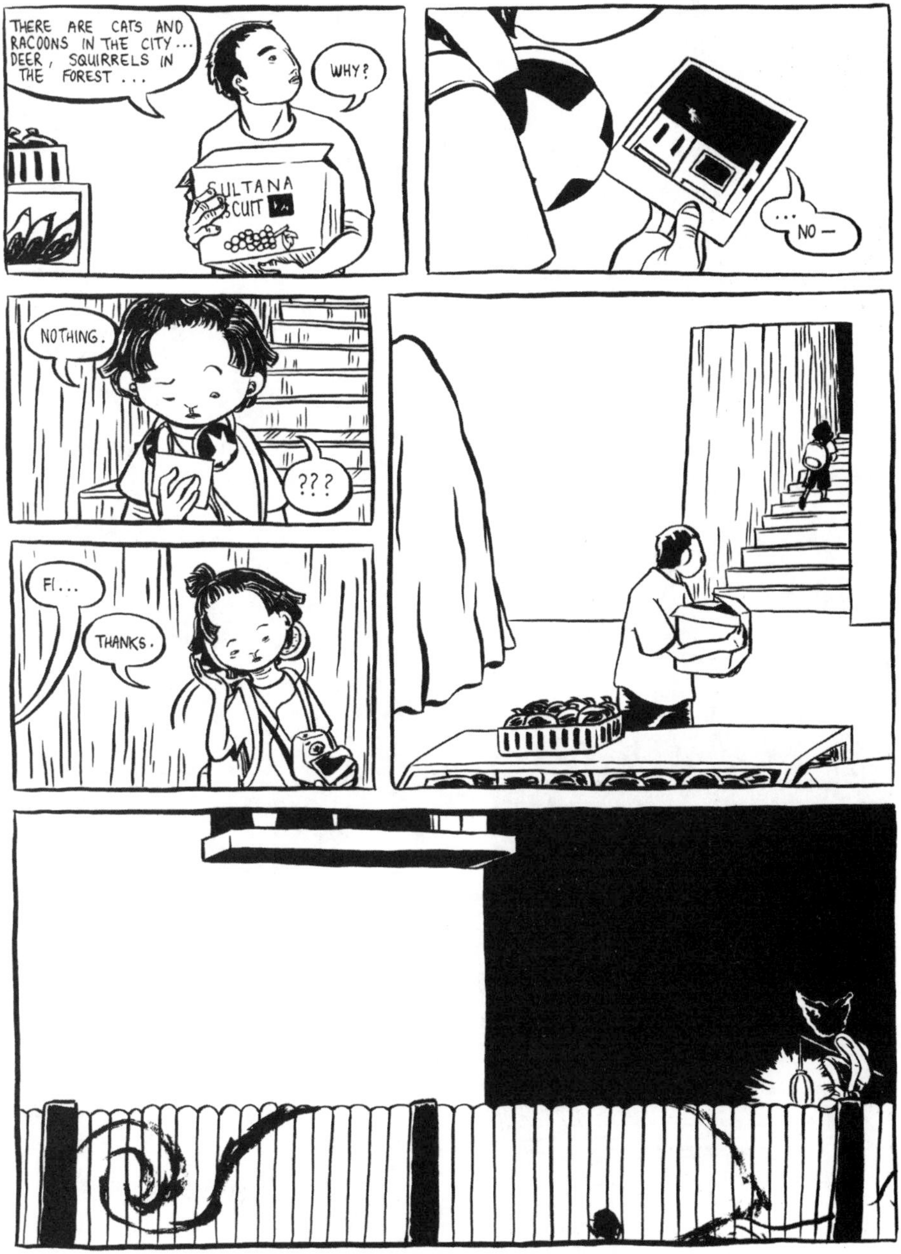
THERE ARE CATS AND RACOONS IN THE CITY... DEER, SQUIRRELS IN THE FOREST...
WHY?
SULTANA
...NO—
NOTHING.
???
FI...
THANKS.

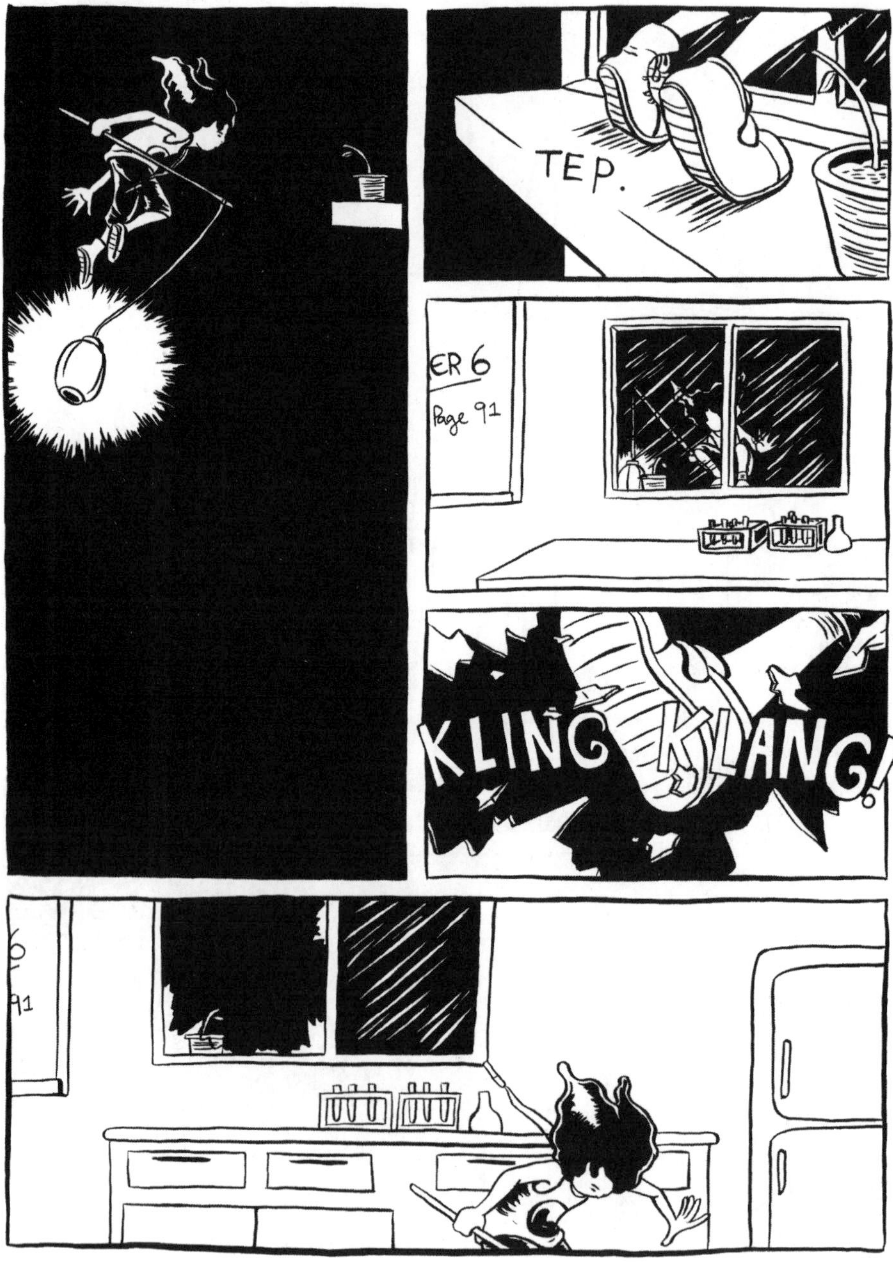
TEP.
ER 6
Page 91
KLING KLANG!
91

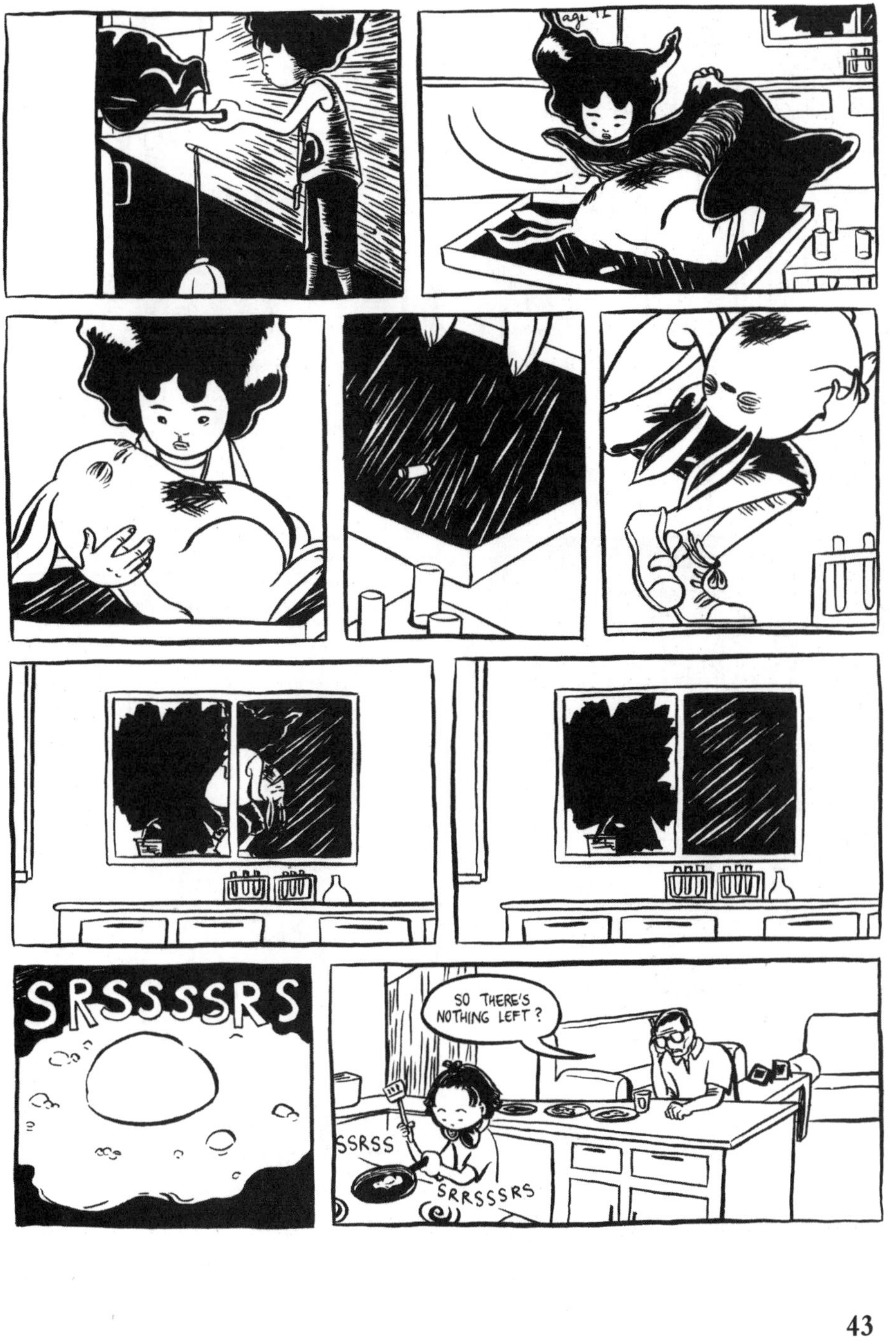
SRSSSSRS
SO THERE'S NOTHING LEFT?
SSRSS
SRRSSSRS

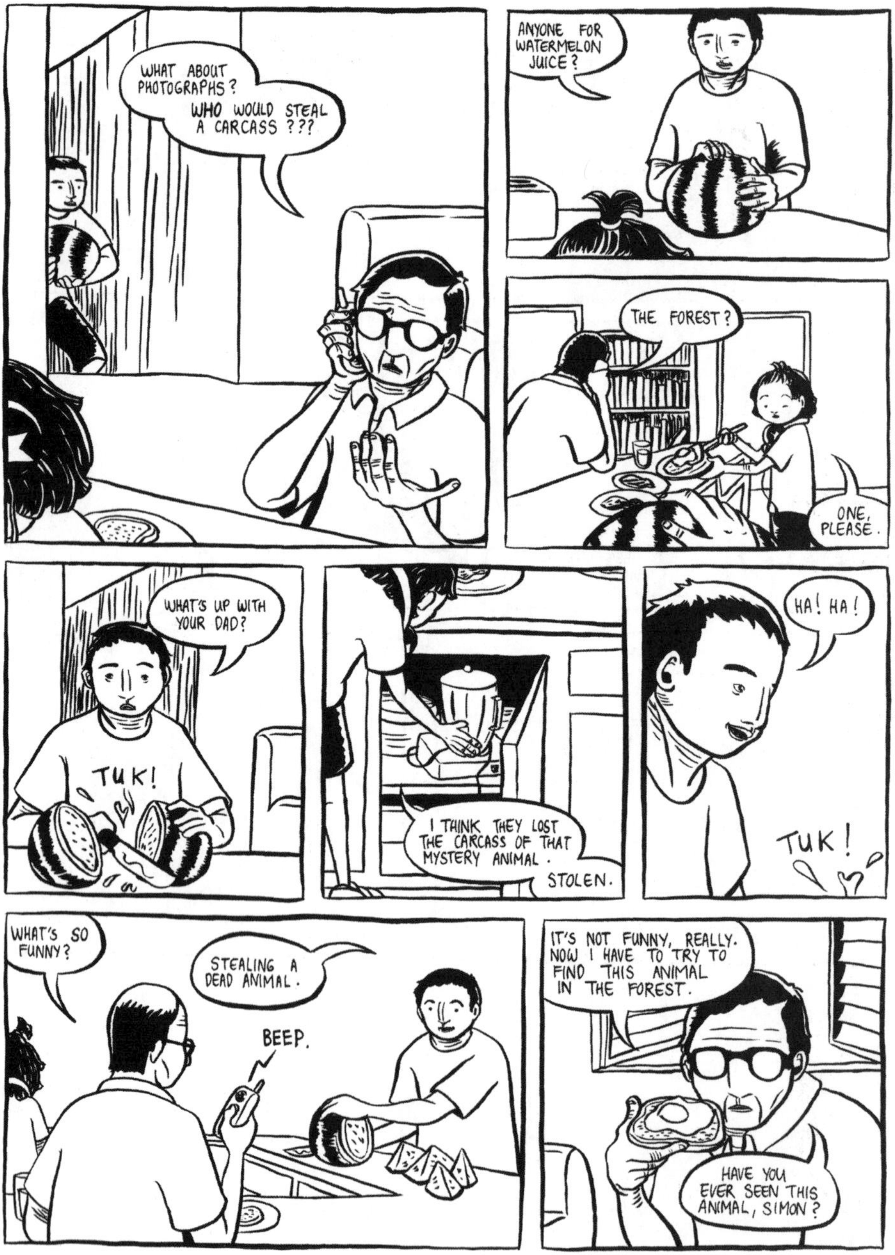

WHAT ABOUT PHOTOGRAPHS?
WHO WOULD STEAL A CARCASS ???
ANYONE FOR WATERMELON JUICE?
THE FOREST?
ONE, PLEASE.
WHAT'S UP WITH YOUR DAD?
TUK!
I THINK THEY LOST THE CARCASS OF THAT MYSTERY ANIMAL.
STOLEN.
HA! HA!
TUK!
WHAT'S SO FUNNY?
STEALING A DEAD ANIMAL.
BEEP.
IT'S NOT FUNNY, REALLY. NOW I HAVE TO TRY TO FIND THIS ANIMAL IN THE FOREST.
HAVE YOU EVER SEEN THIS ANIMAL, SIMON?

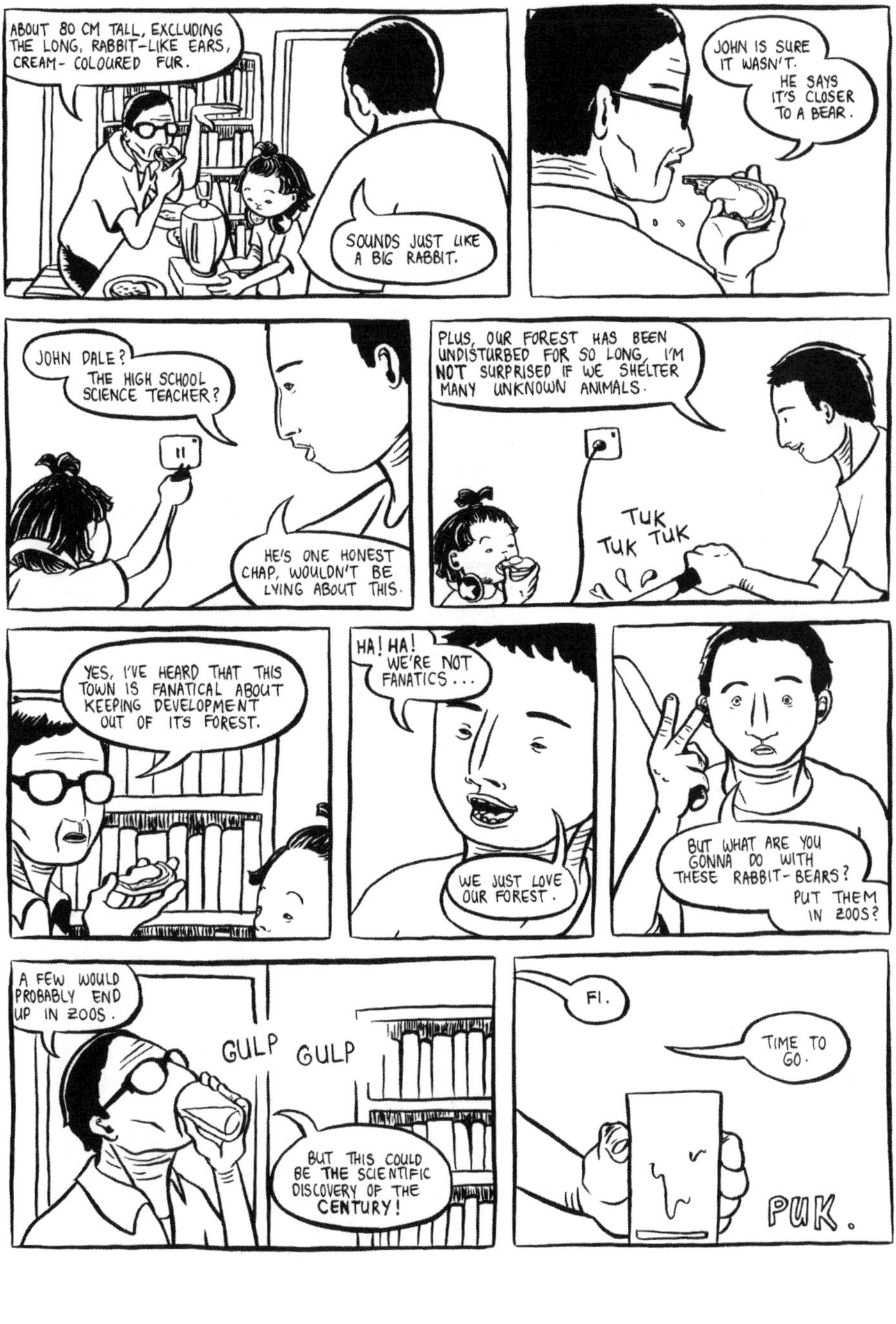
ABOUT 80 CM TALL, EXCLUDING THE LONG, RABBIT-LIKE EARS, CREAM-COLOURED FUR.
SOUNDS JUST LIKE A BIG RABBIT.
JOHN IS SURE IT WASN'T.
HE SAYS IT'S CLOSER TO A BEAR.
JOHN DALE?
THE HIGH SCHOOL SCIENCE TEACHER?
HE'S ONE HONEST CHAP, WOULDN'T BE LYING ABOUT THIS.
PLUS, OUR FOREST HAS BEEN UNDISTURBED FOR SO LONG, I'M NOT SURPRISED IF WE SHELTER MANY UNKNOWN ANIMALS.
TUK TUK TUK
YES, I'VE HEARD THAT THIS TOWN IS FANATICAL ABOUT KEEPING DEVELOPMENT OUT OF ITS FOREST.
HA! HA!
WE'RE NOT FANATICS...
WE JUST LOVE OUR FOREST.
BUT WHAT ARE YOU GONNA DO WITH THESE RABBIT-BEARS?
PUT THEM IN ZOOS?
A FEW WOULD PROBABLY END UP IN ZOOS.
GULP GULP
BUT THIS COULD BE THE SCIENTIFIC DISCOVERY OF THE CENTURY!
FI.
TIME TO GO.
PUK.

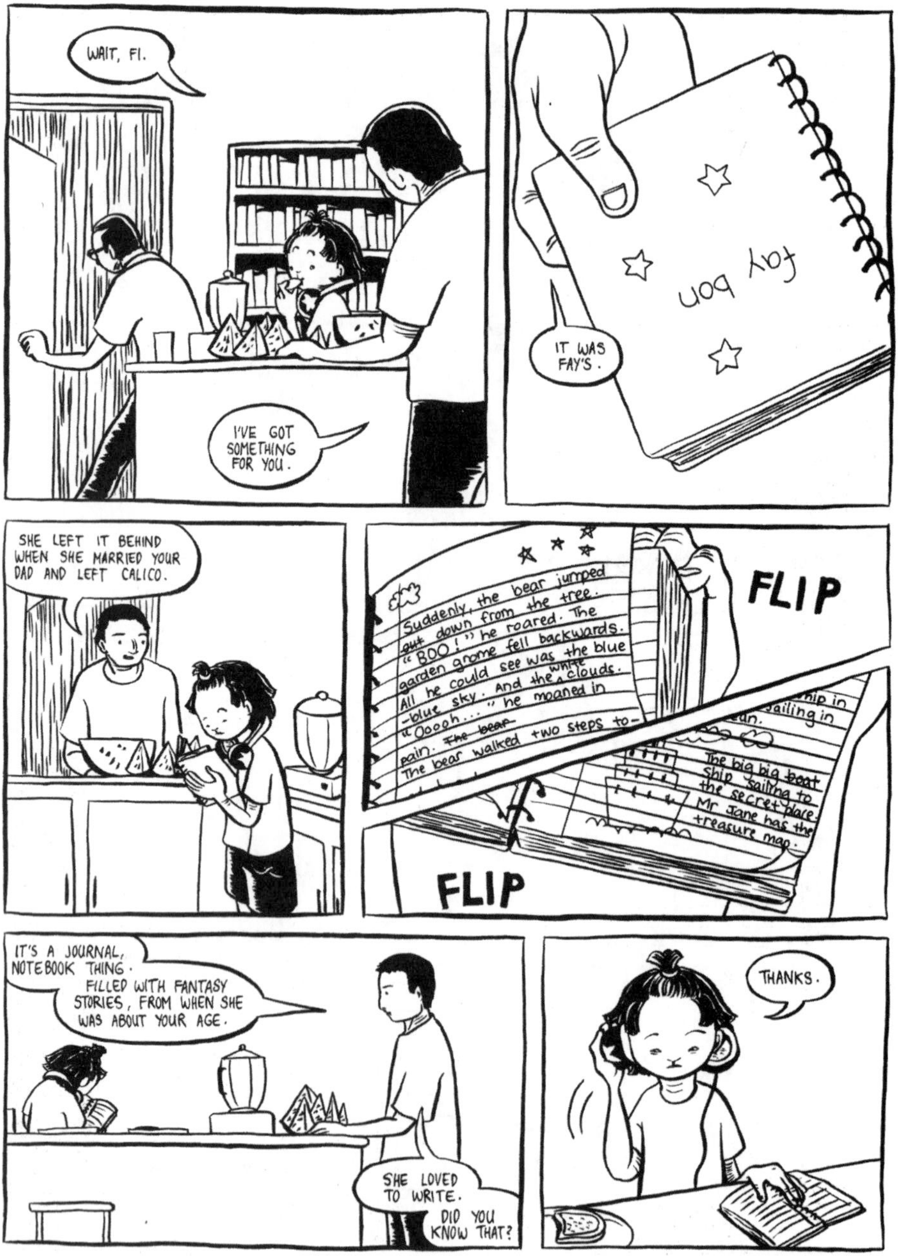
WAIT, FI.
I'VE GOT SOMETHING FOR YOU.
fay bon
IT WAS FAY'S.
SHE LEFT IT BEHIND WHEN SHE MARRIED YOUR DAD AND LEFT CALICO.
Suddenly the bear jumped out down from the tree.
"BOO!" he roared. The garden gnome fell backwards.
All he could see was the blue white clouds.
blue sky. And the
"Ooooh..." he moaned in pain. The bear
The bear walked two steps to-
The big big boat ship sailing to the secret place. Mr Jane has the treasure map.
FLIP
FLIP
IT'S A JOURNAL, NOTEBOOK THING.
FILLED WITH FANTASY STORIES, FROM WHEN SHE WAS ABOUT YOUR AGE.
SHE LOVED TO WRITE.
DID YOU KNOW THAT?
THANKS.

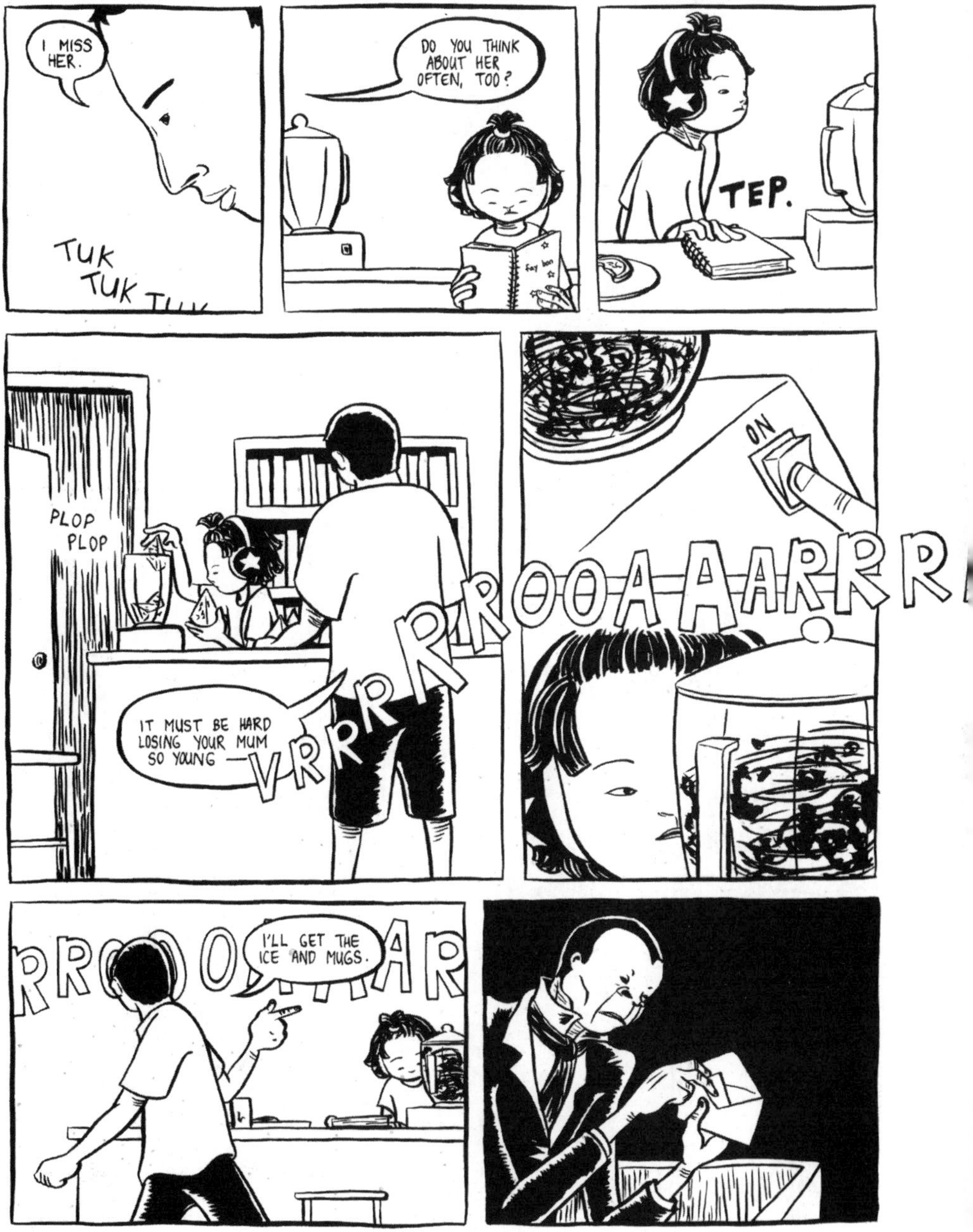
I MISS HER.
TUK TUK
DO YOU THINK ABOUT HER OFTEN, TOO?
TEP.
PLOP PLOP
ON
VRRRRROOAAARRR
IT MUST BE HARD LOSING YOUR MUM SO YOUNG —
I'LL GET THE ICE AND MUGS.

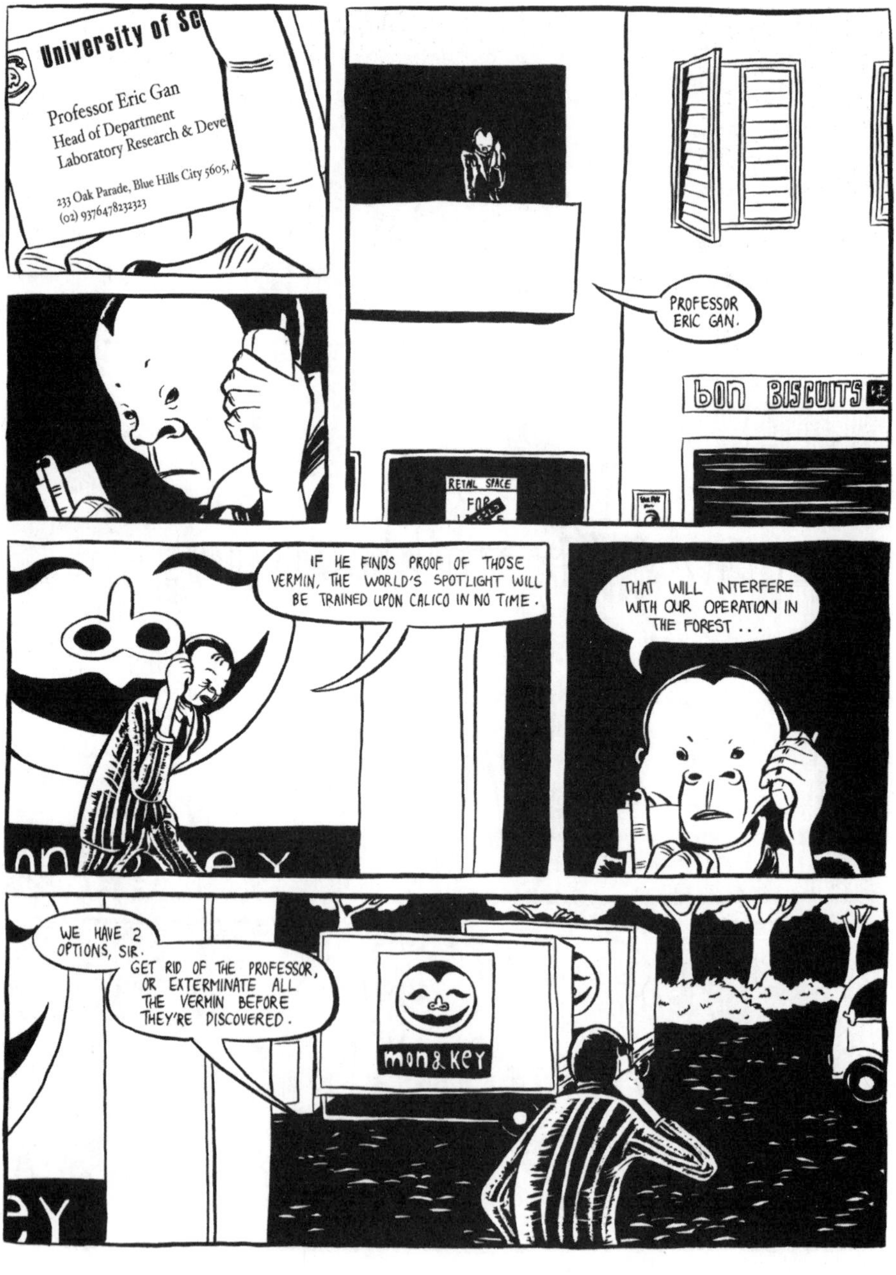
University of Sc
Professor Eric Gan
Head of Department
Laboratory Research & Deve
233 Oak Parade, Blue Hills City 5605, A
(02) 9376478232323
PROFESSOR ERIC GAN.
bon BISCUITS
RETAIL SPACE
IF HE FINDS PROOF OF THOSE VERMIN, THE WORLD'S SPOTLIGHT WILL BE TRAINED UPON CALICO IN NO TIME.
THAT WILL INTERFERE WITH OUR OPERATION IN THE FOREST . . .
WE HAVE 2 OPTIONS, SIR.
GET RID OF THE PROFESSOR, OR EXTERMINATE ALL THE VERMIN BEFORE THEY'RE DISCOVERED.
mon&key

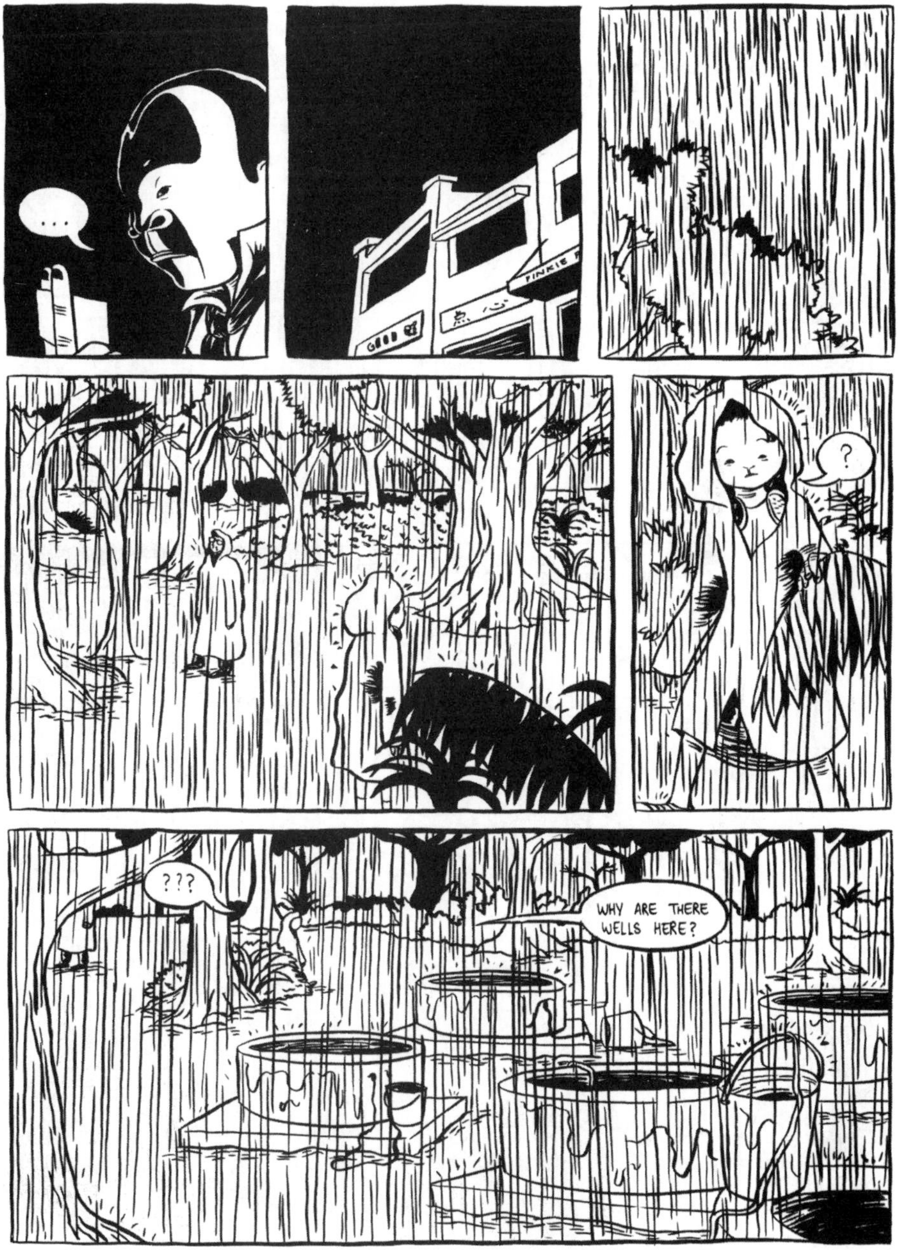
...
PINKIE
点心
GOOD
?
???
WHY ARE THERE WELLS HERE?

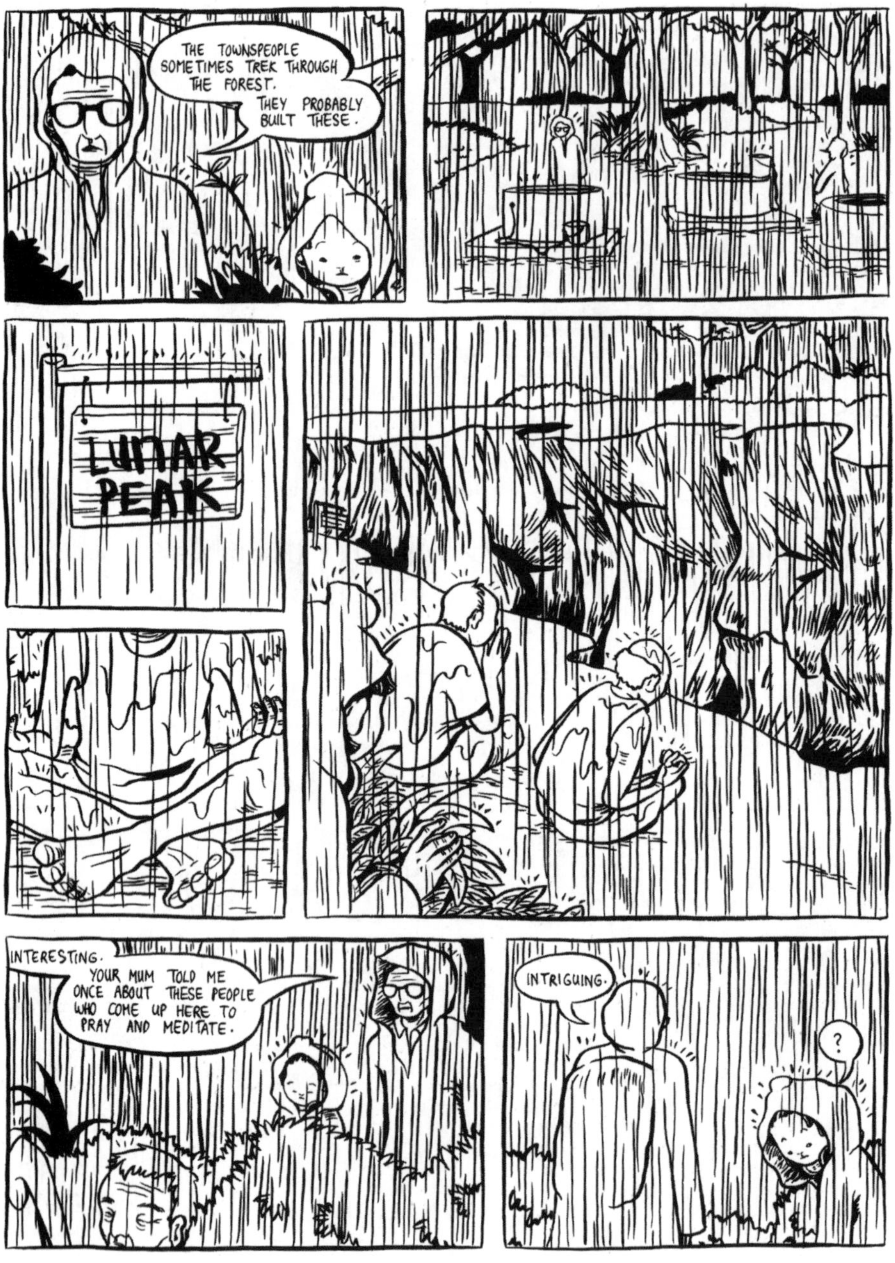
THE TOWNSPEOPLE SOMETIMES TREK THROUGH THE FOREST.
THEY PROBABLY BUILT THESE.
LUNAR PEAK
INTERESTING.
YOUR MUM TOLD ME ONCE ABOUT THESE PEOPLE WHO COME UP HERE TO PRAY AND MEDITATE.
INTRIGUING.
?

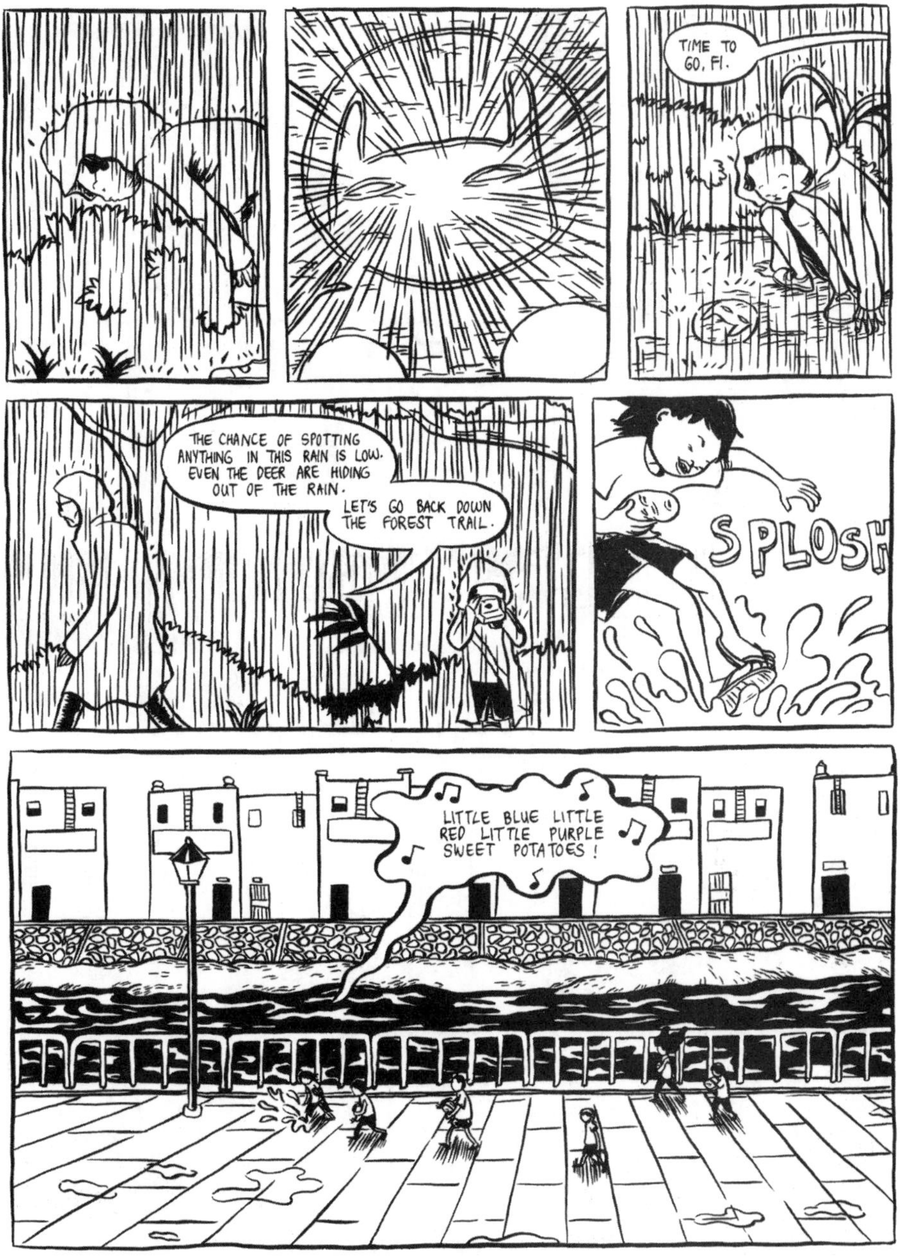
TIME TO GO, FI.
THE CHANCE OF SPOTTING ANYTHING IN THIS RAIN IS LOW. EVEN THE DEER ARE HIDING OUT OF THE RAIN.
LET'S GO BACK DOWN THE FOREST TRAIL.
SPLOSH
LITTLE BLUE LITTLE RED LITTLE PURPLE SWEET POTATOES!

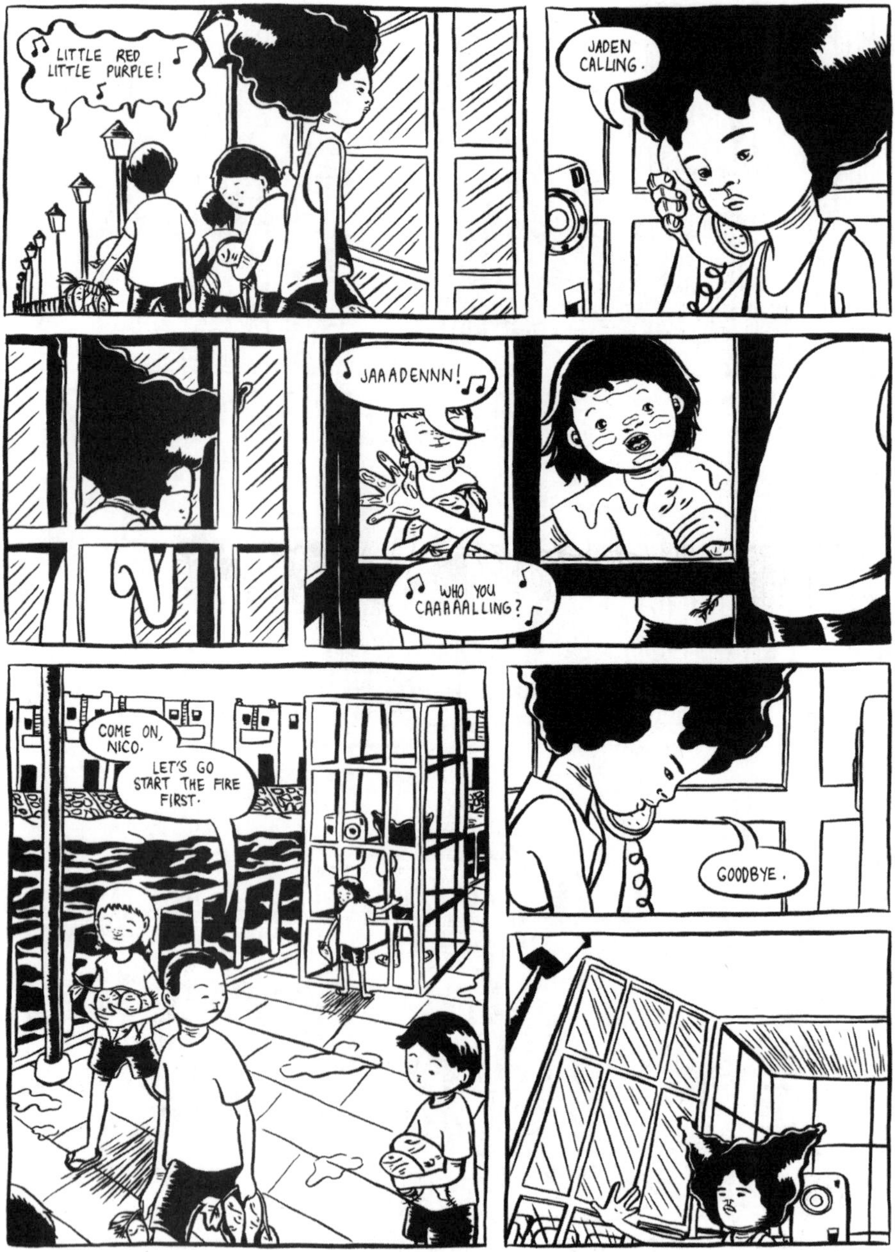
LITTLE RED LITTLE PURPLE!
JADEN CALLING.
JAAADENNN!
WHO YOU CAAAAALLING?
COME ON, NICO.
LET'S GO START THE FIRE FIRST.
GOODBYE.

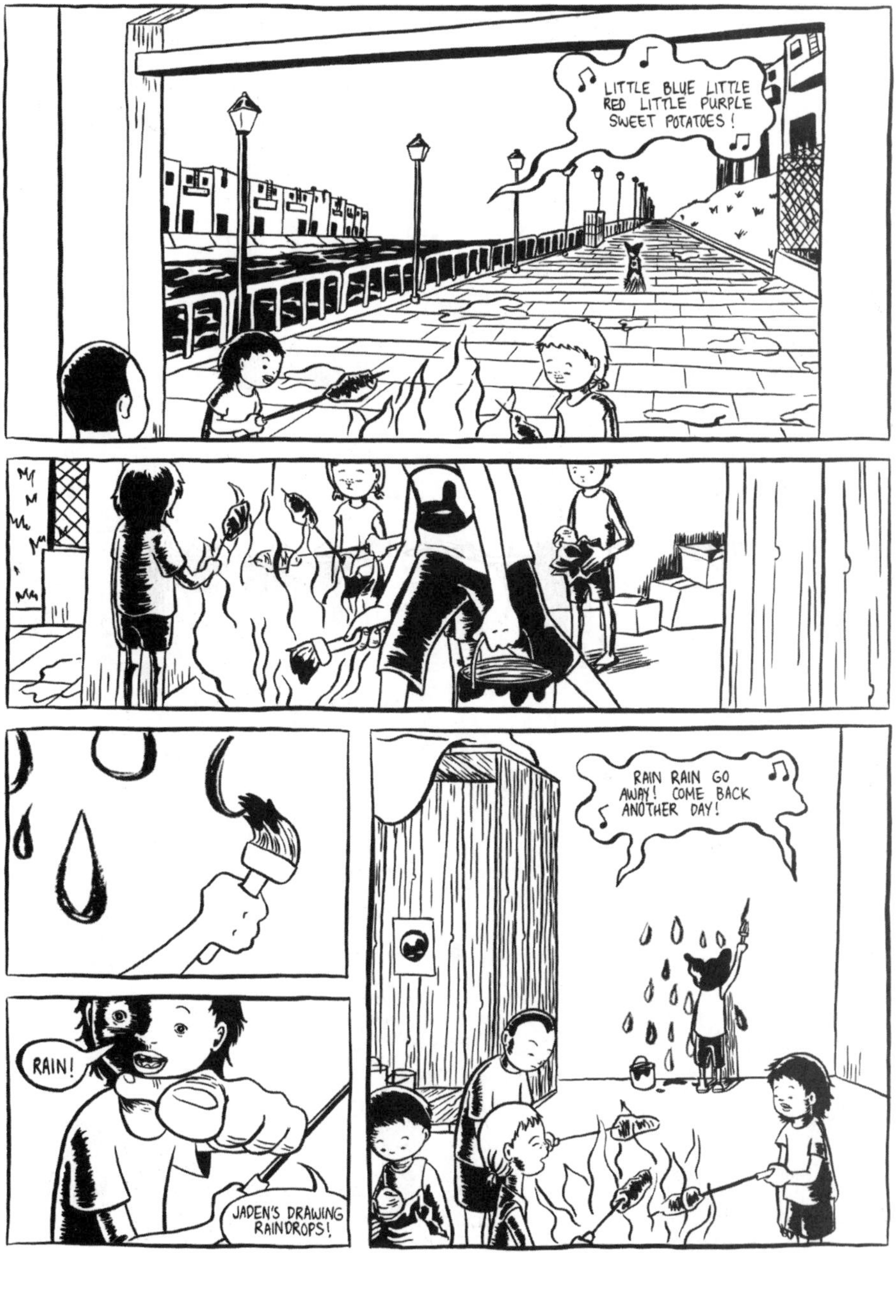
LITTLE BLUE LITTLE RED LITTLE PURPLE SWEET POTATOES!
RAIN!
JADEN'S DRAWING RAINDROPS!
RAIN RAIN GO AWAY! COME BACK ANOTHER DAY!

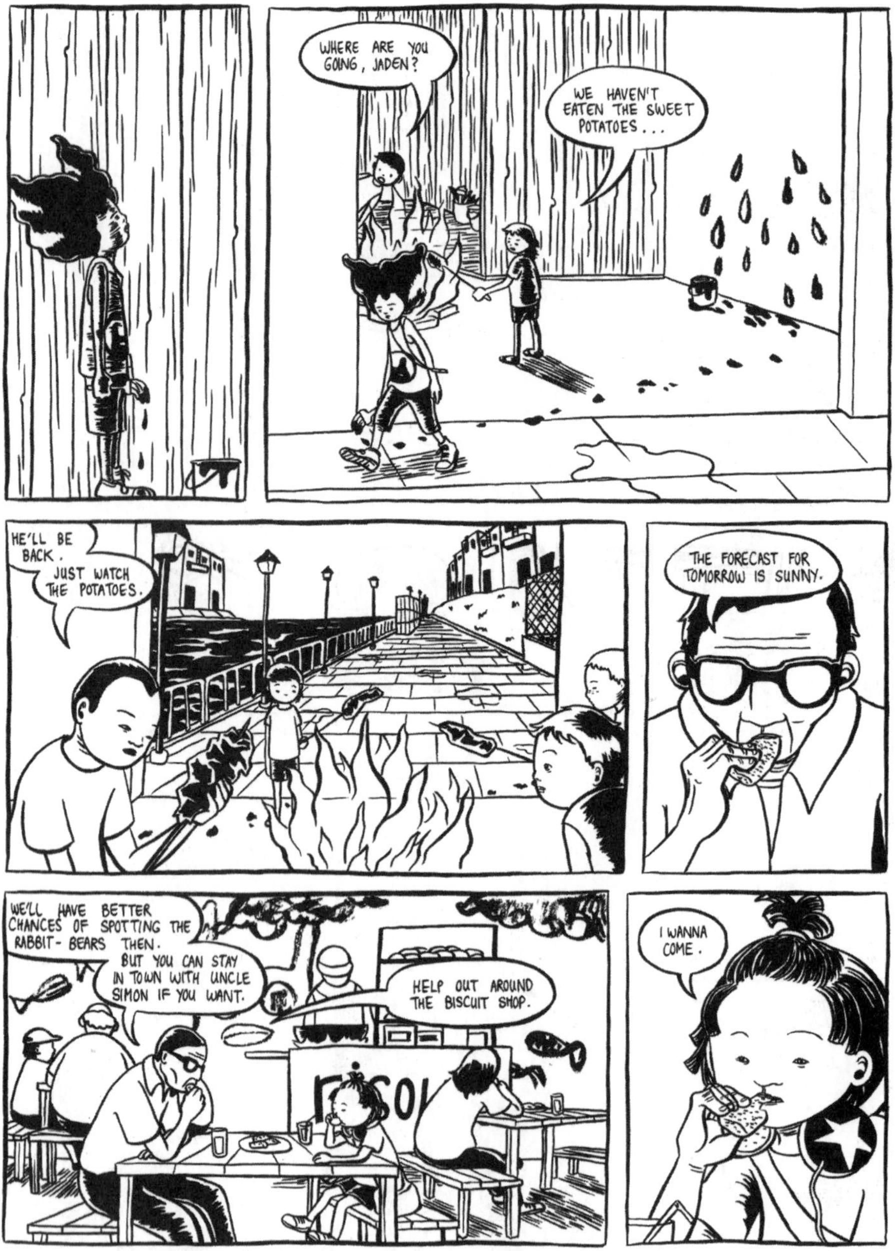
WHERE ARE YOU GOING, JADEN?
WE HAVEN'T EATEN THE SWEET POTATOES...
HE'LL BE BACK.
JUST WATCH THE POTATOES.
THE FORECAST FOR TOMORROW IS SUNNY.
WE'LL HAVE BETTER CHANCES OF SPOTTING THE RABBIT-BEARS THEN.
BUT YOU CAN STAY IN TOWN WITH UNCLE SIMON IF YOU WANT.
HELP OUT AROUND THE BISCUIT SHOP.
I WANNA COME.

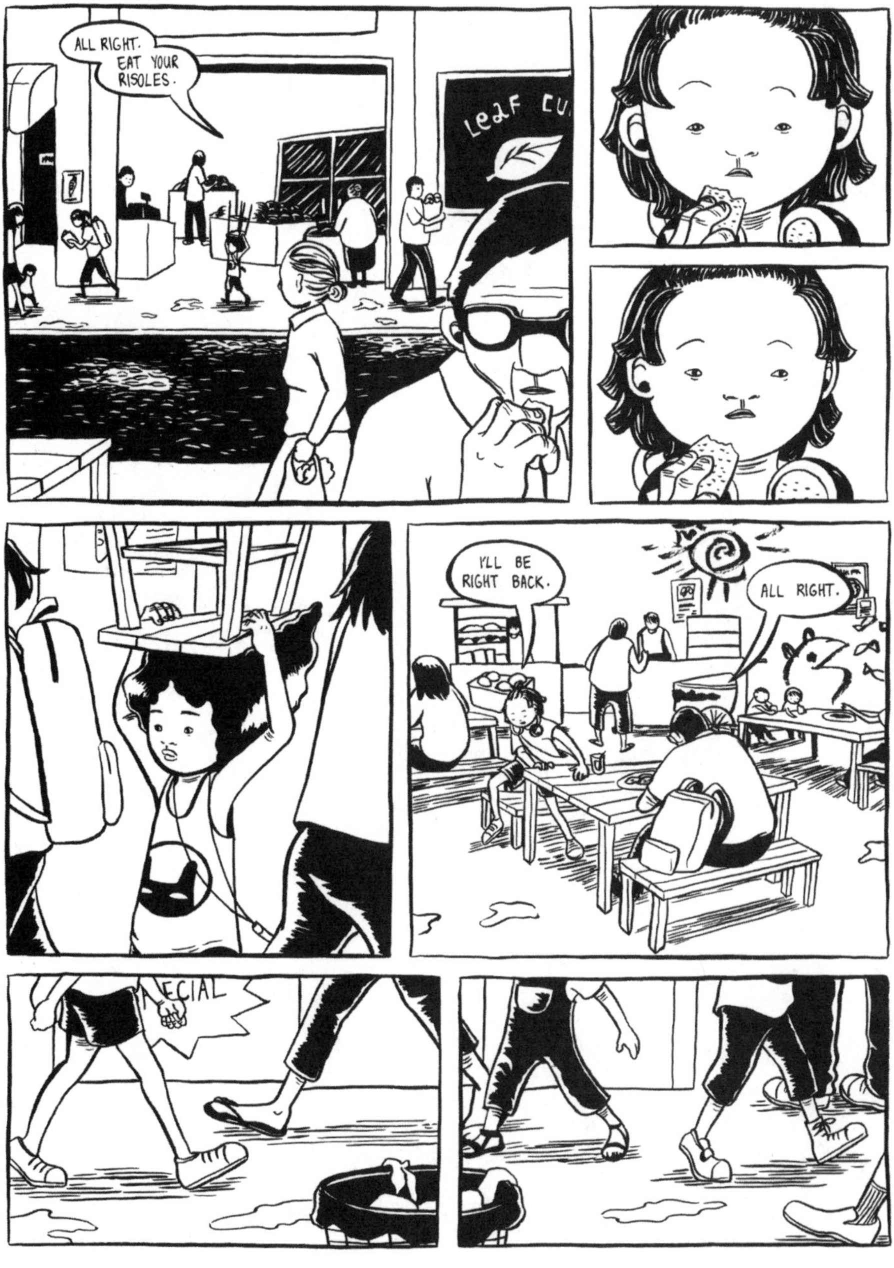
ALL RIGHT. EAT YOUR RISOLES.
LEAF CU
I'LL BE RIGHT BACK.
ALL RIGHT.
ECIAL

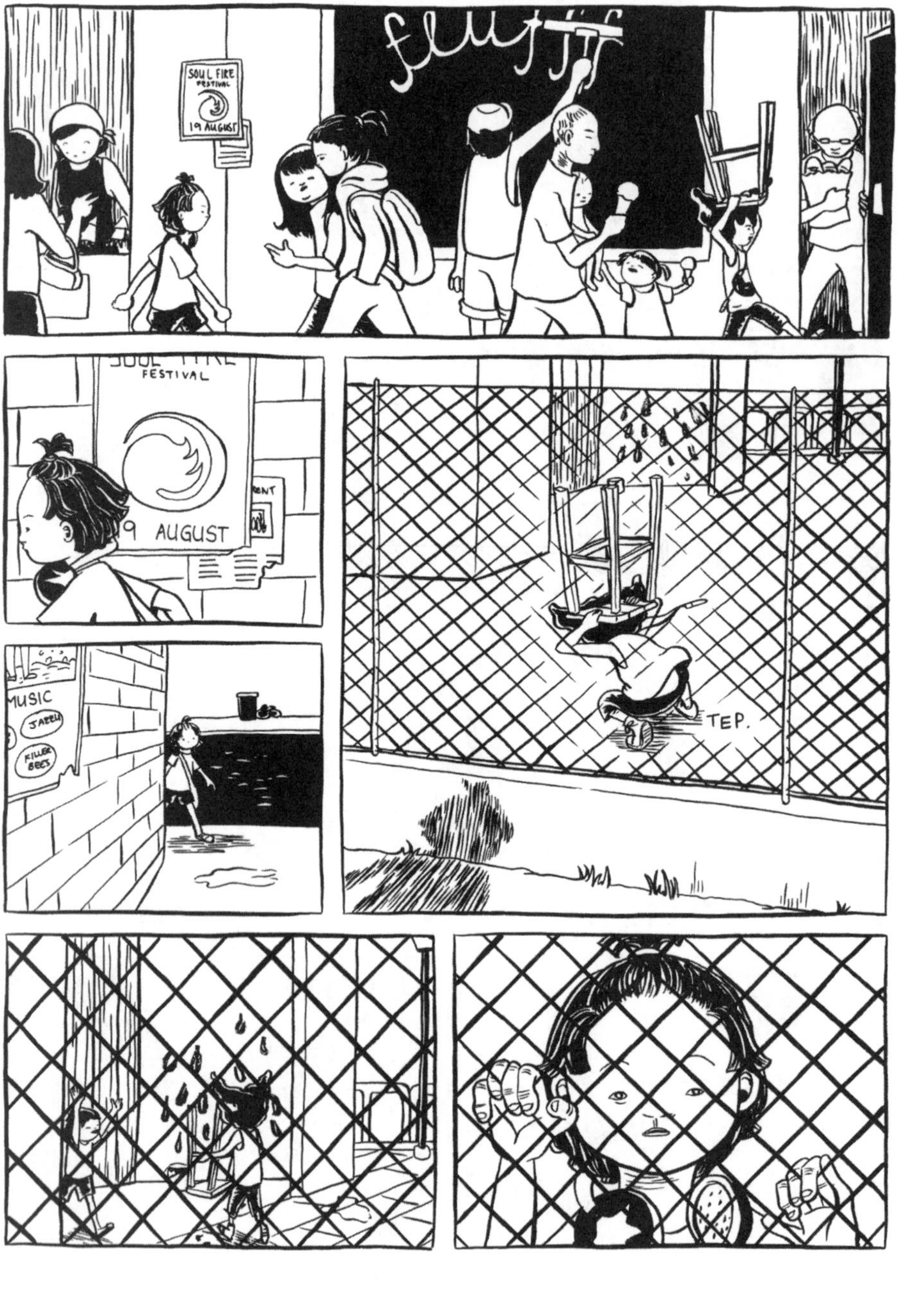
SOUL FIRE FESTIVAL
19 AUGUST
FESTIVAL
9 AUGUST
RENT
MUSIC
KILLER BEES
TEP.

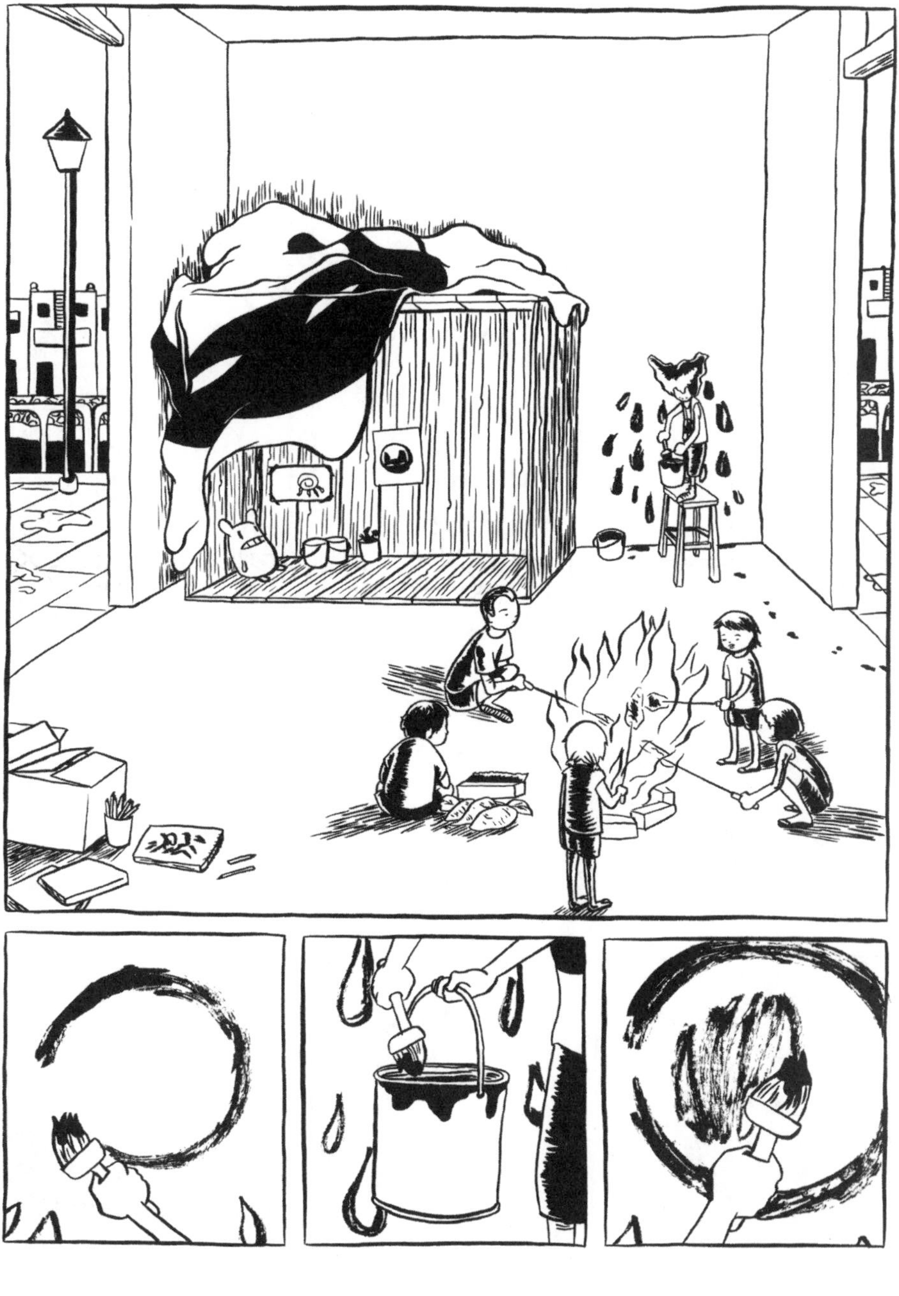

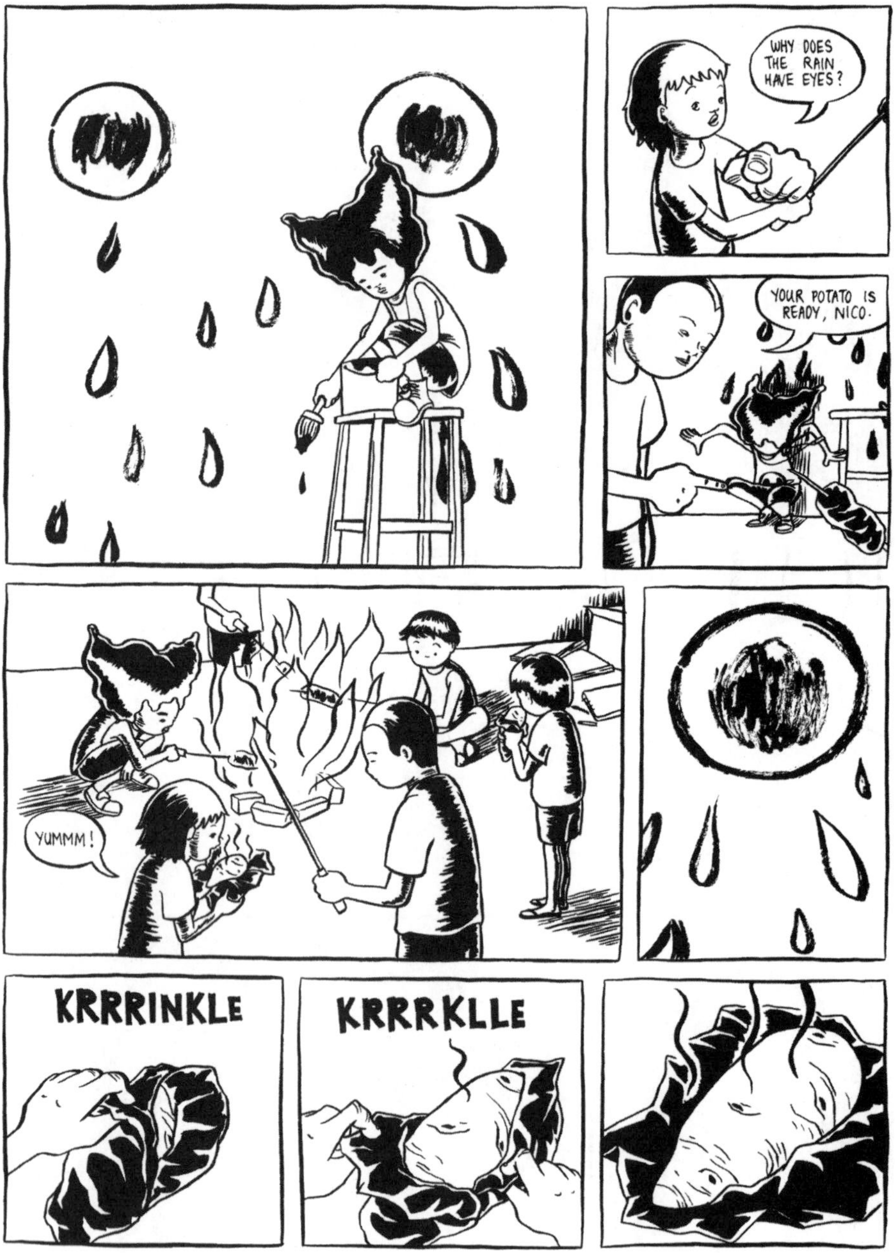
WHY DOES THE RAIN HAVE EYES?
YOUR POTATO IS READY, NICO.
YUMMM!
KRRRINKLE
KRRRKLLE

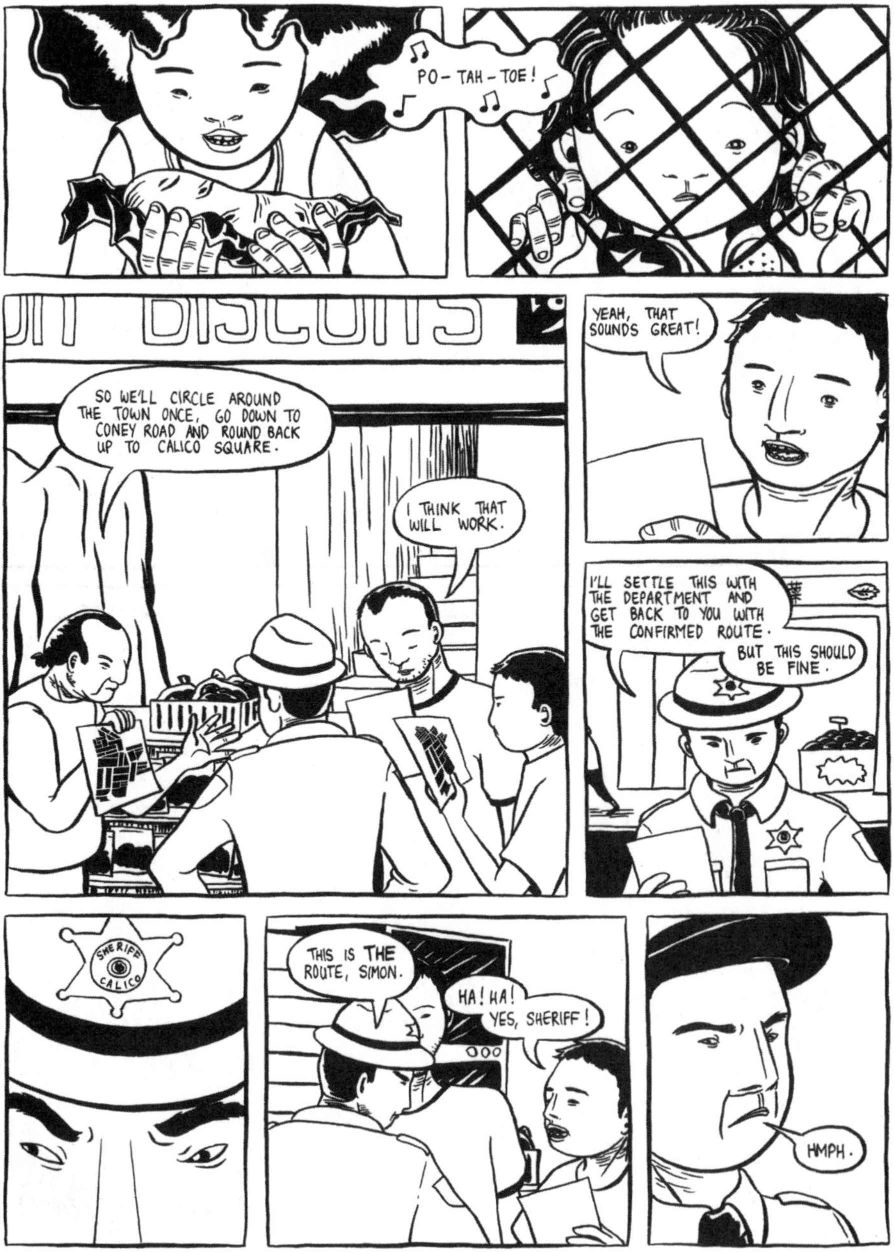
PO-TAH-TOE!
SO WE'LL CIRCLE AROUND THE TOWN ONCE, GO DOWN TO CONEY ROAD AND ROUND BACK UP TO CALICO SQUARE.
I THINK THAT WILL WORK.
YEAH, THAT SOUNDS GREAT!
I'LL SETTLE THIS WITH THE DEPARTMENT AND GET BACK TO YOU WITH THE CONFIRMED ROUTE.
BUT THIS SHOULD BE FINE.
SHERIFF CALICO
THIS IS THE ROUTE, SIMON.
HA! HA! YES, SHERIFF!
HMPH.

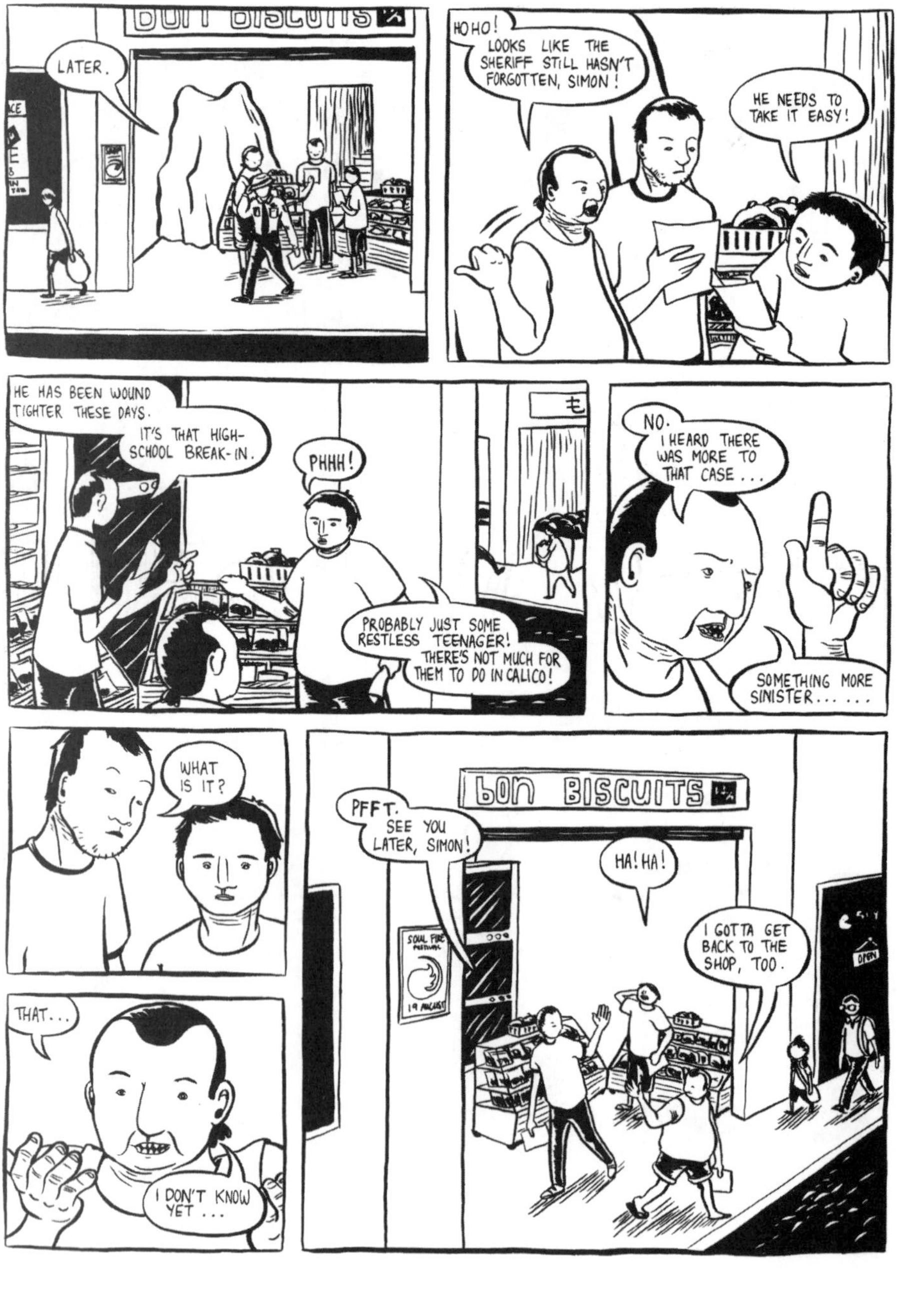
LATER.
HO HO! LOOKS LIKE THE SHERIFF STILL HASN'T FORGOTTEN, SIMON!
HE NEEDS TO TAKE IT EASY!
HE HAS BEEN WOUND TIGHTER THESE DAYS.
IT'S THAT HIGH-SCHOOL BREAK-IN.
PHHH!
PROBABLY JUST SOME RESTLESS TEENAGER!
THERE'S NOT MUCH FOR THEM TO DO IN CALICO!
NO.
I HEARD THERE WAS MORE TO THAT CASE...
SOMETHING MORE SINISTER......
WHAT IS IT?
THAT...
I DON'T KNOW YET...
bon BISCUITS
PFFT.
SEE YOU LATER, SIMON!
HA! HA!
I GOTTA GET BACK TO THE SHOP, TOO.
SOUL FIRE FESTIVAL
19 AUGUST
OPEN

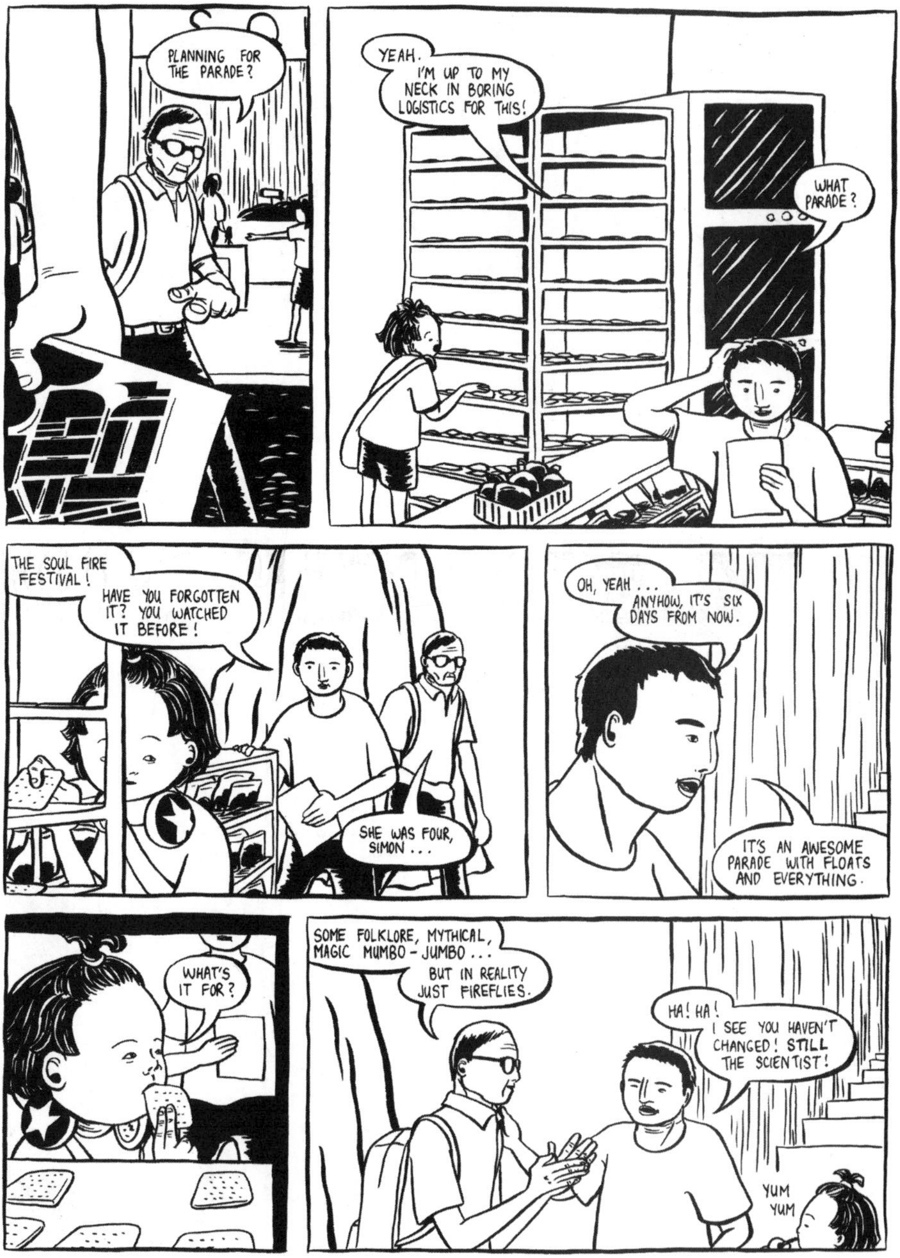
PLANNING FOR THE PARADE?
YEAH.
I'M UP TO MY NECK IN BORING LOGISTICS FOR THIS!
WHAT PARADE?
THE SOUL FIRE FESTIVAL!
HAVE YOU FORGOTTEN IT? YOU WATCHED IT BEFORE!
SHE WAS FOUR, SIMON...
OH, YEAH...
ANYHOW, IT'S SIX DAYS FROM NOW.
IT'S AN AWESOME PARADE WITH FLOATS AND EVERYTHING.
WHAT'S IT FOR?
SOME FOLKLORE, MYTHICAL, MAGIC MUMBO-JUMBO...
BUT IN REALITY JUST FIREFLIES.
HA! HA!
I SEE YOU HAVEN'T CHANGED! **STILL** THE SCIENTIST!
YUM YUM

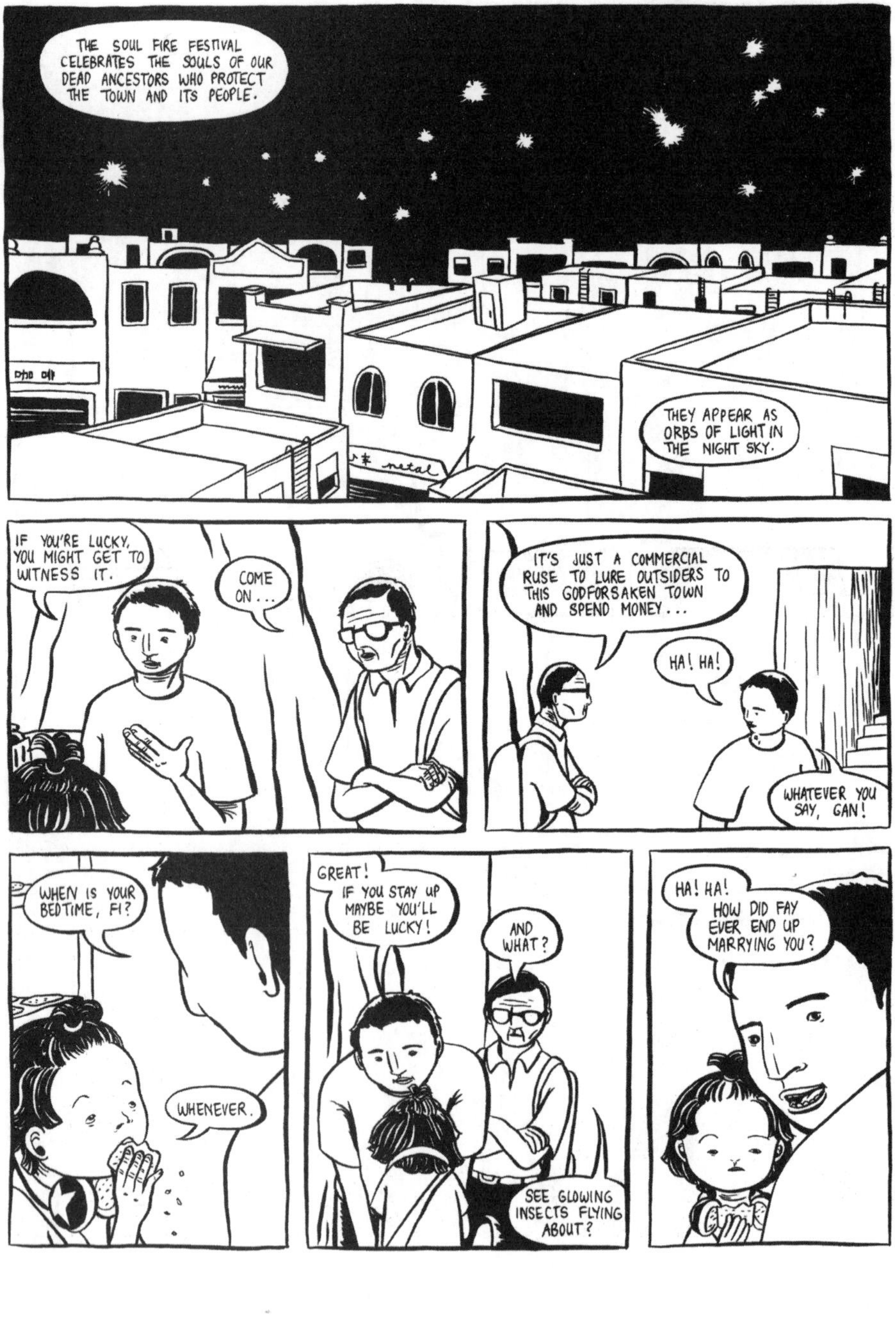
THE SOUL FIRE FESTIVAL CELEBRATES THE SOULS OF OUR DEAD ANCESTORS WHO PROTECT THE TOWN AND ITS PEOPLE.
THEY APPEAR AS ORBS OF LIGHT IN THE NIGHT SKY.
IF YOU'RE LUCKY, YOU MIGHT GET TO WITNESS IT.
COME ON...
IT'S JUST A COMMERCIAL RUSE TO LURE OUTSIDERS TO THIS GODFORSAKEN TOWN AND SPEND MONEY...
HA! HA!
WHATEVER YOU SAY, GAN!
WHEN IS YOUR BEDTIME, FI?
WHENEVER.
GREAT!
IF YOU STAY UP MAYBE YOU'LL BE LUCKY!
AND WHAT?
SEE GLOWING INSECTS FLYING ABOUT?
HA! HA!
HOW DID FAY EVER END UP MARRYING YOU?

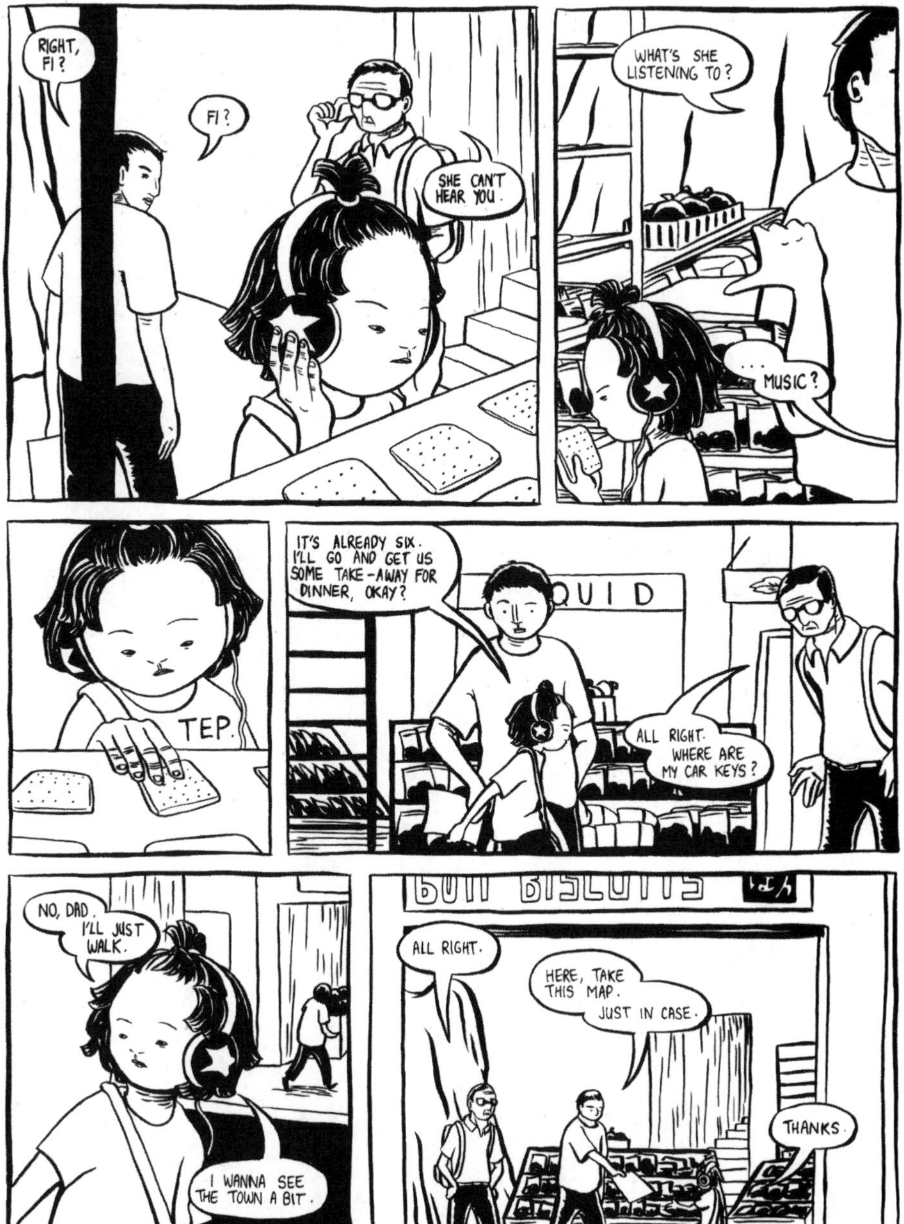
RIGHT, FI?
FI?
SHE CAN'T HEAR YOU.
WHAT'S SHE LISTENING TO?
...MUSIC?
TEP
IT'S ALREADY SIX. I'LL GO AND GET US SOME TAKE-AWAY FOR DINNER, OKAY?
QUID
ALL RIGHT. WHERE ARE MY CAR KEYS?
NO, DAD. I'LL JUST WALK.
I WANNA SEE THE TOWN A BIT.
ALL RIGHT.
HERE, TAKE THIS MAP.
JUST IN CASE.
THANKS.

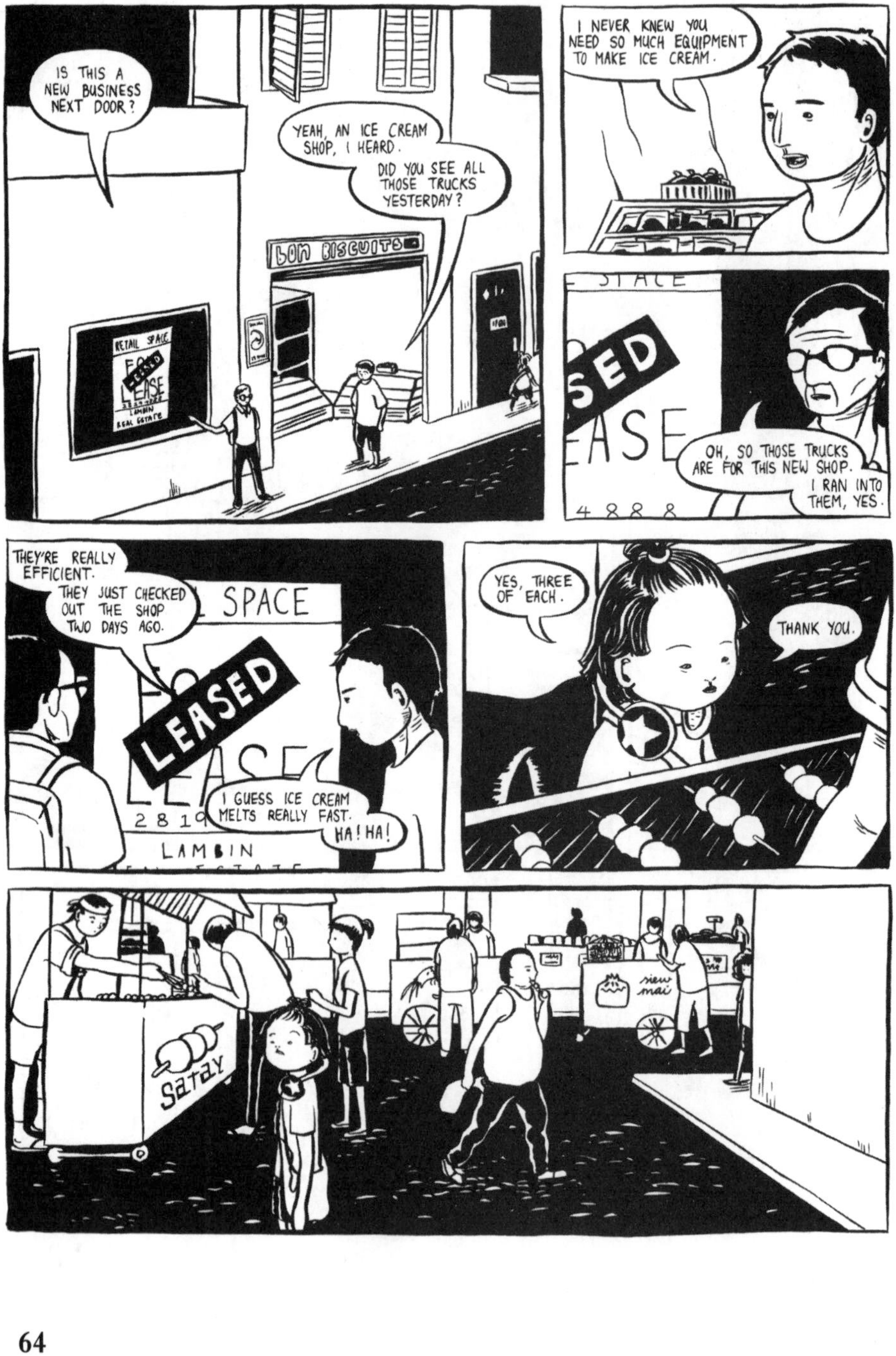
IS THIS A NEW BUSINESS NEXT DOOR?
YEAH, AN ICE CREAM SHOP, I HEARD.
DID YOU SEE ALL THOSE TRUCKS YESTERDAY?
BON BISCUITS
RETAIL SPACE
LEASED
LAMBIN REAL ESTATE
I NEVER KNEW YOU NEED SO MUCH EQUIPMENT TO MAKE ICE CREAM.
SED
EASE
OH, SO THOSE TRUCKS ARE FOR THIS NEW SHOP.
I RAN INTO THEM, YES.
THEY'RE REALLY EFFICIENT.
THEY JUST CHECKED OUT THE SHOP TWO DAYS AGO.
SPACE
LEASED
I GUESS ICE CREAM MELTS REALLY FAST.
HA! HA!
LAMBIN
YES, THREE OF EACH.
THANK YOU.
siew mai
Satay

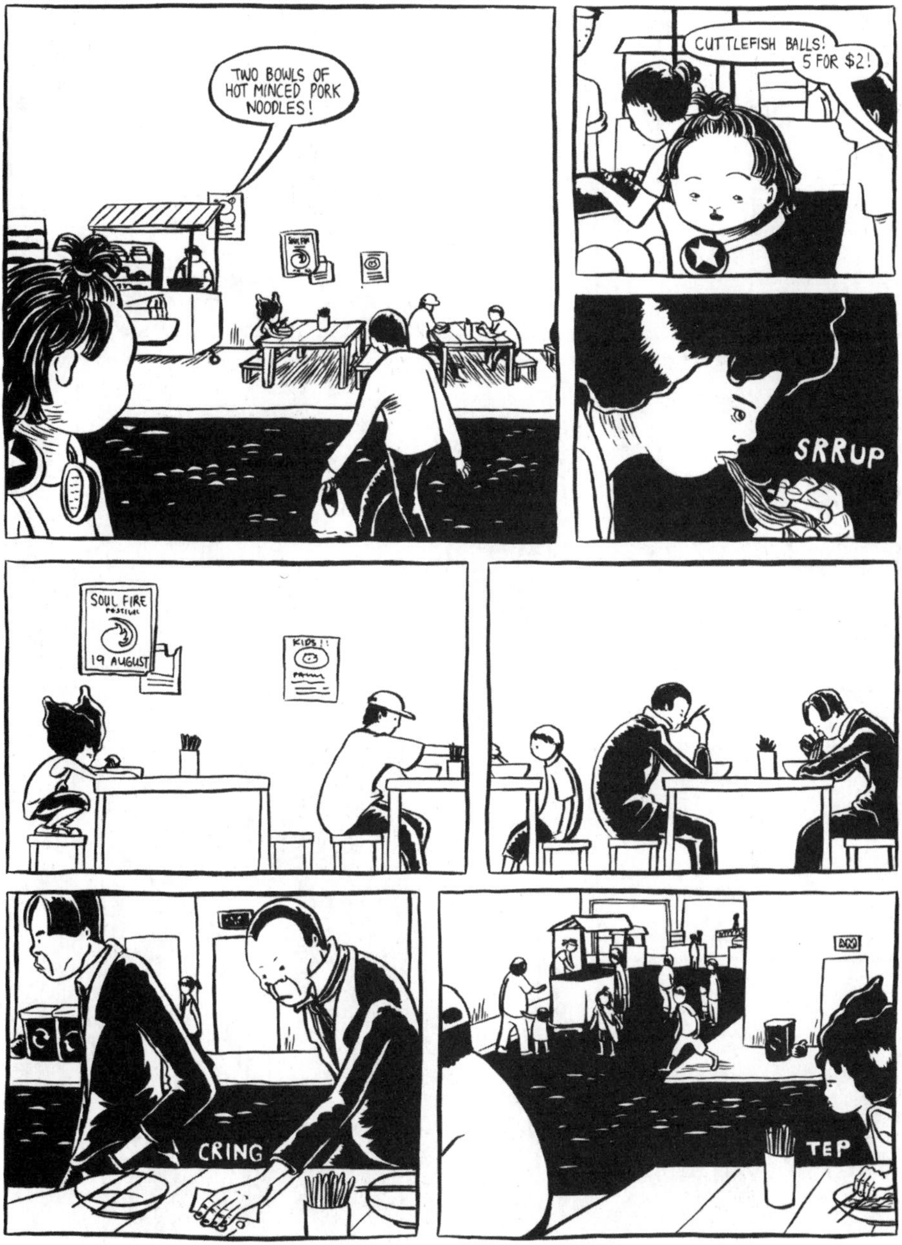
TWO BOWLS OF HOT MINCED PORK NOODLES!
SOUL FIRE
CUTTLEFISH BALLS! 5 FOR $2!
SRRUP
SOUL FIRE
19 AUGUST
KIDS!!
CRING
TEP

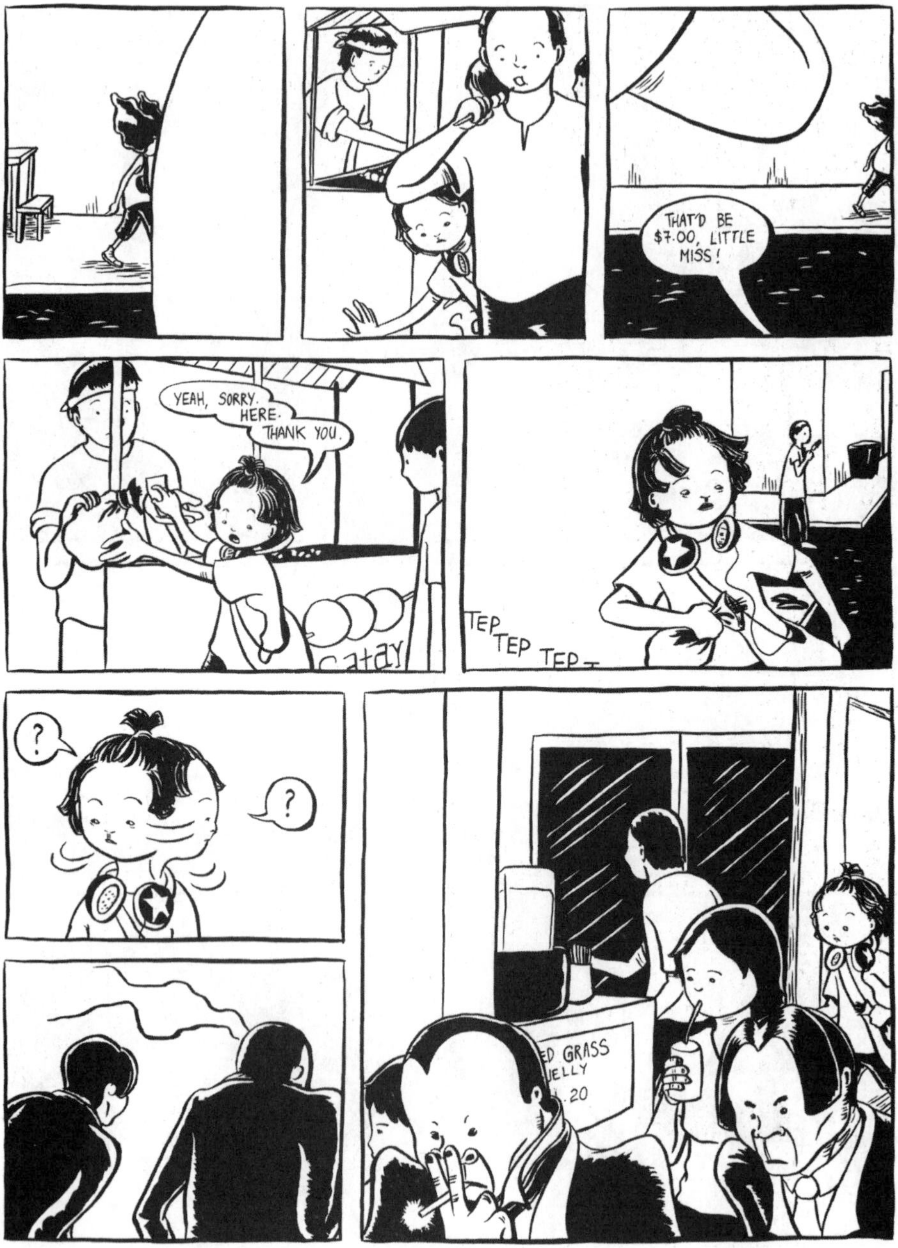
THAT'D BE $7.00, LITTLE MISS!
YEAH, SORRY.
HERE.
THANK YOU.
catay
TEP TEP TEP
?
?
ED GRASS
JELLY
.20

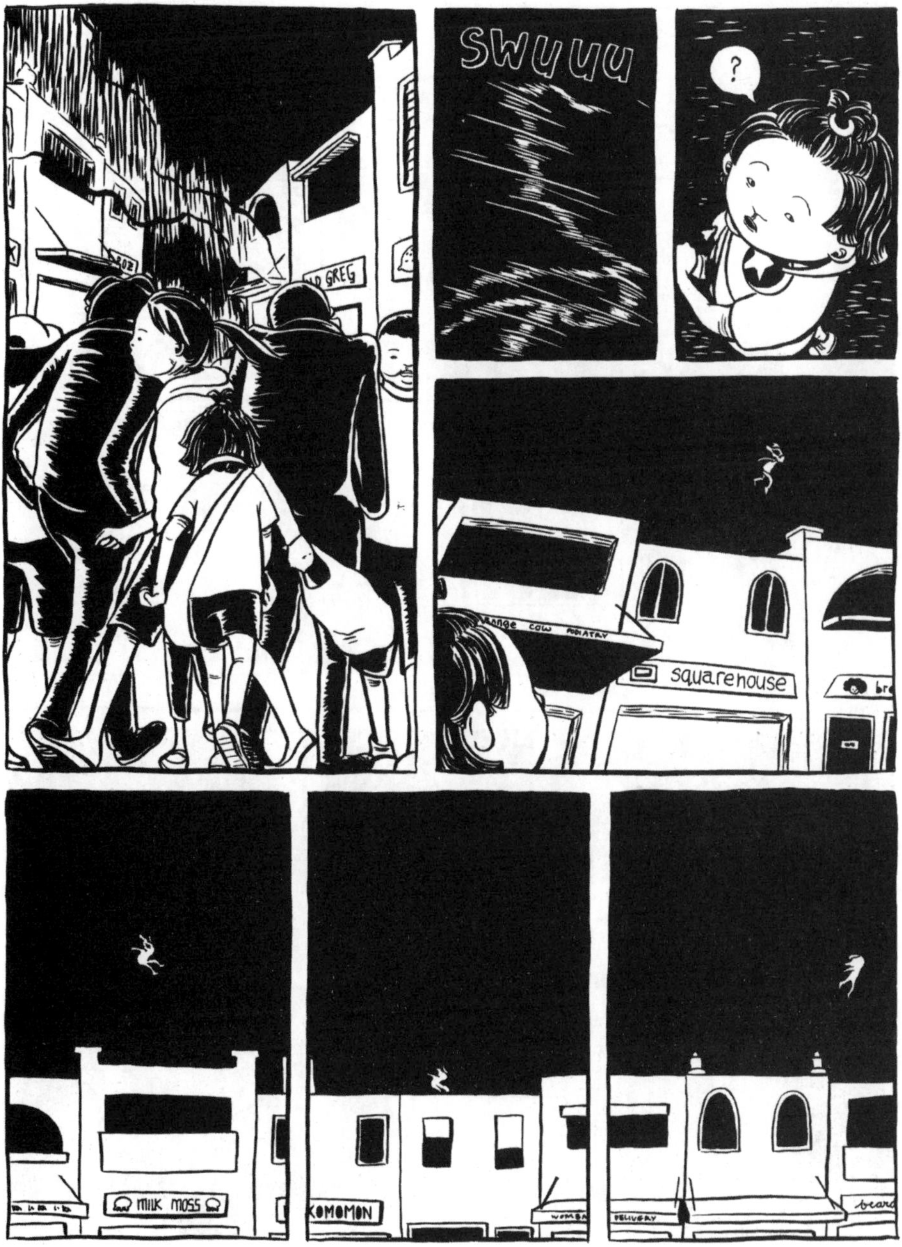
SWUUU
?
squarehouse
MILK MOSS
KOMOMON

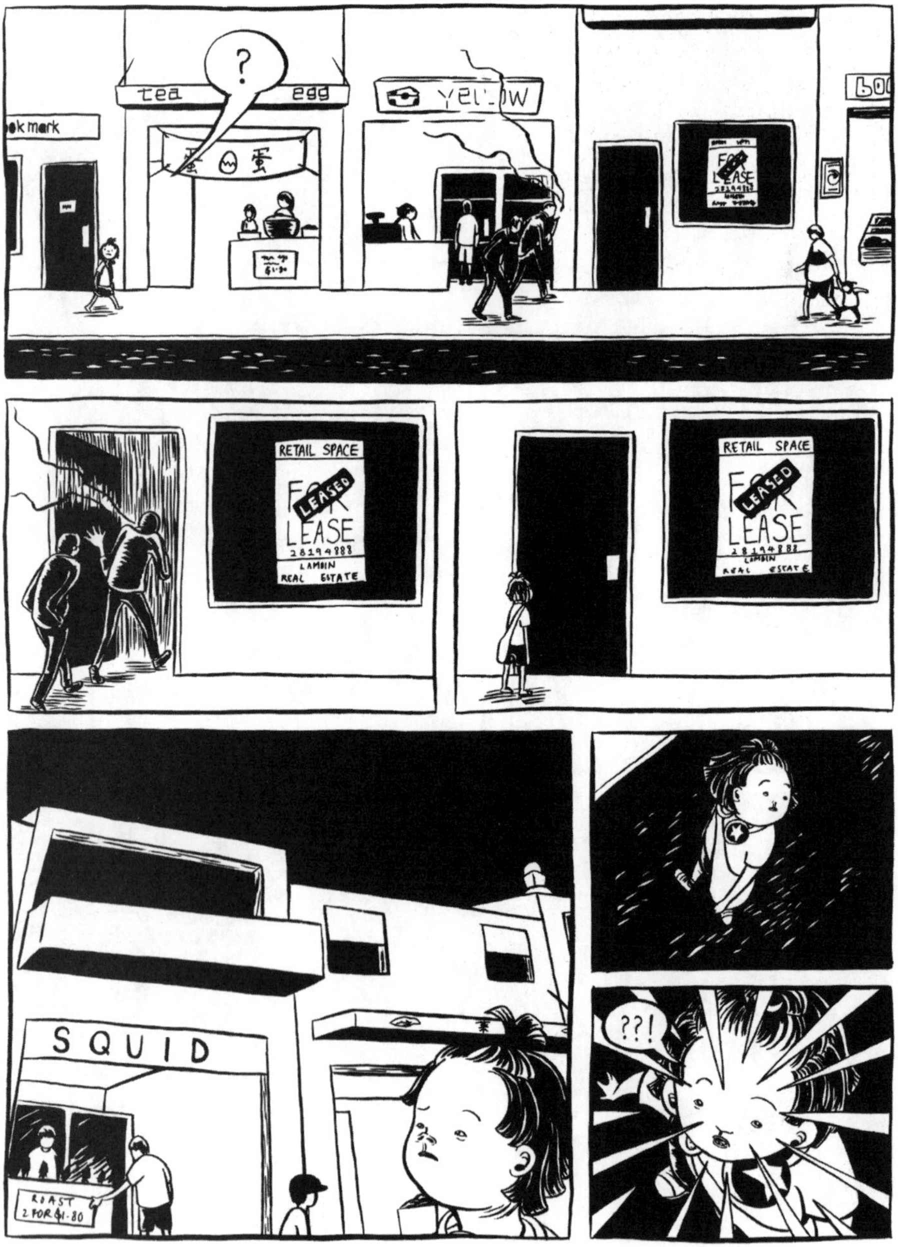

?
tea
egg
蛋 蛋
RETAIL SPACE
FOR LEASE
LEASED
28194888
LAMBIN
REAL ESTATE
RETAIL SPACE
FOR LEASE
LEASED
28194888
LAMBIN
REAL ESTATE
SQUID
ROAST
2 FOR $1.80
??!

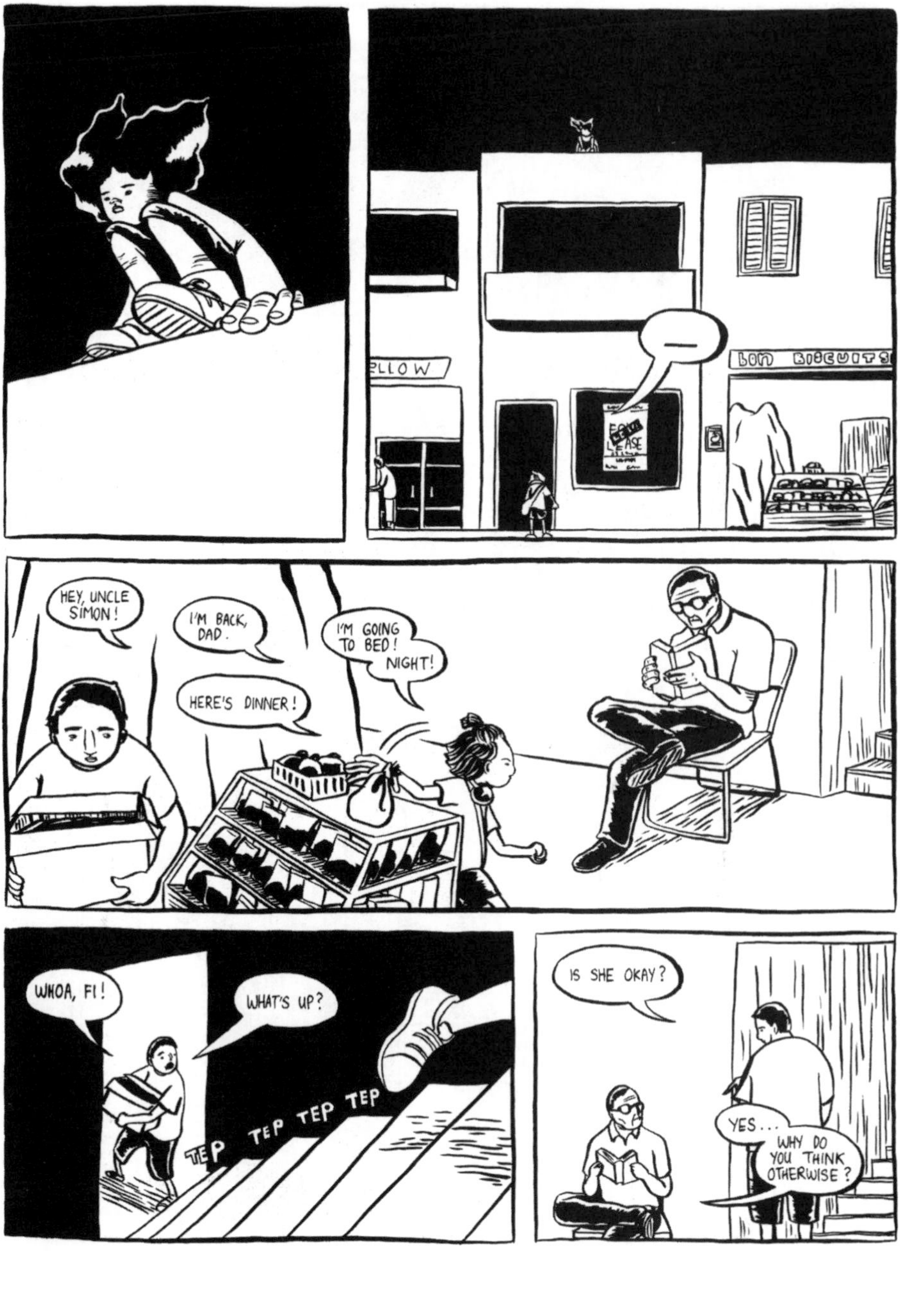

BON BISCUITS
—
HEY, UNCLE SIMON!
I'M BACK, DAD.
HERE'S DINNER!
I'M GOING TO BED! NIGHT!
WHOA, FI!
WHAT'S UP?
TEP TEP TEP TEP
IS SHE OKAY?
YES...
WHY DO YOU THINK OTHERWISE?

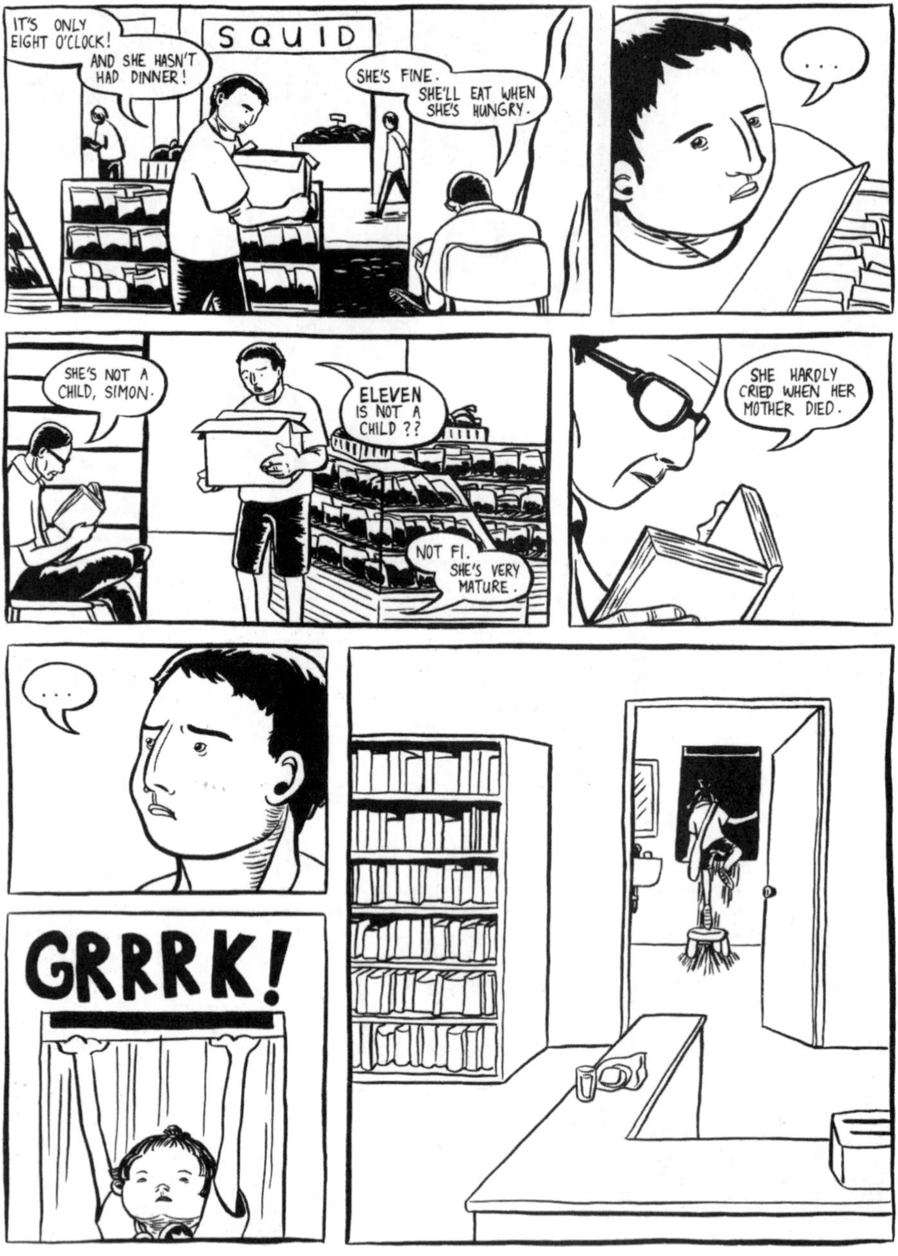
IT'S ONLY EIGHT O'CLOCK!
AND SHE HASN'T HAD DINNER!
SQUID
SHE'S FINE.
SHE'LL EAT WHEN SHE'S HUNGRY.
. . .
SHE'S NOT A CHILD, SIMON.
ELEVEN IS NOT A CHILD ??
NOT FI. SHE'S VERY MATURE.
SHE HARDLY CRIED WHEN HER MOTHER DIED.
. . .
GRRRK!

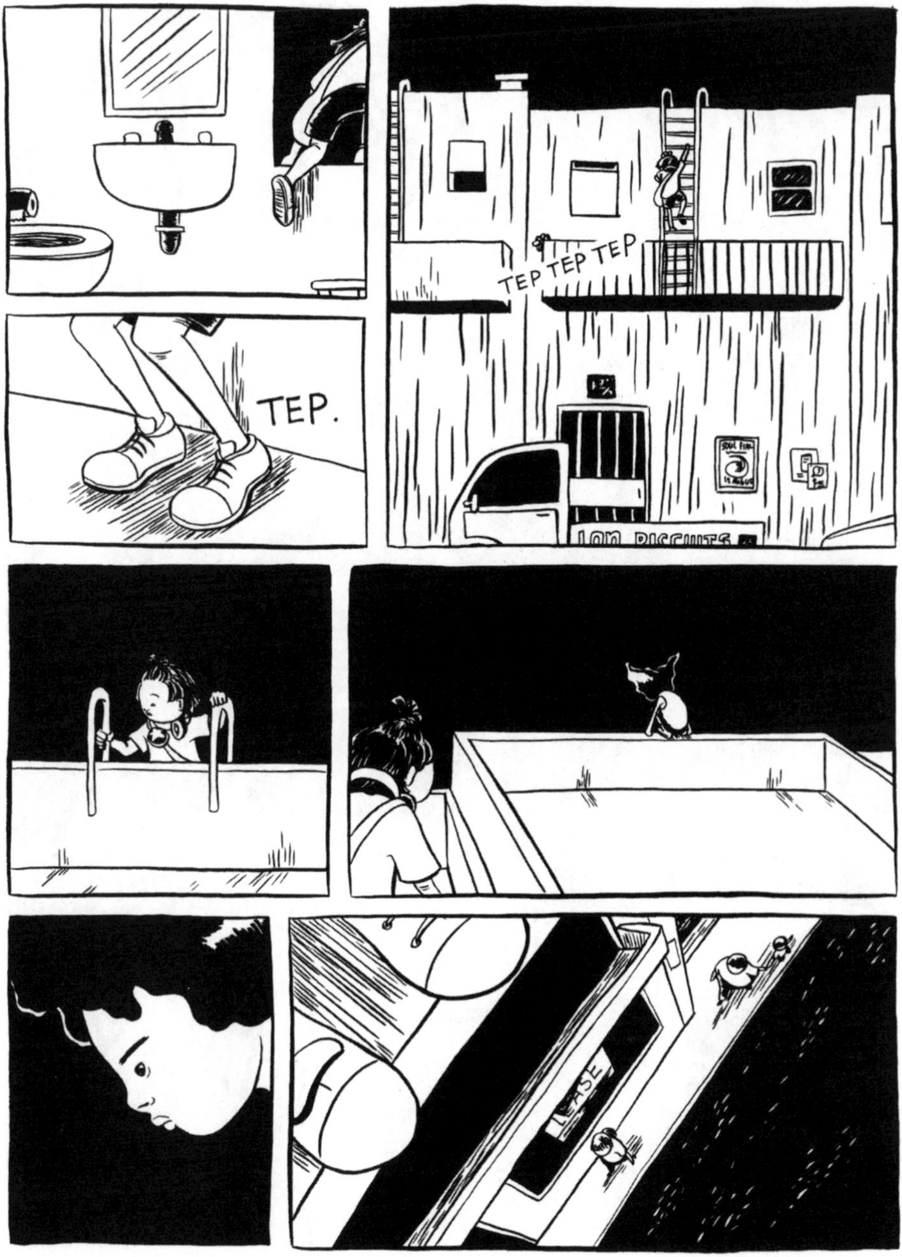
TEP.
TEP TEP TEP
LEASE

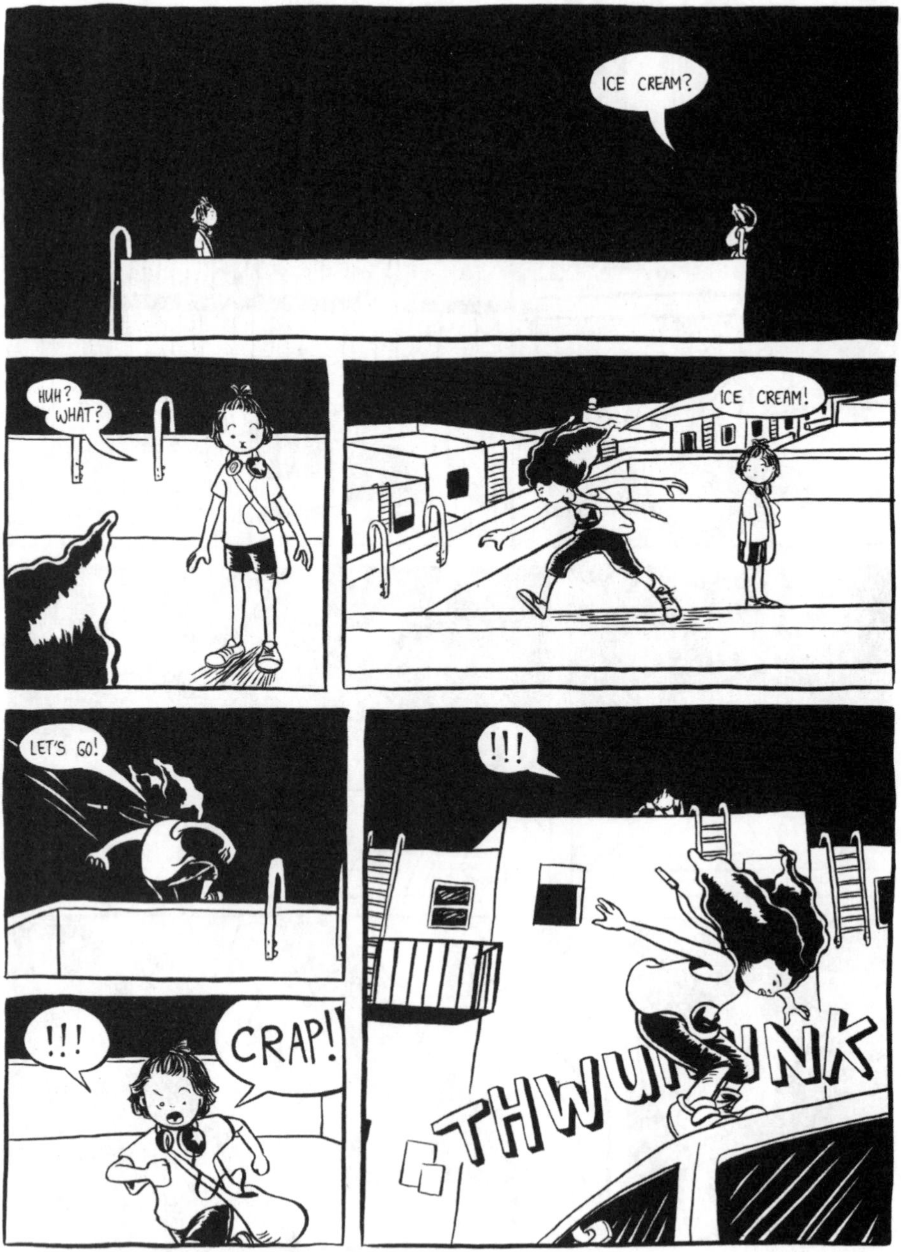
ICE CREAM?
HUH? WHAT?
ICE CREAM!
LET'S GO!
!!!
!!!
CRAP!
THWUNK

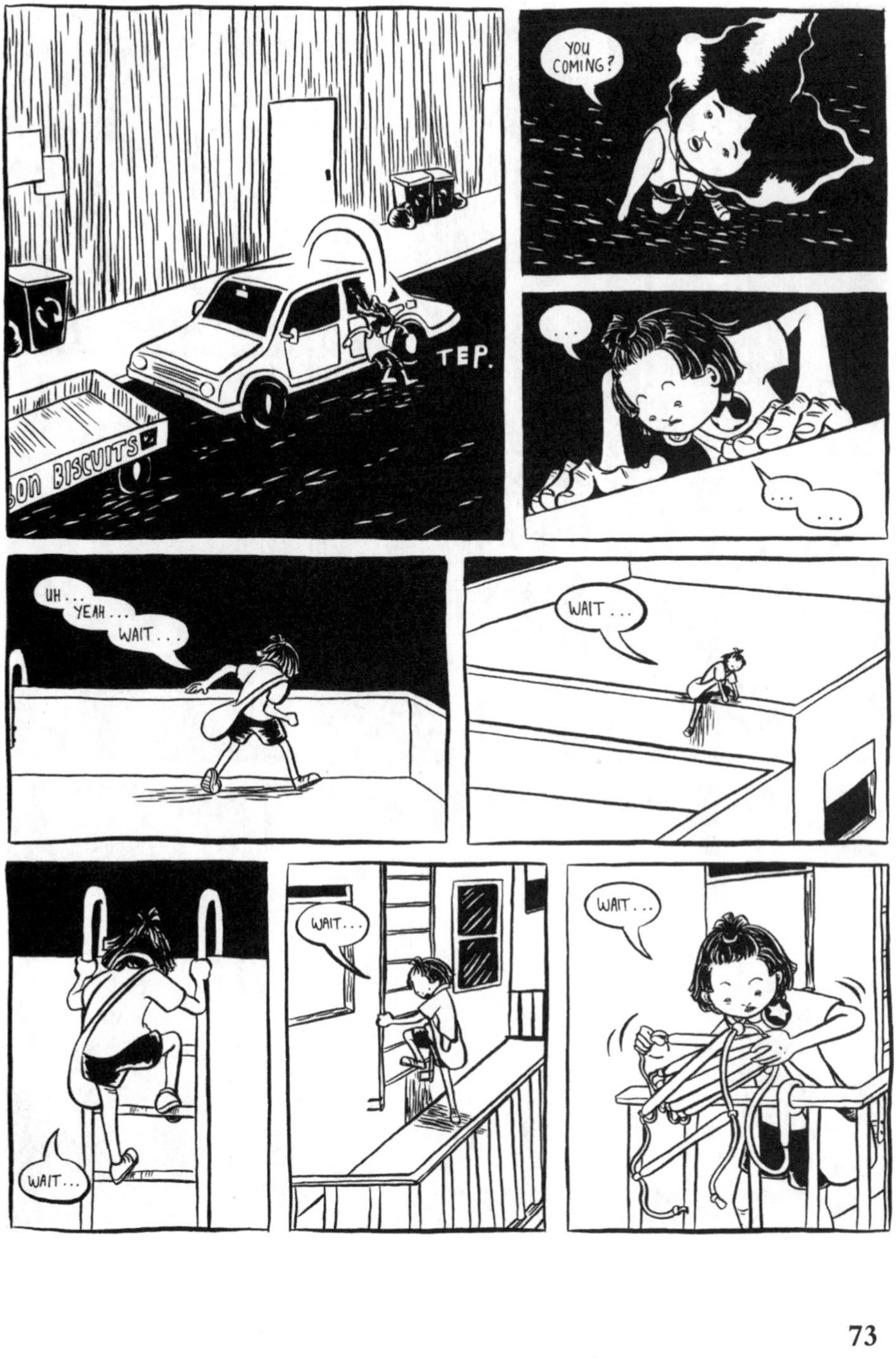
TEP.
ON BISCUITS
YOU COMING?
...
...
...
UH...
YEAH...
WAIT...
WAIT...
WAIT...
WAIT...
WAIT...

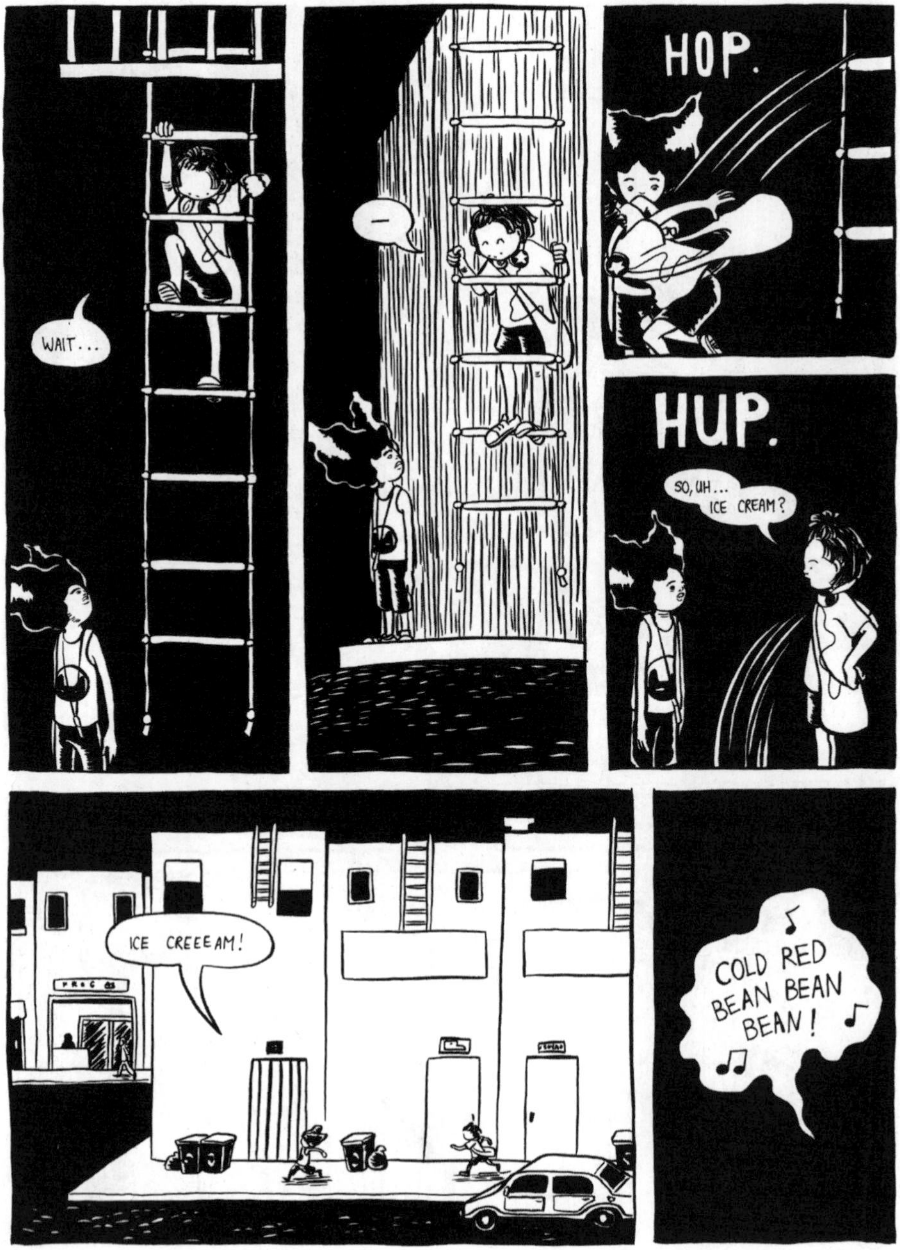

WAIT...
–
HOP.
HUP.
SO, UH... ICE CREAM?
ICE CREEEAM!
COLD RED BEAN BEAN BEAN!

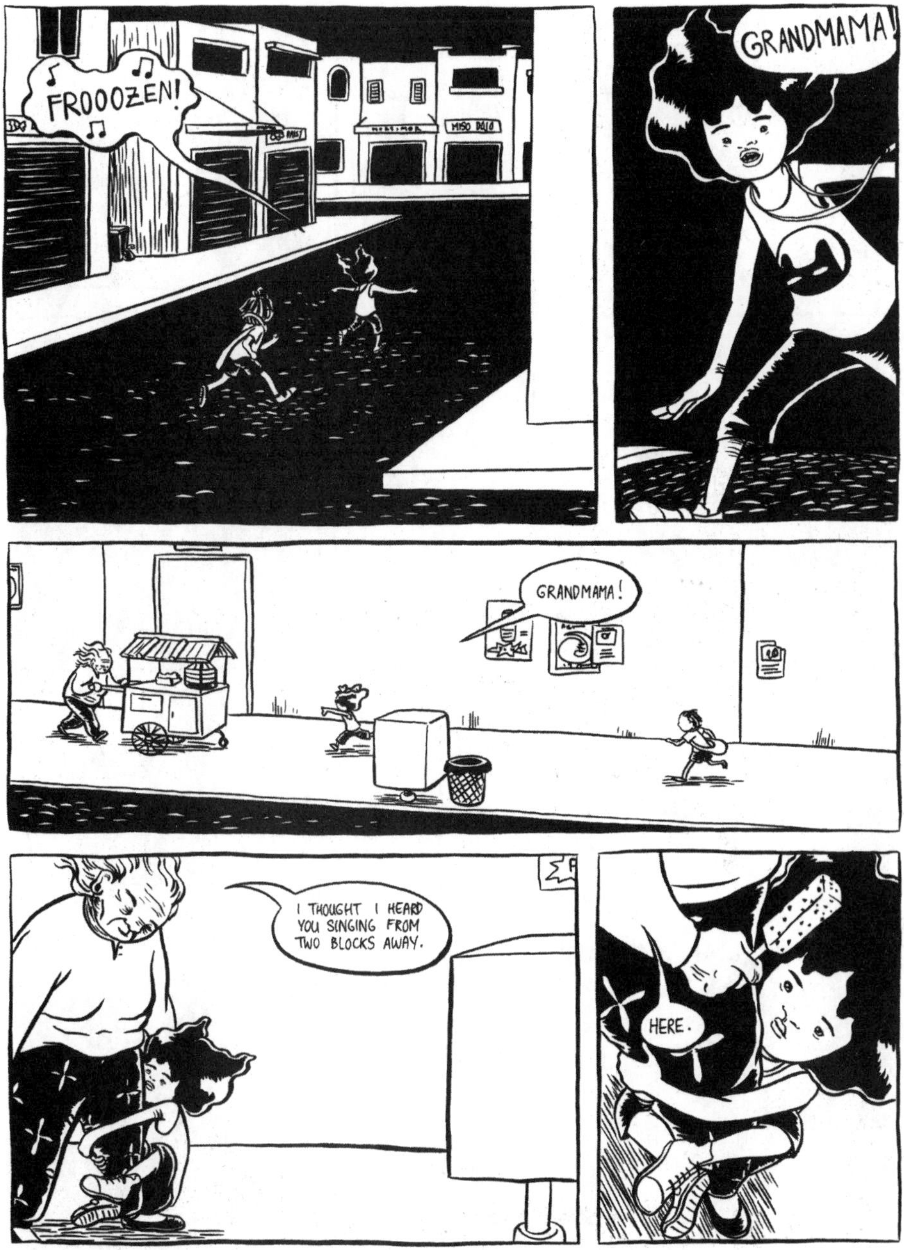
FROOOZEN!
GRANDMAMA!
GRANDMAMA!
I THOUGHT I HEARD YOU SINGING FROM TWO BLOCKS AWAY.
HERE.

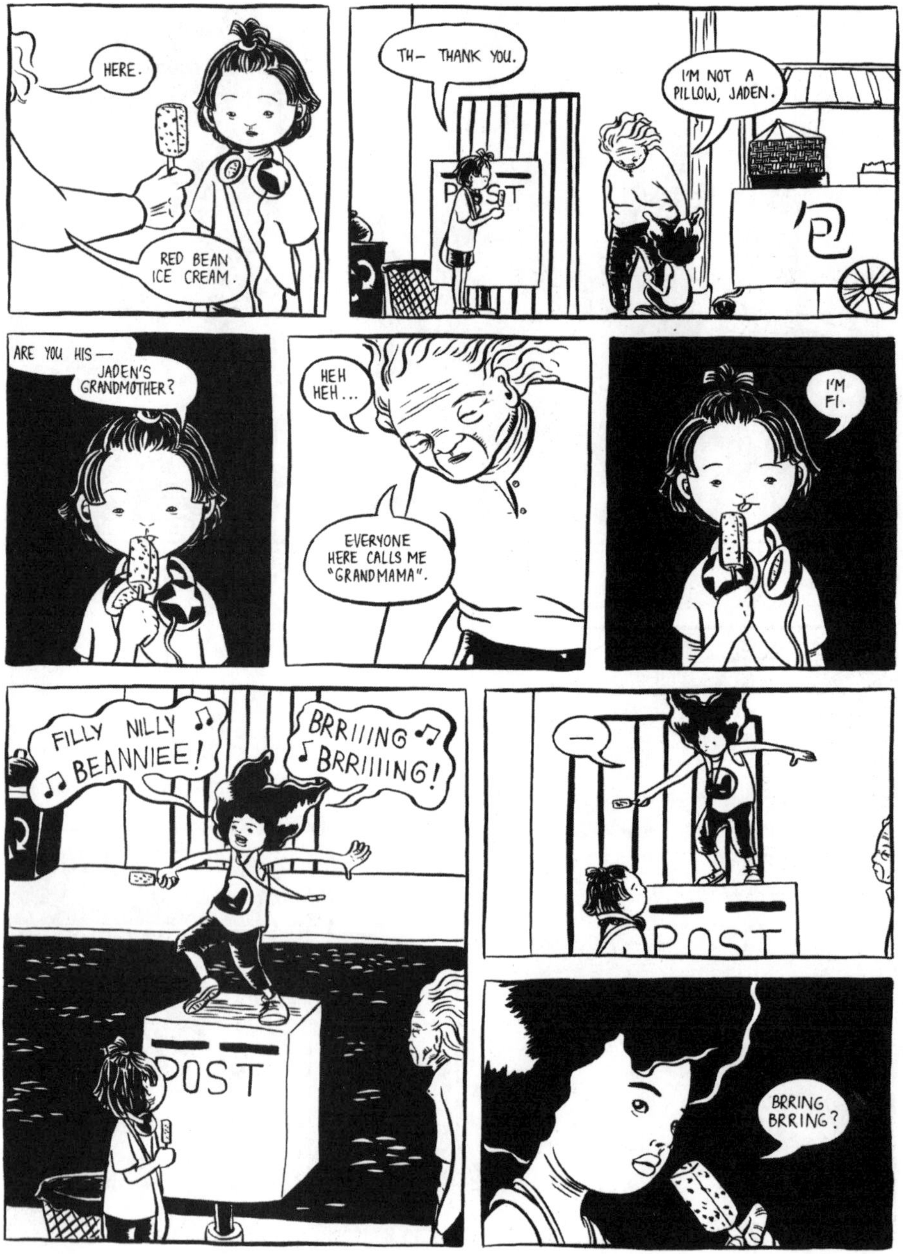
HERE.
RED BEAN ICE CREAM.
TH– THANK YOU.
I'M NOT A PILLOW, JADEN.
包
POST
ARE YOU HIS — JADEN'S GRANDMOTHER?
HEH HEH...
EVERYONE HERE CALLS ME "GRANDMAMA".
I'M FI.
FILLY NILLY ♫ ♫ BEANNIEE!
BRRIIING ♫ ♫ BRRIIIING!
POST
—
POST
BRRING BRRING?

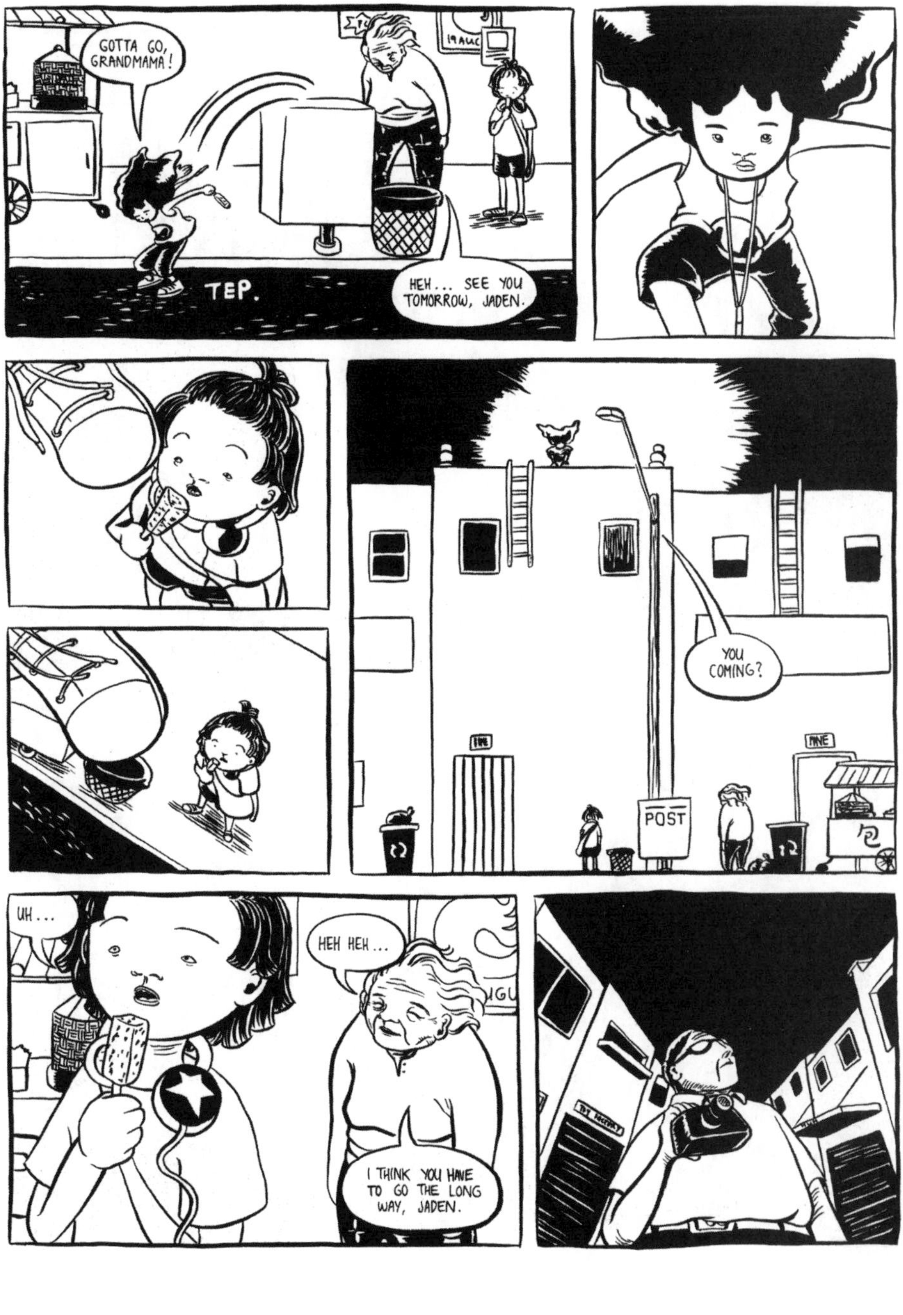
GOTTA GO, GRANDMAMA!
TEP.
HEH... SEE YOU TOMORROW, JADEN.
YOU COMING?
POST
UH...
HEH HEH...
I THINK YOU HAVE TO GO THE LONG WAY, JADEN.

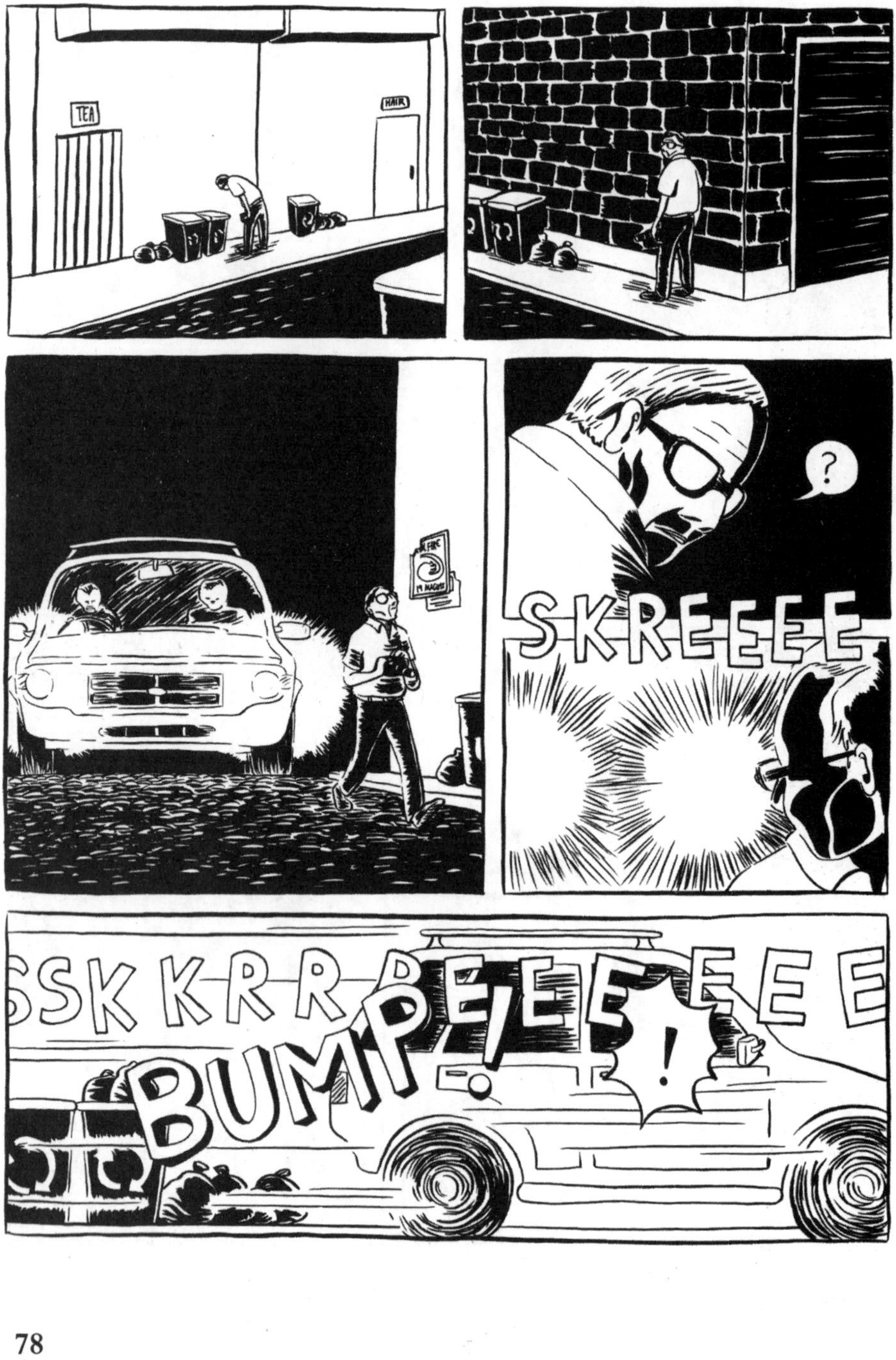
TEA
HAIR
?
SKREEEE
SSKKRREEEEEE
BUMP!
!

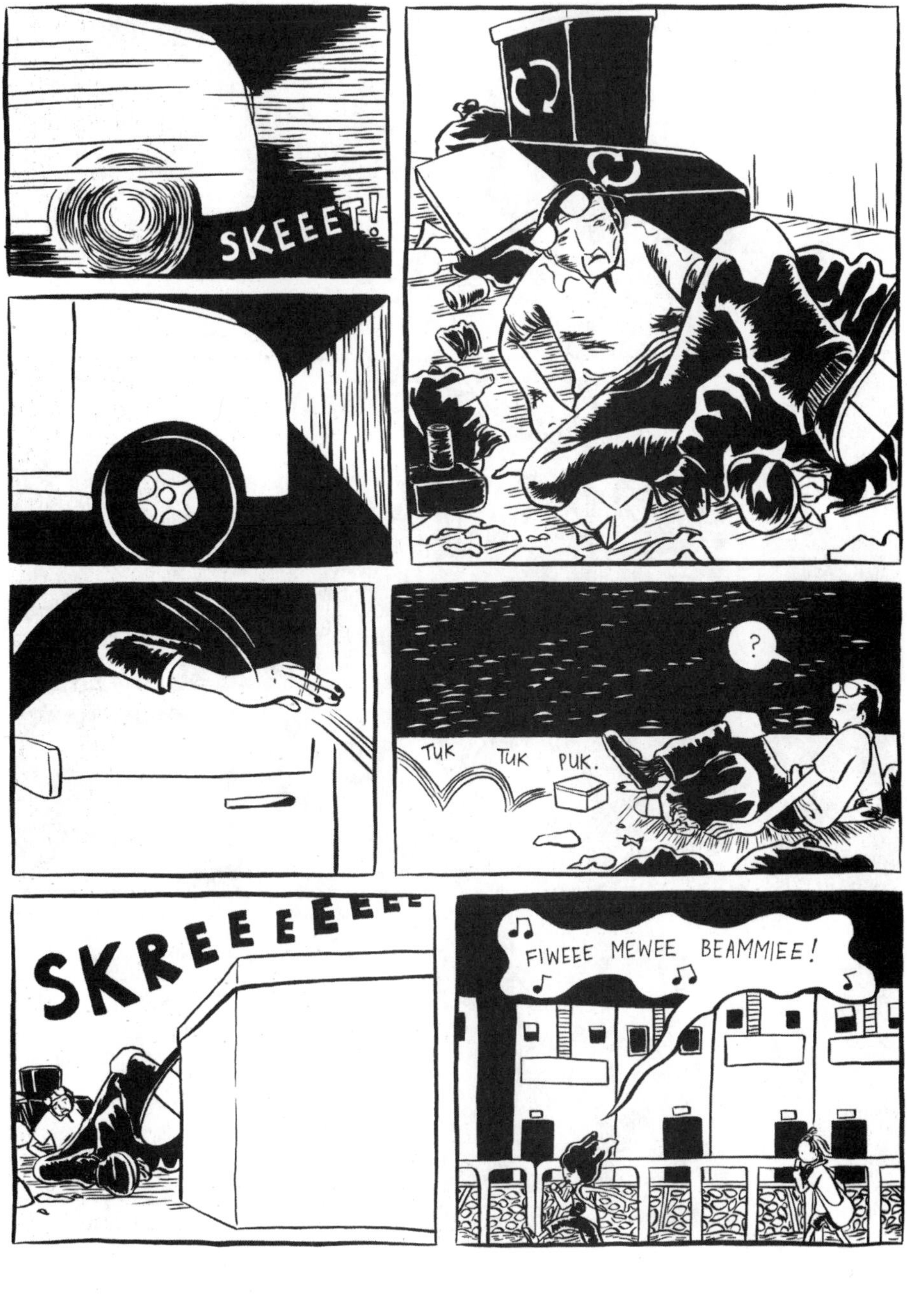
SKEEET!
?
TUK
TUK
PUK.
SKREEEEEEE
FIWEEE MEWEE BEAMMIEE!

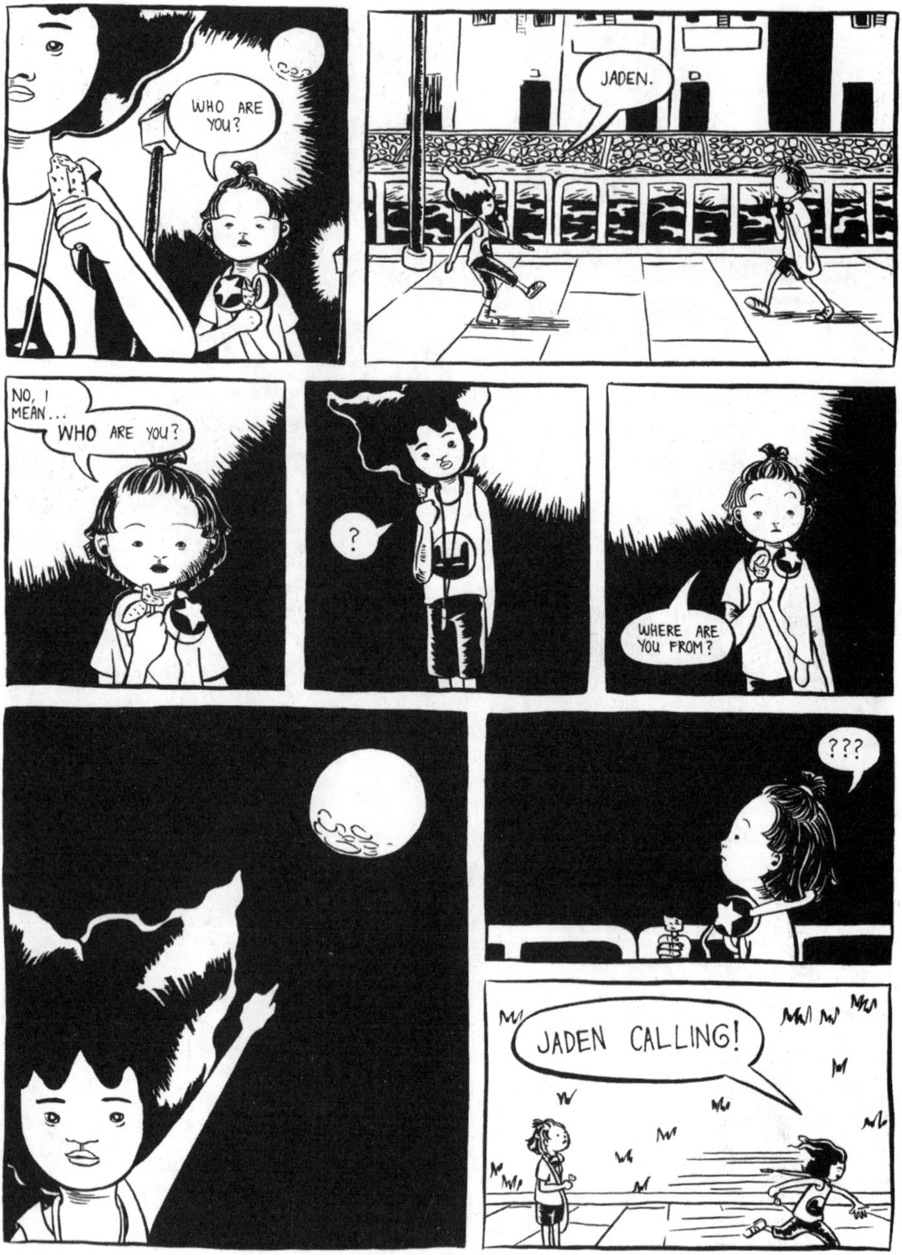
WHO ARE YOU?
JADEN.
NO, I MEAN... WHO ARE YOU?
?
WHERE ARE YOU FROM?
???
JADEN CALLING!

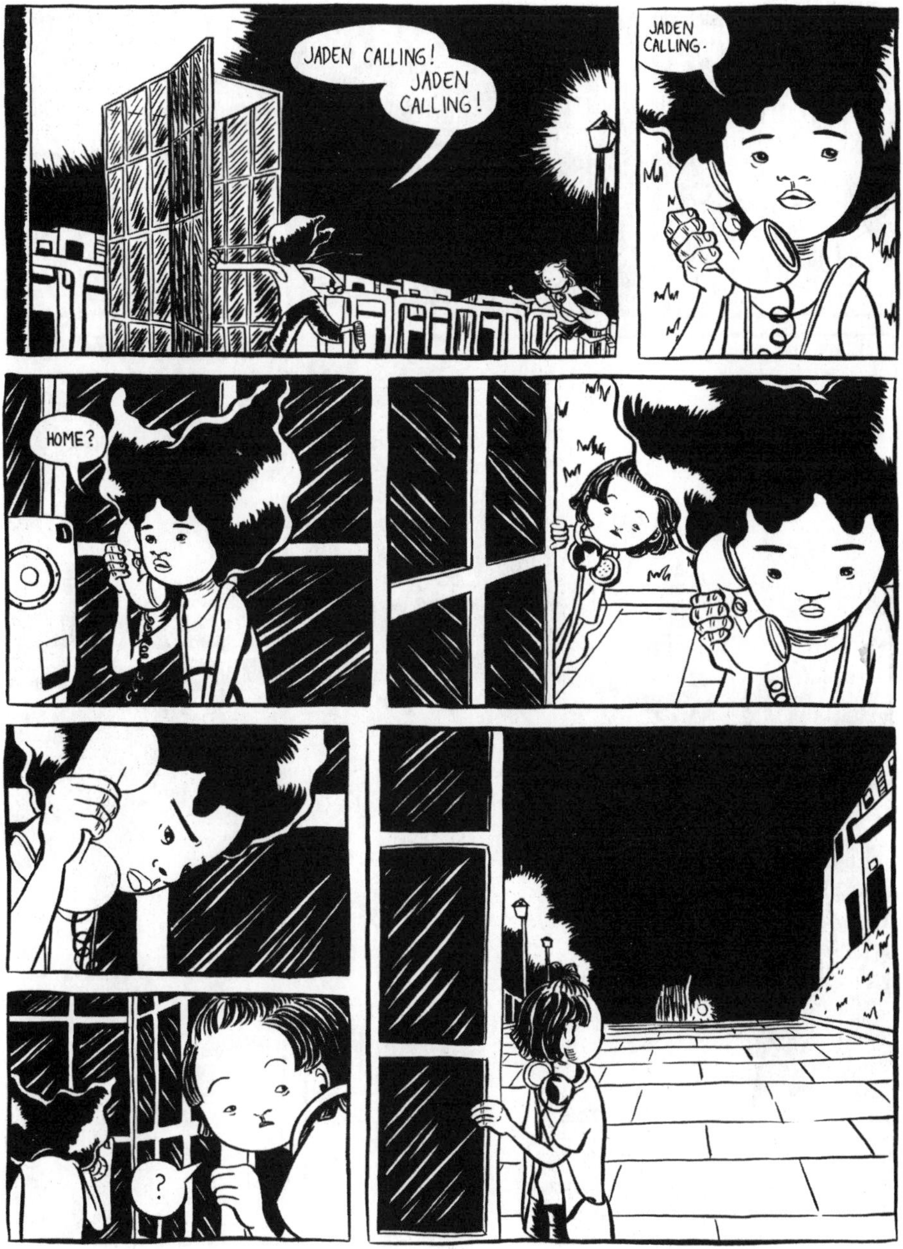
JADEN CALLING!
JADEN CALLING!
JADEN CALLING.
HOME?
?

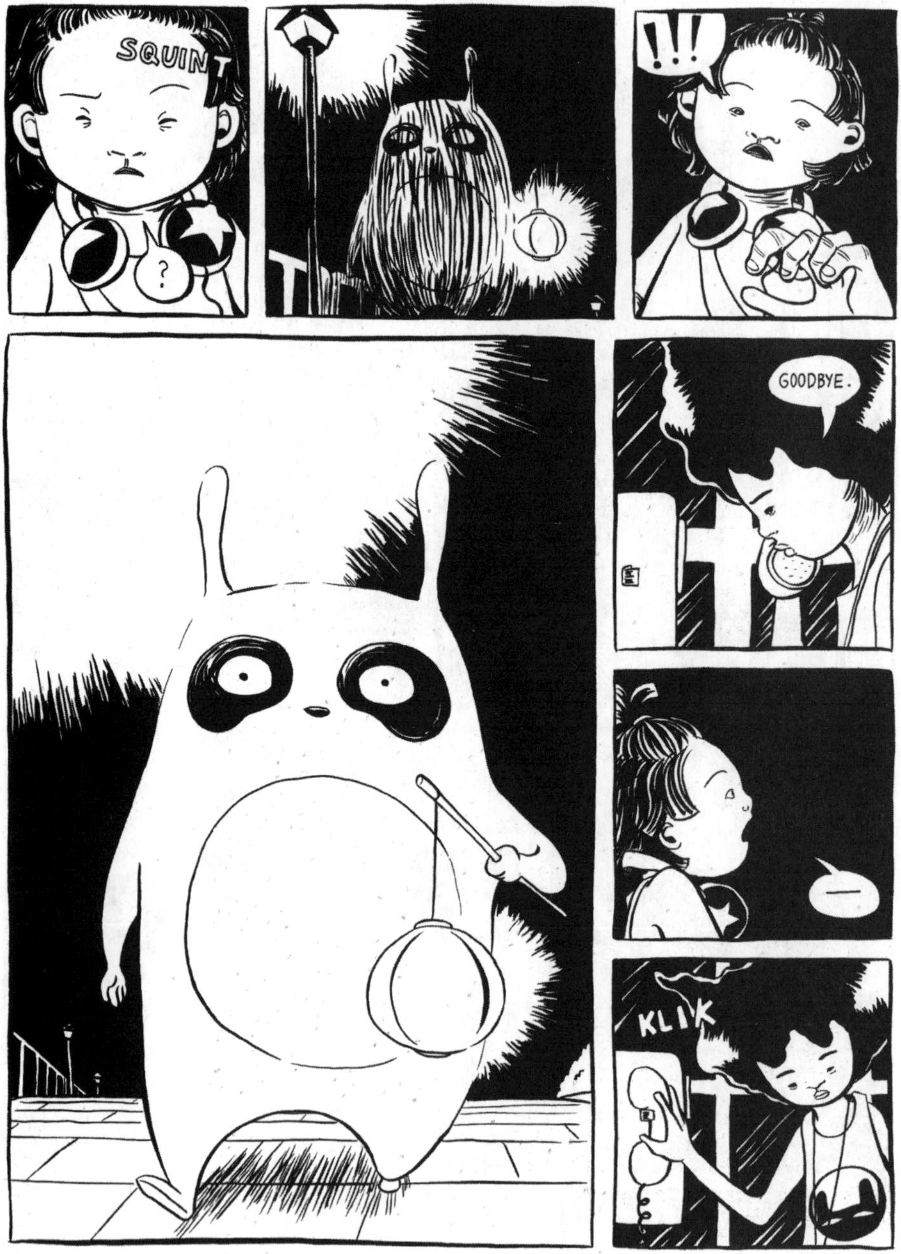
SQUINT
?
!!!
GOODBYE.
—
KLIK

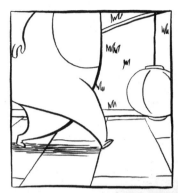

YO, JADEN!

KOO!

WASSUP?

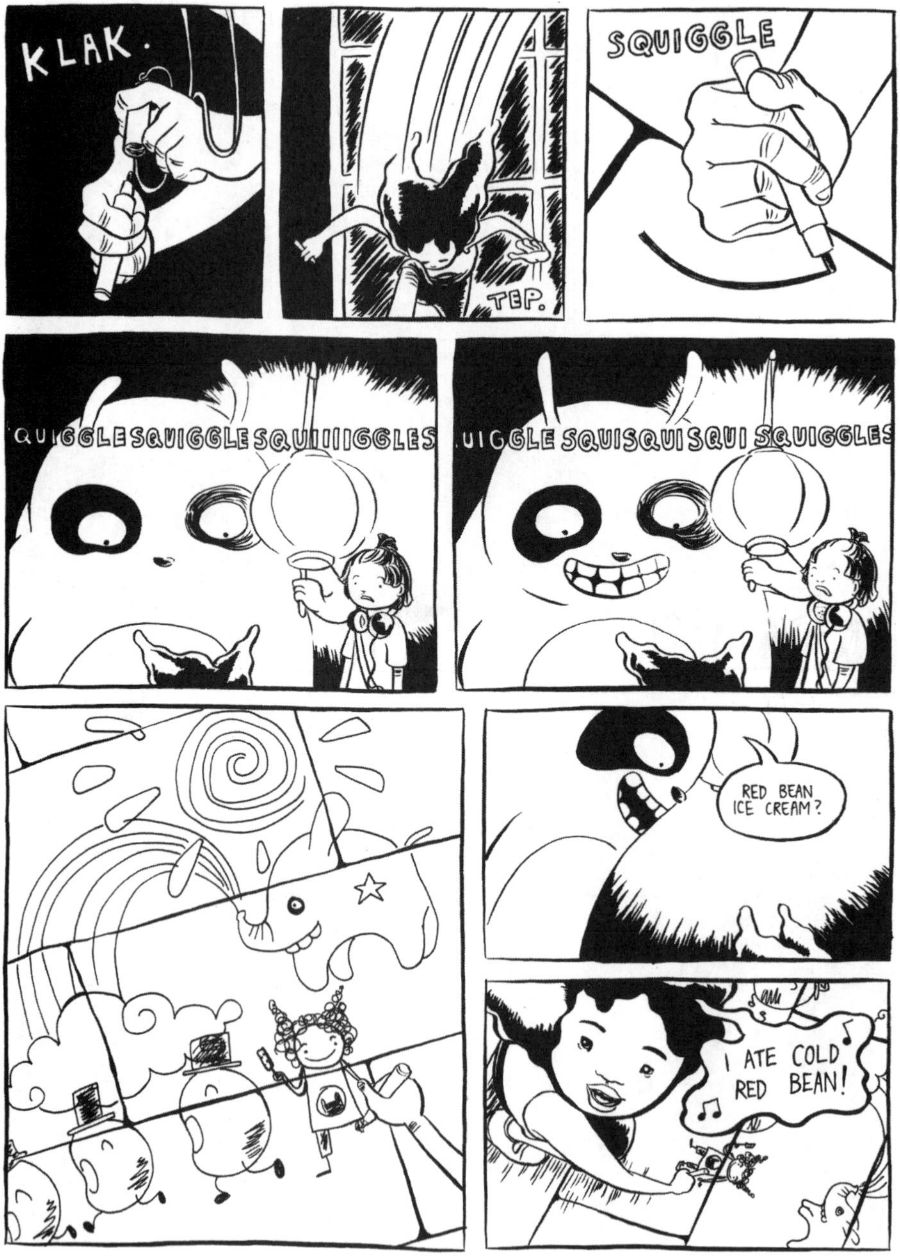
KLAK.
TEP.
SQUIGGLE
QUIGGLESQUIGGLESQUIIIIGGLES
UIGGLE SQUISQUISQUI SQUIGGLES
RED BEAN ICE CREAM?
I ATE COLD RED BEAN!

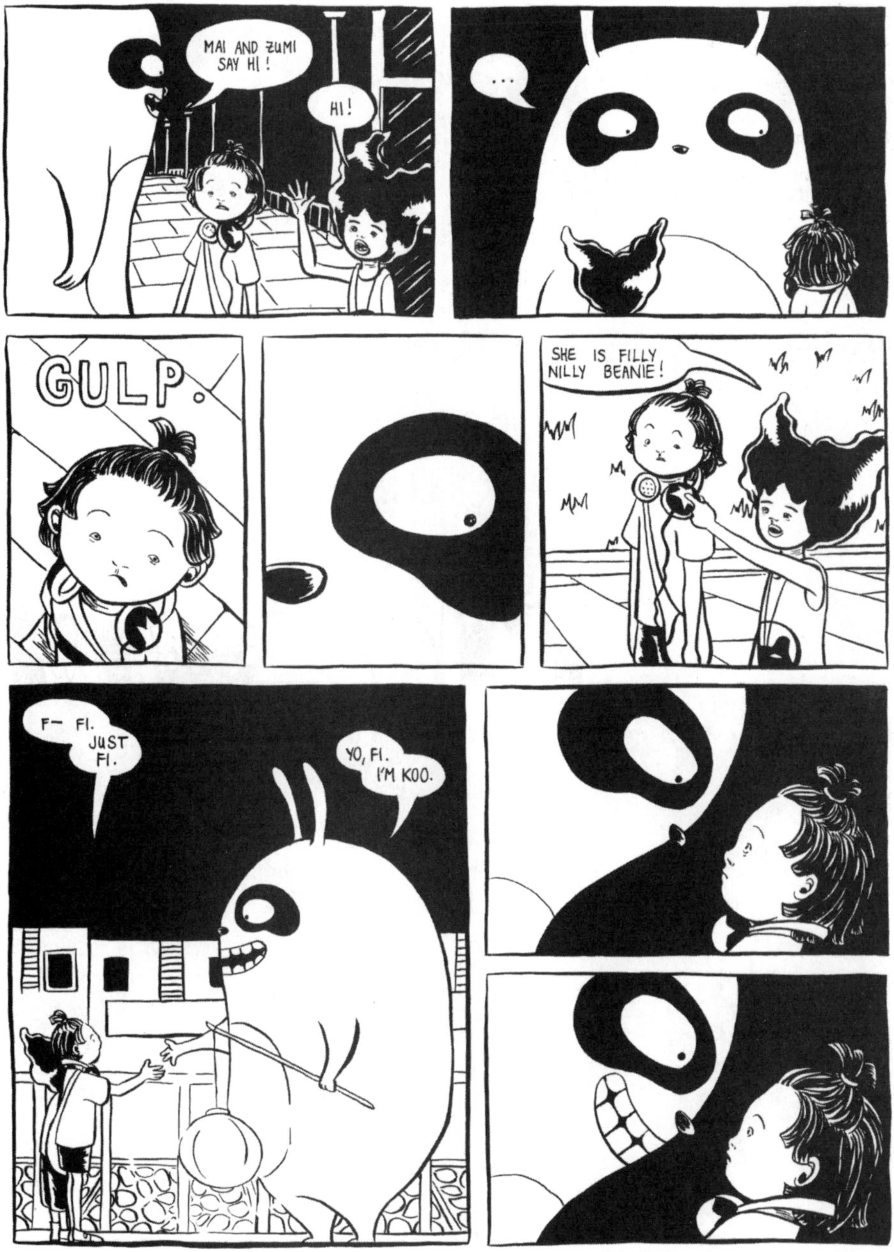
MAI AND ZUMI SAY HI!
HI!
...
GULP.
SHE IS FILLY NILLY BEANIE!
F— FI. JUST FI.
YO, FI. I'M KOO.

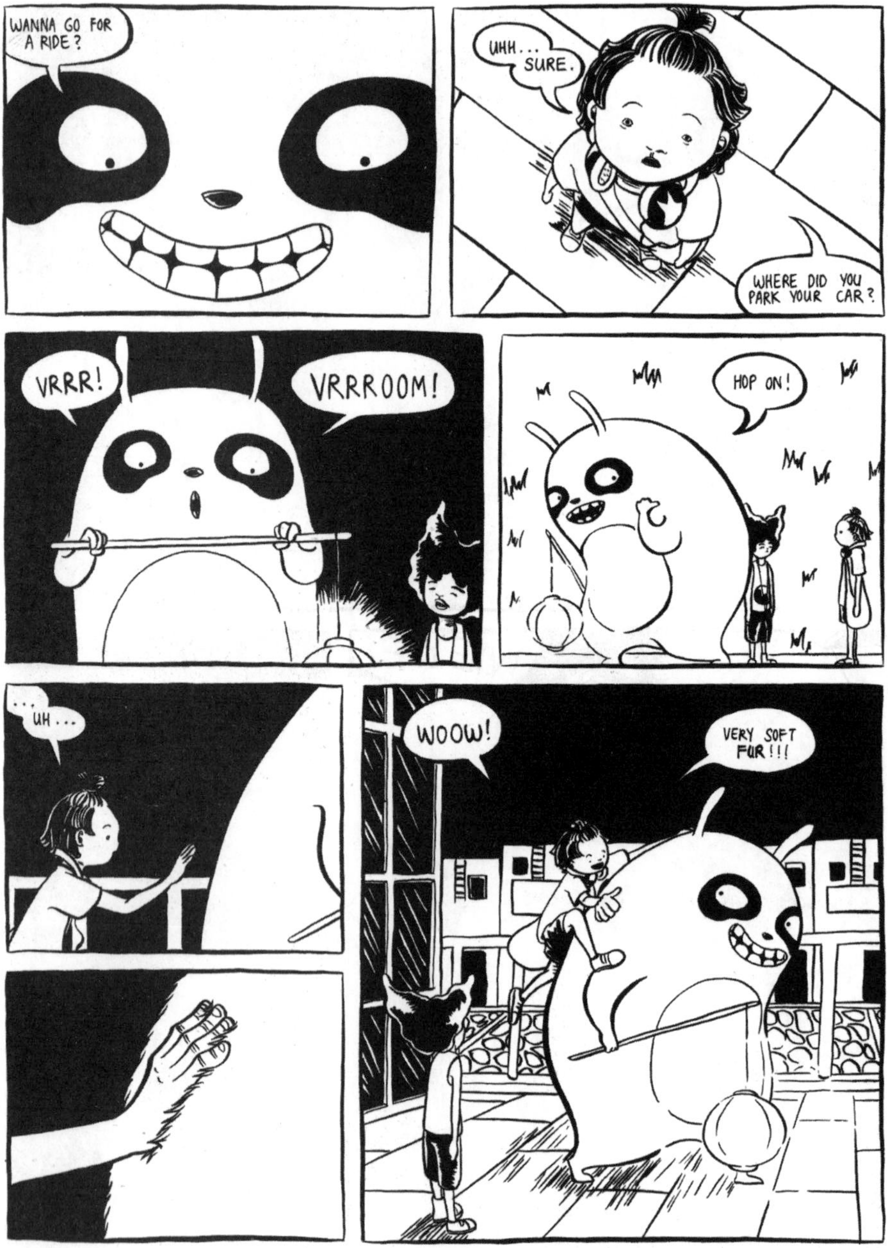
WANNA GO FOR A RIDE?
UHH... SURE.
WHERE DID YOU PARK YOUR CAR?
VRRR!
VRRROOM!
HOP ON!
...UH...
WOOW!
VERY SOFT FUR!!!

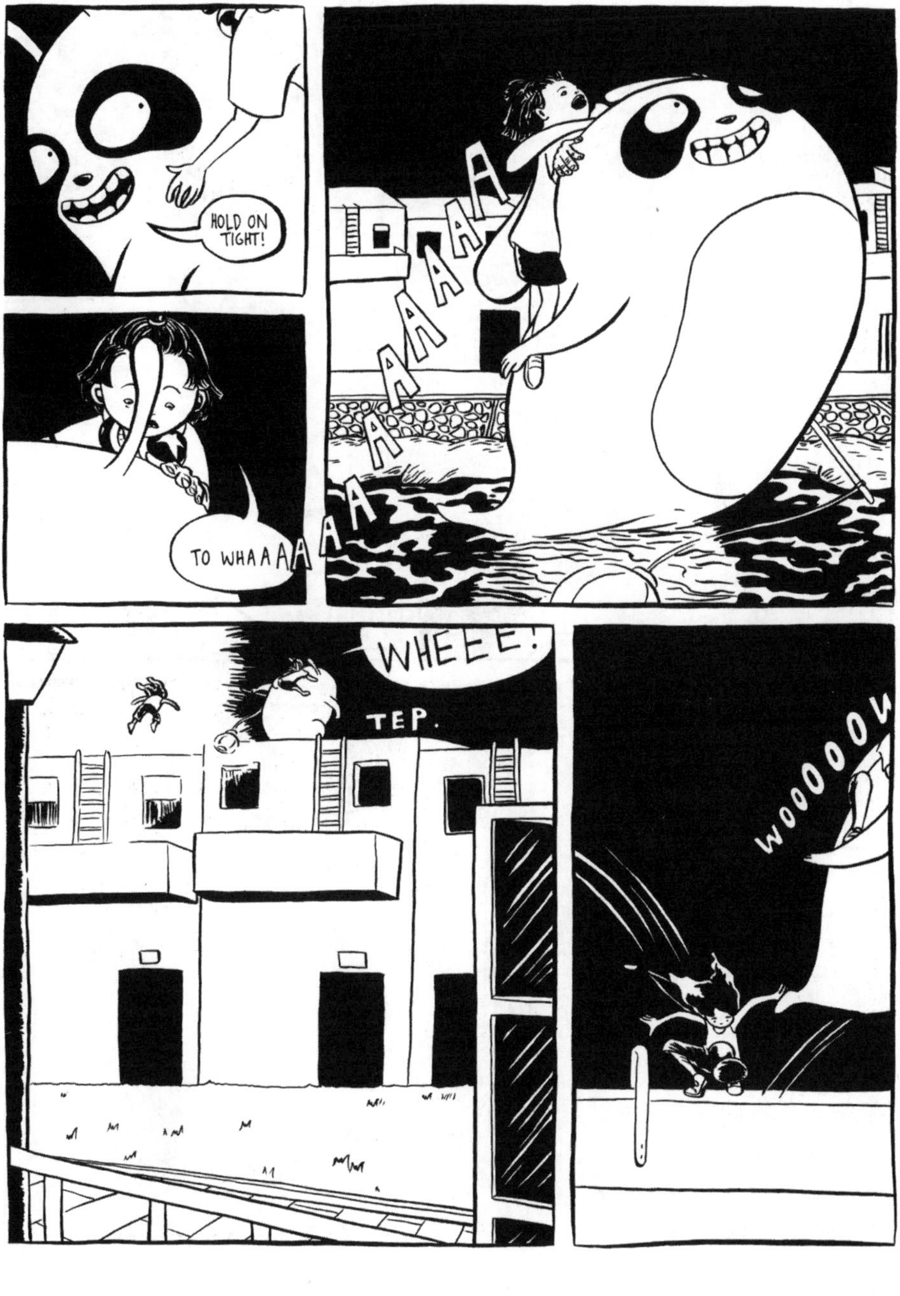
HOLD ON TIGHT!
TO WHAAAAAAAAAAAAAAAAA
WHEEE!
TEP.
WOOOOOW

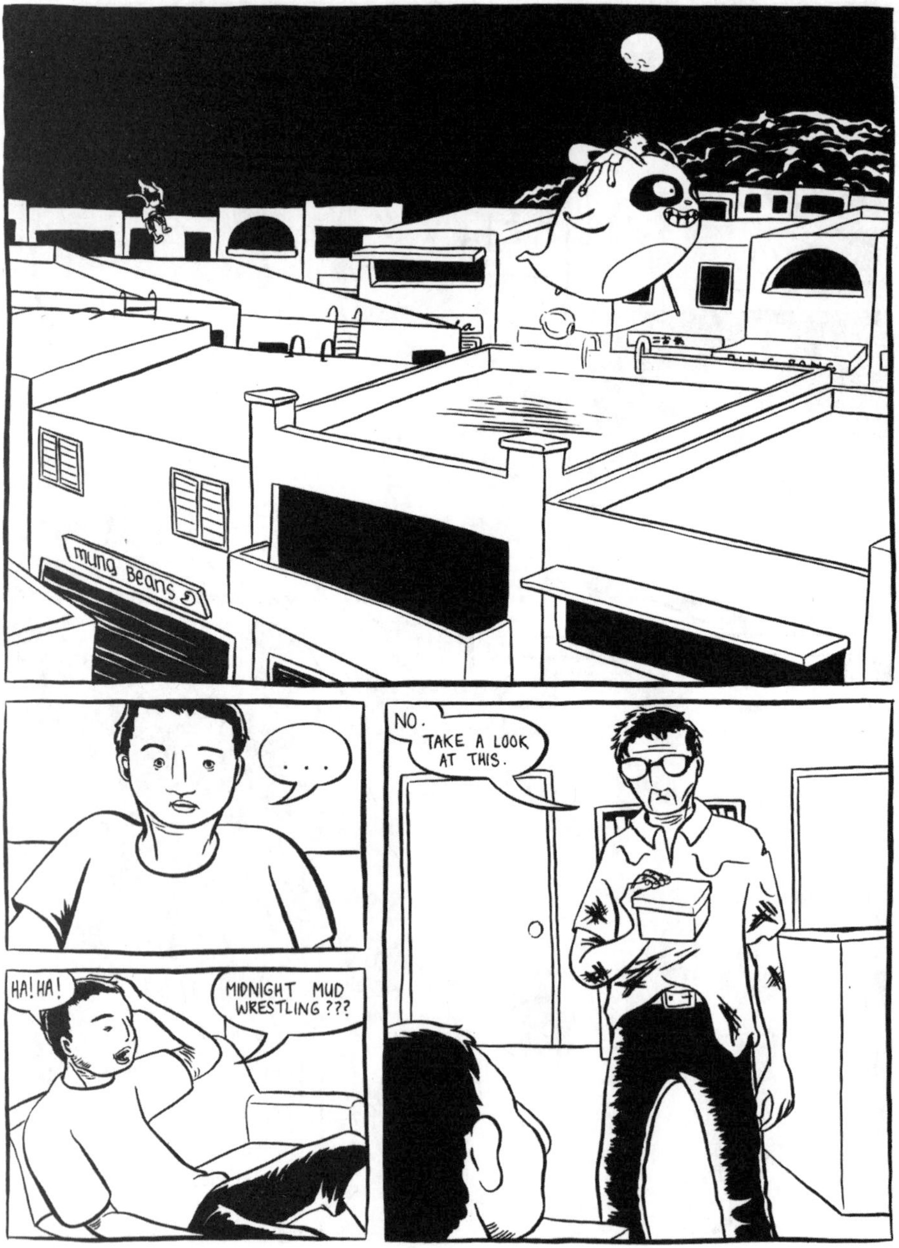
mung Beans
. . .
HA! HA!
MIDNIGHT MUD WRESTLING ???
NO.
TAKE A LOOK AT THIS.

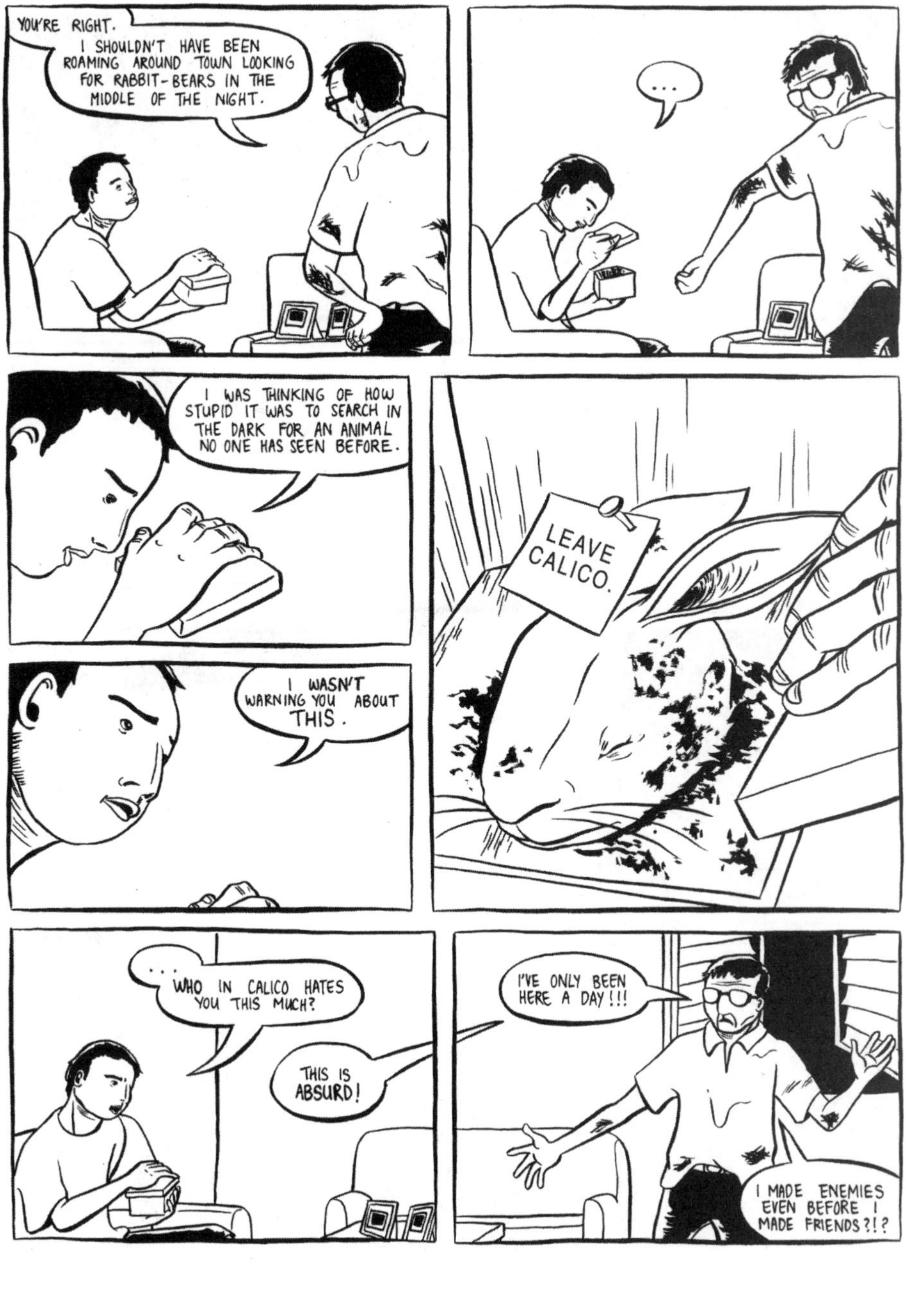
YOU'RE RIGHT.
I SHOULDN'T HAVE BEEN ROAMING AROUND TOWN LOOKING FOR RABBIT-BEARS IN THE MIDDLE OF THE NIGHT.
...
I WAS THINKING OF HOW STUPID IT WAS TO SEARCH IN THE DARK FOR AN ANIMAL NO ONE HAS SEEN BEFORE.
I WASN'T WARNING YOU ABOUT THIS.
LEAVE CALICO.
... WHO IN CALICO HATES YOU THIS MUCH?
THIS IS ABSURD!
I'VE ONLY BEEN HERE A DAY!!!
I MADE ENEMIES EVEN BEFORE I MADE FRIENDS?!?

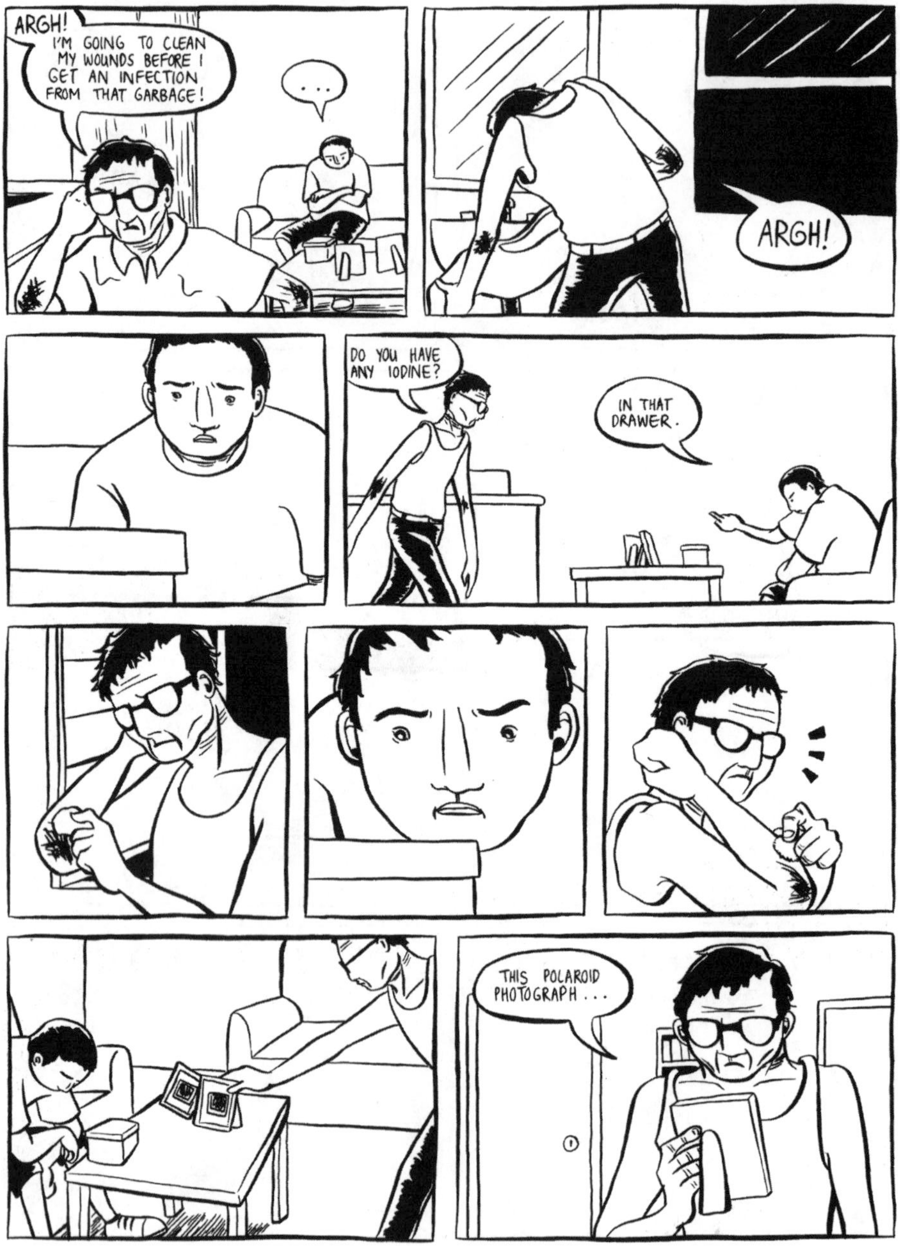
ARGH!
I'M GOING TO CLEAN MY WOUNDS BEFORE I GET AN INFECTION FROM THAT GARBAGE!
. . .
ARGH!
DO YOU HAVE ANY IODINE?
IN THAT DRAWER.
THIS POLAROID PHOTOGRAPH . . .

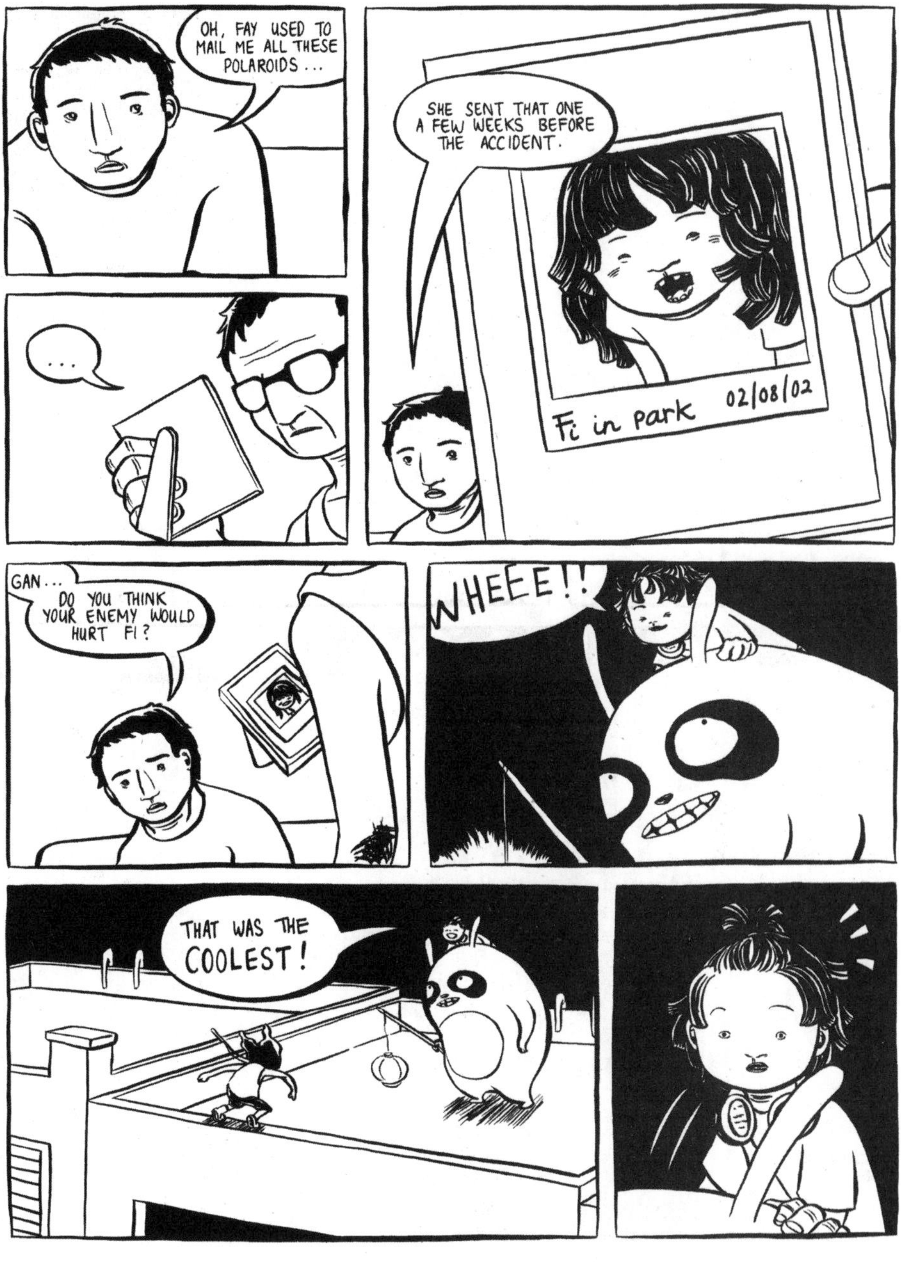
OH, FAY USED TO MAIL ME ALL THESE POLAROIDS...
...
SHE SENT THAT ONE A FEW WEEKS BEFORE THE ACCIDENT.
Fi in park 02/08/02
GAN... DO YOU THINK YOUR ENEMY WOULD HURT FI?
WHEEE!!
THAT WAS THE COOLEST!

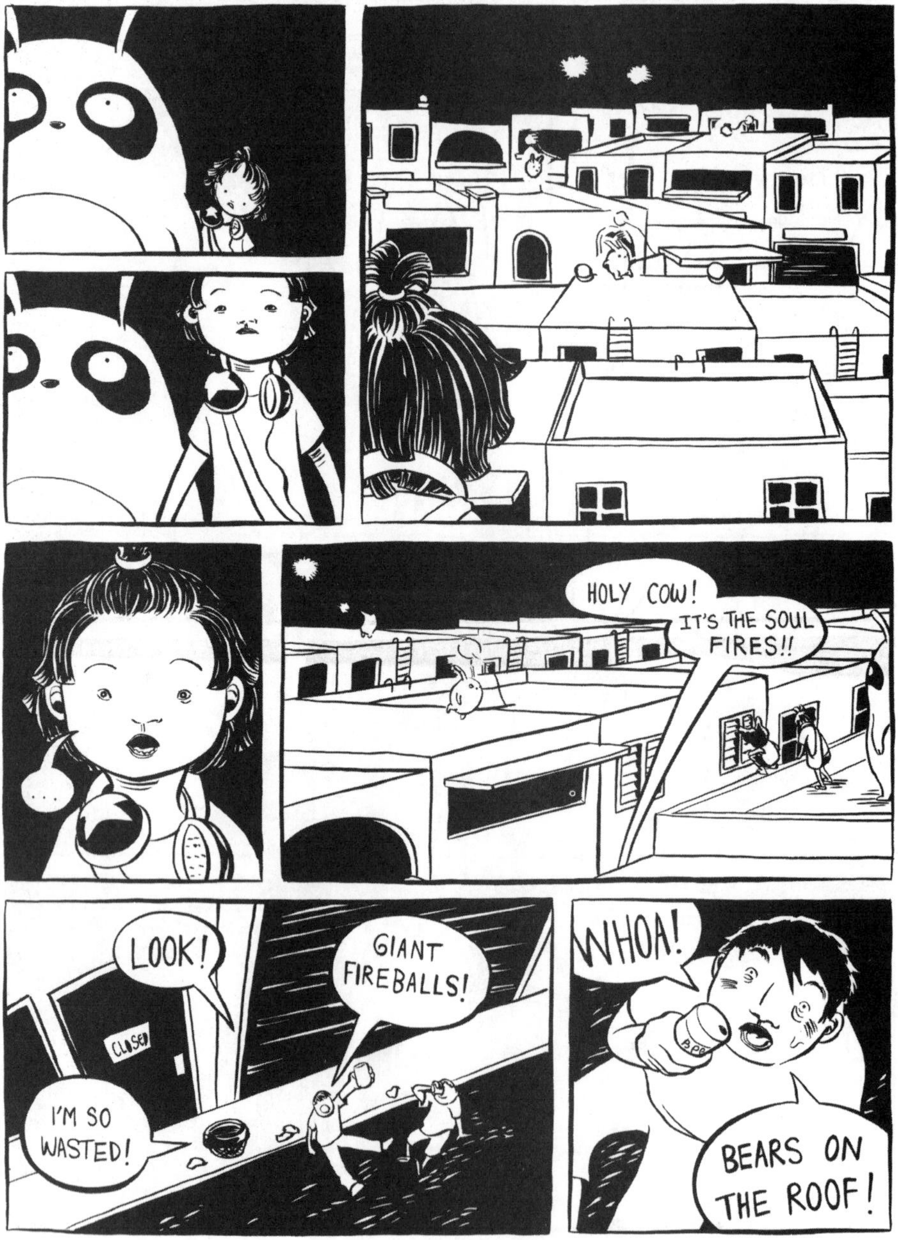
...
HOLY COW!
IT'S THE SOUL FIRES!!
LOOK!
GIANT FIREBALLS!
CLOSED
I'M SO WASTED!
WHOA!
BEARS ON THE ROOF!

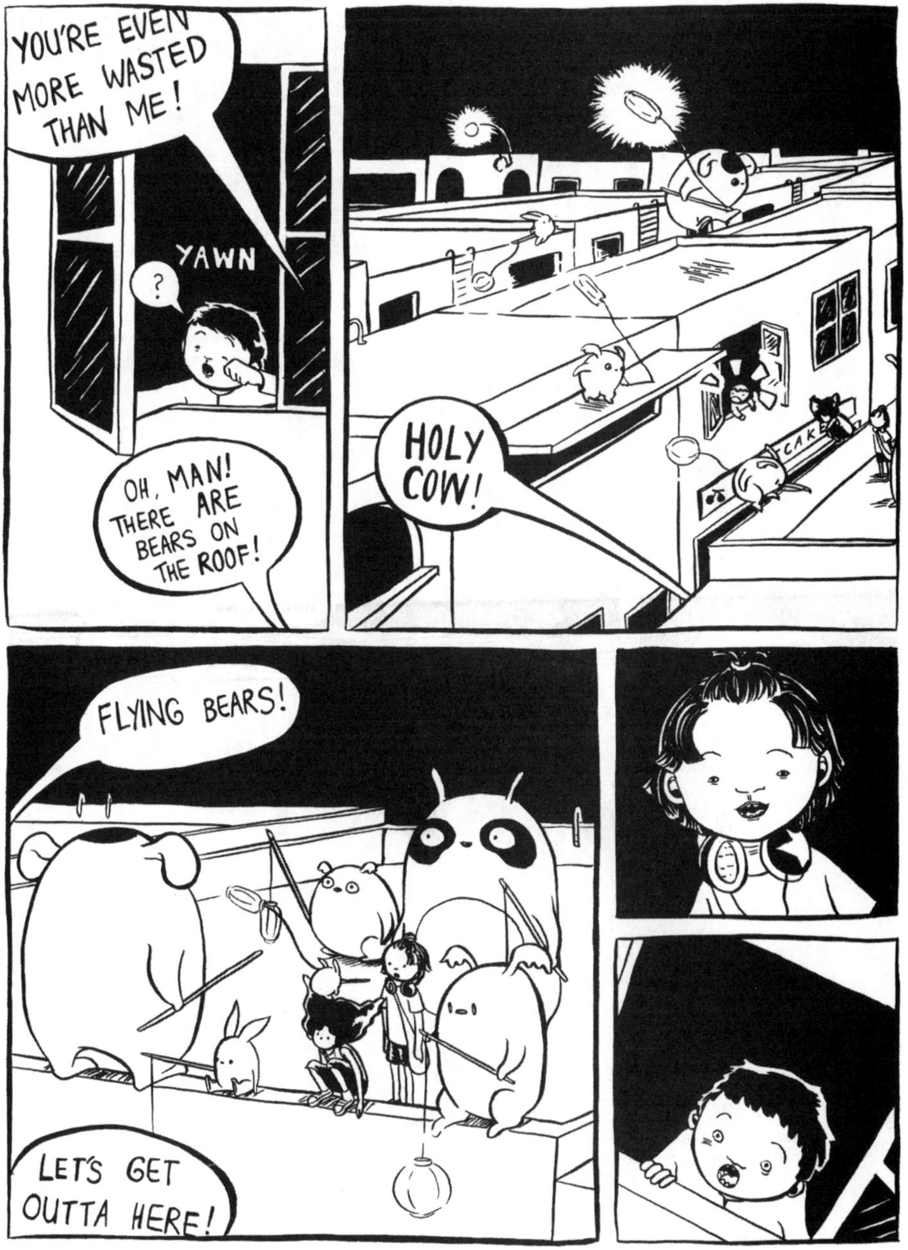
YOU'RE EVEN MORE WASTED THAN ME!
YAWN
?
OH, MAN! THERE ARE BEARS ON THE ROOF!
HOLY COW!
FLYING BEARS!
LET'S GET OUTTA HERE!

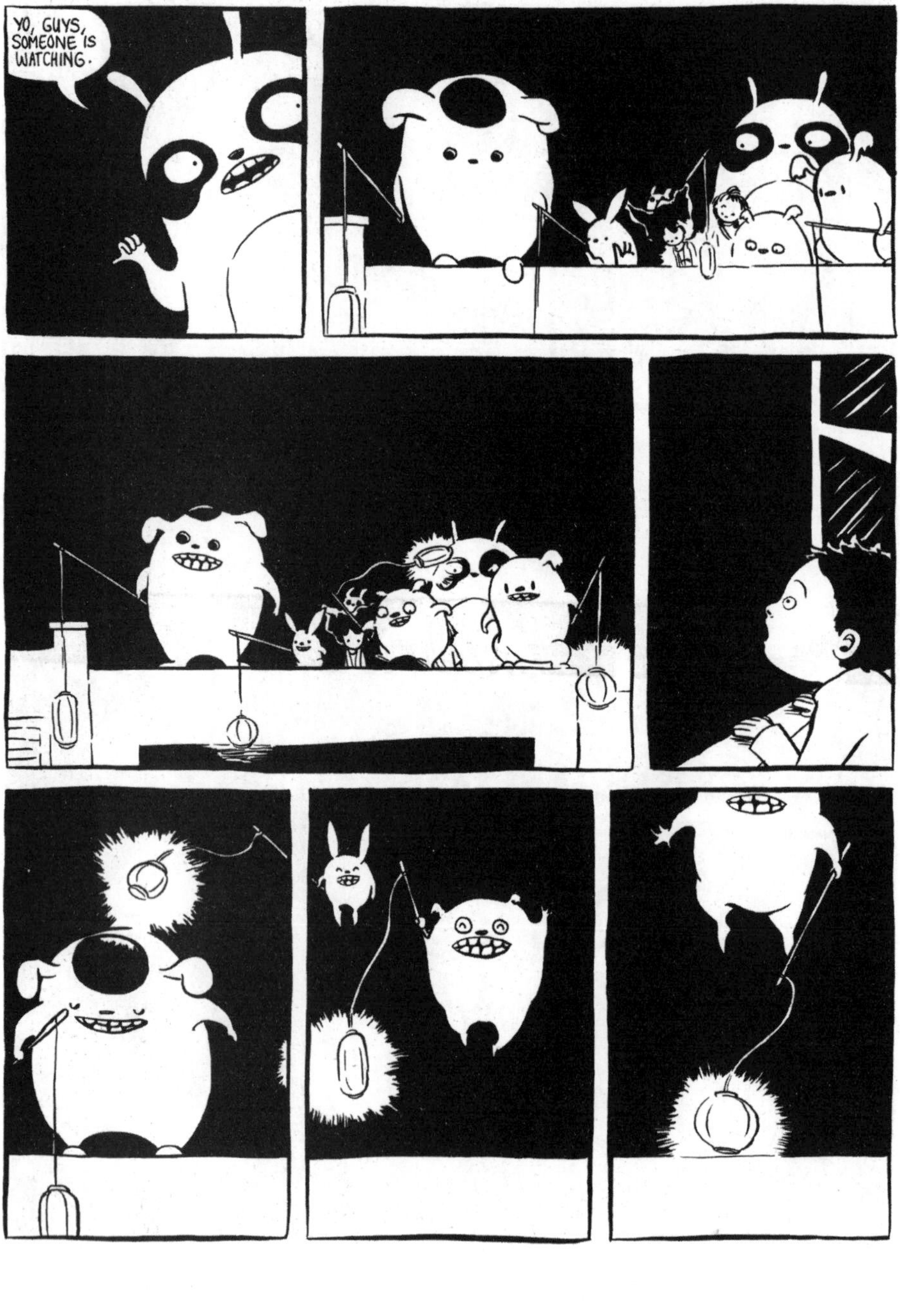
YO, GUYS, SOMEONE IS WATCHING.

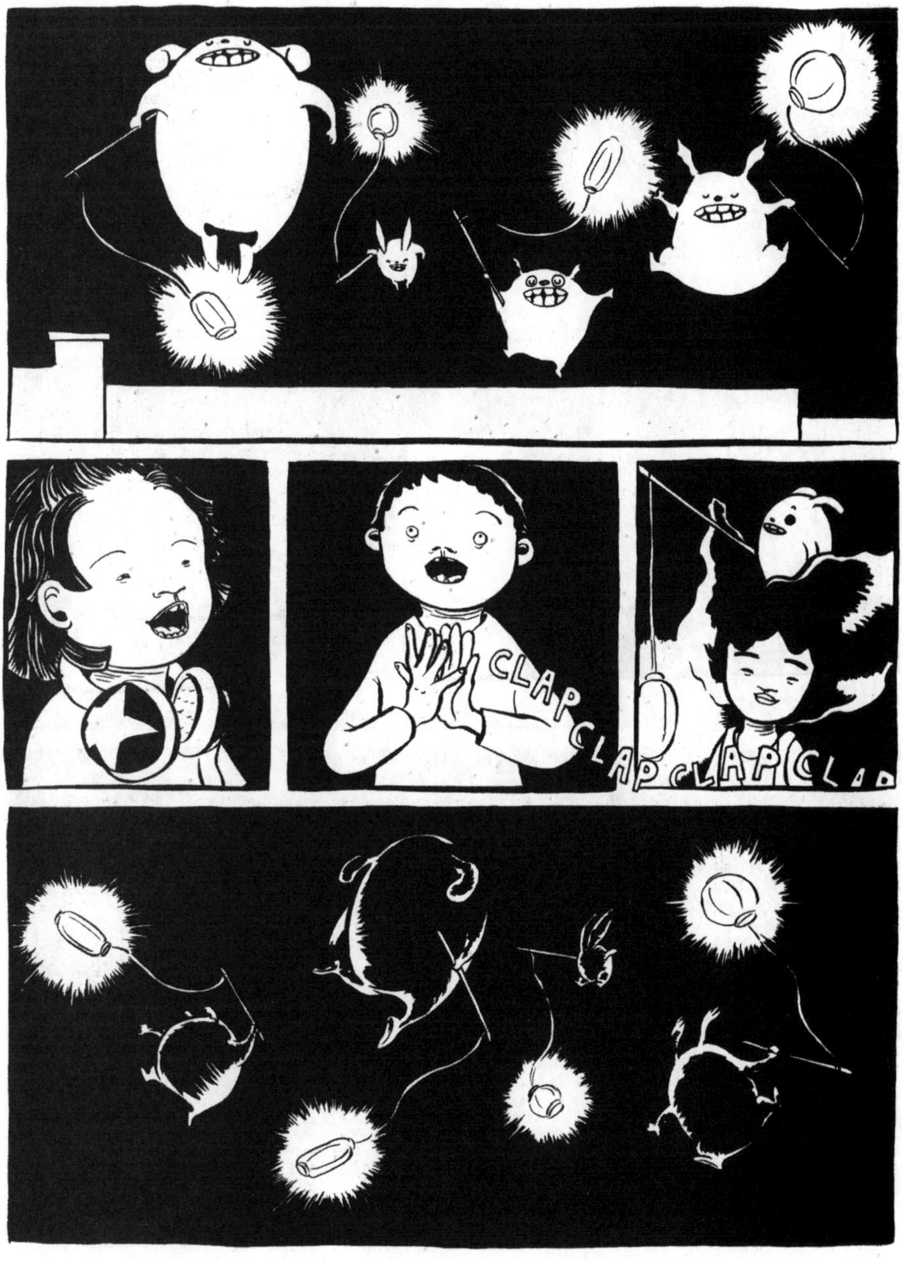
CLAP
CLAP
CLAP
CLAP

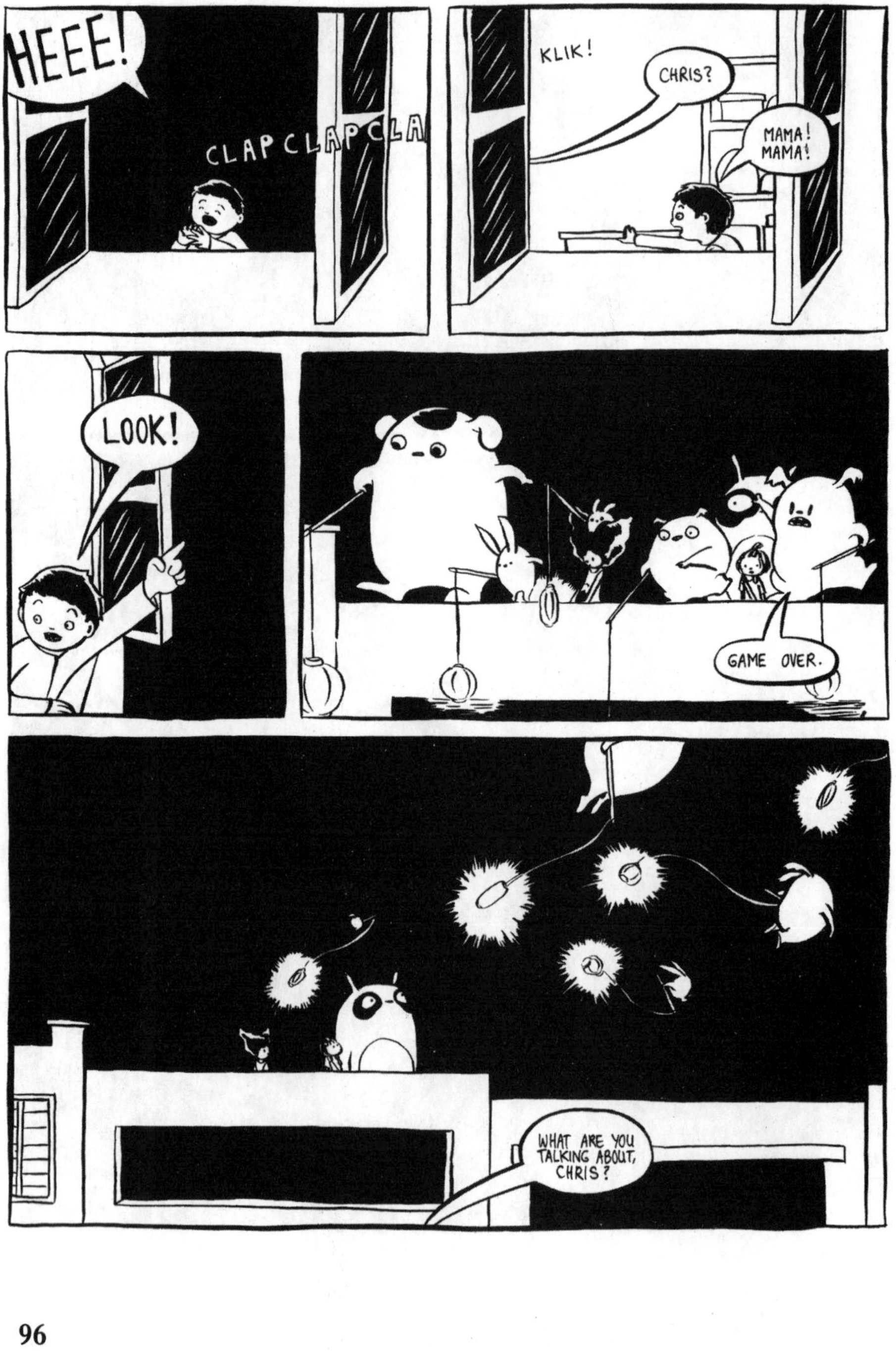
HEEE!
CLAPCLAPCLA
KLIK!
CHRIS?
MAMA! MAMA!
LOOK!
GAME OVER.
WHAT ARE YOU TALKING ABOUT, CHRIS?

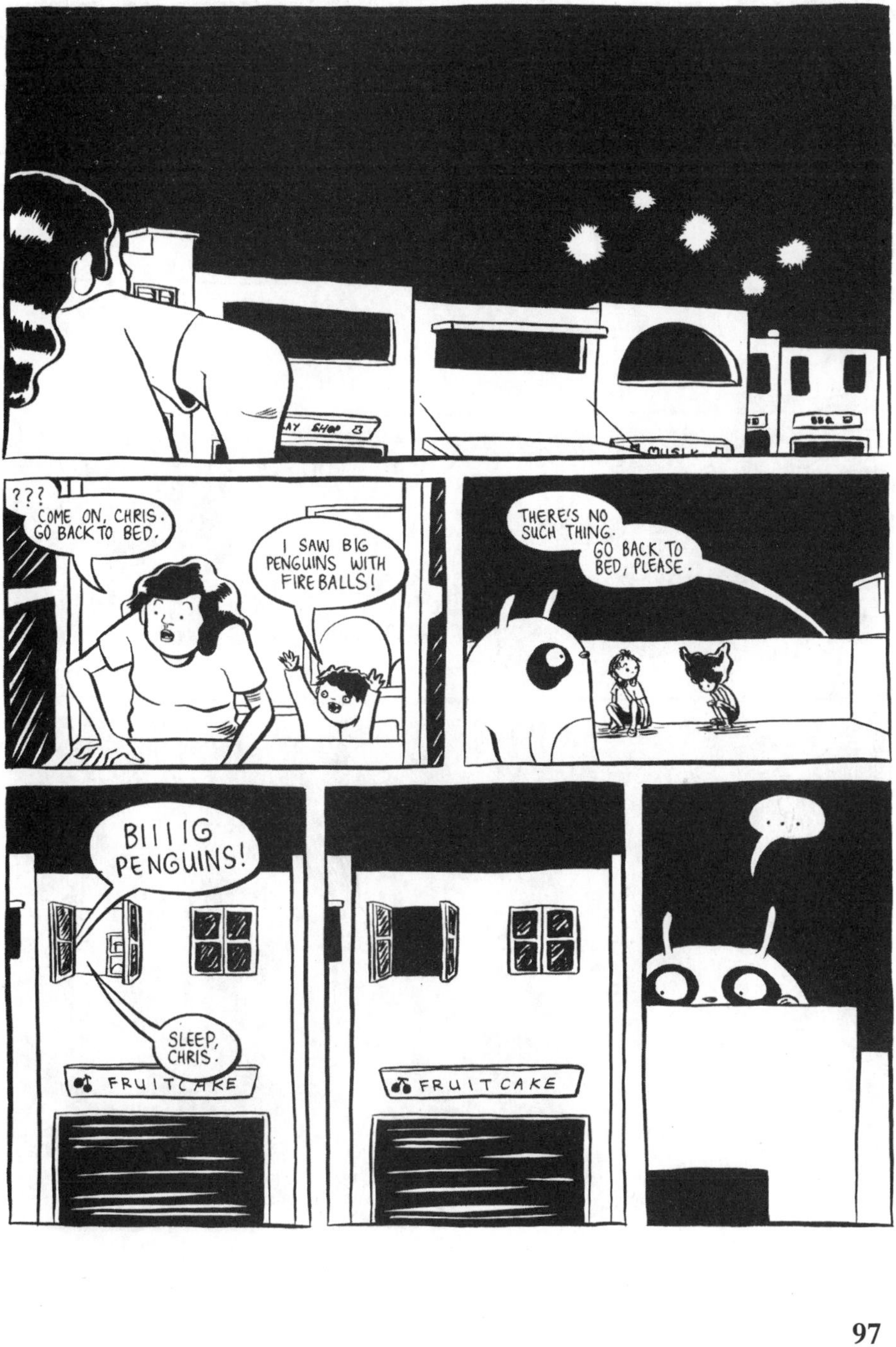
???
COME ON, CHRIS. GO BACK TO BED.
I SAW BIG PENGUINS WITH FIRE BALLS!
THERE'S NO SUCH THING.
GO BACK TO BED, PLEASE.
BIIIIG PENGUINS!
SLEEP, CHRIS.
FRUITCAKE
FRUITCAKE

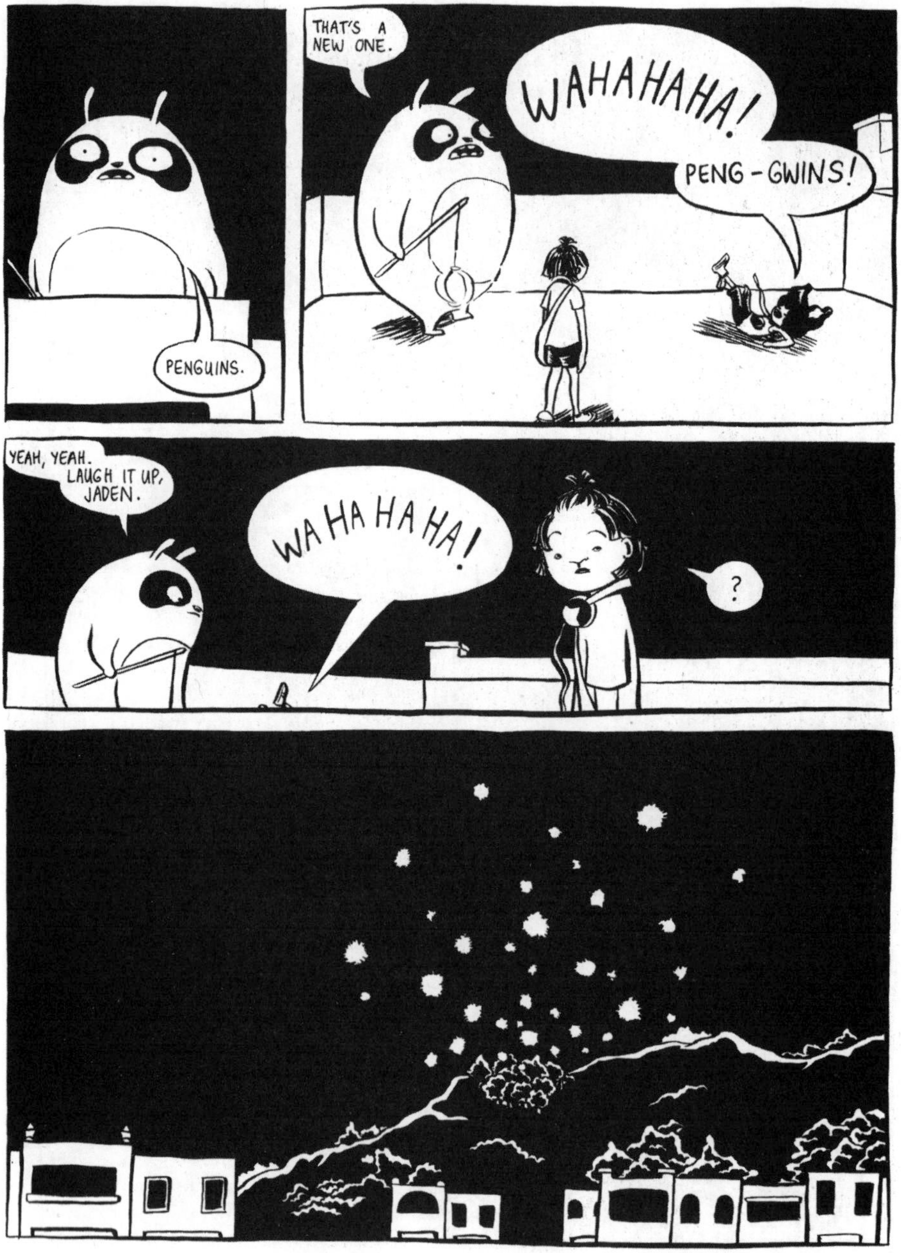
PENGUINS.
THAT'S A NEW ONE.
WAHAHAHA!
PENG-GWINS!
YEAH, YEAH. LAUGH IT UP, JADEN.
WAHAHAHA!
?

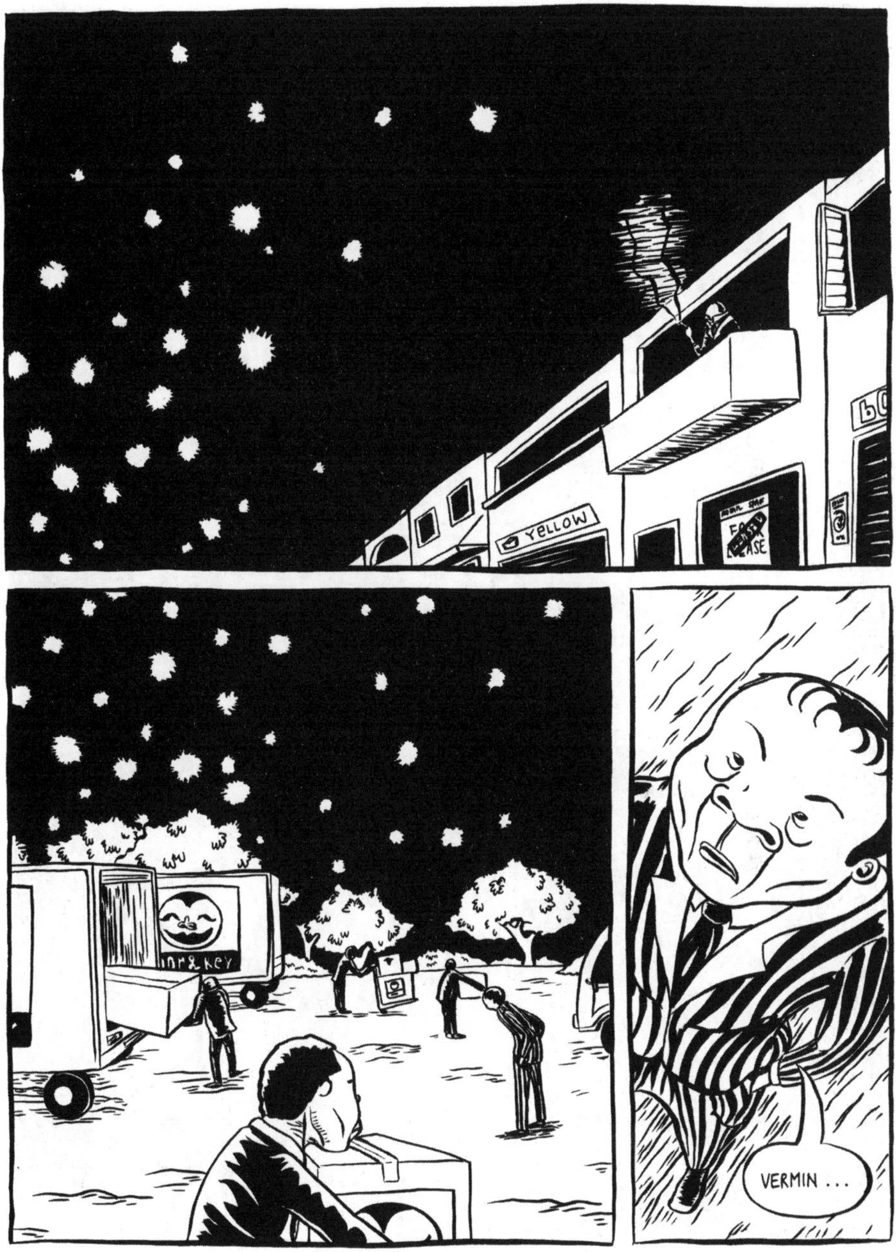
YELLOW
VERMIN . . .

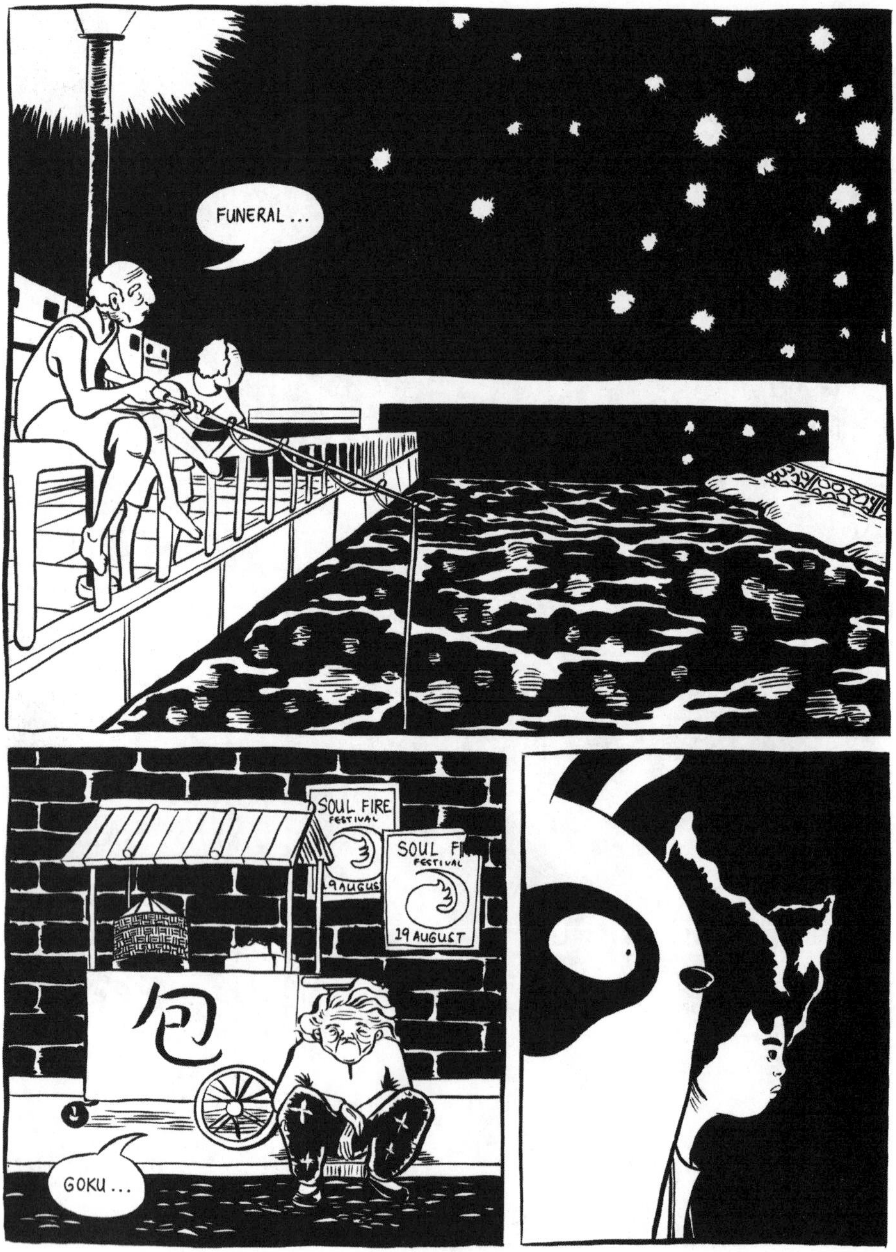
FUNERAL...
SOUL FIRE
FESTIVAL
19 AUGUST
SOUL FI
FESTIVAL
19 AUGUST
包
GOKU...

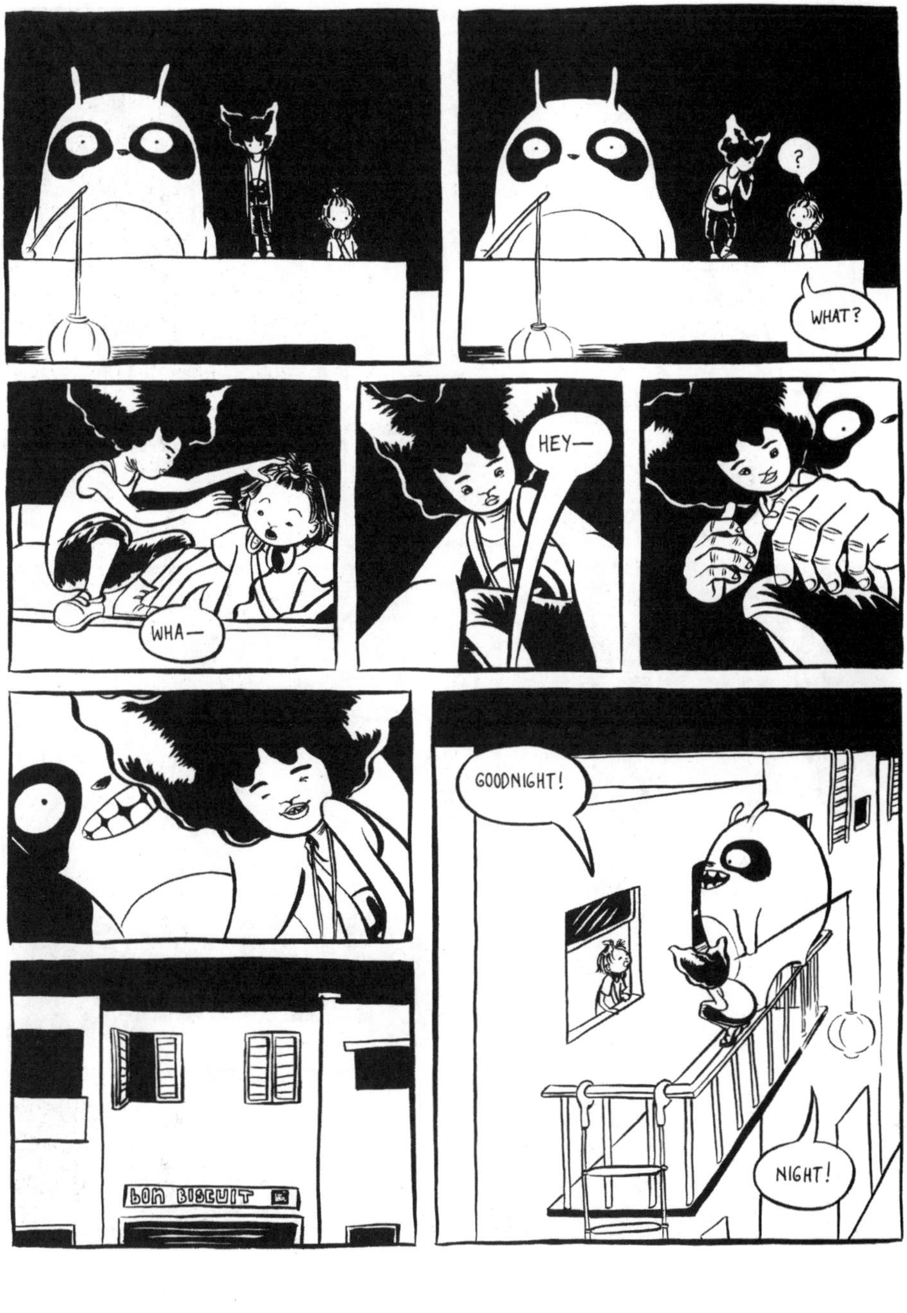
?
WHAT?
WHA—
HEY—
GOODNIGHT!
NIGHT!
BON BISCUIT

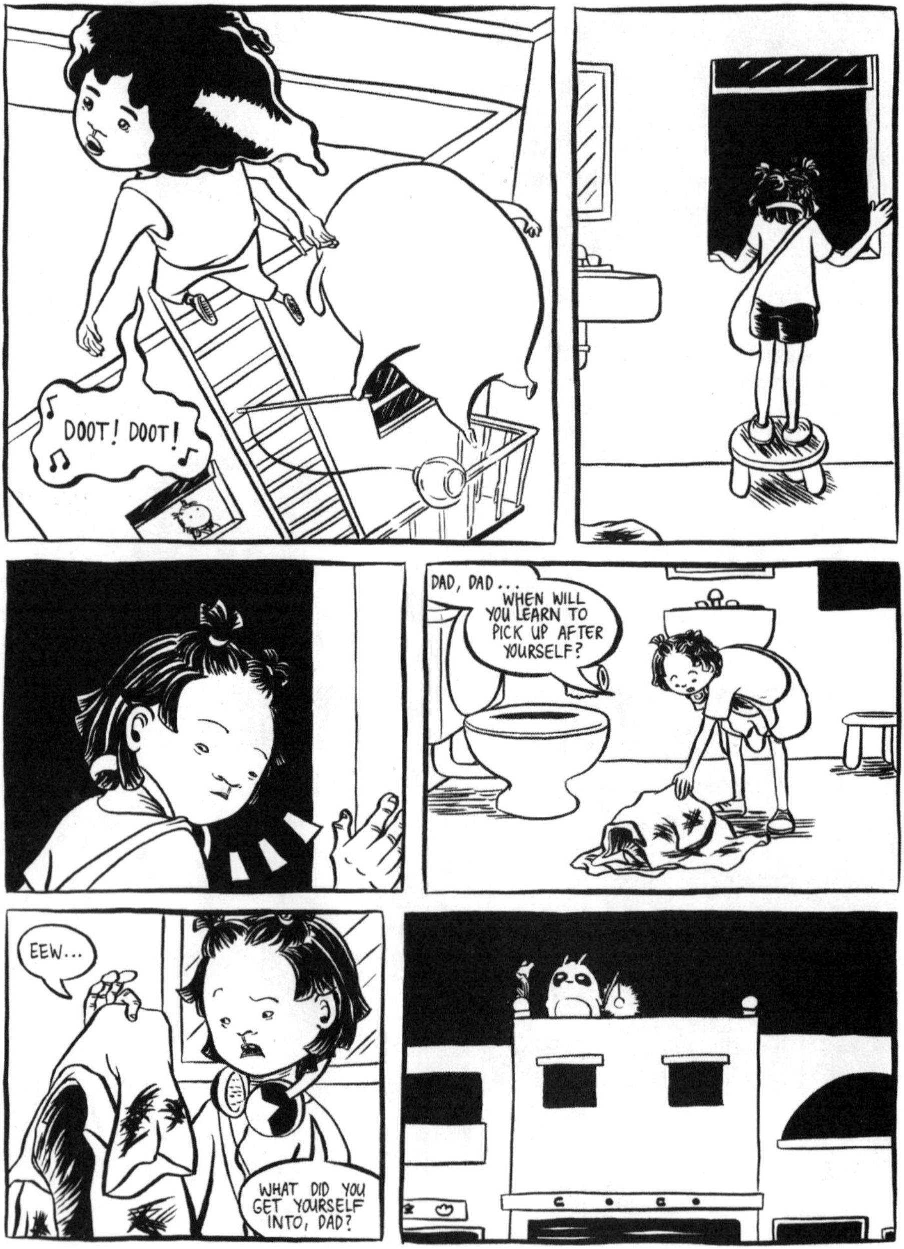
DOOT! DOOT!
DAD, DAD...
WHEN WILL YOU LEARN TO PICK UP AFTER YOURSELF?
EEW...
WHAT DID YOU GET YOURSELF INTO, DAD?

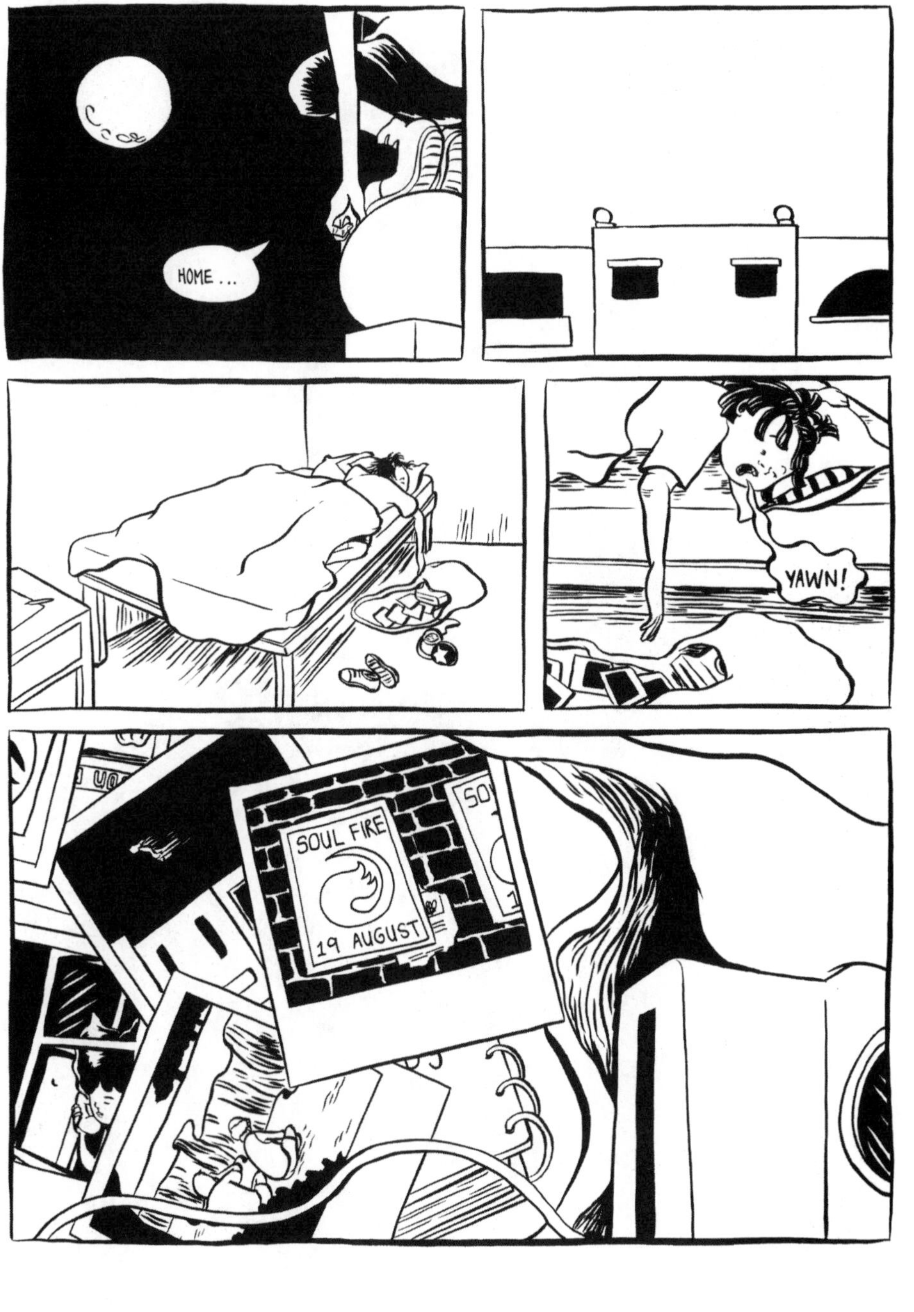
HOME...
YAWN!
SOUL FIRE
19 AUGUST

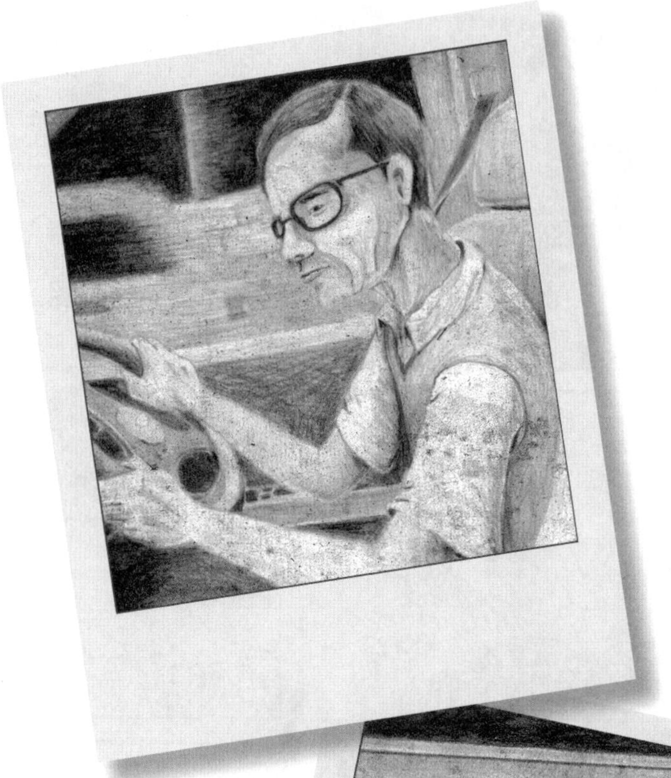

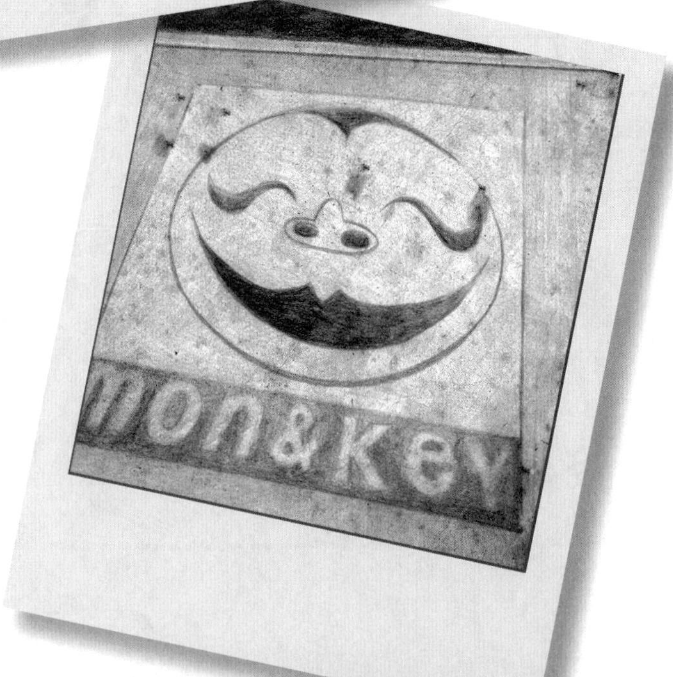
mon&key

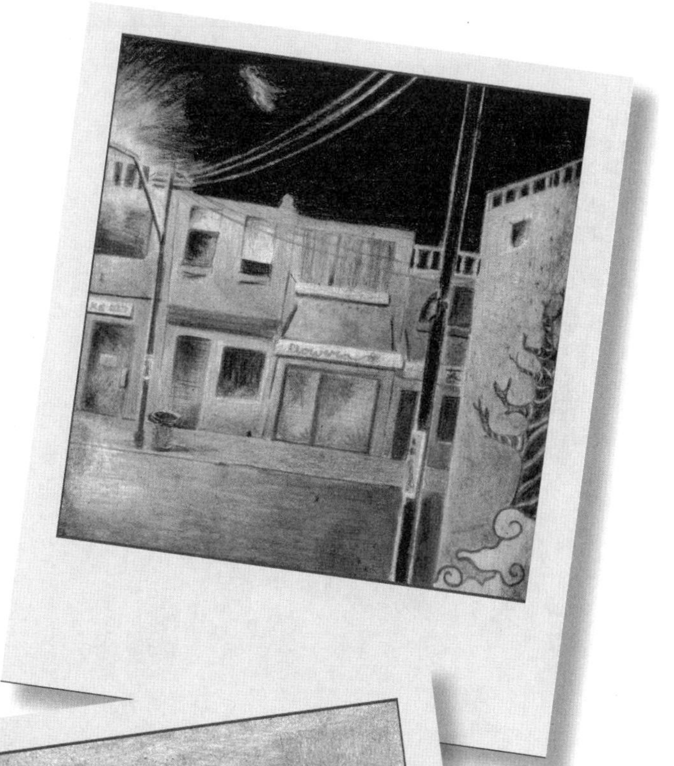

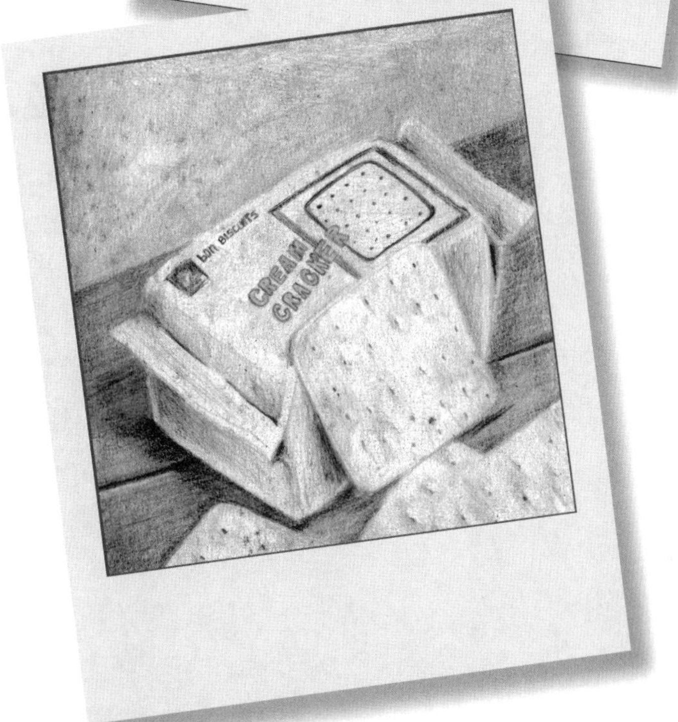
bon biscuits
CREAM

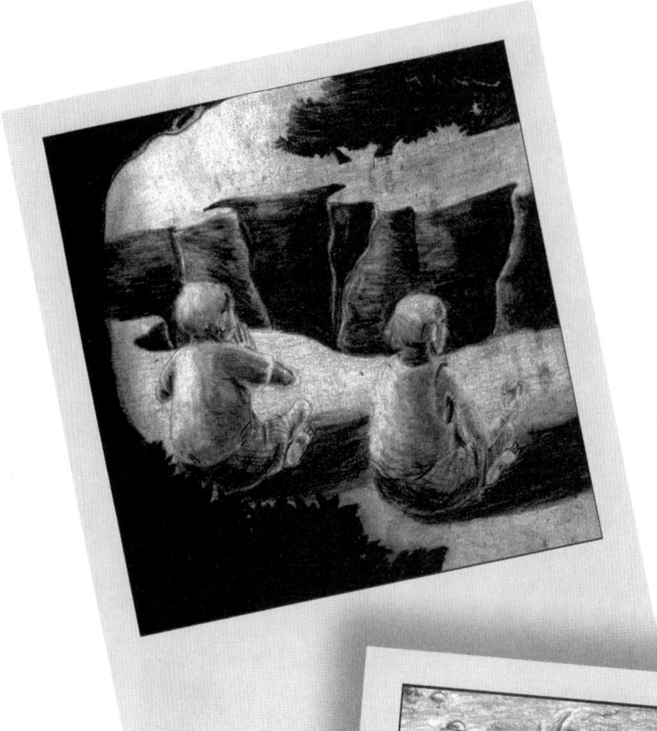

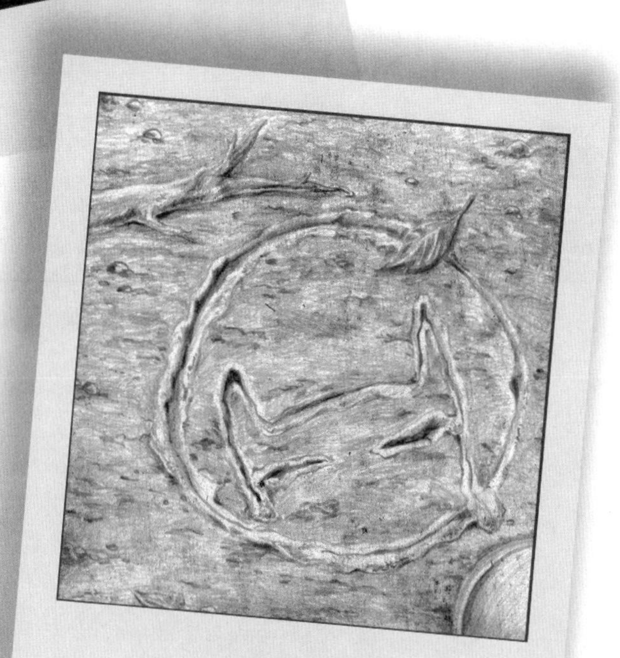

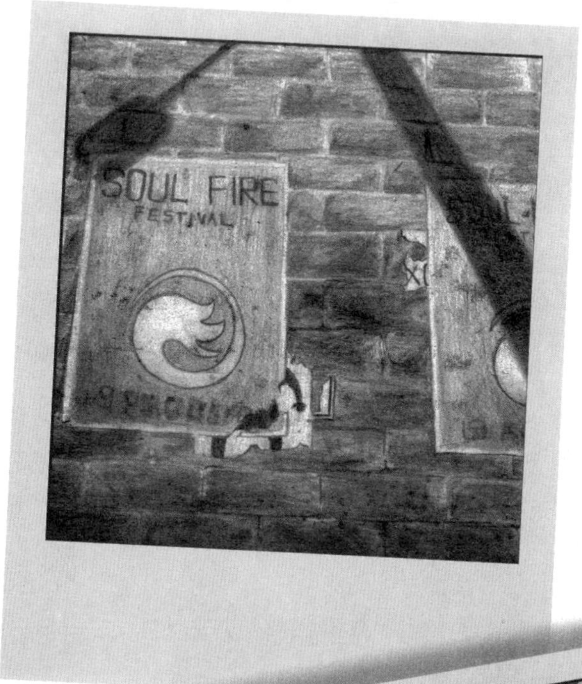
SOUL FIRE
FESTIVAL

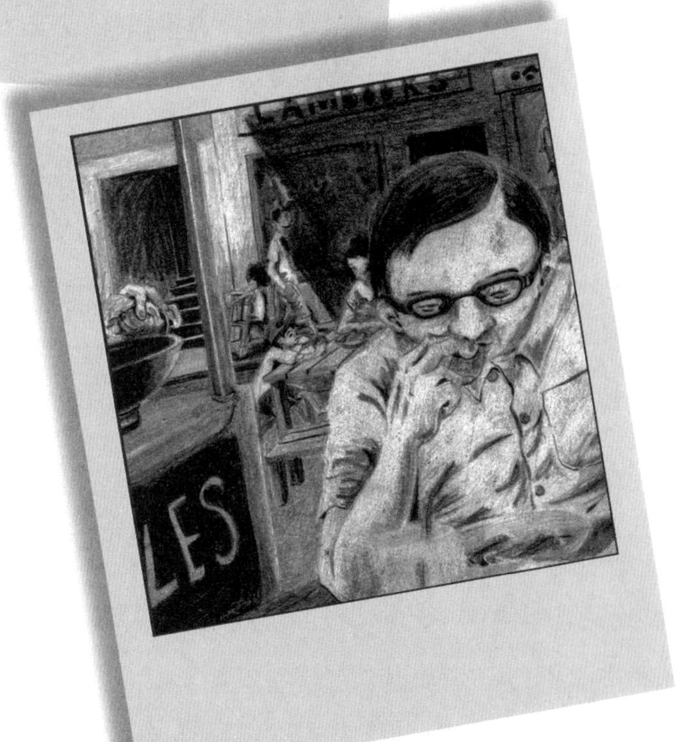
LES

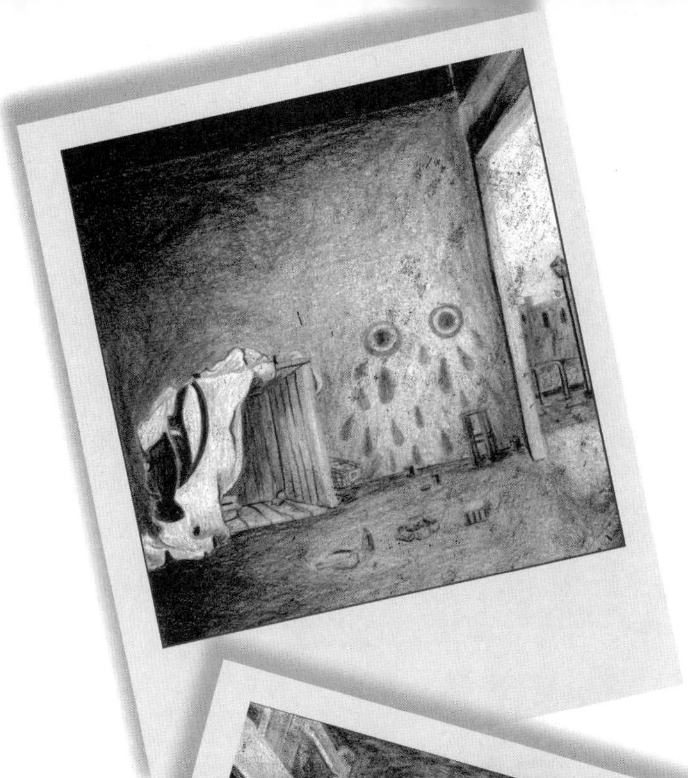

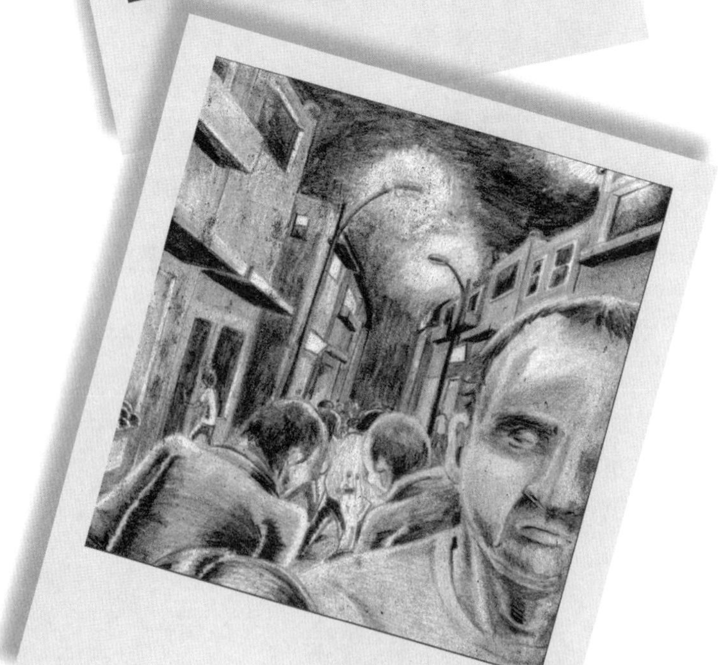

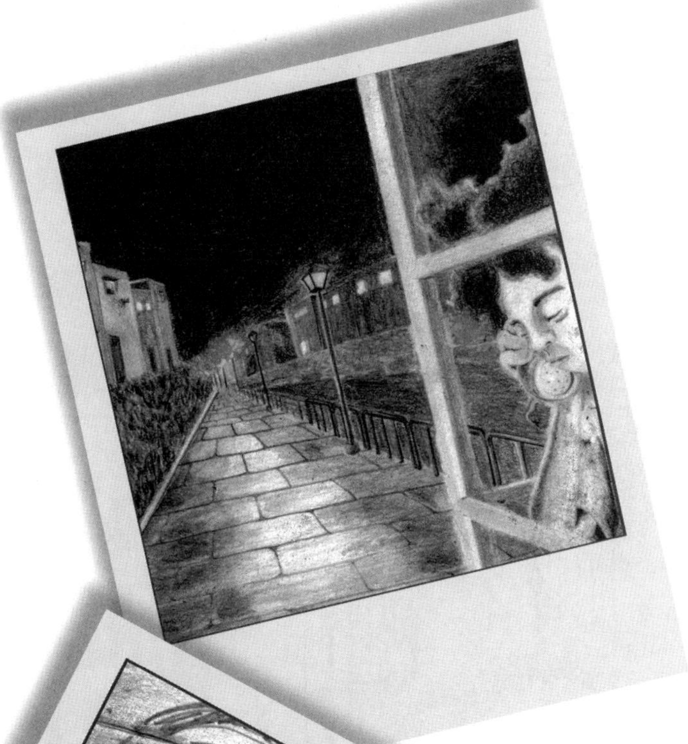

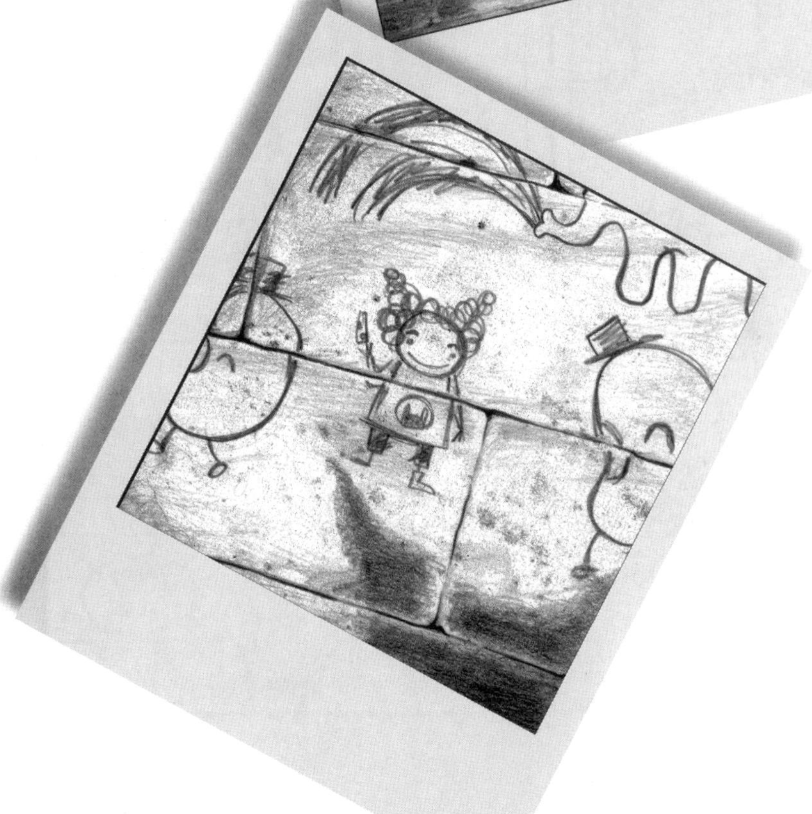

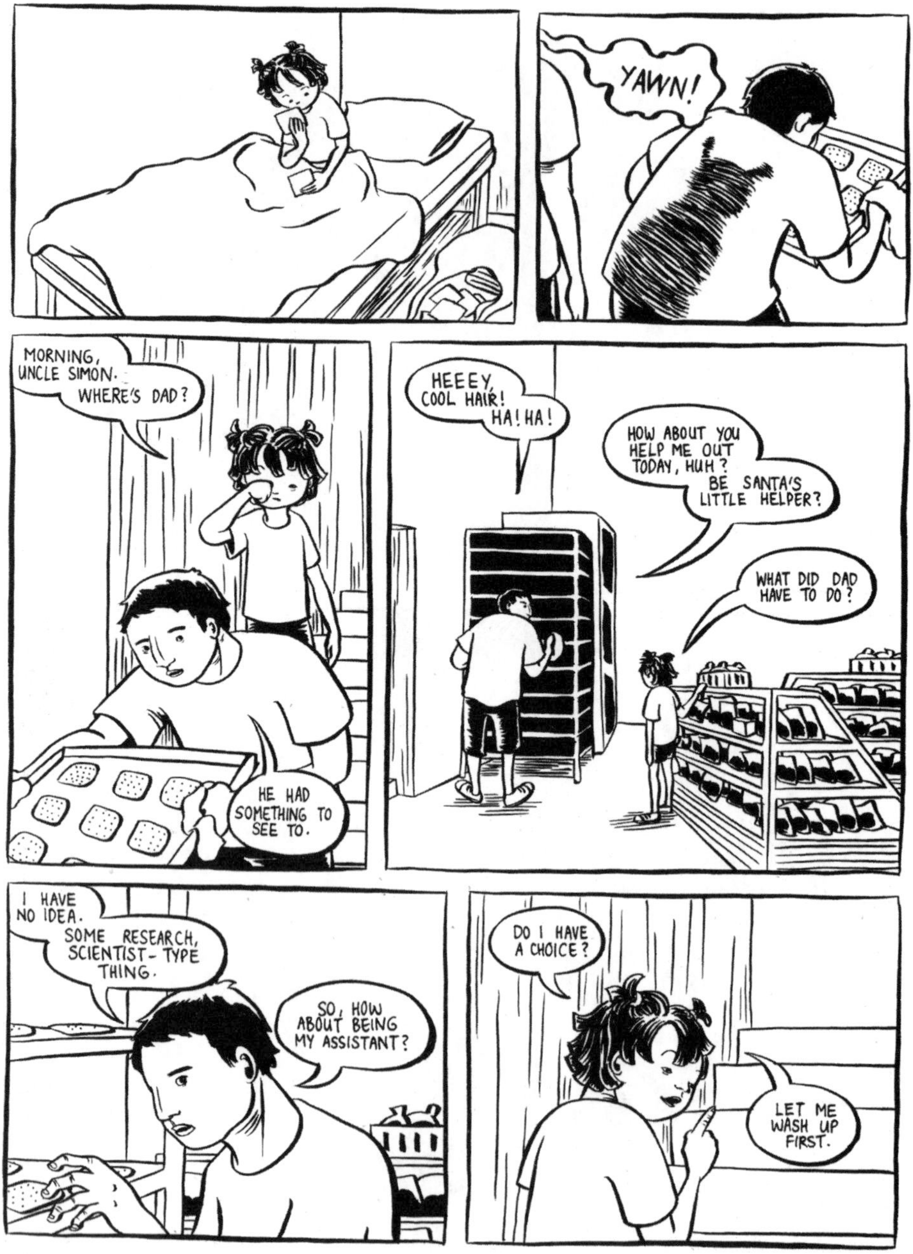
YAWN!
MORNING, UNCLE SIMON. WHERE'S DAD?
HE HAD SOMETHING TO SEE TO.
HEEEY, COOL HAIR! HA! HA!
HOW ABOUT YOU HELP ME OUT TODAY, HUH? BE SANTA'S LITTLE HELPER?
WHAT DID DAD HAVE TO DO?
I HAVE NO IDEA. SOME RESEARCH, SCIENTIST-TYPE THING.
SO, HOW ABOUT BEING MY ASSISTANT?
DO I HAVE A CHOICE?
LET ME WASH UP FIRST.

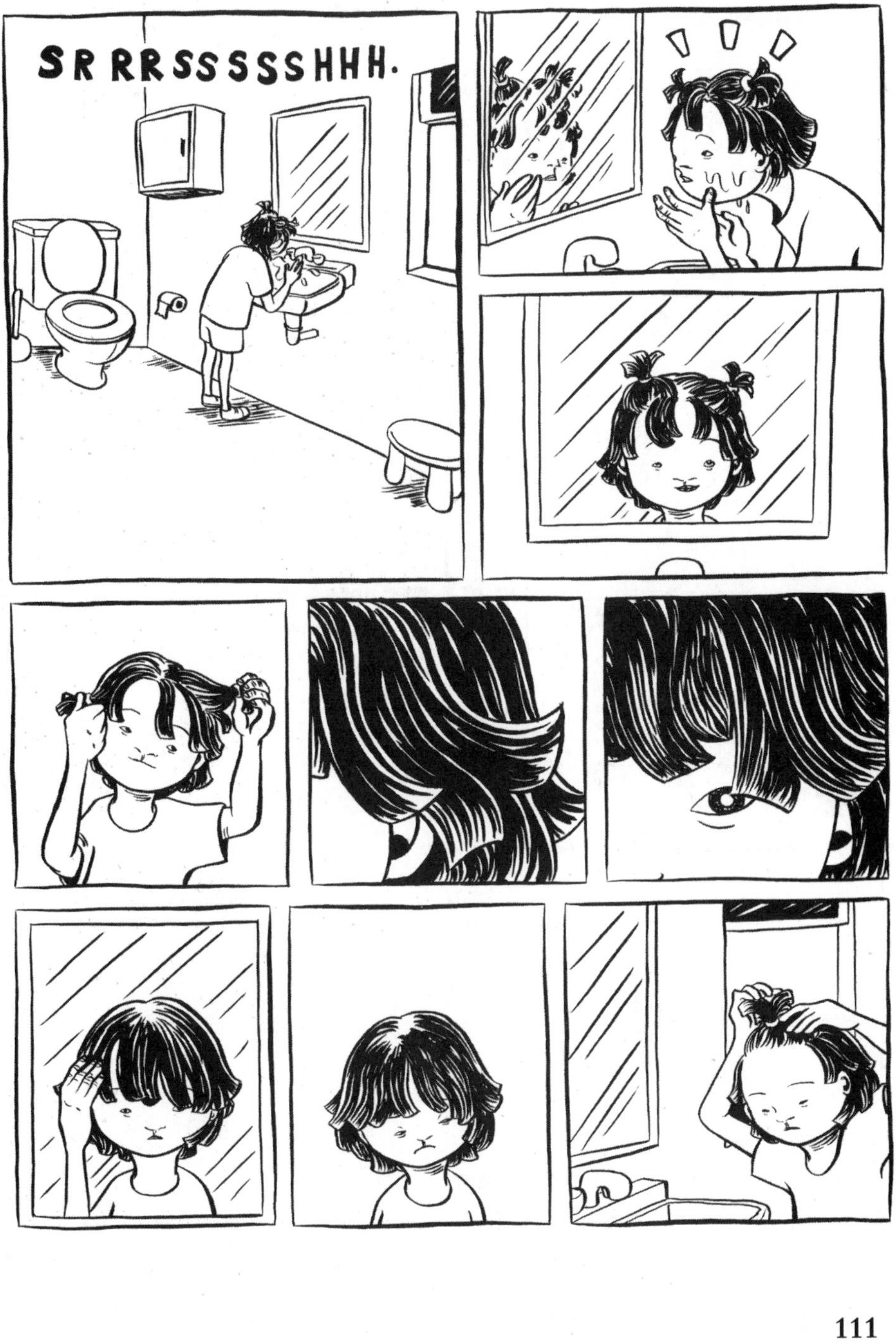
SRRRSSSSSHHH.

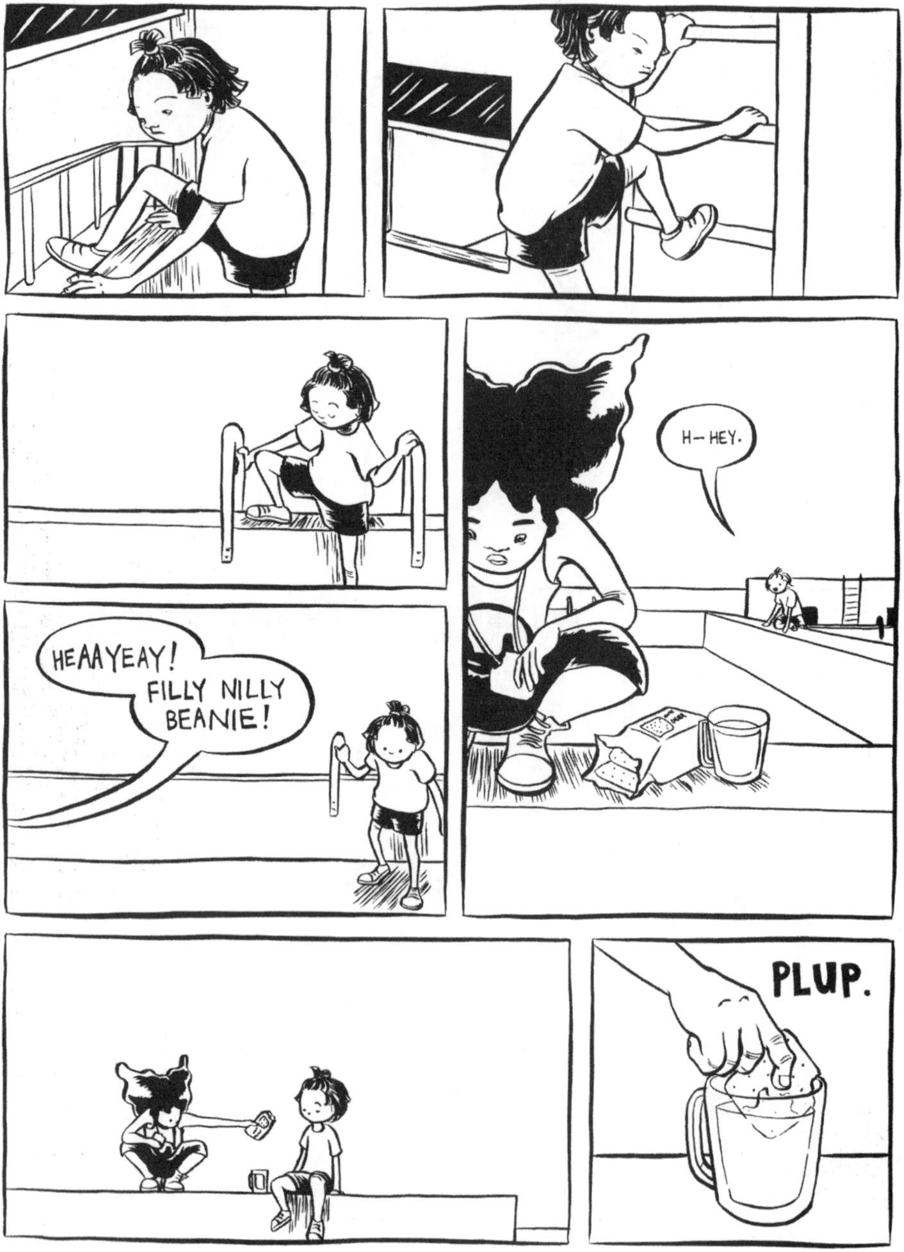
H— HEY.
HEAAYEAY! FILLY NILLY BEANIE!
PLUP.

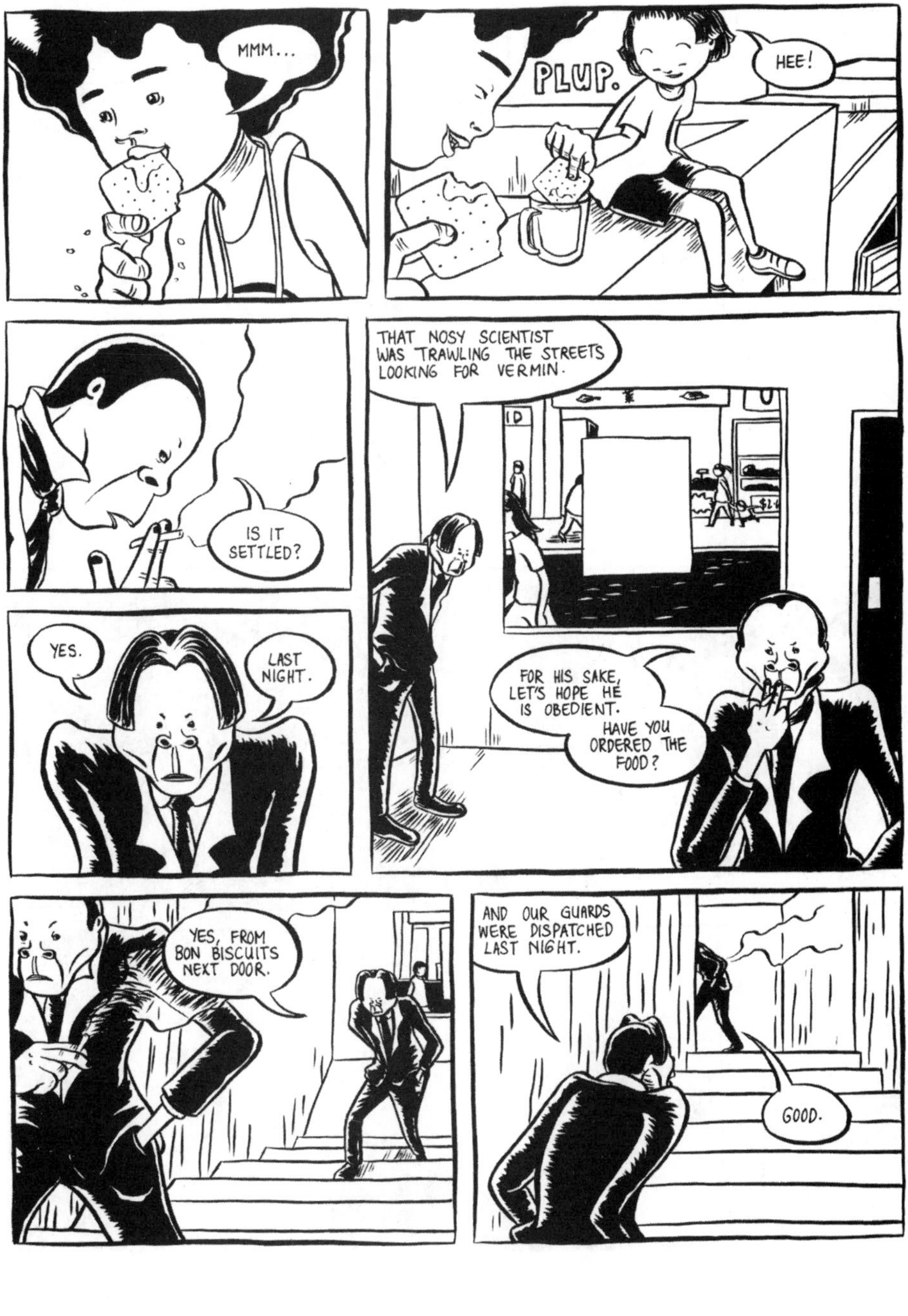
MMM...
PLUP.
HEE!
IS IT SETTLED?
THAT NOSY SCIENTIST WAS TRAWLING THE STREETS LOOKING FOR VERMIN.
YES.
LAST NIGHT.
FOR HIS SAKE, LET'S HOPE HE IS OBEDIENT.
HAVE YOU ORDERED THE FOOD?
YES, FROM BON BISCUITS NEXT DOOR.
AND OUR GUARDS WERE DISPATCHED LAST NIGHT.
GOOD.

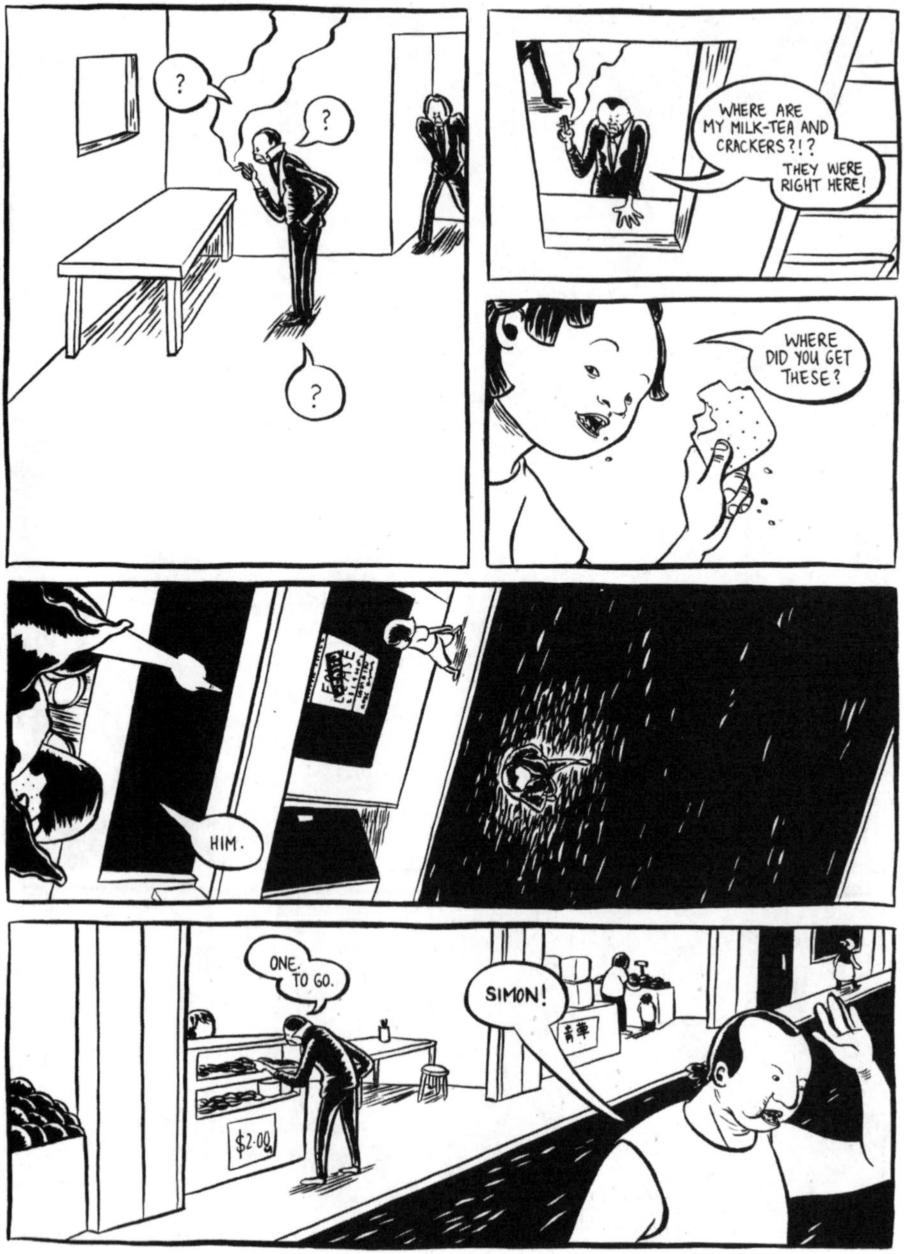
?
?
?
WHERE ARE MY MILK-TEA AND CRACKERS?!?
THEY WERE RIGHT HERE!
WHERE DID YOU GET THESE?
HIM.
ONE. TO GO.
SIMON!
$2.00

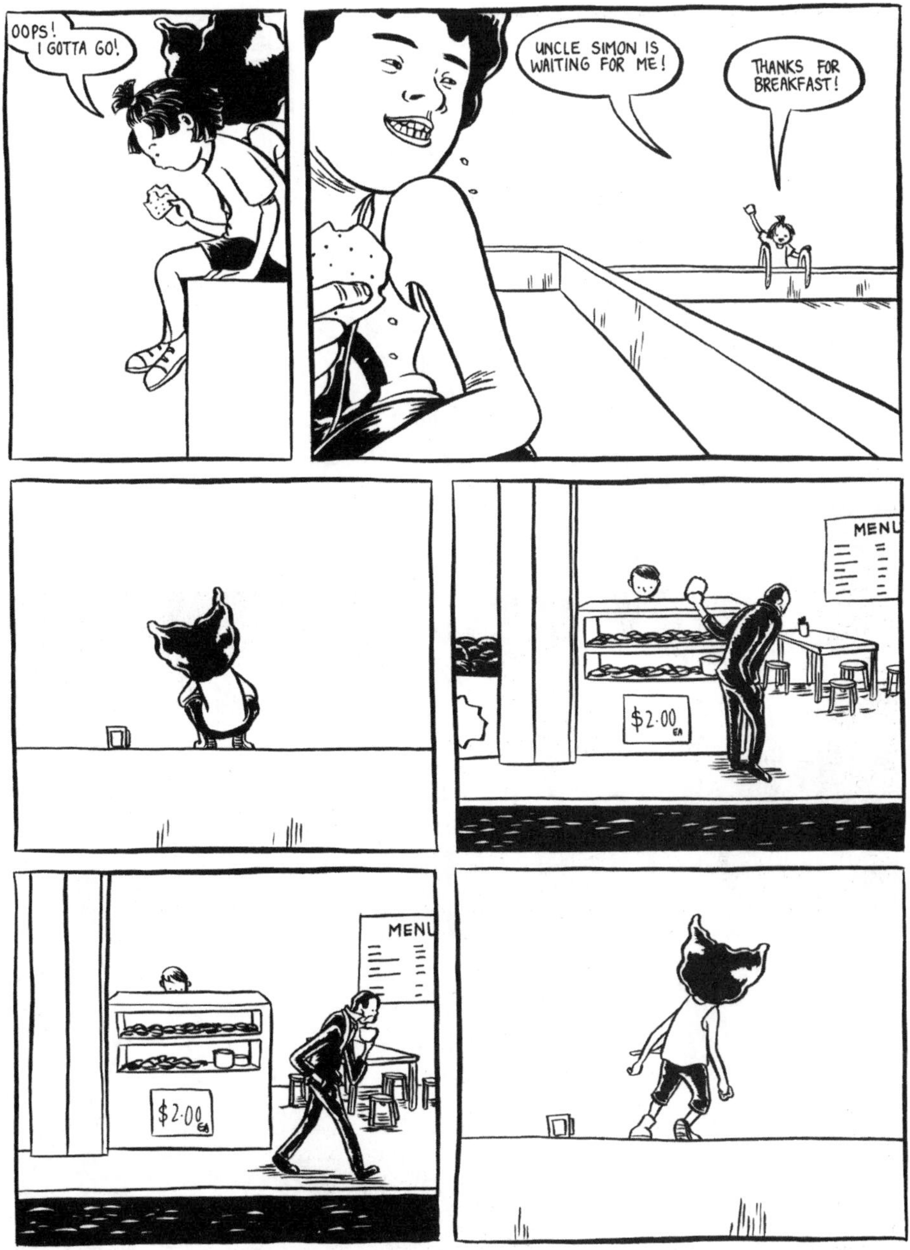
OOPS! I GOTTA GO!
UNCLE SIMON IS WAITING FOR ME!
THANKS FOR BREAKFAST!
MENU
$2.00 EA
MENU
$2.00 EA

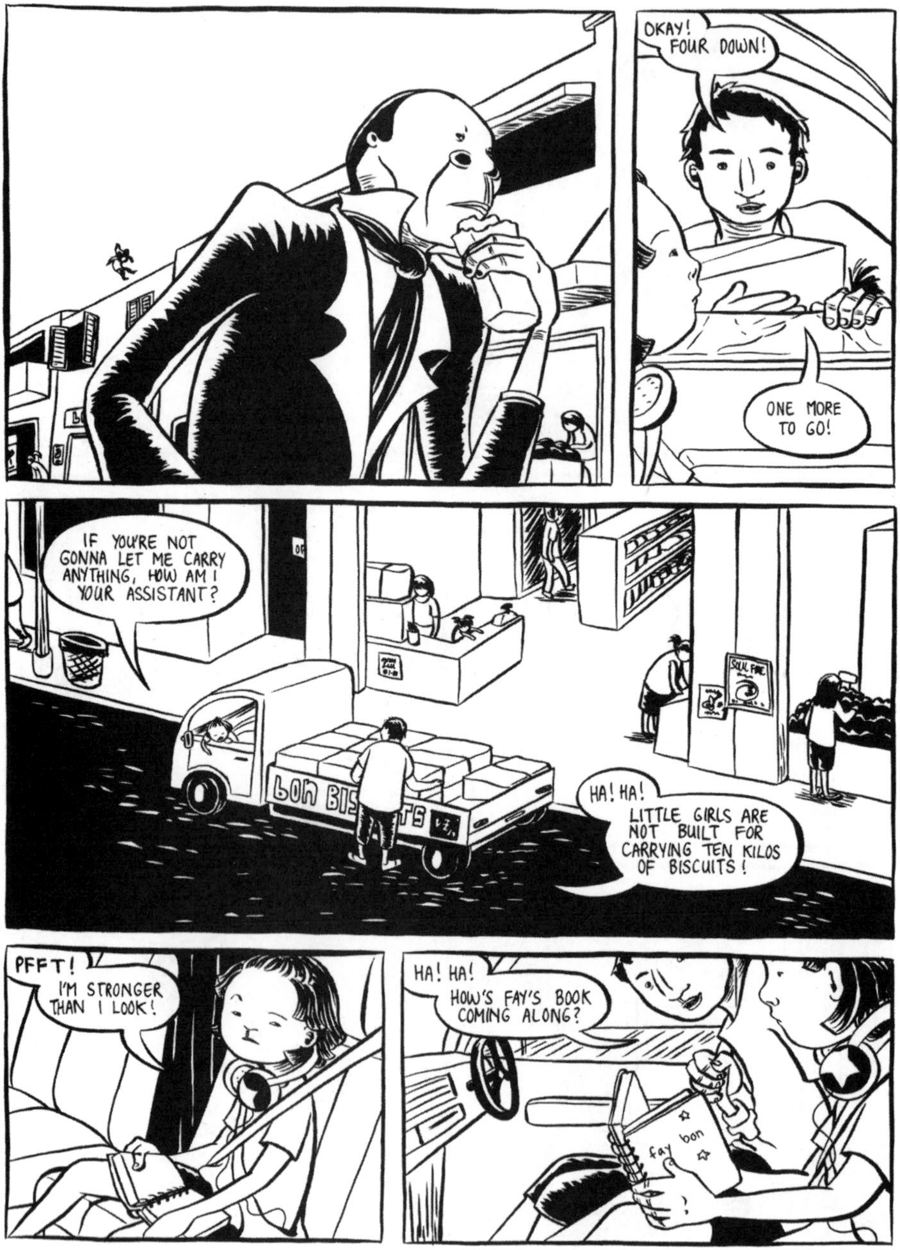
OKAY! FOUR DOWN!
ONE MORE TO GO!
IF YOU'RE NOT GONNA LET ME CARRY ANYTHING, HOW AM I YOUR ASSISTANT?
bon BISCUITS
SOUL FIRE
HA! HA! LITTLE GIRLS ARE NOT BUILT FOR CARRYING TEN KILOS OF BISCUITS!
PFFT! I'M STRONGER THAN I LOOK!
HA! HA! HOW'S FAY'S BOOK COMING ALONG?
fay bon

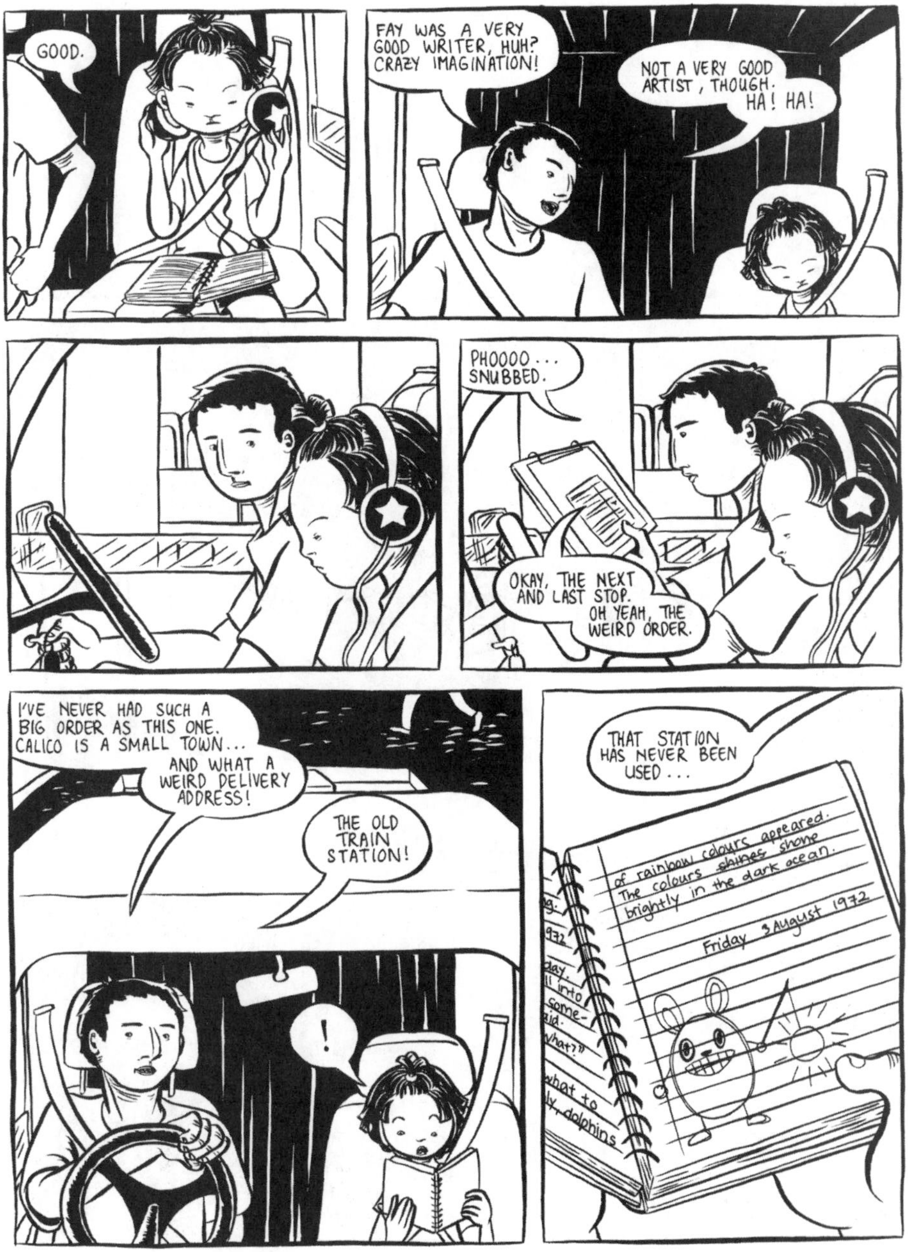
GOOD.
FAY WAS A VERY GOOD WRITER, HUH? CRAZY IMAGINATION!
NOT A VERY GOOD ARTIST, THOUGH. HA! HA!
PHOOOO... SNUBBED.
OKAY, THE NEXT AND LAST STOP.
OH YEAH, THE WEIRD ORDER.
I'VE NEVER HAD SUCH A BIG ORDER AS THIS ONE. CALICO IS A SMALL TOWN...
AND WHAT A WEIRD DELIVERY ADDRESS!
THE OLD TRAIN STATION!
!
THAT STATION HAS NEVER BEEN USED...
of rainbow colours appeared. The colours shines shone brightly in the dark ocean.
Friday 3 August 1972

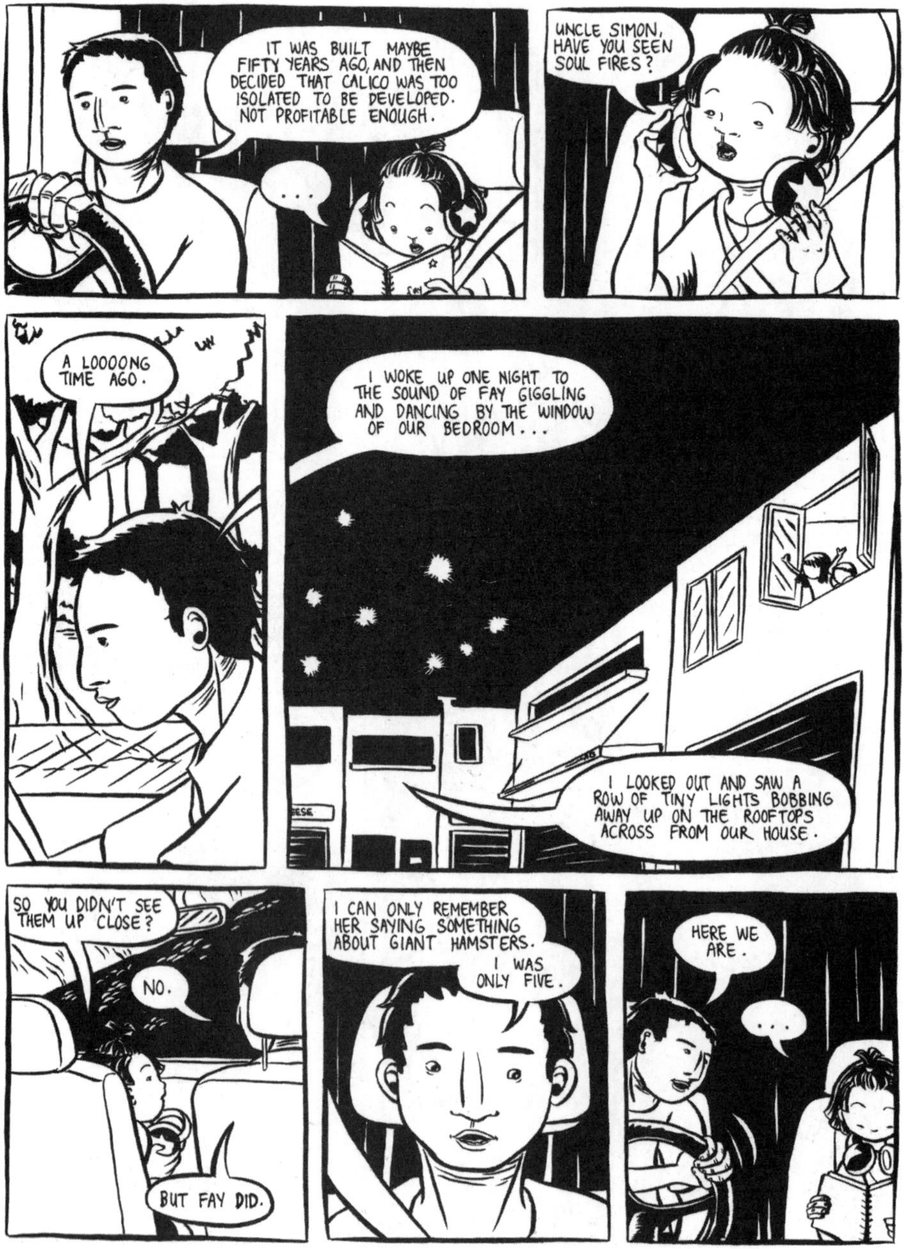
IT WAS BUILT MAYBE FIFTY YEARS AGO, AND THEN DECIDED THAT CALICO WAS TOO ISOLATED TO BE DEVELOPED. NOT PROFITABLE ENOUGH.
...
UNCLE SIMON, HAVE YOU SEEN SOUL FIRES?
A LOOOONG TIME AGO.
I WOKE UP ONE NIGHT TO THE SOUND OF FAY GIGGLING AND DANCING BY THE WINDOW OF OUR BEDROOM...
I LOOKED OUT AND SAW A ROW OF TINY LIGHTS BOBBING AWAY UP ON THE ROOFTOPS ACROSS FROM OUR HOUSE.
SO YOU DIDN'T SEE THEM UP CLOSE?
NO.
BUT FAY DID.
I CAN ONLY REMEMBER HER SAYING SOMETHING ABOUT GIANT HAMSTERS.
I WAS ONLY FIVE.
HERE WE ARE.
...

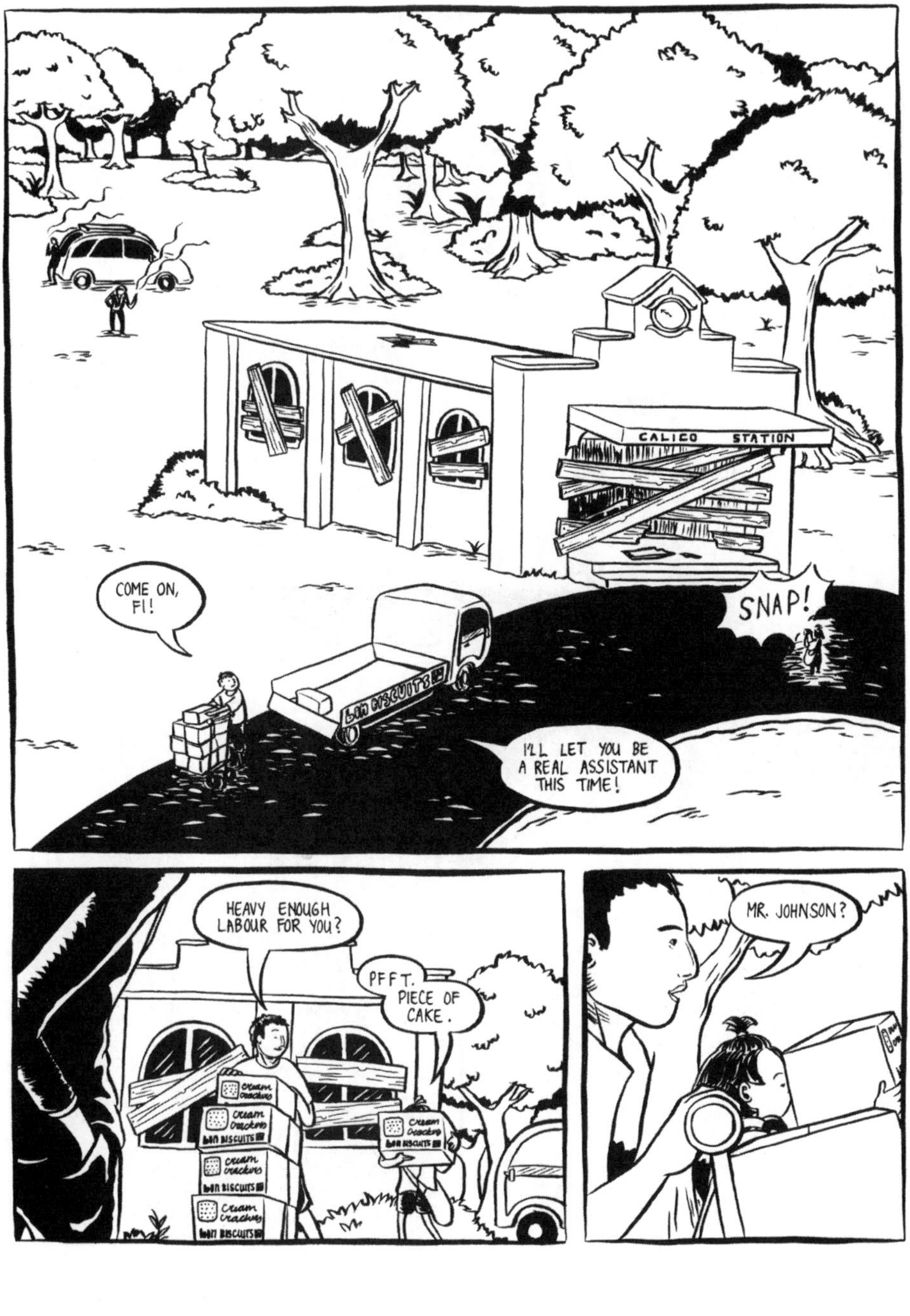
CALICO STATION
COME ON, FI!
SNAP!
bon BISCUITS
I'LL LET YOU BE A REAL ASSISTANT THIS TIME!
HEAVY ENOUGH LABOUR FOR YOU?
PFFT. PIECE OF CAKE.
cream crackers
bon BISCUITS
MR. JOHNSON?

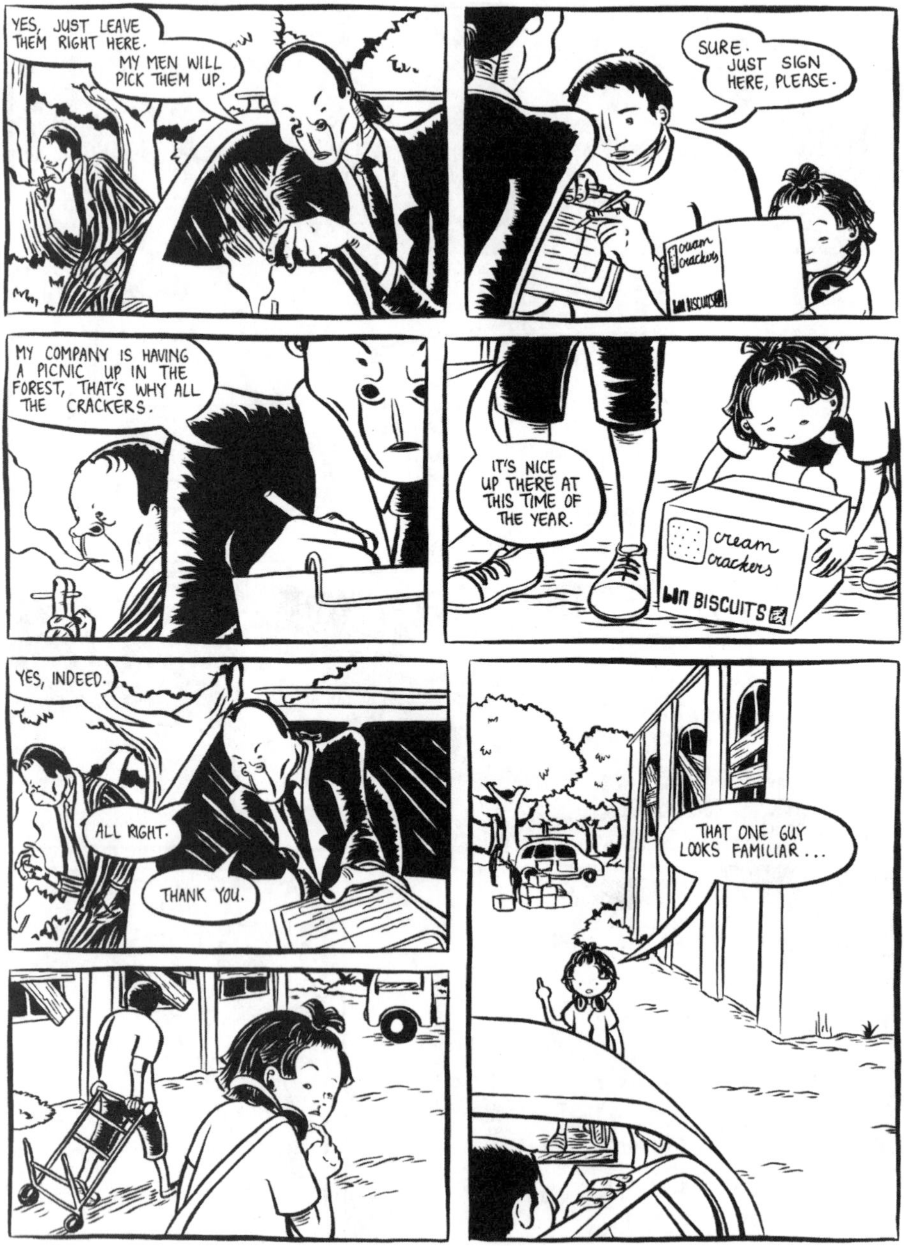
YES, JUST LEAVE THEM RIGHT HERE.
MY MEN WILL PICK THEM UP.
SURE. JUST SIGN HERE, PLEASE.
cream crackers
MY COMPANY IS HAVING A PICNIC UP IN THE FOREST, THAT'S WHY ALL THE CRACKERS.
IT'S NICE UP THERE AT THIS TIME OF THE YEAR.
cream crackers
BISCUITS
YES, INDEED.
ALL RIGHT.
THANK YOU.
THAT ONE GUY LOOKS FAMILIAR...

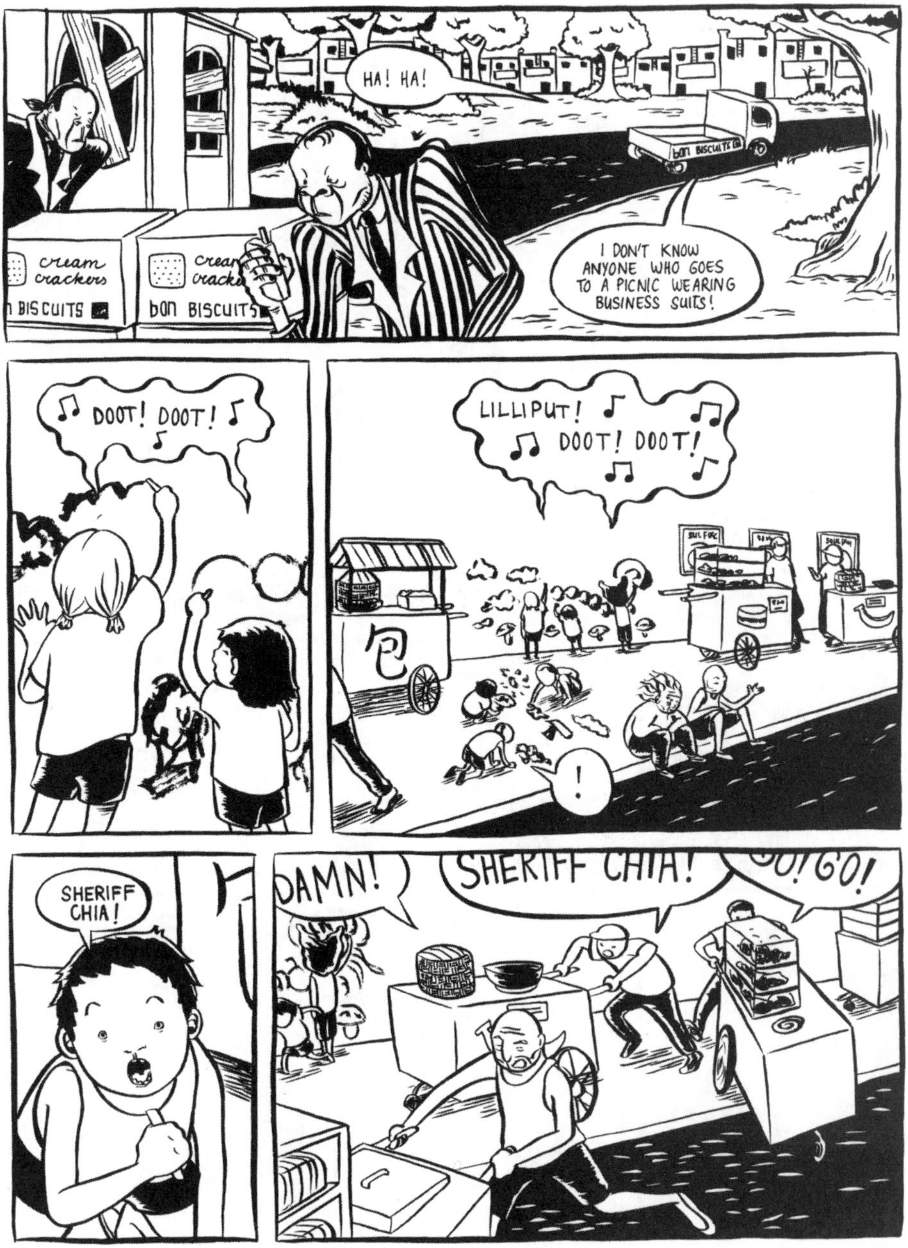
HA! HA!
I DON'T KNOW ANYONE WHO GOES TO A PICNIC WEARING BUSINESS SUITS!
cream crackers
BISCUITS
cream crackers
bon BISCUITS
bon BISCUITS
DOOT! DOOT!
LILLIPUT! DOOT! DOOT!
!
SHERIFF CHIA!
DAMN!
SHERIFF CHIA!
GO! GO!

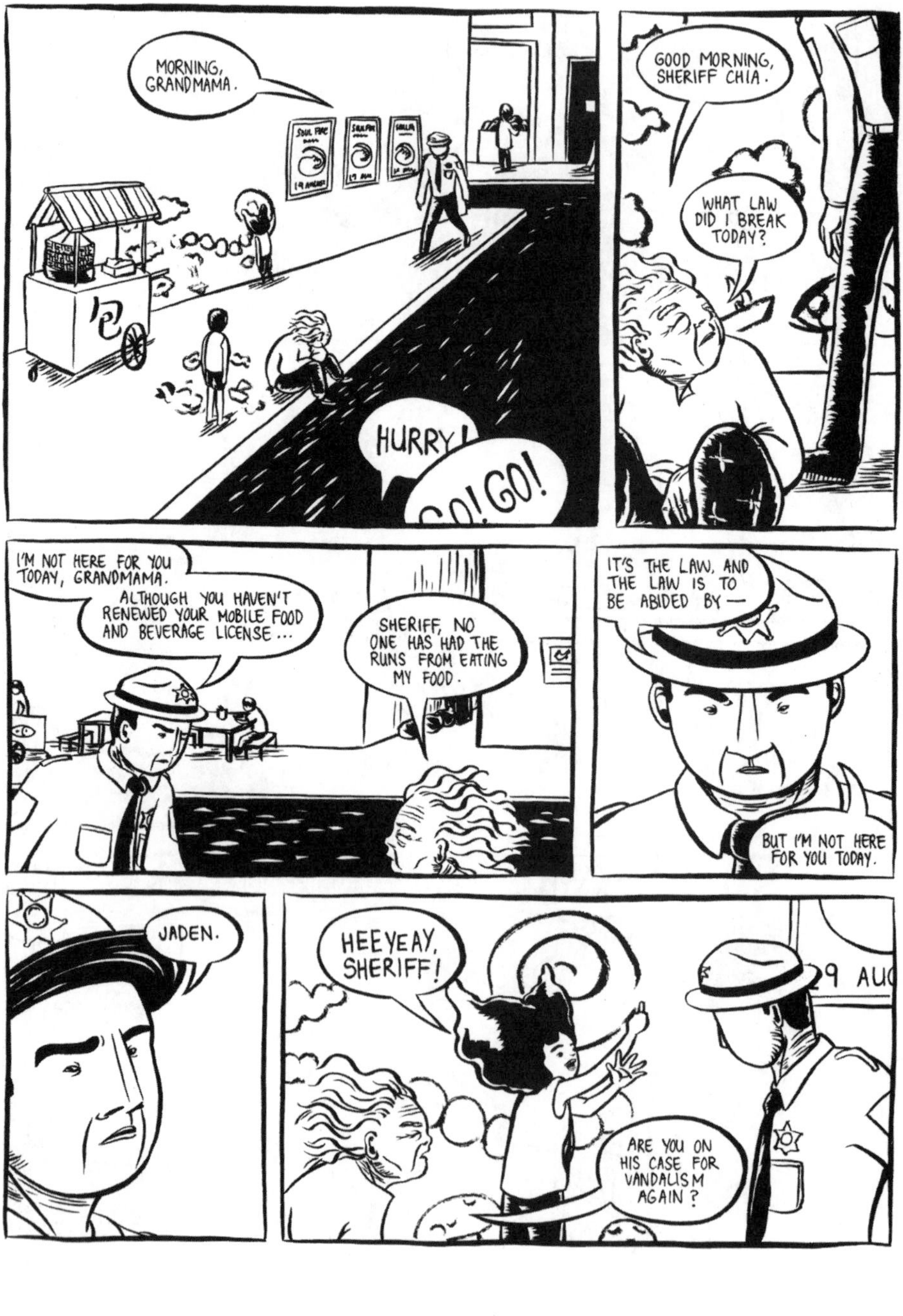
MORNING, GRANDMAMA.
HURRY!
GO! GO!
GOOD MORNING, SHERIFF CHIA.
WHAT LAW DID I BREAK TODAY?
I'M NOT HERE FOR YOU TODAY, GRANDMAMA.
ALTHOUGH YOU HAVEN'T RENEWED YOUR MOBILE FOOD AND BEVERAGE LICENSE...
SHERIFF, NO ONE HAS HAD THE RUNS FROM EATING MY FOOD.
IT'S THE LAW, AND THE LAW IS TO BE ABIDED BY—
BUT I'M NOT HERE FOR YOU TODAY.
JADEN.
HEEYEAY, SHERIFF!
ARE YOU ON HIS CASE FOR VANDALISM AGAIN?

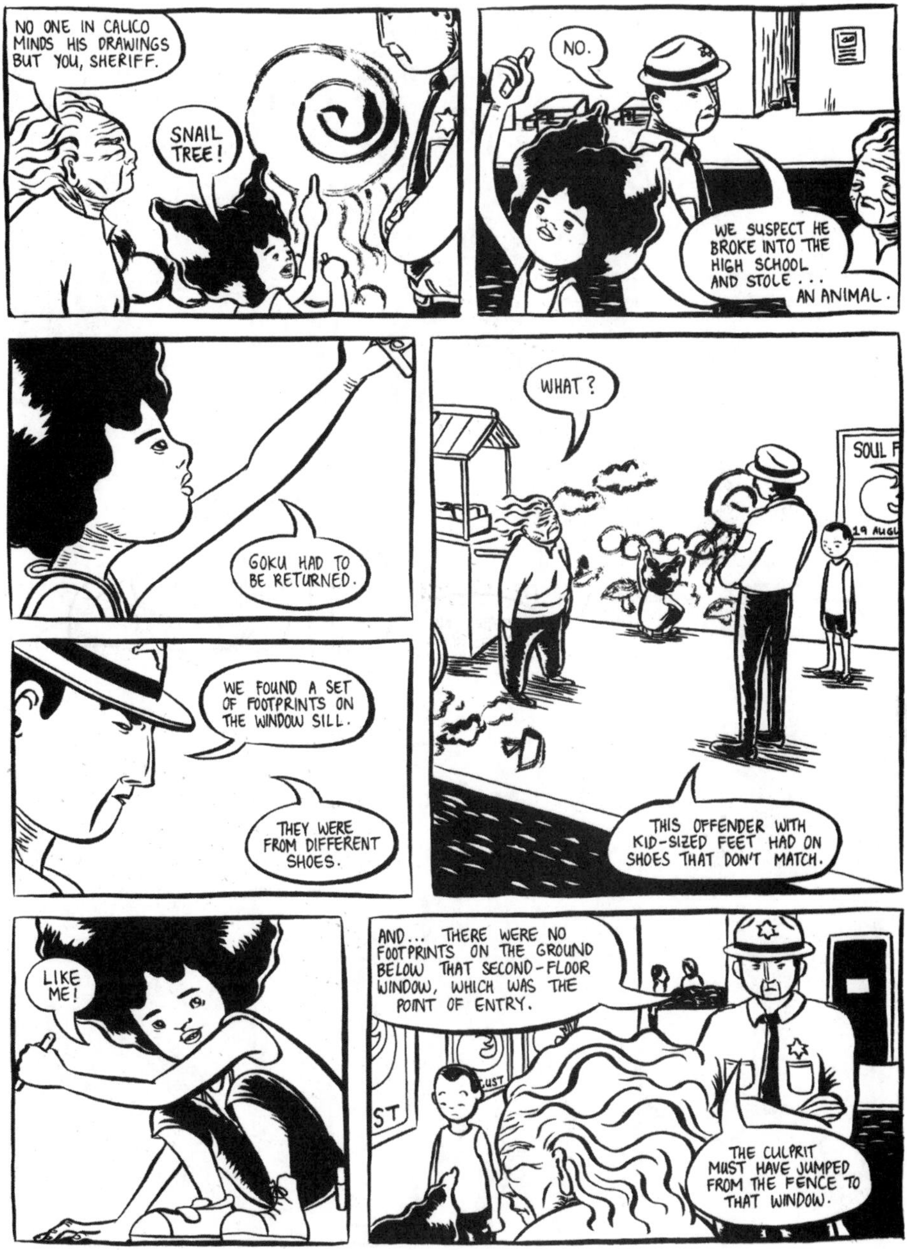

NO ONE IN CALICO MINDS HIS DRAWINGS BUT YOU, SHERIFF.
SNAIL TREE!
NO.
WE SUSPECT HE BROKE INTO THE HIGH SCHOOL AND STOLE . . .
AN ANIMAL.
GOKU HAD TO BE RETURNED.
WHAT?
SOUL F
19 AUGU
WE FOUND A SET OF FOOTPRINTS ON THE WINDOW SILL.
THEY WERE FROM DIFFERENT SHOES.
THIS OFFENDER WITH KID-SIZED FEET HAD ON SHOES THAT DON'T MATCH.
LIKE ME!
AND... THERE WERE NO FOOTPRINTS ON THE GROUND BELOW THAT SECOND-FLOOR WINDOW, WHICH WAS THE POINT OF ENTRY.
THE CULPRIT MUST HAVE JUMPED FROM THE FENCE TO THAT WINDOW.

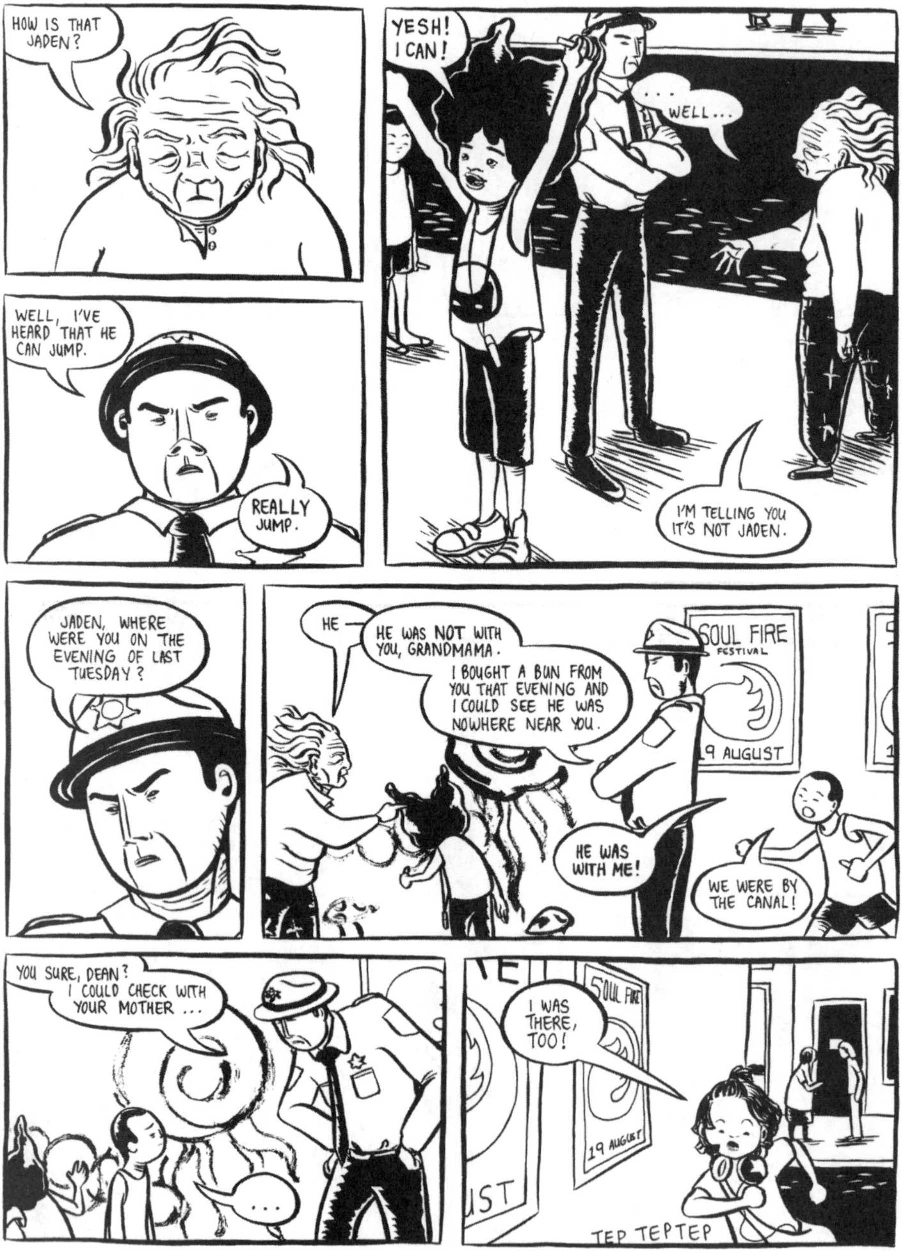
HOW IS THAT JADEN?
WELL, I'VE HEARD THAT HE CAN JUMP.
REALLY JUMP.
YESH! I CAN!
. . .
WELL...
I'M TELLING YOU IT'S NOT JADEN.
JADEN, WHERE WERE YOU ON THE EVENING OF LAST TUESDAY?
HE —
HE WAS NOT WITH YOU, GRANDMAMA.
I BOUGHT A BUN FROM YOU THAT EVENING AND I COULD SEE HE WAS NOWHERE NEAR YOU.
SOUL FIRE FESTIVAL
19 AUGUST
HE WAS WITH ME!
WE WERE BY THE CANAL!
YOU SURE, DEAN?
I COULD CHECK WITH YOUR MOTHER ...
...
SOUL FIRE
I WAS THERE, TOO!
19 AUGUST
UST
TEP TEPTEP

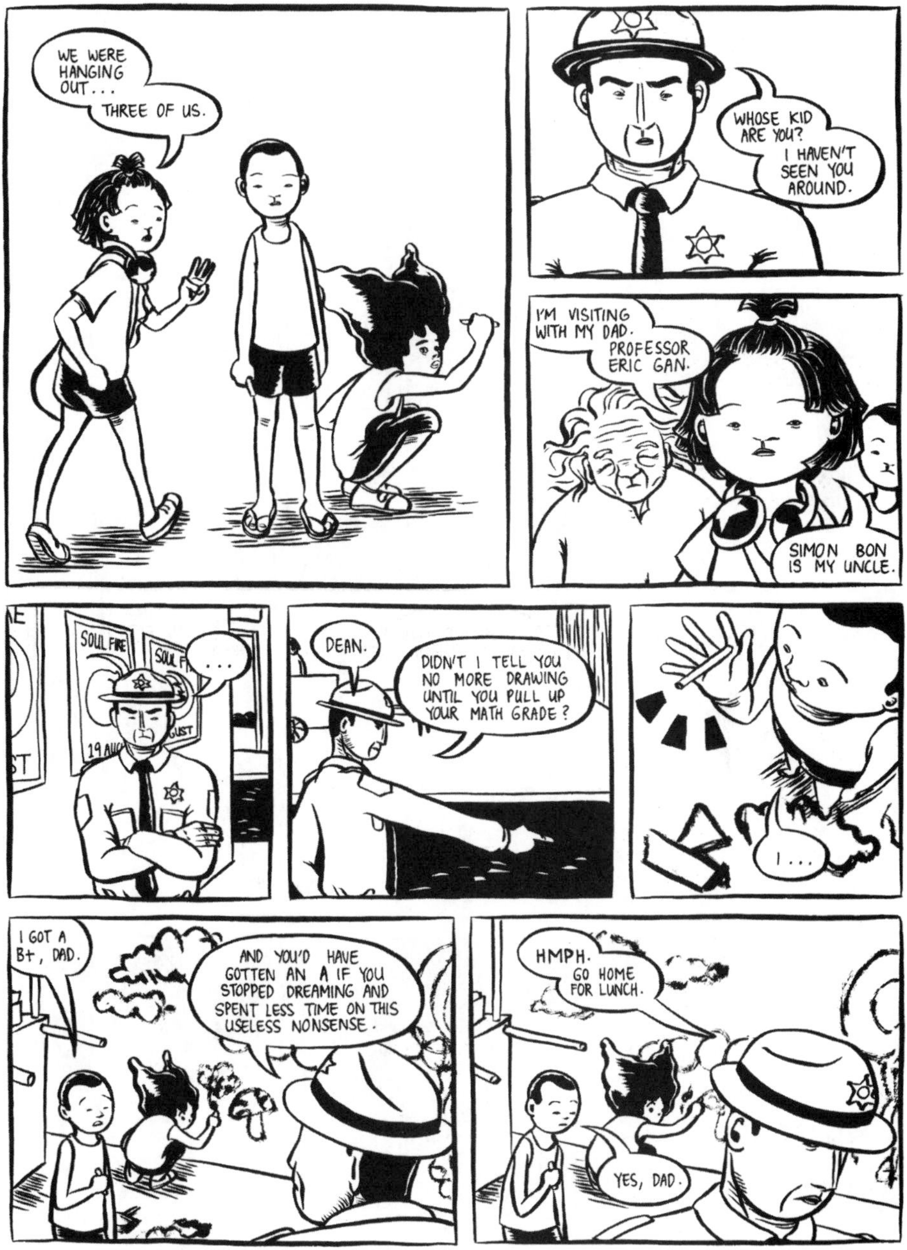
WE WERE HANGING OUT...
THREE OF US.
WHOSE KID ARE YOU?
I HAVEN'T SEEN YOU AROUND.
I'M VISITING WITH MY DAD.
PROFESSOR ERIC GAN.
SIMON BON IS MY UNCLE.
SOUL FIRE
19 AUG
...
DEAN.
DIDN'T I TELL YOU NO MORE DRAWING UNTIL YOU PULL UP YOUR MATH GRADE?
I...
I GOT A B+, DAD.
AND YOU'D HAVE GOTTEN AN A IF YOU STOPPED DREAMING AND SPENT LESS TIME ON THIS USELESS NONSENSE.
HMPH.
GO HOME FOR LUNCH.
YES, DAD.

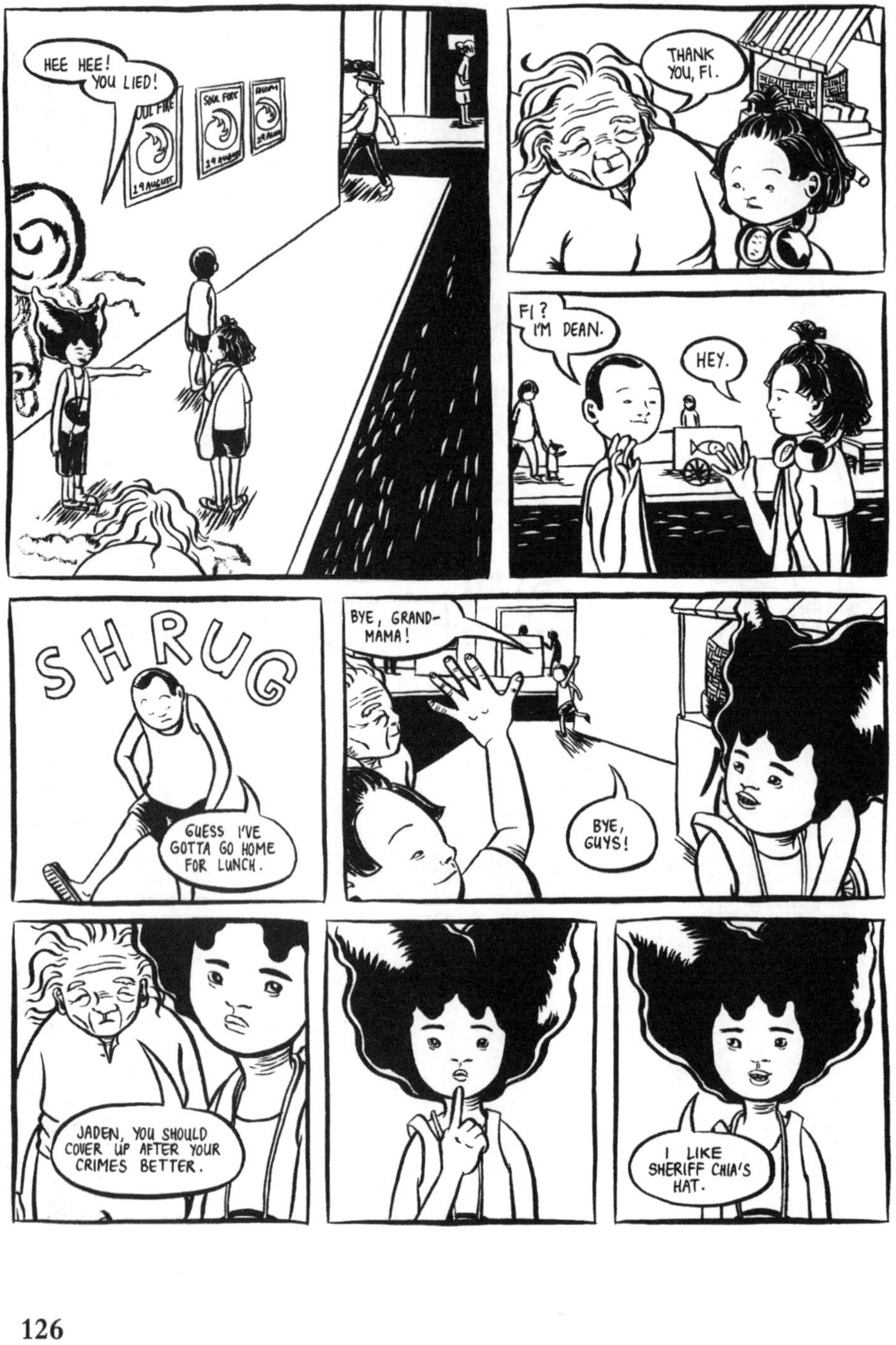
HEE HEE! YOU LIED!
SOUL FIRE
19 AUGUST
SOUL FIRE
19 AUGUST
THANK YOU, FI.
FI? I'M DEAN.
HEY.
SHRUG
GUESS I'VE GOTTA GO HOME FOR LUNCH.
BYE, GRAND-MAMA!
BYE, GUYS!
JADEN, YOU SHOULD COVER UP AFTER YOUR CRIMES BETTER.
I LIKE SHERIFF CHIA'S HAT.

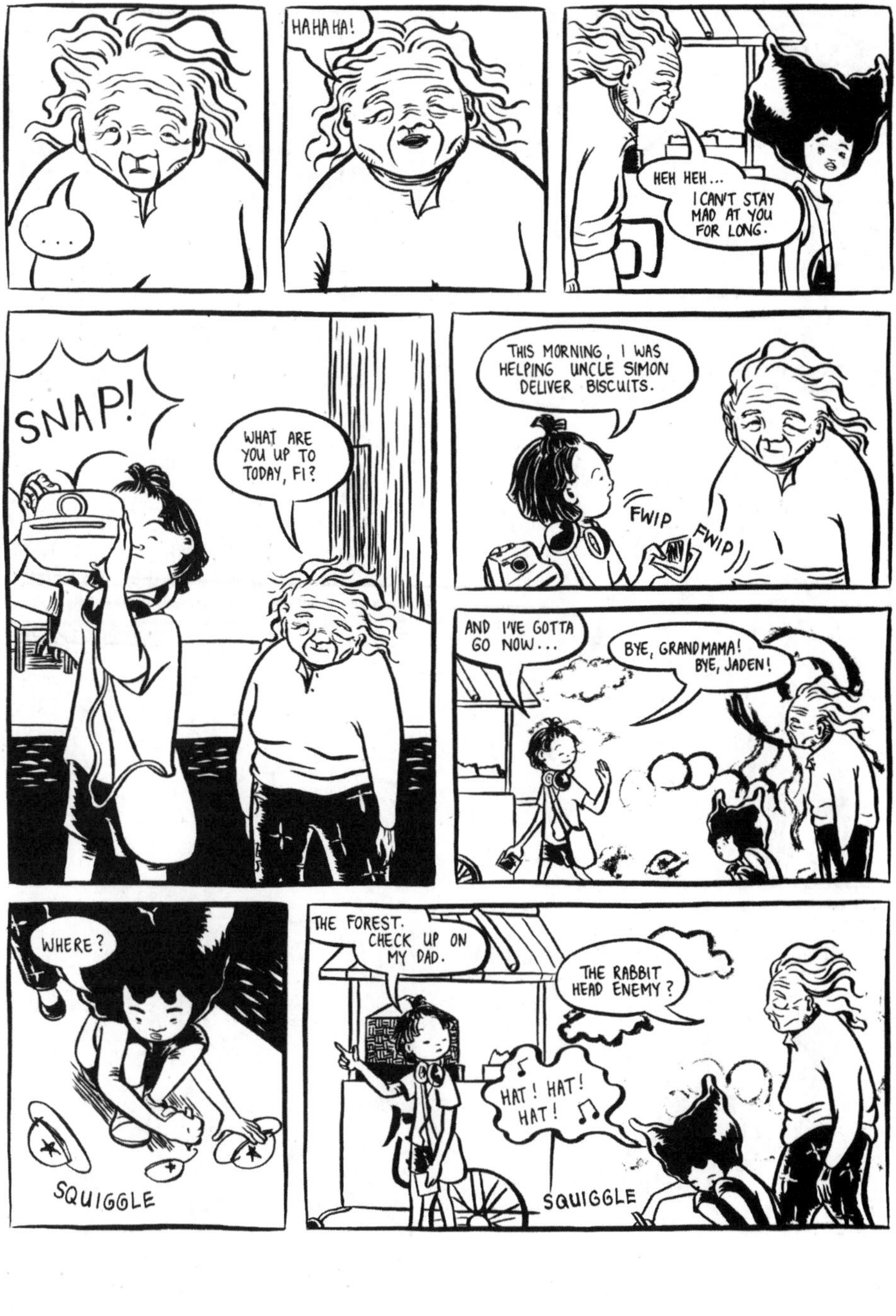
...
HA HA HA!
HEH HEH...
I CAN'T STAY MAD AT YOU FOR LONG.
SNAP!
WHAT ARE YOU UP TO TODAY, FI?
THIS MORNING, I WAS HELPING UNCLE SIMON DELIVER BISCUITS.
FWIP
FWIP
AND I'VE GOTTA GO NOW...
BYE, GRANDMAMA!
BYE, JADEN!
WHERE?
SQUIGGLE
THE FOREST.
CHECK UP ON MY DAD.
THE RABBIT HEAD ENEMY?
HAT! HAT! HAT!
SQUIGGLE

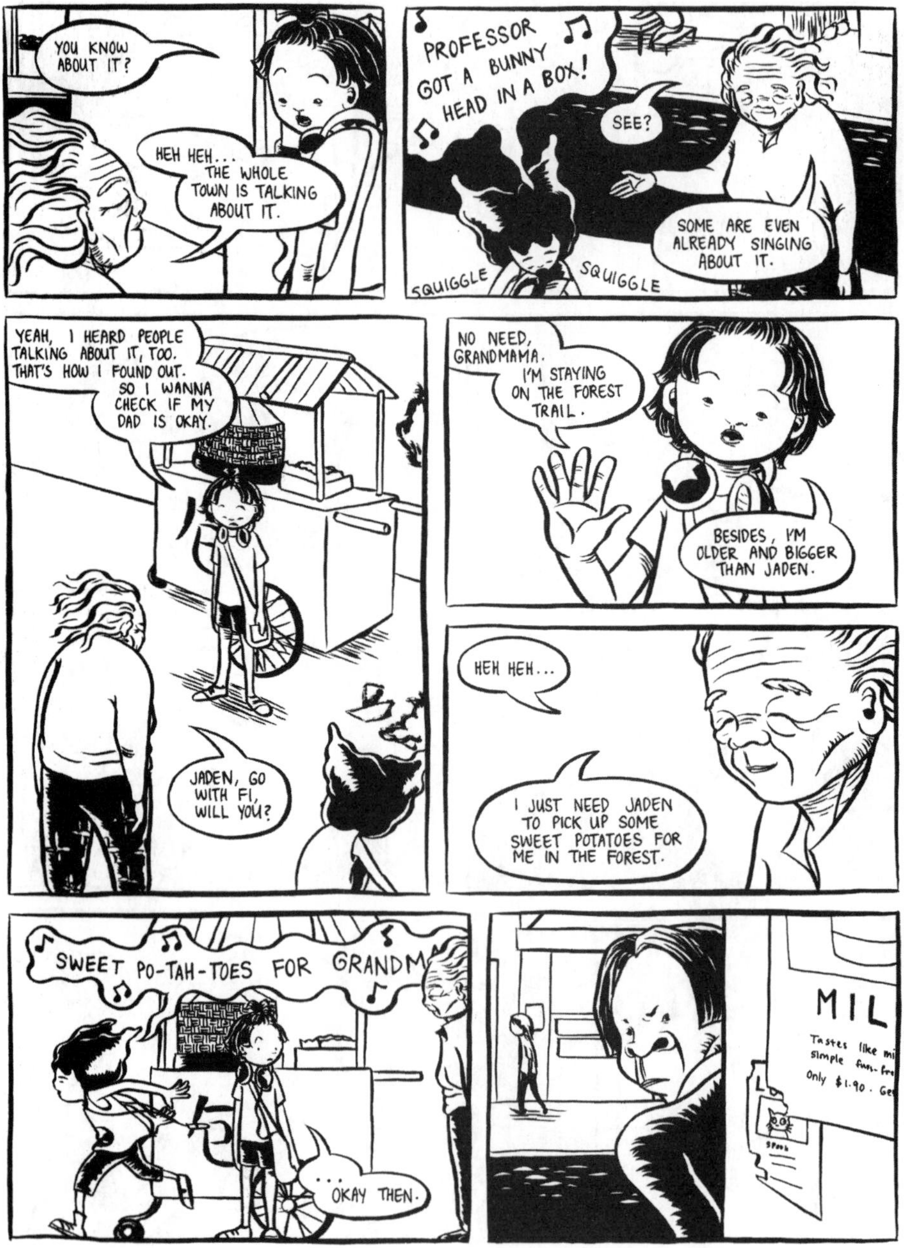
YOU KNOW ABOUT IT?
HEH HEH... THE WHOLE TOWN IS TALKING ABOUT IT.
PROFESSOR GOT A BUNNY HEAD IN A BOX!
SEE?
SOME ARE EVEN ALREADY SINGING ABOUT IT.
SQUIGGLE SQUIGGLE
YEAH, I HEARD PEOPLE TALKING ABOUT IT, TOO. THAT'S HOW I FOUND OUT.
SO I WANNA CHECK IF MY DAD IS OKAY.
JADEN, GO WITH FI, WILL YOU?
NO NEED, GRANDMAMA.
I'M STAYING ON THE FOREST TRAIL.
BESIDES, I'M OLDER AND BIGGER THAN JADEN.
HEH HEH...
I JUST NEED JADEN TO PICK UP SOME SWEET POTATOES FOR ME IN THE FOREST.
SWEET PO-TAH-TOES FOR GRANDM
... OKAY THEN.
MIL
Tastes like mi
simple fun-fre
Only $1.90. Ge

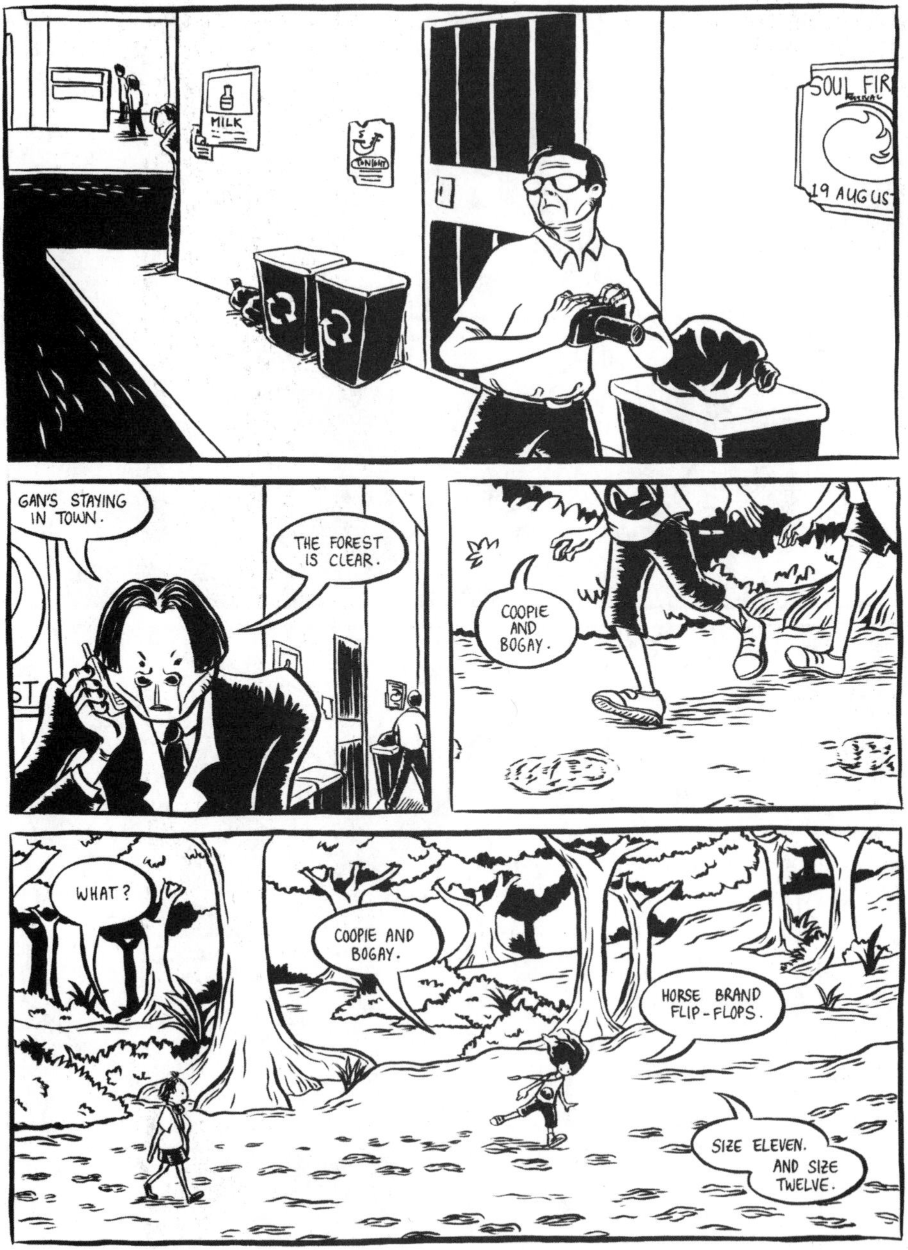
MILK
TONIGHT
SOUL FIR
19 AUGUST
GAN'S STAYING IN TOWN.
THE FOREST IS CLEAR.
COOPIE AND BOGAY.
WHAT?
COOPIE AND BOGAY.
HORSE BRAND FLIP-FLOPS.
SIZE ELEVEN. AND SIZE TWELVE.

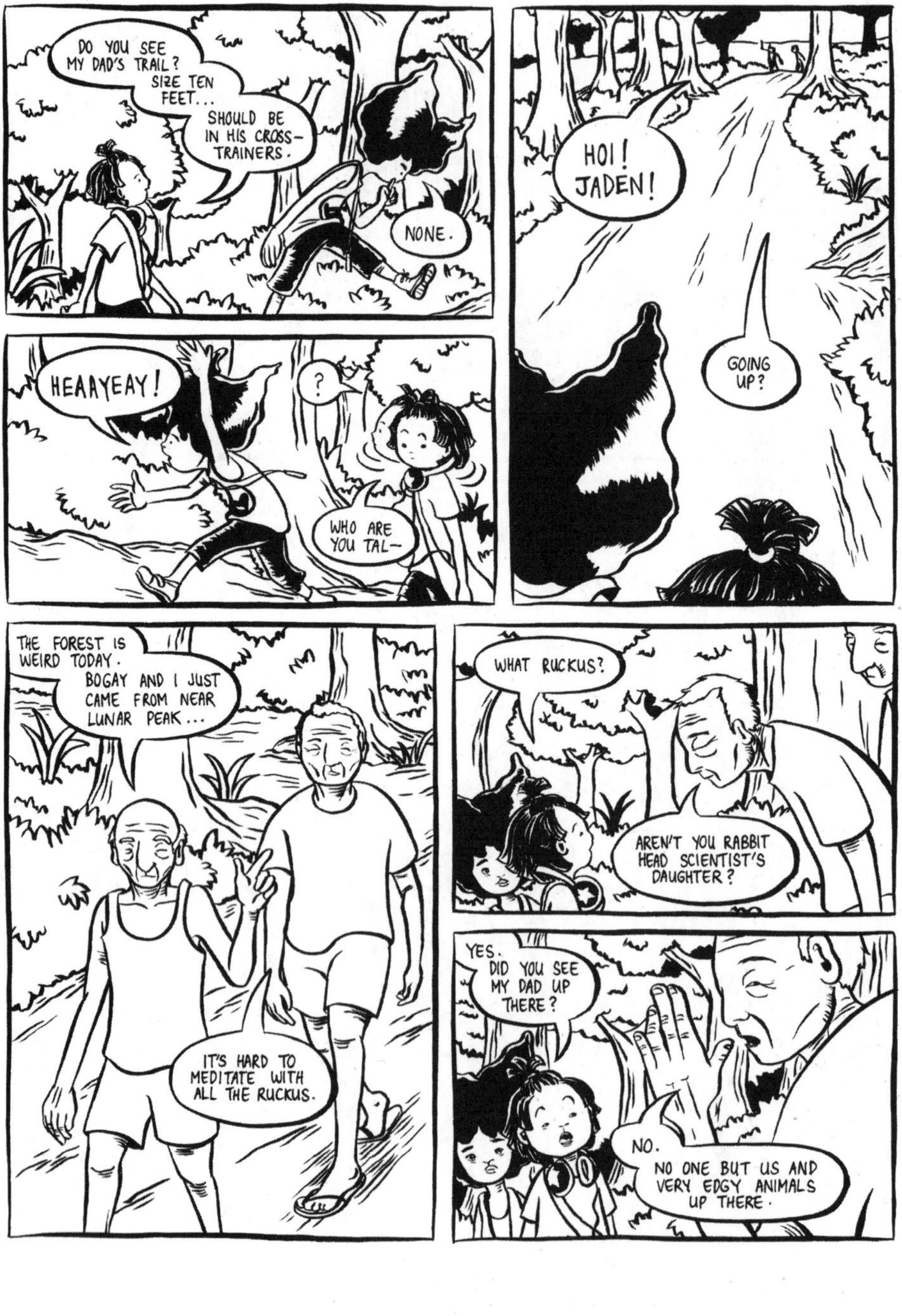
DO YOU SEE MY DAD'S TRAIL? SIZE TEN FEET... SHOULD BE IN HIS CROSS-TRAINERS.
NONE.
HOI! JADEN!
HEAAYEAY!
?
WHO ARE YOU TAL—
GOING UP?
THE FOREST IS WEIRD TODAY.
BOGAY AND I JUST CAME FROM NEAR LUNAR PEAK...
IT'S HARD TO MEDITATE WITH ALL THE RUCKUS.
WHAT RUCKUS?
AREN'T YOU RABBIT HEAD SCIENTIST'S DAUGHTER?
YES.
DID YOU SEE MY DAD UP THERE?
NO.
NO ONE BUT US AND VERY EDGY ANIMALS UP THERE.

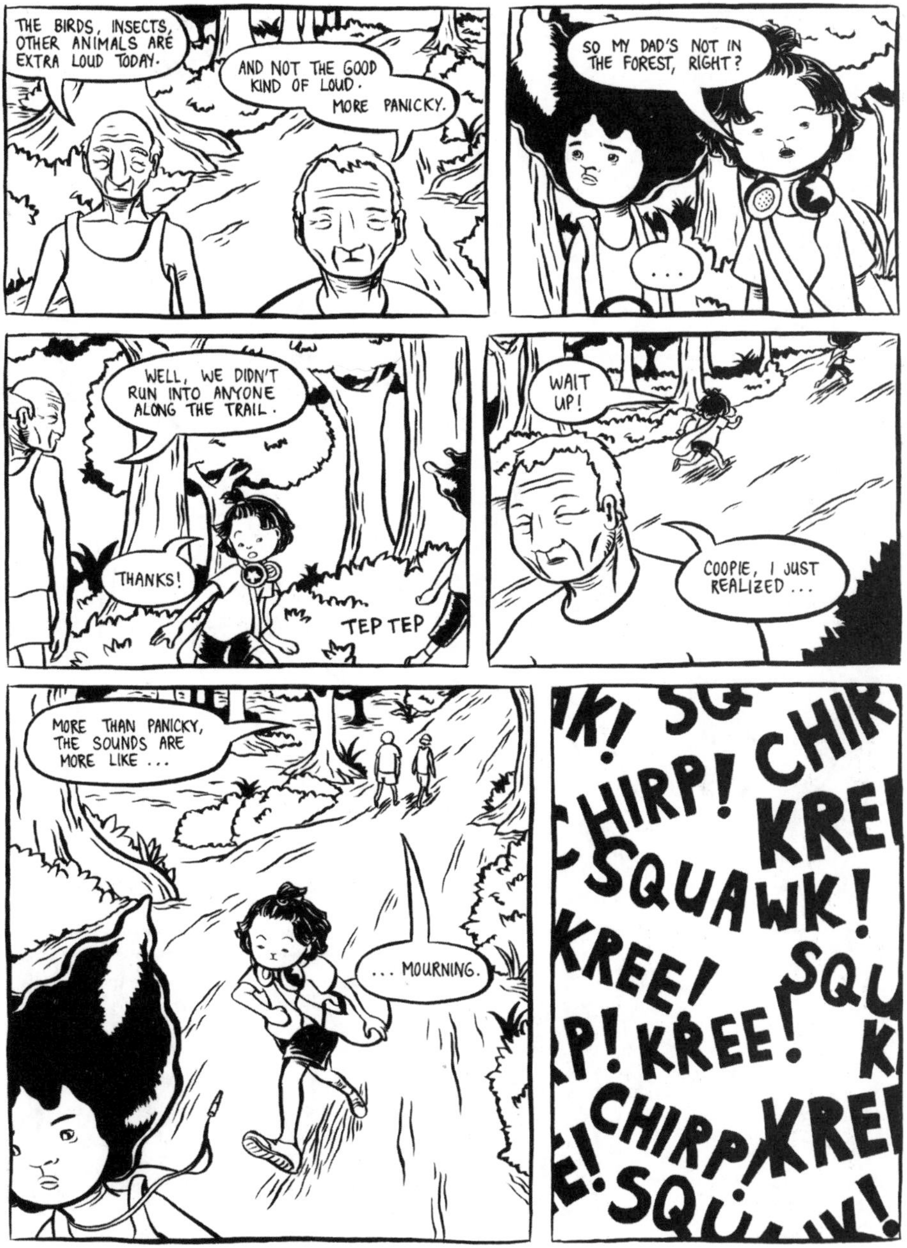
THE BIRDS, INSECTS, OTHER ANIMALS ARE EXTRA LOUD TODAY.
AND NOT THE GOOD KIND OF LOUD. MORE PANICKY.
SO MY DAD'S NOT IN THE FOREST, RIGHT?
...
WELL, WE DIDN'T RUN INTO ANYONE ALONG THE TRAIL.
THANKS!
TEP TEP
WAIT UP!
COOPIE, I JUST REALIZED ...
MORE THAN PANICKY, THE SOUNDS ARE MORE LIKE ...
... MOURNING.
CHIRP! CHIR KREE SQUAWK! KREE! SQU P! KREE! K CHIRP! KREE! SQUAWK!

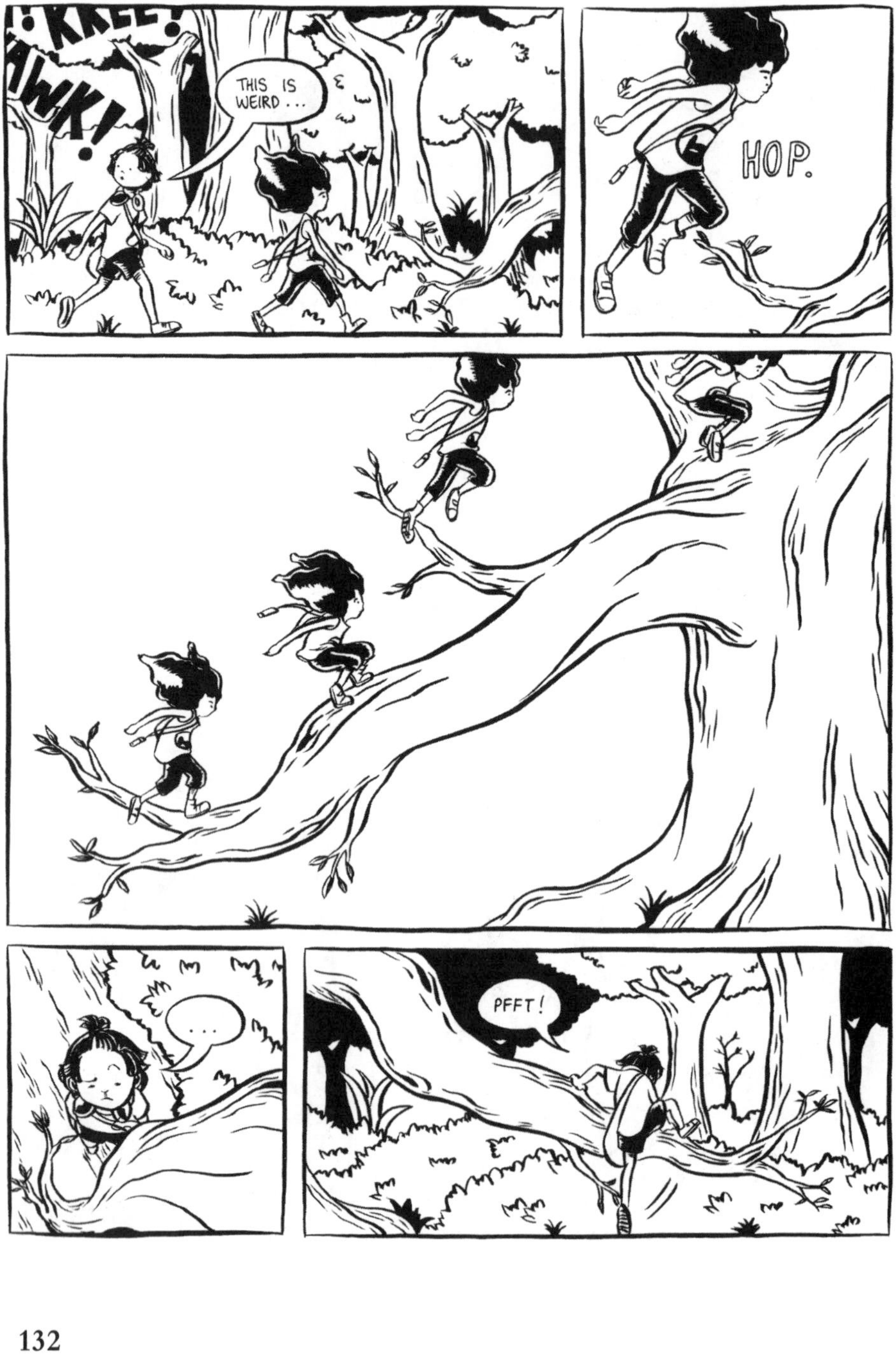
THIS IS WEIRD ...
HOP.
...
PFFT!

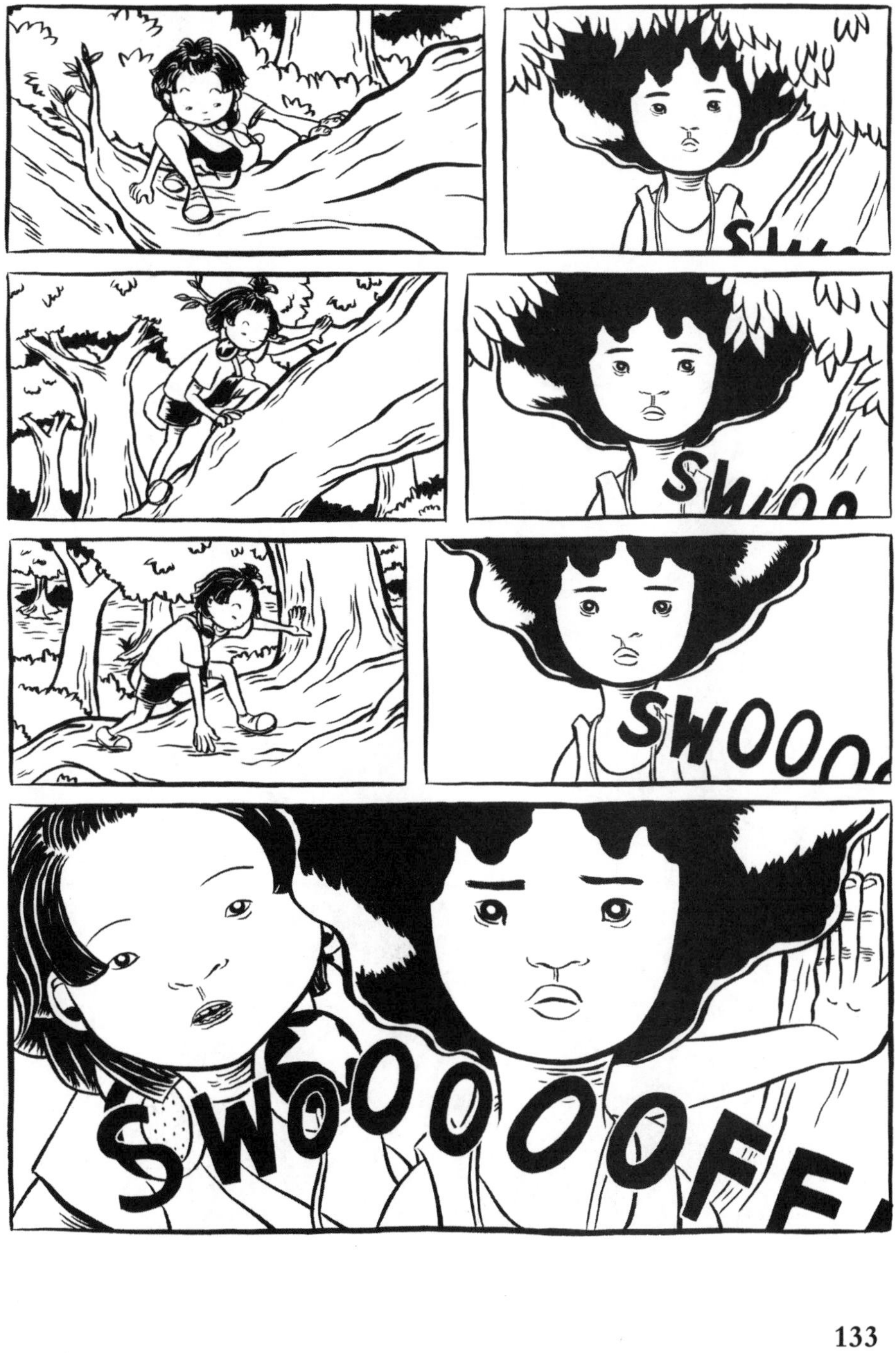
SWOO
SWOOO
SWOOOOOOFF

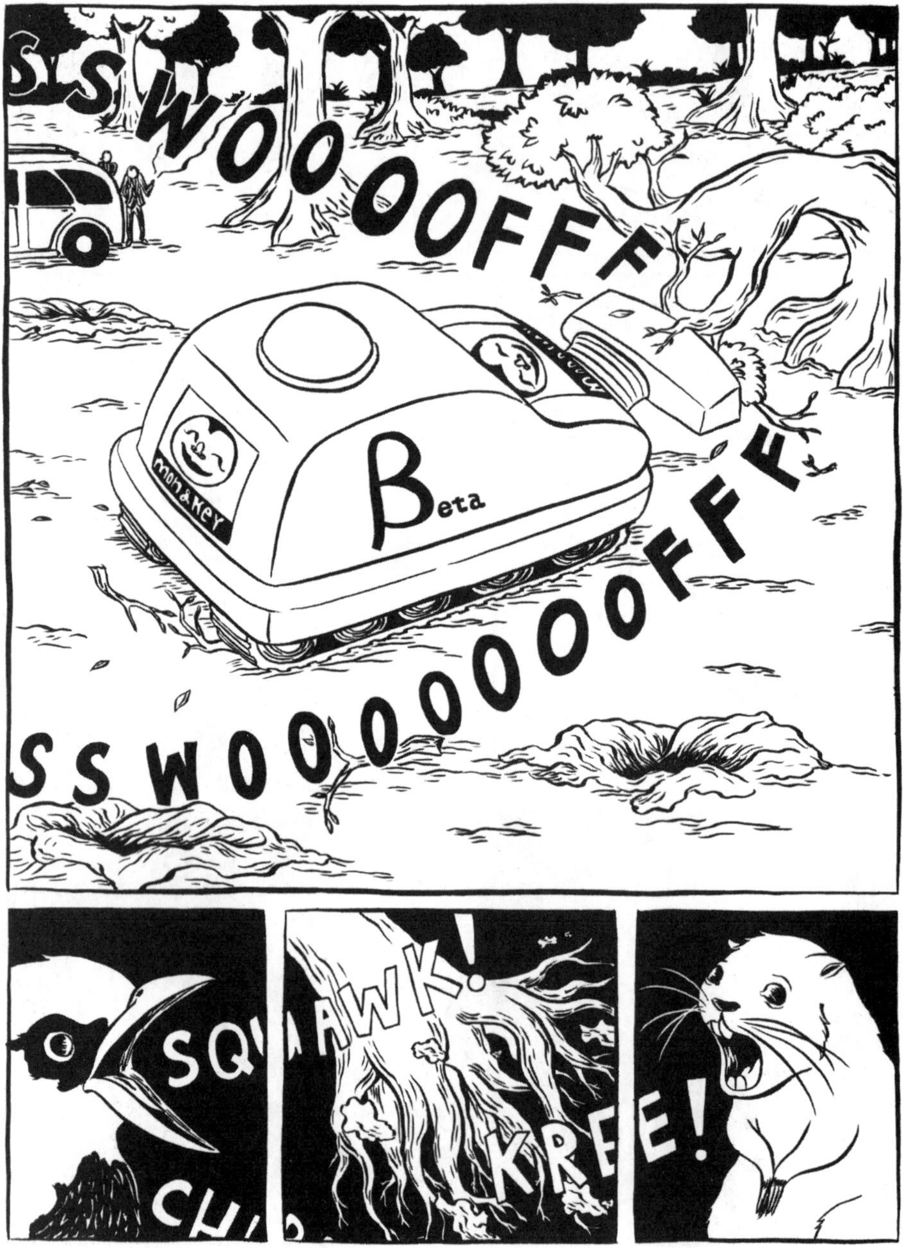
SSWOOOOFFFF
mon&key
Beta
SSWOOOOOOOOFFFF
SQUAWK!
CHI
KREE!

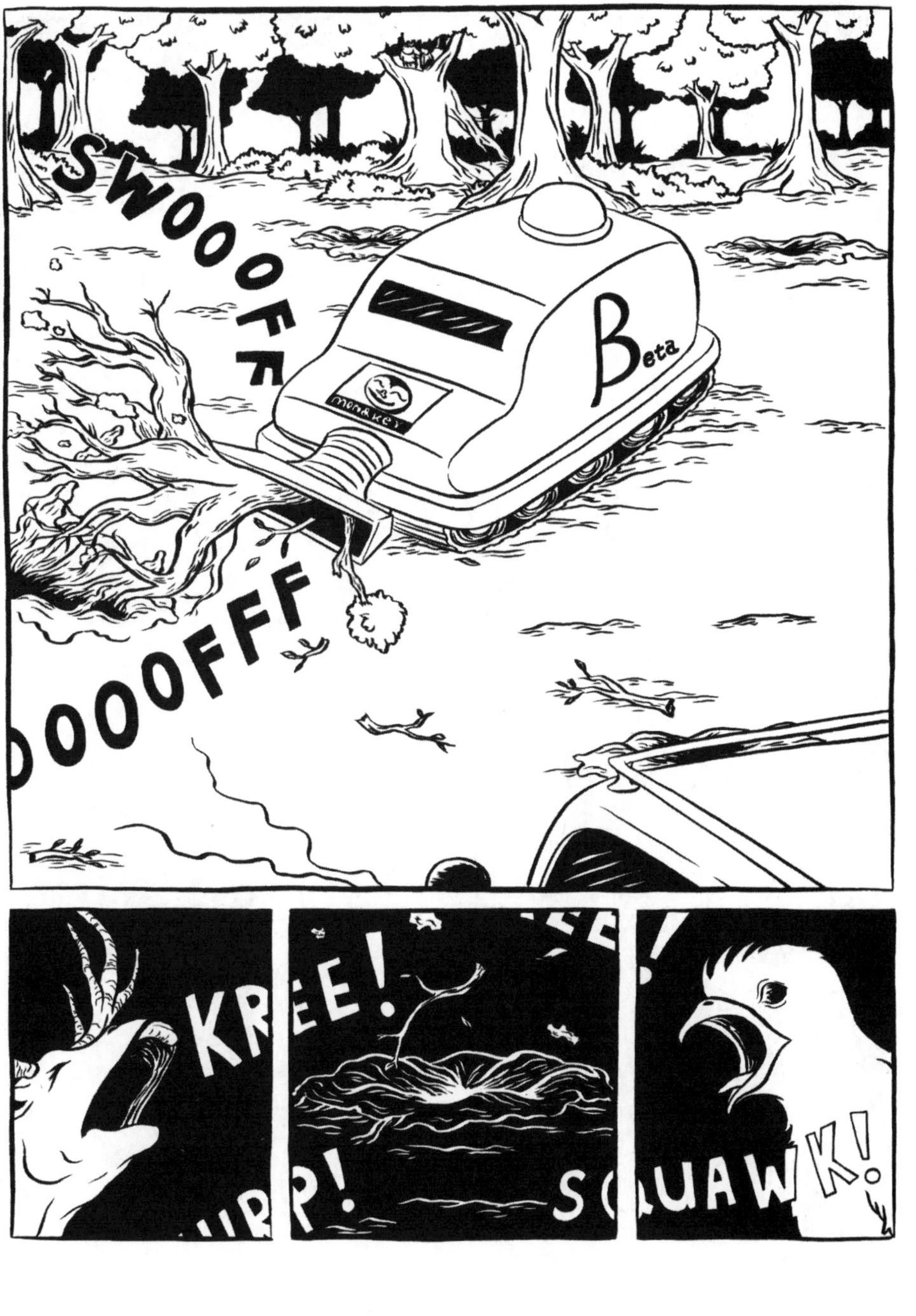

SWOOOFF
OOOOFFF
Beta
KREE!
SQUAWK!

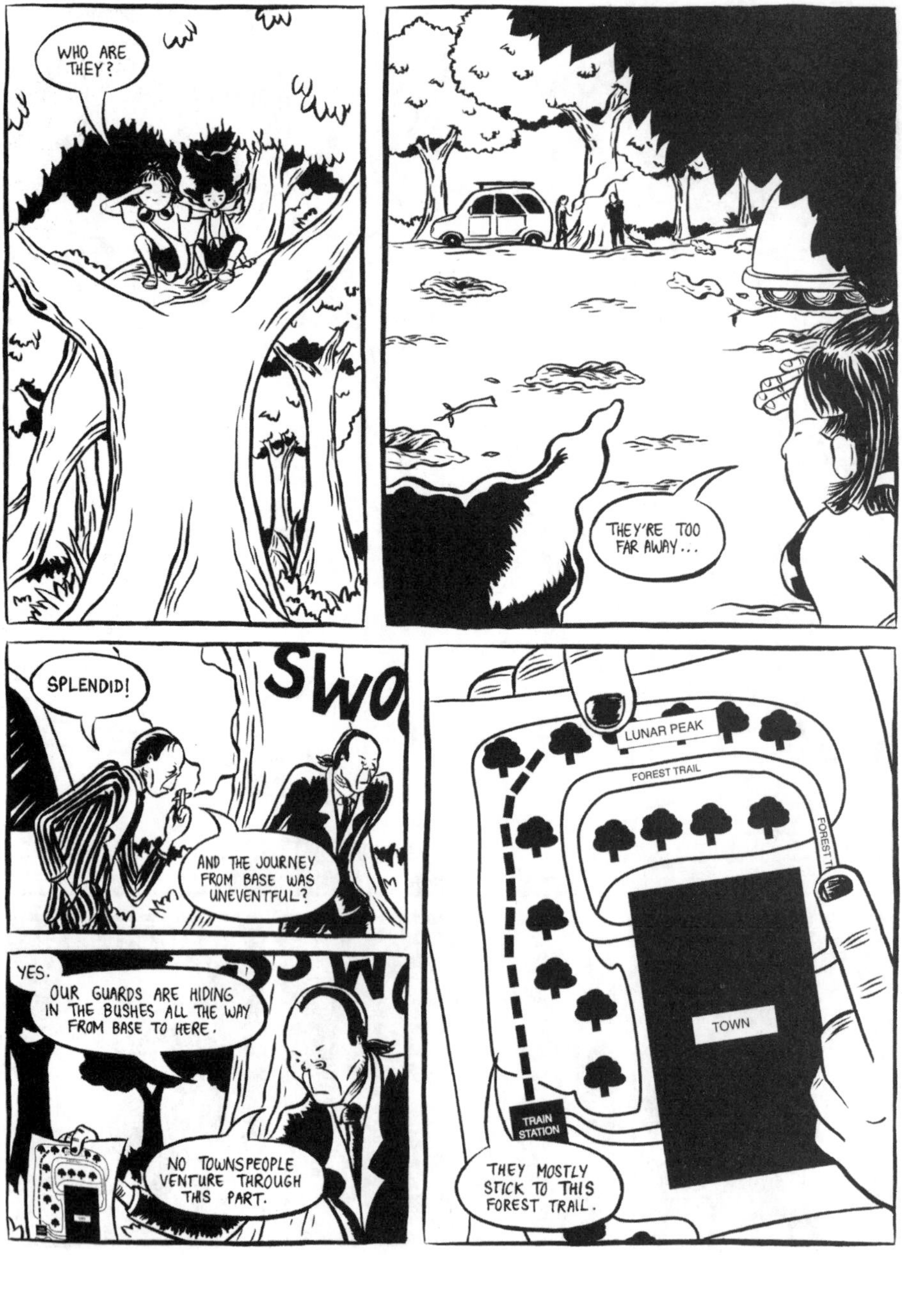
WHO ARE THEY?
THEY'RE TOO FAR AWAY...
SPLENDID!
SWO
AND THE JOURNEY FROM BASE WAS UNEVENTFUL?
YES.
OUR GUARDS ARE HIDING IN THE BUSHES ALL THE WAY FROM BASE TO HERE.
NO TOWNSPEOPLE VENTURE THROUGH THIS PART.
LUNAR PEAK
FOREST TRAIL
TOWN
TRAIN STATION
THEY MOSTLY STICK TO THIS FOREST TRAIL.

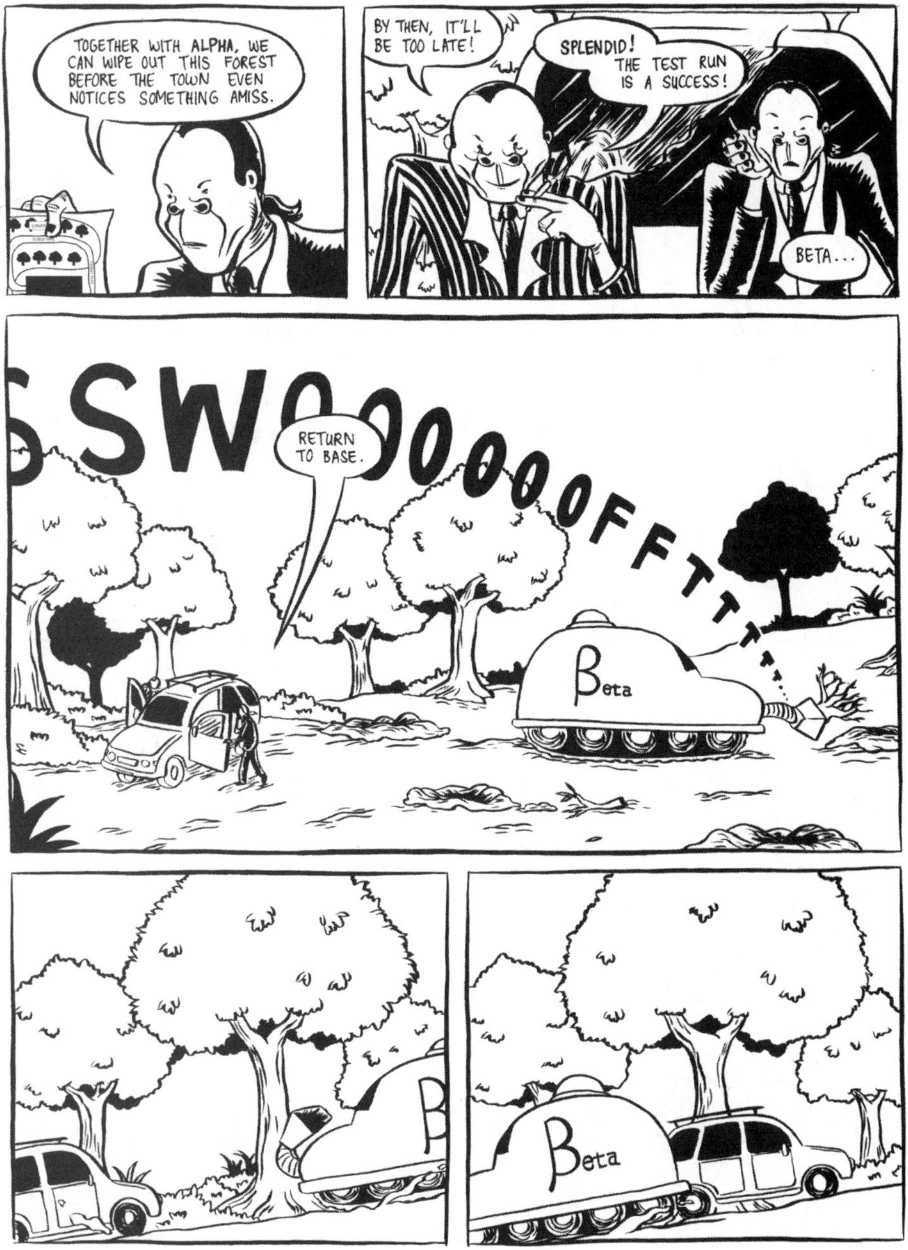
TOGETHER WITH ALPHA, WE CAN WIPE OUT THIS FOREST BEFORE THE TOWN EVEN NOTICES SOMETHING AMISS.
BY THEN, IT'LL BE TOO LATE!
SPLENDID! THE TEST RUN IS A SUCCESS!
BETA...
SSWOOOOOOOFFTTT...
RETURN TO BASE.
Beta
Beta

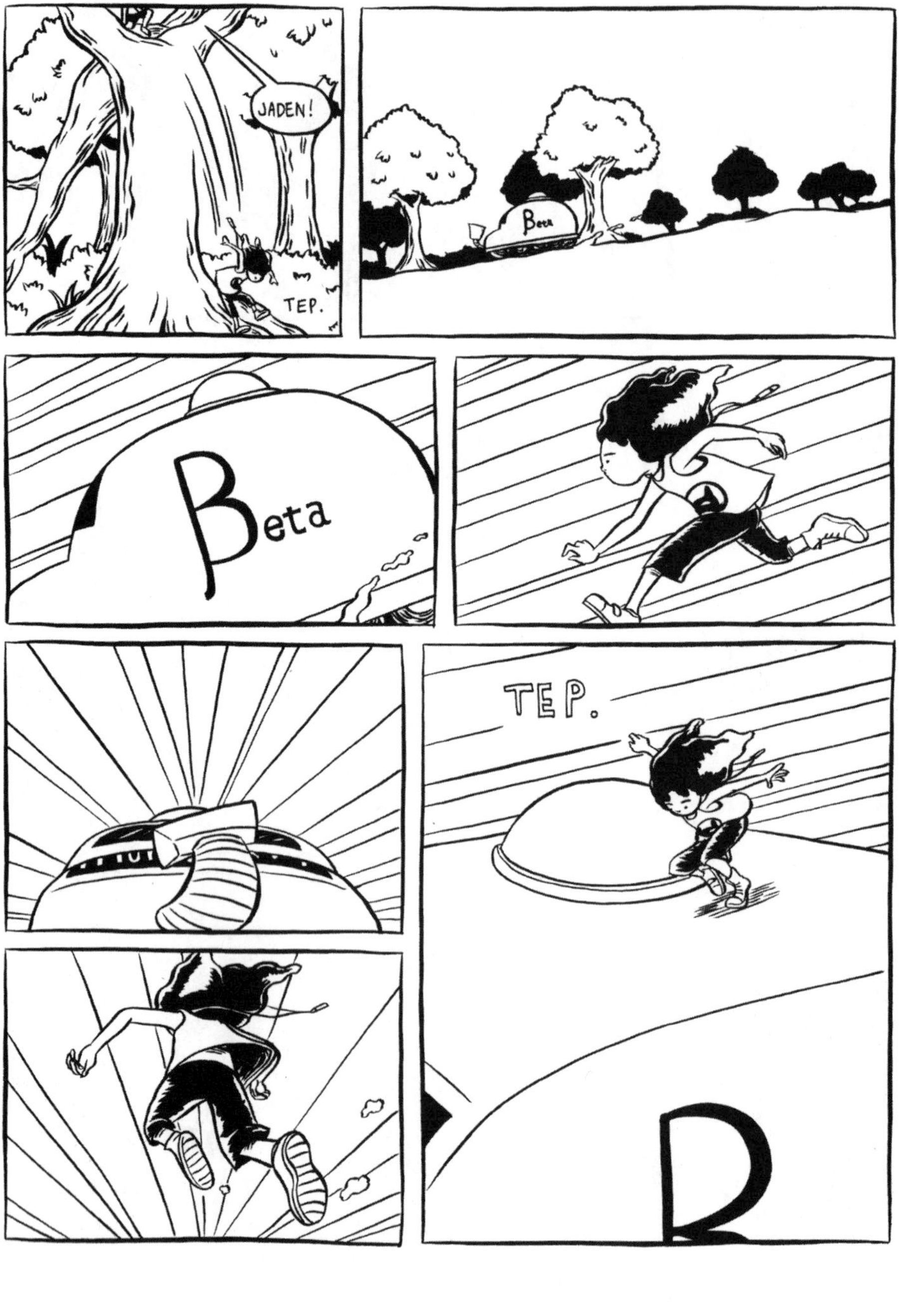
JADEN!
TEP.
Beta
Beta
TEP.

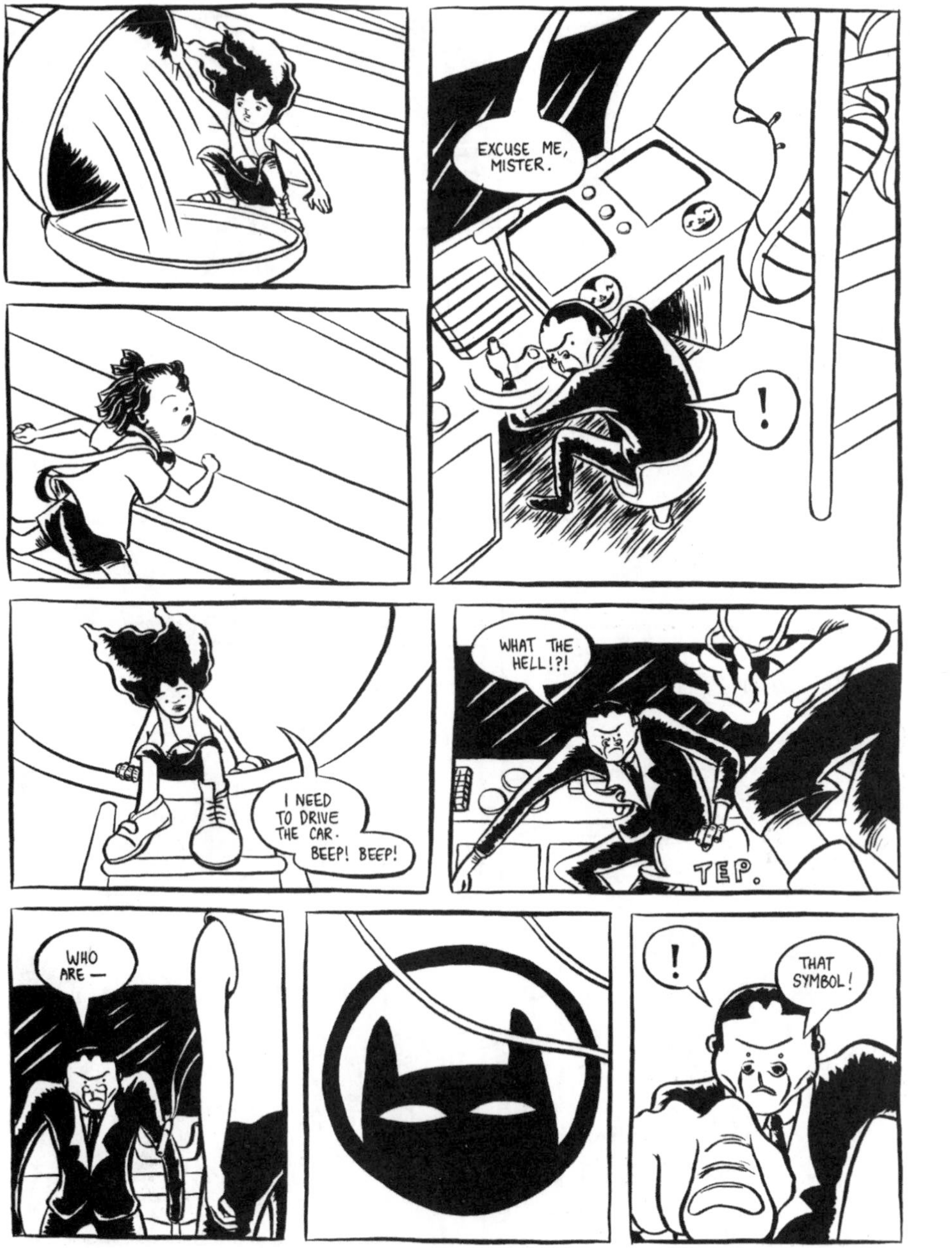
EXCUSE ME, MISTER.
!
WHAT THE HELL!?!
I NEED TO DRIVE THE CAR. BEEP! BEEP!
TEP.
WHO ARE —
!
THAT SYMBOL!

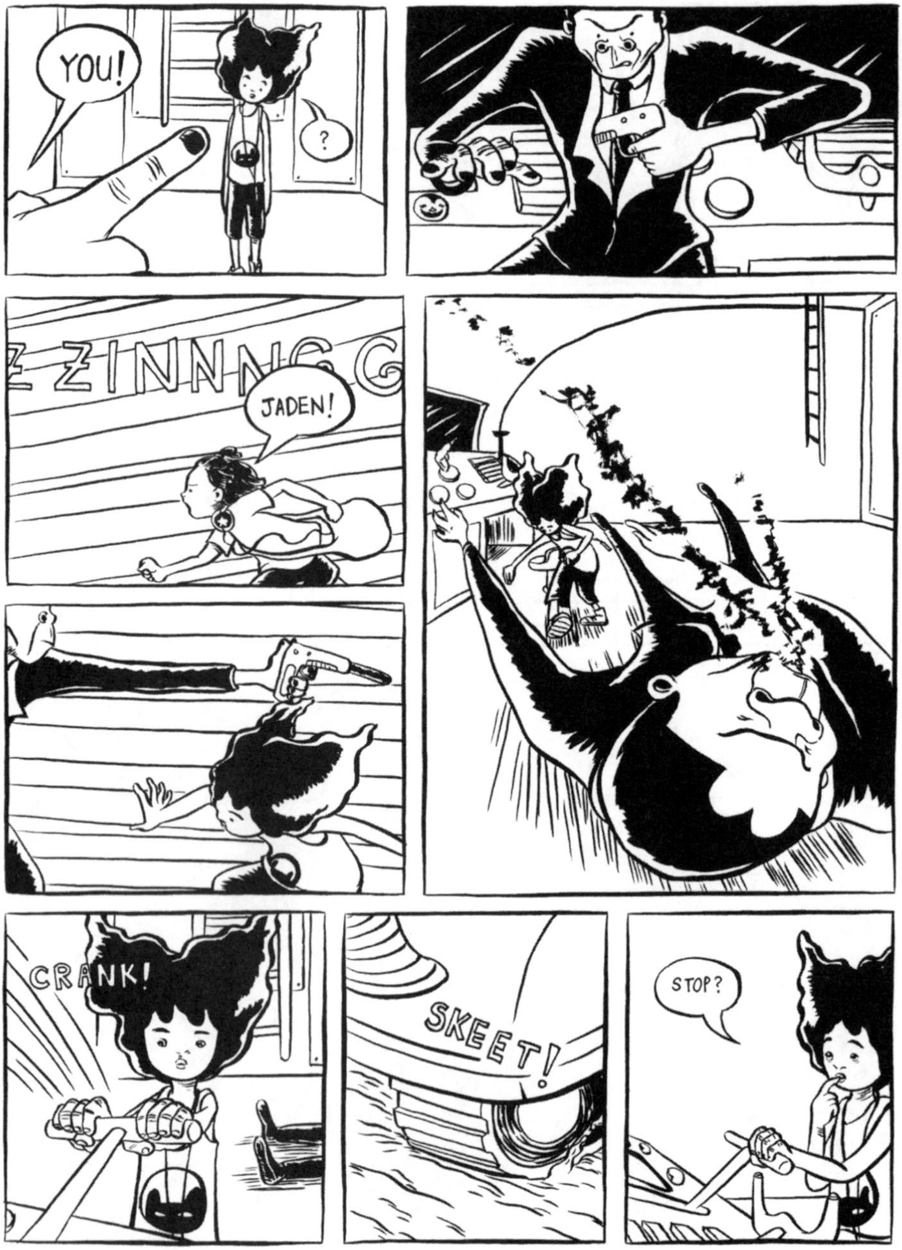
YOU!
?
ZZINNNGG
JADEN!
CRANK!
SKEET!
STOP?

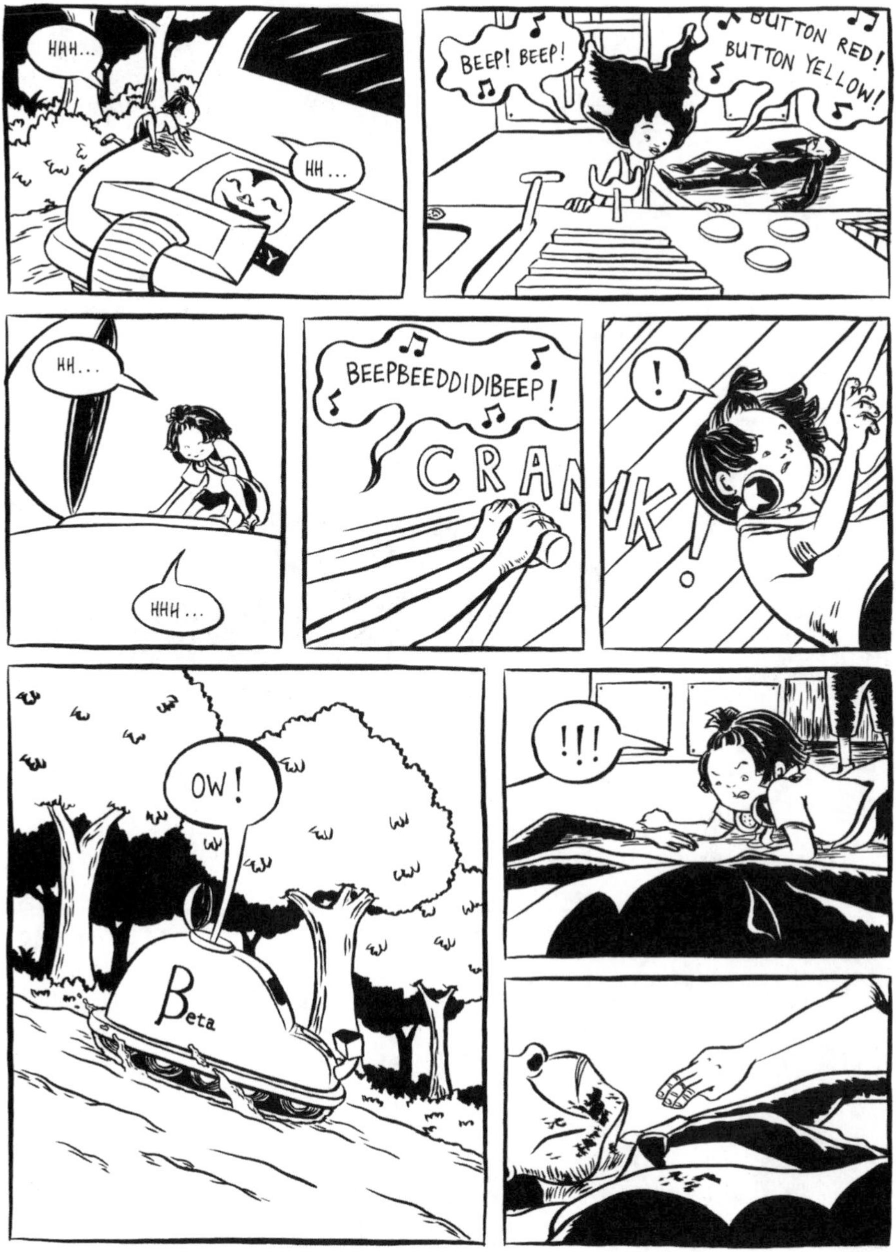
HHH...
HH...
BEEP! BEEP!
BUTTON RED!
BUTTON YELLOW!
HH...
HHH...
BEEPBEEDDIDIBEEP!
CRANK!
!
OW!
Beta
!!!

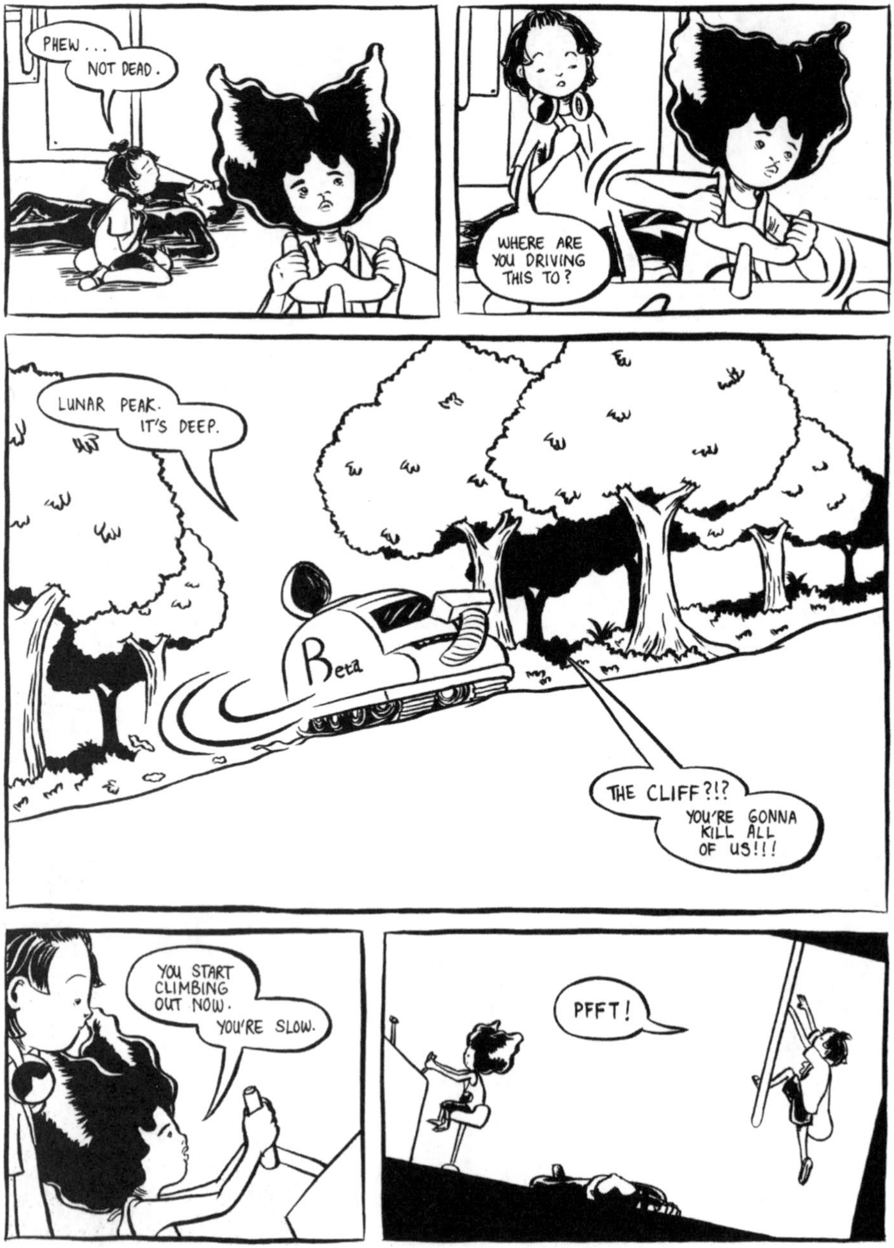
PHEW . . . NOT DEAD .
WHERE ARE YOU DRIVING THIS TO ?
LUNAR PEAK. IT'S DEEP.
Beta
THE CLIFF?!? YOU'RE GONNA KILL ALL OF US!!!
YOU START CLIMBING OUT NOW. YOU'RE SLOW.
PFFT!

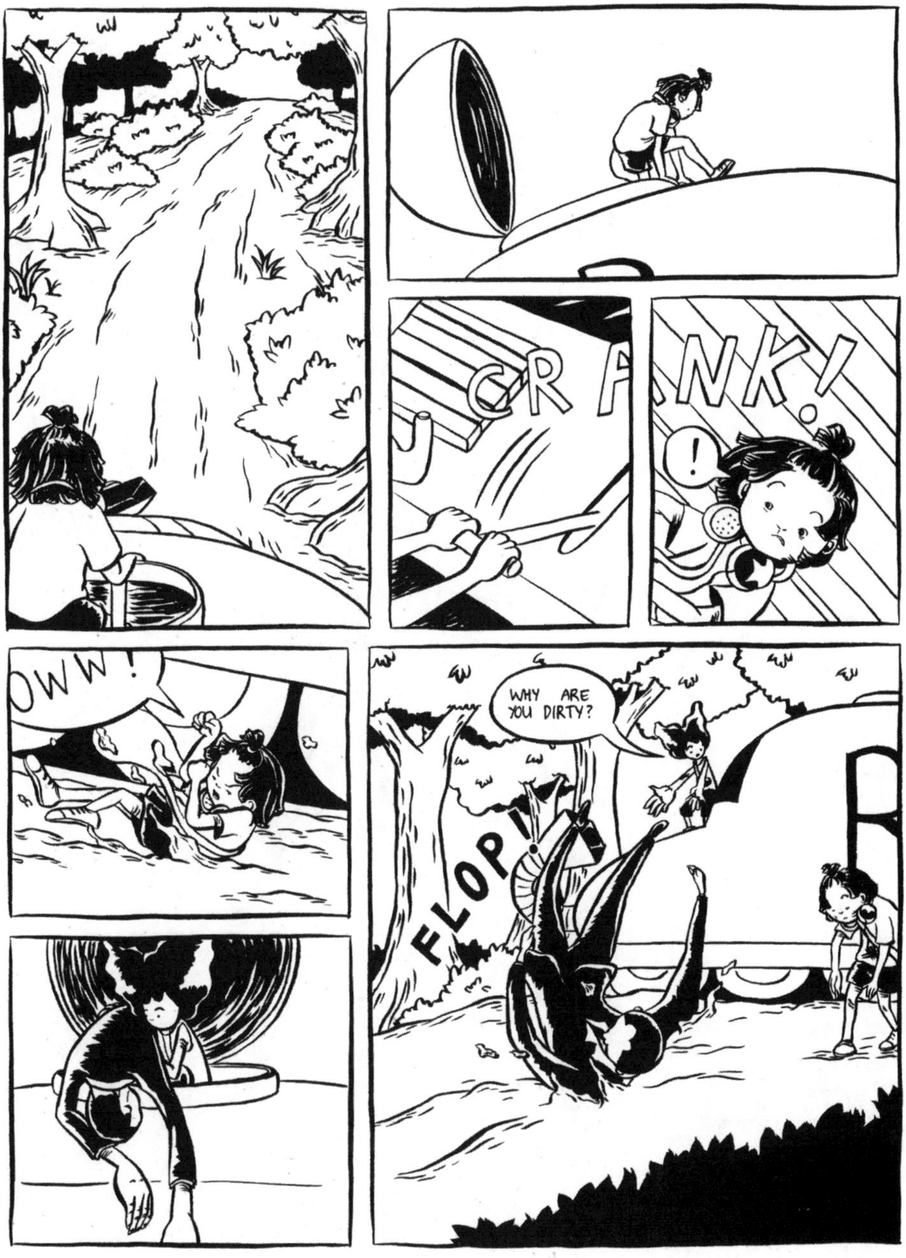
CRANK!
!
OWW!
WHY ARE YOU DIRTY?
FLOP!

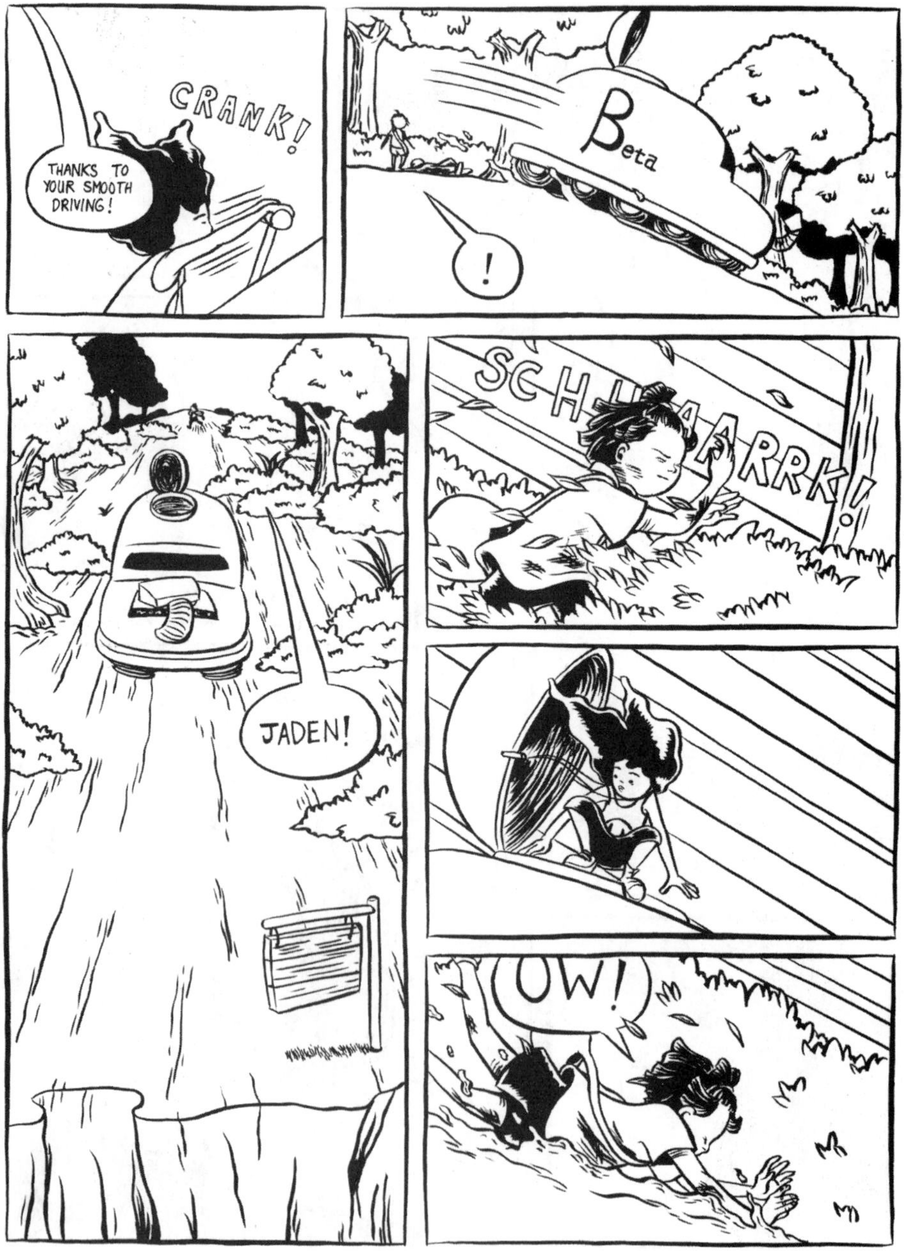

CRANK!
THANKS TO YOUR SMOOTH DRIVING!
Beta
!
JADEN!
SCHHAARRK!
OW!

KRAK!
Lunar PEAK
TEP.
BLOOD.
ARE YOU CRAZY?!?
I THOUGHT YOU WERE GOING KAMIKAZE!
BLOOD.

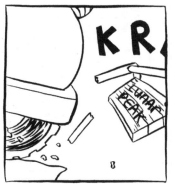

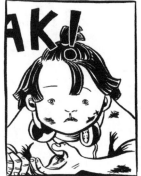

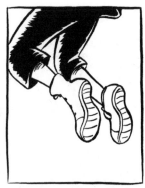

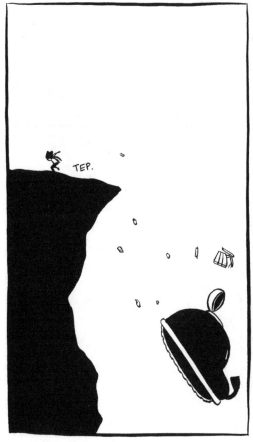

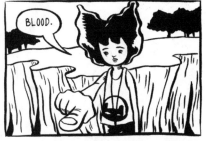

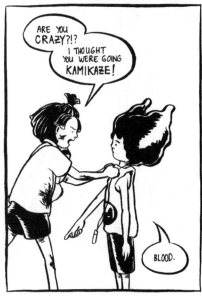

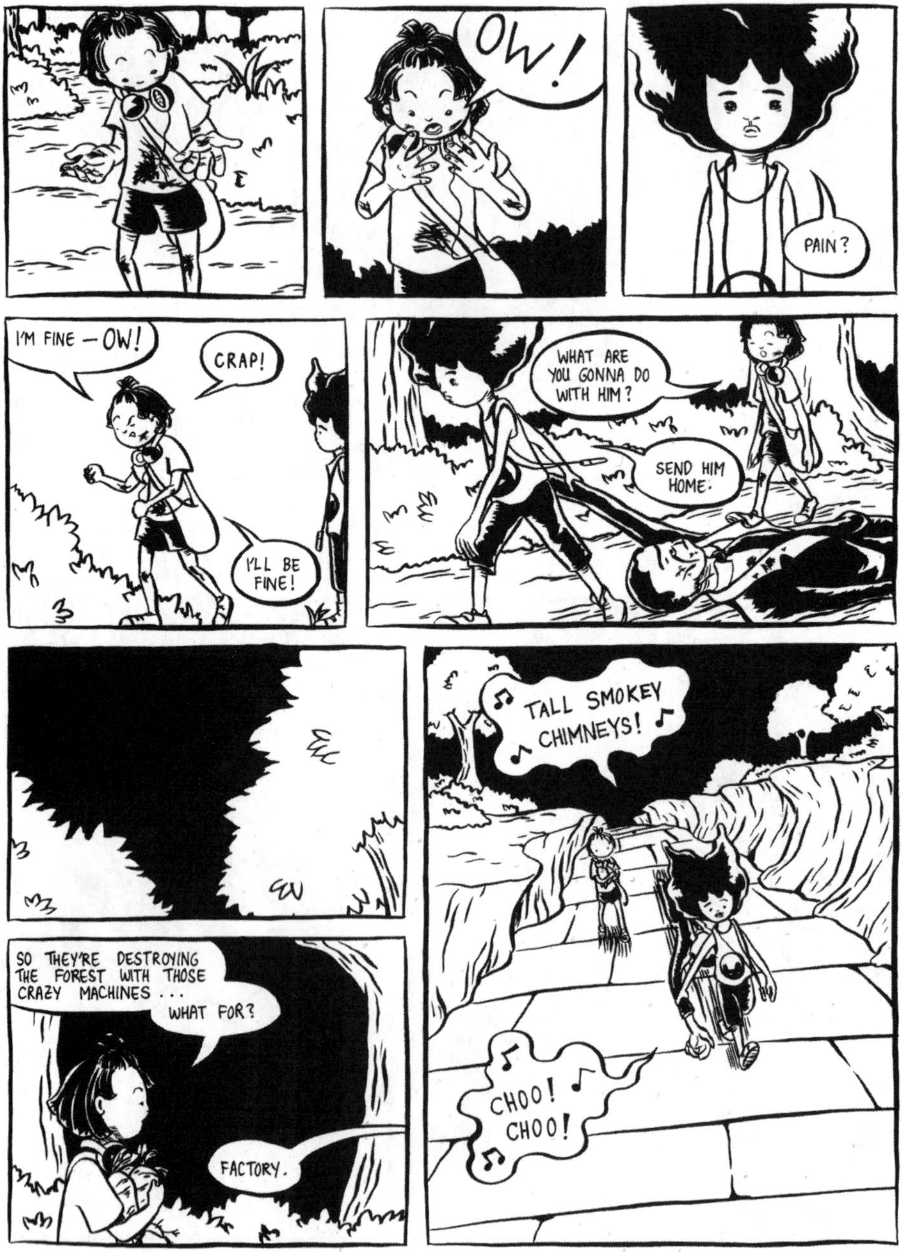
OW!
PAIN?
I'M FINE — OW!
CRAP!
I'LL BE FINE!
WHAT ARE YOU GONNA DO WITH HIM?
SEND HIM HOME.
SO THEY'RE DESTROYING THE FOREST WITH THOSE CRAZY MACHINES . . .
WHAT FOR?
FACTORY.
TALL SMOKEY CHIMNEYS!
CHOO! CHOO!

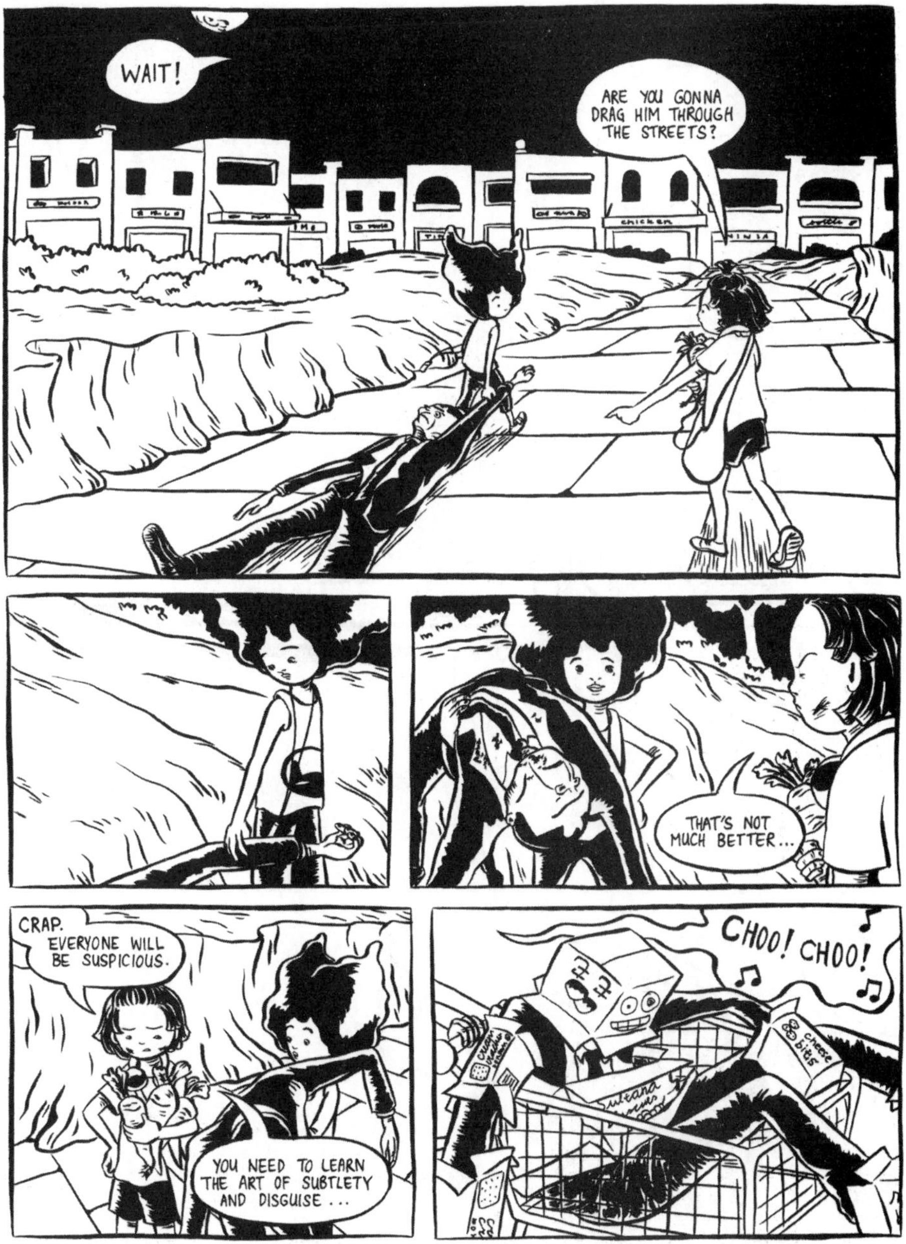
WAIT!
ARE YOU GONNA DRAG HIM THROUGH THE STREETS?
THAT'S NOT MUCH BETTER...
CRAP. EVERYONE WILL BE SUSPICIOUS.
YOU NEED TO LEARN THE ART OF SUBTLETY AND DISGUISE...
CHOO! CHOO!

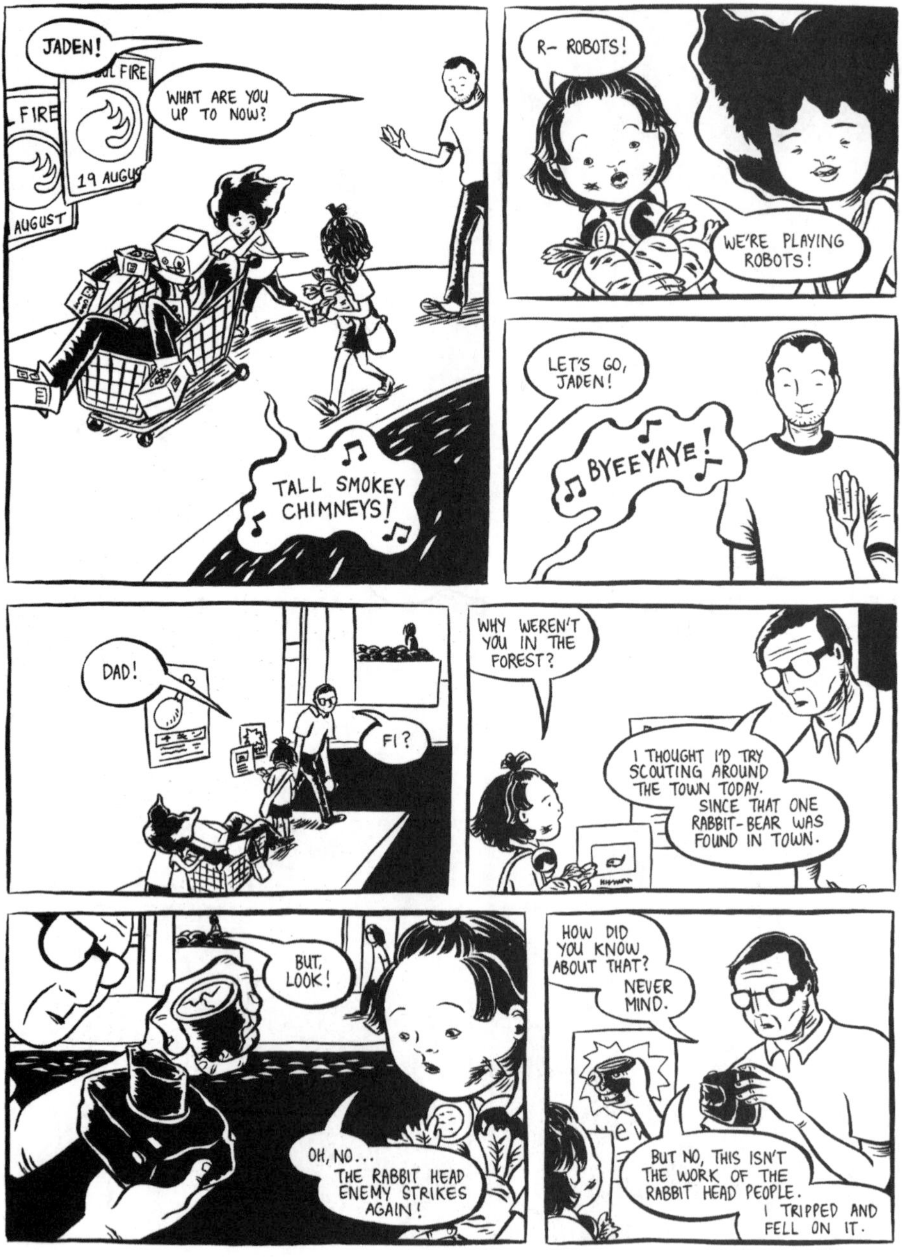
JADEN!
WHAT ARE YOU UP TO NOW?
TALL SMOKEY CHIMNEYS!
R- ROBOTS!
WE'RE PLAYING ROBOTS!
LET'S GO, JADEN!
BYEEYAYE!
DAD!
FI?
WHY WEREN'T YOU IN THE FOREST?
I THOUGHT I'D TRY SCOUTING AROUND THE TOWN TODAY.
SINCE THAT ONE RABBIT-BEAR WAS FOUND IN TOWN.
BUT, LOOK!
OH, NO...
THE RABBIT HEAD ENEMY STRIKES AGAIN!
HOW DID YOU KNOW ABOUT THAT?
NEVER MIND.
BUT NO, THIS ISN'T THE WORK OF THE RABBIT HEAD PEOPLE.
I TRIPPED AND FELL ON IT.

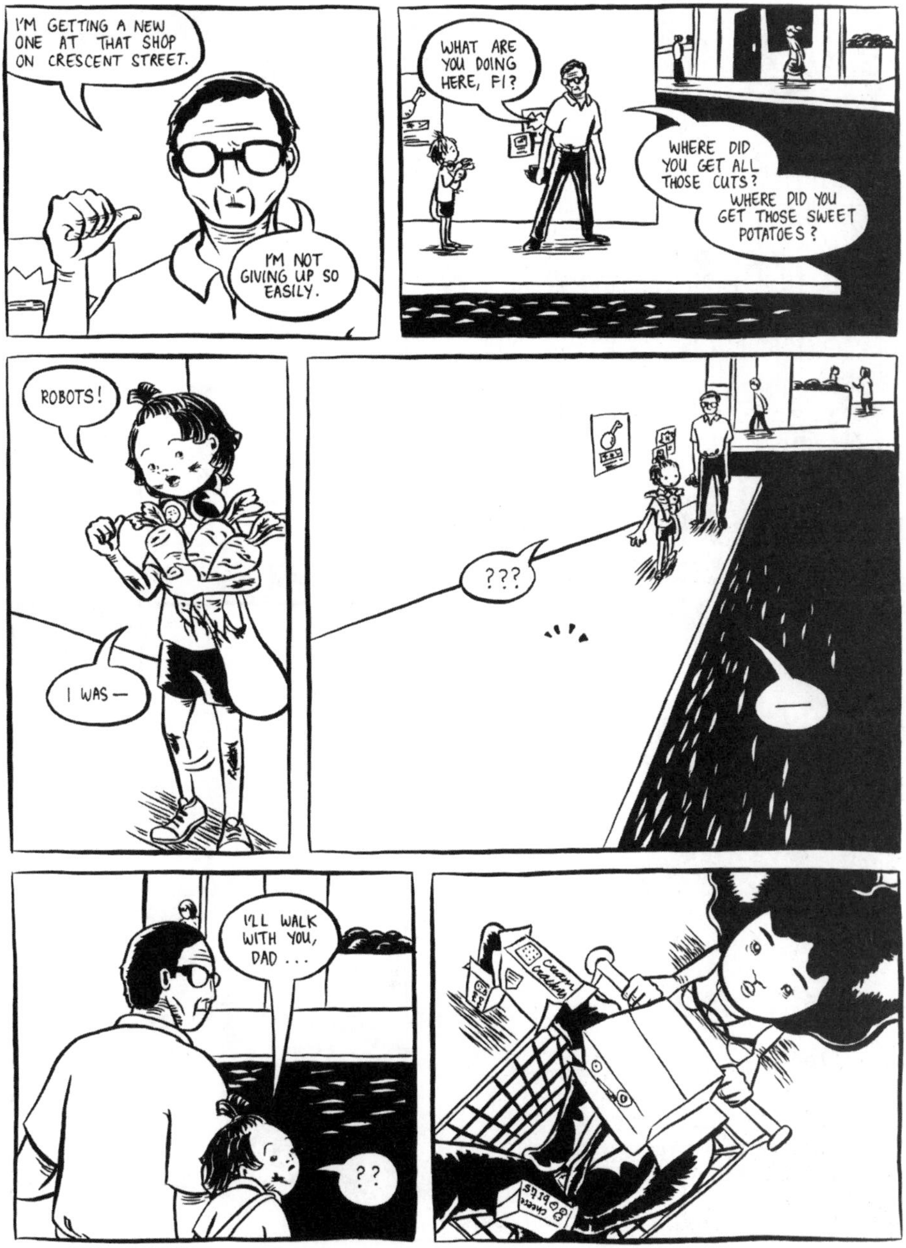
I'M GETTING A NEW ONE AT THAT SHOP ON CRESCENT STREET.
I'M NOT GIVING UP SO EASILY.
WHAT ARE YOU DOING HERE, FI?
WHERE DID YOU GET ALL THOSE CUTS?
WHERE DID YOU GET THOSE SWEET POTATOES?
ROBOTS!
I WAS—
???
—
I'LL WALK WITH YOU, DAD . . .
??

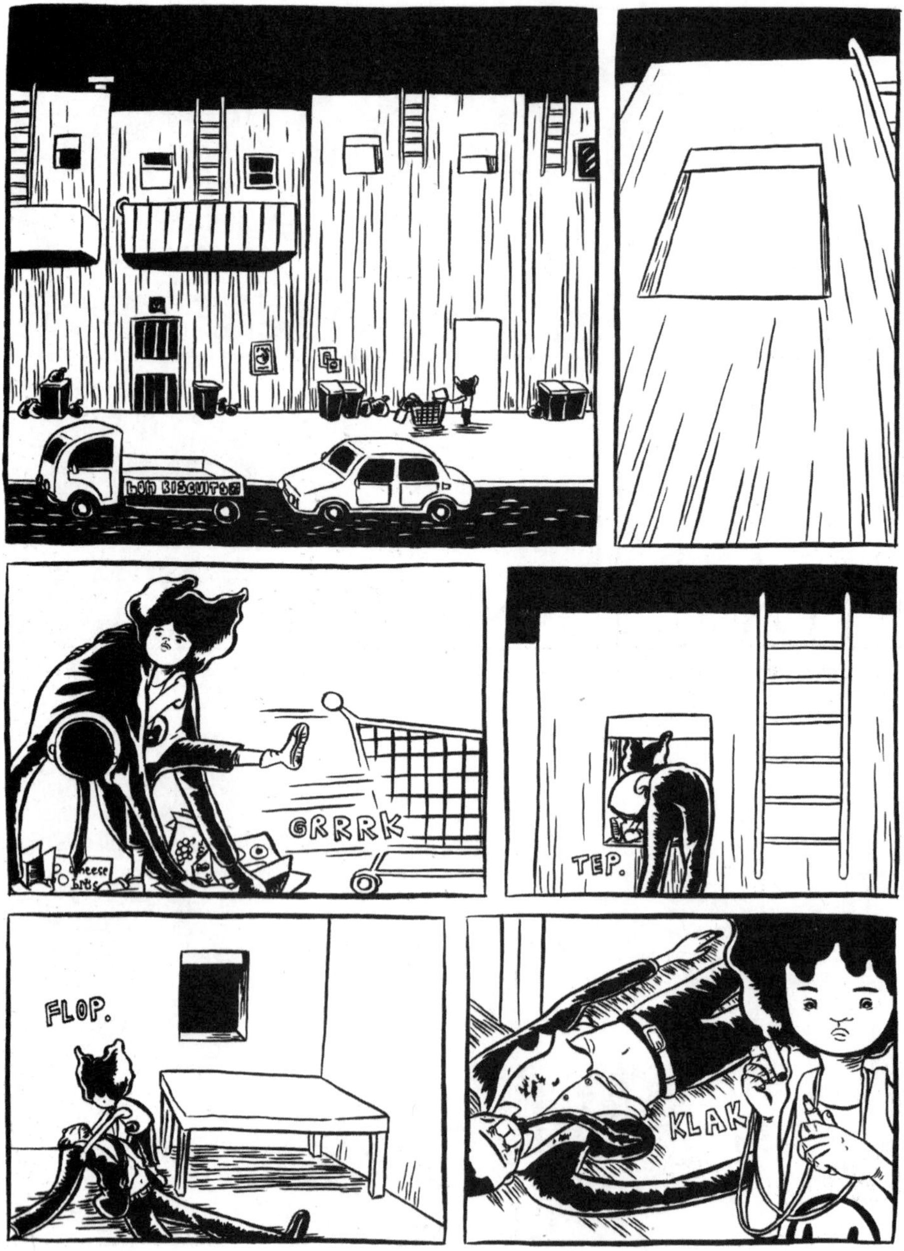
GRRRK
TEP.
FLOP.
KLAK

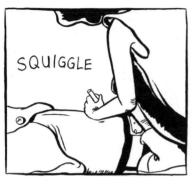

SQUIGGLE

SO, FI...

DO YOU DO THE DISHES AT HOME?

I LOAD THE DISHWASHER.

SO YOU AND YOUR DAD ARE DOING OKAY?

WE'RE OKAY.

YOU KNOW, YOU REMIND ME SO MUCH OF FAY.

SHE WOULD BE PROUD TO SEE YOU ALL GROWN UP.

...

SOMETIMES I LOOK AT YOU AND FEEL THAT SHE'S AROUND, WATCHING YOU...

SIMON, SIMON.

NONE OF THAT IN FRONT OF FI.

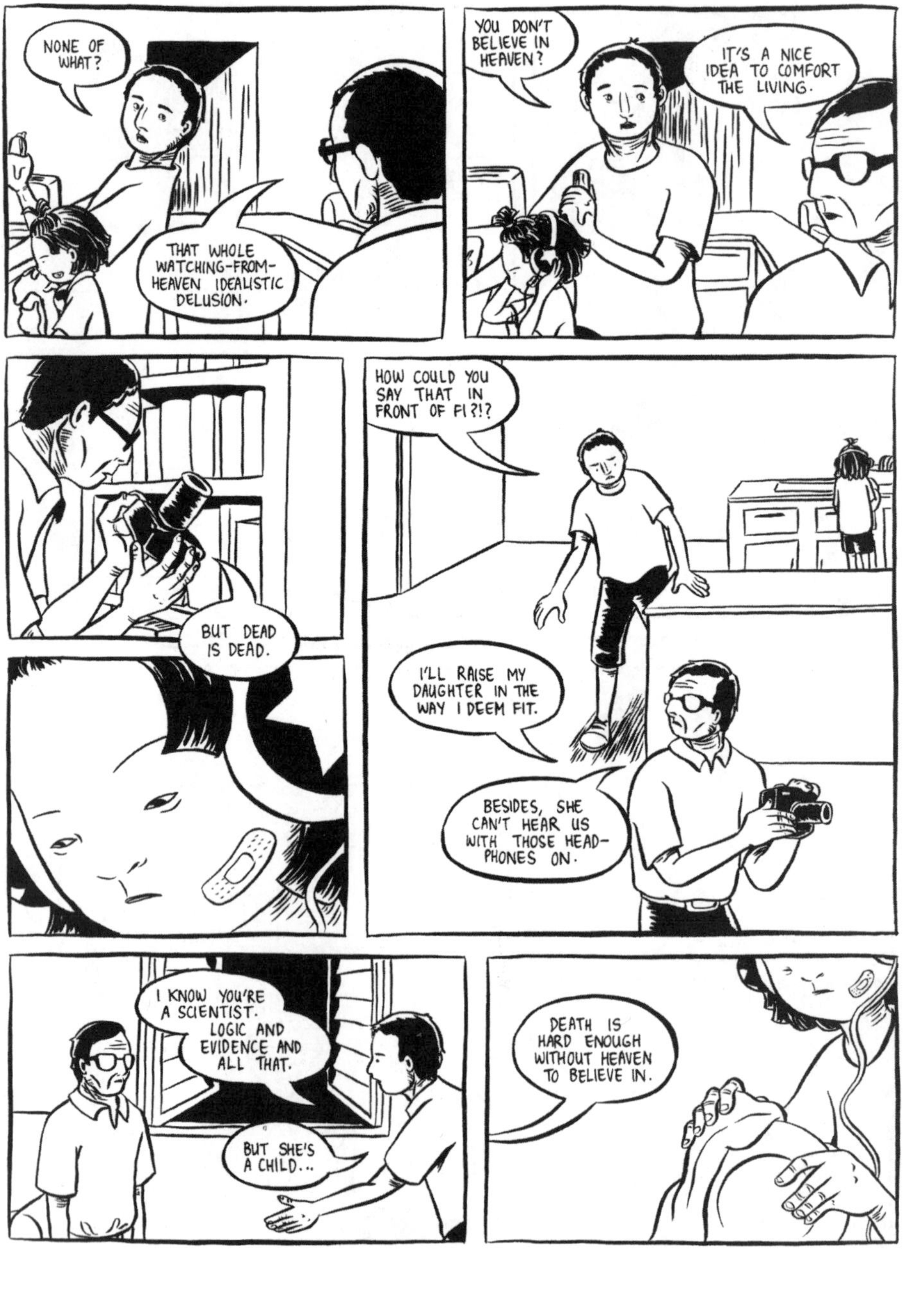

NONE OF WHAT?
THAT WHOLE WATCHING-FROM-HEAVEN IDEALISTIC DELUSION.
YOU DON'T BELIEVE IN HEAVEN?
IT'S A NICE IDEA TO COMFORT THE LIVING.
BUT DEAD IS DEAD.
HOW COULD YOU SAY THAT IN FRONT OF FI?!?
I'LL RAISE MY DAUGHTER IN THE WAY I DEEM FIT.
BESIDES, SHE CAN'T HEAR US WITH THOSE HEAD-PHONES ON.
I KNOW YOU'RE A SCIENTIST. LOGIC AND EVIDENCE AND ALL THAT.
BUT SHE'S A CHILD...
DEATH IS HARD ENOUGH WITHOUT HEAVEN TO BELIEVE IN.

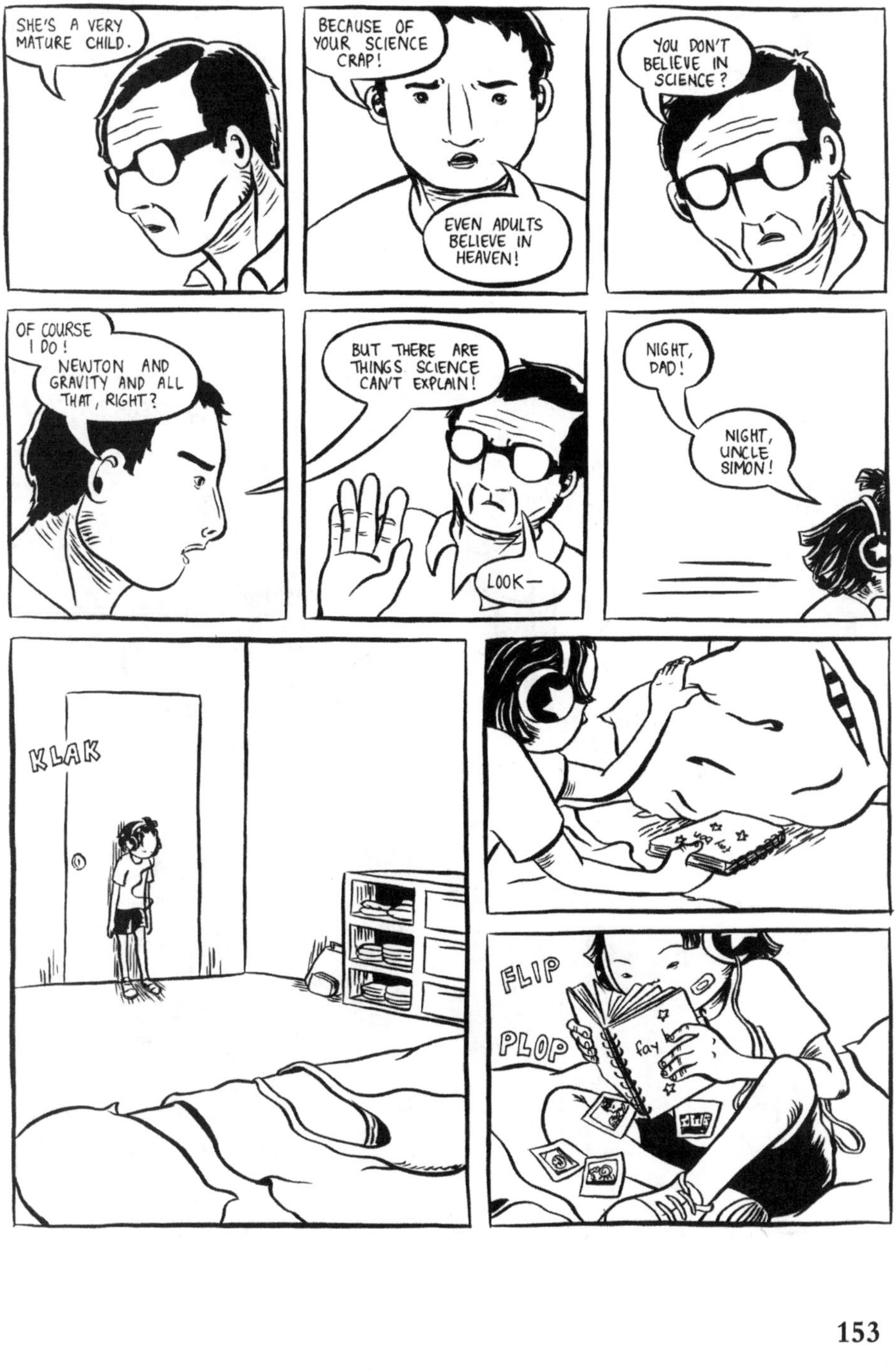
SHE'S A VERY MATURE CHILD.
BECAUSE OF YOUR SCIENCE CRAP!
EVEN ADULTS BELIEVE IN HEAVEN!
YOU DON'T BELIEVE IN SCIENCE?
OF COURSE I DO!
NEWTON AND GRAVITY AND ALL THAT, RIGHT?
BUT THERE ARE THINGS SCIENCE CAN'T EXPLAIN!
LOOK—
NIGHT, DAD!
NIGHT, UNCLE SIMON!
KLAK
FLIP
PLOP

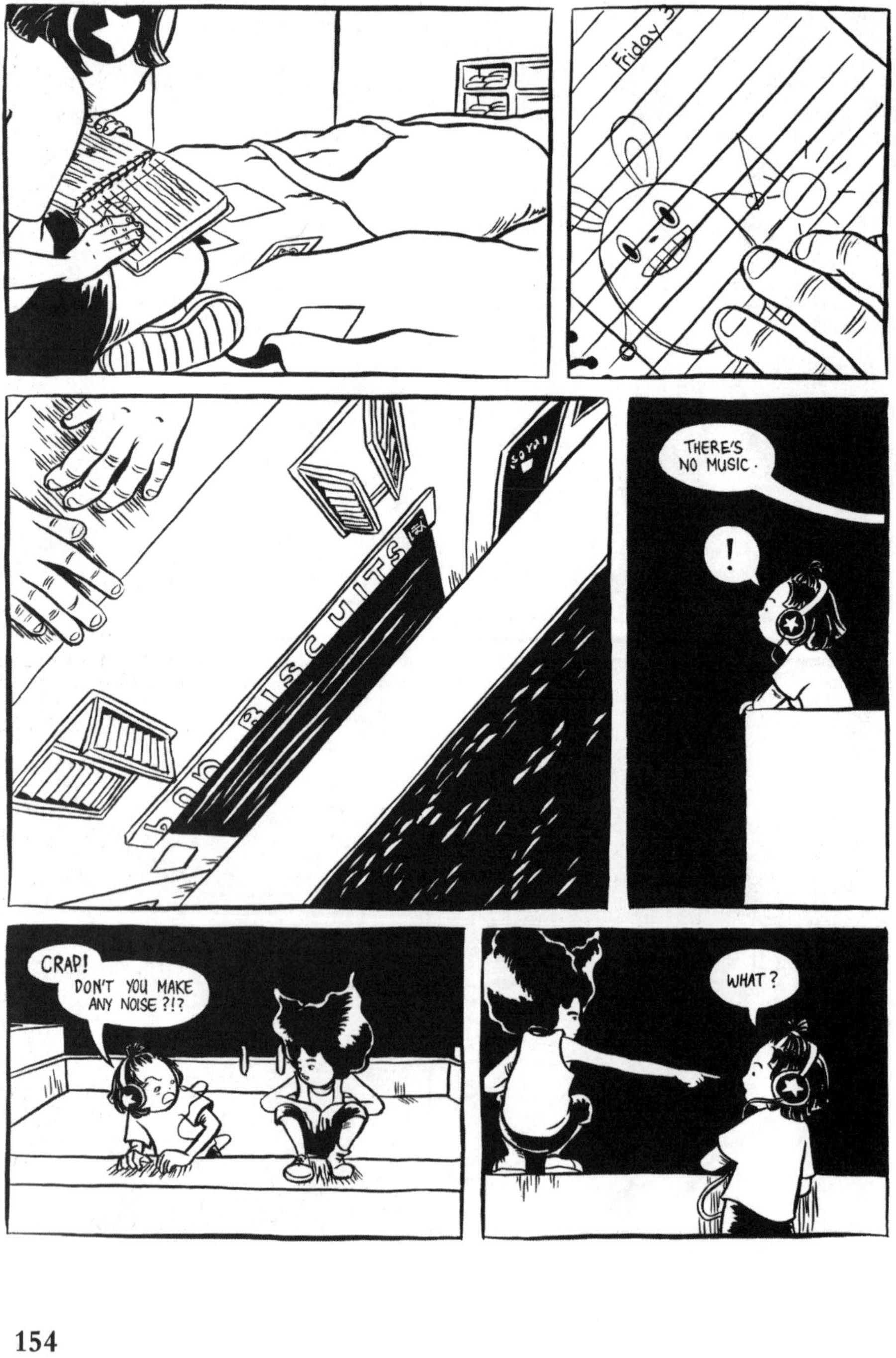
Friday 3
bob BISCUITS
THERE'S NO MUSIC.
!
CRAP!
DON'T YOU MAKE ANY NOISE?!?
WHAT?

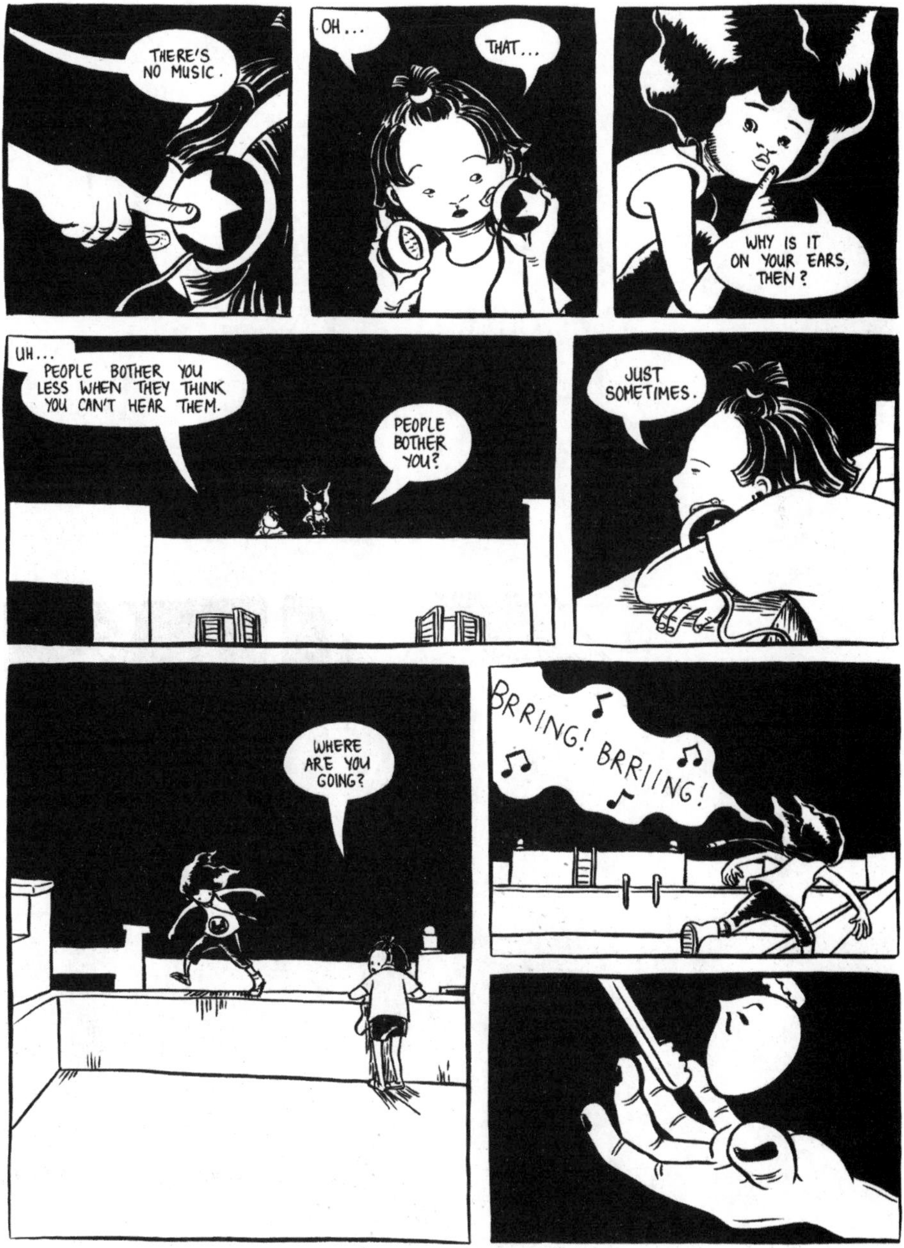
THERE'S NO MUSIC.
OH...
THAT...
WHY IS IT ON YOUR EARS, THEN?
UH... PEOPLE BOTHER YOU LESS WHEN THEY THINK YOU CAN'T HEAR THEM.
PEOPLE BOTHER YOU?
JUST SOMETIMES.
WHERE ARE YOU GOING?
BRRING! BRRIING!

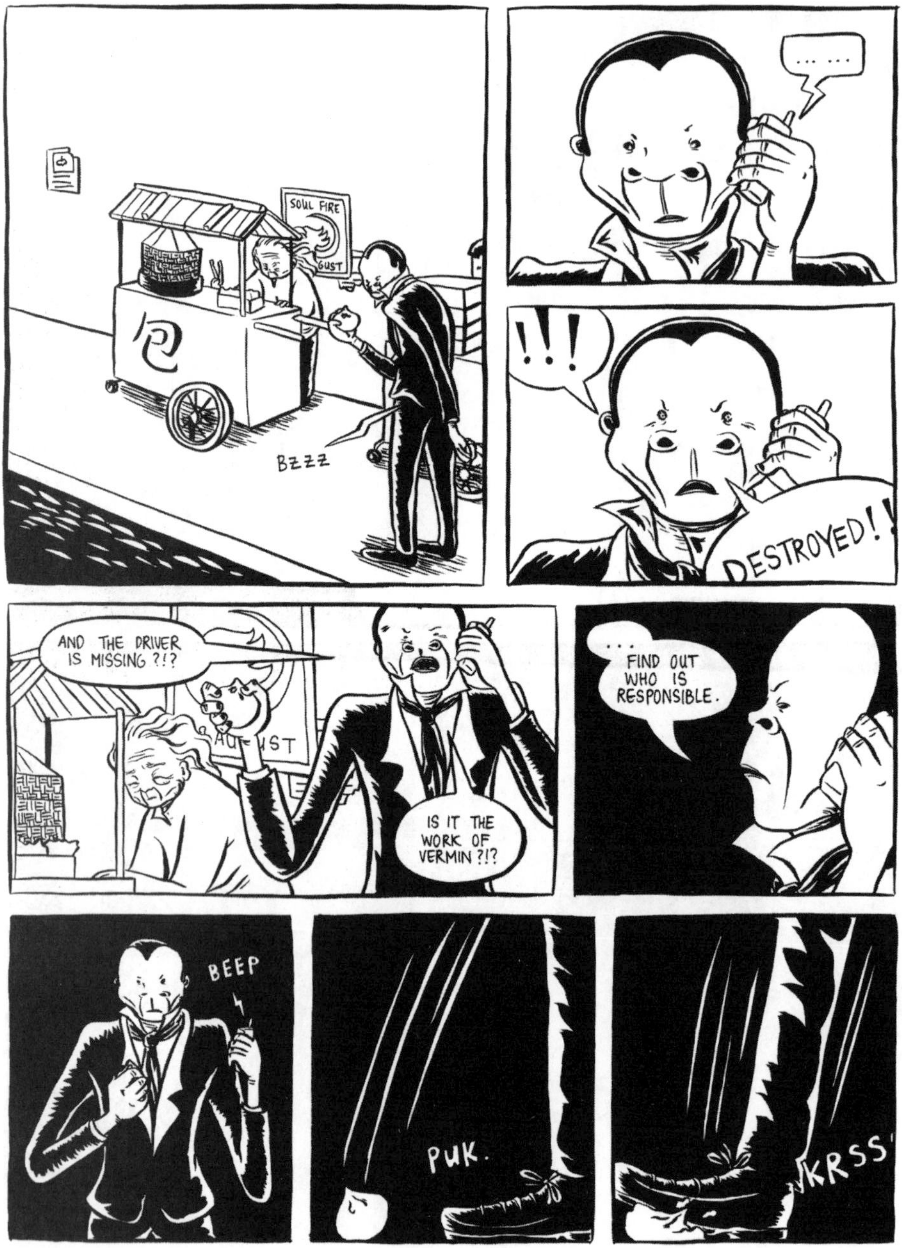
SOUL FIRE
GUST
BZZZ
... ...
!!!
DESTROYED!!
AND THE DRIVER IS MISSING ?!?
IS IT THE WORK OF VERMIN ?!?
... FIND OUT WHO IS RESPONSIBLE.
BEEP
PUK.
KRSS

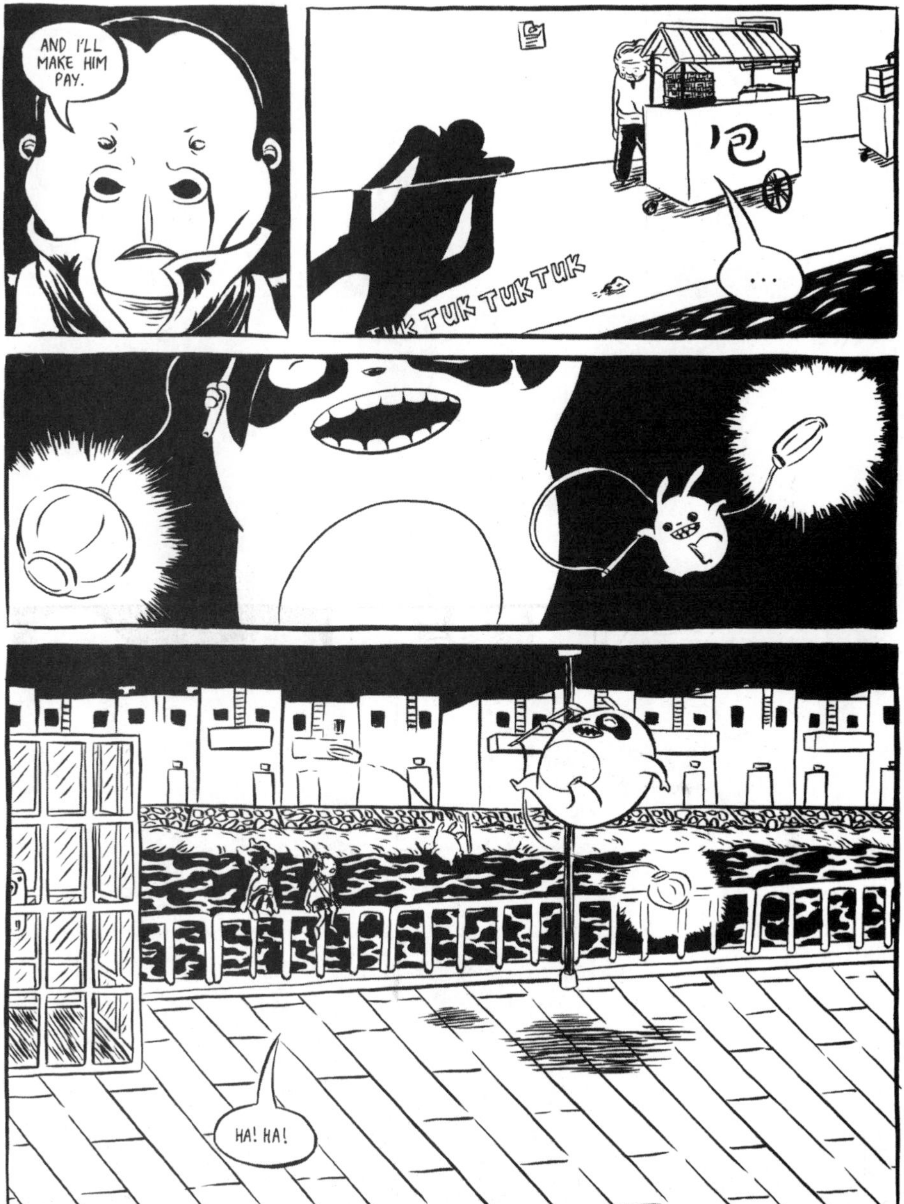
AND I'LL MAKE HIM PAY.
包
TUK TUK TUK TUK
...
HA! HA!

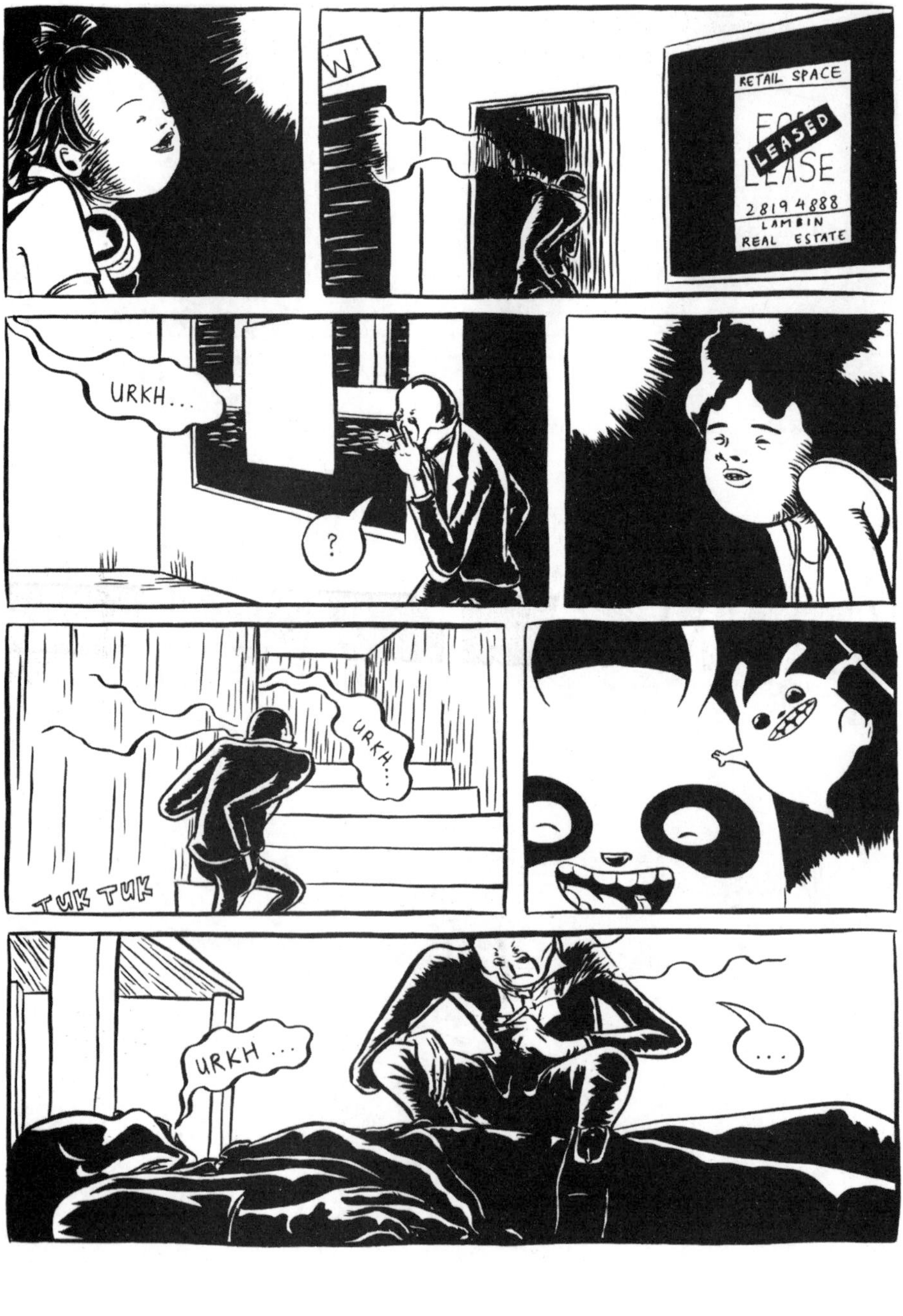
W
RETAIL SPACE
FOR LEASE
LEASED
2819 4888
LAMBIN
REAL ESTATE
URKH...
?
URKH...
TUK TUK
URKH....
...

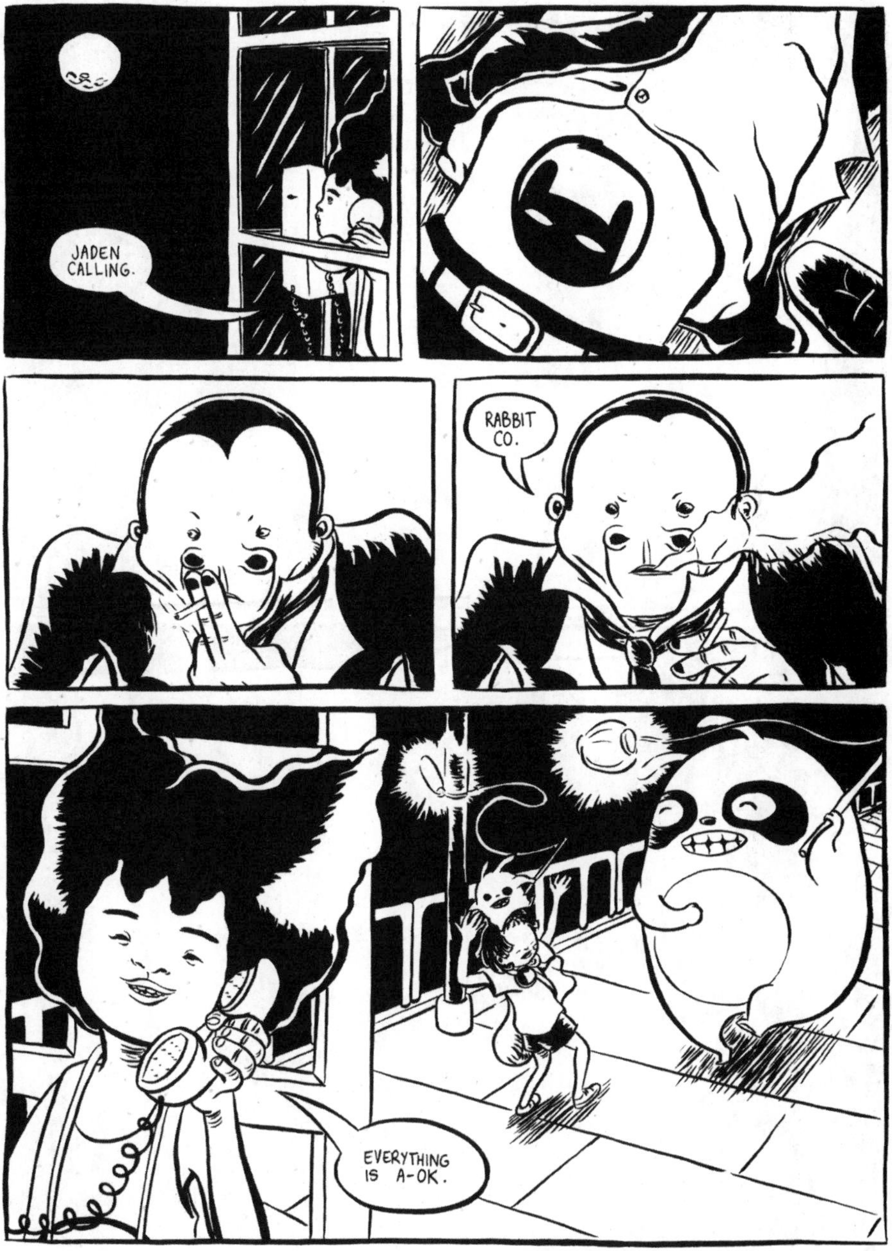
JADEN CALLING.
RABBIT CO.
EVERYTHING IS A-OK.

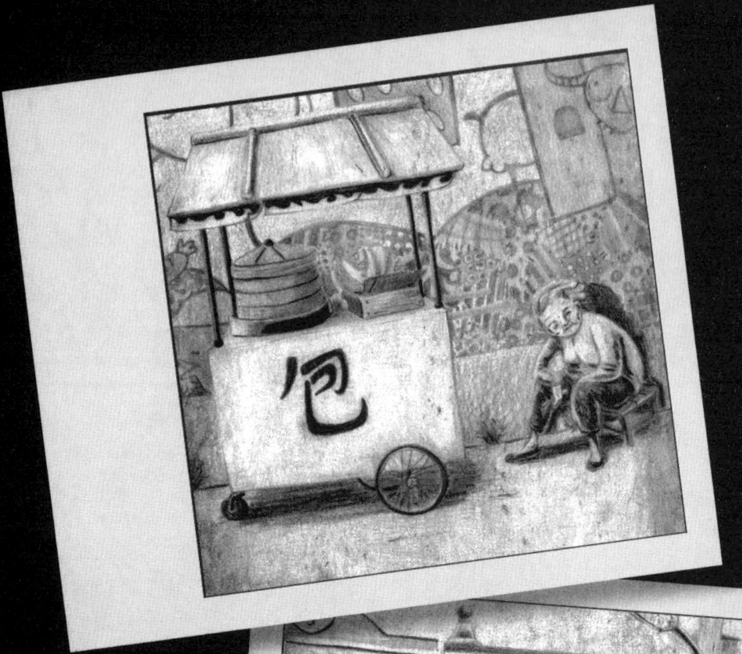
包

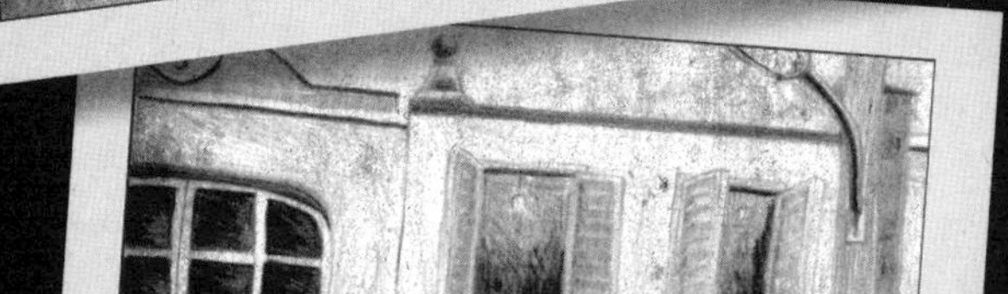
BON BISCUITS
FOR LEASE
LEASED

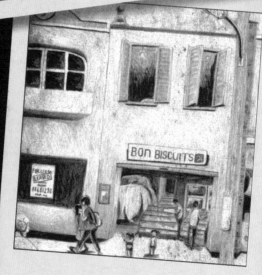

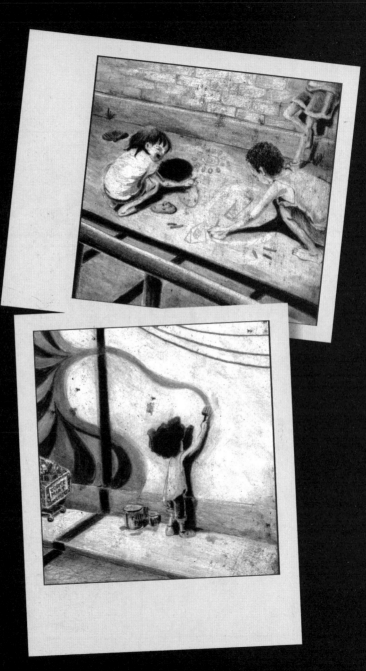

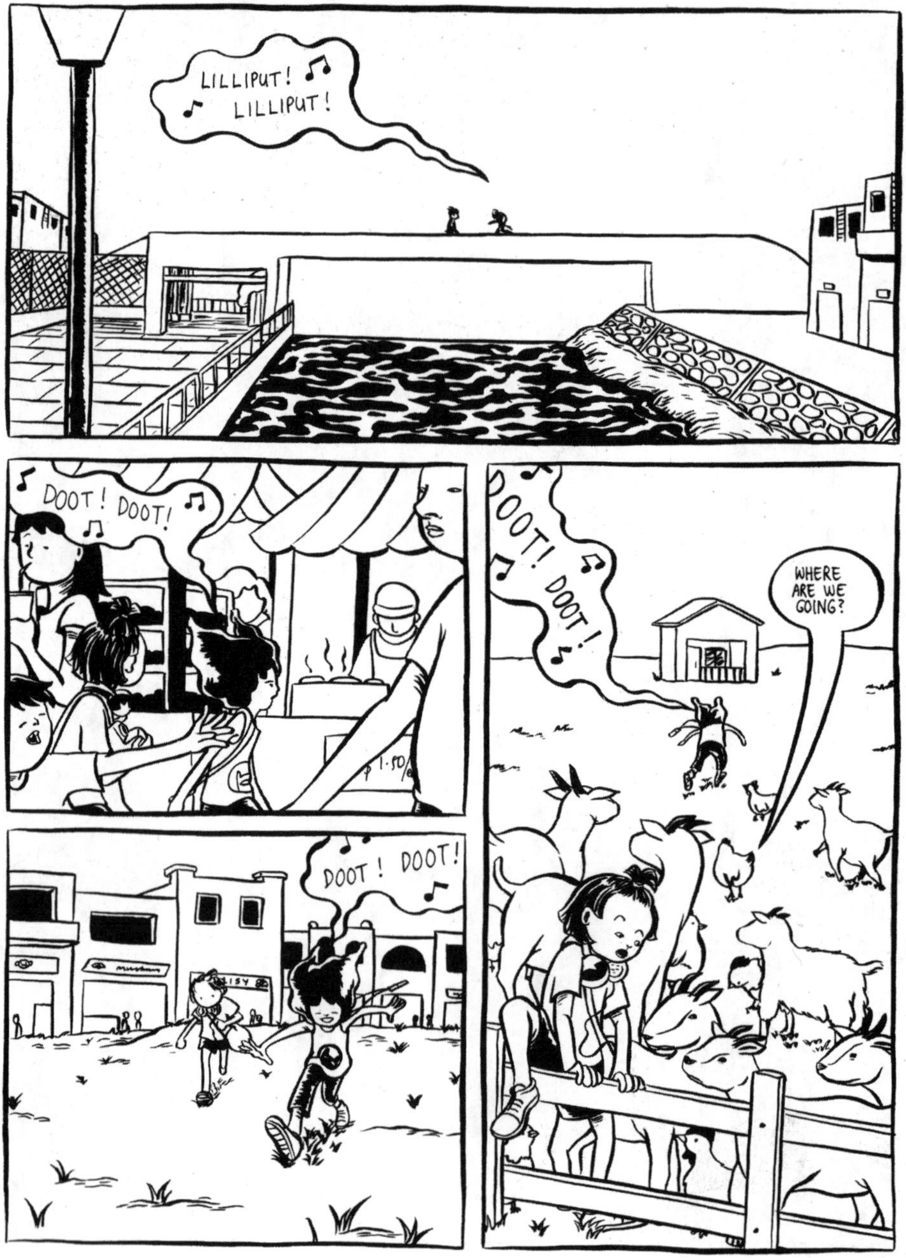
LILLIPUT! LILLIPUT!
DOOT! DOOT!
DOOT! DOOT!
DOOT! DOOT!
WHERE ARE WE GOING?

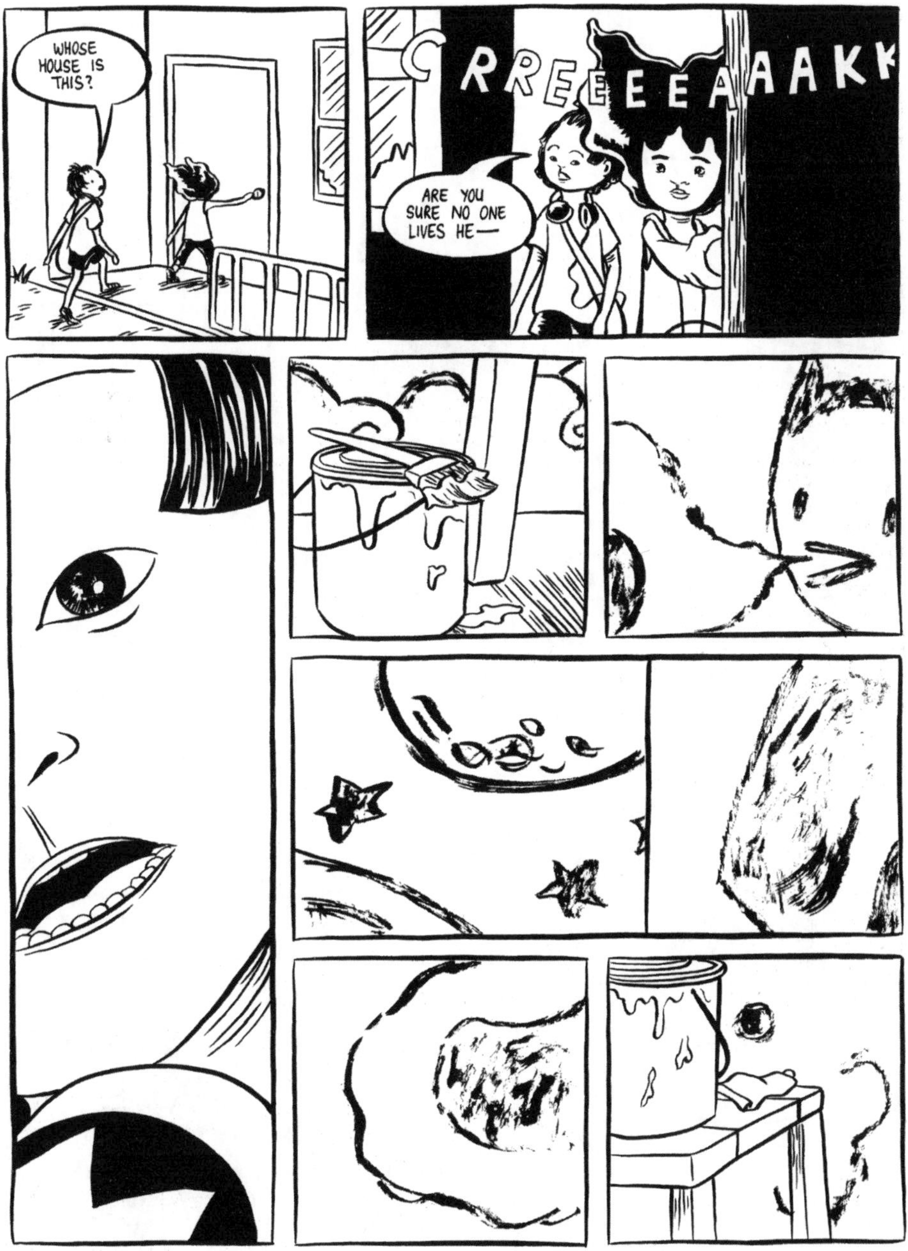
WHOSE HOUSE IS THIS?
CRREEEEEAAAKK
ARE YOU SURE NO ONE LIVES HE—

...
LILLIPUT!
...

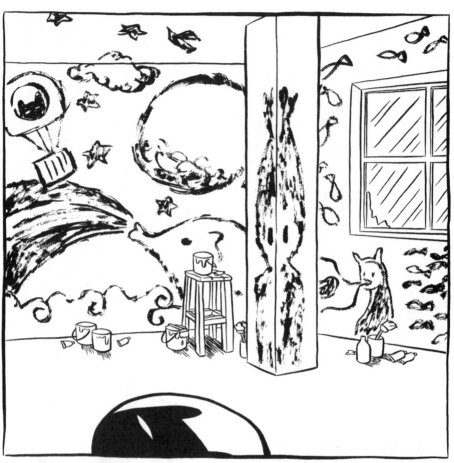

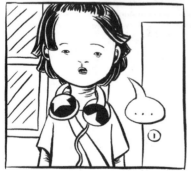

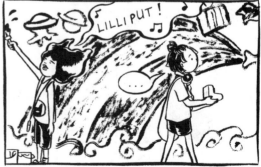

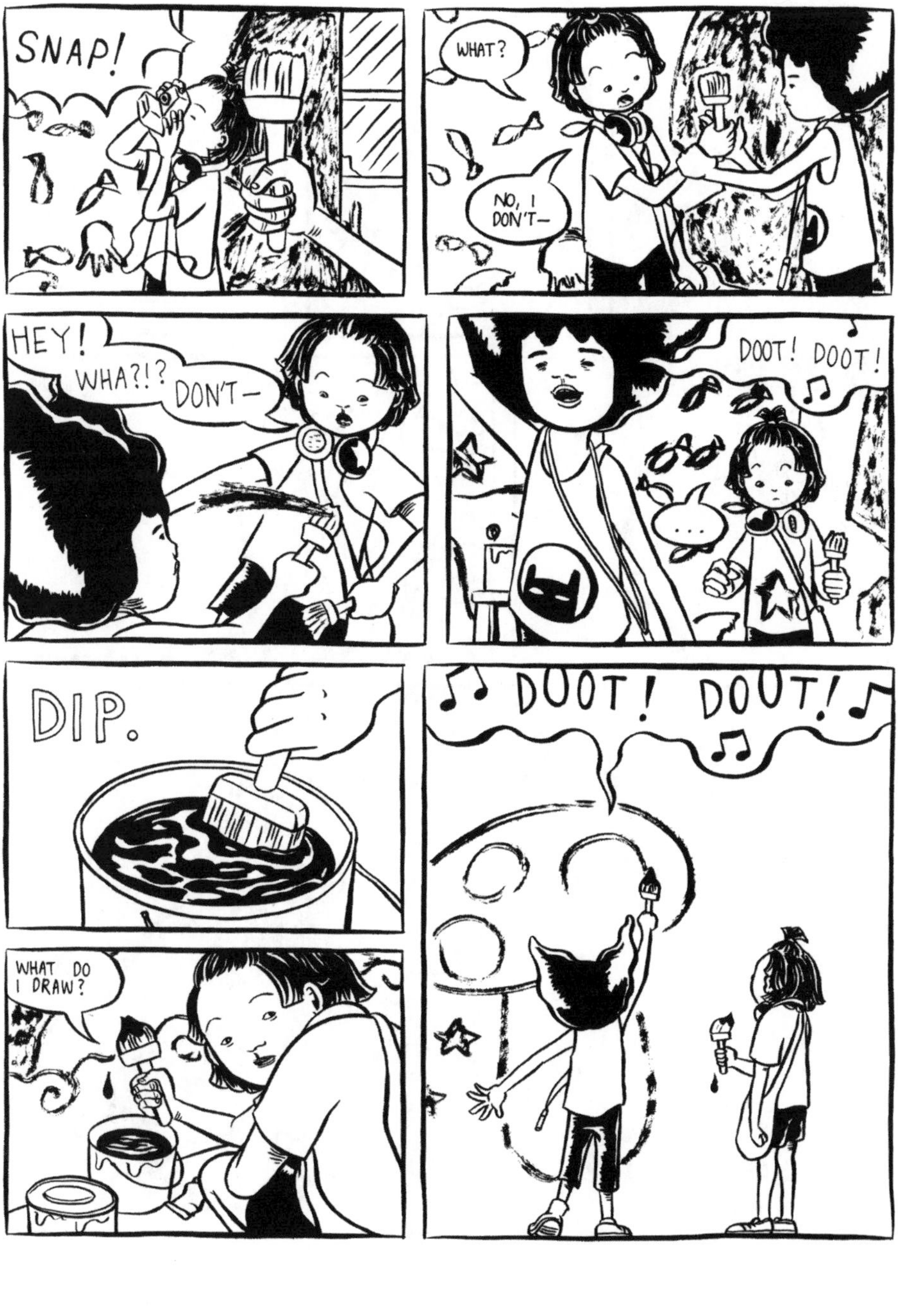
SNAP!
WHAT?
NO, I DON'T—
HEY!
WHA?!?
DON'T—
DOOT! DOOT!
...
DIP.
WHAT DO I DRAW?
DOOT! DOUT!

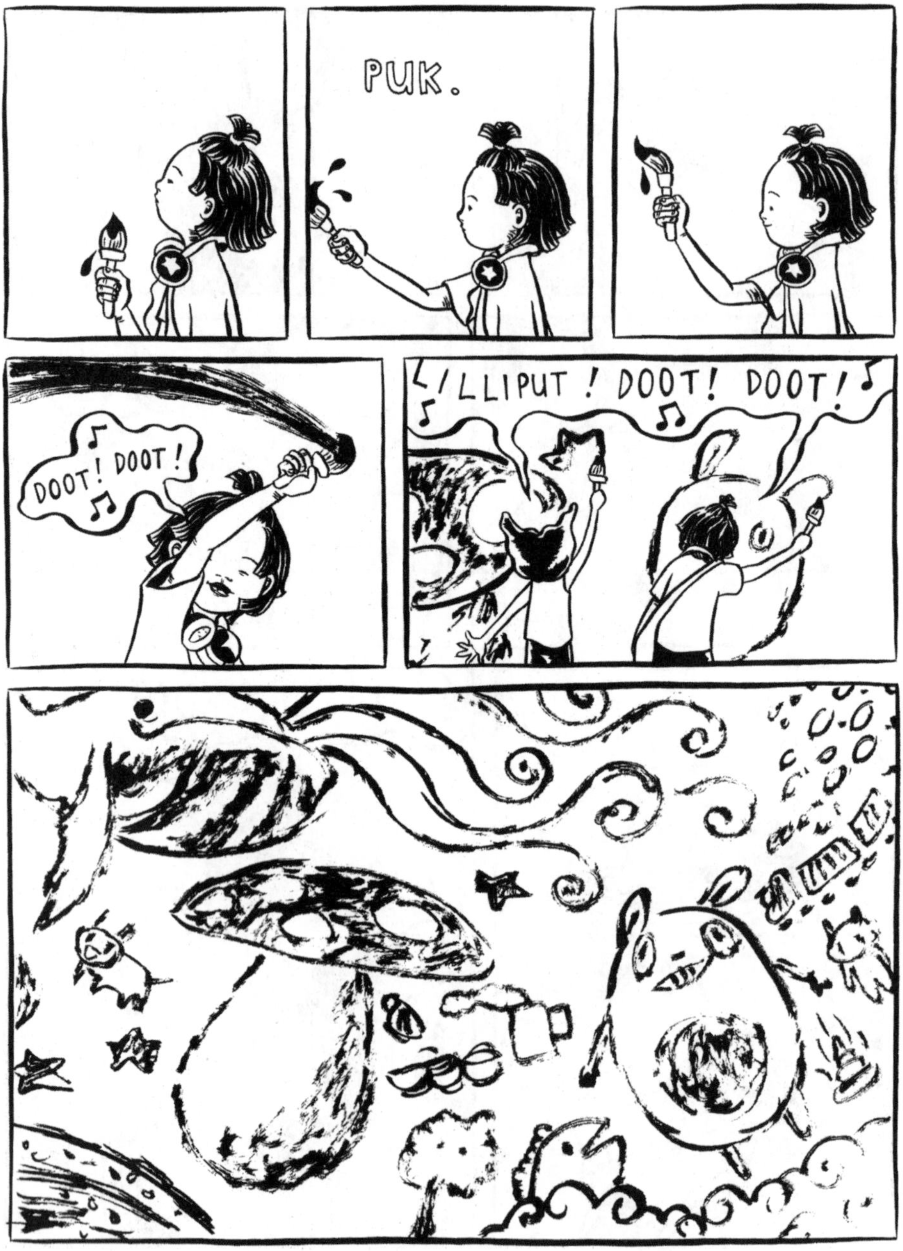

PUK.
DOOT! DOOT!
LILLIPUT! DOOT! DOOT!

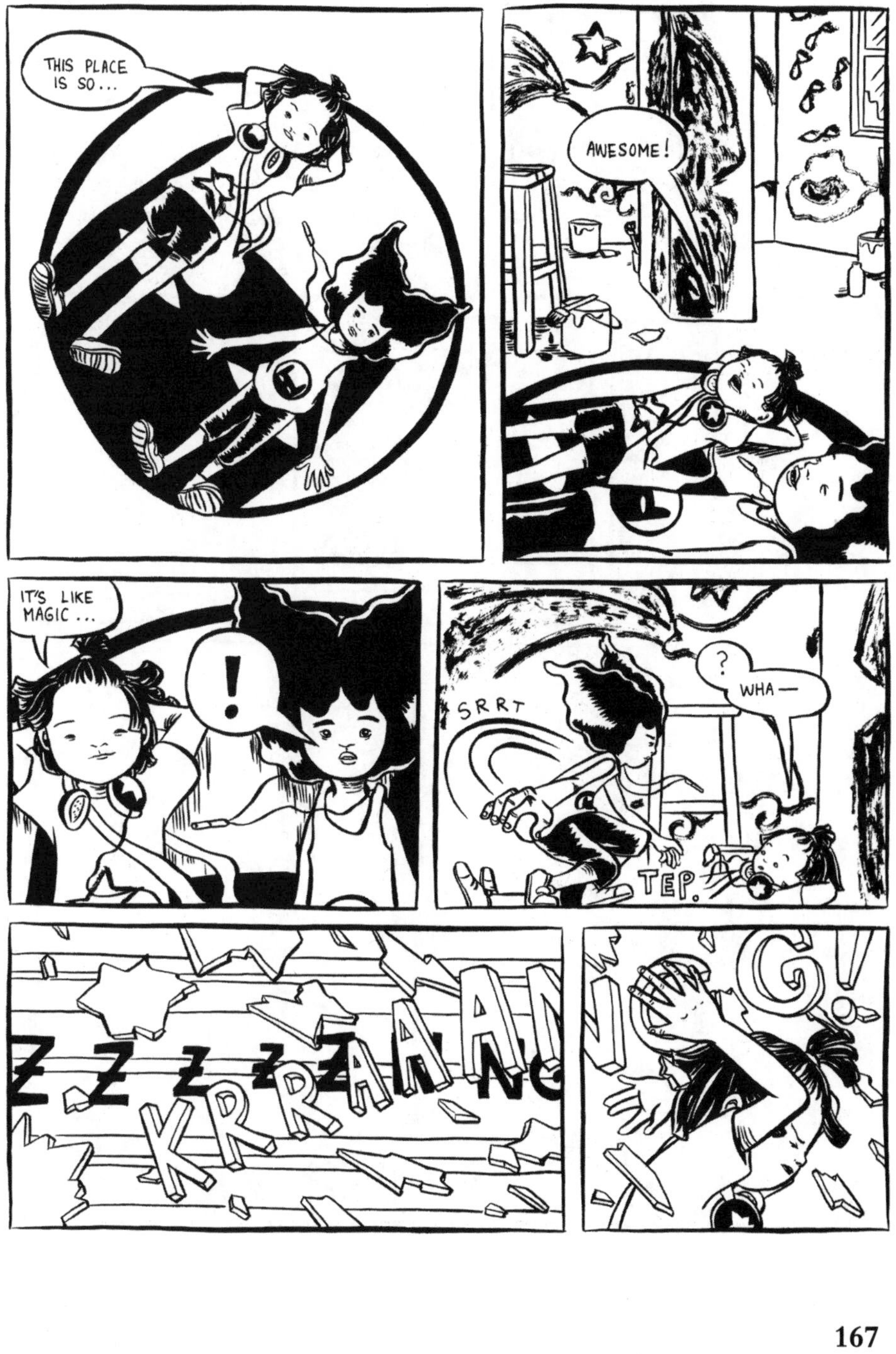
THIS PLACE IS SO...
AWESOME!
IT'S LIKE MAGIC...
!
SRRT
?
WHA—
TEP.
ZZZZZ
KRRZAAANG!

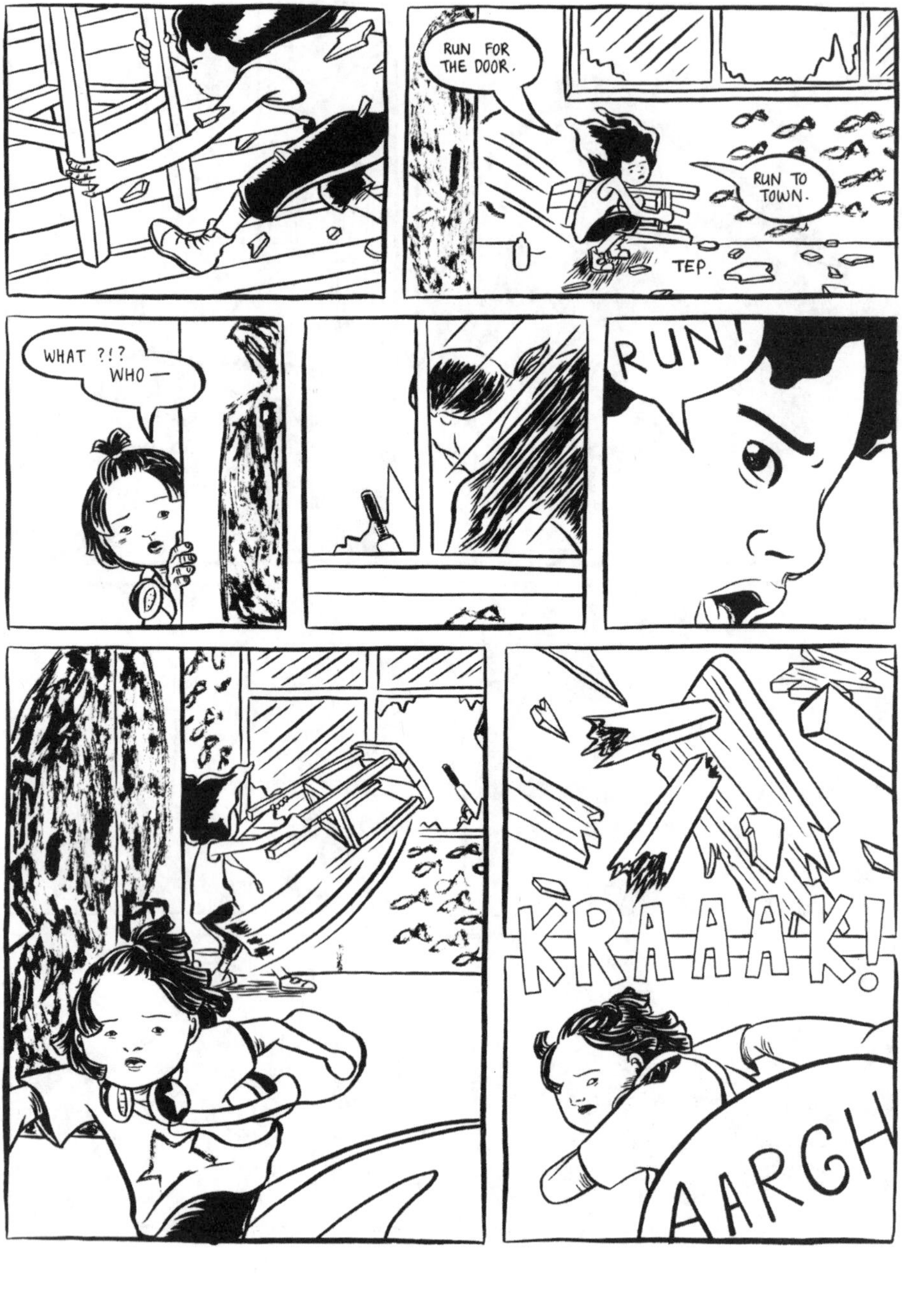

RUN FOR THE DOOR.
RUN TO TOWN.
TEP.
WHAT ?!? WHO—
RUN!
KRAAAK!
AARGH

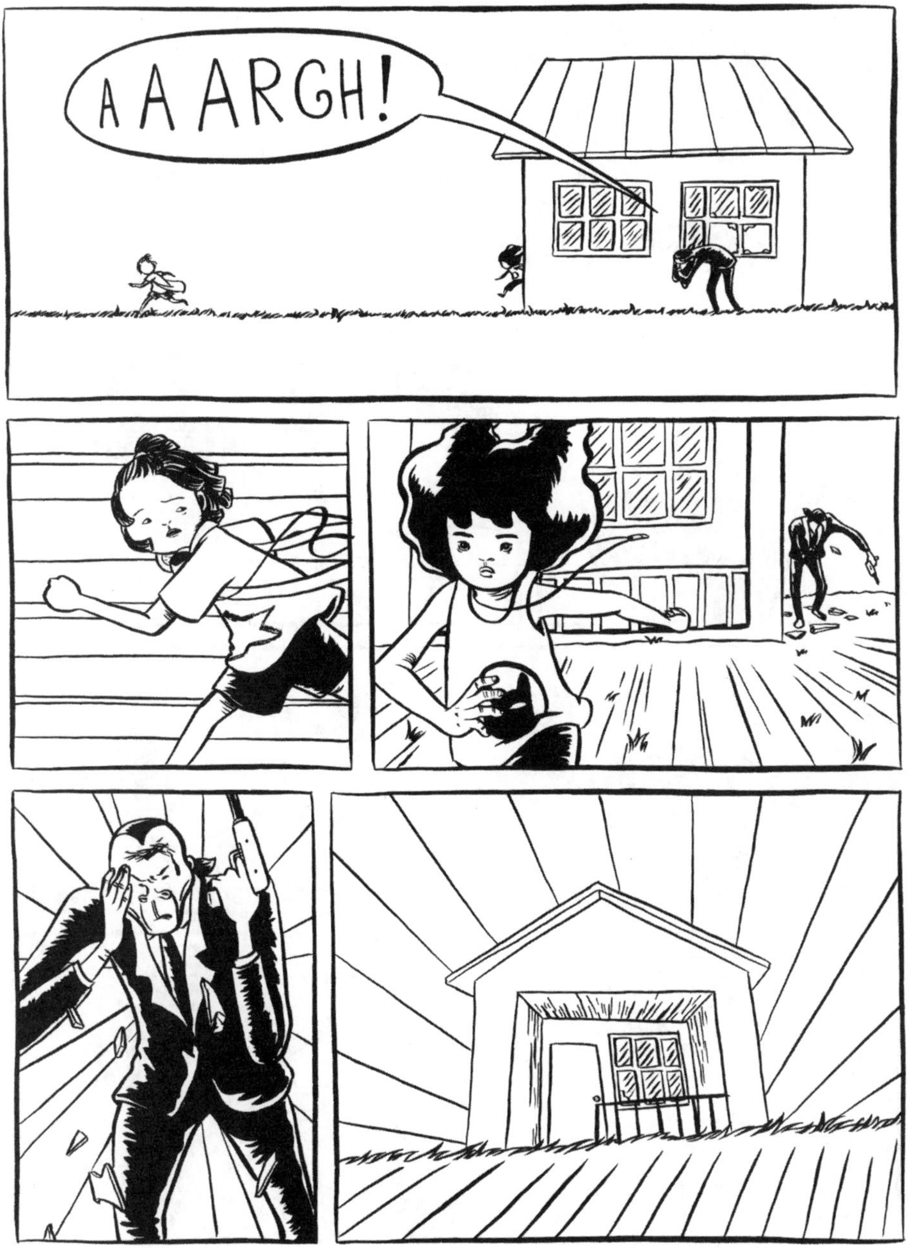
AAARGH!

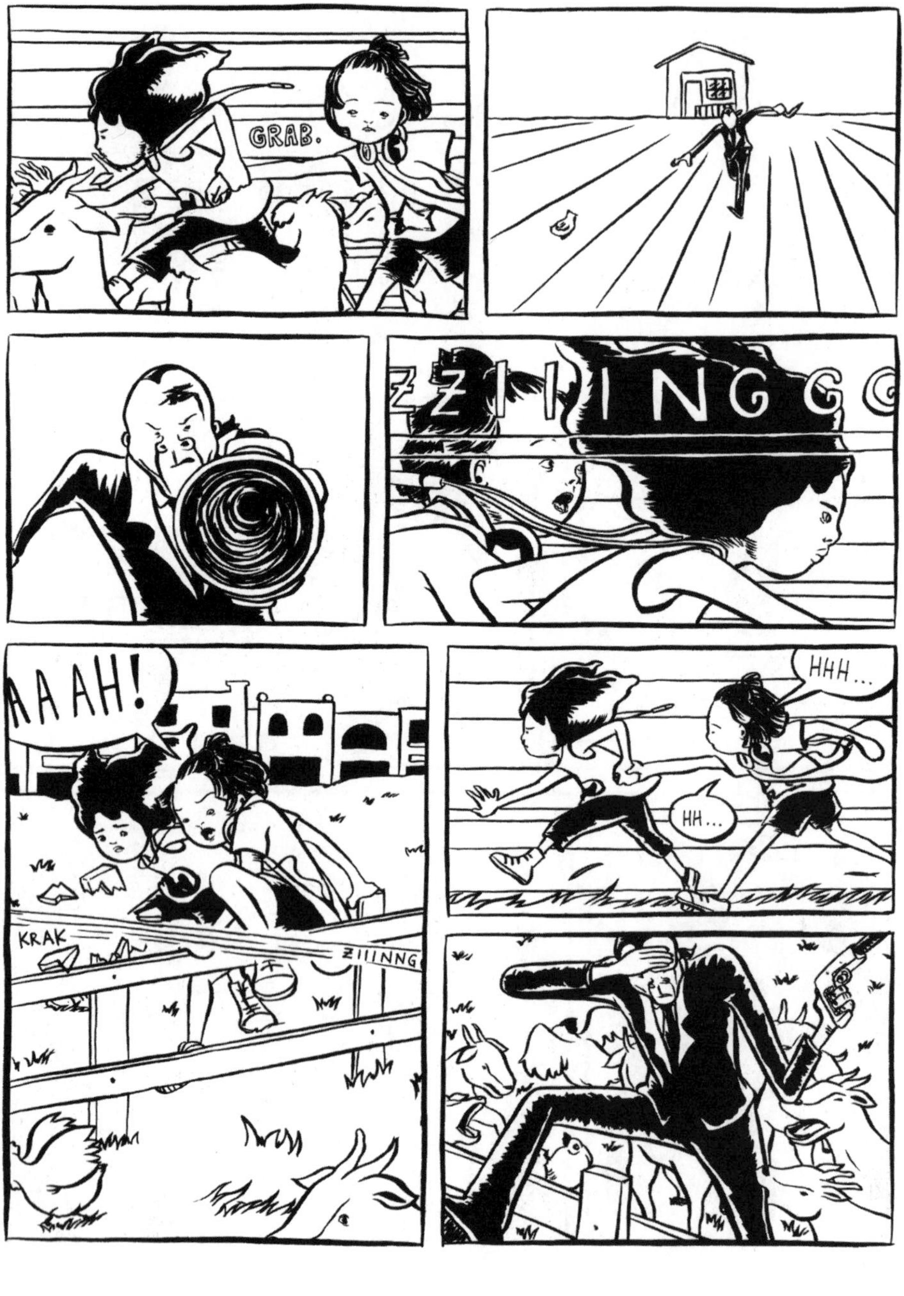
GRAB.
ZZIIINGG
AAAH!
KRAK
ZIIINNG
HHH...
HH...

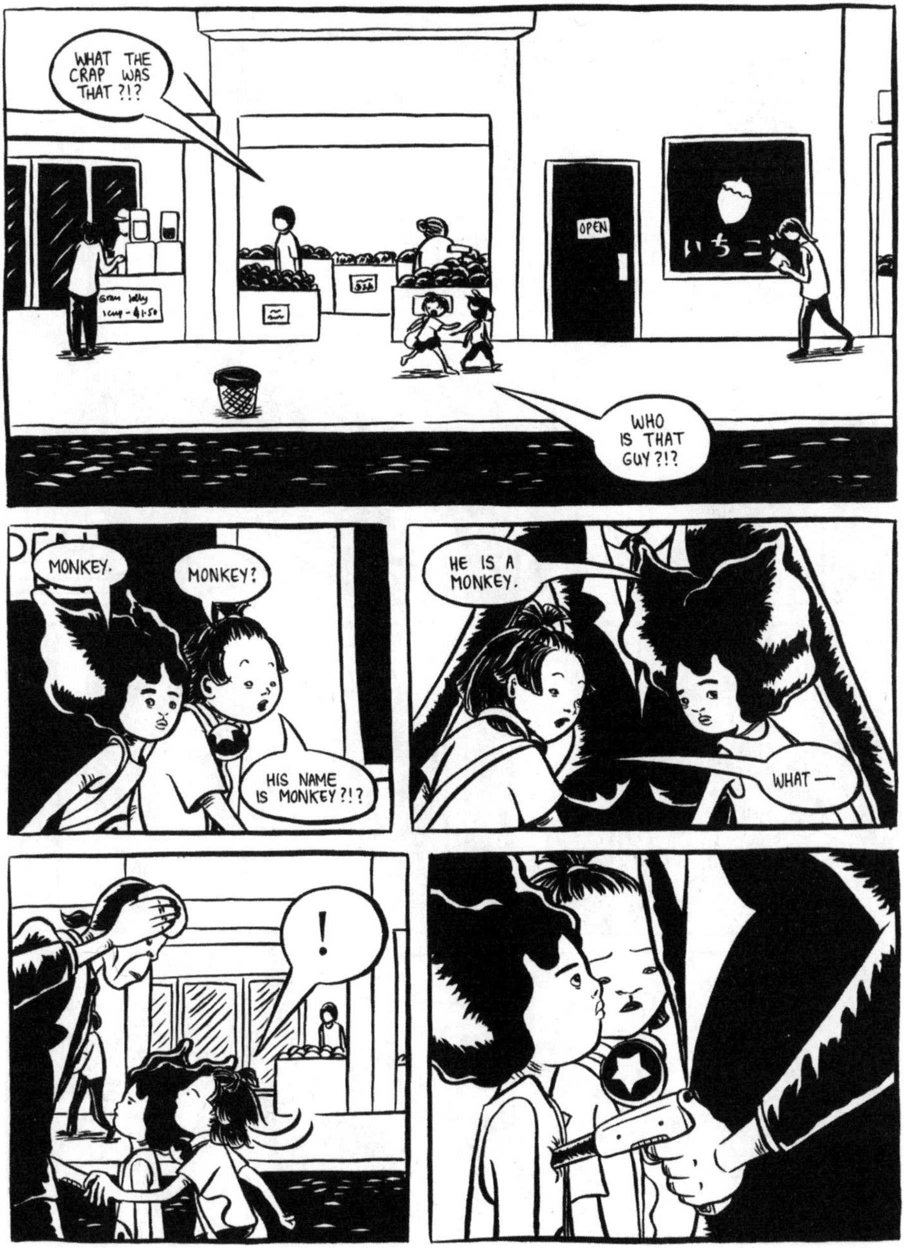
WHAT THE CRAP WAS THAT ?!?
OPEN
WHO IS THAT GUY ?!?
MONKEY.
MONKEY?
HIS NAME IS MONKEY ?!?
HE IS A MONKEY.
WHAT—
!

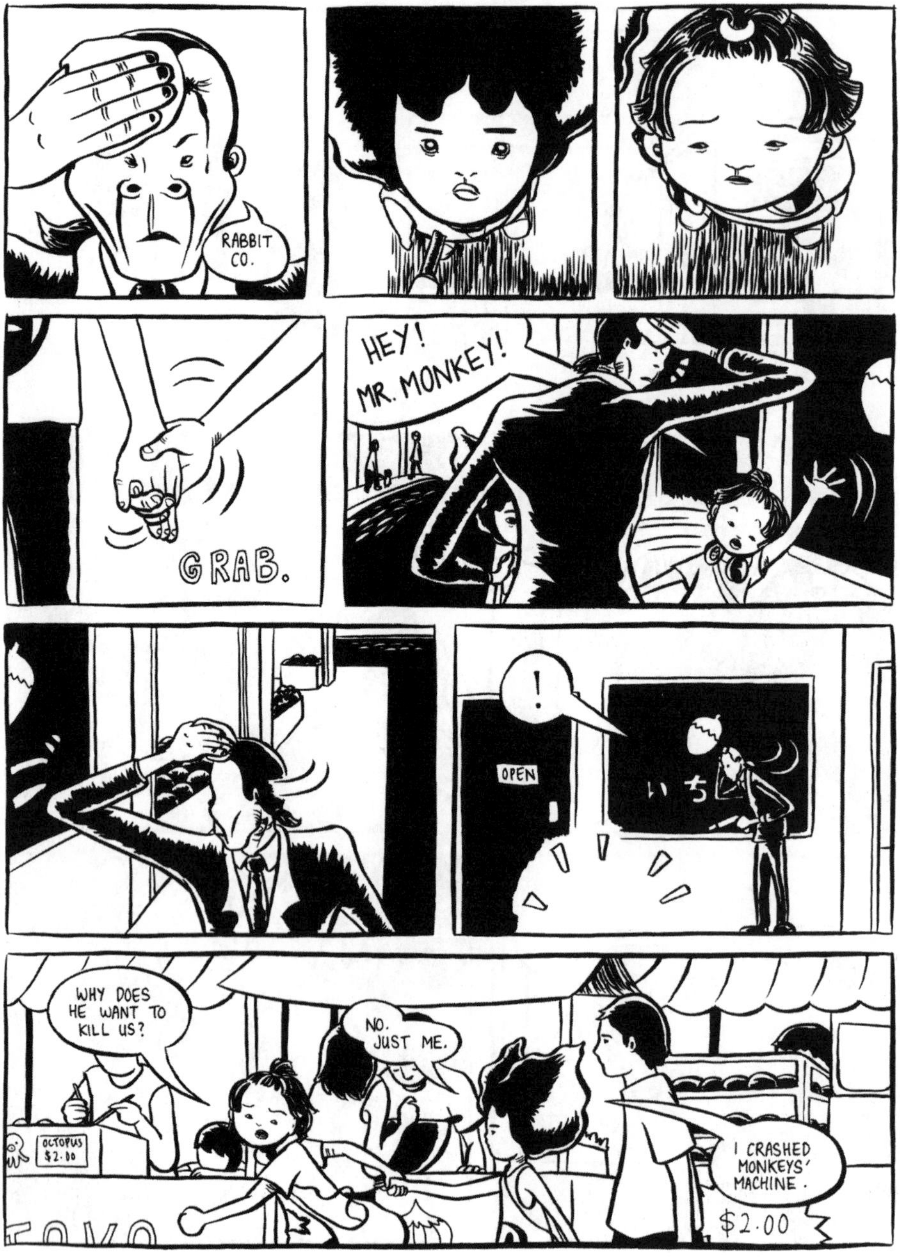
RABBIT CO.
HEY! MR. MONKEY!
GRAB.
!
OPEN
いち
WHY DOES HE WANT TO KILL US?
NO. JUST ME.
I CRASHED MONKEYS' MACHINE.
OCTOPUS $2.00
$2.00

WHAT?!? HE'S ONE OF THEM?!?
COSTUME
CRAP! HE'S STILL RIGHT BEHIND US!
I'VE GOT AN IDEA! COME, QUICK!
??
?
COSTUME
?
?

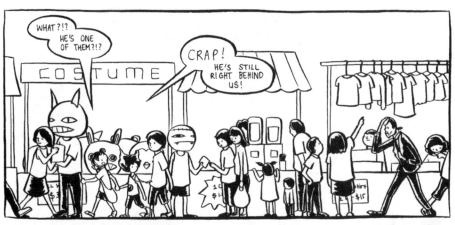

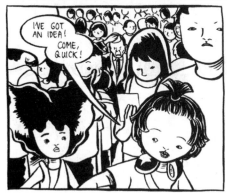

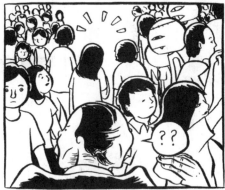

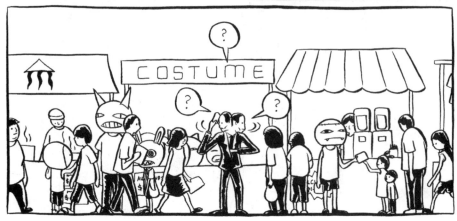

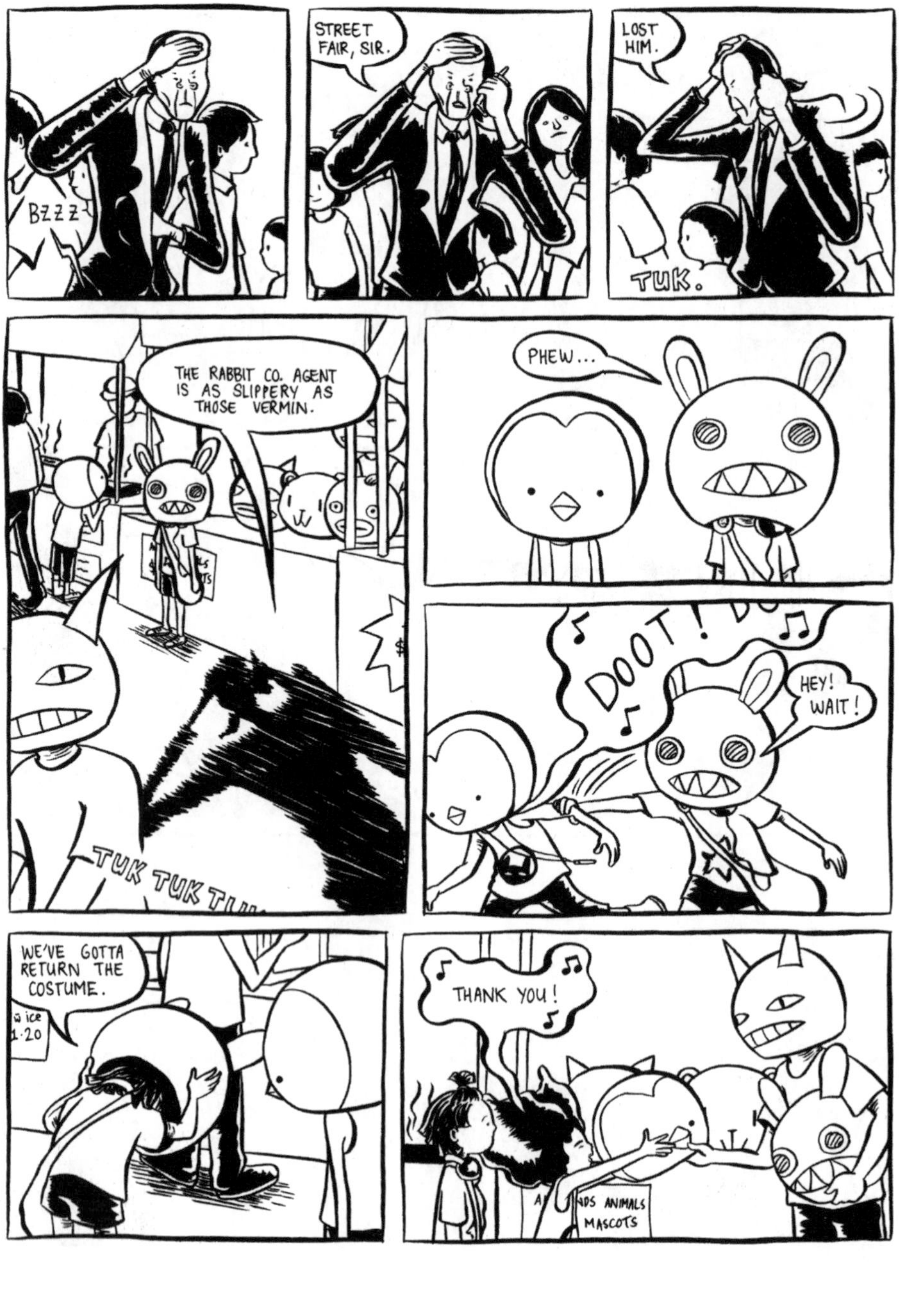
BZZZ
STREET FAIR, SIR.
LOST HIM.
TUK.
THE RABBIT CO. AGENT IS AS SLIPPERY AS THOSE VERMIN.
TUK TUK
PHEW...
DOOT!
HEY! WAIT!
WE'VE GOTTA RETURN THE COSTUME.
THANK YOU!
ANIMALS
MASCOTS

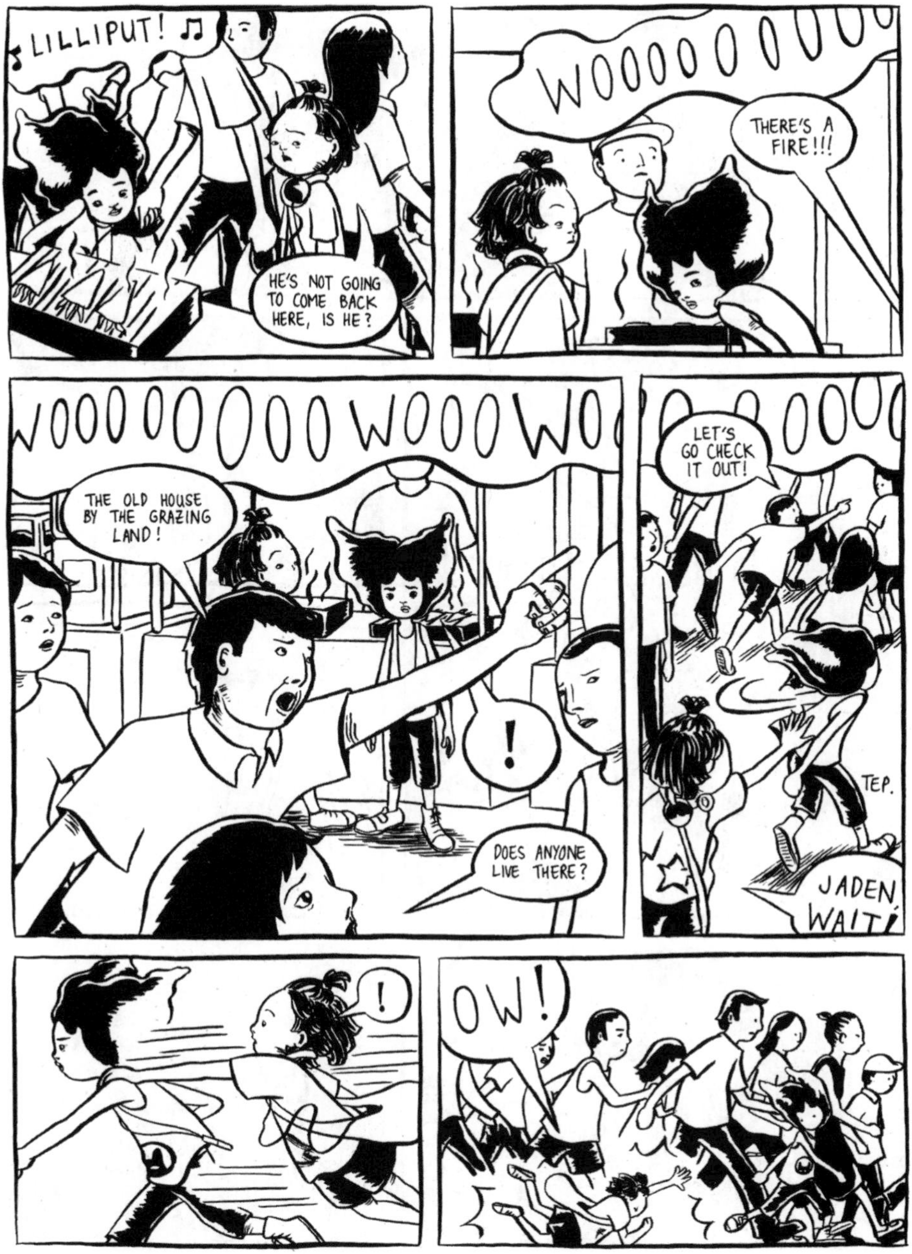
♪ LILLIPUT! ♫
HE'S NOT GOING TO COME BACK HERE, IS HE?
WOOOOOOOO
THERE'S A FIRE!!!
WOOOOOOOOOWOOOWO
THE OLD HOUSE BY THE GRAZING LAND!
!
DOES ANYONE LIVE THERE?
LET'S GO CHECK IT OUT!
TEP.
JADEN WAIT!
!
OW!

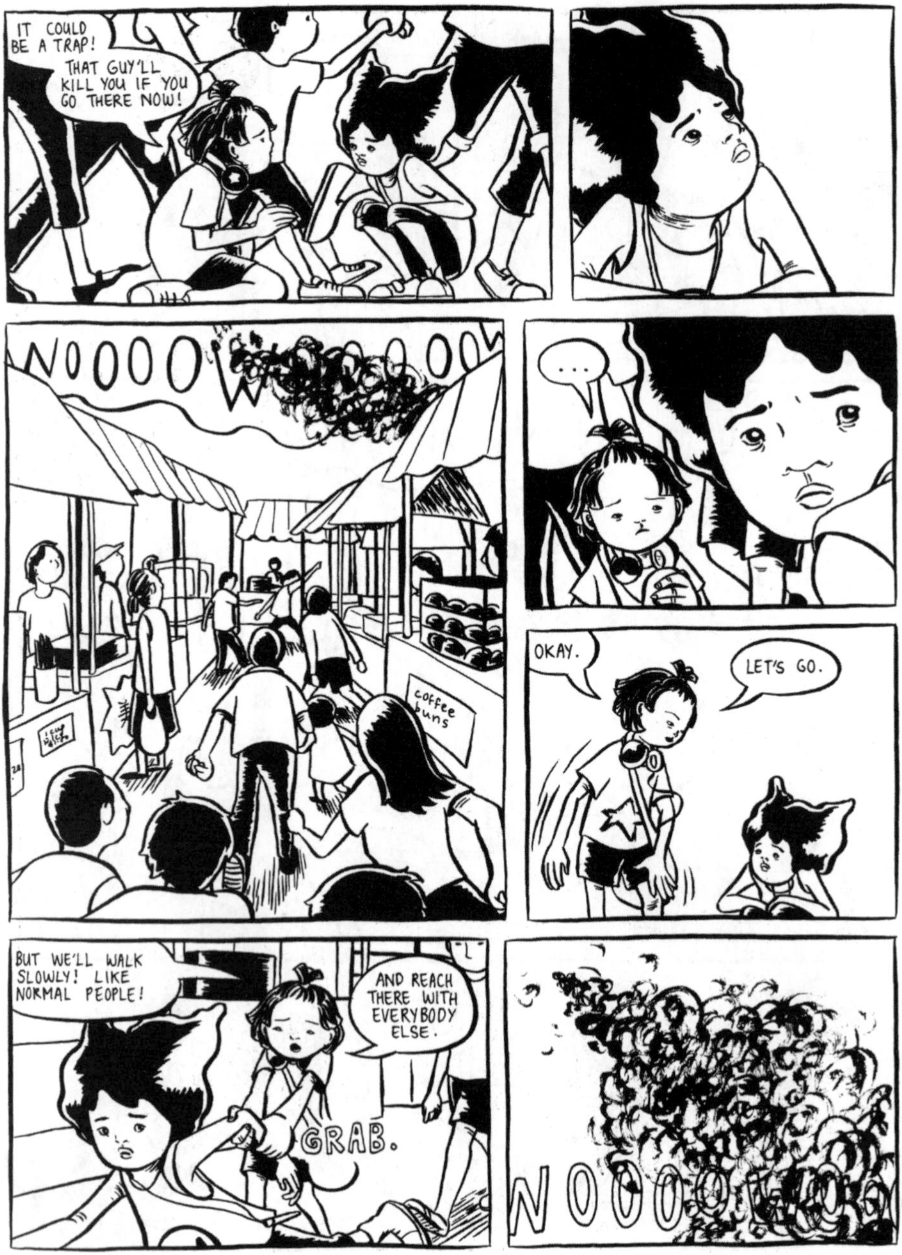
IT COULD BE A TRAP!
THAT GUY'LL KILL YOU IF YOU GO THERE NOW!
NOOOOW
...
coffee buns
OKAY.
LET'S GO.
BUT WE'LL WALK SLOWLY! LIKE NORMAL PEOPLE!
AND REACH THERE WITH EVERYBODY ELSE.
GRAB.
NOOOO

TEP.
DO NOT CROSS
POLICE LINE DO NOT CROSS
POLICE LINE
POLICE LINE DO NOT CROSS

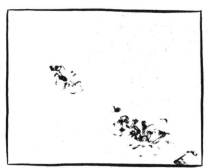

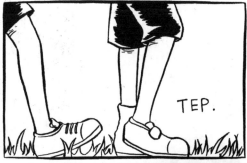

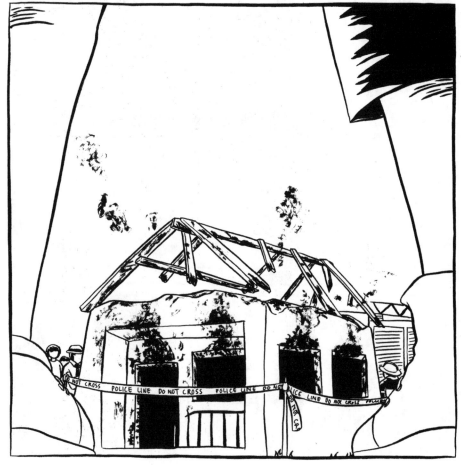

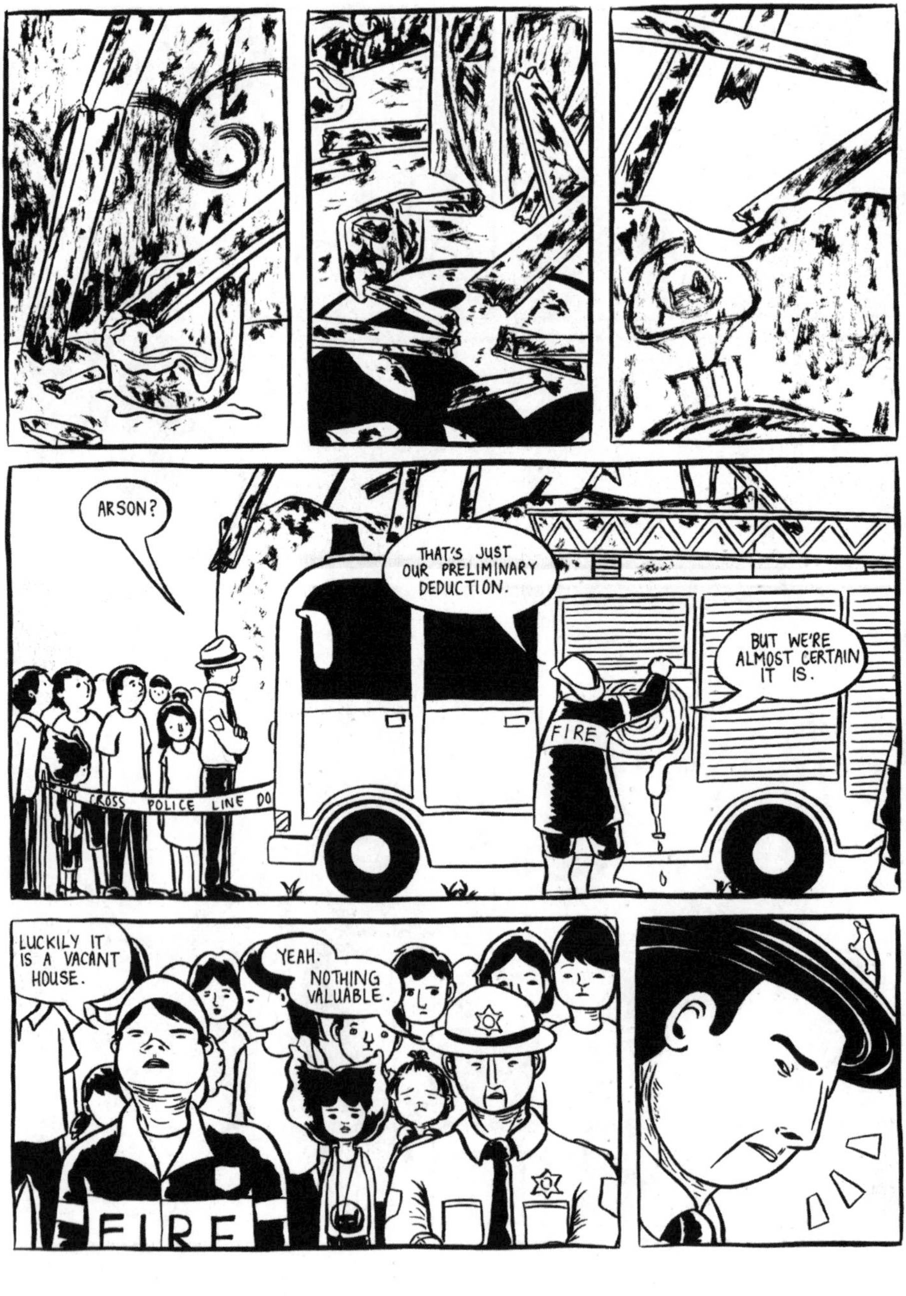
ARSON?
THAT'S JUST OUR PRELIMINARY DEDUCTION.
BUT WE'RE ALMOST CERTAIN IT IS.
POLICE LINE DO
FIRE
LUCKILY IT IS A VACANT HOUSE.
YEAH. NOTHING VALUABLE.
FIRE

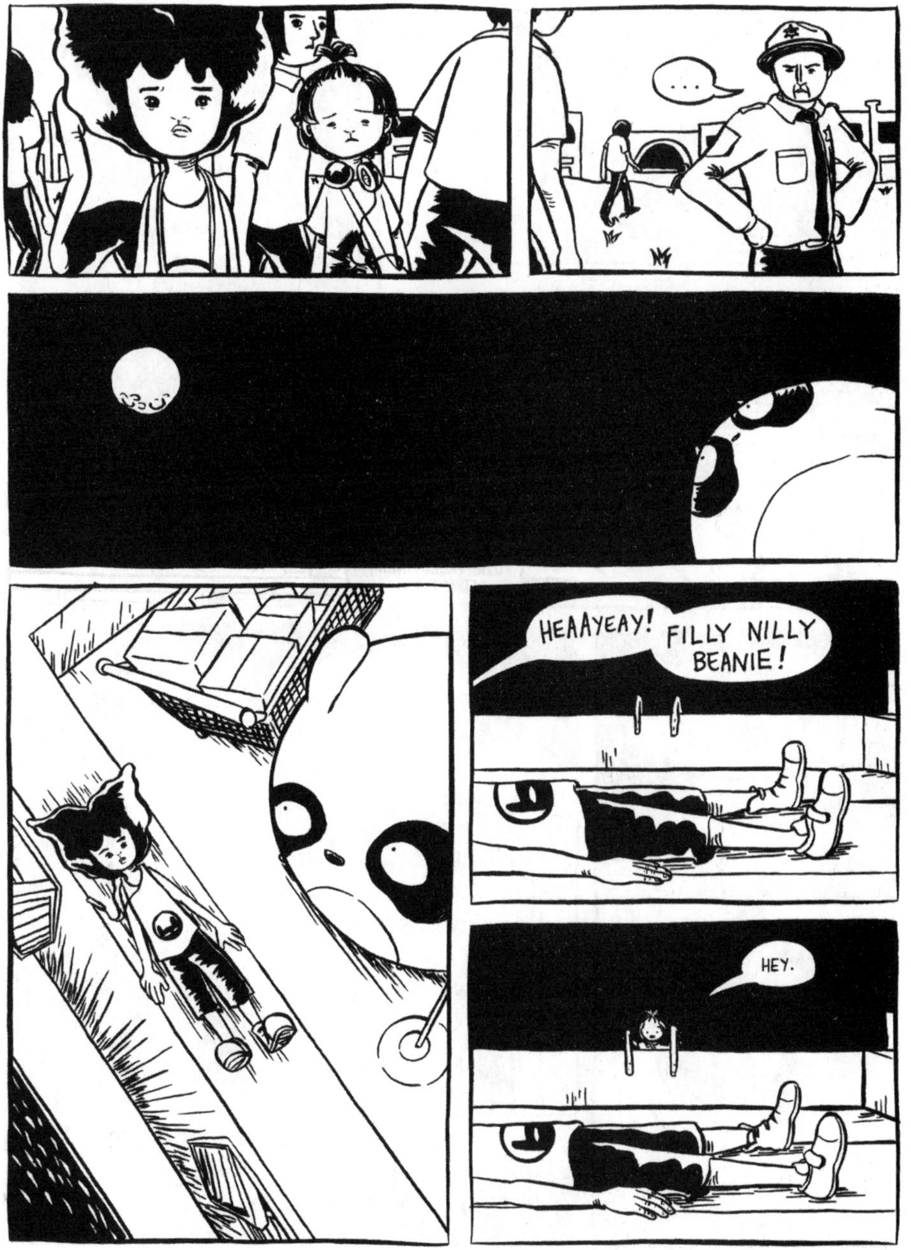
. . .
HEAAYEAY!
FILLY NILLY BEANIE!
HEY.

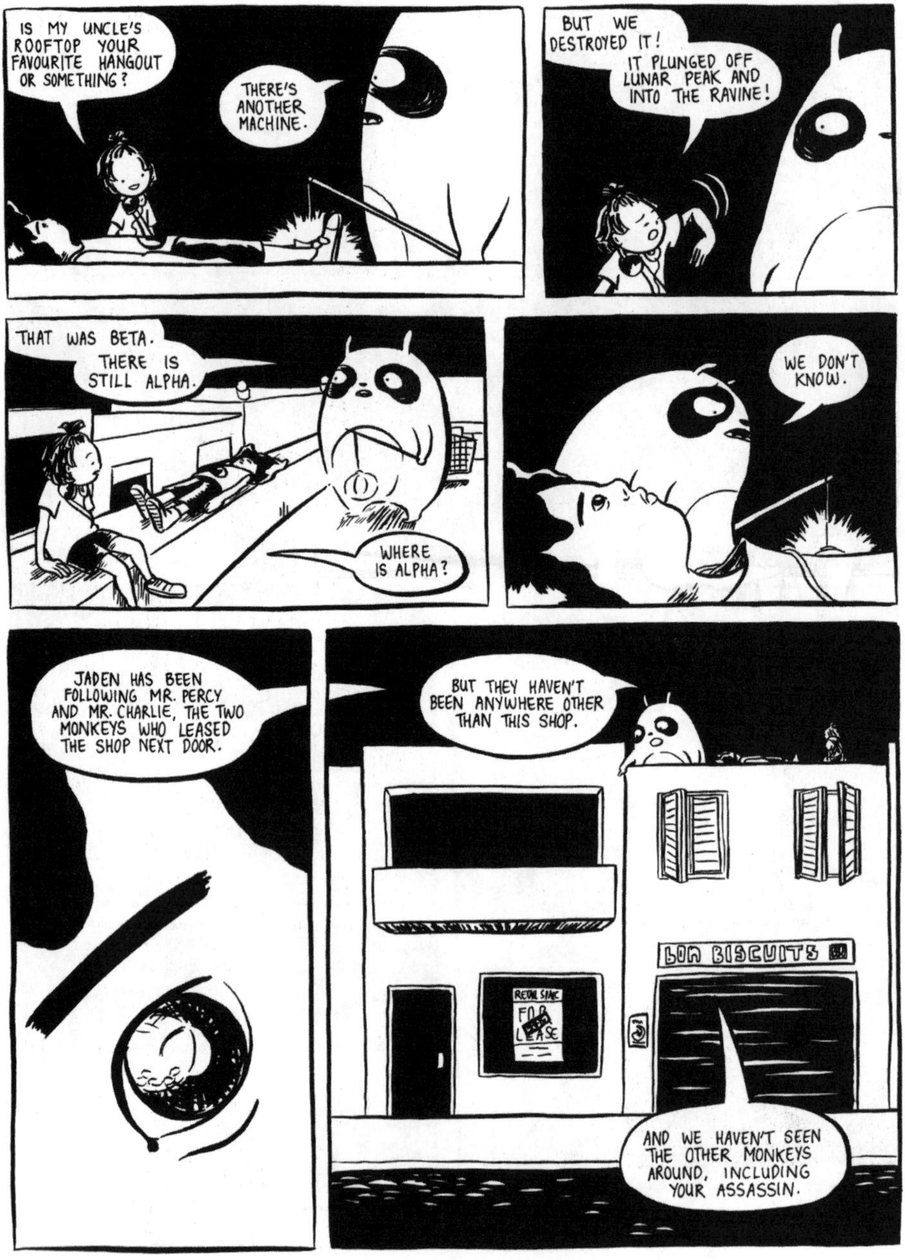
IS MY UNCLE'S ROOFTOP YOUR FAVOURITE HANGOUT OR SOMETHING?
THERE'S ANOTHER MACHINE.
BUT WE DESTROYED IT!
IT PLUNGED OFF LUNAR PEAK AND INTO THE RAVINE!
THAT WAS BETA.
THERE IS STILL ALPHA.
WHERE IS ALPHA?
WE DON'T KNOW.
JADEN HAS BEEN FOLLOWING MR. PERCY AND MR. CHARLIE, THE TWO MONKEYS WHO LEASED THE SHOP NEXT DOOR.
BUT THEY HAVEN'T BEEN ANYWHERE OTHER THAN THIS SHOP.
BON BISCUITS
FOR LEASE
AND WE HAVEN'T SEEN THE OTHER MONKEYS AROUND, INCLUDING YOUR ASSASSIN.

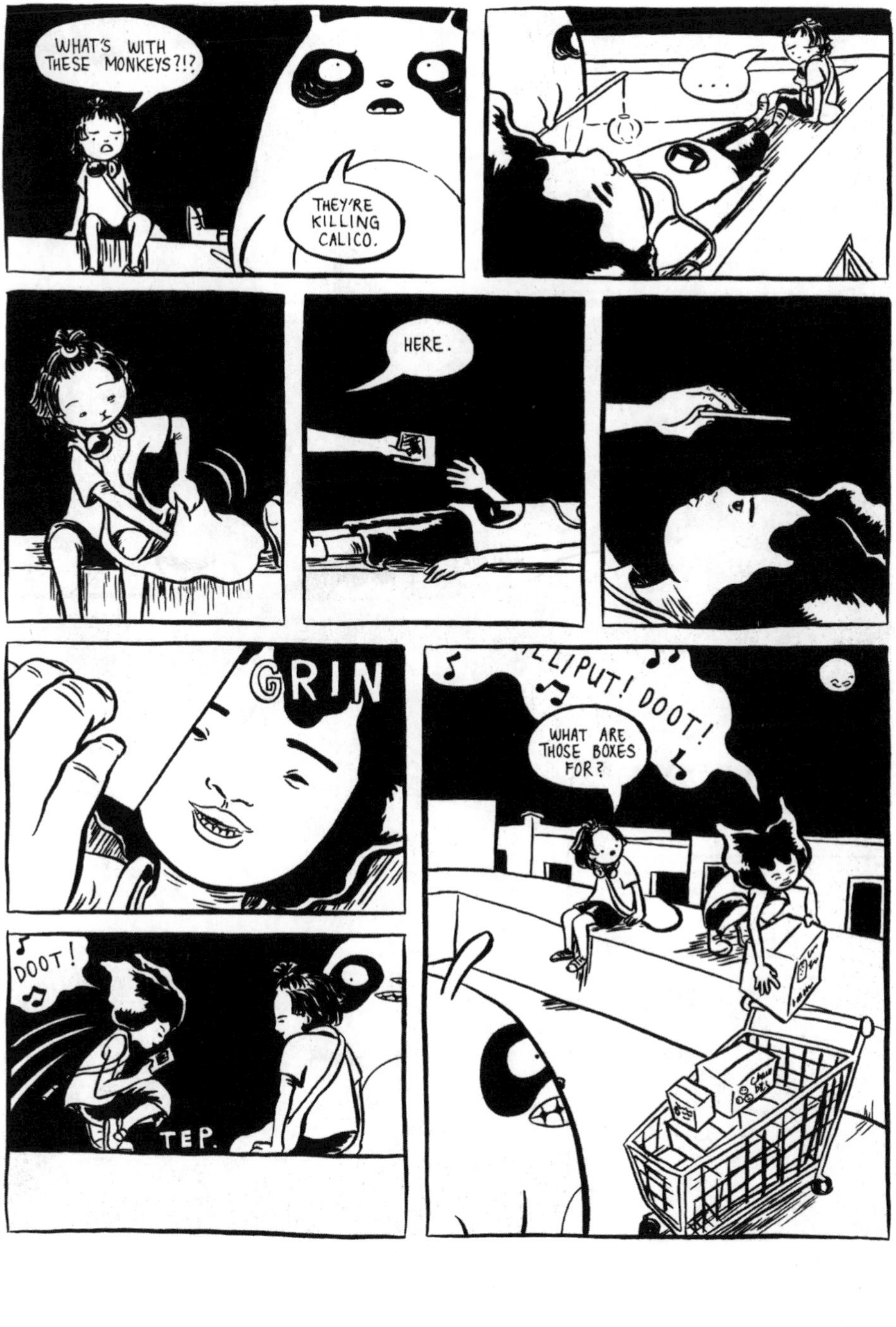
WHAT'S WITH THESE MONKEYS?!?
THEY'RE KILLING CALICO.
...
HERE.
GRIN
ILLIPUT! DOOT!
WHAT ARE THOSE BOXES FOR?
DOOT!
TEP.

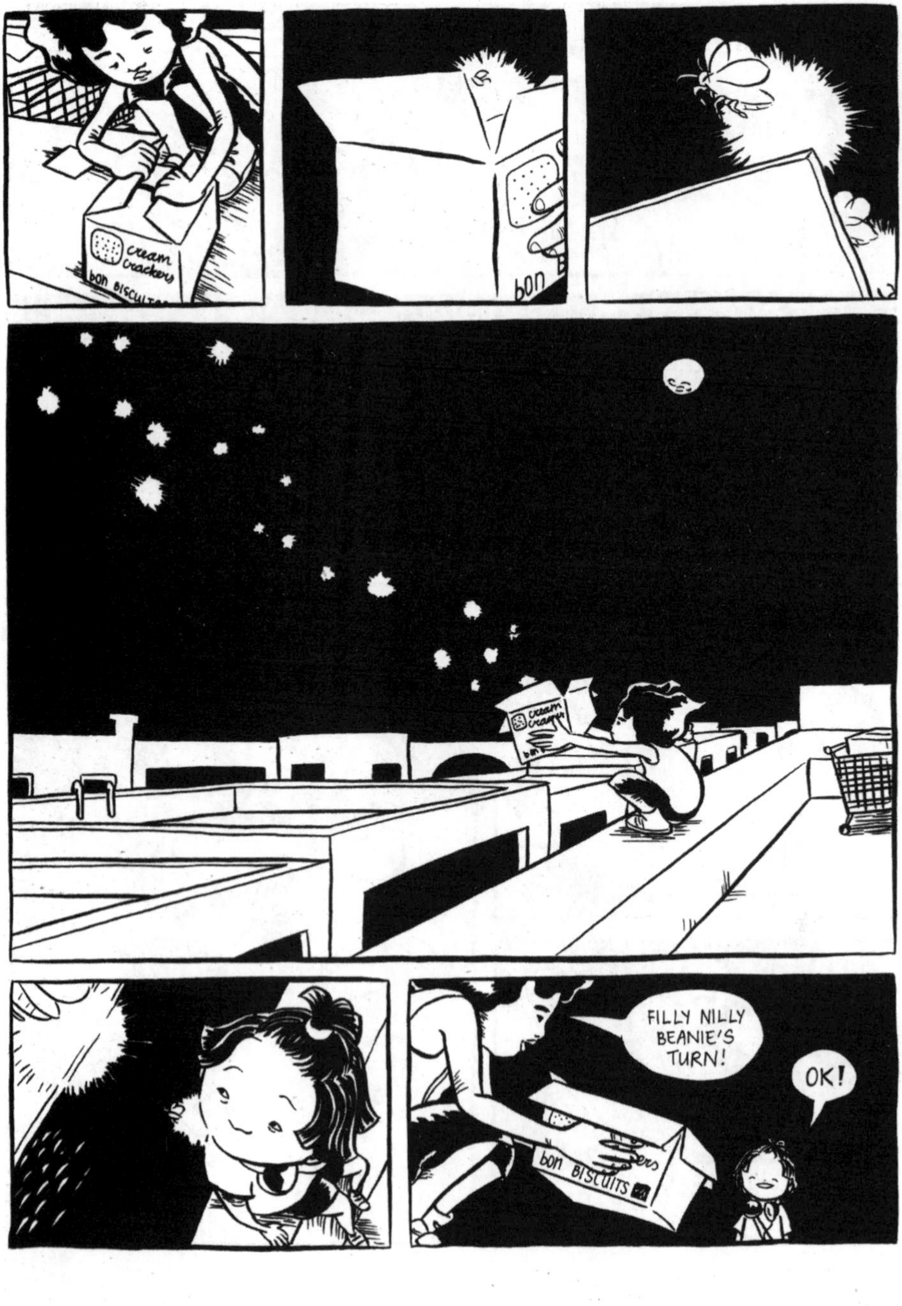
cream crackers
bon BISCUITS
bon
FILLY NILLY BEANIE'S TURN!
OK!
bon BISCUITS

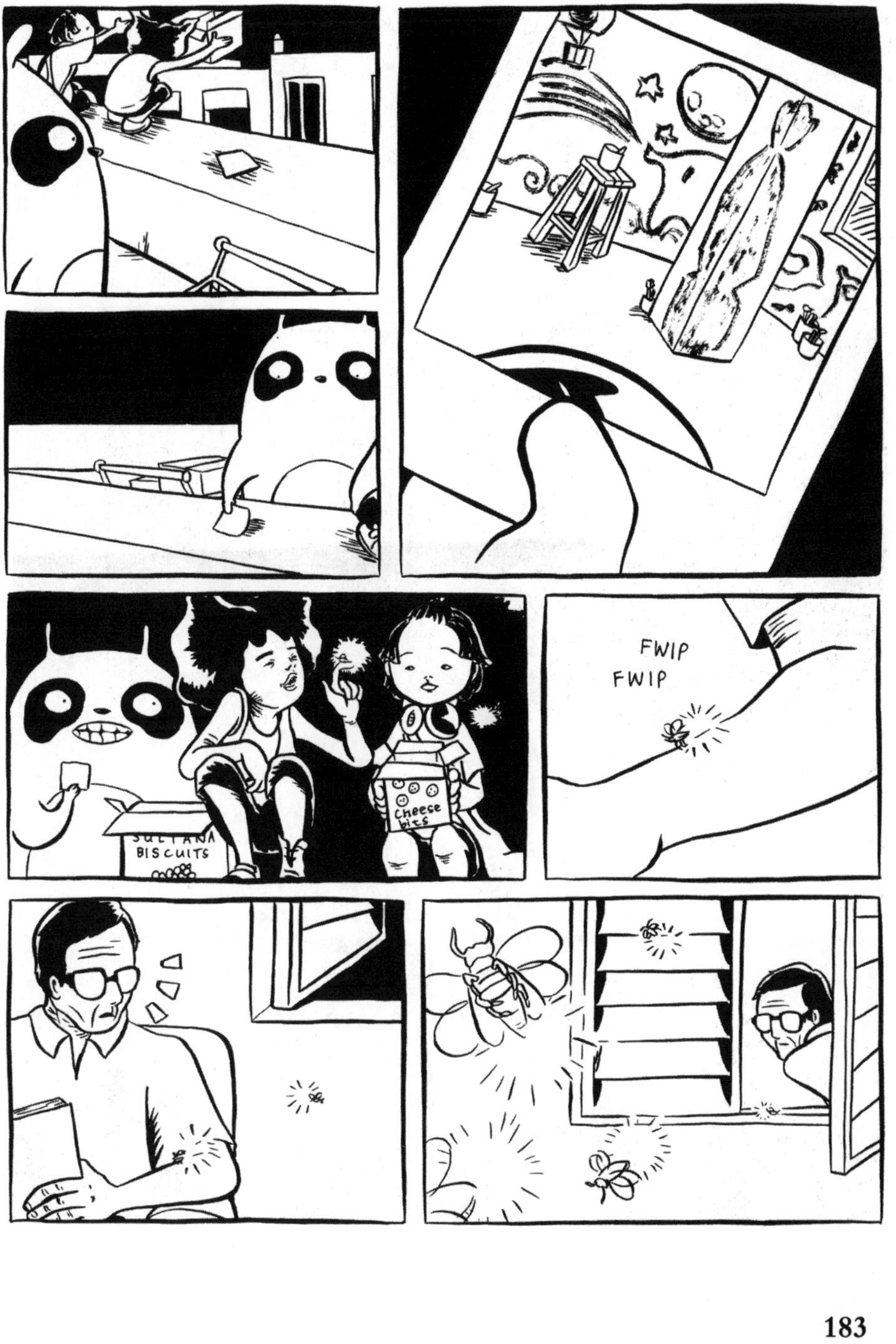

SULTANA BISCUITS
Cheese bits
FWIP
FWIP

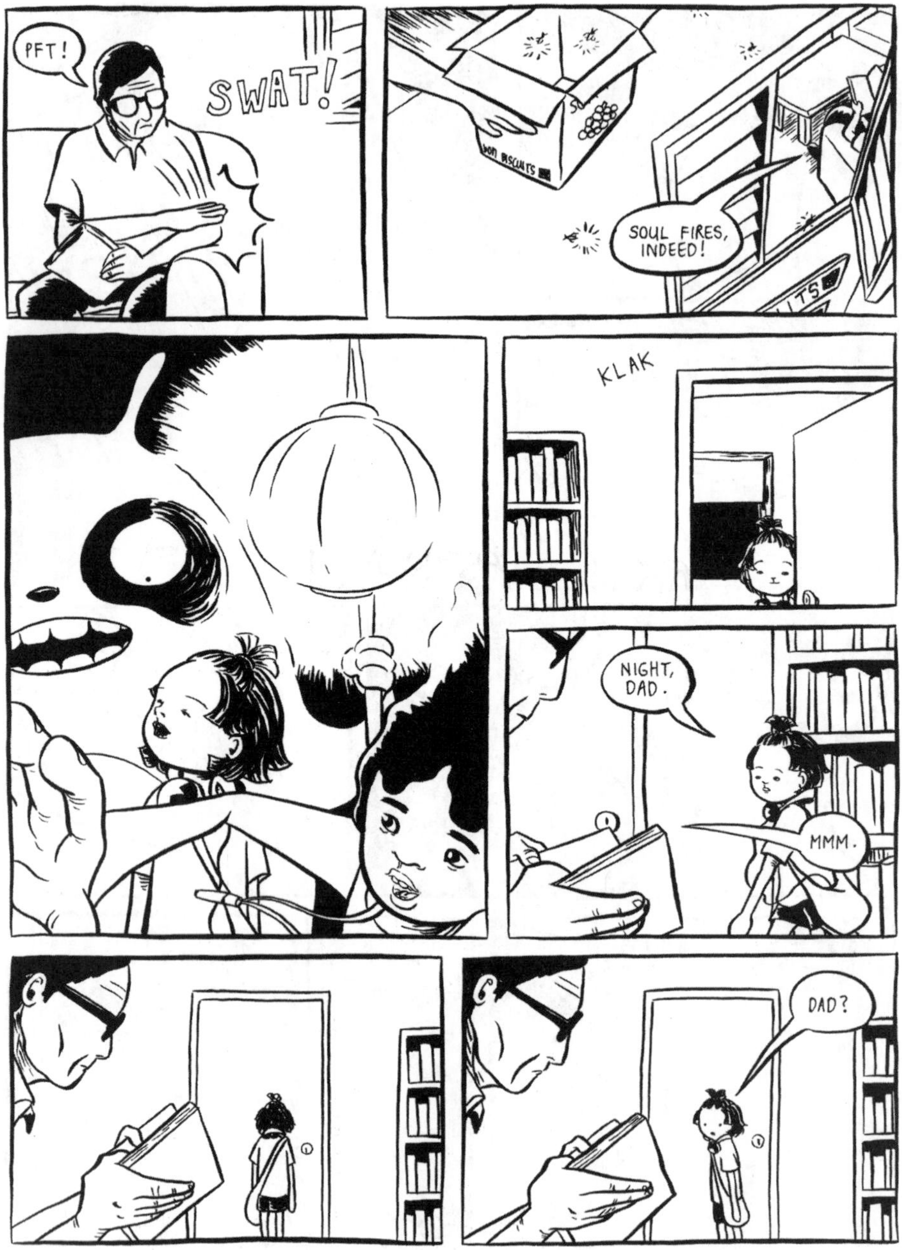
PFT!
SWAT!
SOUL FIRES, INDEED!
KLAK
NIGHT, DAD.
MMM.
DAD?

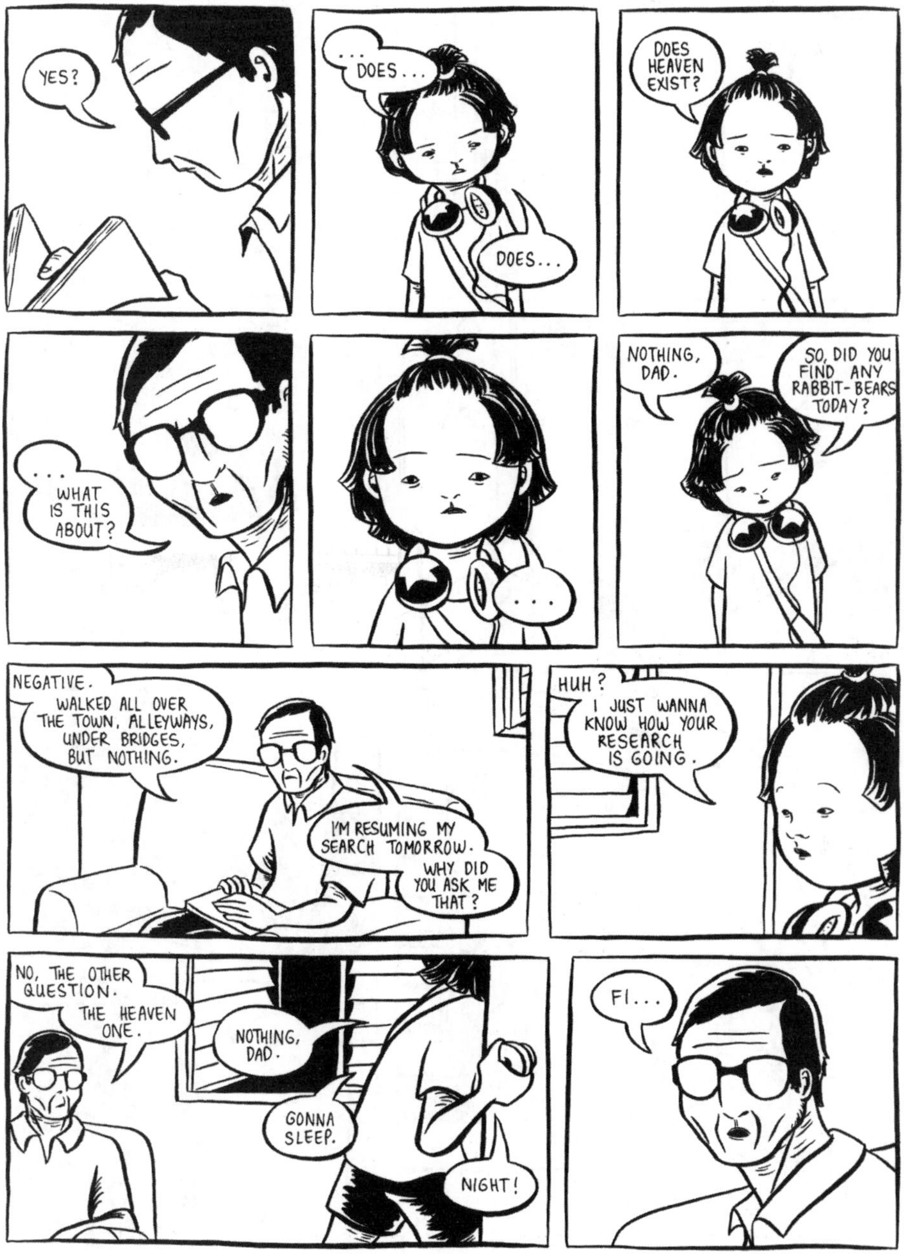
YES?
... DOES...
DOES...
DOES HEAVEN EXIST?
... WHAT IS THIS ABOUT?
...
NOTHING, DAD.
SO, DID YOU FIND ANY RABBIT-BEARS TODAY?
NEGATIVE.
WALKED ALL OVER THE TOWN, ALLEYWAYS, UNDER BRIDGES, BUT NOTHING.
I'M RESUMING MY SEARCH TOMORROW.
WHY DID YOU ASK ME THAT?
HUH?
I JUST WANNA KNOW HOW YOUR RESEARCH IS GOING.
NO, THE OTHER QUESTION.
THE HEAVEN ONE.
NOTHING, DAD.
GONNA SLEEP.
NIGHT!
FI...

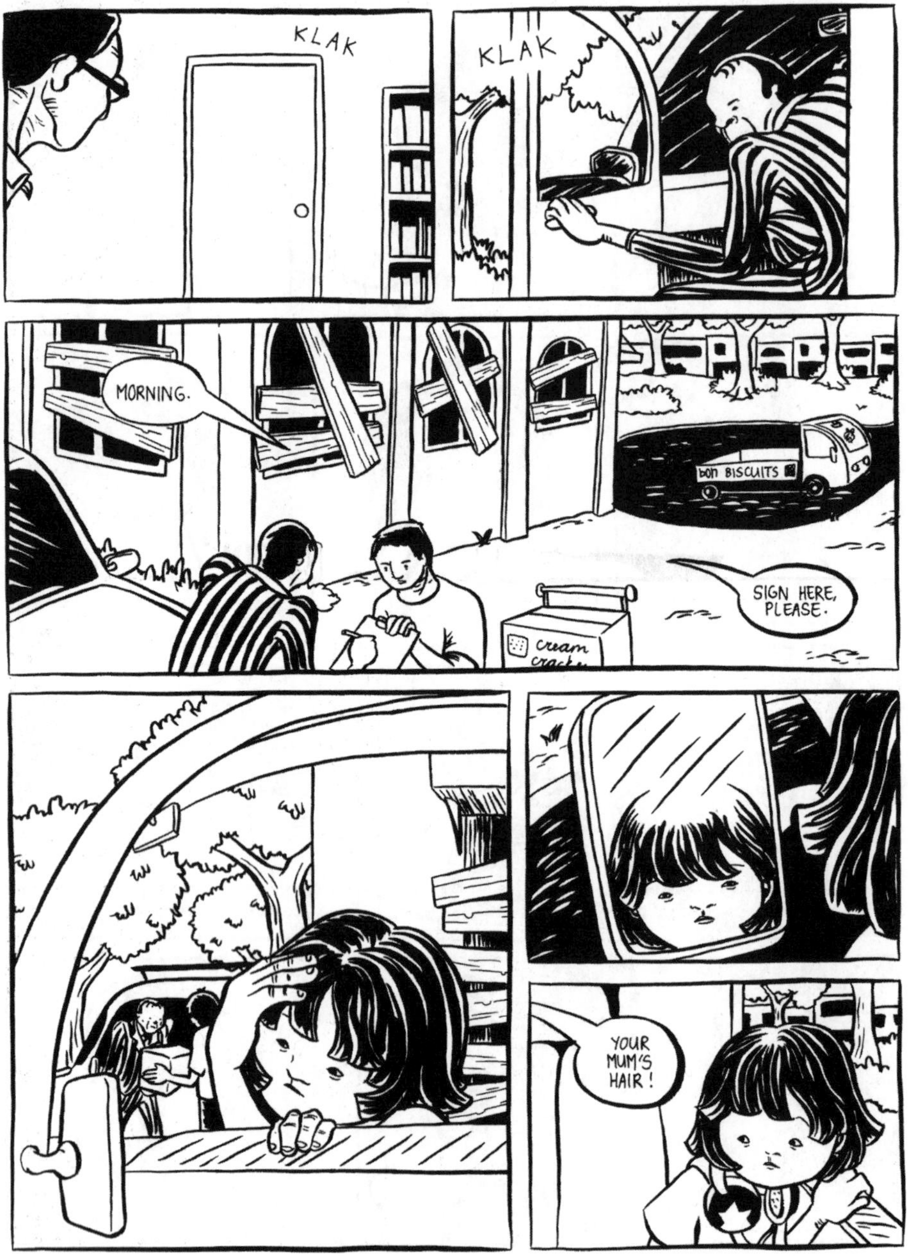
KLAK
KLAK
MORNING.
bon BISCUITS
SIGN HERE, PLEASE.
cream
YOUR MUM'S HAIR!

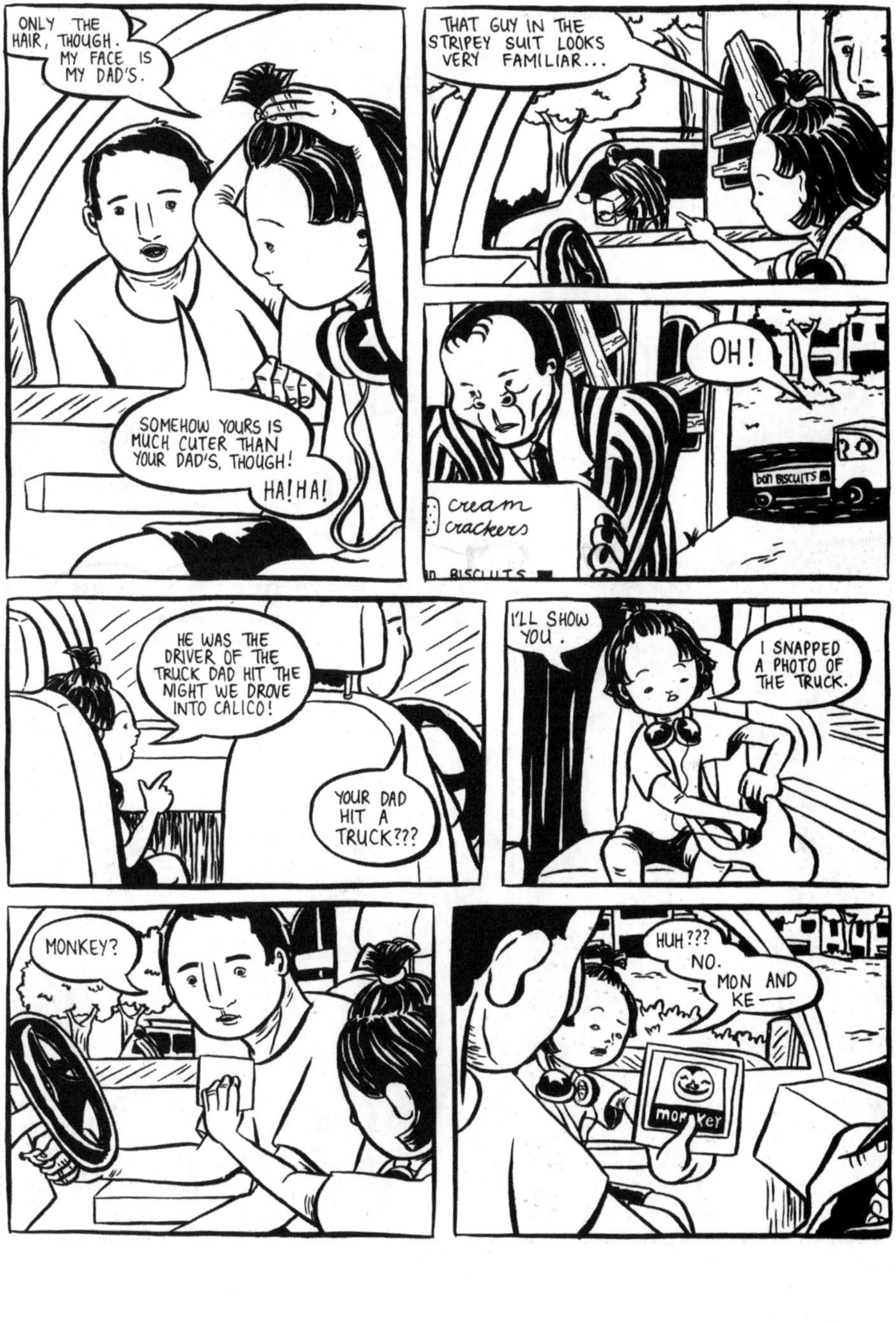
ONLY THE HAIR, THOUGH. MY FACE IS MY DAD'S.
SOMEHOW YOURS IS MUCH CUTER THAN YOUR DAD'S, THOUGH! HA! HA!
THAT GUY IN THE STRIPEY SUIT LOOKS VERY FAMILIAR...
OH!
cream crackers
bon BISCUITS
HE WAS THE DRIVER OF THE TRUCK DAD HIT THE NIGHT WE DROVE INTO CALICO!
YOUR DAD HIT A TRUCK???
I'LL SHOW YOU.
I SNAPPED A PHOTO OF THE TRUCK.
MONKEY?
HUH??? NO. MON AND KE—
monkey

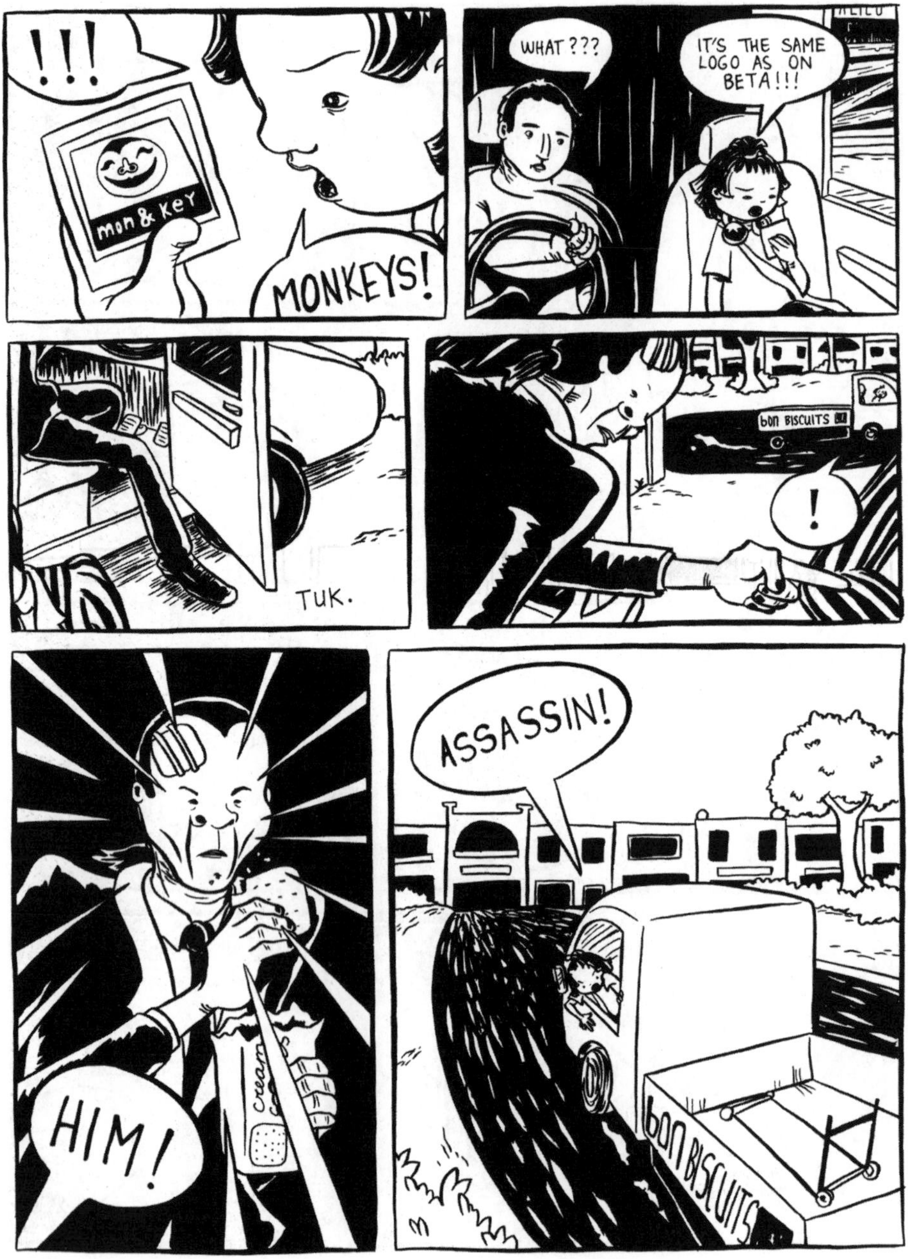
!!!
mon & key
MONKEYS!
WHAT???
IT'S THE SAME LOGO AS ON BETA!!!
TUK.
bon BISCUITS
!
HIM!
cream
ASSASSIN!
bon BISCUITS

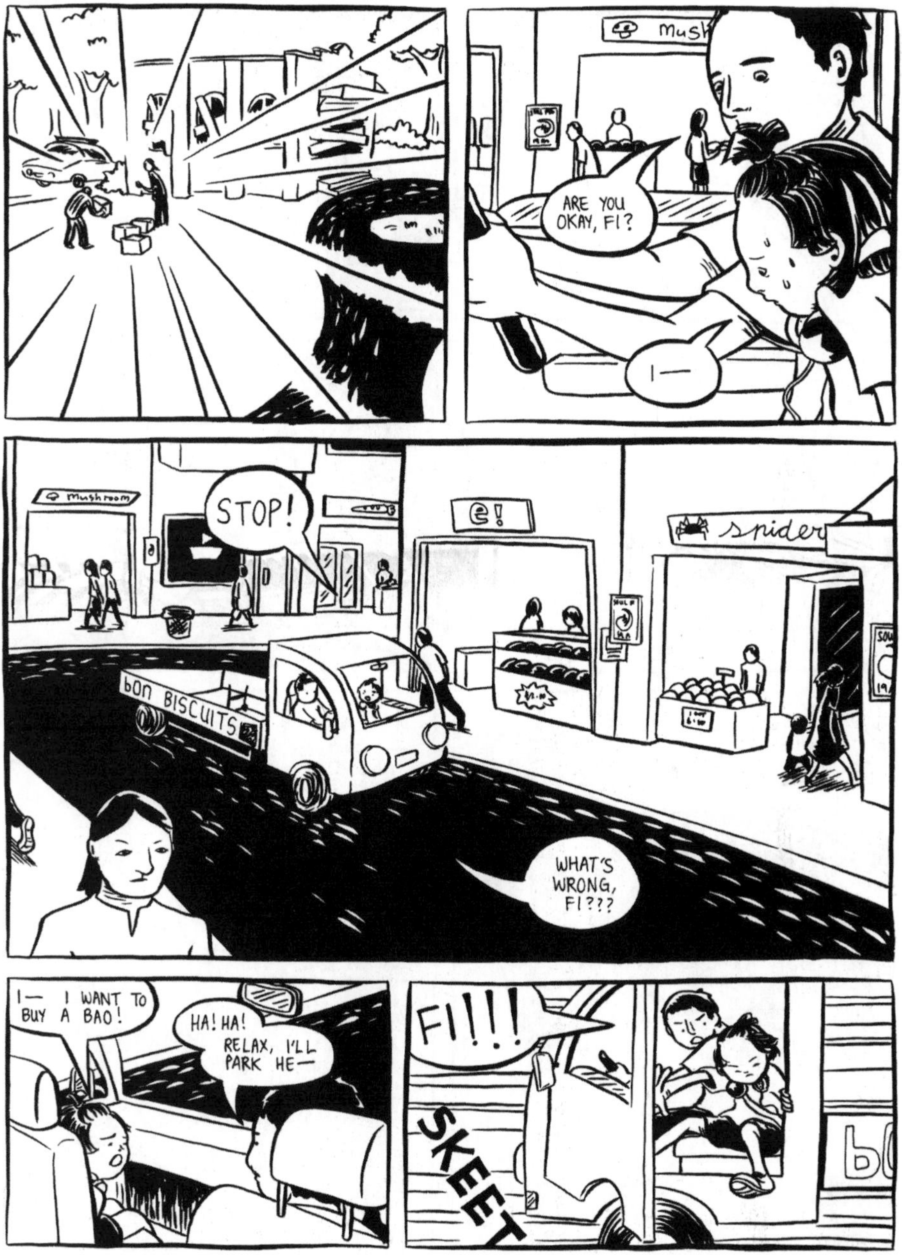
ARE YOU OKAY, FI?
I—
STOP!
WHAT'S WRONG, FI???
I— I WANT TO BUY A BAO!
HA! HA! RELAX, I'LL PARK HE—
FI!!!
SKEET

FI—

SLAM!

I'LL WALK HOME MYSELF, UNCLE SIMON!

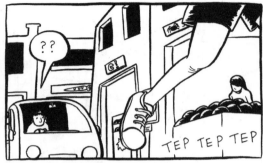

??

TEP TEP TEP

I TOLD YOU, SHERIFF!

I DON'T KNOW WHERE HE IS.

GRANDMAMA, PLEASE.

I CAN ARREST YOU FOR OBSTRUCTION OF JUSTICE.

YOU CAN'T ARREST ME FOR NOT KNOWING WHERE HE IS.

THIS IS A MUCH GRAVER ISSUE THAN YOU THINK, GRANDMAMA.

IT WAS JUST A HIGH-SCHOOL BREAK-IN.

NO ONE WAS HURT AND YOU HAVE NO REAL PROOF IT WAS JADEN.

IT'S NOT JUST THAT, GRANDMAMA.

THAT BOY IS NOT JUST A HARMLESS VANDAL.

HE IS A . . .

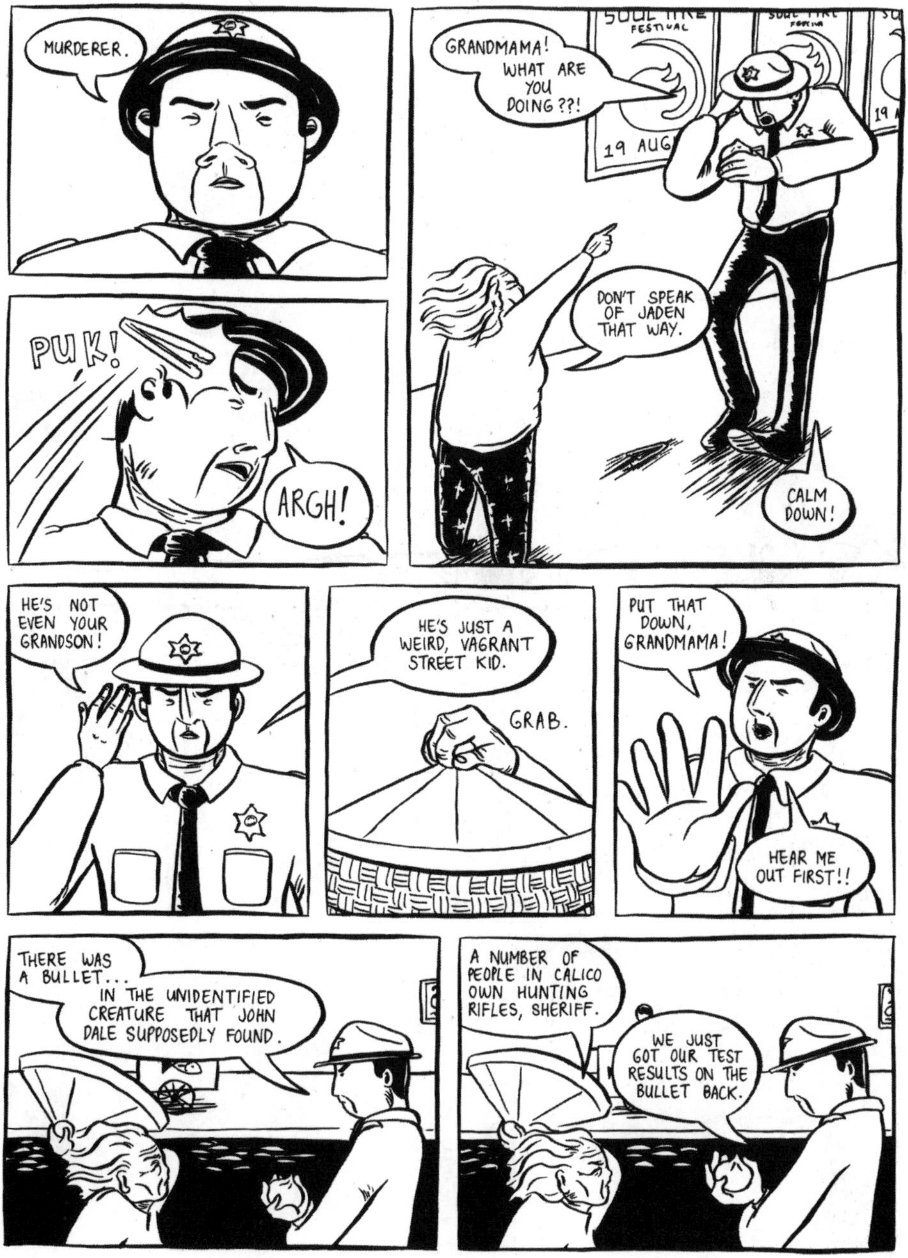
MURDERER.
GRANDMAMA! WHAT ARE YOU DOING??!
SOUL FIRE FESTIVAL
19 AUG
PUK!
ARGH!
DON'T SPEAK OF JADEN THAT WAY.
CALM DOWN!
HE'S NOT EVEN YOUR GRANDSON!
HE'S JUST A WEIRD, VAGRANT STREET KID.
GRAB.
PUT THAT DOWN, GRANDMAMA!
HEAR ME OUT FIRST!!
THERE WAS A BULLET... IN THE UNIDENTIFIED CREATURE THAT JOHN DALE SUPPOSEDLY FOUND.
A NUMBER OF PEOPLE IN CALICO OWN HUNTING RIFLES, SHERIFF.
WE JUST GOT OUR TEST RESULTS ON THE BULLET BACK.

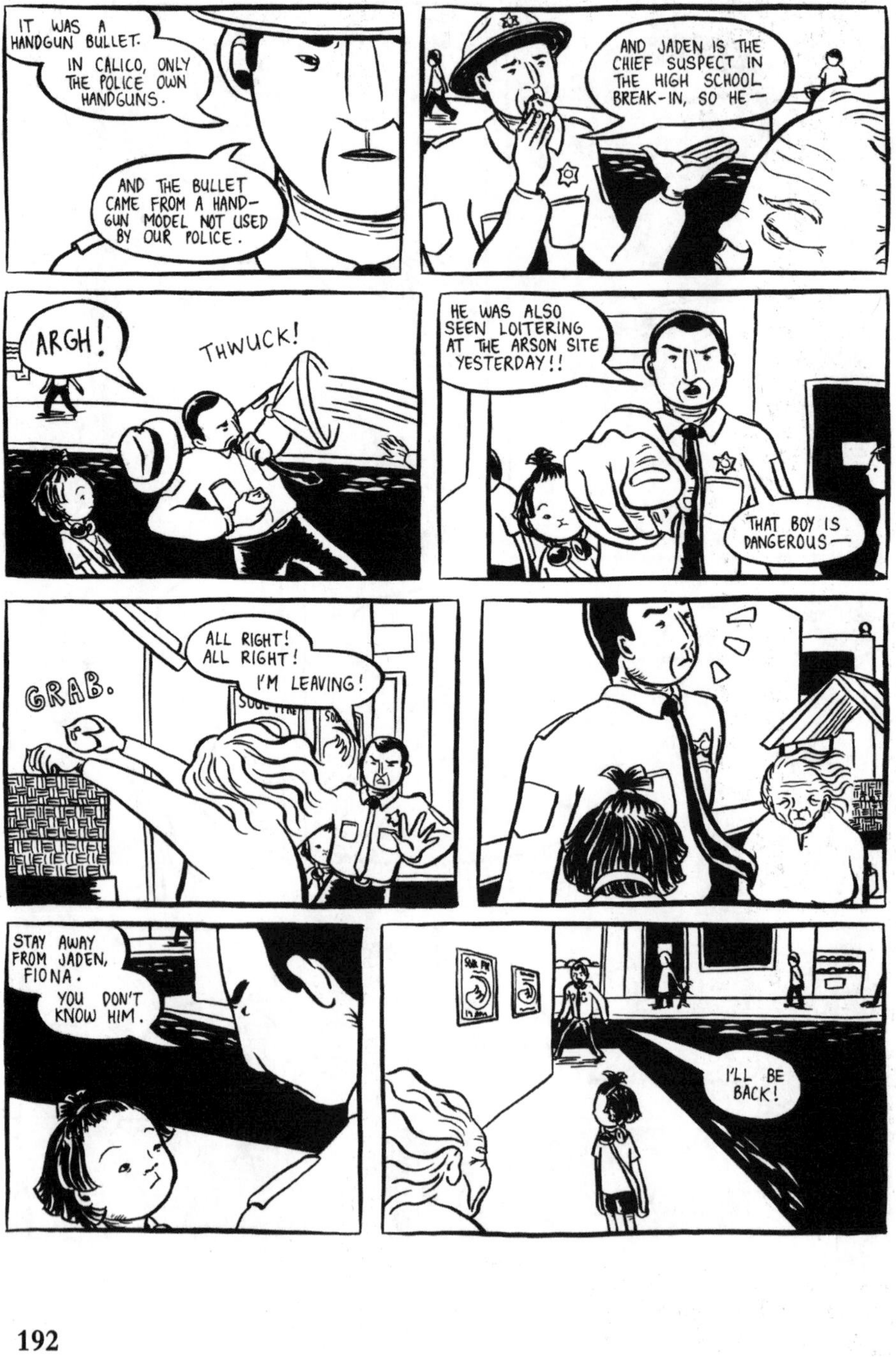
IT WAS A HANDGUN BULLET.
IN CALICO, ONLY THE POLICE OWN HANDGUNS.
AND THE BULLET CAME FROM A HAND-GUN MODEL NOT USED BY OUR POLICE.
AND JADEN IS THE CHIEF SUSPECT IN THE HIGH SCHOOL BREAK-IN, SO HE—
ARGH!
THWUCK!
HE WAS ALSO SEEN LOITERING AT THE ARSON SITE YESTERDAY!!
THAT BOY IS DANGEROUS—
GRAB.
ALL RIGHT! ALL RIGHT!
I'M LEAVING!
STAY AWAY FROM JADEN, FIONA.
YOU DON'T KNOW HIM.
I'LL BE BACK!

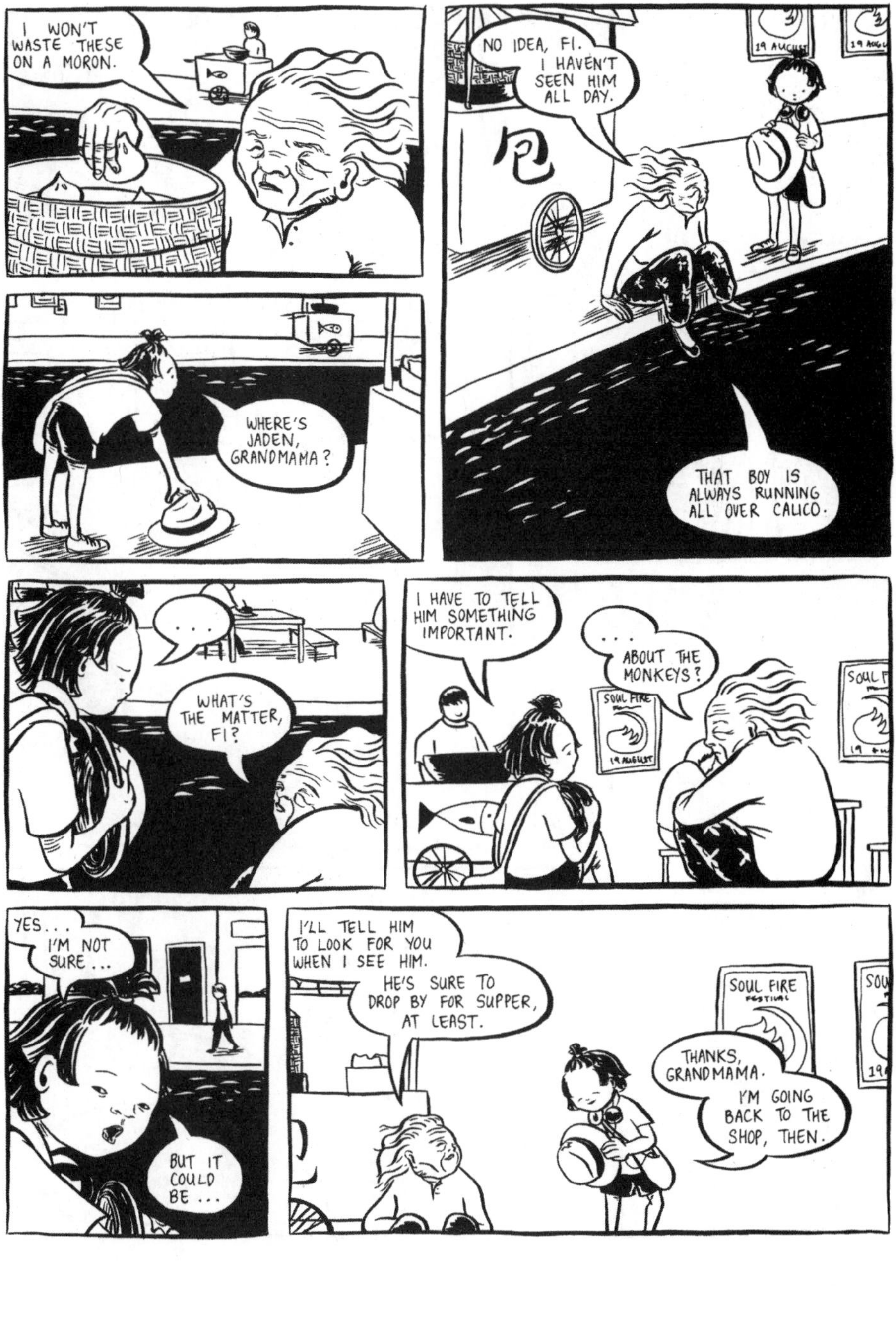
I WON'T WASTE THESE ON A MORON.
WHERE'S JADEN, GRANDMAMA?
NO IDEA, FI. I HAVEN'T SEEN HIM ALL DAY.
THAT BOY IS ALWAYS RUNNING ALL OVER CALICO.
. . .
WHAT'S THE MATTER, FI?
I HAVE TO TELL HIM SOMETHING IMPORTANT.
. . . ABOUT THE MONKEYS?
SOUL FIRE
19 AUGUST
YES . . . I'M NOT SURE . . .
BUT IT COULD BE . . .
I'LL TELL HIM TO LOOK FOR YOU WHEN I SEE HIM.
HE'S SURE TO DROP BY FOR SUPPER, AT LEAST.
SOUL FIRE FESTIVAL
THANKS, GRANDMAMA.
I'M GOING BACK TO THE SHOP, THEN.

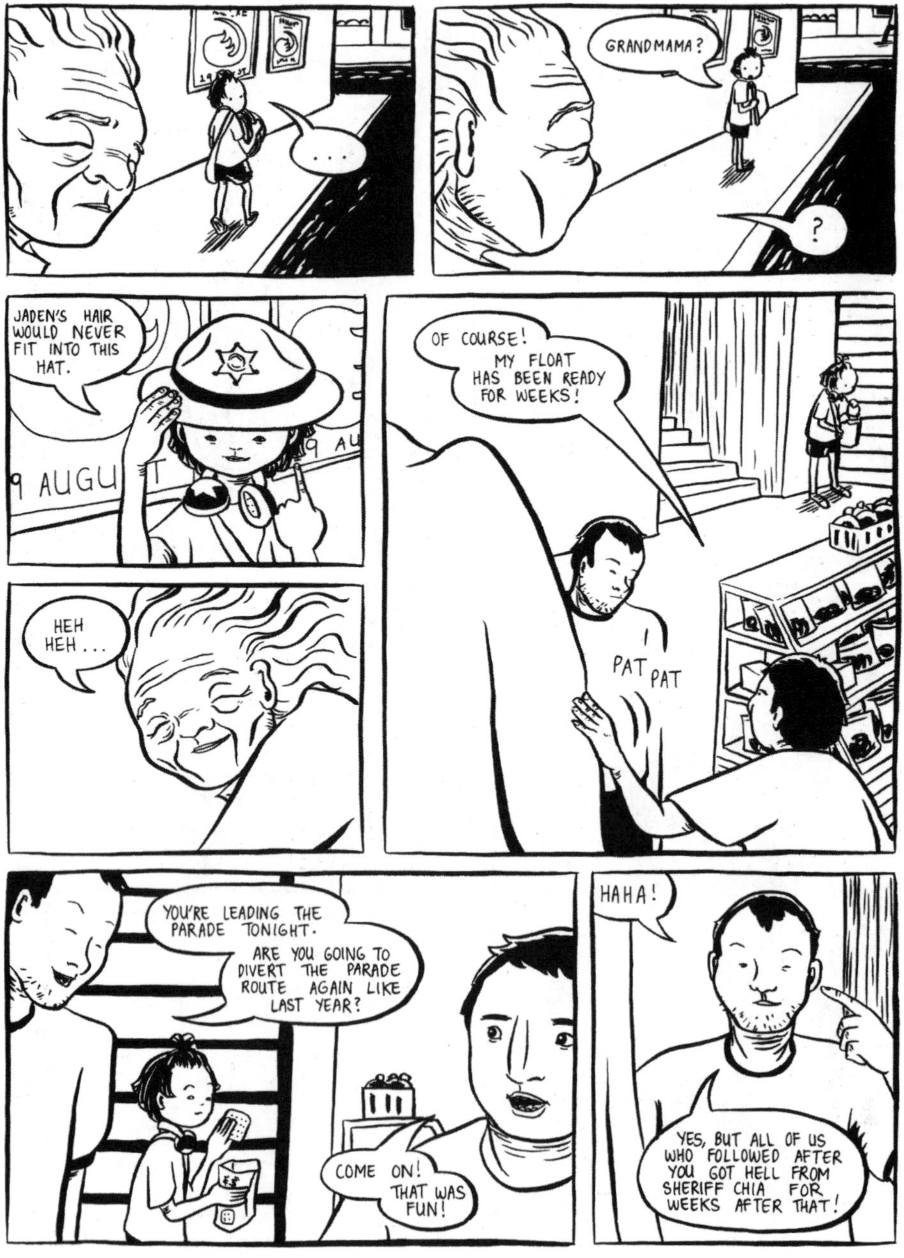

...
GRANDMAMA?
?
JADEN'S HAIR WOULD NEVER FIT INTO THIS HAT.
9 AUGU
9 AU
HEH HEH...
OF COURSE! MY FLOAT HAS BEEN READY FOR WEEKS!
PAT PAT
YOU'RE LEADING THE PARADE TONIGHT.
ARE YOU GOING TO DIVERT THE PARADE ROUTE AGAIN LIKE LAST YEAR?
COME ON! THAT WAS FUN!
HAHA!
YES, BUT ALL OF US WHO FOLLOWED AFTER YOU GOT HELL FROM SHERIFF CHIA FOR WEEKS AFTER THAT!

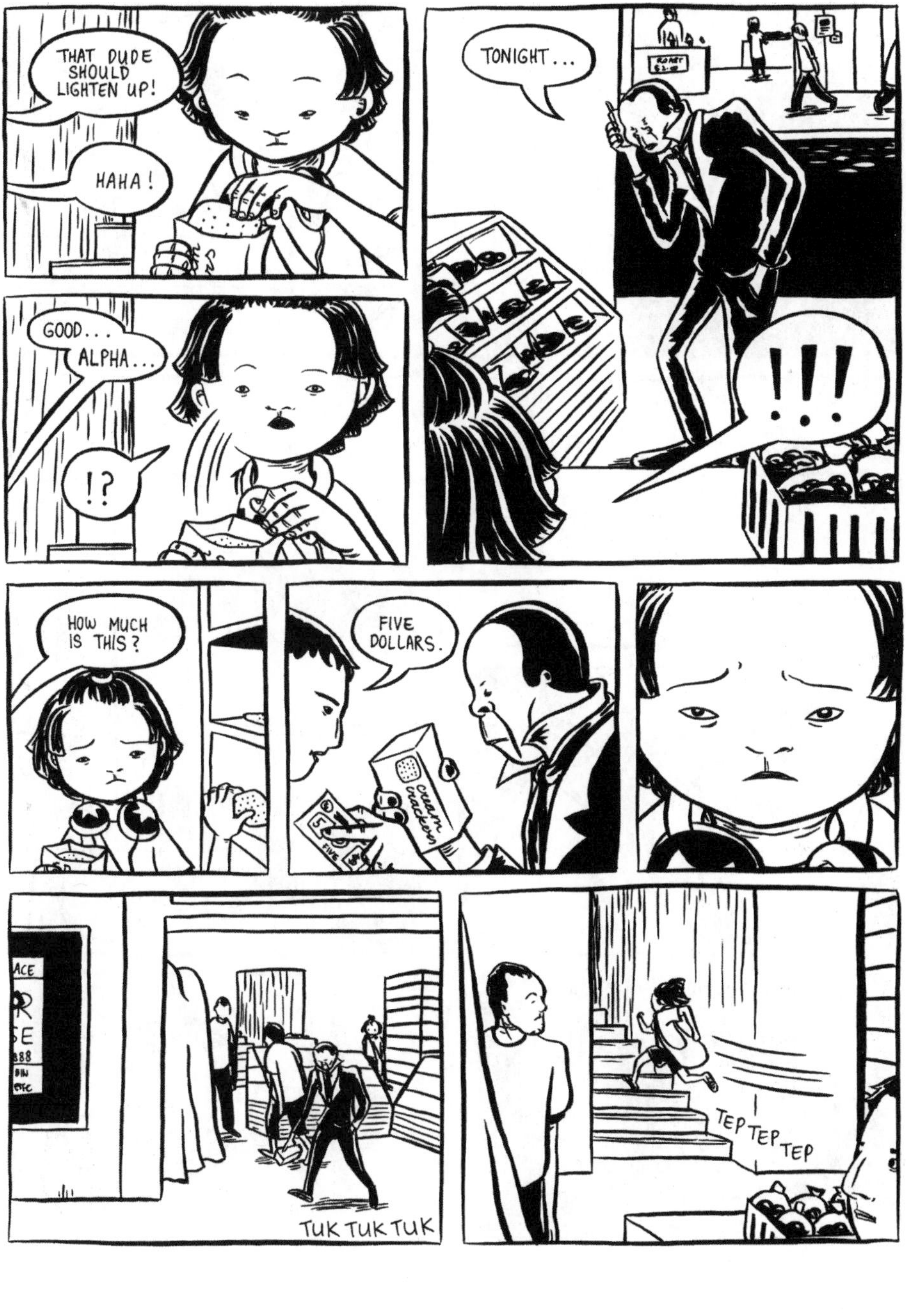
THAT DUDE SHOULD LIGHTEN UP!
HAHA!
TONIGHT...
GOOD...
ALPHA...
!?
!!!
HOW MUCH IS THIS?
FIVE DOLLARS.
cream crackers
TUK TUK TUK
TEP TEP TEP

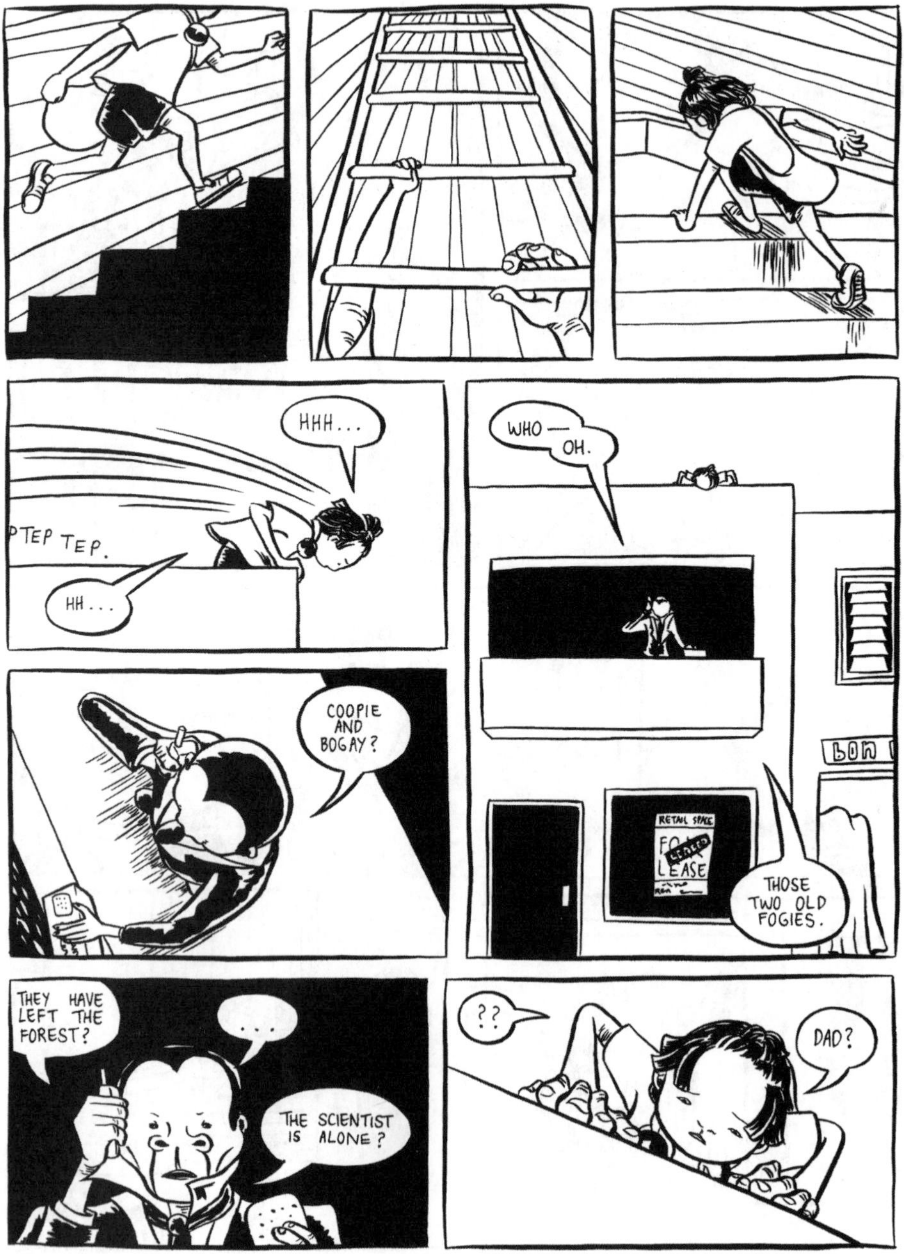
HHH...
TEP TEP.
HH...
WHO —
OH.
COOPIE AND BOGAY?
THOSE TWO OLD FOGIES.
RETAIL SPACE
LEASE
THEY HAVE LEFT THE FOREST?
...
THE SCIENTIST IS ALONE?
??
DAD?

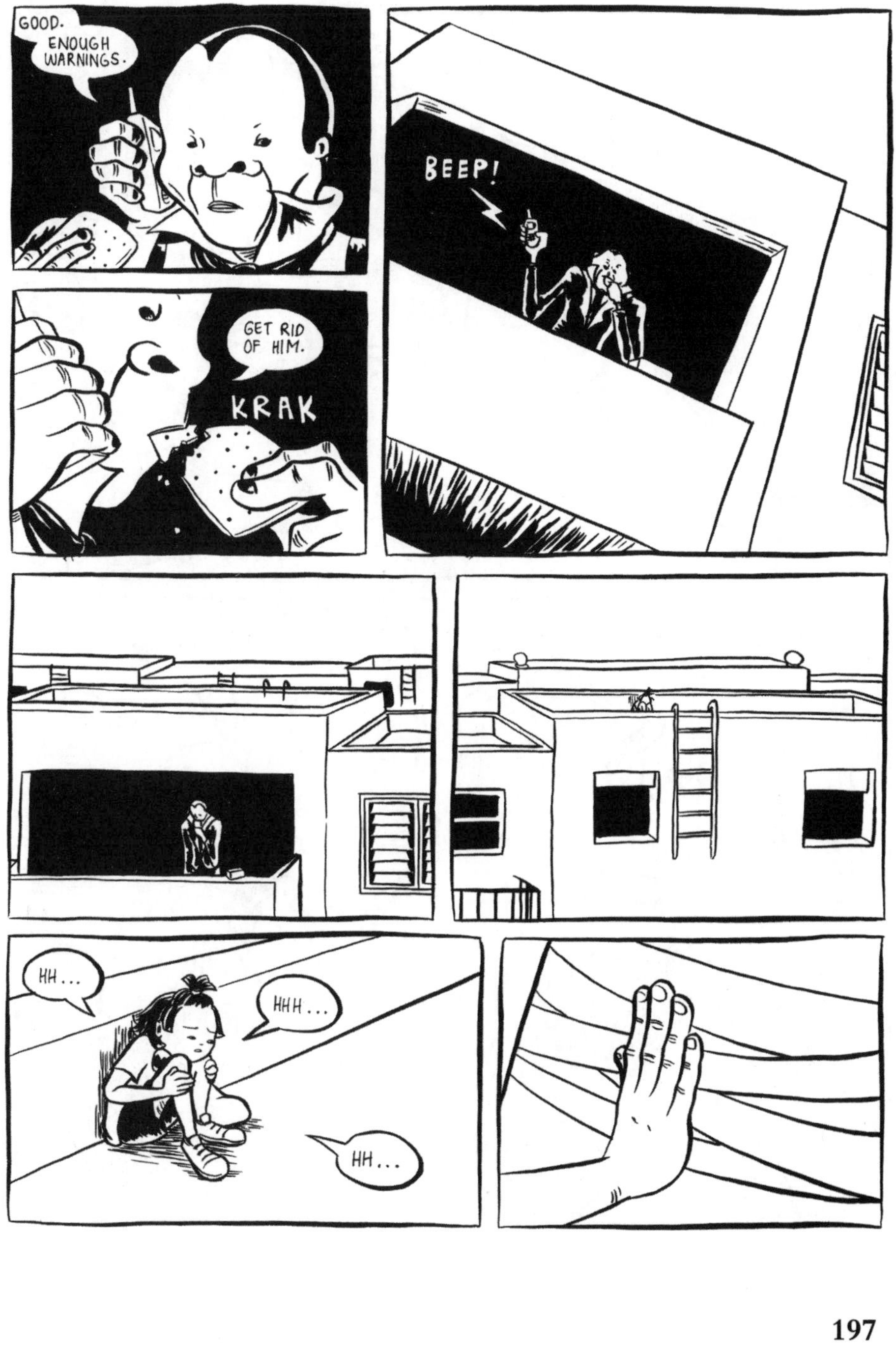
GOOD.
ENOUGH WARNINGS.
BEEP!
GET RID OF HIM.
KRAK
HH...
HHH...
HH...

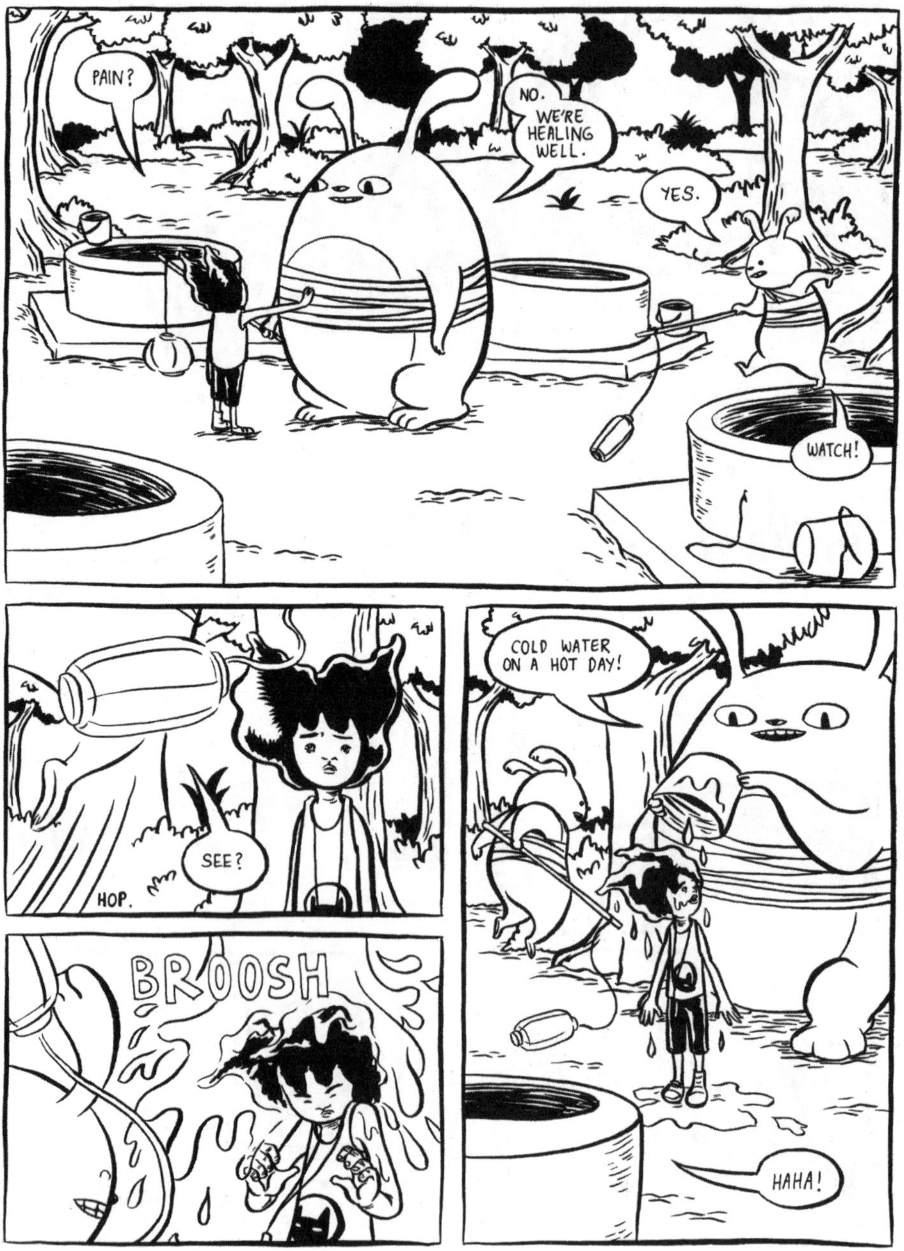
PAIN?
NO. WE'RE HEALING WELL.
YES.
WATCH!
HOP.
SEE?
BROOSH
COLD WATER ON A HOT DAY!
HAHA!

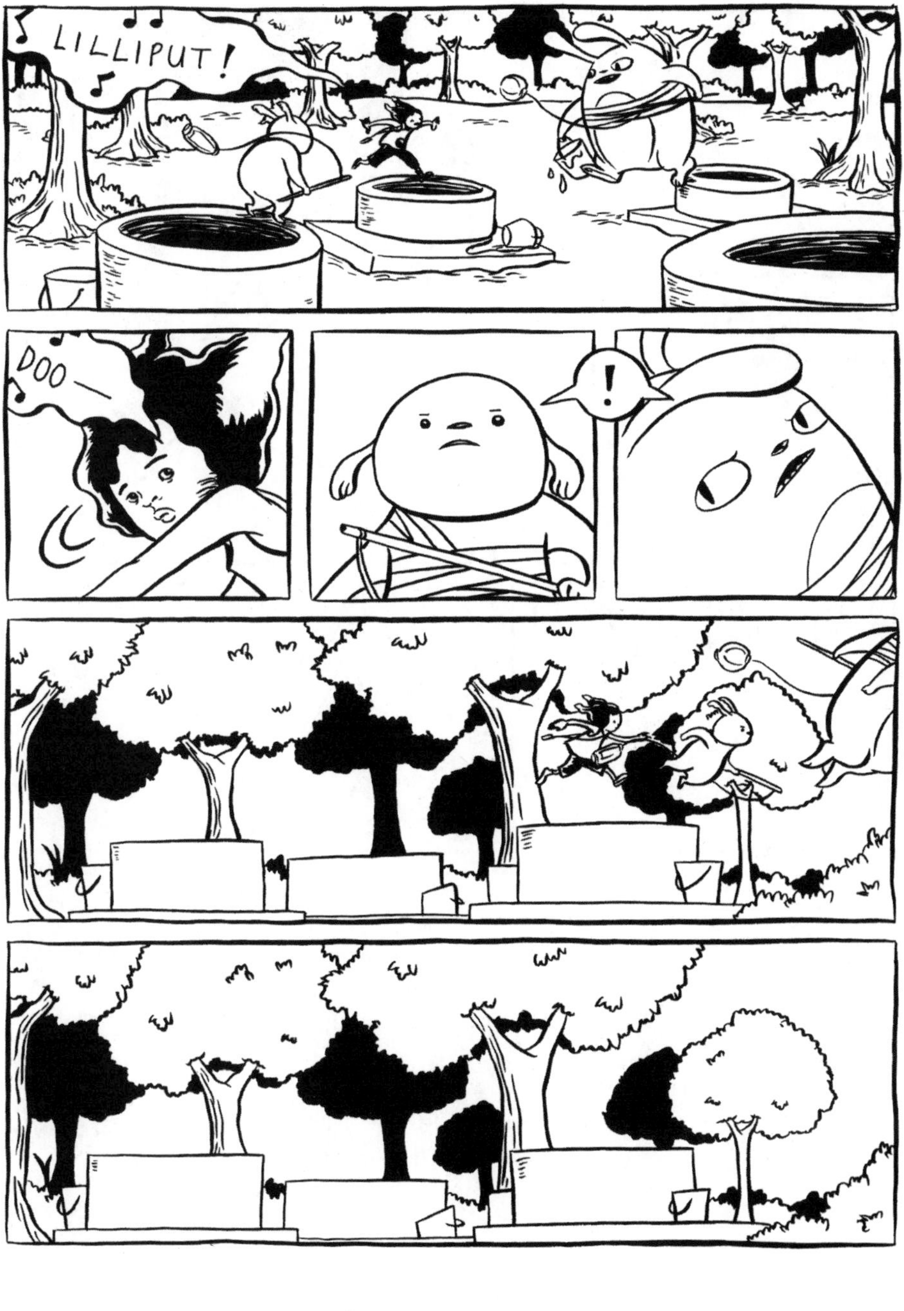
LILLIPUT!
DOO—
!

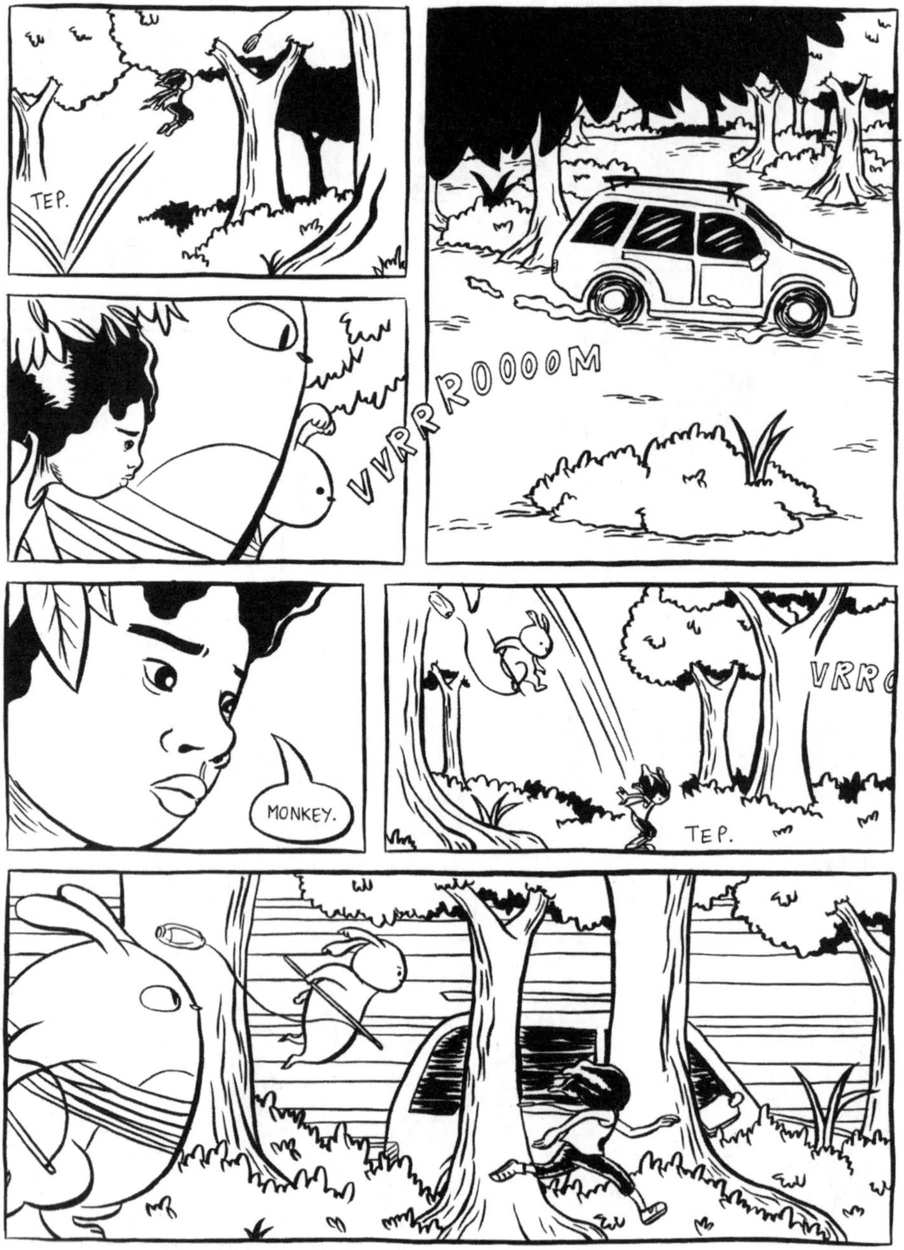
TEP.
VVRRROOOOM
MONKEY.
VRRO
TEP.

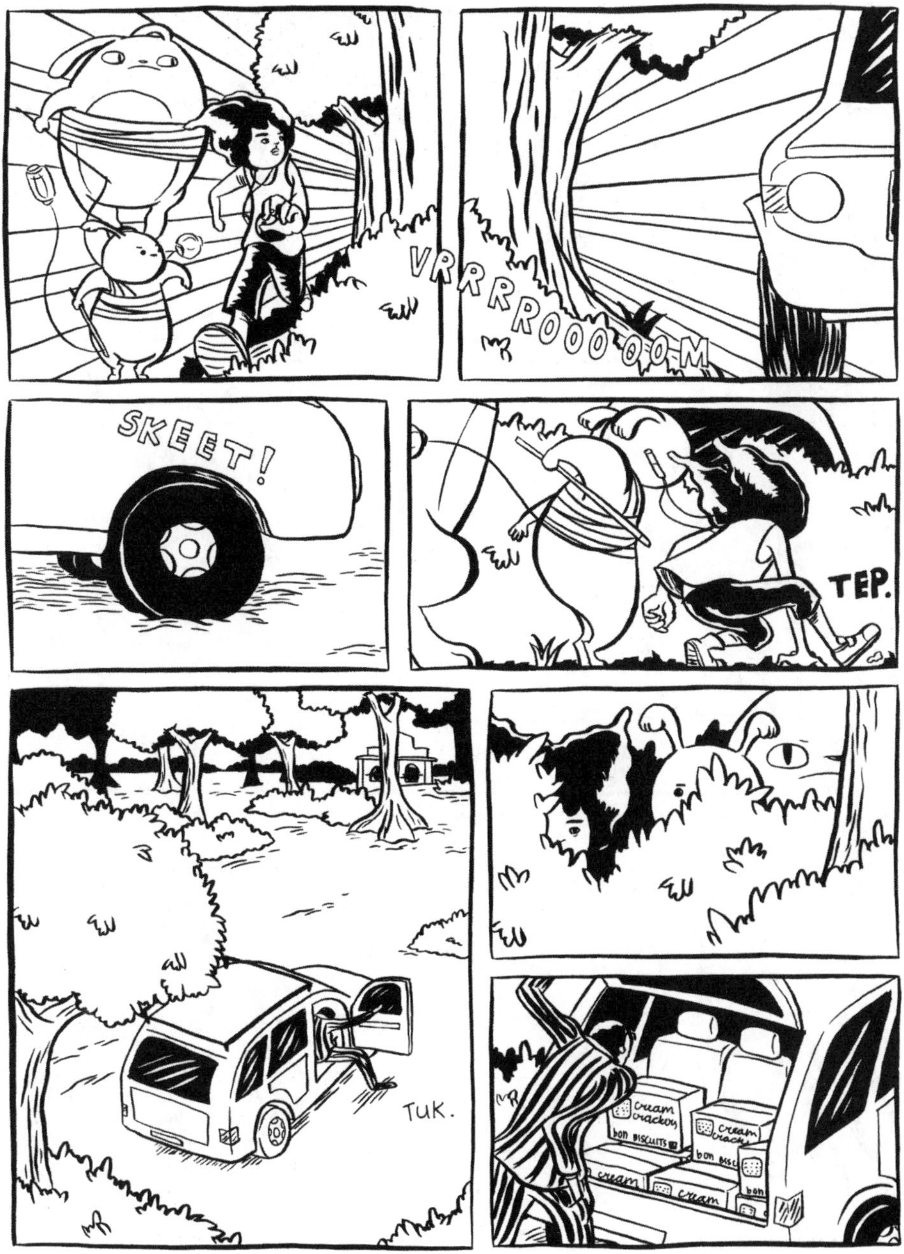
VRRRROOOOOM
SKEET!
TEP.
TUK.
bon BISCUITS

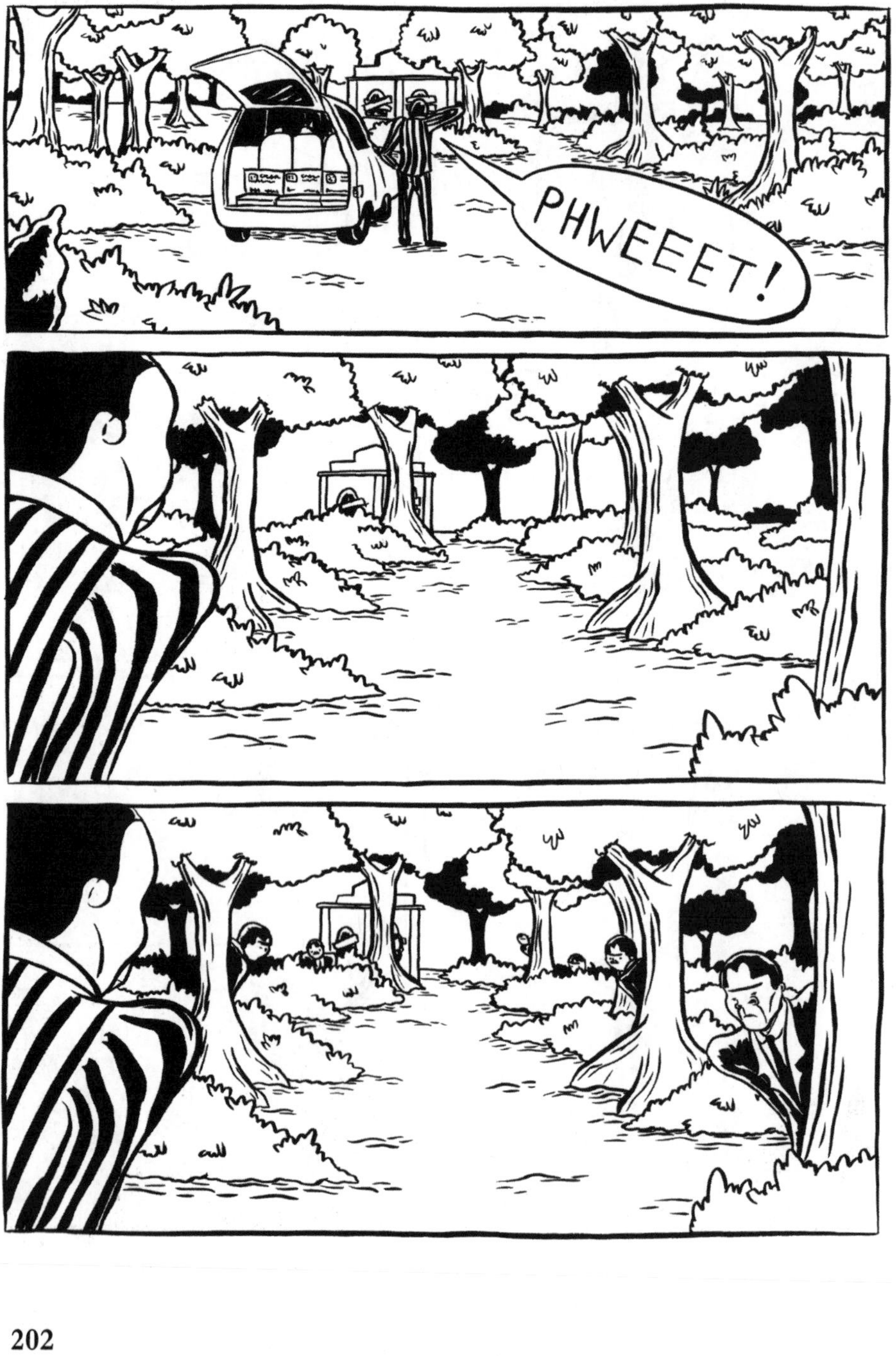
PHWEEEET!

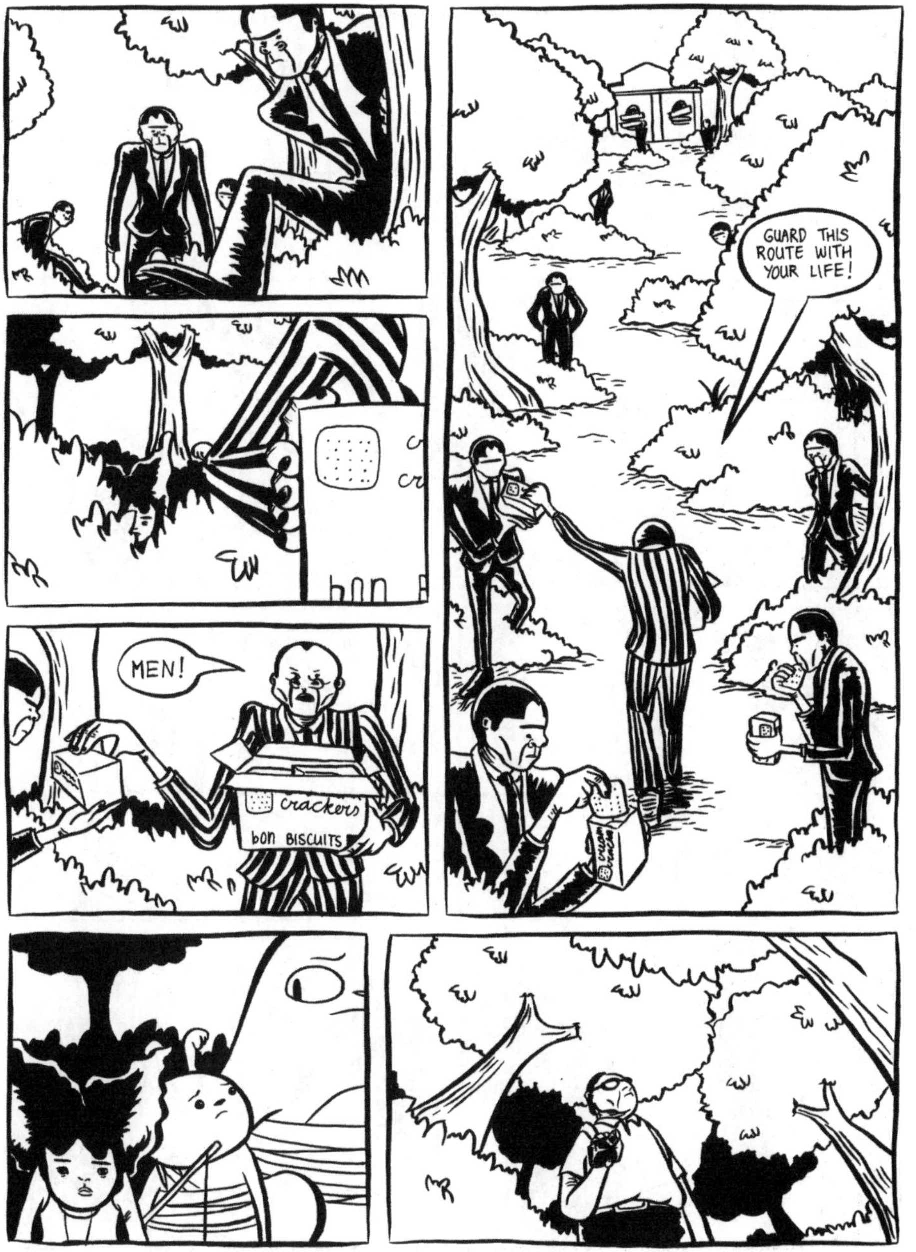
GUARD THIS ROUTE WITH YOUR LIFE!
MEN!
crackers
bon BISCUITS

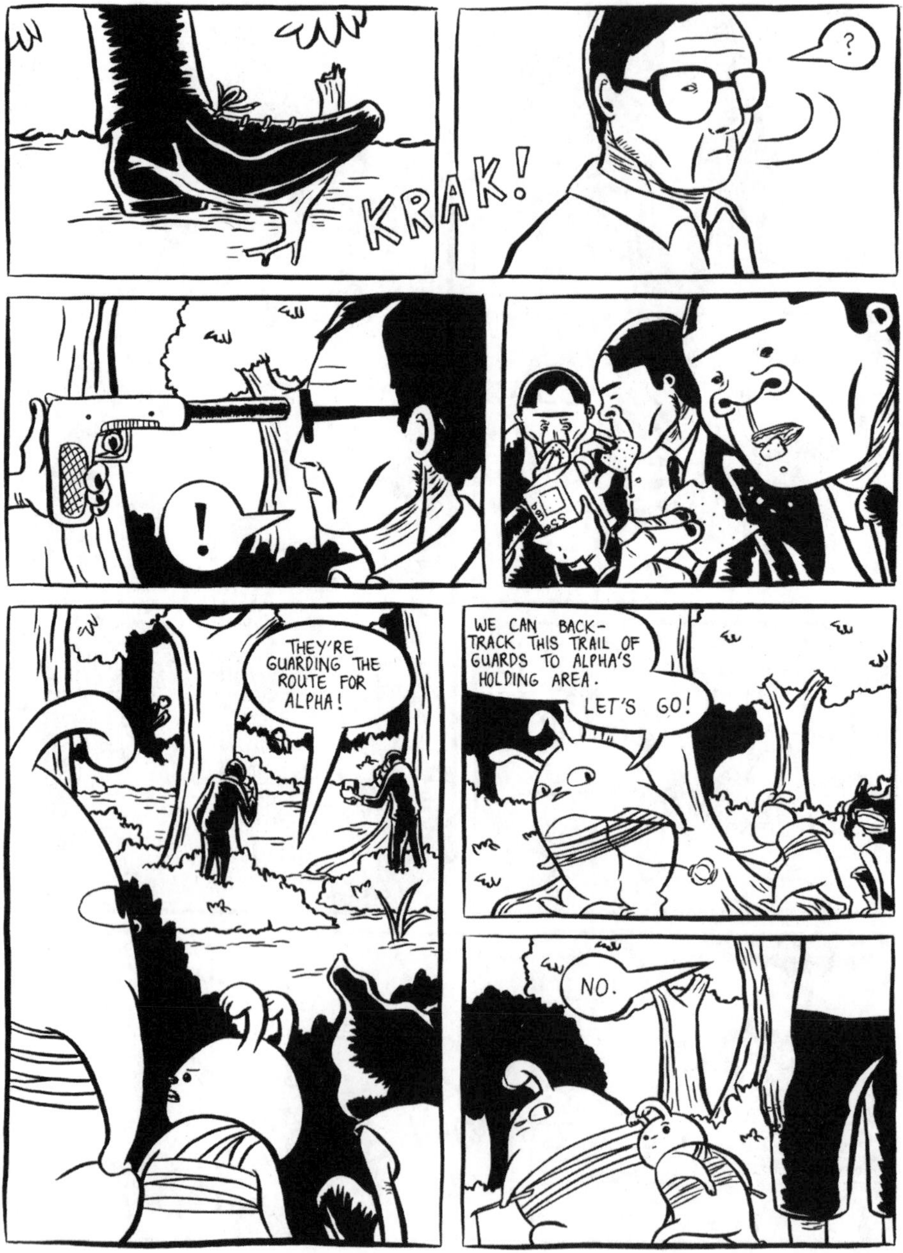
KRAK!
?
!
THEY'RE GUARDING THE ROUTE FOR ALPHA!
WE CAN BACK-TRACK THIS TRAIL OF GUARDS TO ALPHA'S HOLDING AREA.
LET'S GO!
NO.

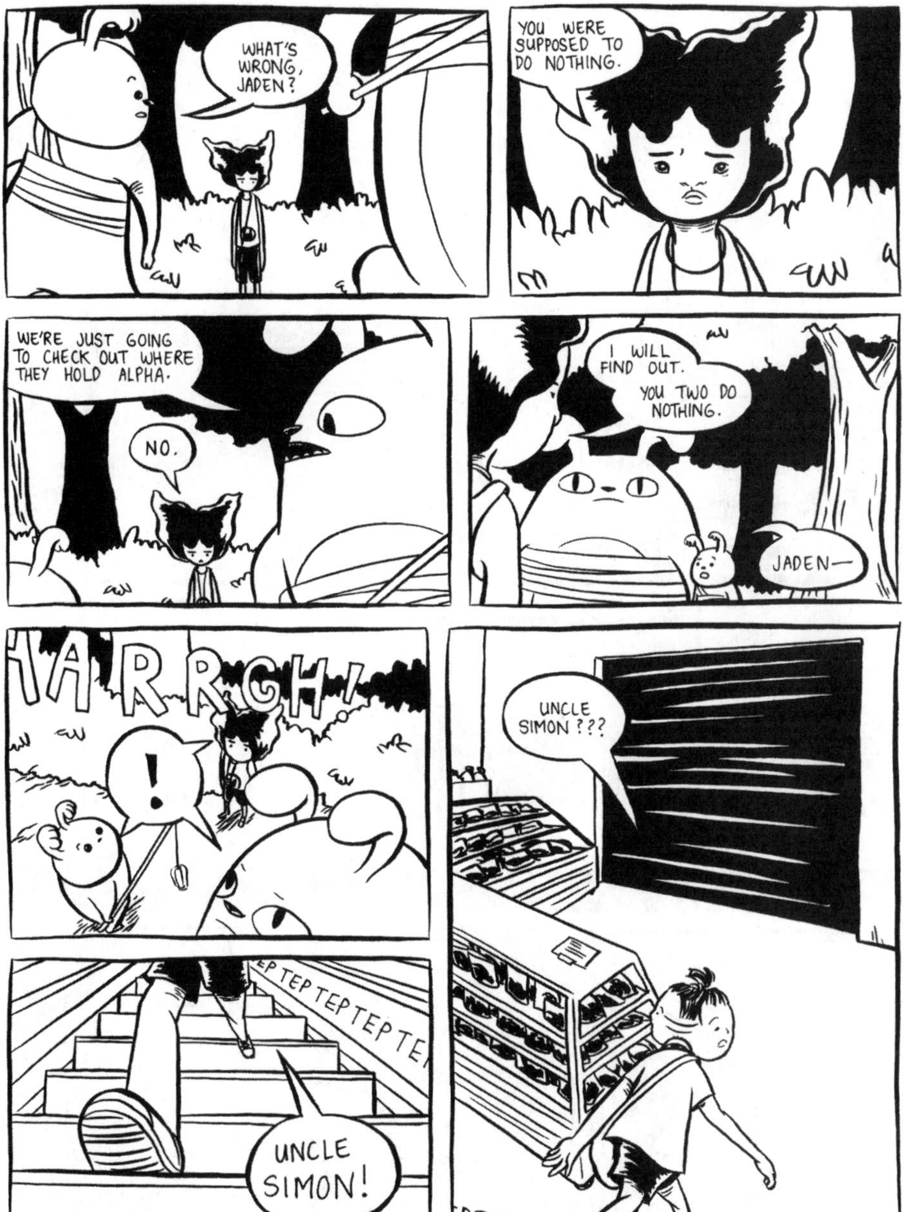
WHAT'S WRONG, JADEN?
YOU WERE SUPPOSED TO DO NOTHING.
WE'RE JUST GOING TO CHECK OUT WHERE THEY HOLD ALPHA.
NO.
I WILL FIND OUT.
YOU TWO DO NOTHING.
JADEN—
HARRGH!
!
UNCLE SIMON???
TEP TEP TEP TEP TE
UNCLE SIMON!
TEP TEP TEP

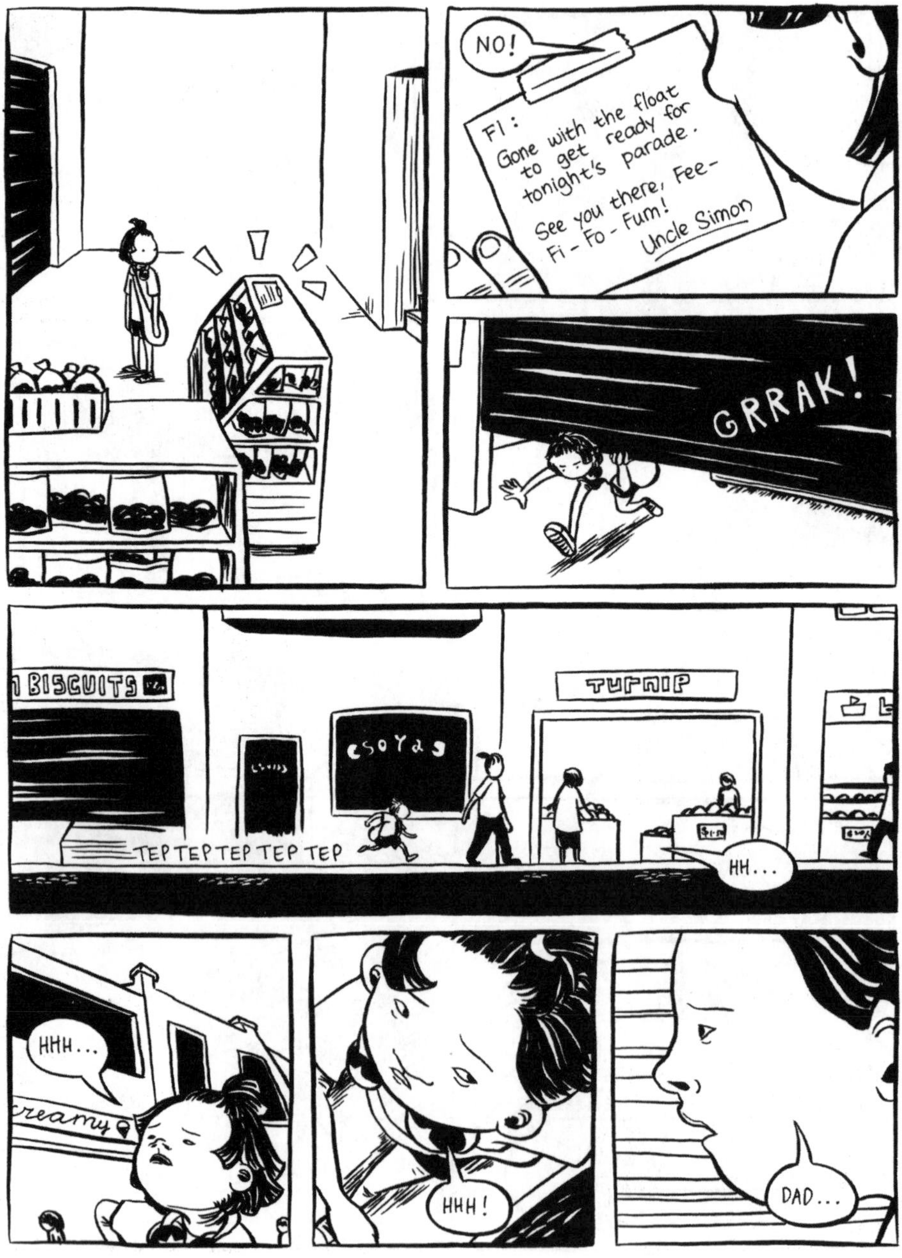
NO!
FI :
Gone with the float
to get ready for
tonight's parade.
See you there, Fee-
Fi - Fo - Fum!
Uncle Simon
GRRAK!
BISCUITS
TURNIP
TEP TEP TEP TEP TEP
HH...
HHH...
creamy
HHH!
DAD...

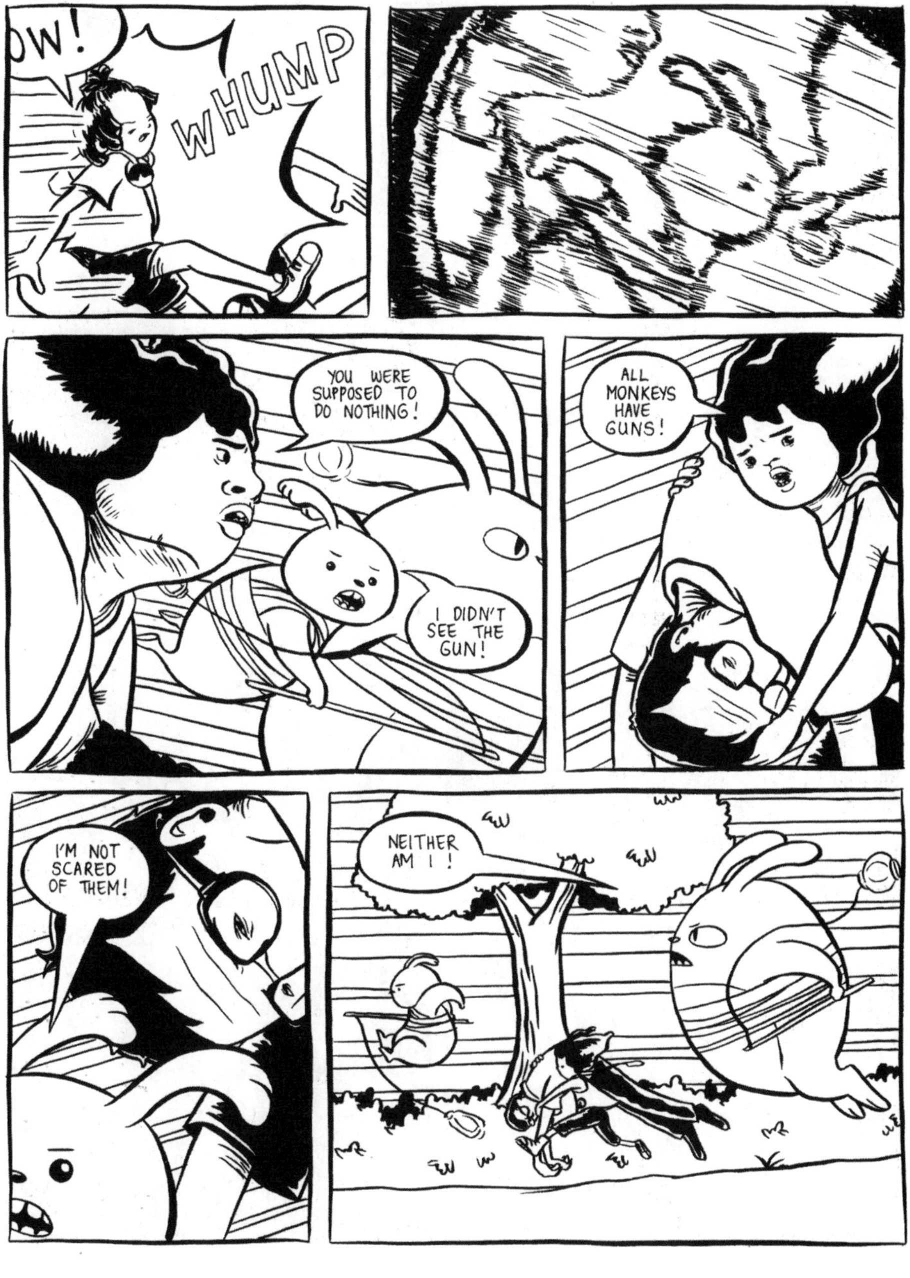
OW!
WHUMP
YOU WERE SUPPOSED TO DO NOTHING!
I DIDN'T SEE THE GUN!
ALL MONKEYS HAVE GUNS!
I'M NOT SCARED OF THEM!
NEITHER AM I!

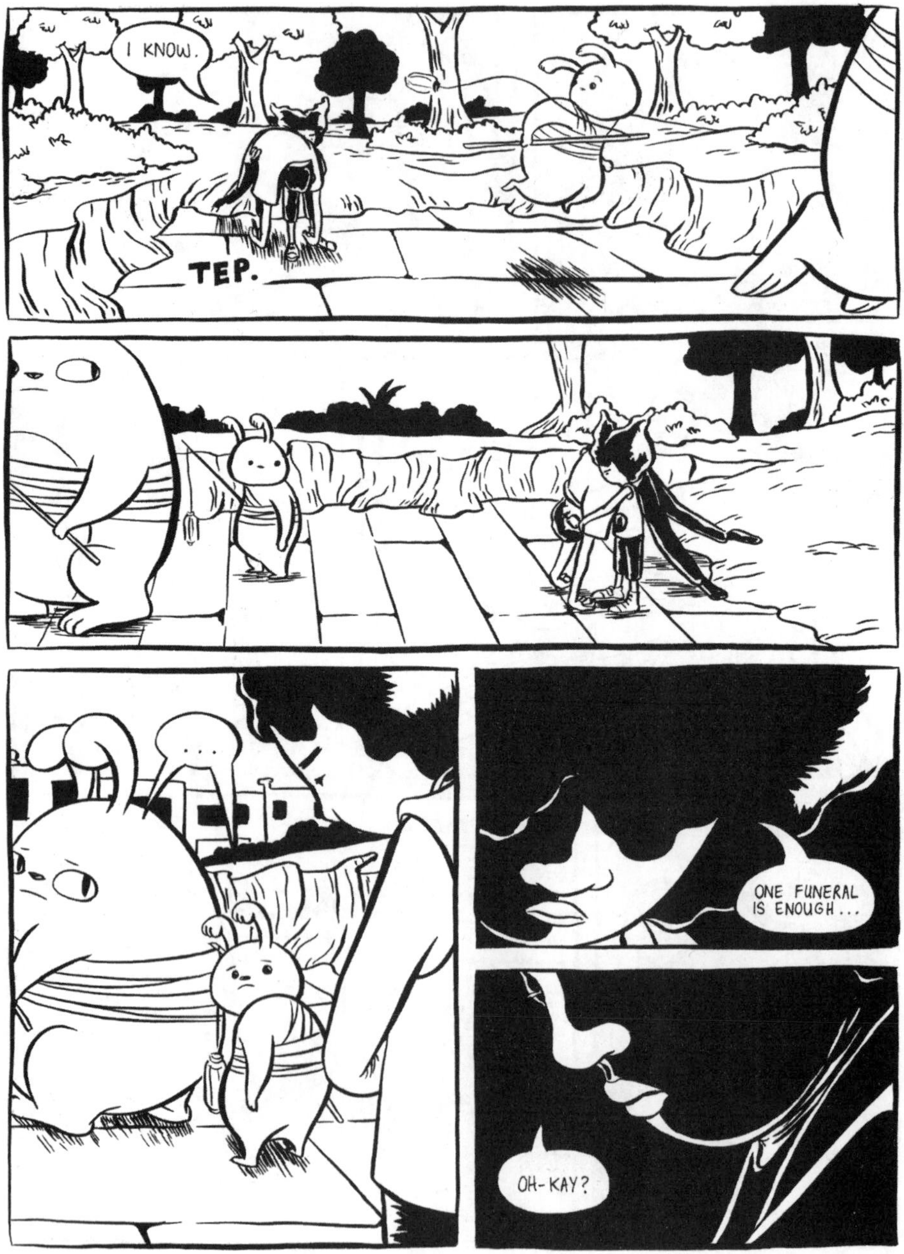
I KNOW.
TEP.
...
ONE FUNERAL IS ENOUGH...
OH-KAY?

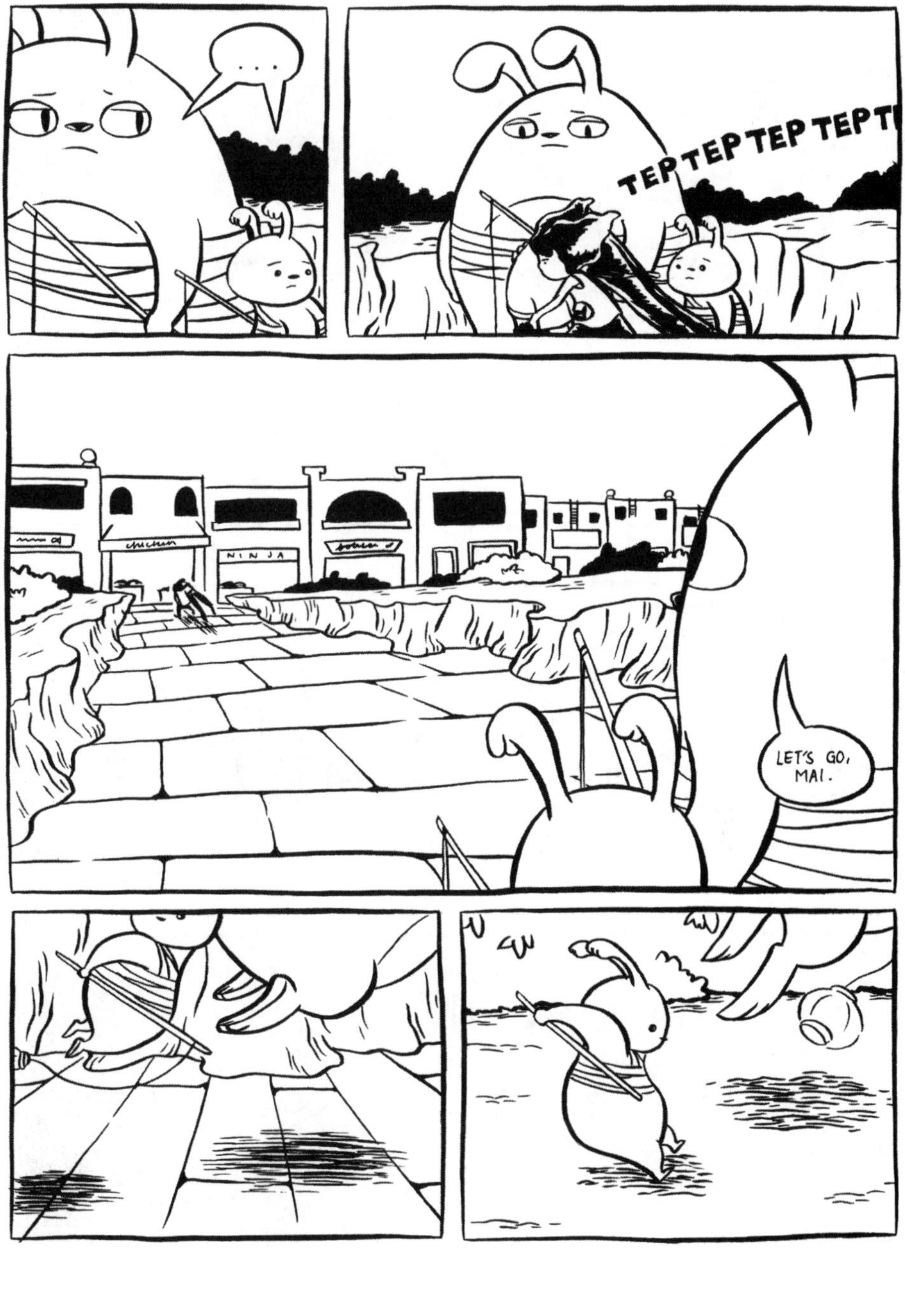
. . .
TEP TEP TEP TEP TEP
NINJA
LET'S GO, MAI.

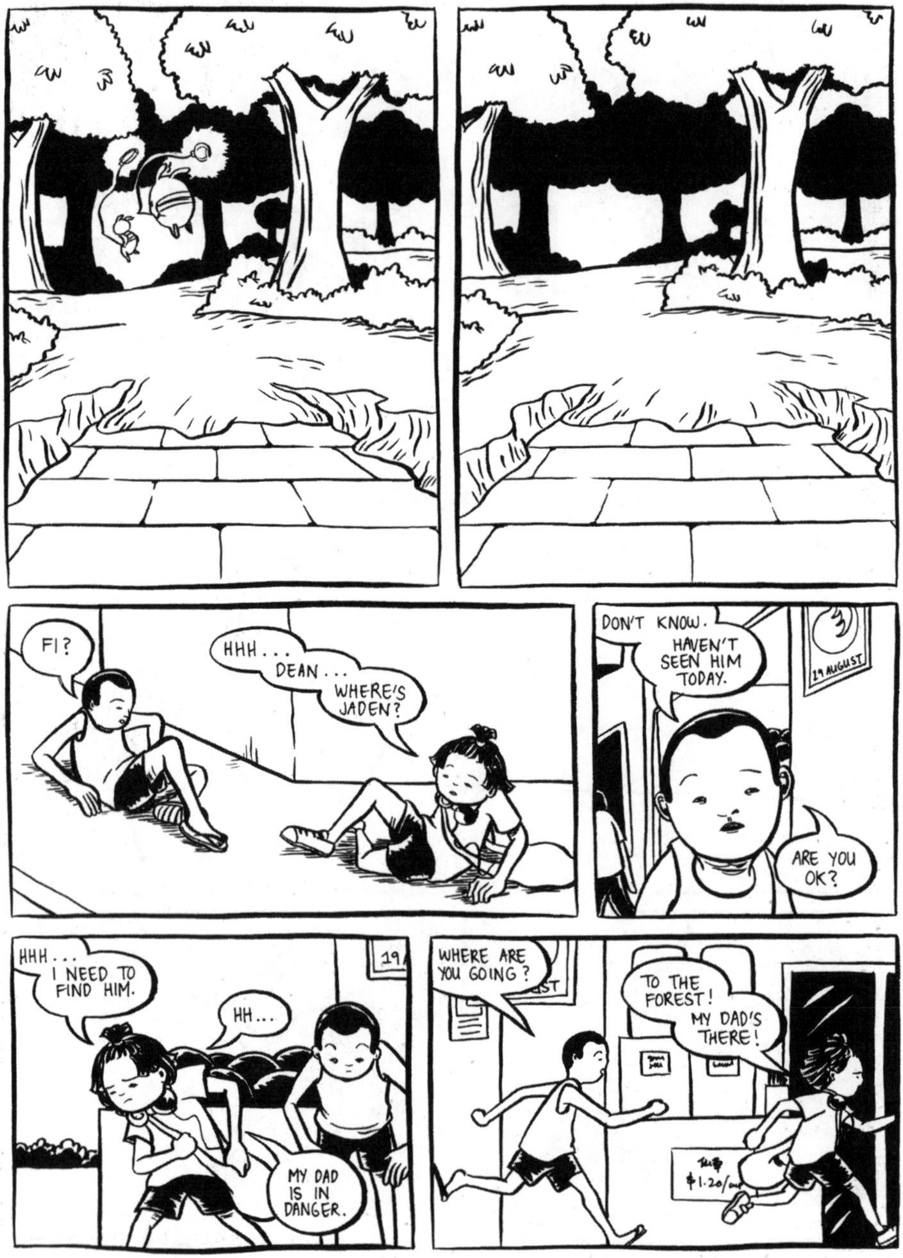
FI?
HHH . . . DEAN . . . WHERE'S JADEN?
DON'T KNOW. HAVEN'T SEEN HIM TODAY.
29 AUGUST
ARE YOU OK?
HHH . . . I NEED TO FIND HIM.
HH . . .
MY DAD IS IN DANGER.
WHERE ARE YOU GOING?
TO THE FOREST! MY DAD'S THERE!

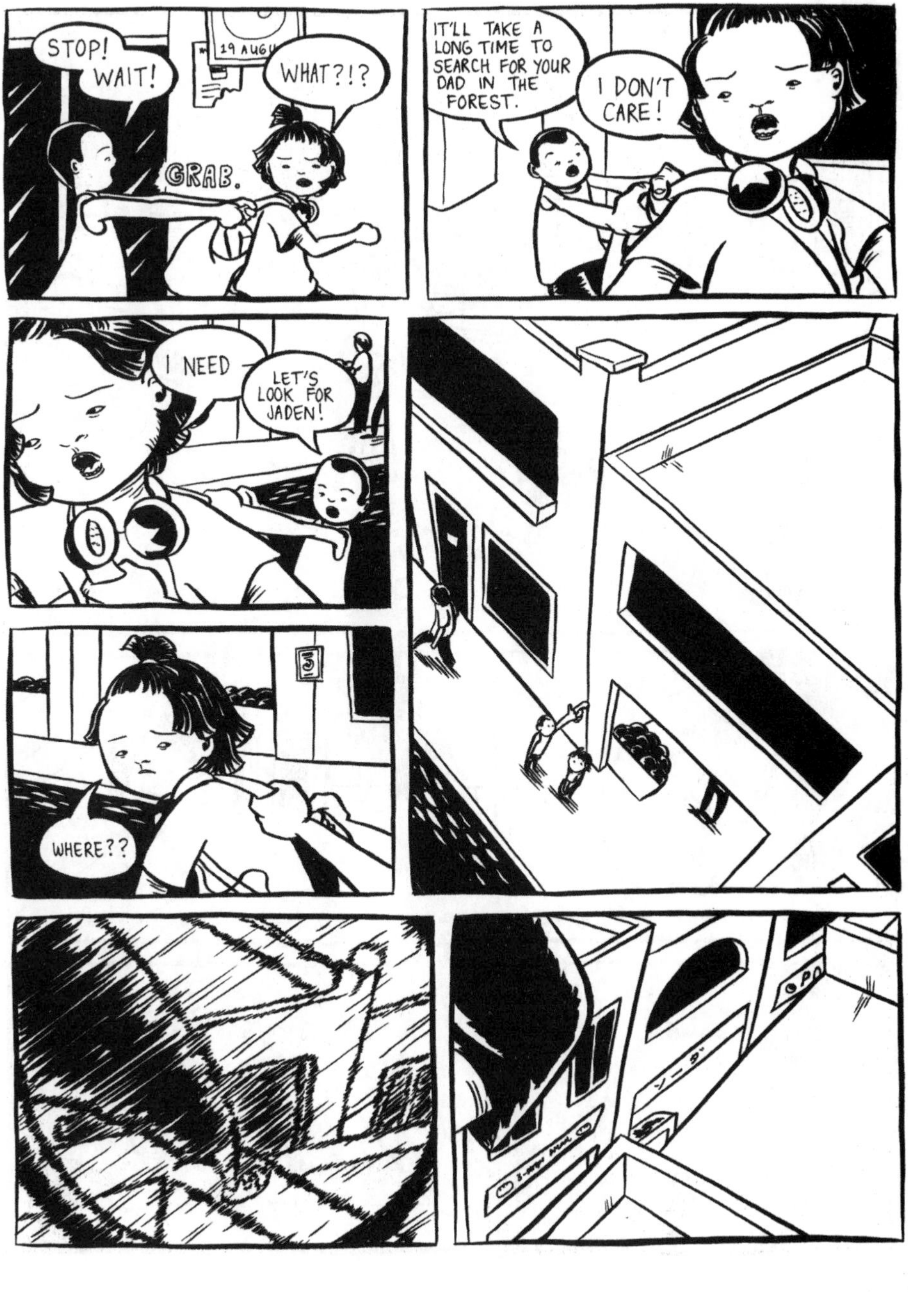
STOP!
WAIT!
19 AUG
WHAT?!?
GRAB.
IT'LL TAKE A LONG TIME TO SEARCH FOR YOUR DAD IN THE FOREST.
I DON'T CARE!
I NEED
LET'S LOOK FOR JADEN!
WHERE??

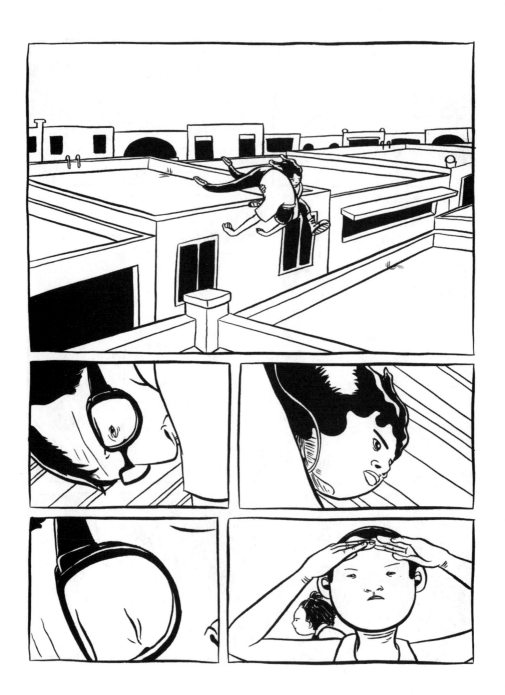

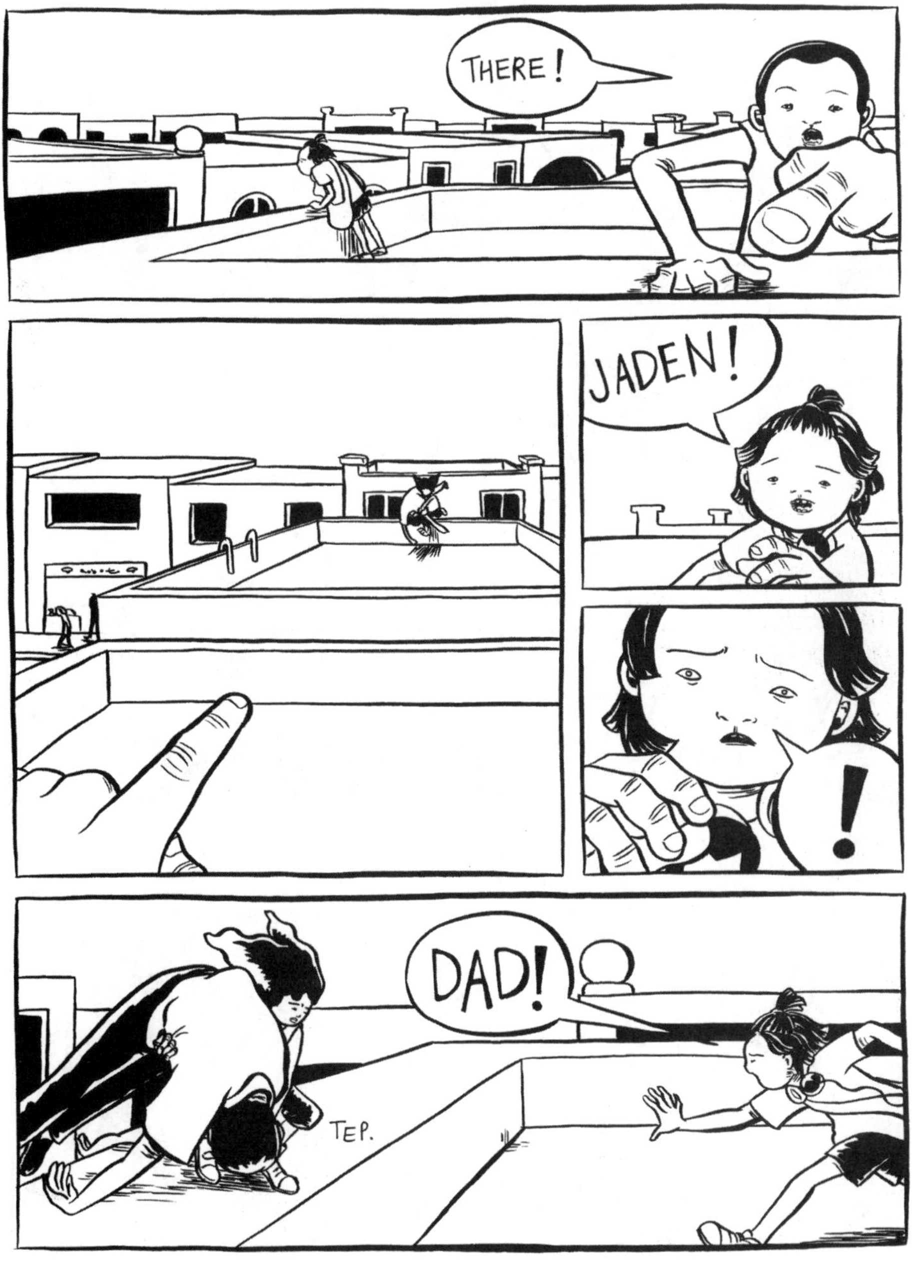
THERE!
JADEN!
!
DAD!
TEP.

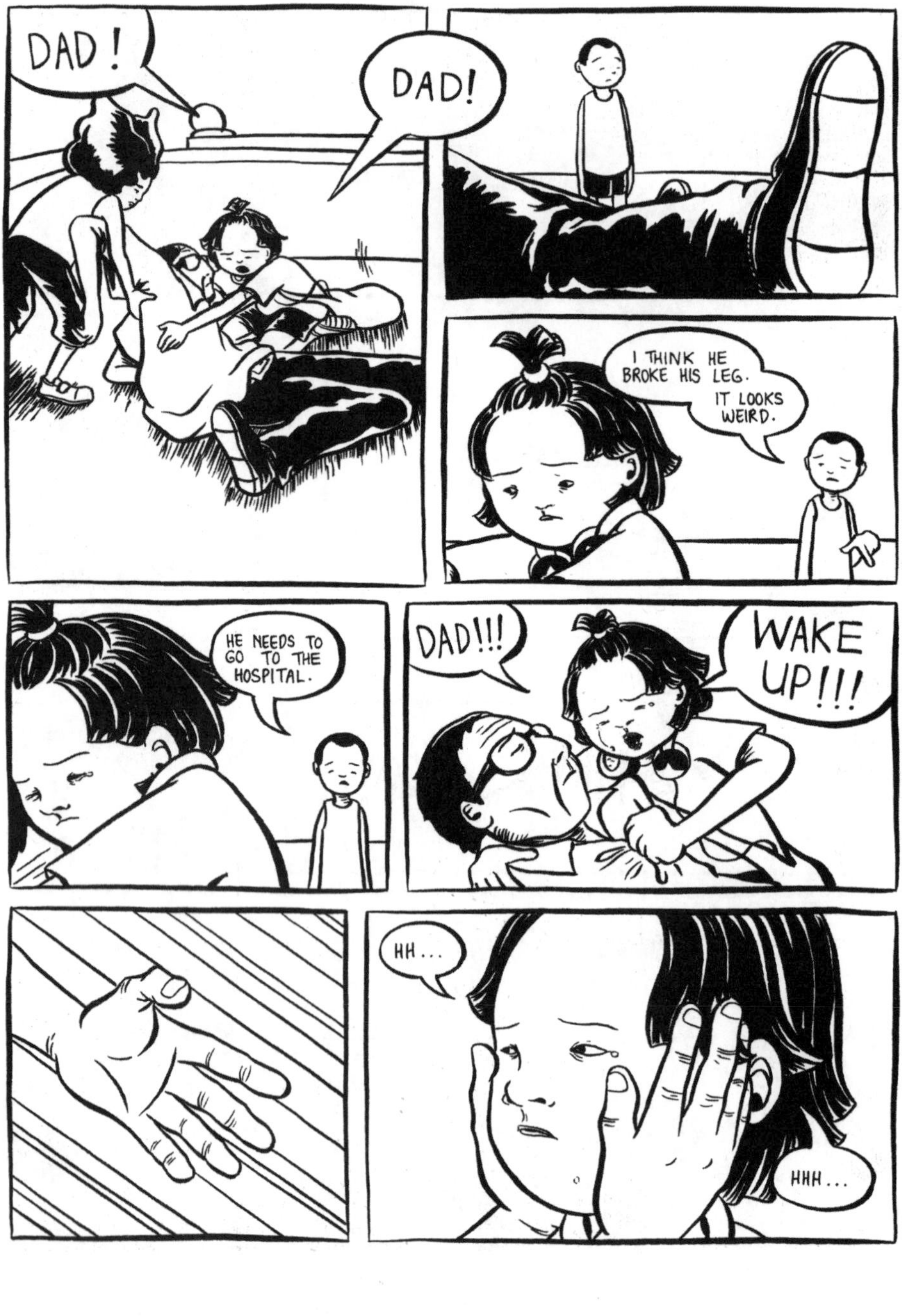
DAD!
DAD!
I THINK HE BROKE HIS LEG.
IT LOOKS WEIRD.
HE NEEDS TO GO TO THE HOSPITAL.
DAD!!!
WAKE UP!!!
HH...
HHH...

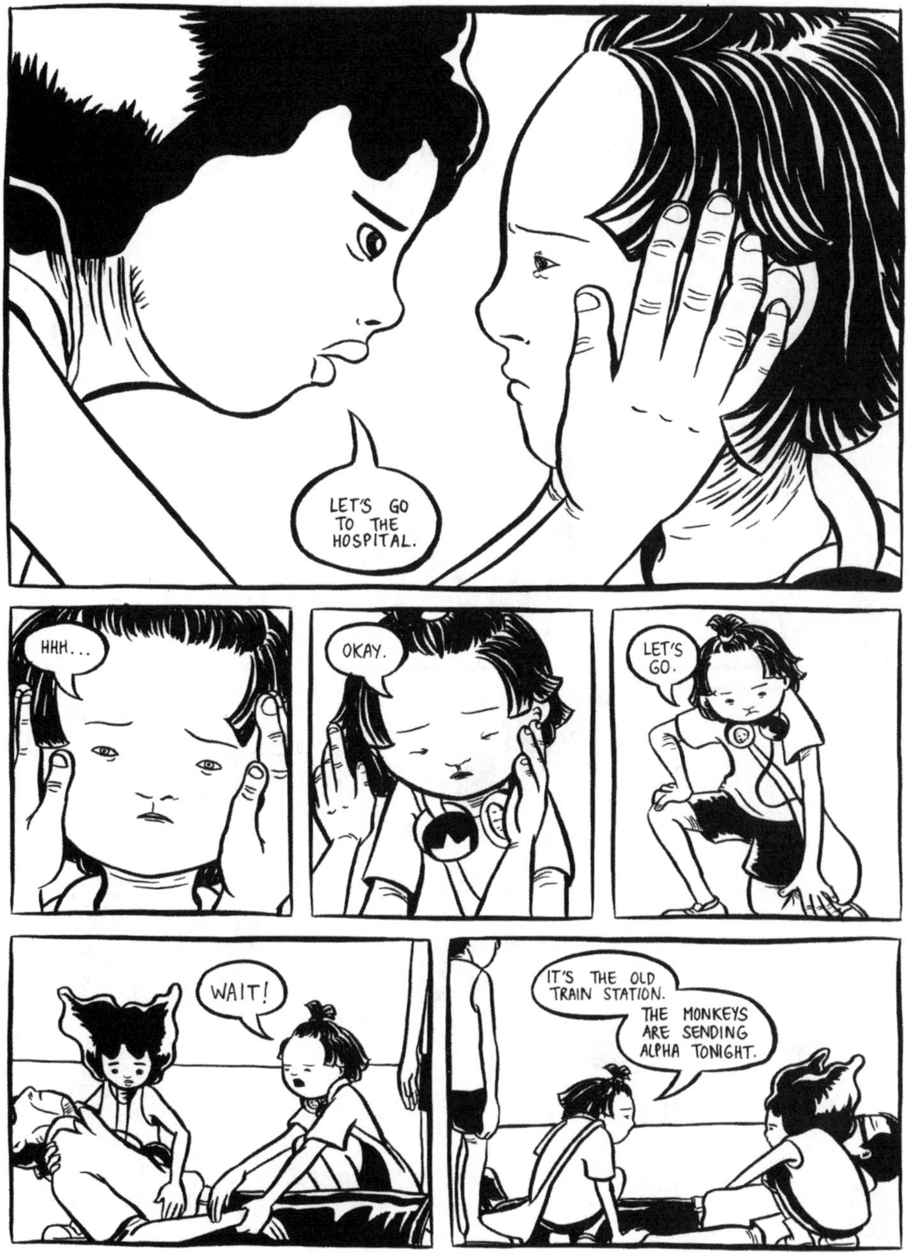
LET'S GO TO THE HOSPITAL.
HHH...
OKAY.
LET'S GO.
WAIT!
IT'S THE OLD TRAIN STATION.
THE MONKEYS ARE SENDING ALPHA TONIGHT.

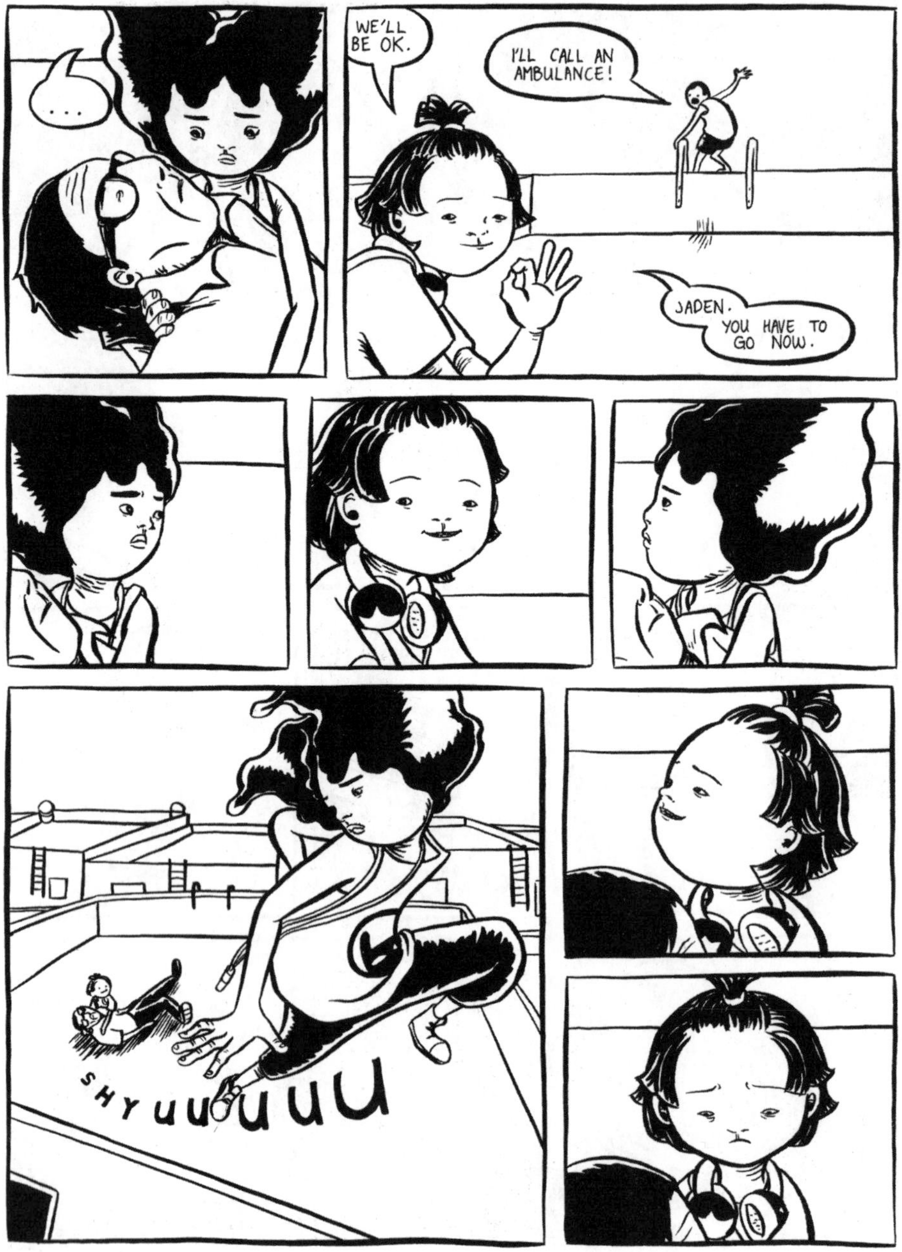
. . .
WE'LL BE OK.
I'LL CALL AN AMBULANCE!
JADEN. YOU HAVE TO GO NOW.
SHYUUUUUU

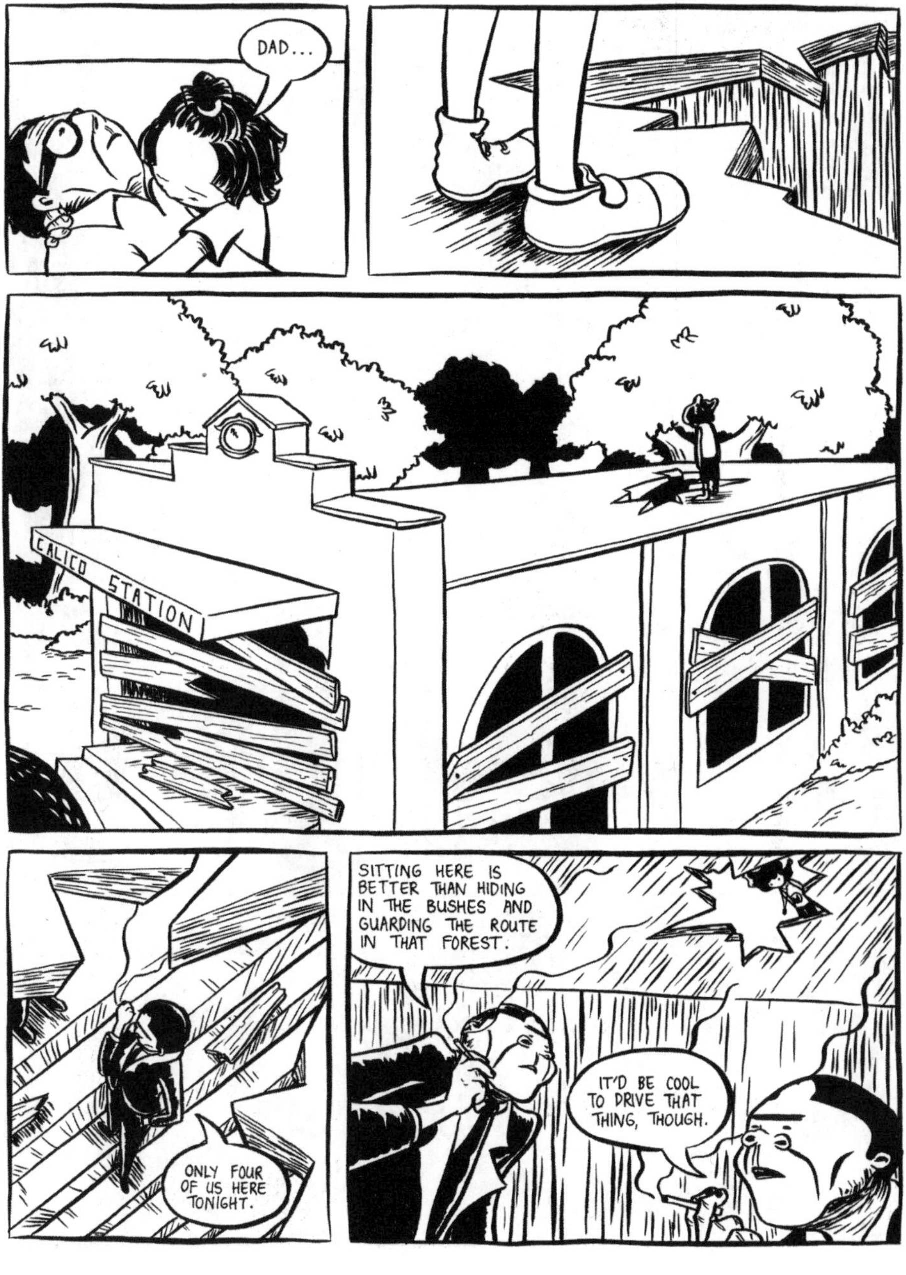
DAD...
CALICO STATION
ONLY FOUR OF US HERE TONIGHT.
SITTING HERE IS BETTER THAN HIDING IN THE BUSHES AND GUARDING THE ROUTE IN THAT FOREST.
IT'D BE COOL TO DRIVE THAT THING, THOUGH.

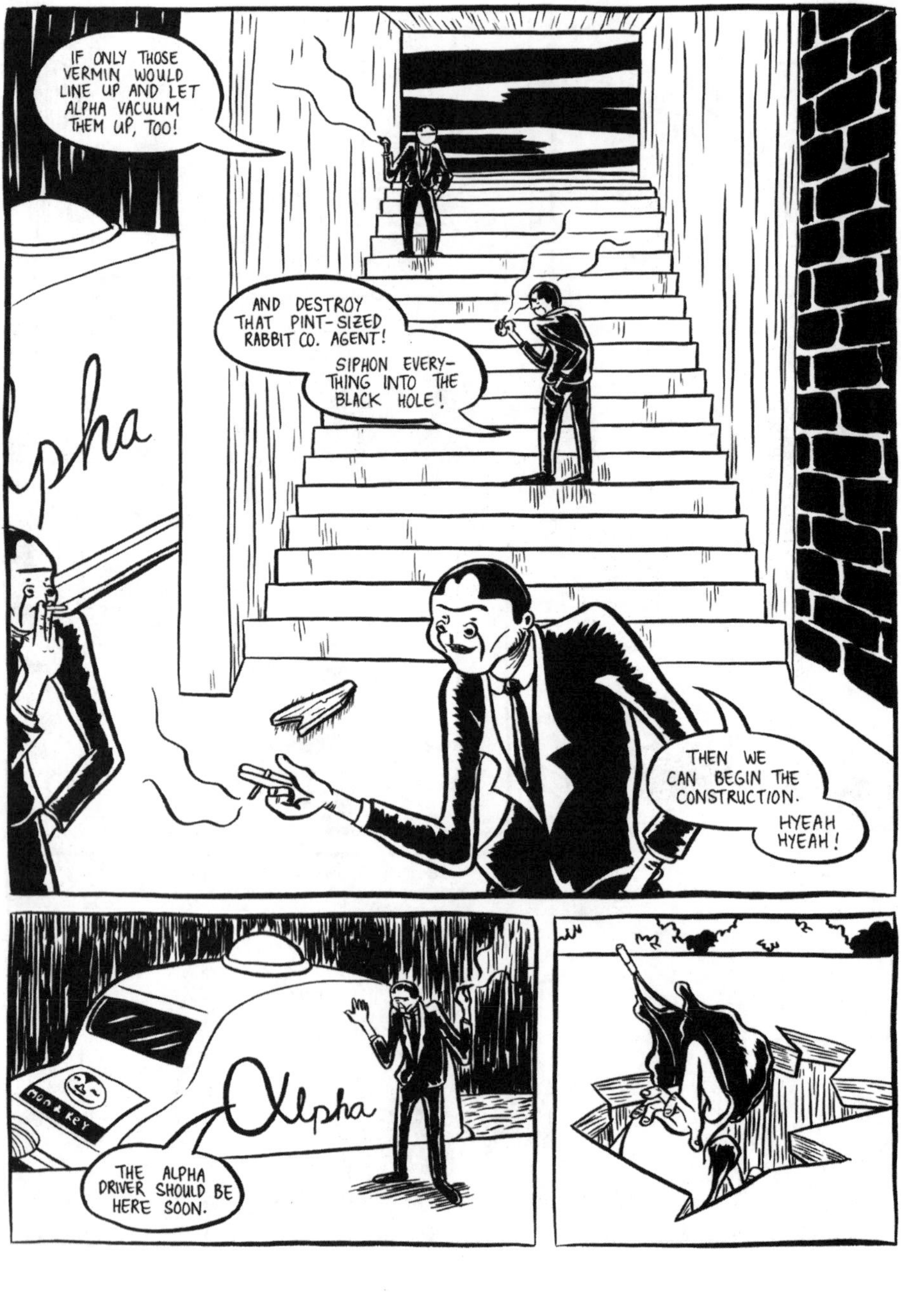
IF ONLY THOSE VERMIN WOULD LINE UP AND LET ALPHA VACUUM THEM UP, TOO!
AND DESTROY THAT PINT-SIZED RABBIT CO. AGENT!
SIPHON EVERY-THING INTO THE BLACK HOLE!
Alpha
THEN WE CAN BEGIN THE CONSTRUCTION.
HYEAH HYEAH!
Alpha
THE ALPHA DRIVER SHOULD BE HERE SOON.

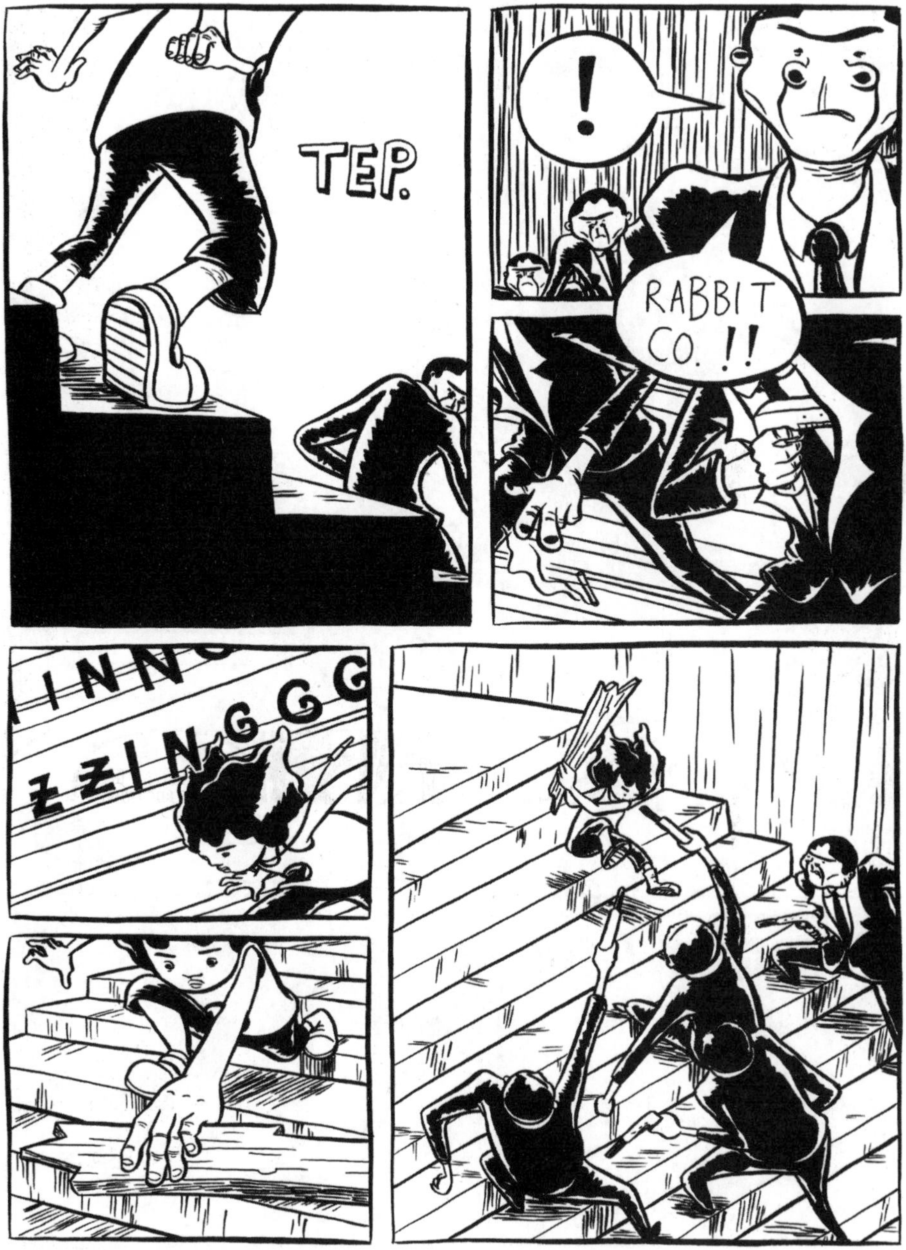
TEP.
!
RABBIT CO. !!
INNG
ZZINGGG

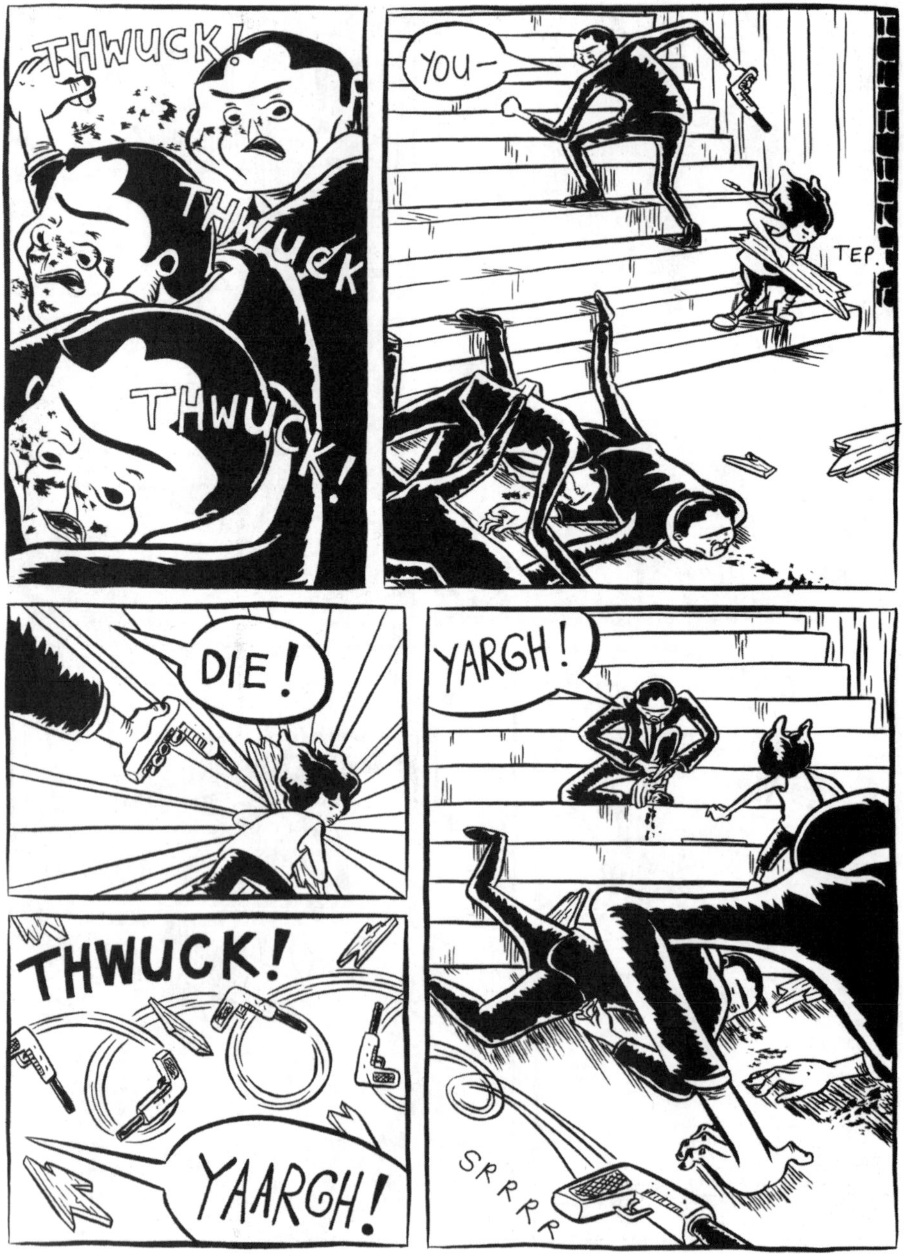
THWUCK!
THWUCK
THWUCK!
YOU-
TEP.
DIE!
THWUCK!
YAARGH!
YARGH!
SRRRR

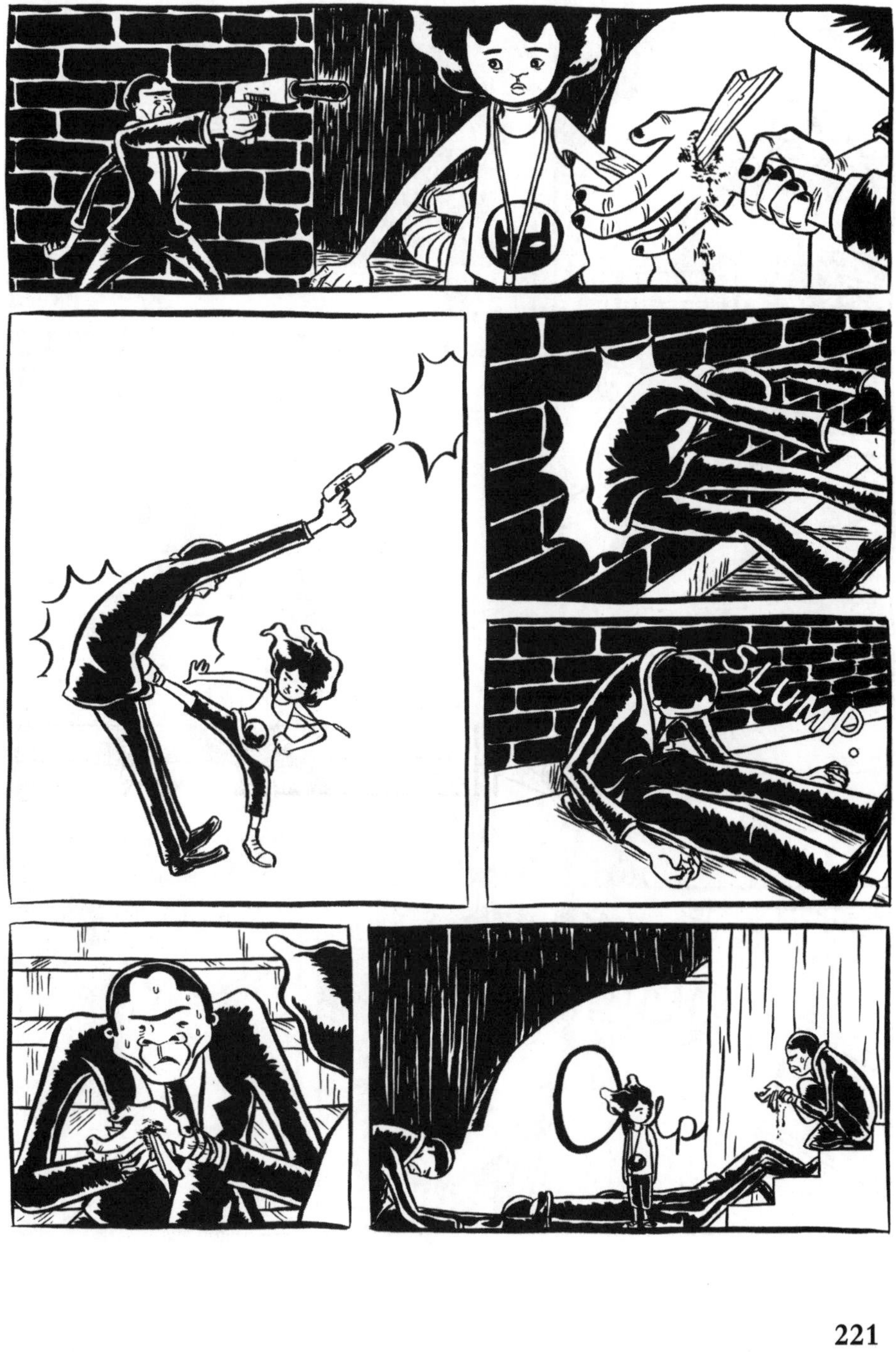
SLUMP.

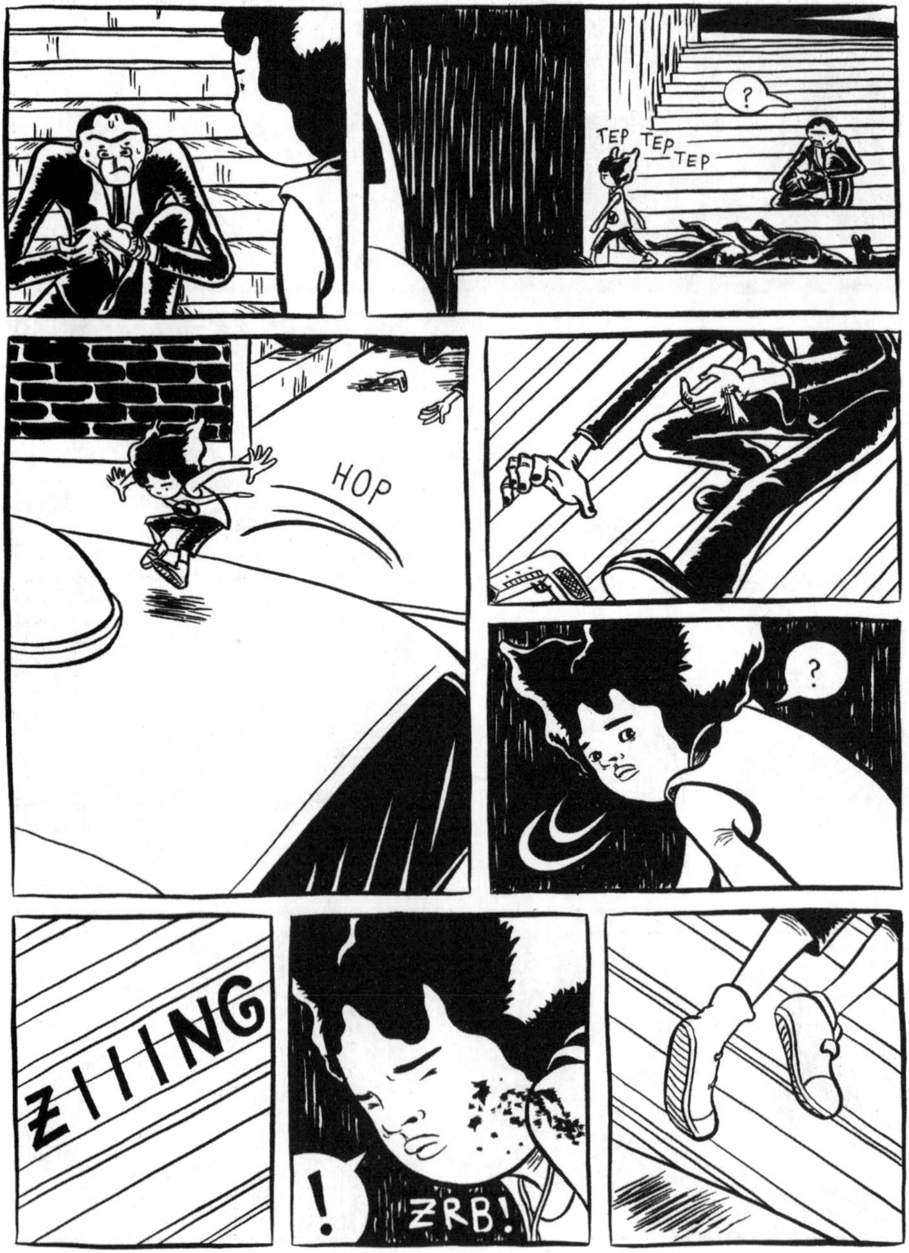
?
TEP TEP TEP
HOP
?
ZIIING
!
ZRB!

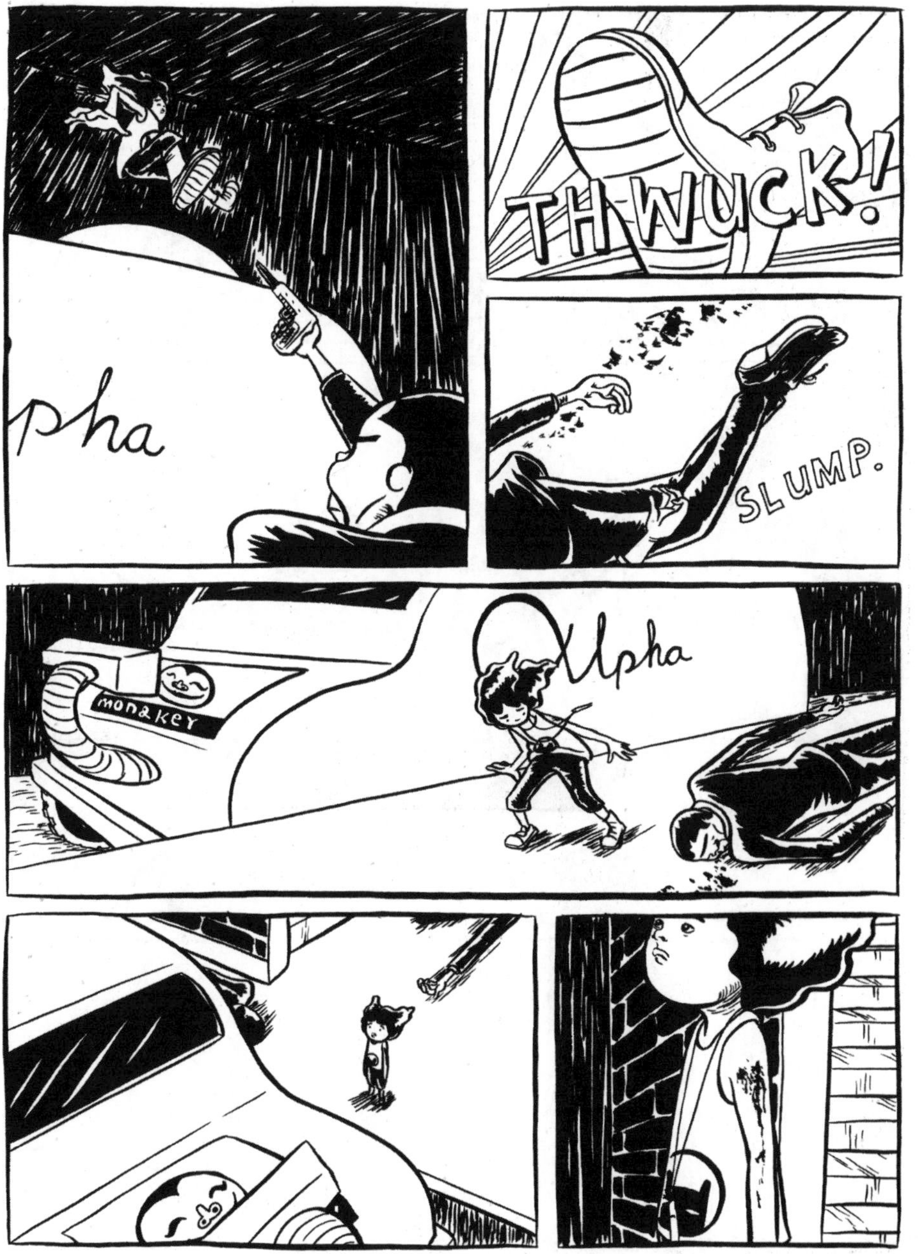
pha
THWUCK!
SLUMP.
Upha
mon&key

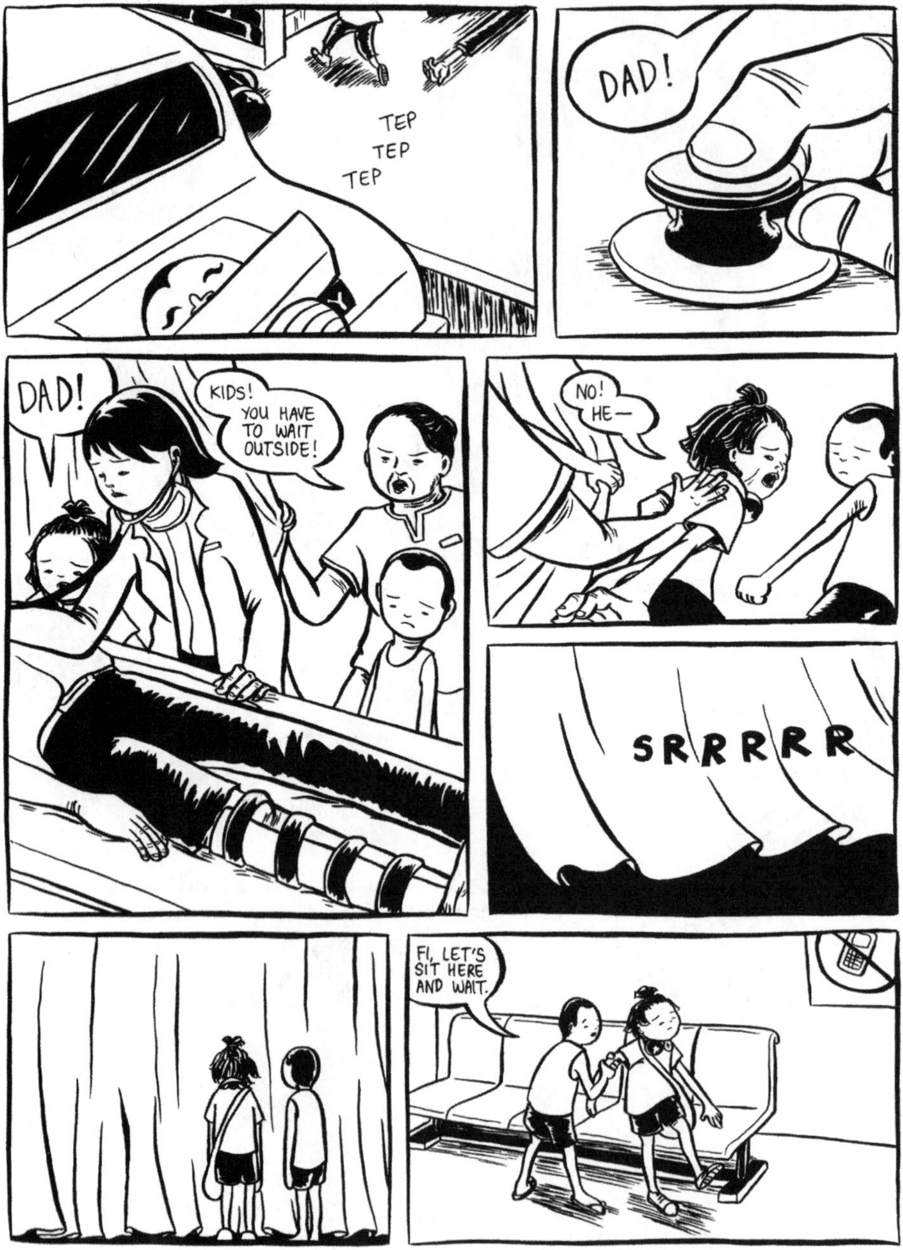
TEP
TEP
TEP
DAD!
DAD!
KIDS! YOU HAVE TO WAIT OUTSIDE!
NO! HE—
SRRRRR
FI, LET'S SIT HERE AND WAIT.

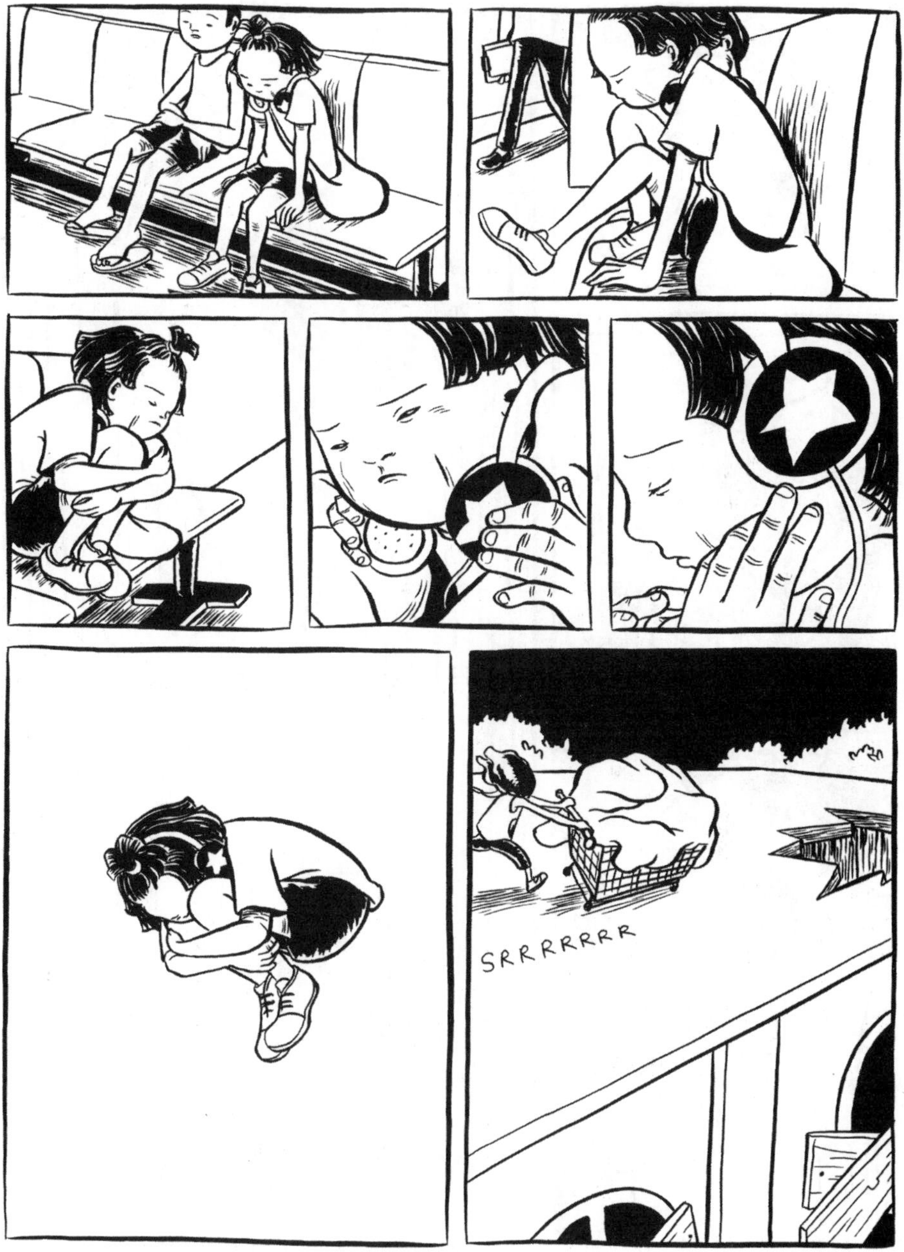
SRRRRRRR

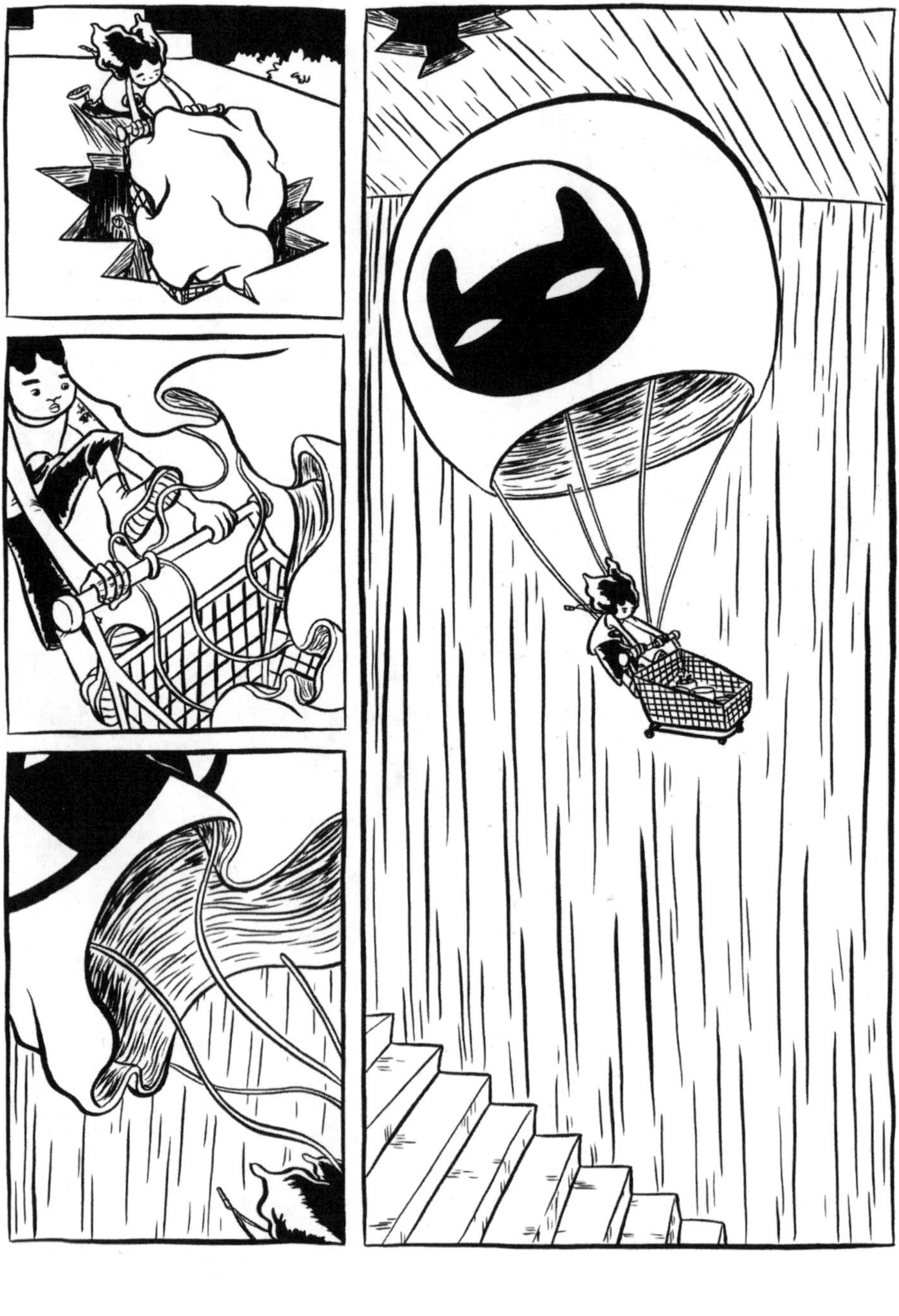

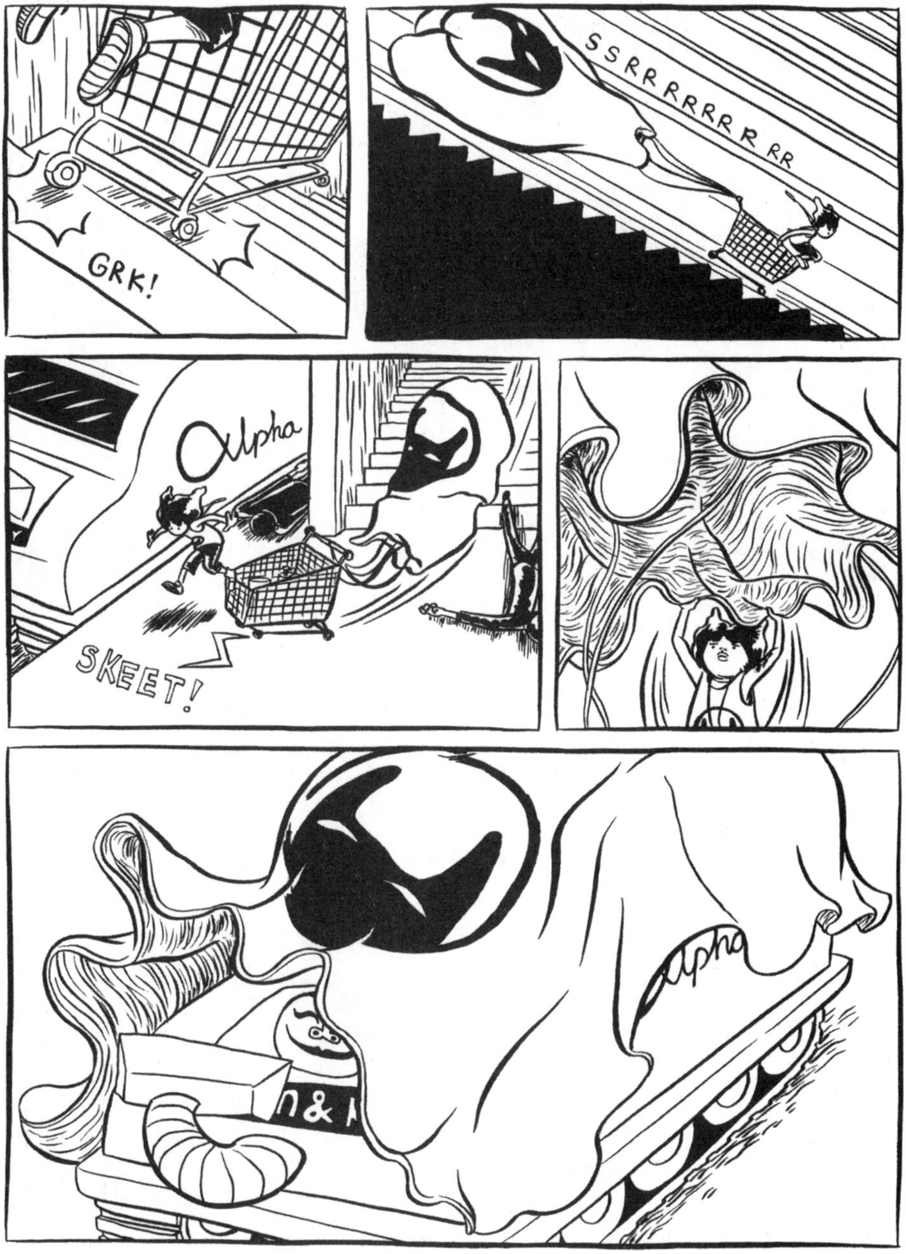
GRK!
SSRRRRRRRRRRR
Alpha
SKEET!
Alpha
n&

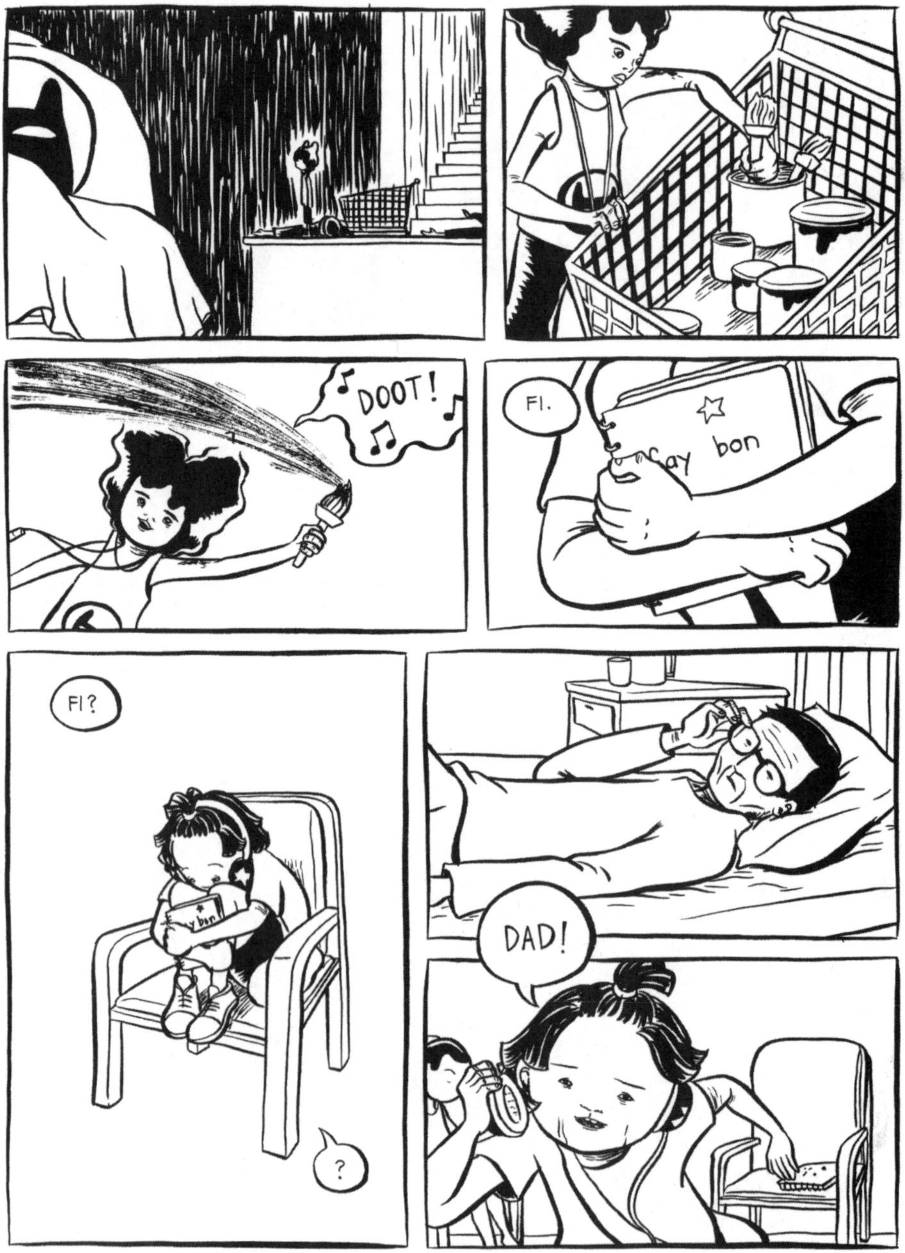
DOOT!
FI.
Cay bon
FI?
?
DAD!

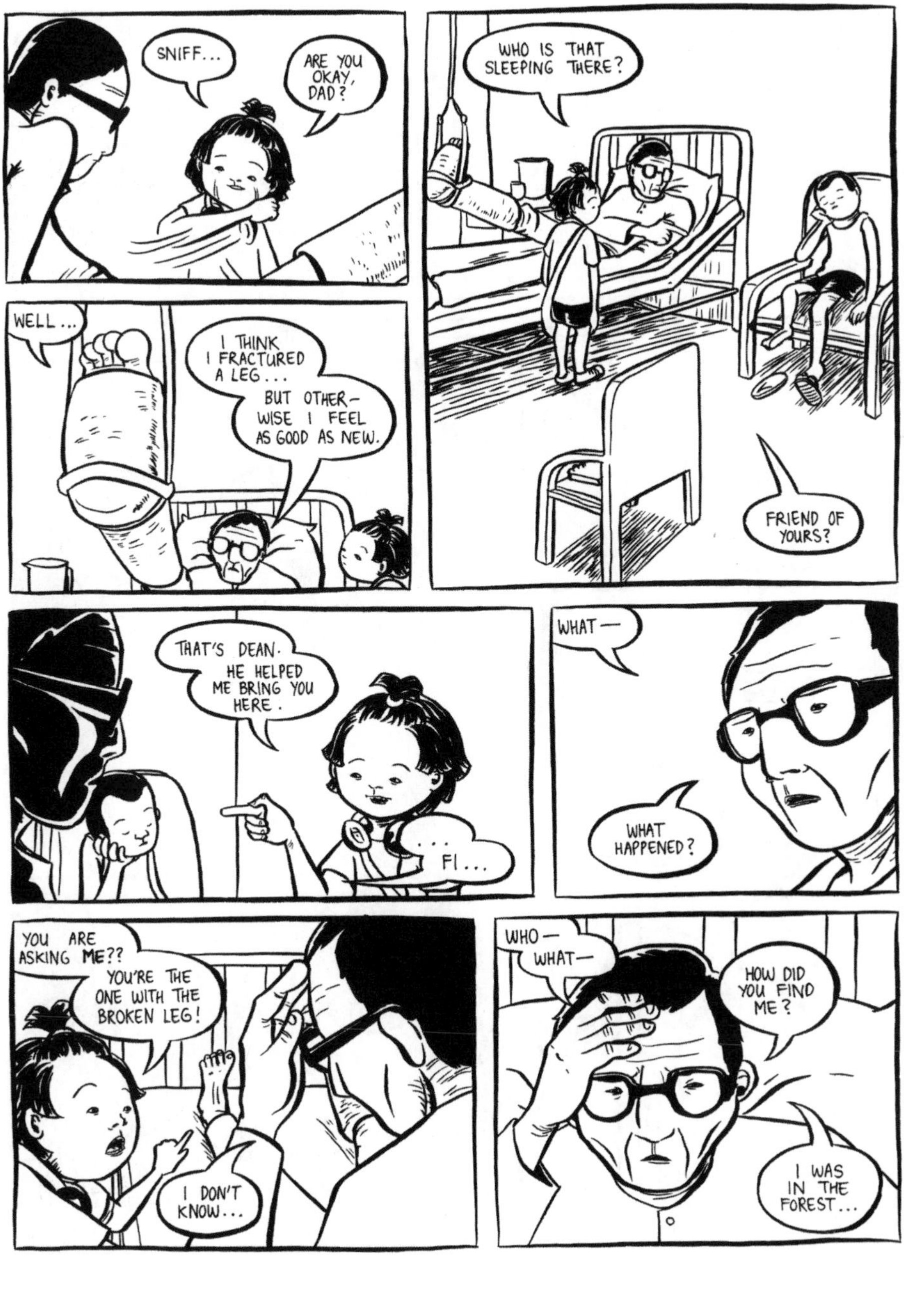
SNIFF...
ARE YOU OKAY, DAD?
WHO IS THAT SLEEPING THERE?
WELL...
I THINK I FRACTURED A LEG...
BUT OTHER-WISE I FEEL AS GOOD AS NEW.
FRIEND OF YOURS?
THAT'S DEAN.
HE HELPED ME BRING YOU HERE.
... FI...
WHAT—
WHAT HAPPENED?
YOU ARE ASKING **ME**??
YOU'RE THE ONE WITH THE BROKEN LEG!
I DON'T KNOW...
WHO—
WHAT—
HOW DID YOU FIND ME?
I WAS IN THE FOREST...

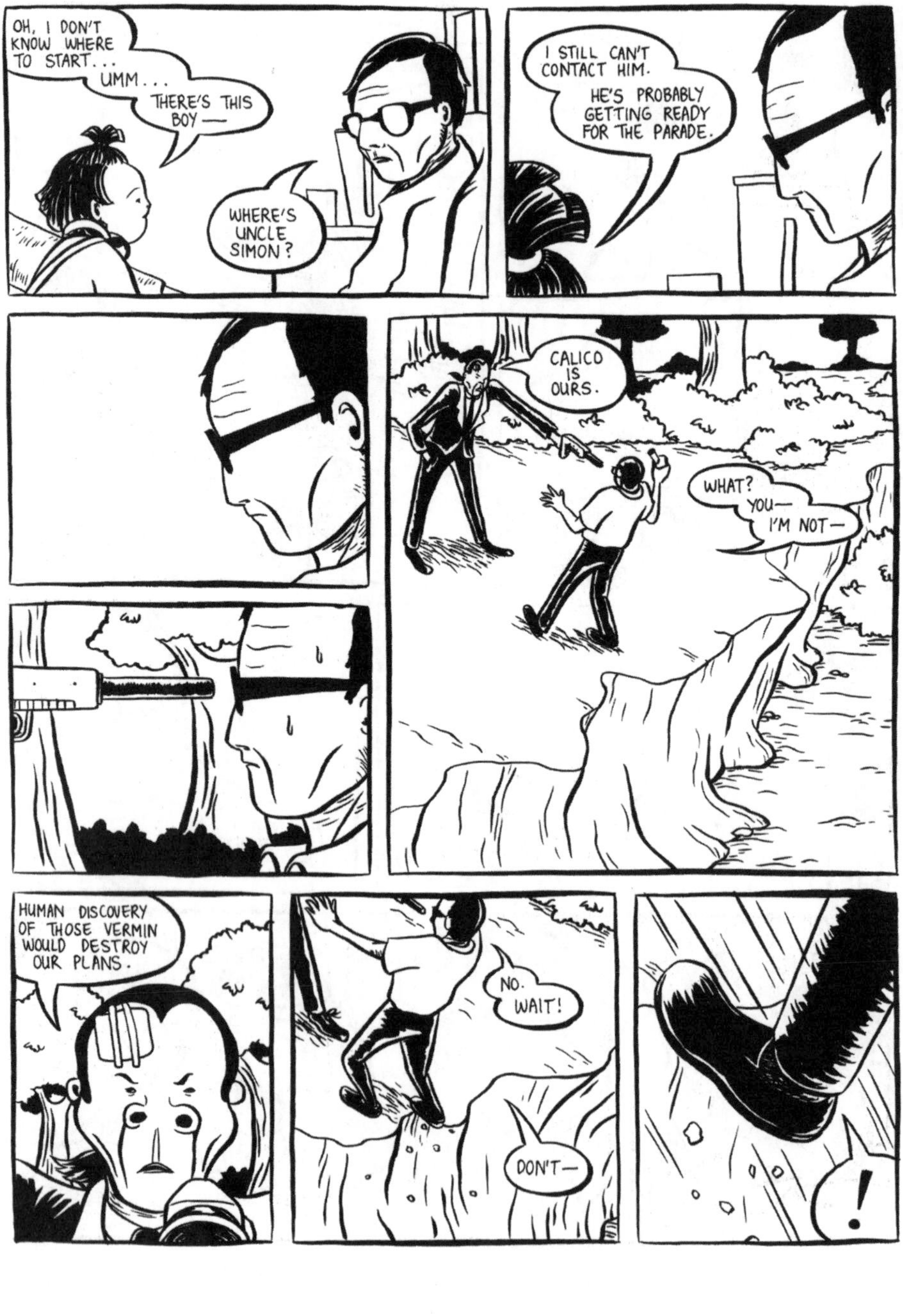
OH, I DON'T KNOW WHERE TO START...
UMM...
THERE'S THIS BOY—
WHERE'S UNCLE SIMON?
I STILL CAN'T CONTACT HIM.
HE'S PROBABLY GETTING READY FOR THE PARADE.
CALICO IS OURS.
WHAT? YOU—
I'M NOT—
HUMAN DISCOVERY OF THOSE VERMIN WOULD DESTROY OUR PLANS.
NO. WAIT!
DON'T—
!

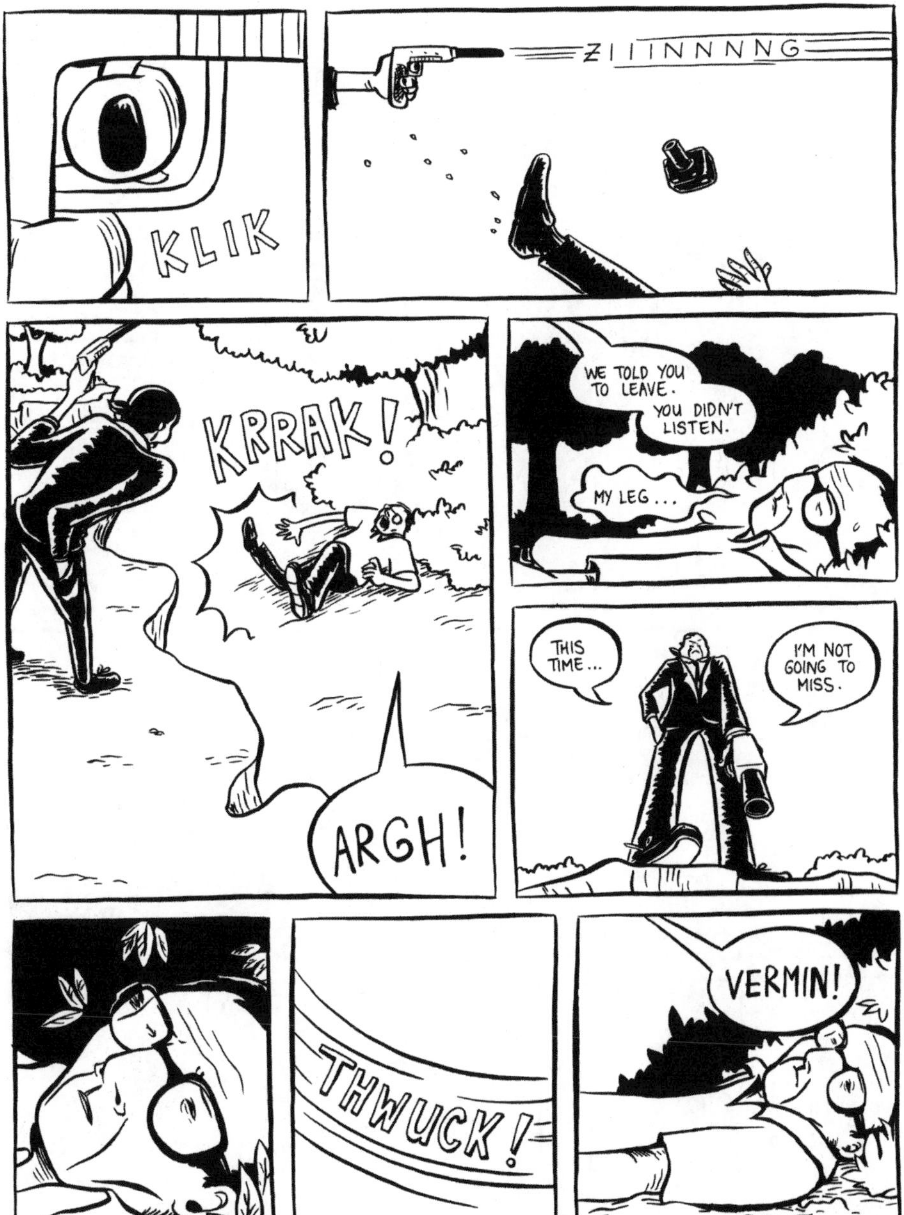
KLIK
ZIIINNNNG
KRRAK!
ARGH!
WE TOLD YOU TO LEAVE.
YOU DIDN'T LISTEN.
MY LEG...
THIS TIME...
I'M NOT GOING TO MISS.
THWUCK!
VERMIN!

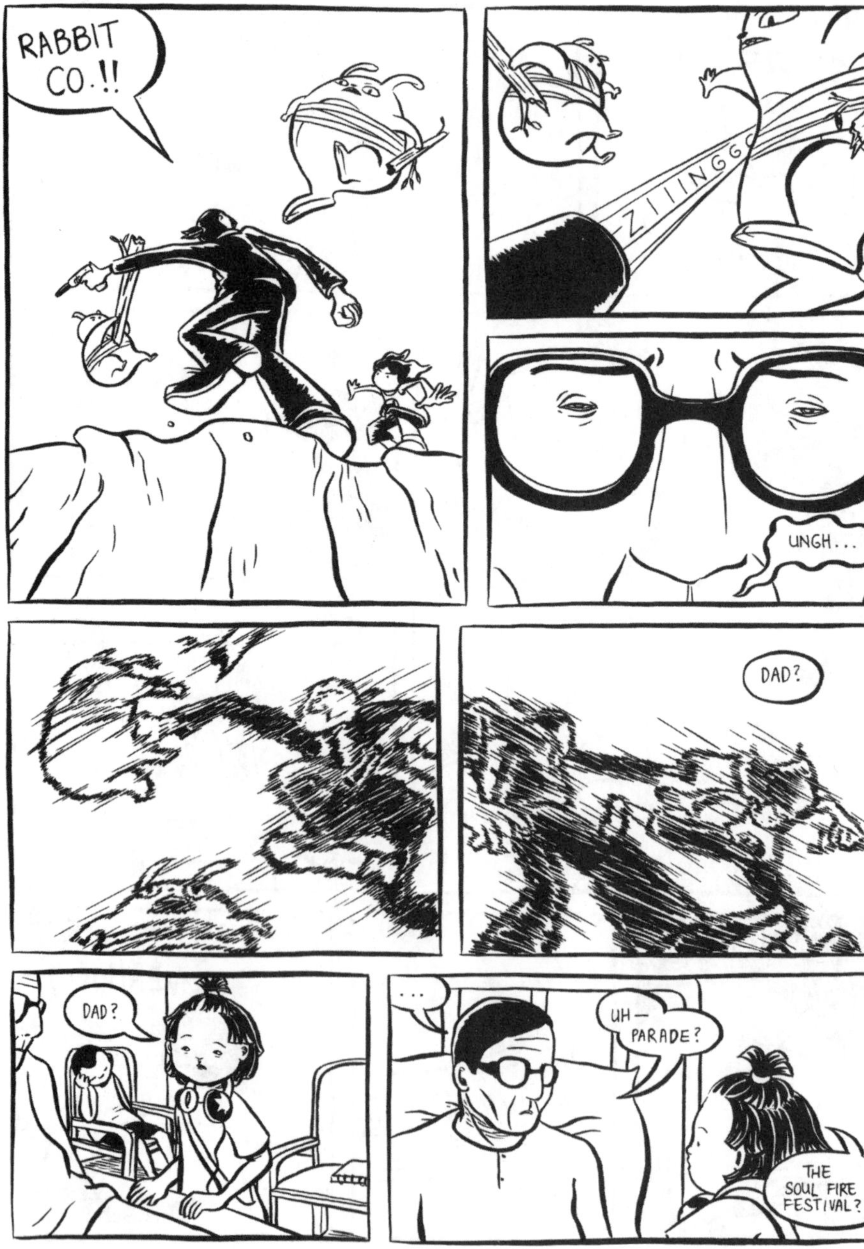
RABBIT CO.!!
ZIIINGG
UNGH...
DAD?
DAD?
...
UH— PARADE?
THE SOUL FIRE FESTIVAL?

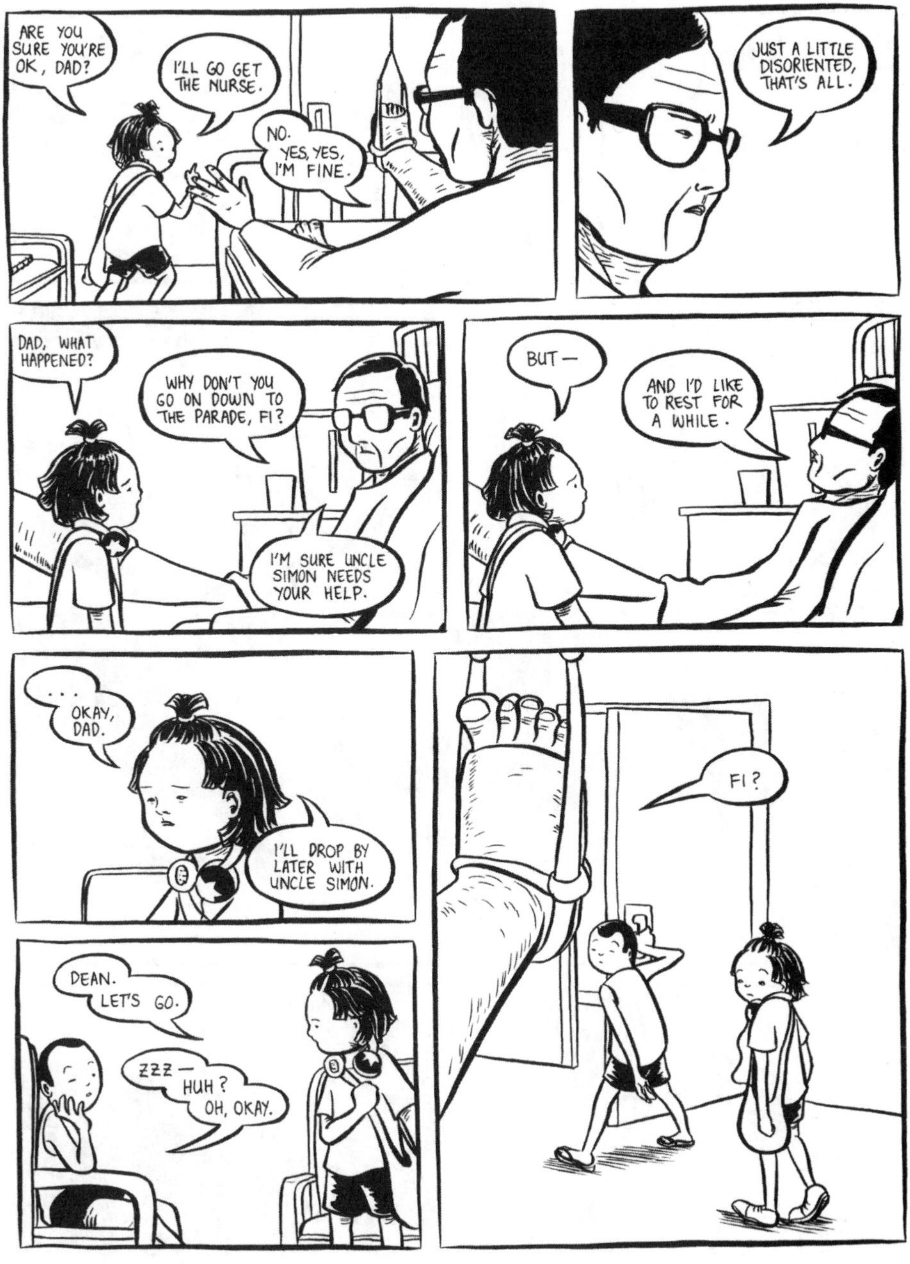
ARE YOU SURE YOU'RE OK, DAD?
I'LL GO GET THE NURSE.
NO. YES, YES, I'M FINE.
JUST A LITTLE DISORIENTED, THAT'S ALL.
DAD, WHAT HAPPENED?
WHY DON'T YOU GO ON DOWN TO THE PARADE, FI?
I'M SURE UNCLE SIMON NEEDS YOUR HELP.
BUT—
AND I'D LIKE TO REST FOR A WHILE.
... OKAY, DAD.
I'LL DROP BY LATER WITH UNCLE SIMON.
DEAN. LET'S GO.
ZZZ— HUH? OH, OKAY.
FI?

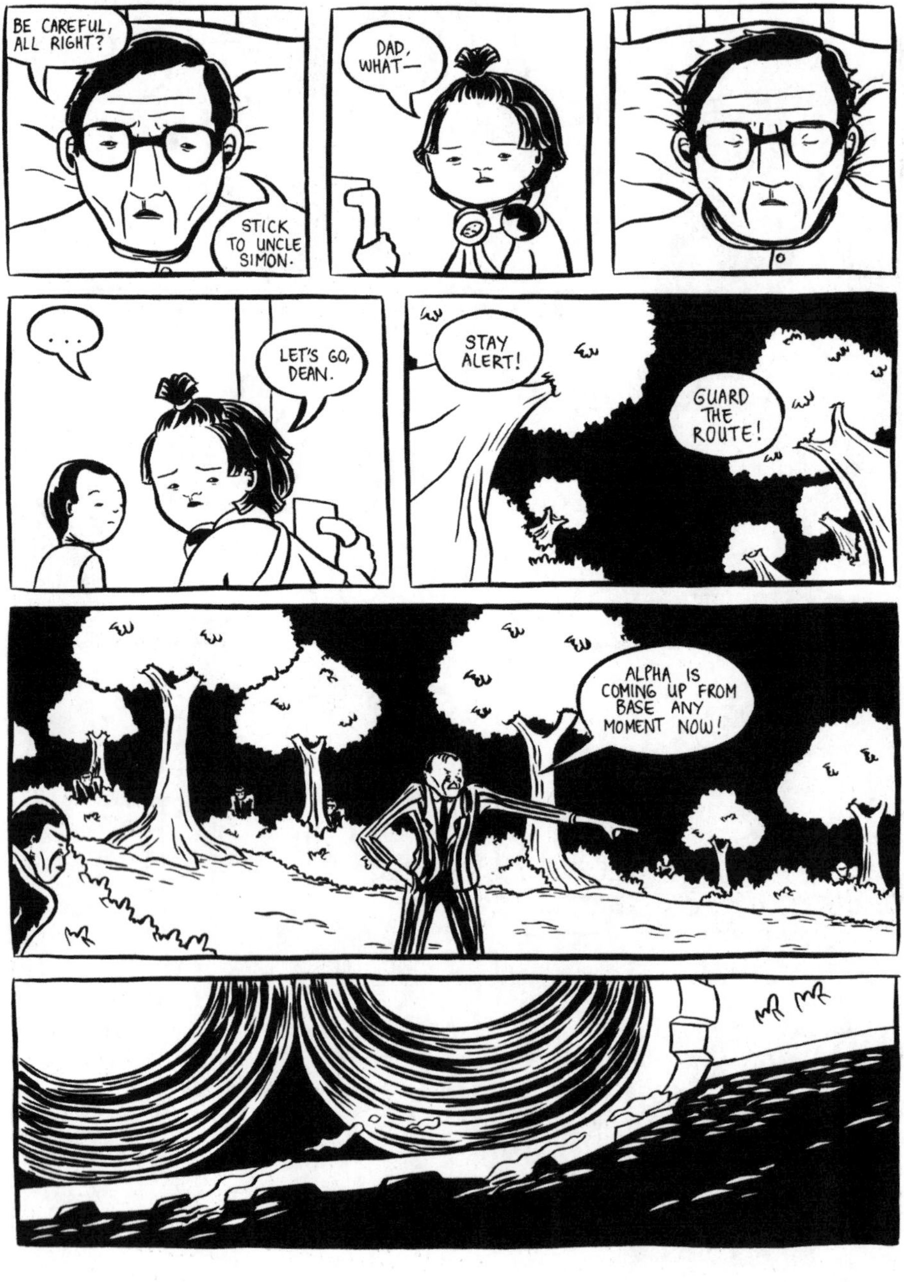
BE CAREFUL, ALL RIGHT?
STICK TO UNCLE SIMON.
DAD, WHAT—
. . .
LET'S GO, DEAN.
STAY ALERT!
GUARD THE ROUTE!
ALPHA IS COMING UP FROM BASE ANY MOMENT NOW!

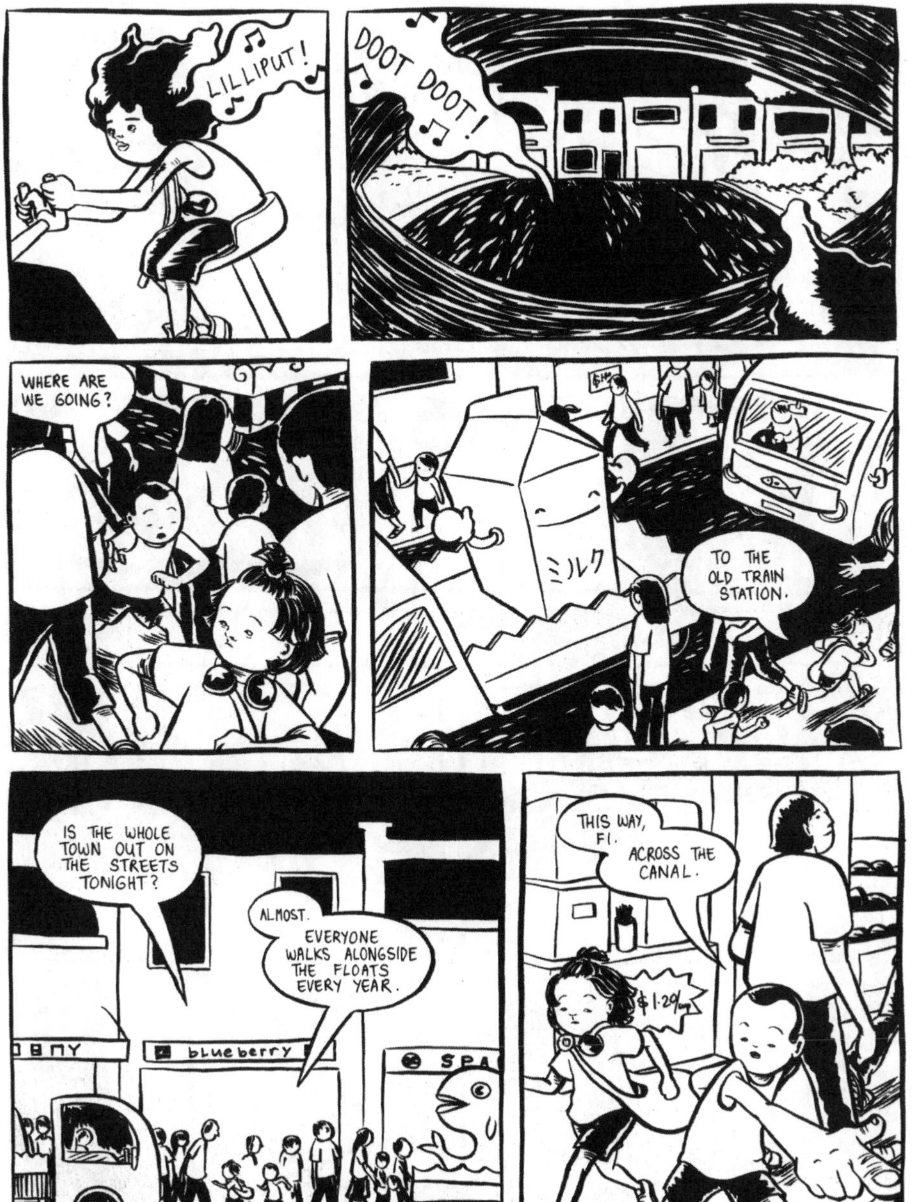
LILLIPUT!
DOOT DOOT!
WHERE ARE WE GOING?
ミルク
TO THE OLD TRAIN STATION.
IS THE WHOLE TOWN OUT ON THE STREETS TONIGHT?
ALMOST.
EVERYONE WALKS ALONGSIDE THE FLOATS EVERY YEAR.
blueberry
THIS WAY, FI.
ACROSS THE CANAL.
$1.29

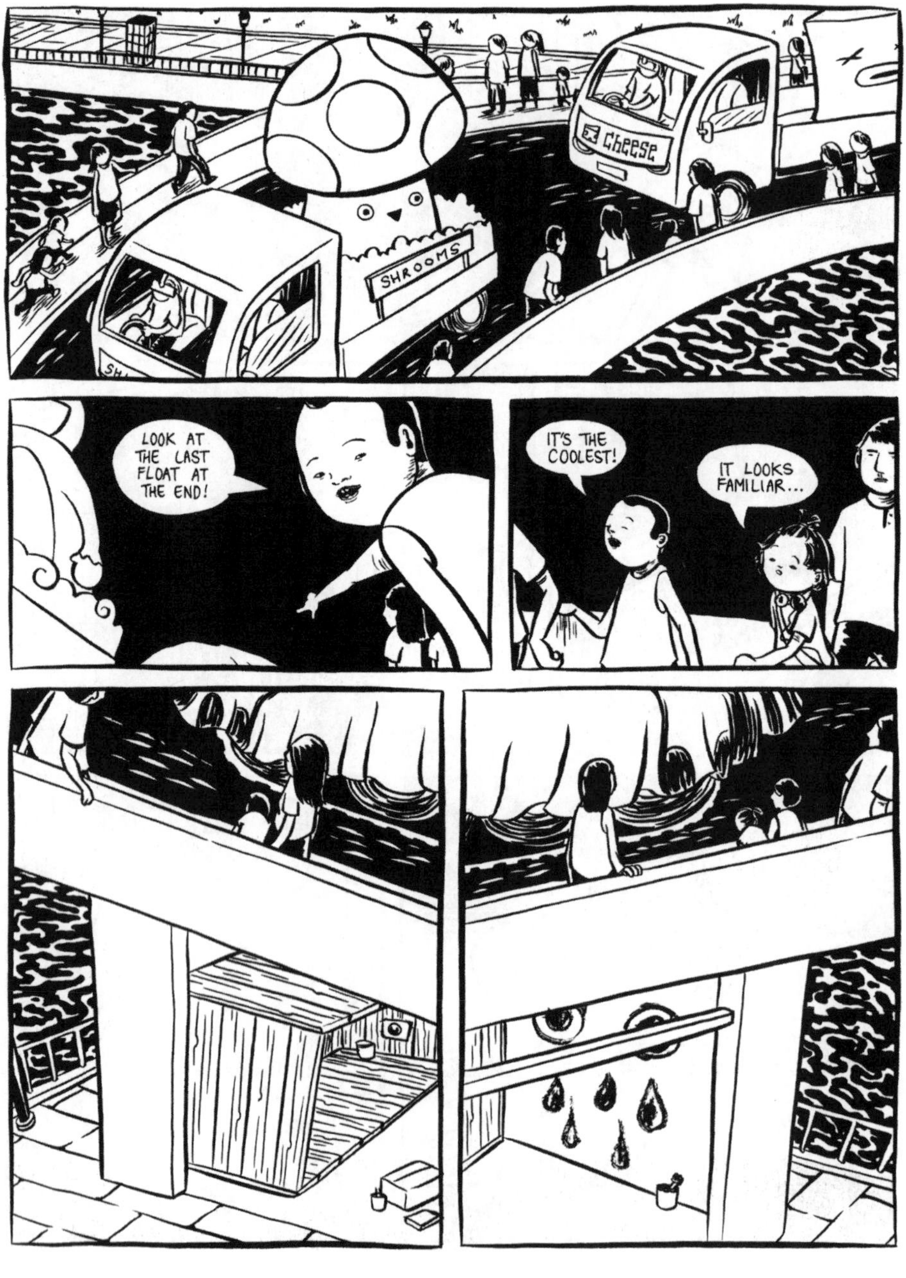
SHROOMS
Cheese
LOOK AT THE LAST FLOAT AT THE END!
IT'S THE COOLEST!
IT LOOKS FAMILIAR...

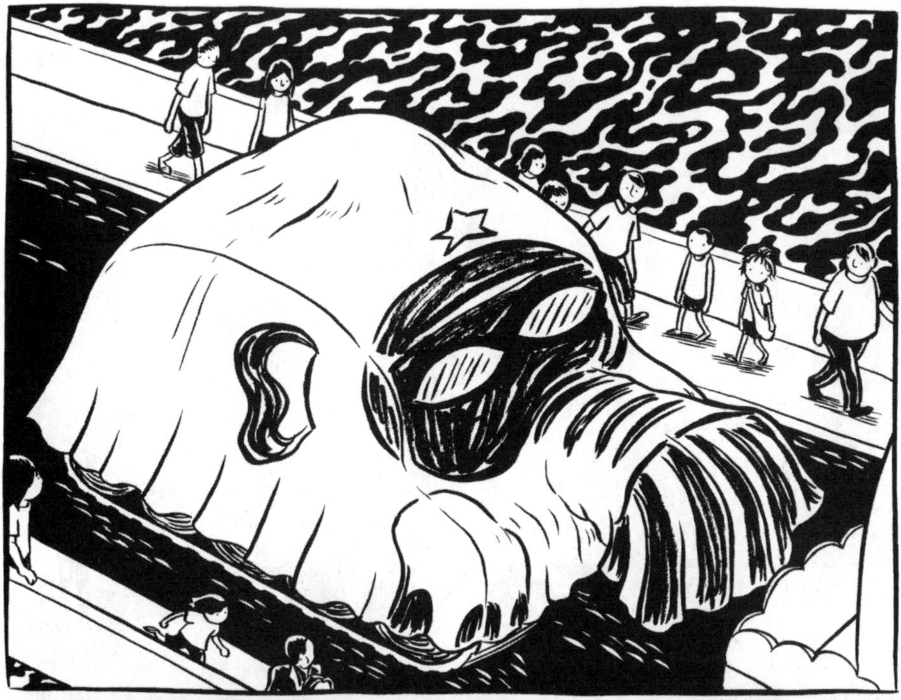

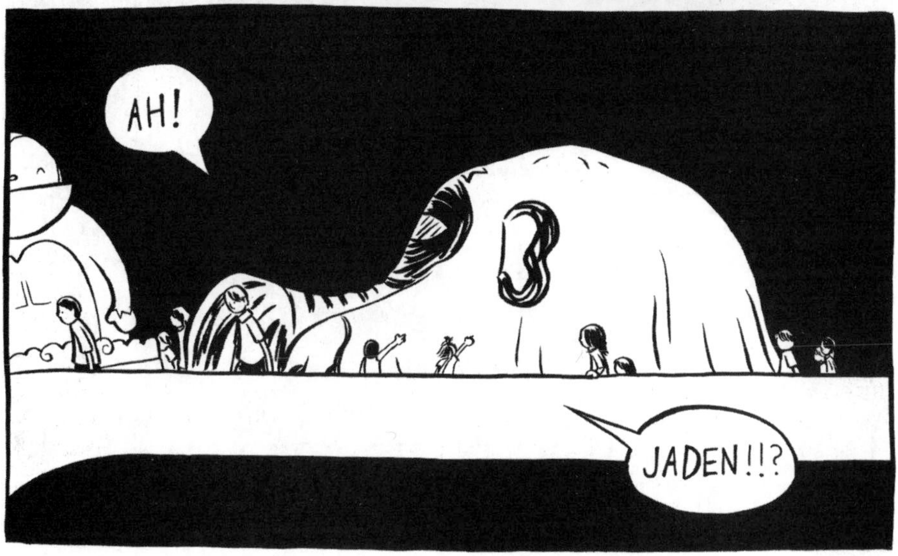
AH!
JADEN!!?

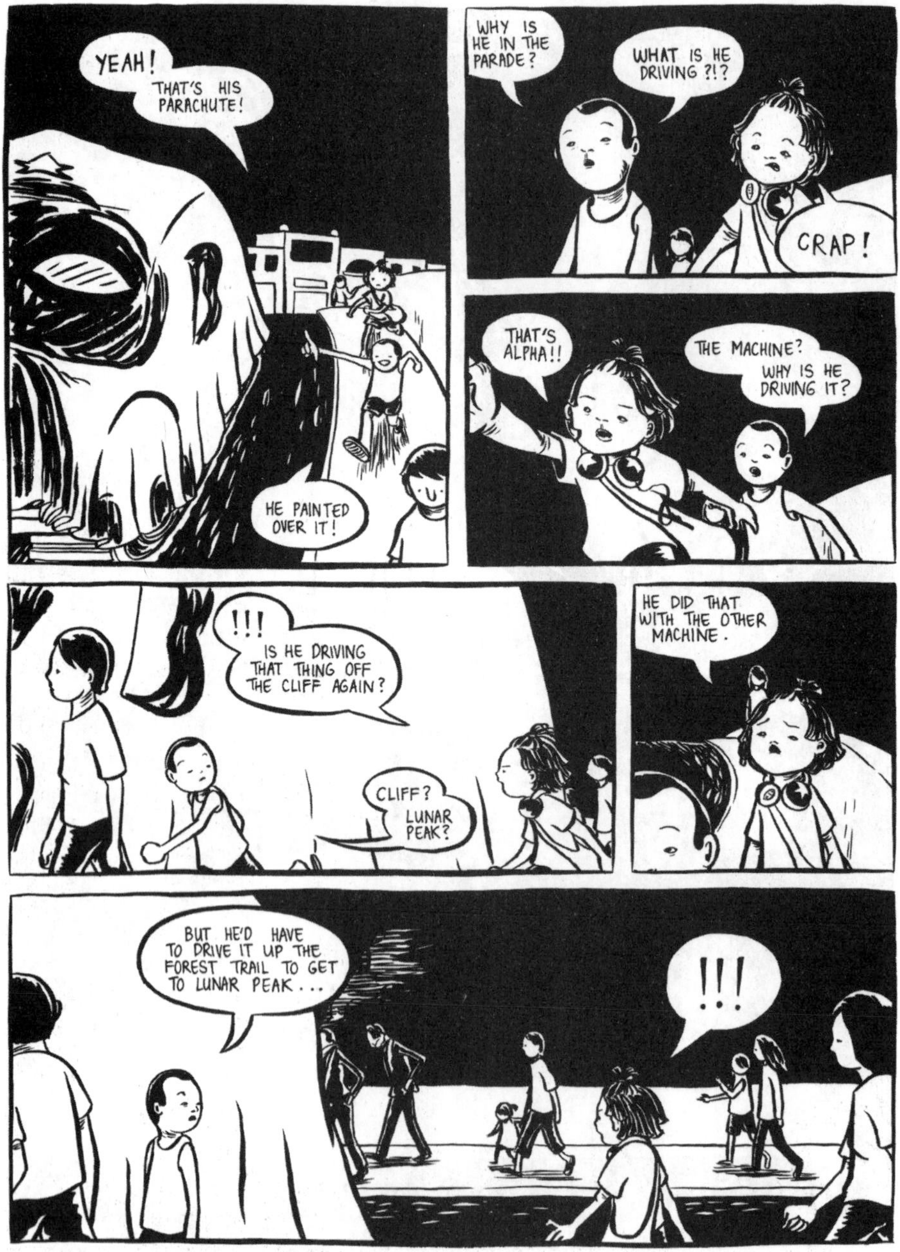
YEAH!
THAT'S HIS PARACHUTE!
HE PAINTED OVER IT!
WHY IS HE IN THE PARADE?
WHAT IS HE DRIVING ?!?
CRAP!
THAT'S ALPHA!!
THE MACHINE?
WHY IS HE DRIVING IT?
!!!
IS HE DRIVING THAT THING OFF THE CLIFF AGAIN?
CLIFF?
LUNAR PEAK?
HE DID THAT WITH THE OTHER MACHINE.
BUT HE'D HAVE TO DRIVE IT UP THE FOREST TRAIL TO GET TO LUNAR PEAK...
!!!

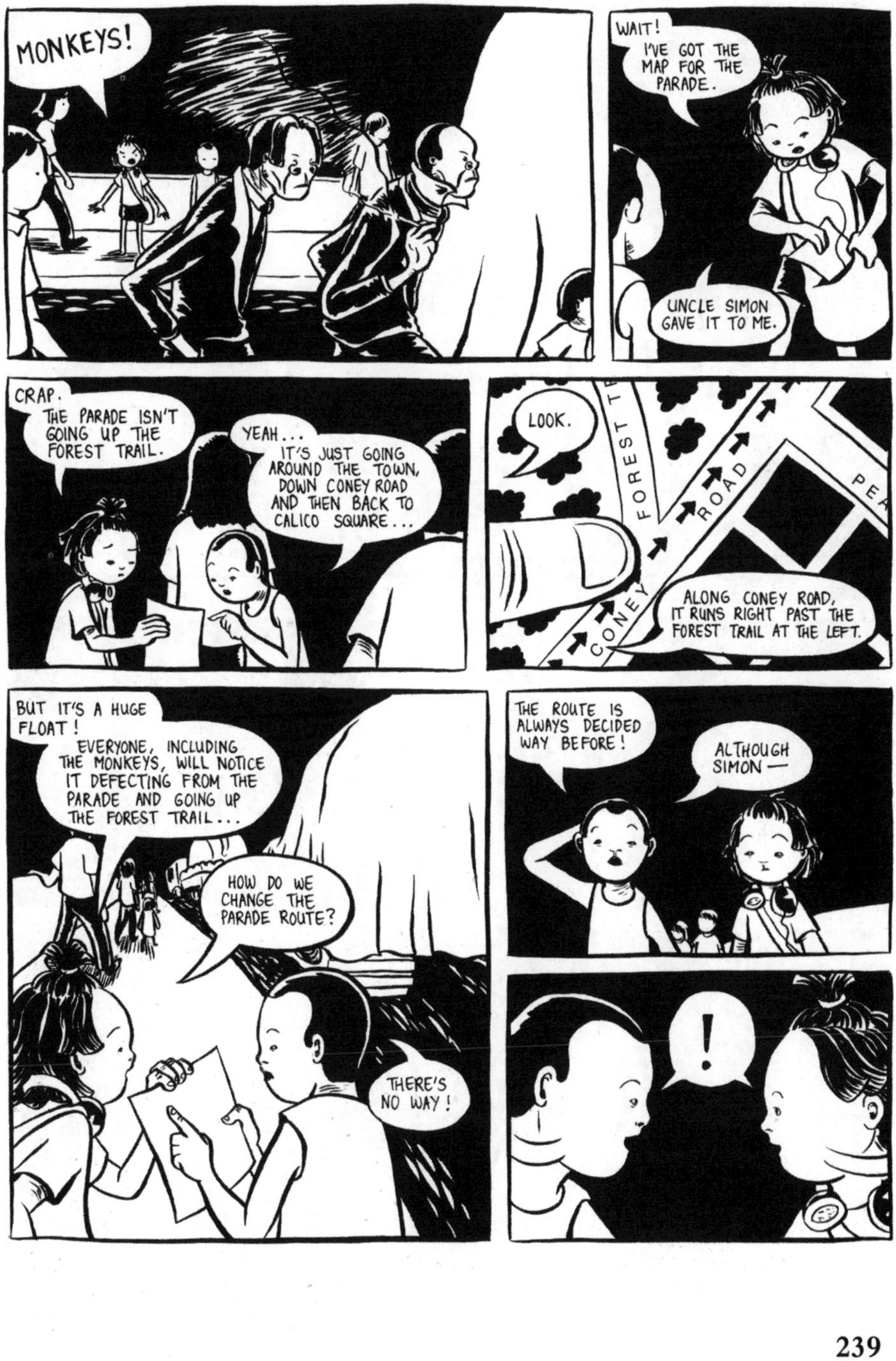
MONKEYS!
WAIT!
I'VE GOT THE MAP FOR THE PARADE.
UNCLE SIMON GAVE IT TO ME.
CRAP.
THE PARADE ISN'T GOING UP THE FOREST TRAIL.
YEAH...
IT'S JUST GOING AROUND THE TOWN, DOWN CONEY ROAD AND THEN BACK TO CALICO SQUARE...
LOOK.
FOREST T
ROAD
PEA
CONEY
ALONG CONEY ROAD, IT RUNS RIGHT PAST THE FOREST TRAIL AT THE LEFT.
BUT IT'S A HUGE FLOAT!
EVERYONE, INCLUDING THE MONKEYS, WILL NOTICE IT DEFECTING FROM THE PARADE AND GOING UP THE FOREST TRAIL...
HOW DO WE CHANGE THE PARADE ROUTE?
THERE'S NO WAY!
THE ROUTE IS ALWAYS DECIDED WAY BEFORE!
ALTHOUGH SIMON —
!

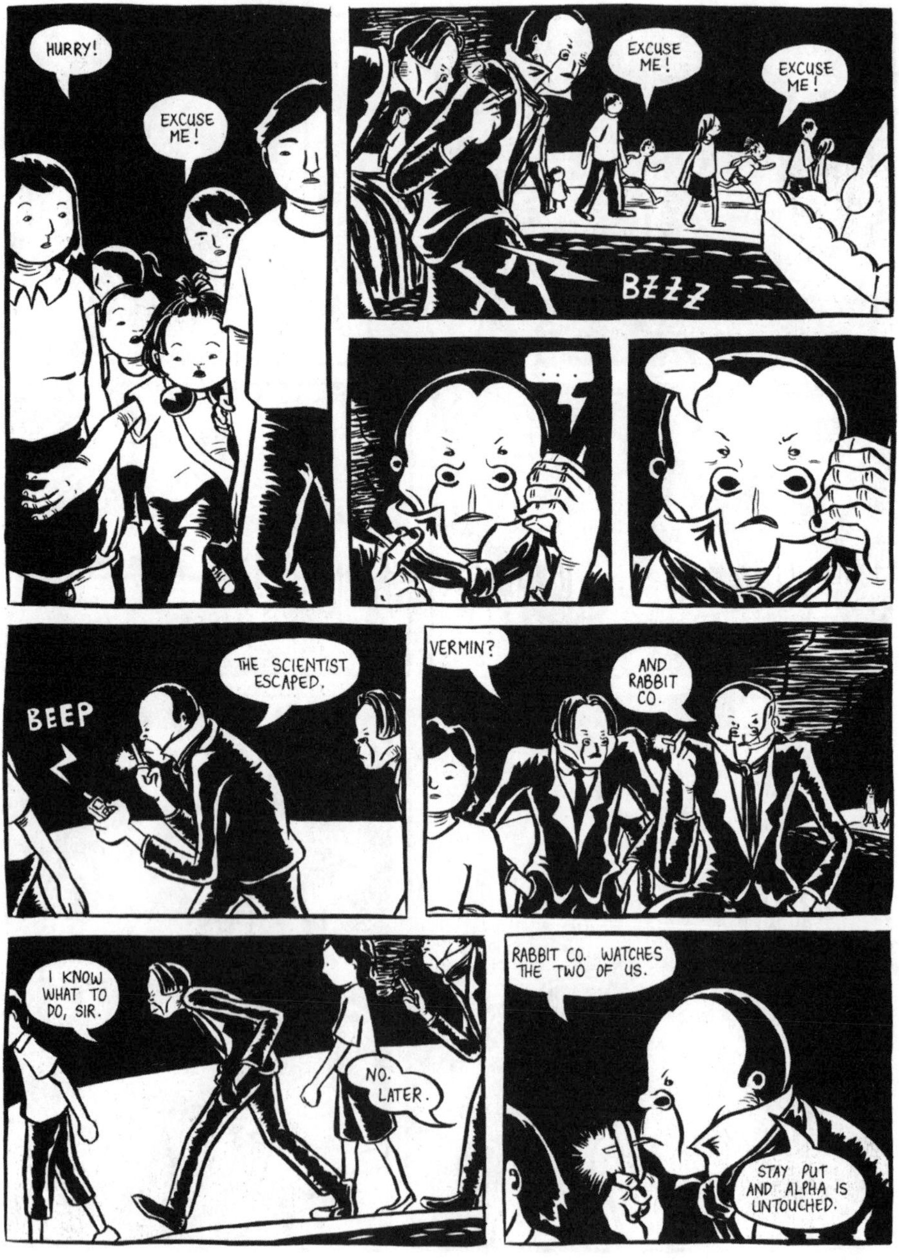
HURRY!
EXCUSE ME!
EXCUSE ME!
EXCUSE ME!
BZZZ
...
—
BEEP
THE SCIENTIST ESCAPED.
VERMIN?
AND RABBIT CO.
I KNOW WHAT TO DO, SIR.
NO. LATER.
RABBIT CO. WATCHES THE TWO OF US.
STAY PUT AND ALPHA IS UNTOUCHED.

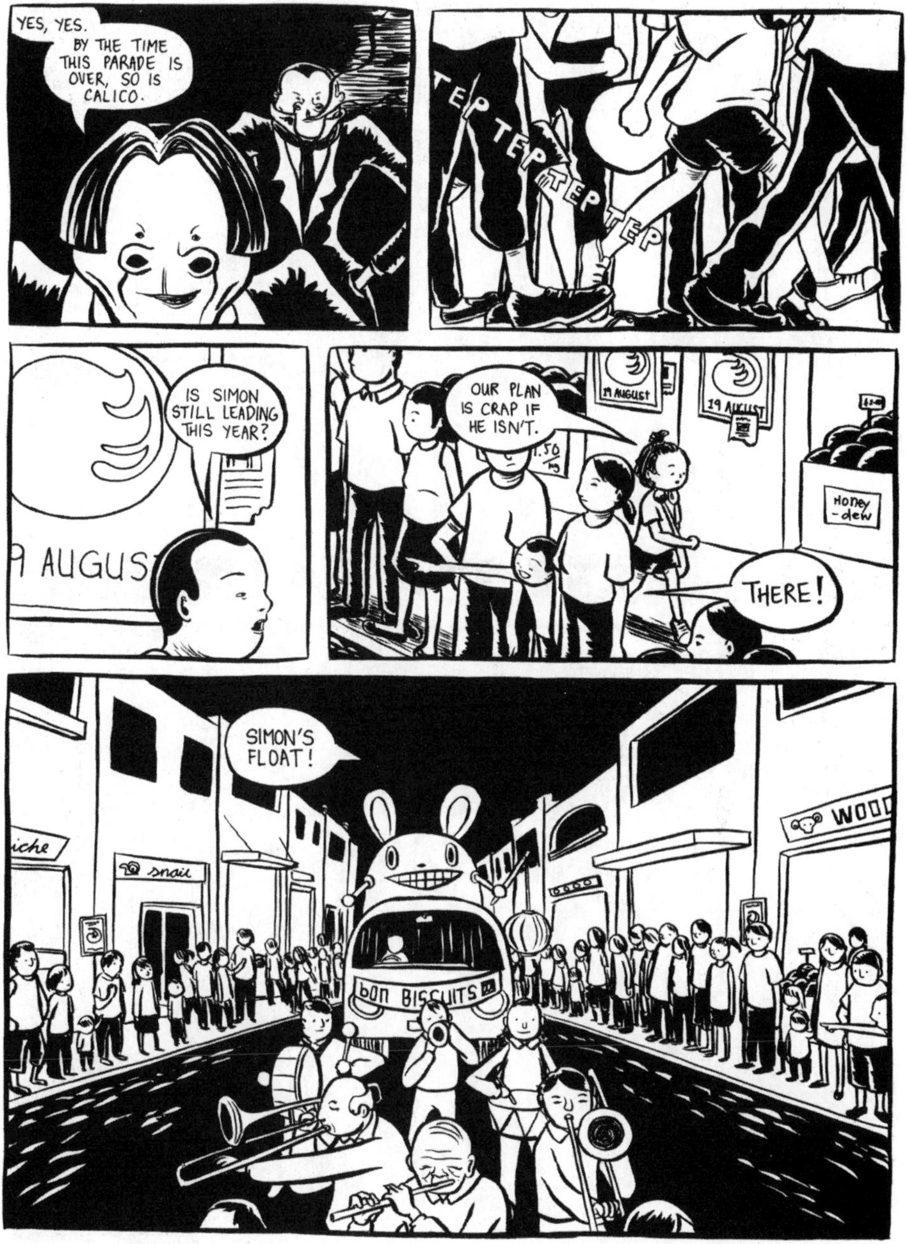
YES, YES.
BY THE TIME THIS PARADE IS OVER, SO IS CALICO.
TEP TEP TEP TEP TEP TEP
IS SIMON STILL LEADING THIS YEAR?
9 AUGUS
OUR PLAN IS CRAP IF HE ISN'T.
19 AUGUST
19 AUGUST
Honey -dew
THERE!
SIMON'S FLOAT!
snail
WOOD
BON BISCUITS

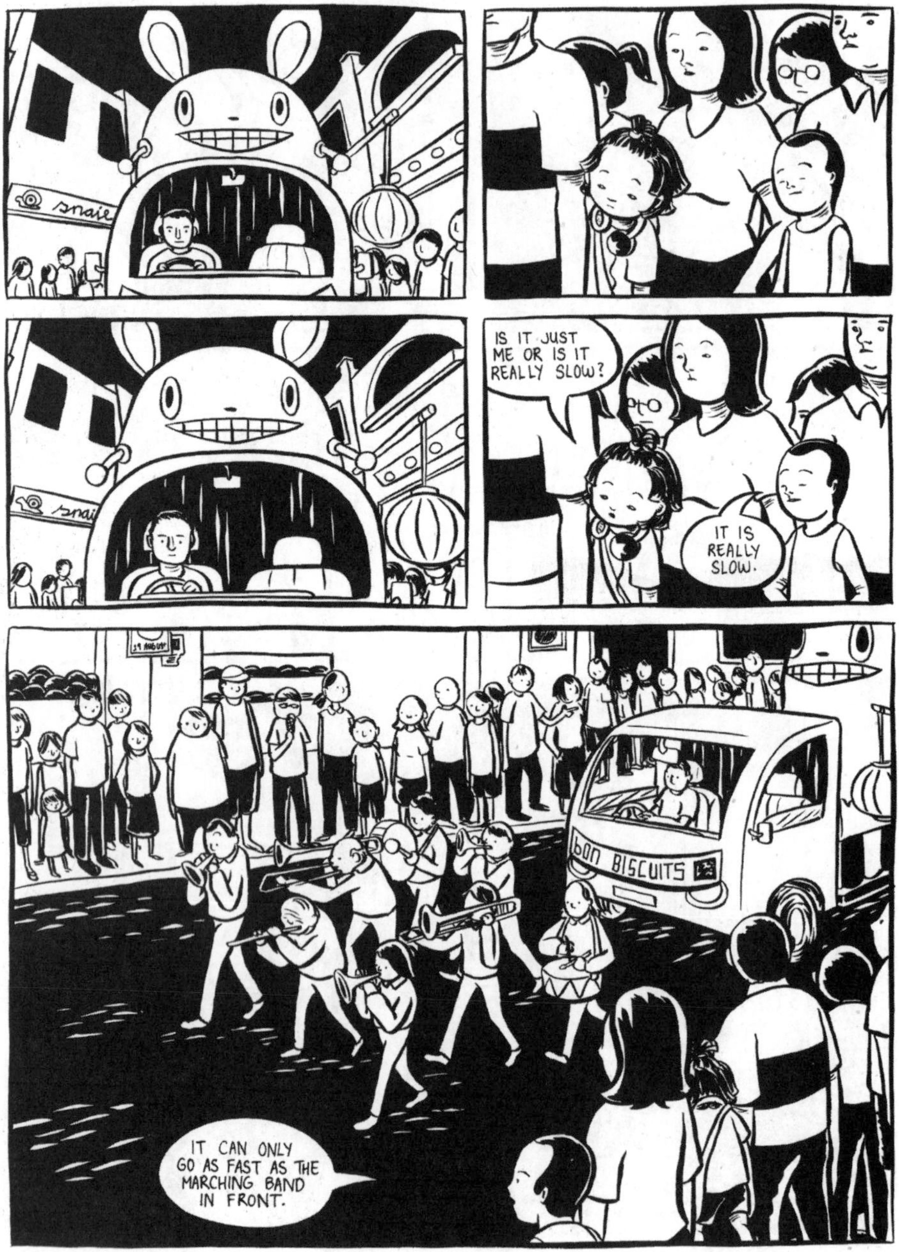
snail
snail
IS IT JUST ME OR IS IT REALLY SLOW?
IT IS REALLY SLOW.
bon BISCUITS
IT CAN ONLY GO AS FAST AS THE MARCHING BAND IN FRONT.

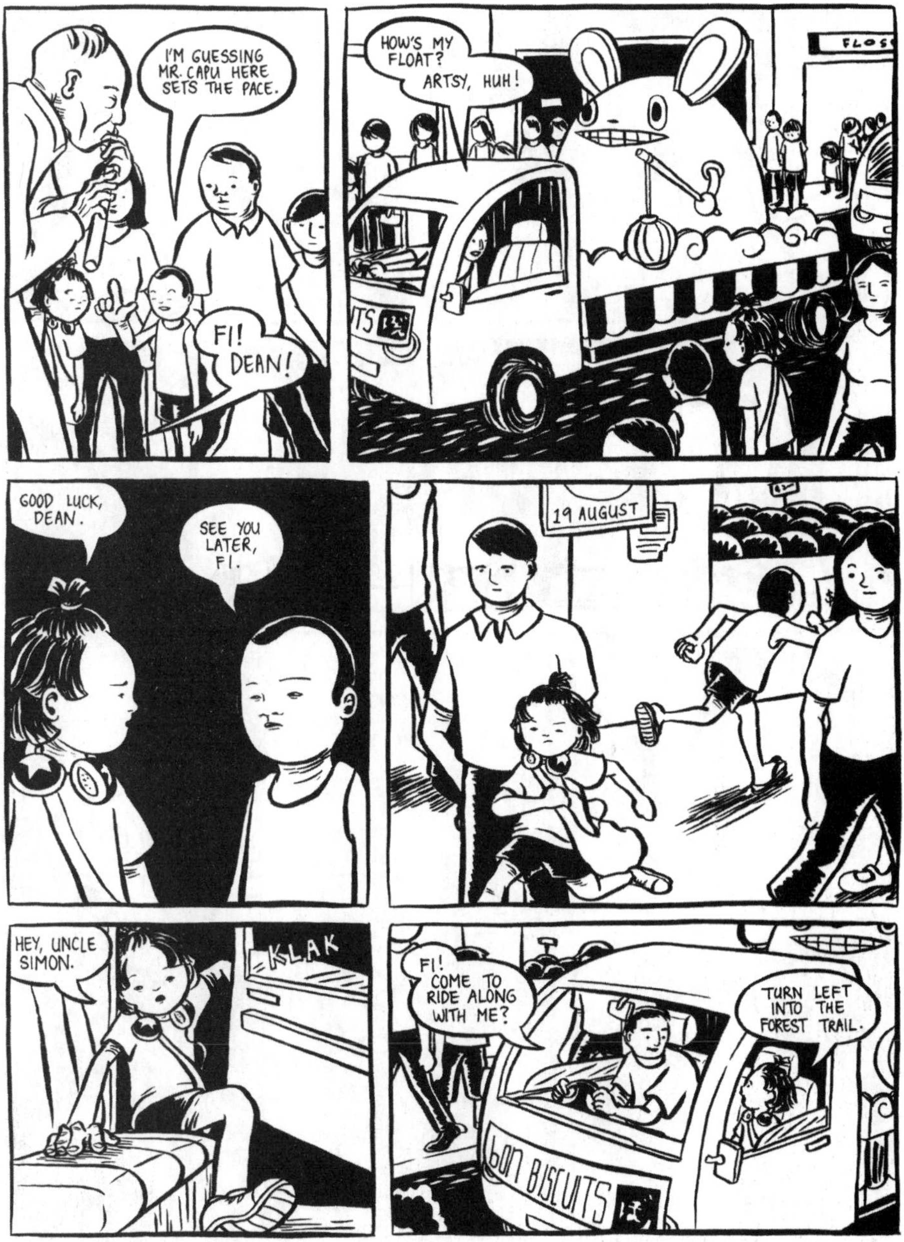
I'M GUESSING MR. CAPU HERE SETS THE PACE.
FI! DEAN!
HOW'S MY FLOAT?
ARTSY, HUH!
FLOS
GOOD LUCK, DEAN.
SEE YOU LATER, FI.
19 AUGUST
HEY, UNCLE SIMON.
KLAK
FI! COME TO RIDE ALONG WITH ME?
TURN LEFT INTO THE FOREST TRAIL.
BON BISCUITS

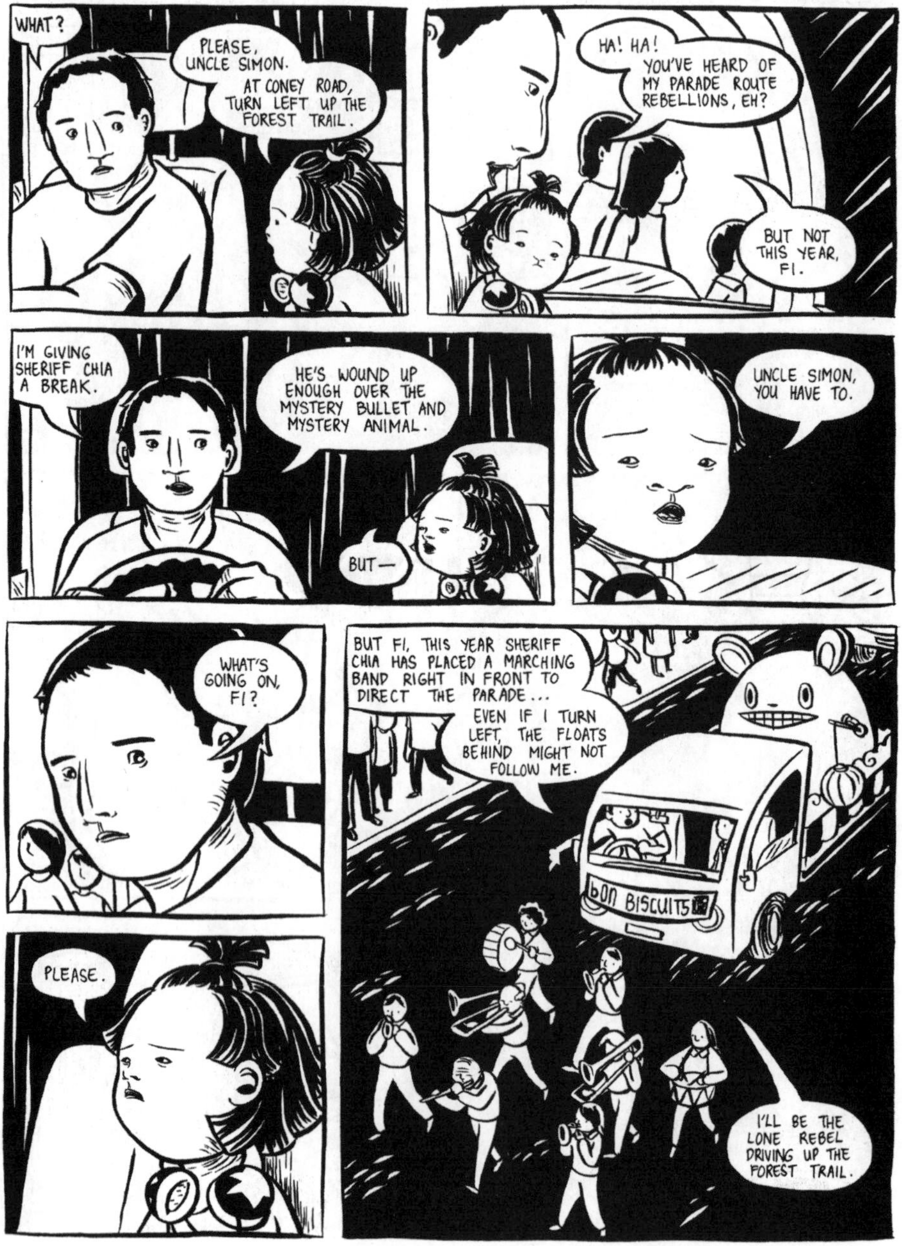
WHAT?
PLEASE, UNCLE SIMON.
AT CONEY ROAD, TURN LEFT UP THE FOREST TRAIL.
HA! HA!
YOU'VE HEARD OF MY PARADE ROUTE REBELLIONS, EH?
BUT NOT THIS YEAR, FI.
I'M GIVING SHERIFF CHIA A BREAK.
HE'S WOUND UP ENOUGH OVER THE MYSTERY BULLET AND MYSTERY ANIMAL.
BUT—
UNCLE SIMON, YOU HAVE TO.
WHAT'S GOING ON, FI?
PLEASE.
BUT FI, THIS YEAR SHERIFF CHIA HAS PLACED A MARCHING BAND RIGHT IN FRONT TO DIRECT THE PARADE...
EVEN IF I TURN LEFT, THE FLOATS BEHIND MIGHT NOT FOLLOW ME.
BON BISCUITS
I'LL BE THE LONE REBEL DRIVING UP THE FOREST TRAIL.

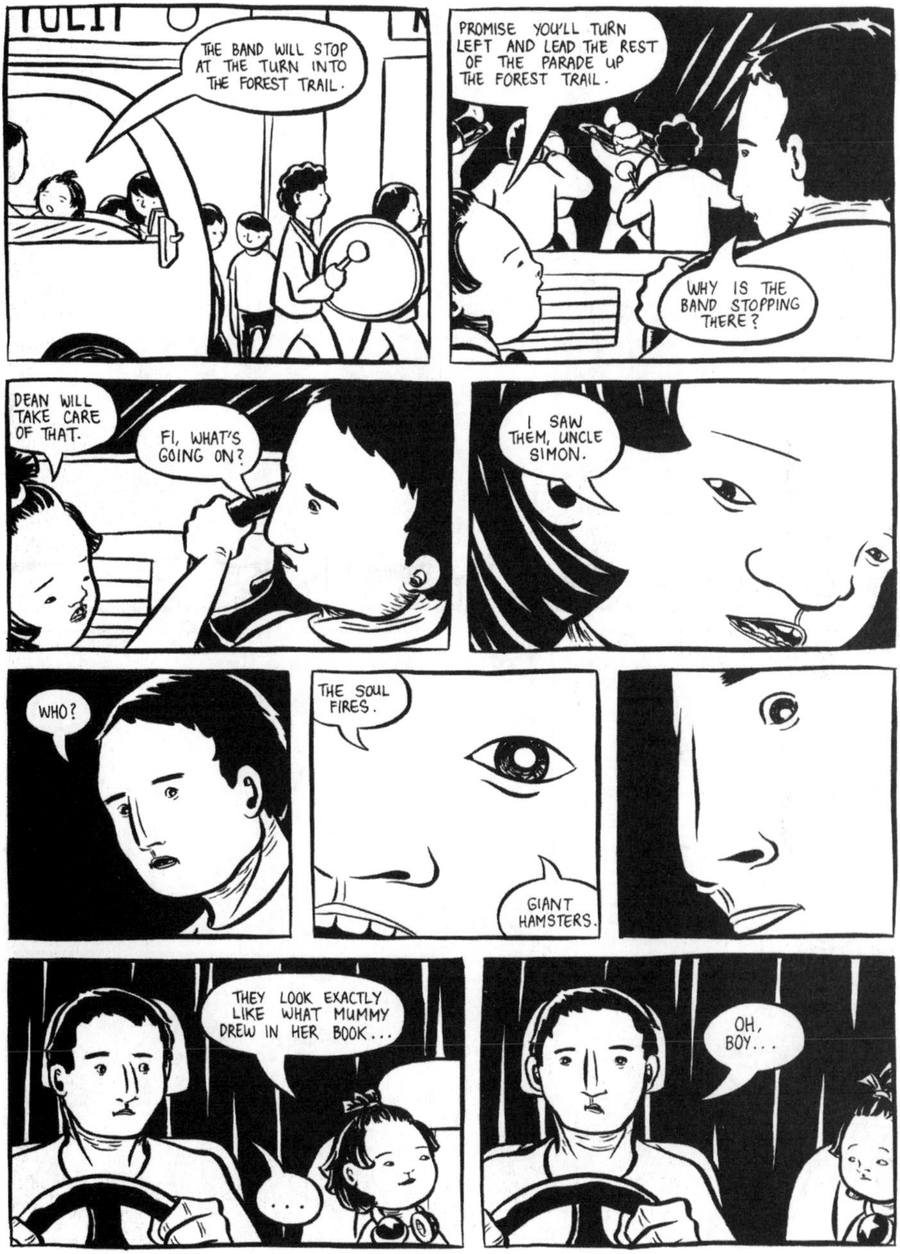
THE BAND WILL STOP AT THE TURN INTO THE FOREST TRAIL.
PROMISE YOU'LL TURN LEFT AND LEAD THE REST OF THE PARADE UP THE FOREST TRAIL.
WHY IS THE BAND STOPPING THERE?
DEAN WILL TAKE CARE OF THAT.
FI, WHAT'S GOING ON?
I SAW THEM, UNCLE SIMON.
WHO?
THE SOUL FIRES.
GIANT HAMSTERS.
THEY LOOK EXACTLY LIKE WHAT MUMMY DREW IN HER BOOK...
...
OH, BOY...

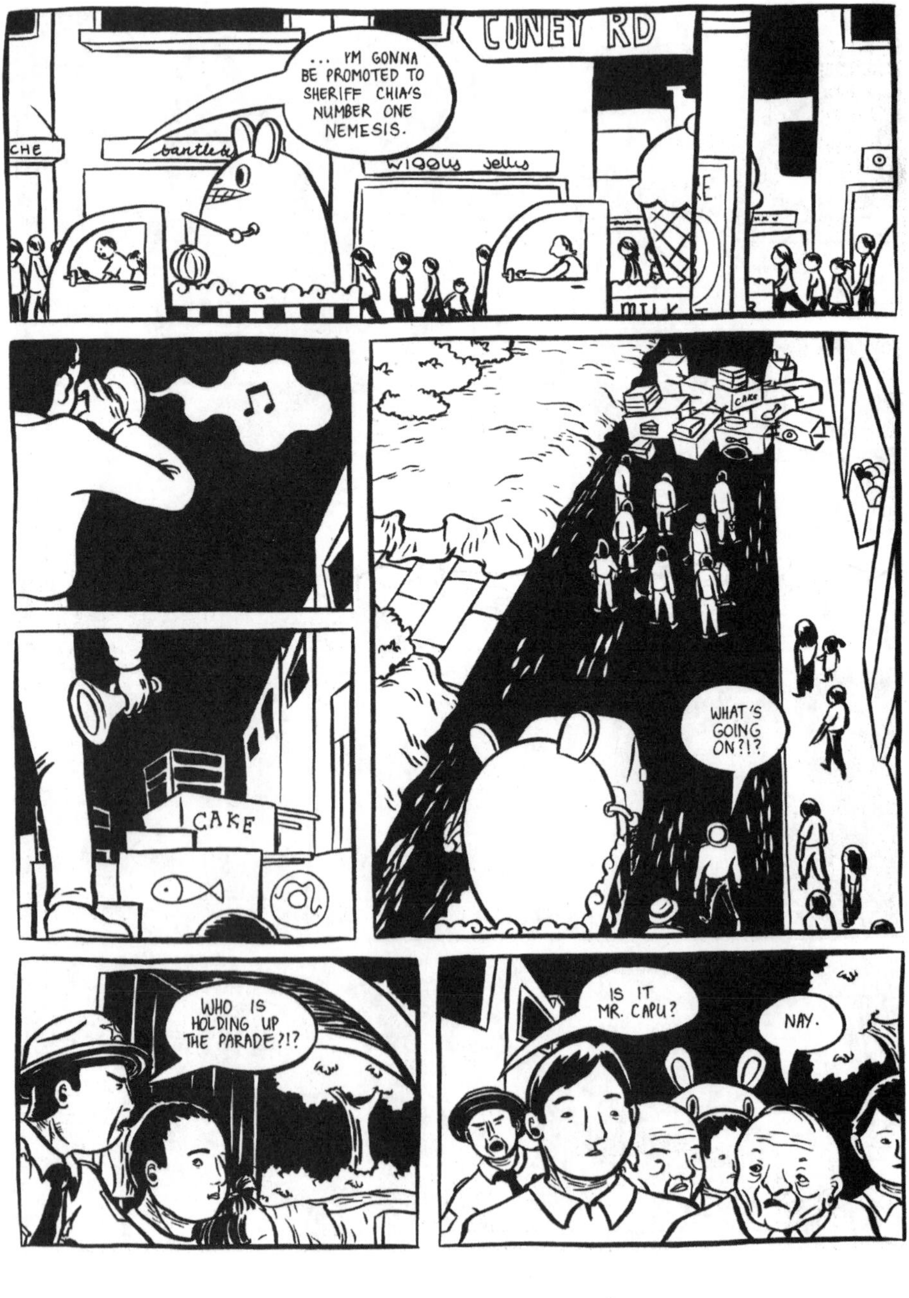
CONEY RD
... I'M GONNA BE PROMOTED TO SHERIFF CHIA'S NUMBER ONE NEMESIS.
CHE
wiggly jelly
MILK
CAKE
CAKE
WHAT'S GOING ON?!?
WHO IS HOLDING UP THE PARADE?!?
IS IT MR. CAPU?
NAY.

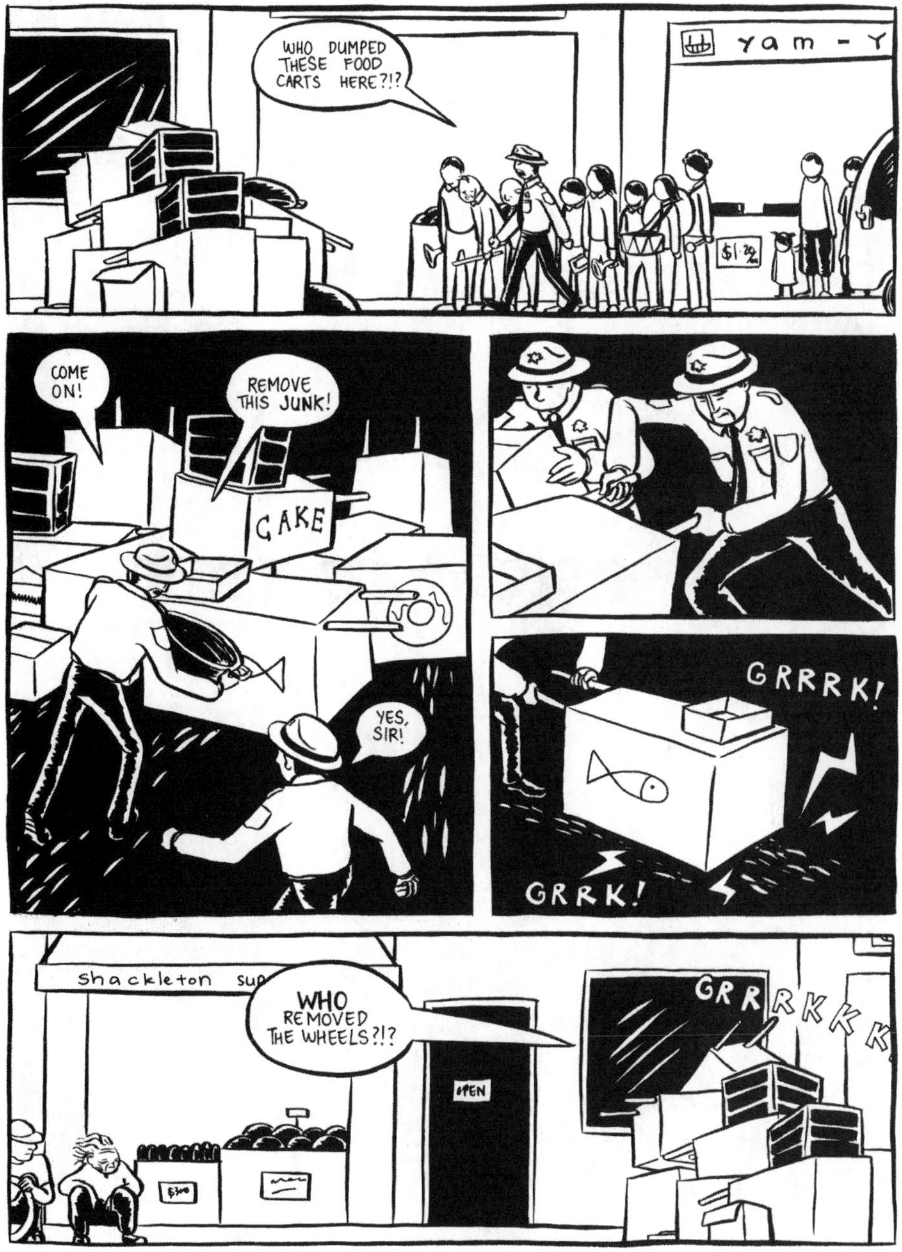
WHO DUMPED THESE FOOD CARTS HERE?!?
yam - Y
$1.20
COME ON!
REMOVE THIS JUNK!
CAKE
YES, SIR!
GRRRK!
GRRK!
shackleton su
WHO REMOVED THE WHEELS?!?
OPEN
GRRRKKKK

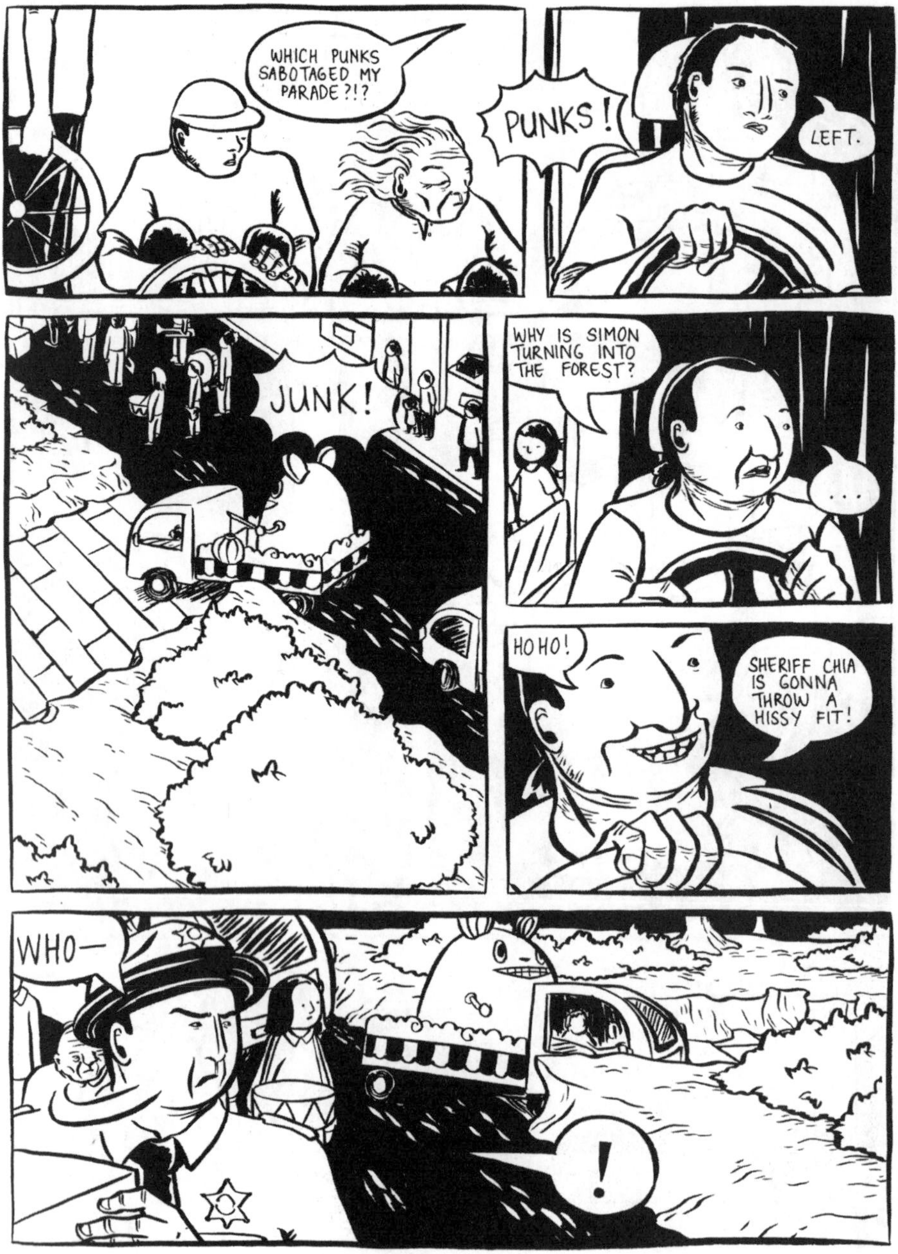
WHICH PUNKS SABOTAGED MY PARADE?!?
PUNKS!
LEFT.
JUNK!
WHY IS SIMON TURNING INTO THE FOREST?
...
HO HO!
SHERIFF CHIA IS GONNA THROW A HISSY FIT!
WHO—
!

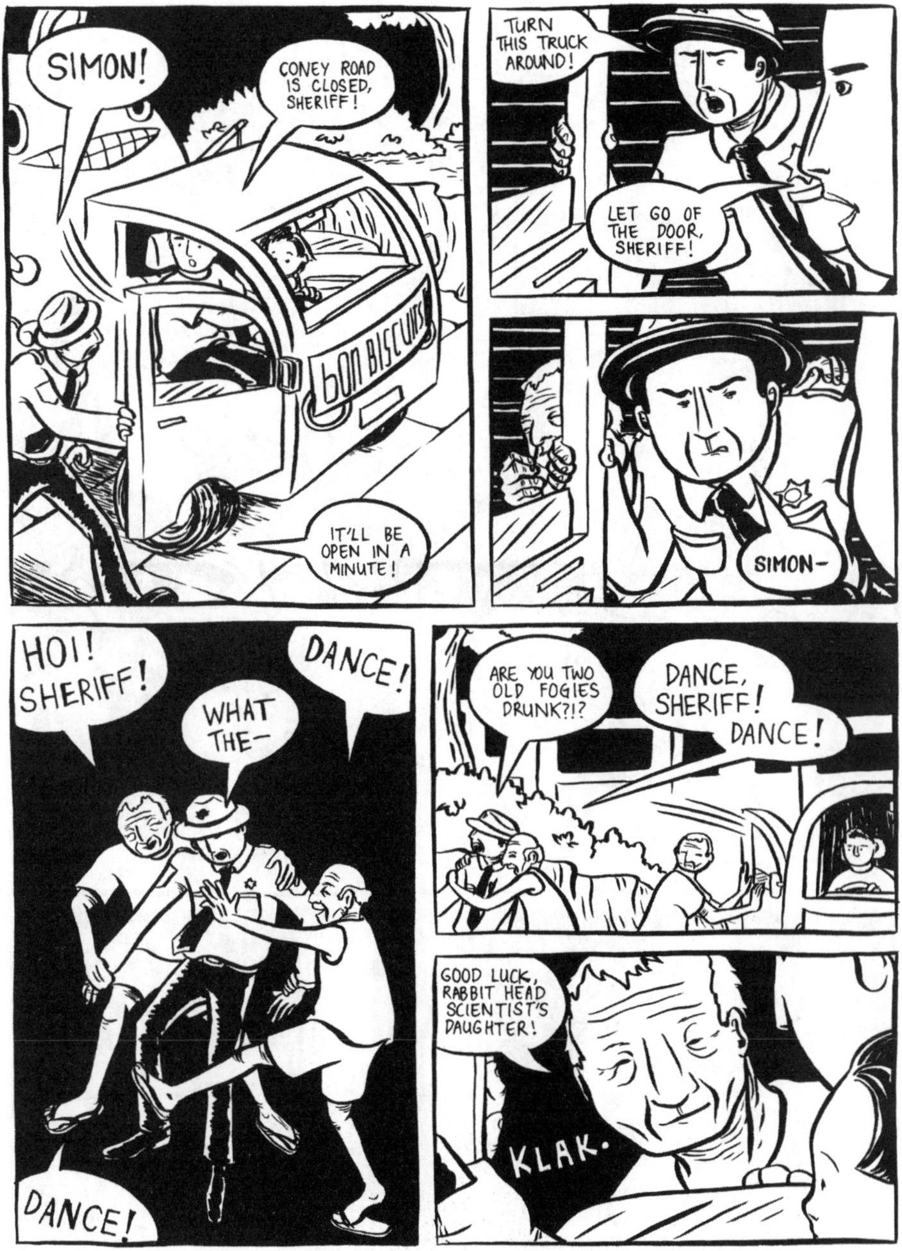
SIMON!
CONEY ROAD IS CLOSED, SHERIFF!
bon BISCUITS
IT'LL BE OPEN IN A MINUTE!
TURN THIS TRUCK AROUND!
LET GO OF THE DOOR, SHERIFF!
SIMON-
HOI! SHERIFF!
WHAT THE-
DANCE!
DANCE!
ARE YOU TWO OLD FOGIES DRUNK?!?
DANCE, SHERIFF! DANCE!
GOOD LUCK, RABBIT HEAD SCIENTIST'S DAUGHTER!
KLAK.

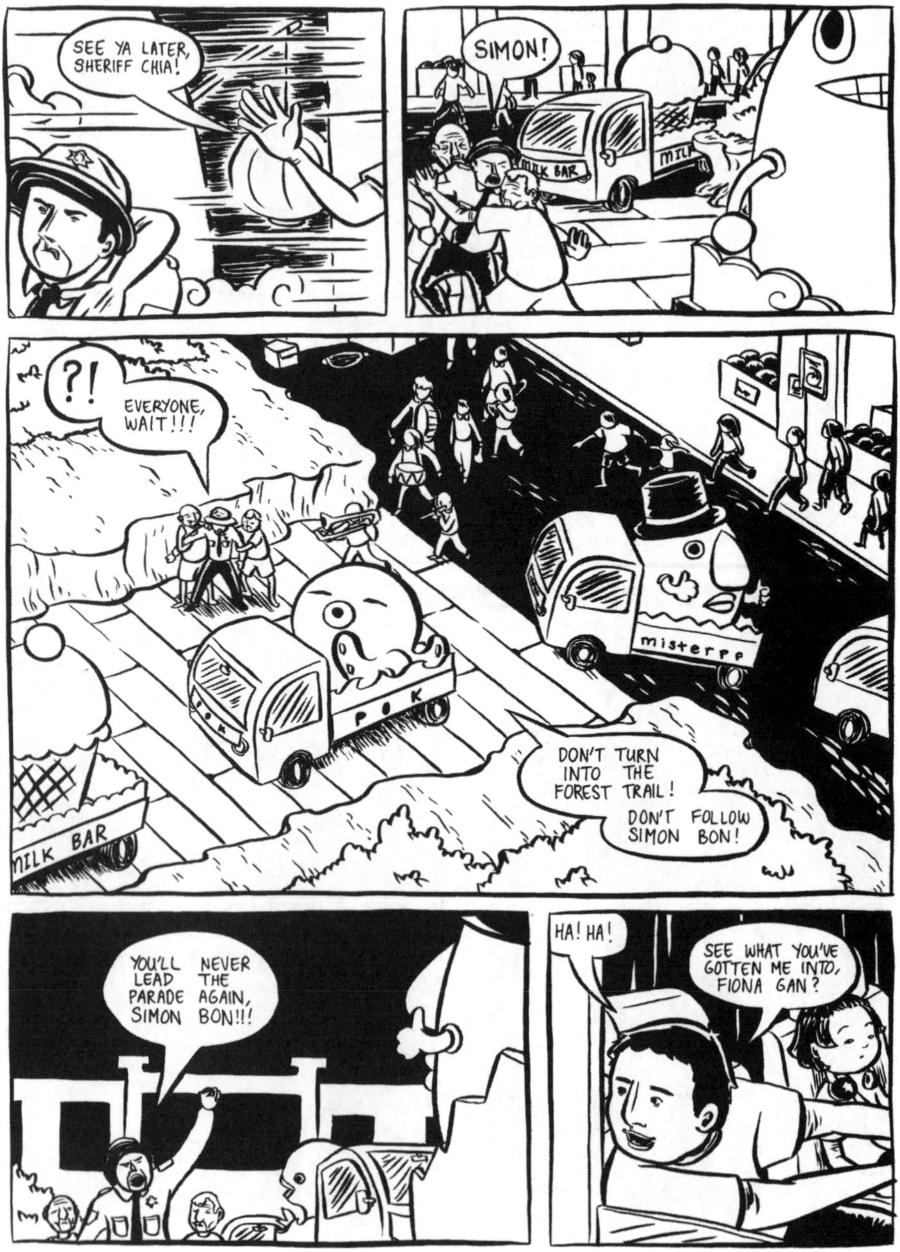
SEE YA LATER, SHERIFF CHIA!
SIMON!
?!
EVERYONE, WAIT!!!
MILK BAR
POK
misterpp
DON'T TURN INTO THE FOREST TRAIL!
DON'T FOLLOW SIMON BON!
YOU'LL NEVER LEAD THE PARADE AGAIN, SIMON BON!!!
HA! HA!
SEE WHAT YOU'VE GOTTEN ME INTO, FIONA GAN?

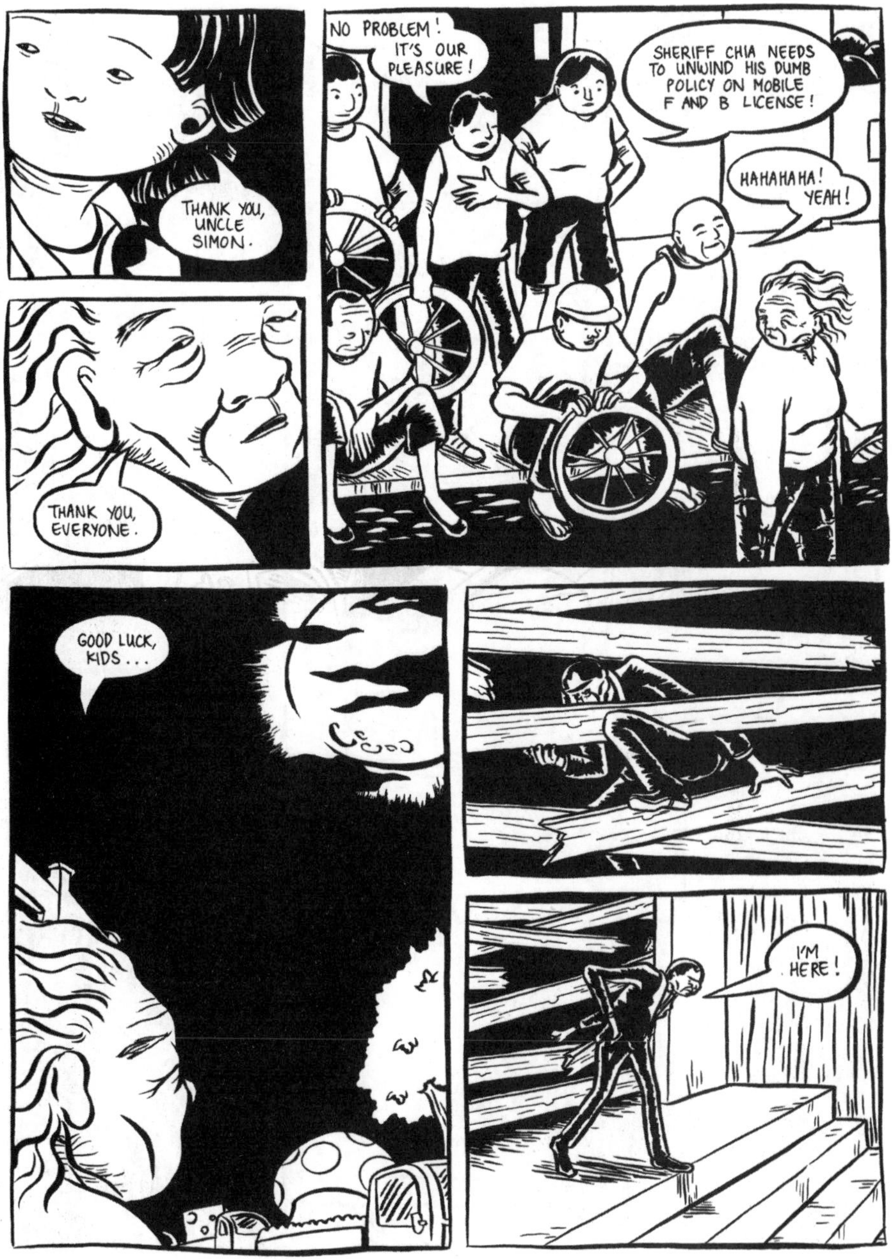
THANK YOU, UNCLE SIMON.
THANK YOU, EVERYONE.
NO PROBLEM! IT'S OUR PLEASURE!
SHERIFF CHIA NEEDS TO UNWIND HIS DUMB POLICY ON MOBILE F AND B LICENSE!
HAHAHAHA! YEAH!
GOOD LUCK, KIDS...
I'M HERE!

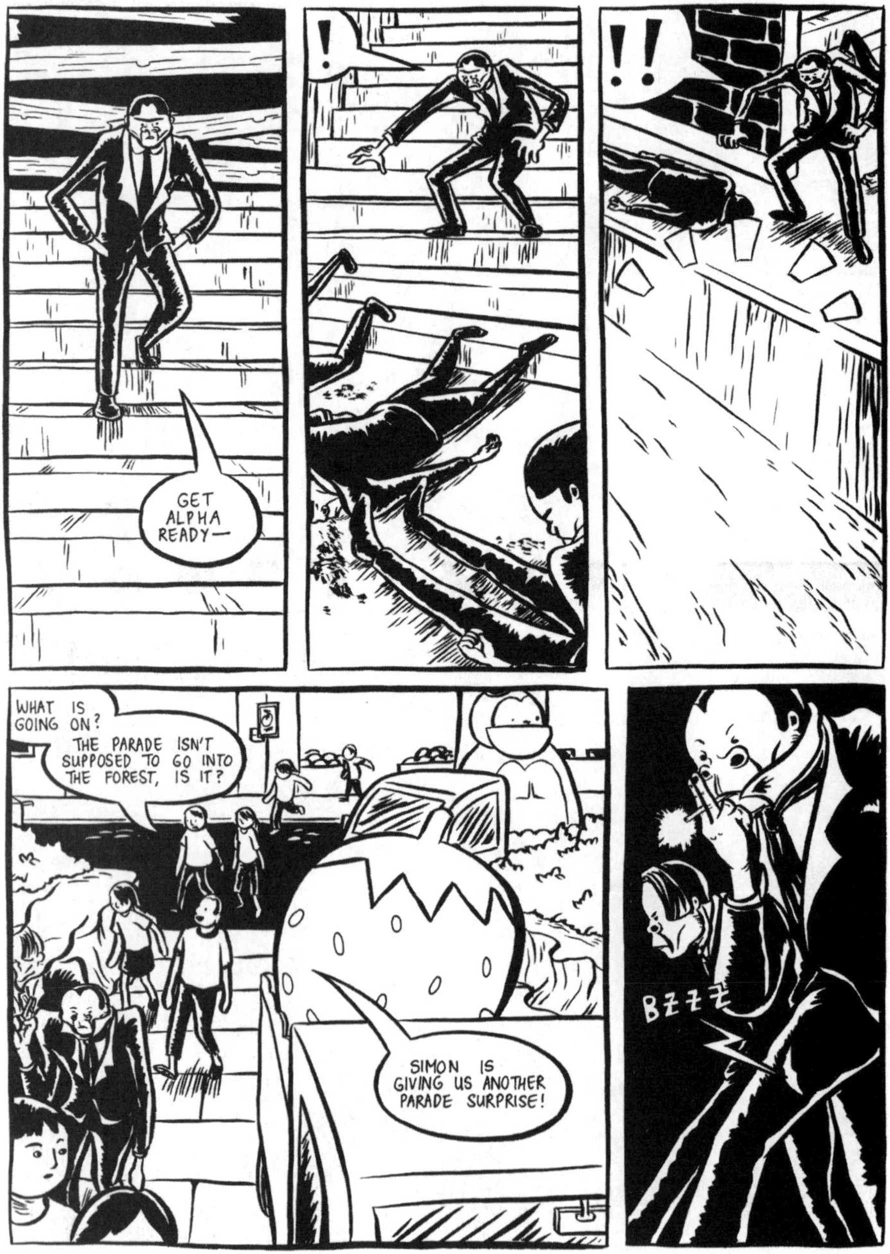
!
!!
GET ALPHA READY—
WHAT IS GOING ON?
THE PARADE ISN'T SUPPOSED TO GO INTO THE FOREST, IS IT?
SIMON IS GIVING US ANOTHER PARADE SURPRISE!
BZZZ

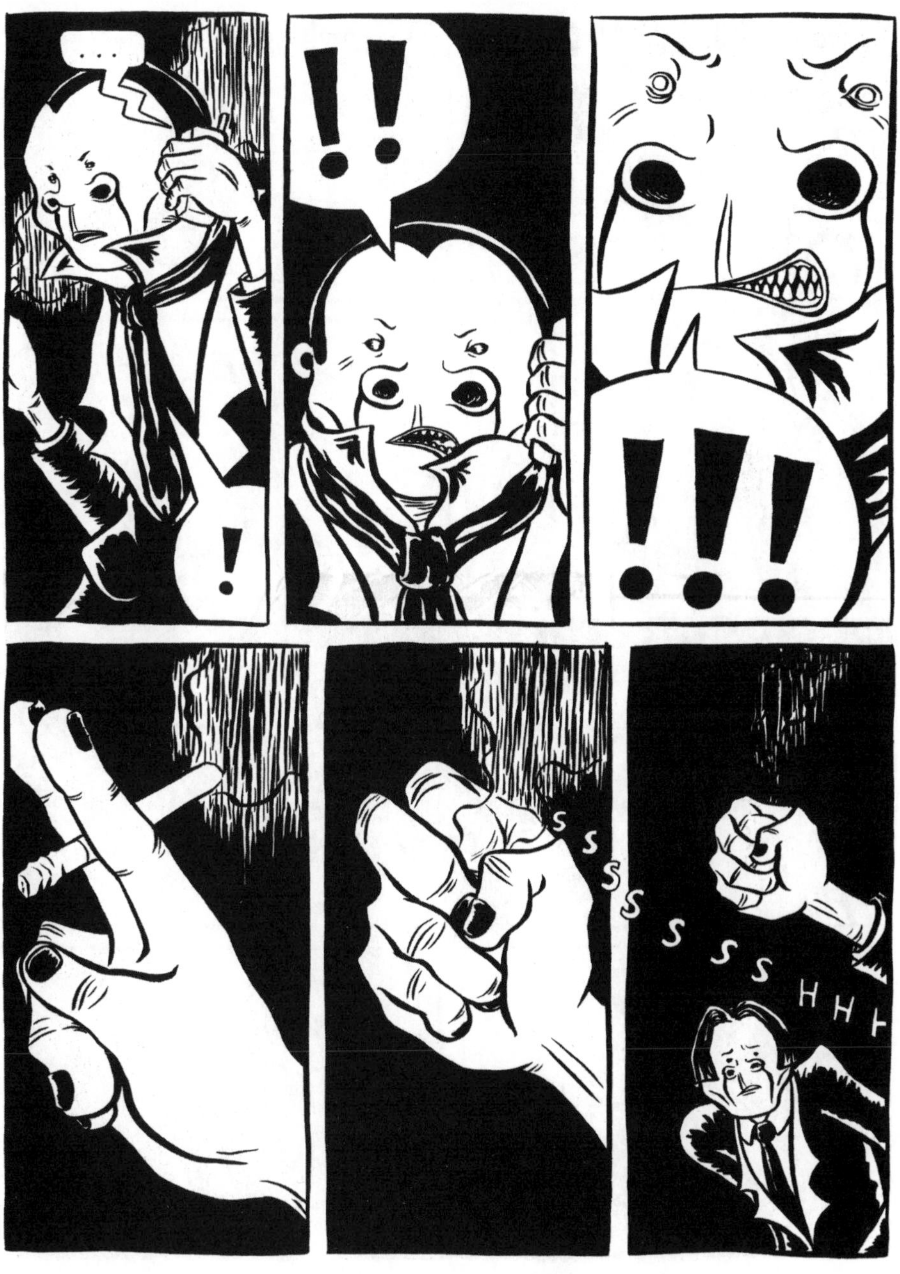
...
!
!!
!!!
SSSSSSSSHHHH

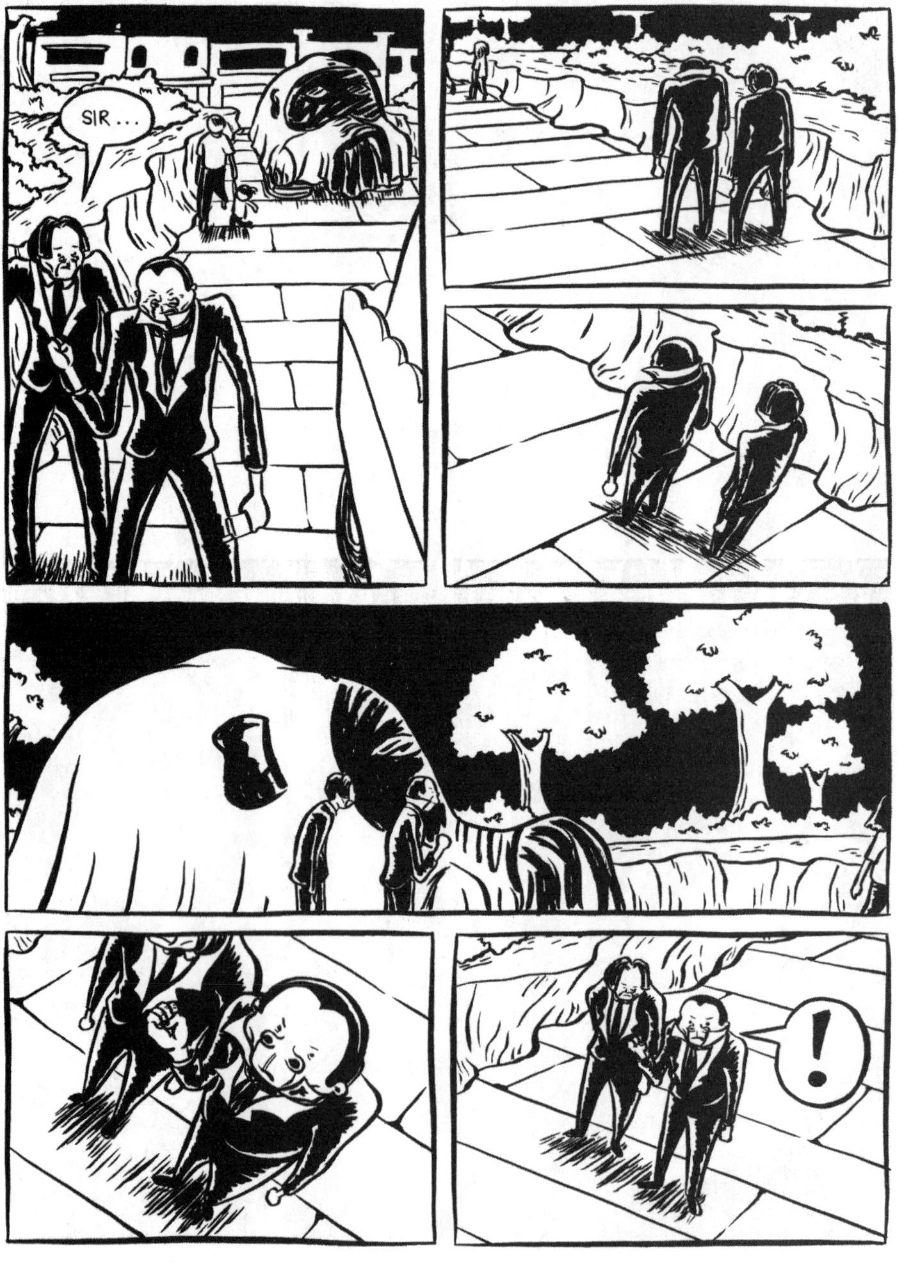
SIR...
!

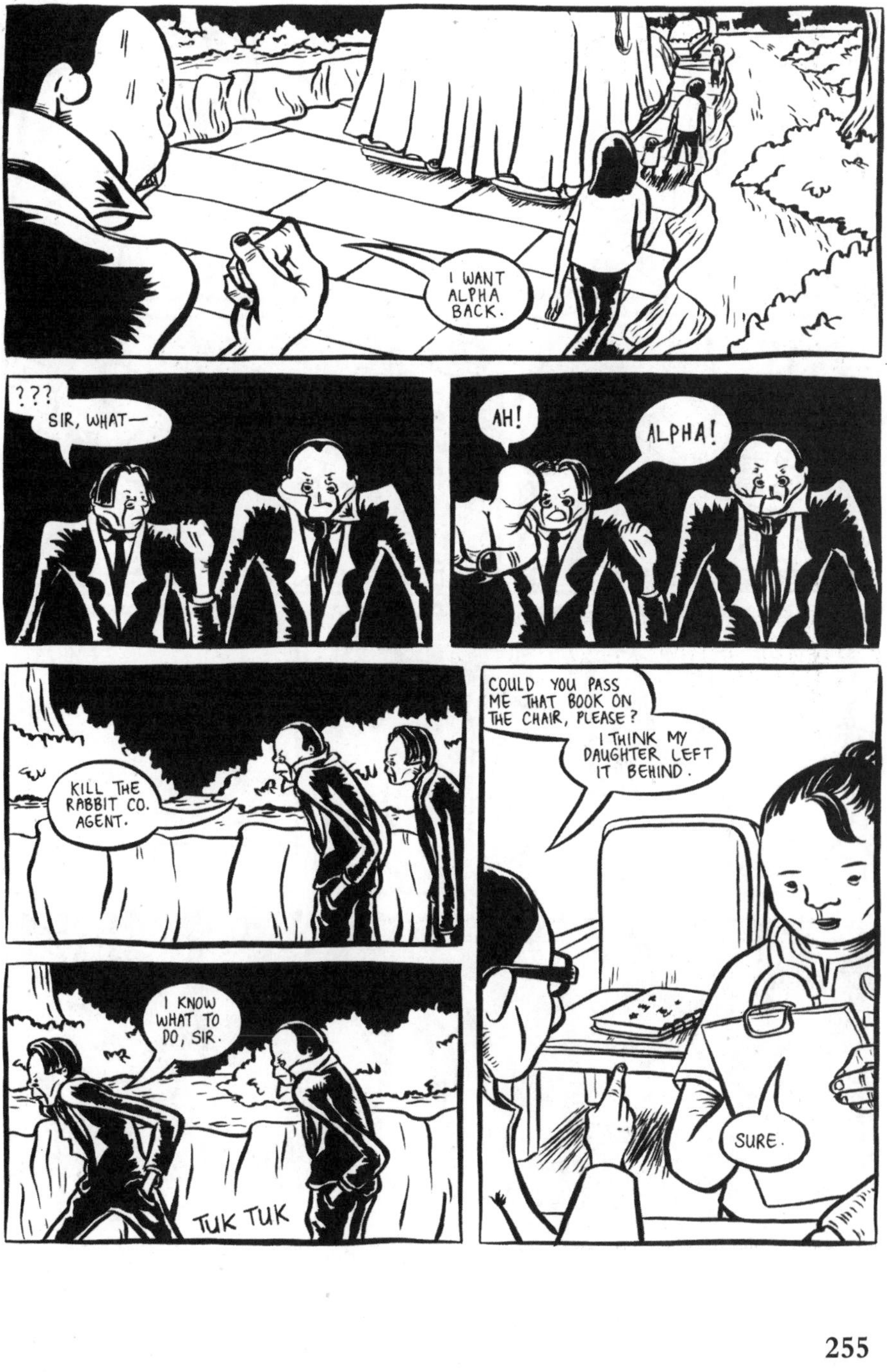
I WANT ALPHA BACK.
???
SIR, WHAT—
AH!
ALPHA!
KILL THE RABBIT CO. AGENT.
I KNOW WHAT TO DO, SIR.
TUK TUK
COULD YOU PASS ME THAT BOOK ON THE CHAIR, PLEASE?
I THINK MY DAUGHTER LEFT IT BEHIND.
SURE.

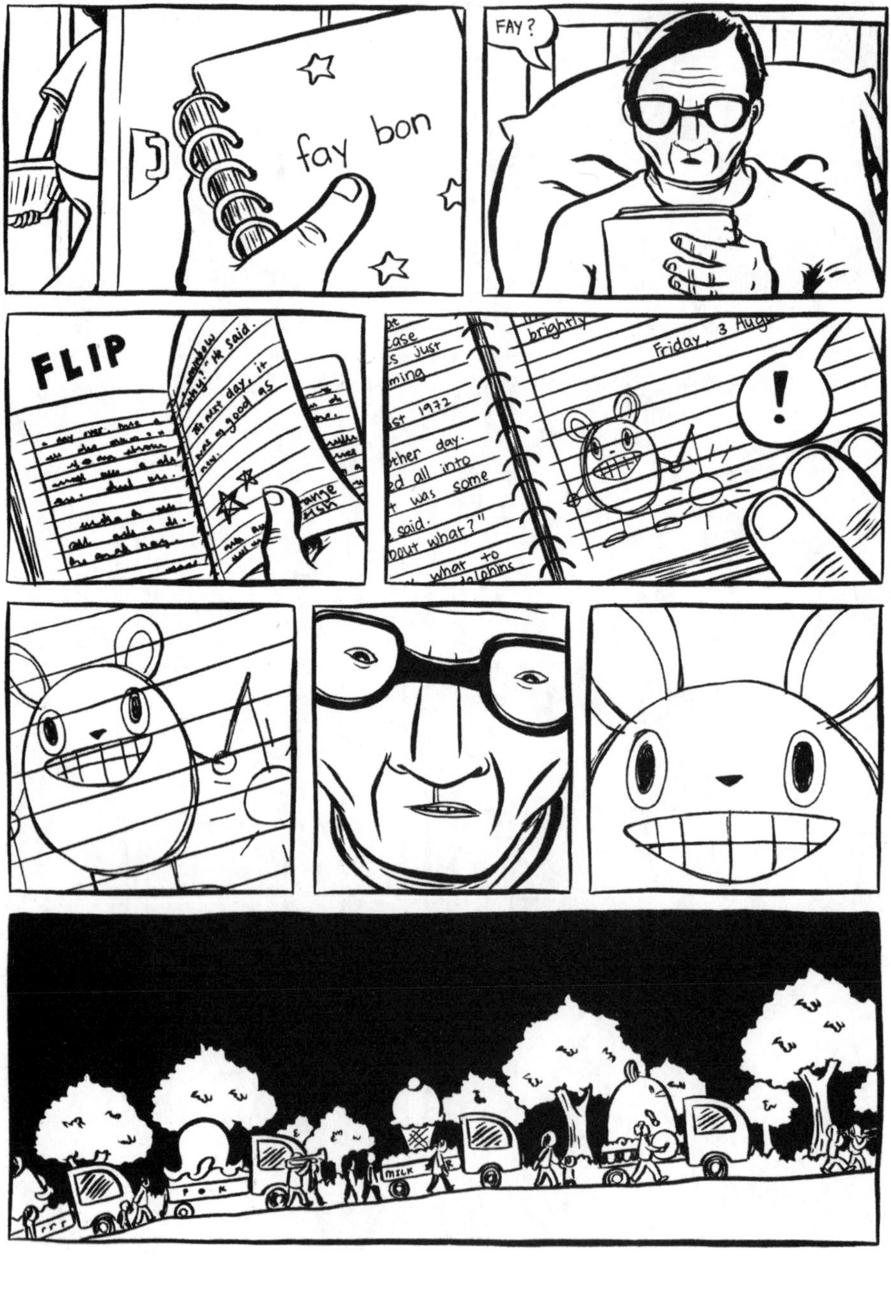
fay bon
FAY?
FLIP
!

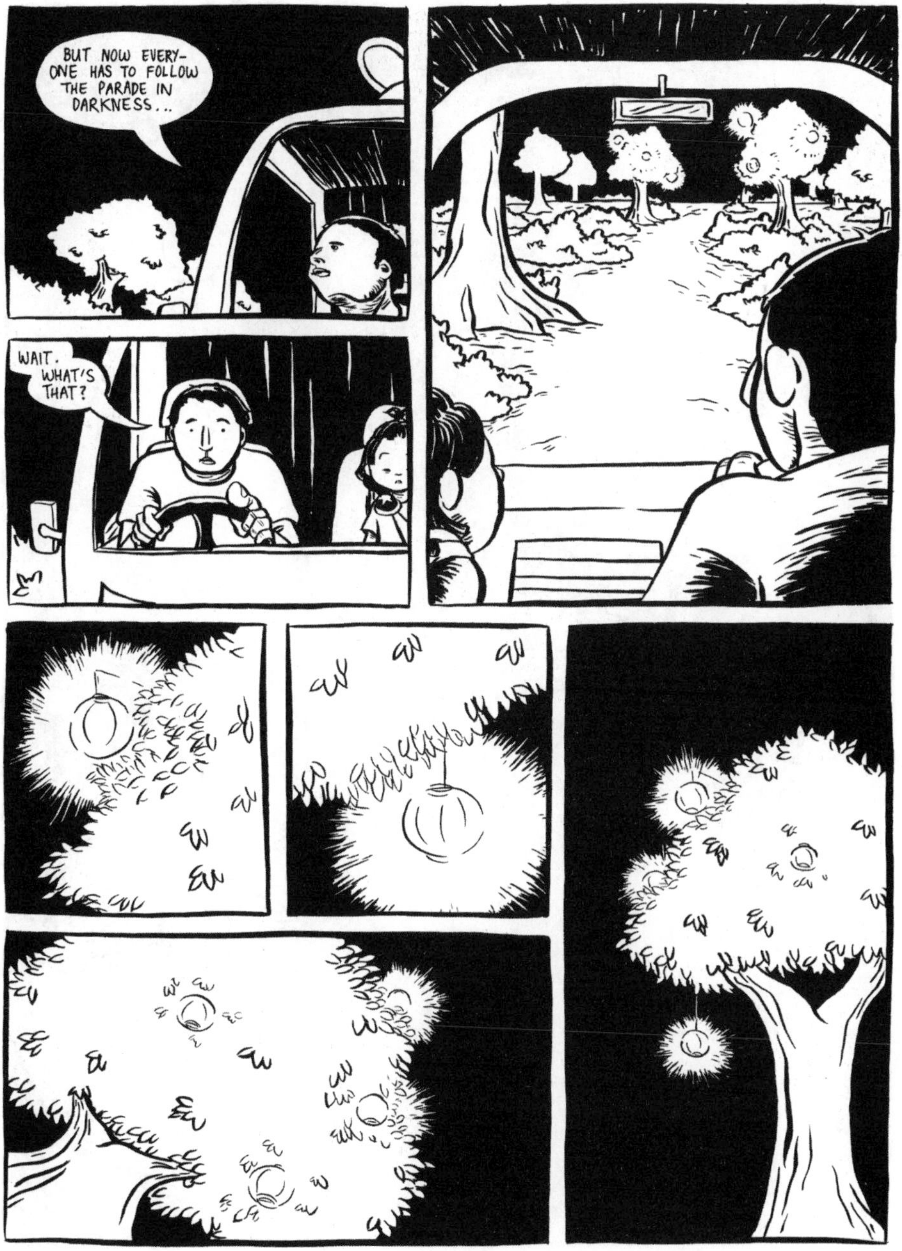
BUT NOW EVERY-ONE HAS TO FOLLOW THE PARADE IN DARKNESS...
WAIT. WHAT'S THAT?

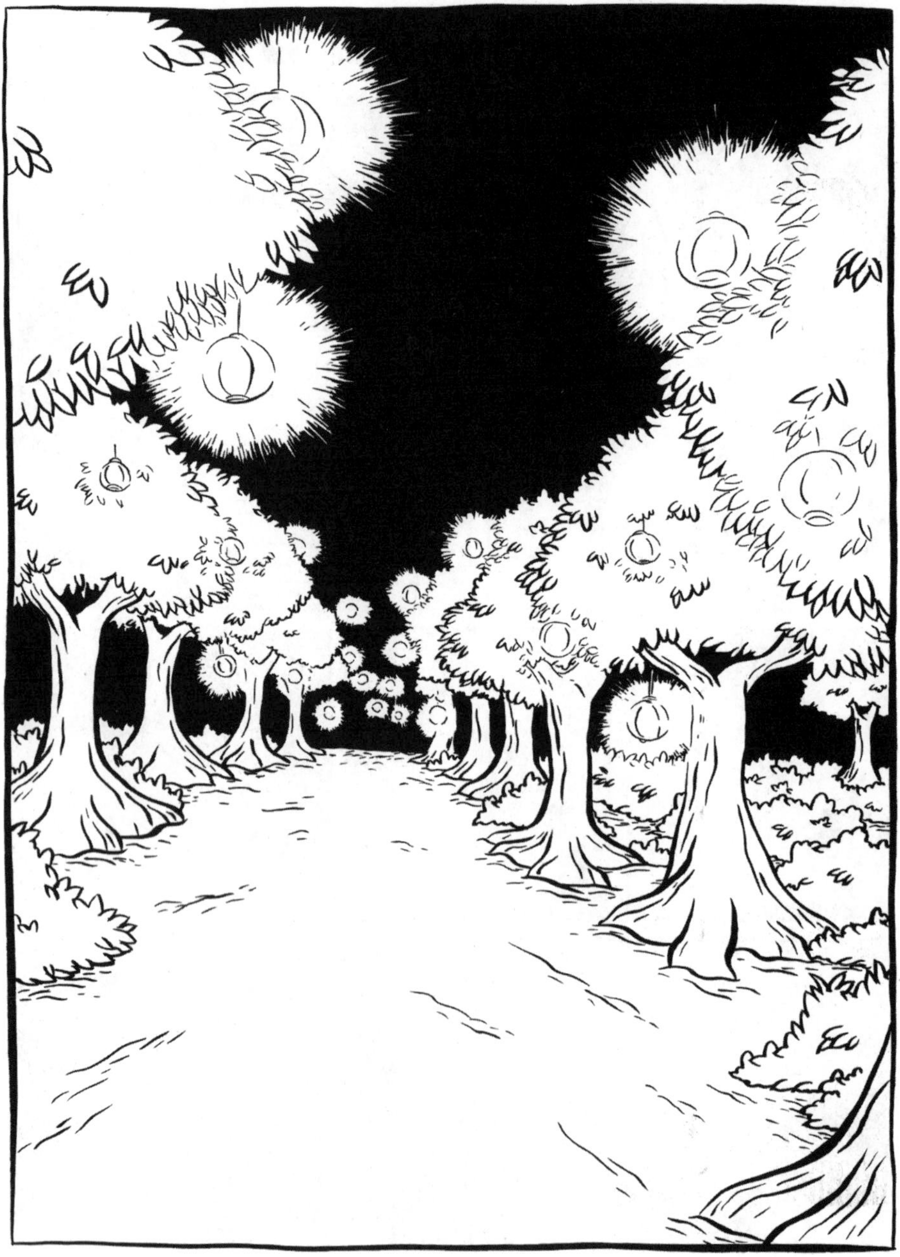

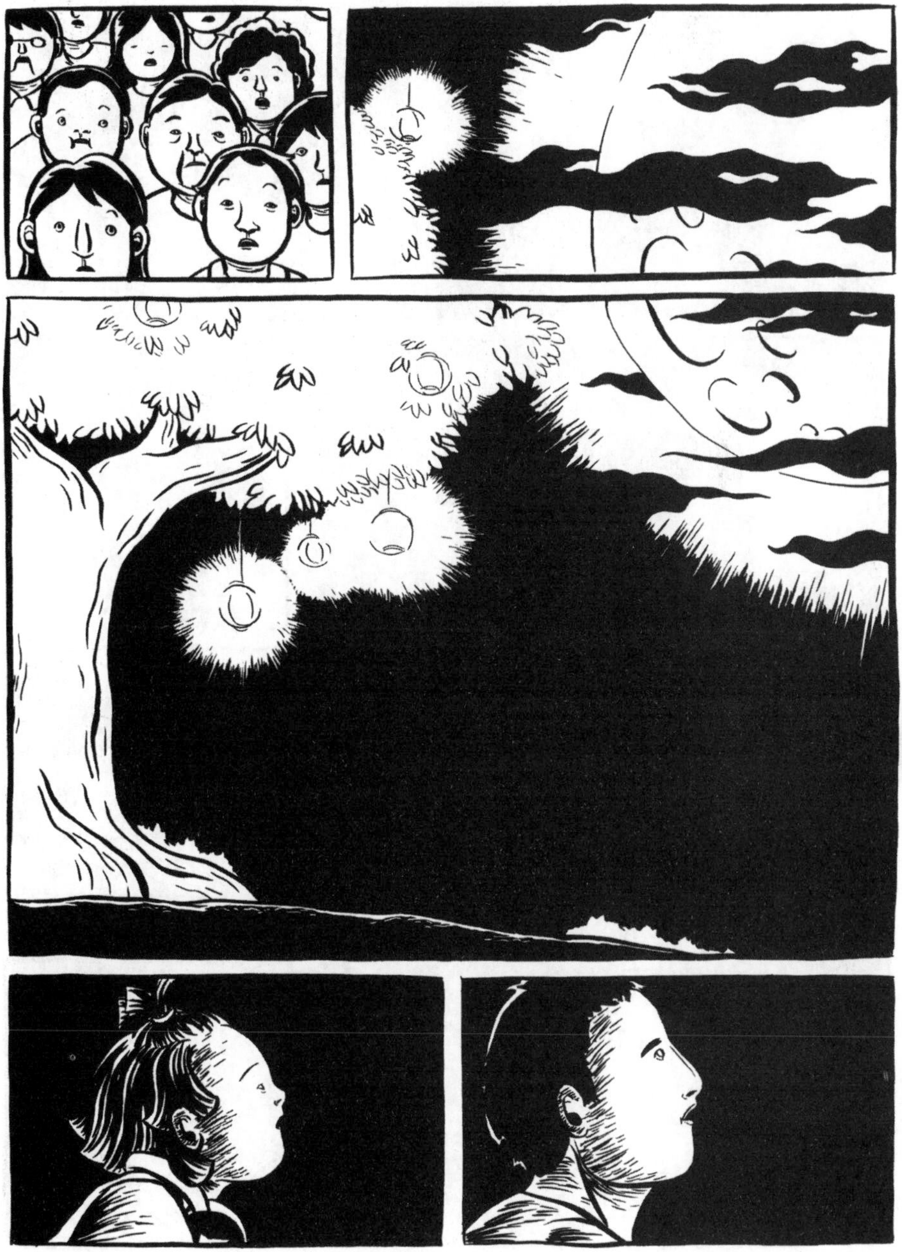

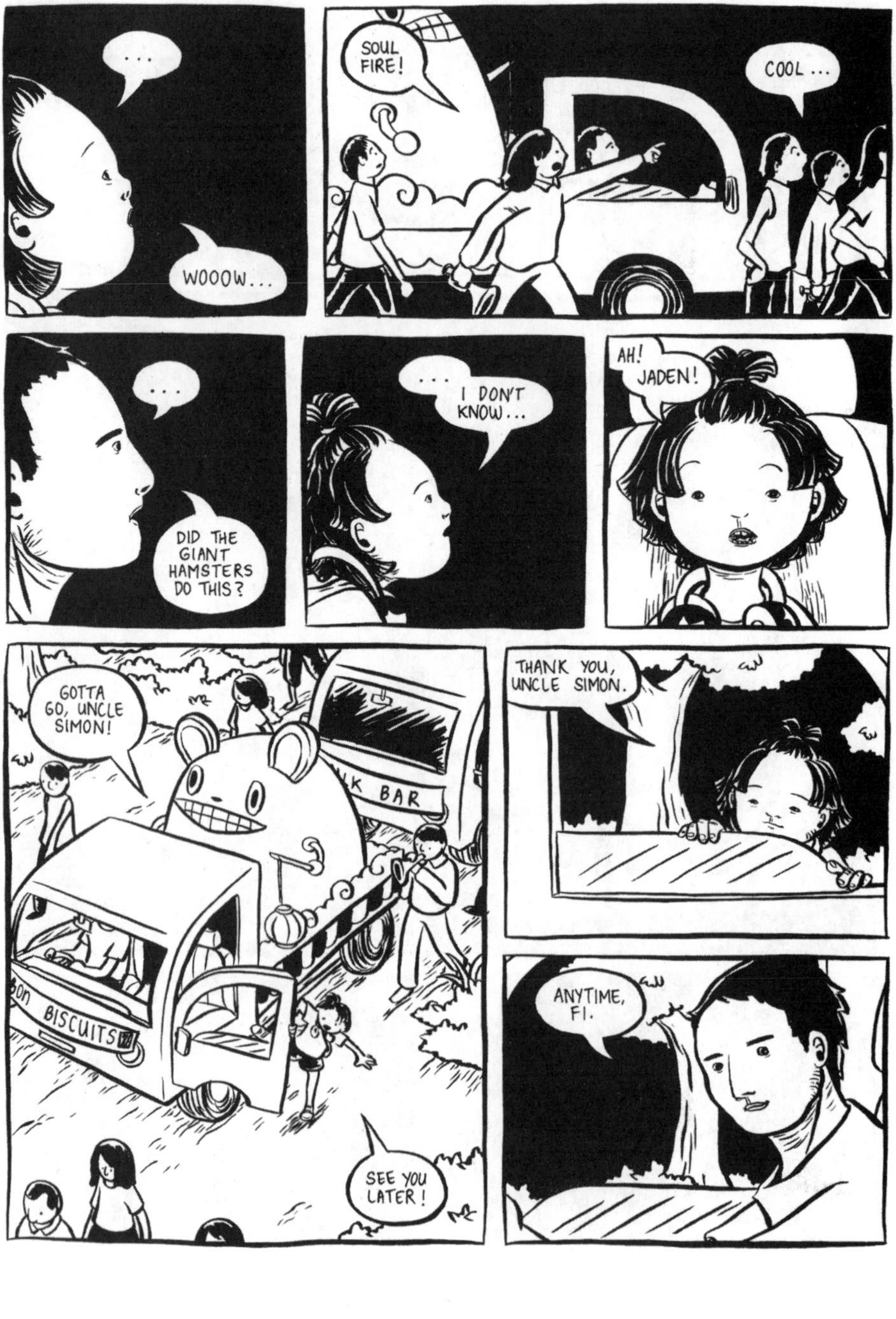
. . .
WOOOW...
SOUL FIRE!
COOL...
. . .
DID THE GIANT HAMSTERS DO THIS?
. . .
I DON'T KNOW...
AH! JADEN!
GOTTA GO, UNCLE SIMON!
K BAR
BISCUITS
SEE YOU LATER!
THANK YOU, UNCLE SIMON.
ANYTIME, FI.

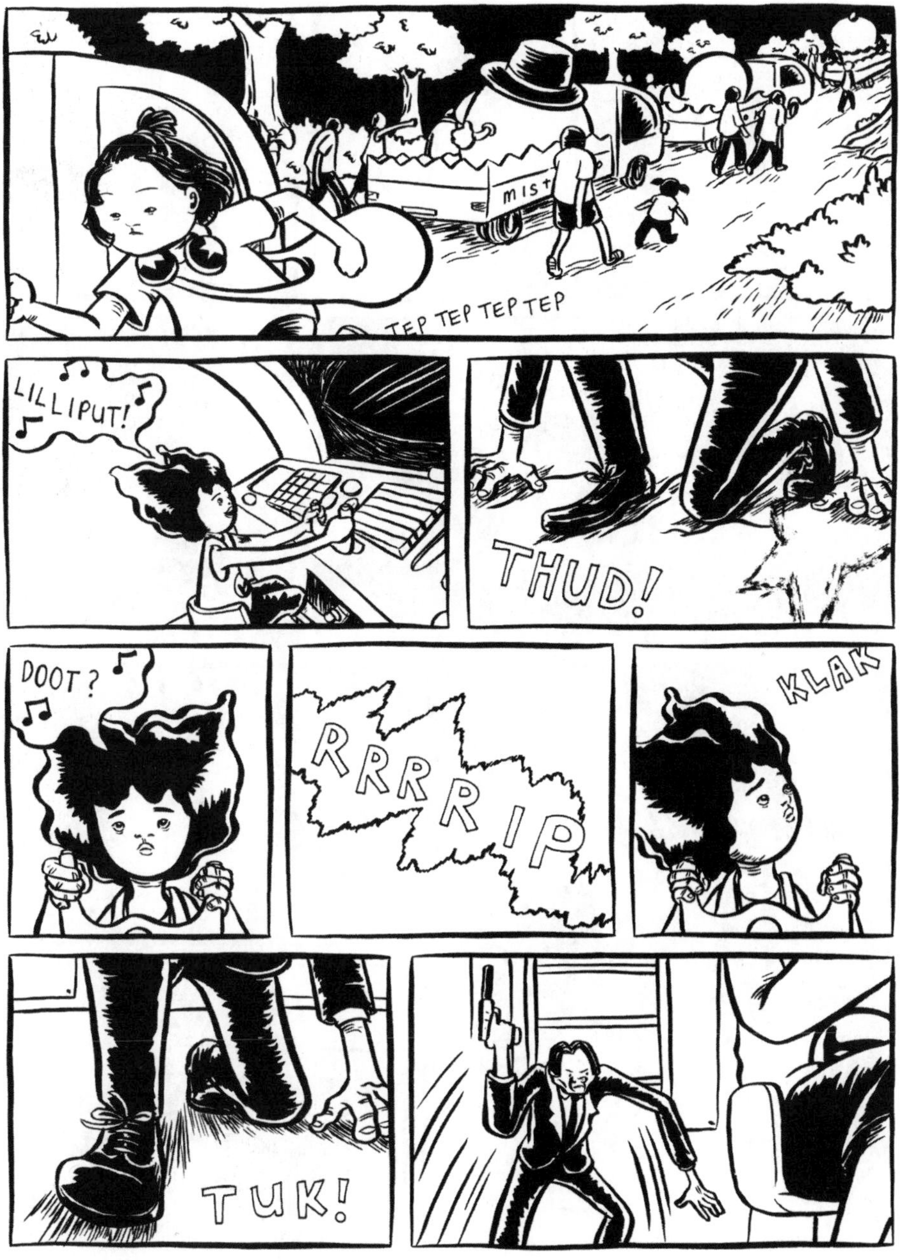
mist
TEP TEP TEP TEP
LILLIPUT!
THUD!
DOOT?
RRRRRIP
KLAK
TUK!

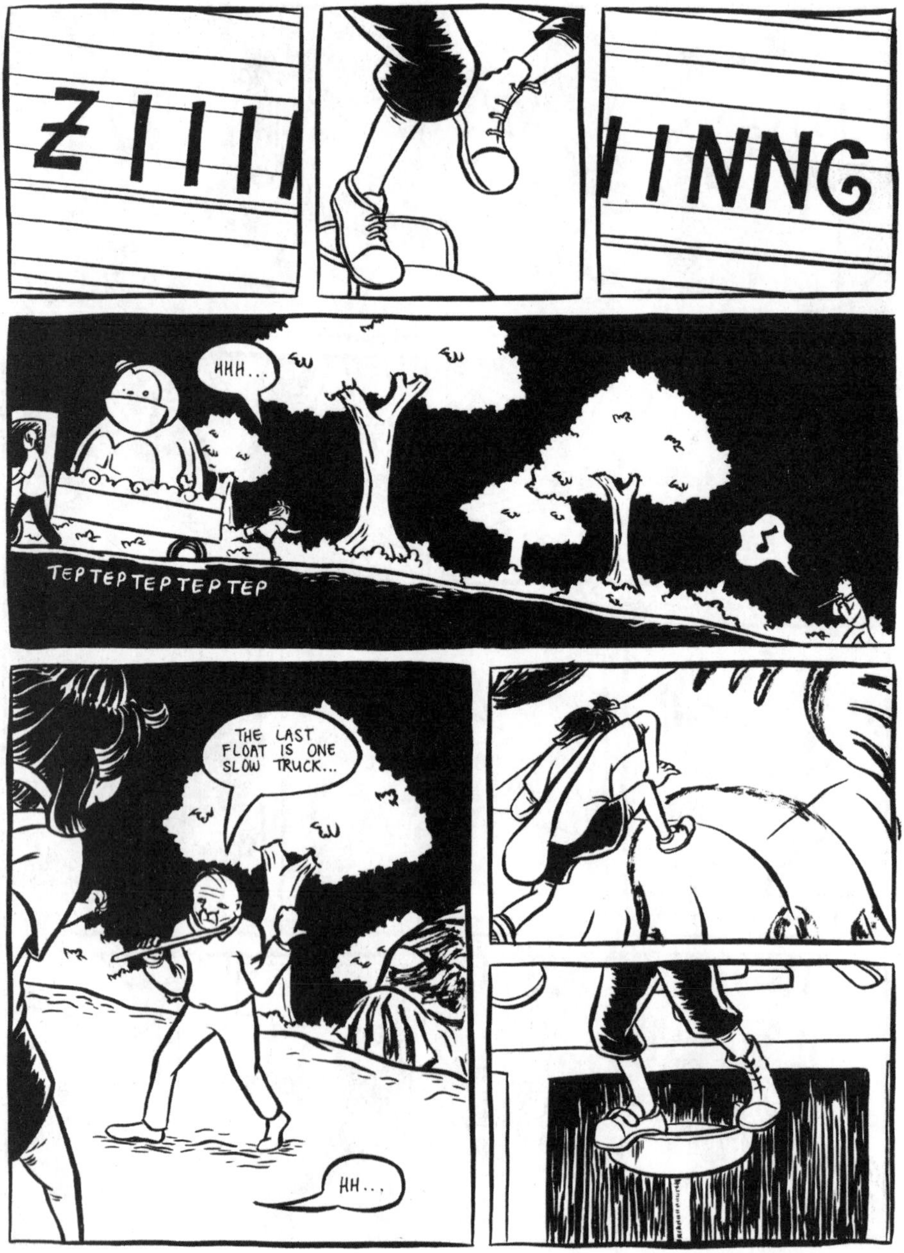
ZIIII
IINNG
HHH...
TEPTEPTEPTEPTEP
THE LAST FLOAT IS ONE SLOW TRUCK...
HH...

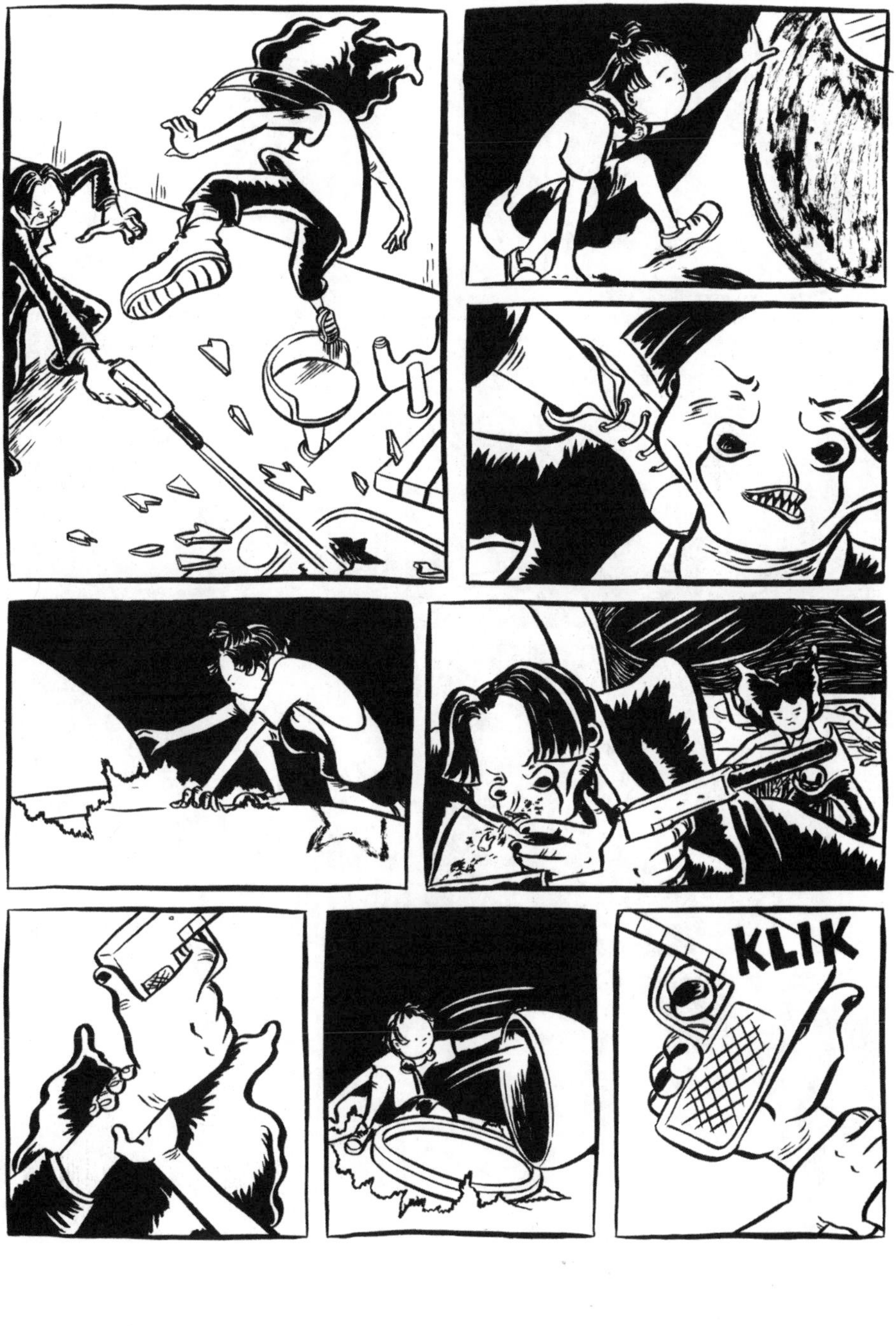
KLIK

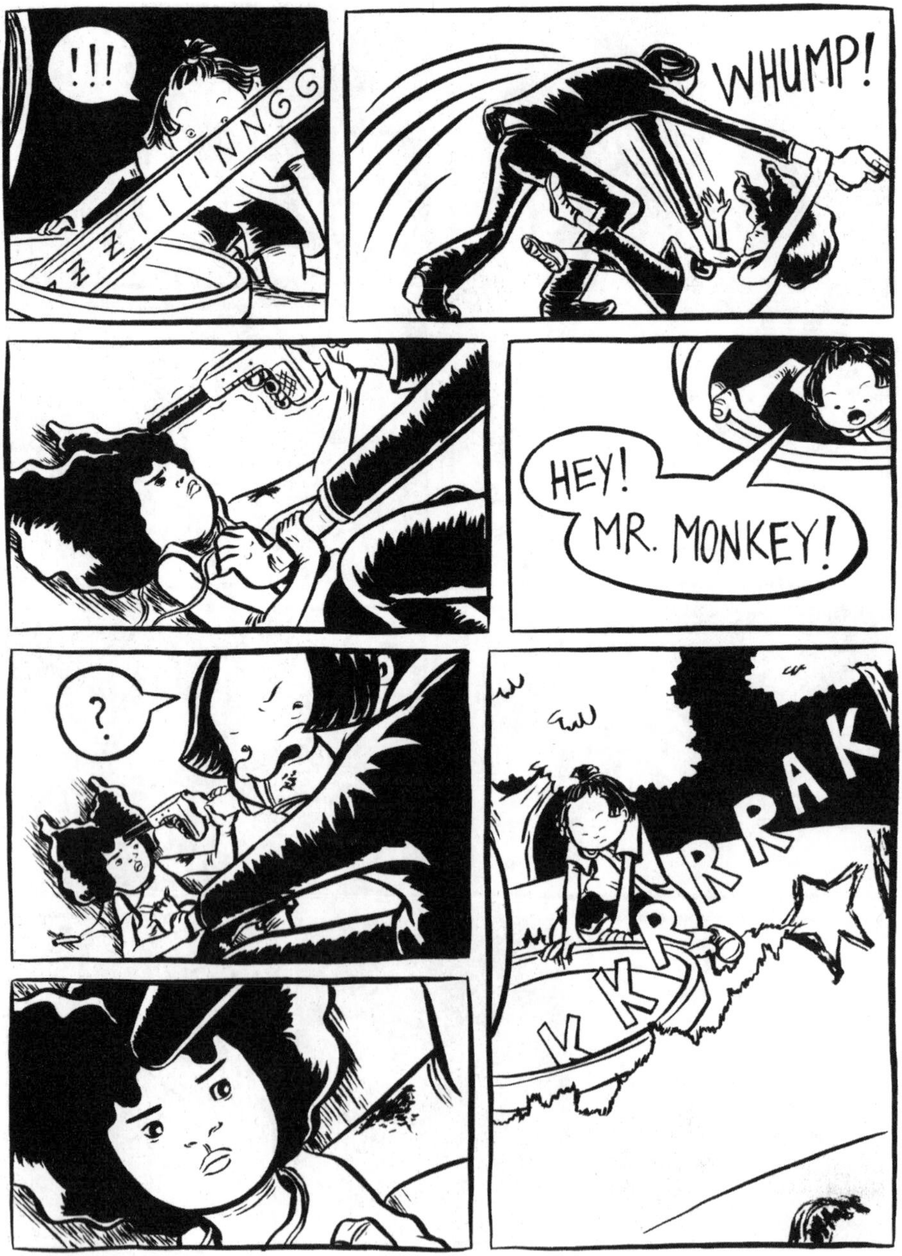
!!!
ZZZIIIINNGG
WHUMP!
HEY! MR. MONKEY!
?
KKRRRRAK

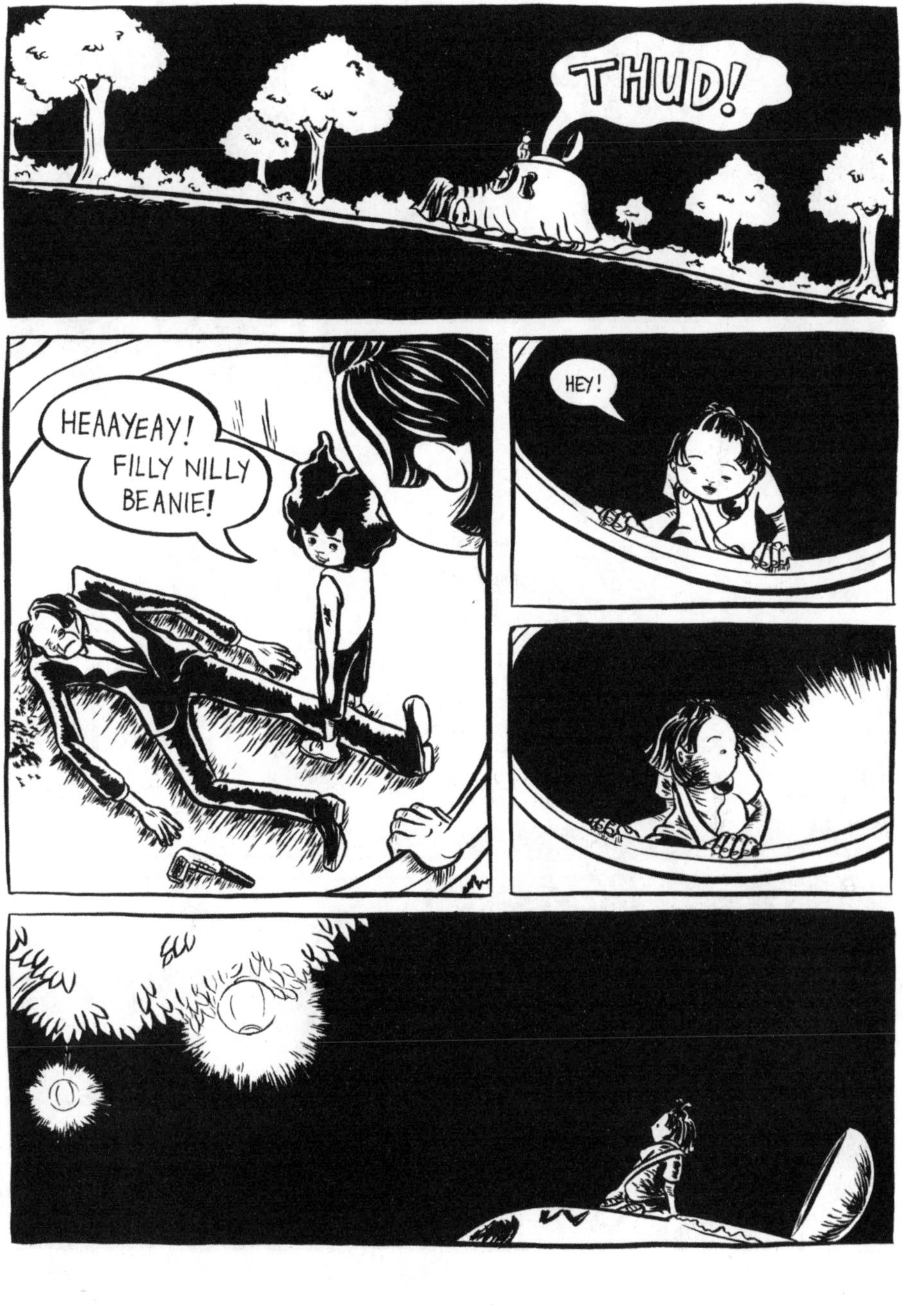
THUD!
HEAAYEAY! FILLY NILLY BEANIE!
HEY!

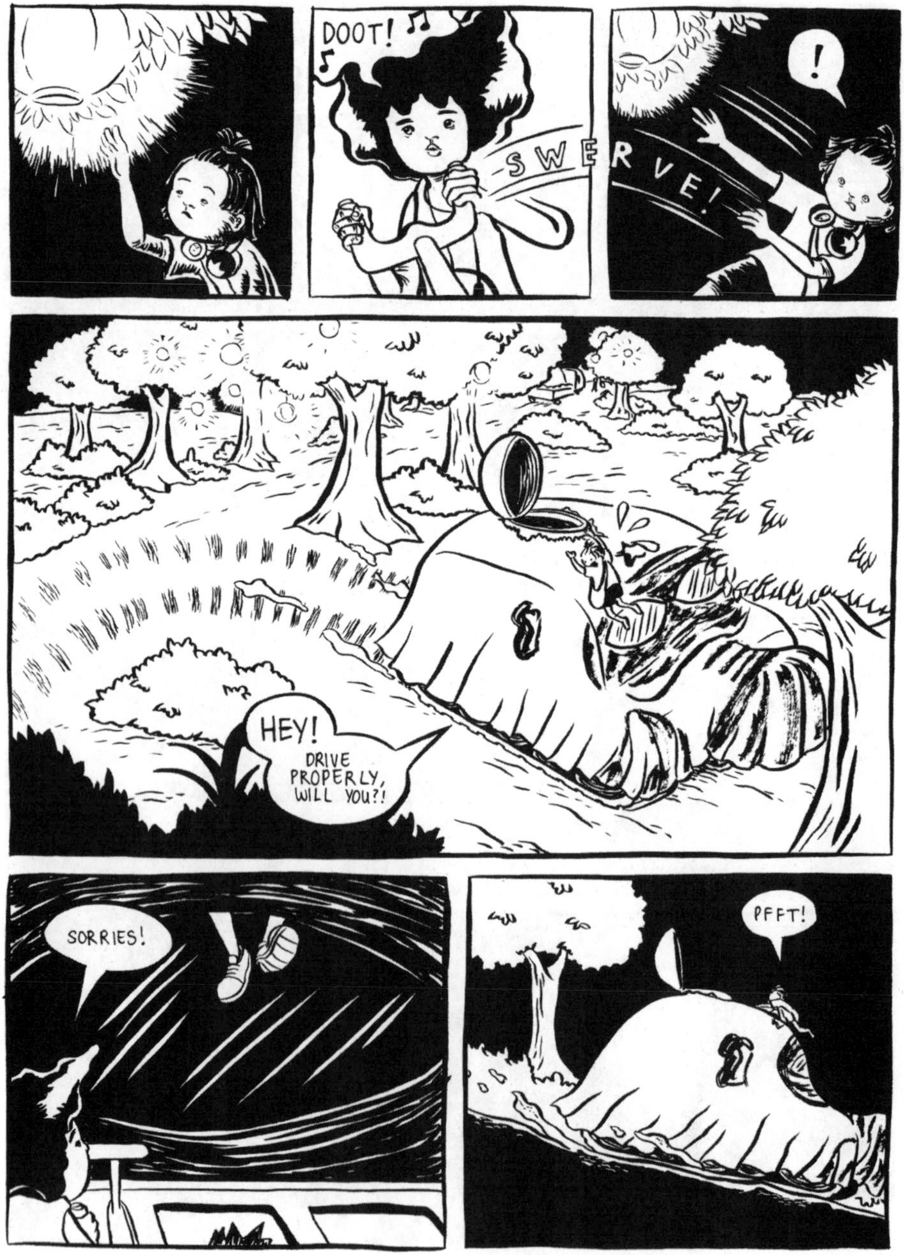
DOOT!
SWERVE!
!
HEY!
DRIVE PROPERLY, WILL YOU?!
SORRIES!
PFFT!

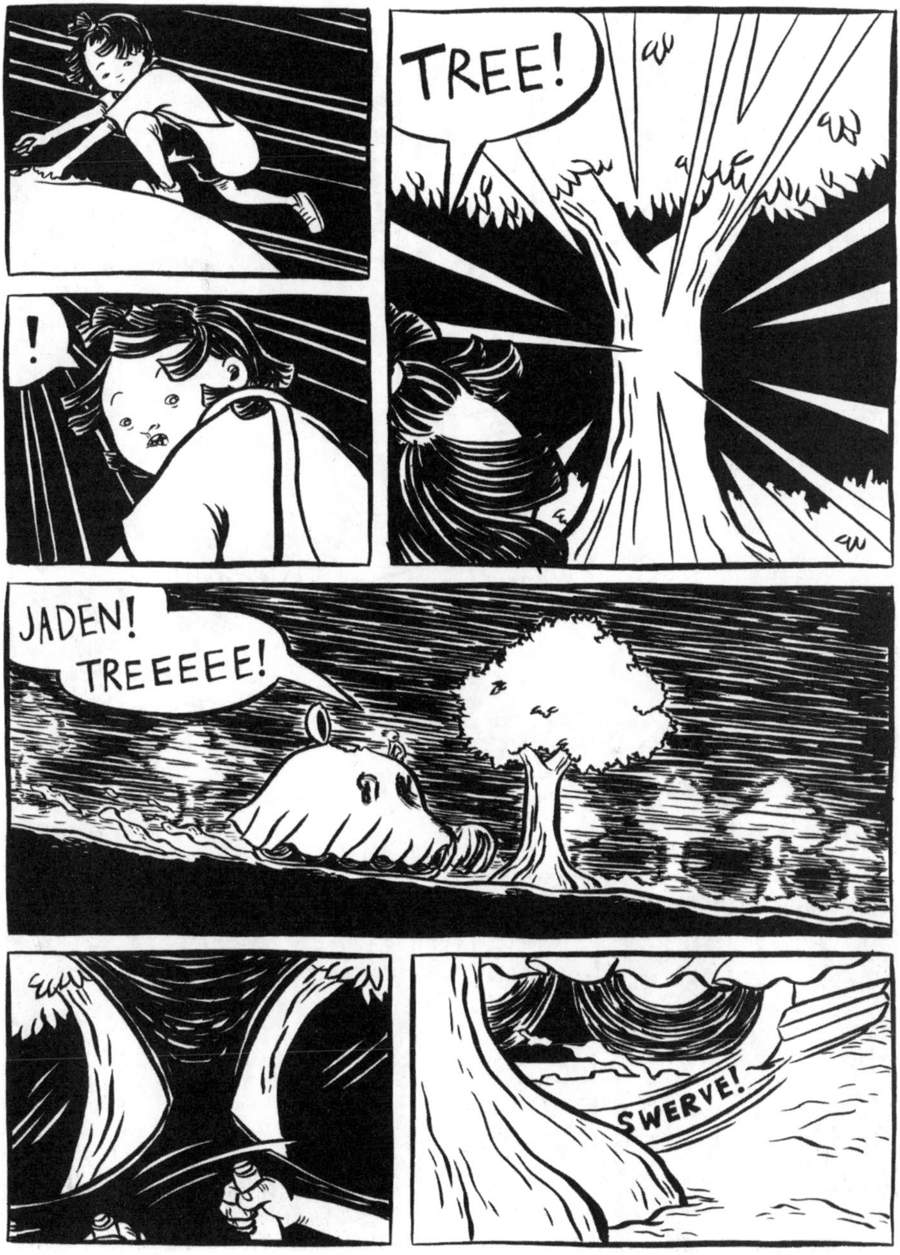
TREE!
!
JADEN! TREEEEE!
SWERVE!

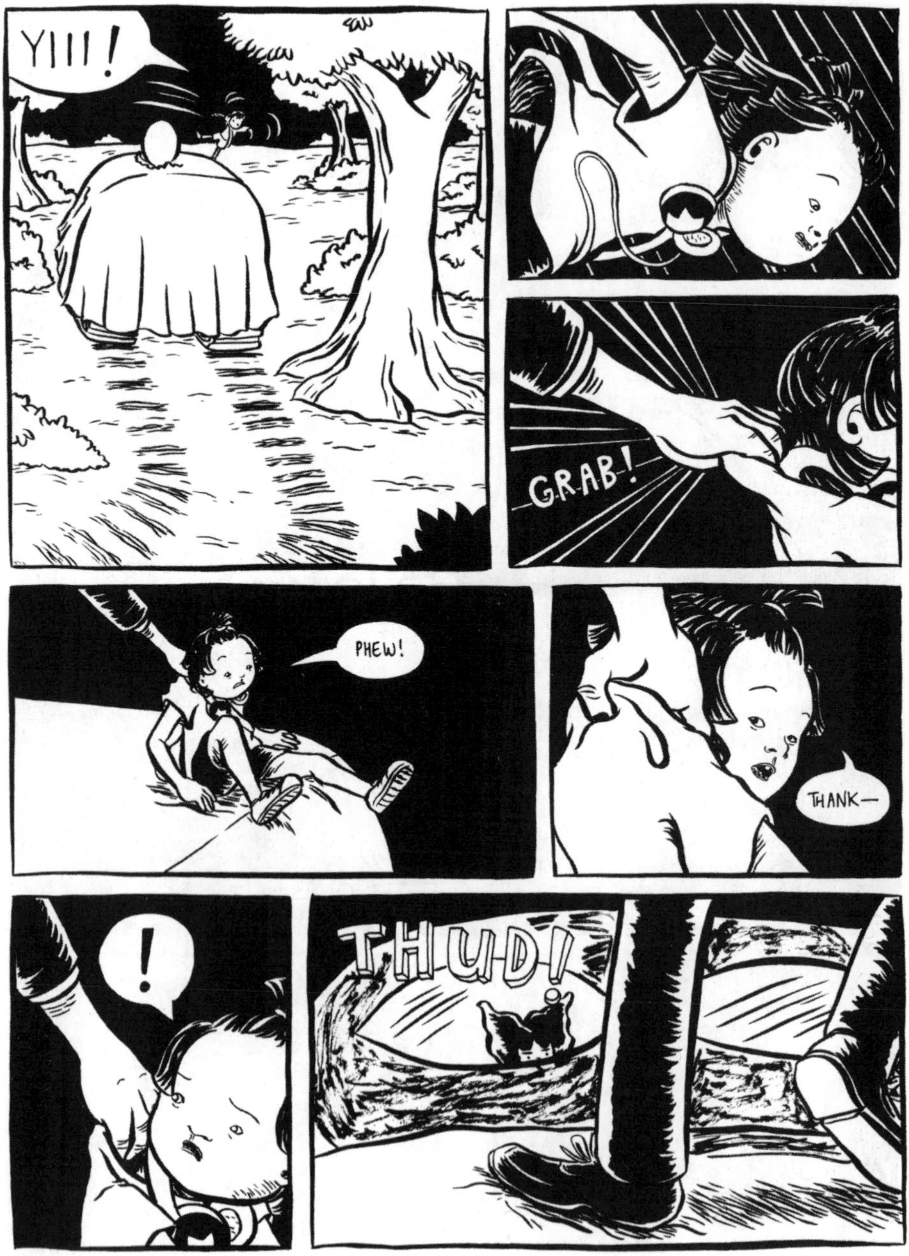
YIII!
GRAB!
PHEW!
THANK—
!
THUD!

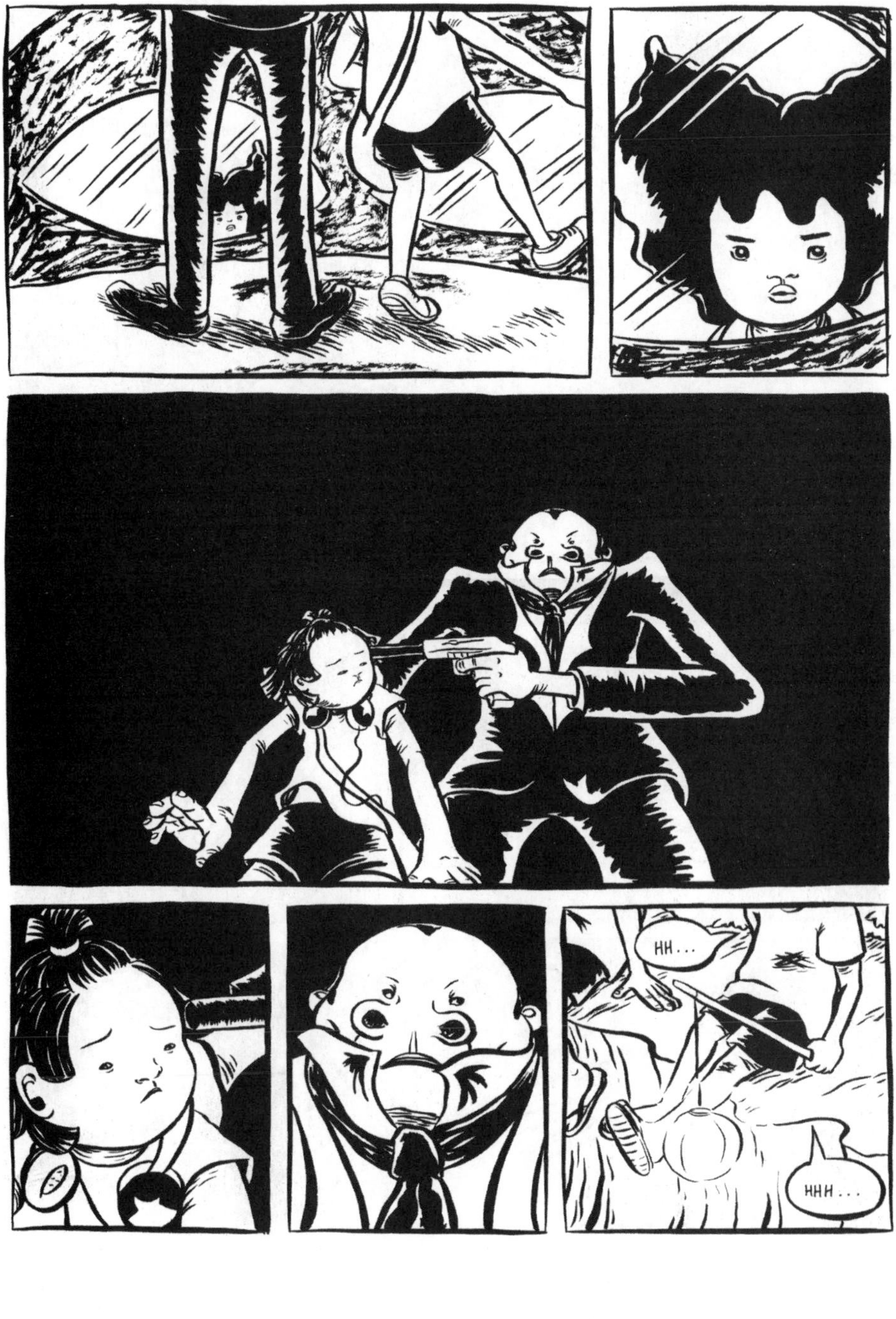
HH...
HHH...

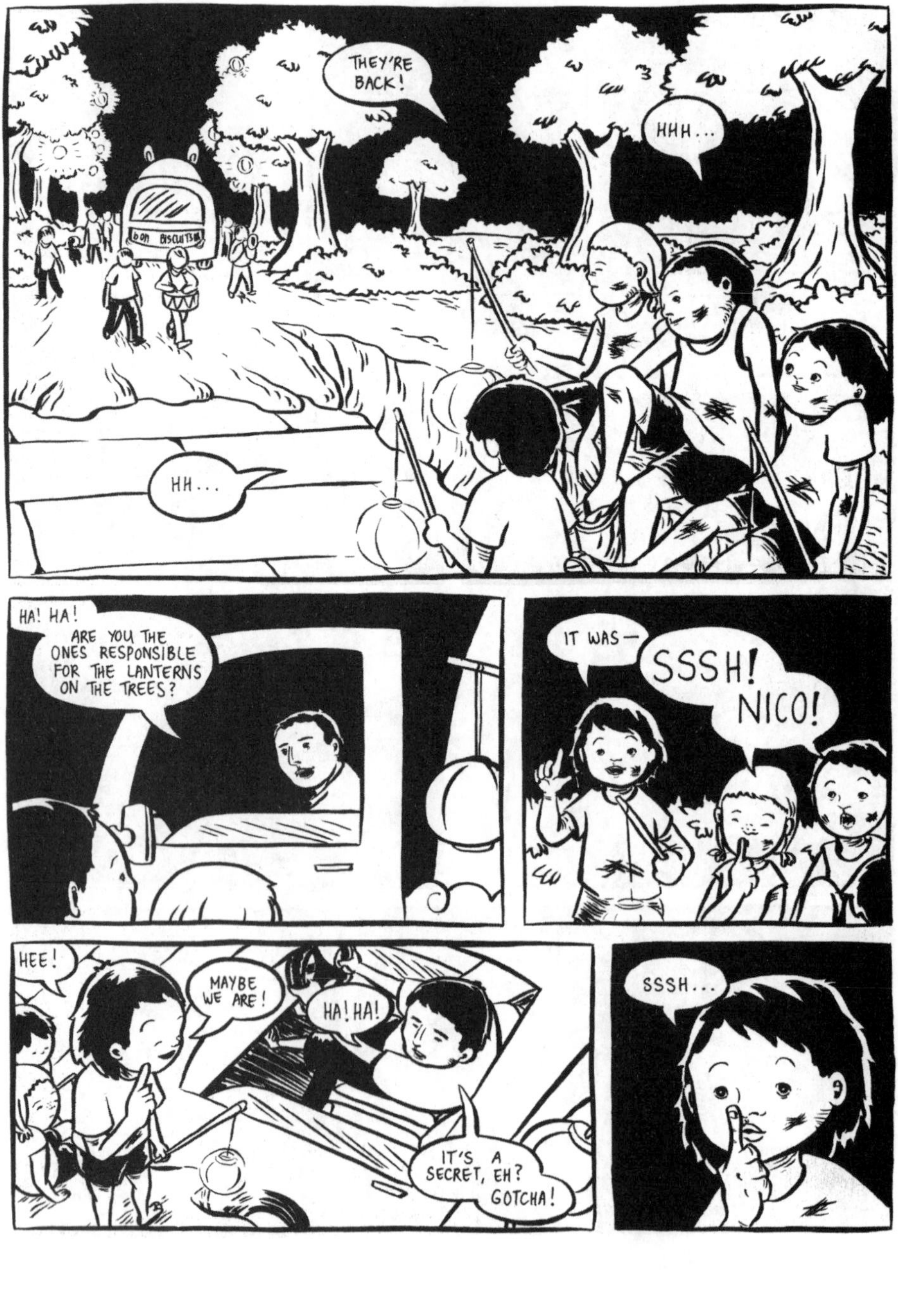
THEY'RE BACK!
HHH...
BON BISCUITS
HH...
HA! HA!
ARE YOU THE ONES RESPONSIBLE FOR THE LANTERNS ON THE TREES?
IT WAS—
SSSH! NICO!
HEE!
MAYBE WE ARE!
HA! HA!
IT'S A SECRET, EH? GOTCHA!
SSSH...

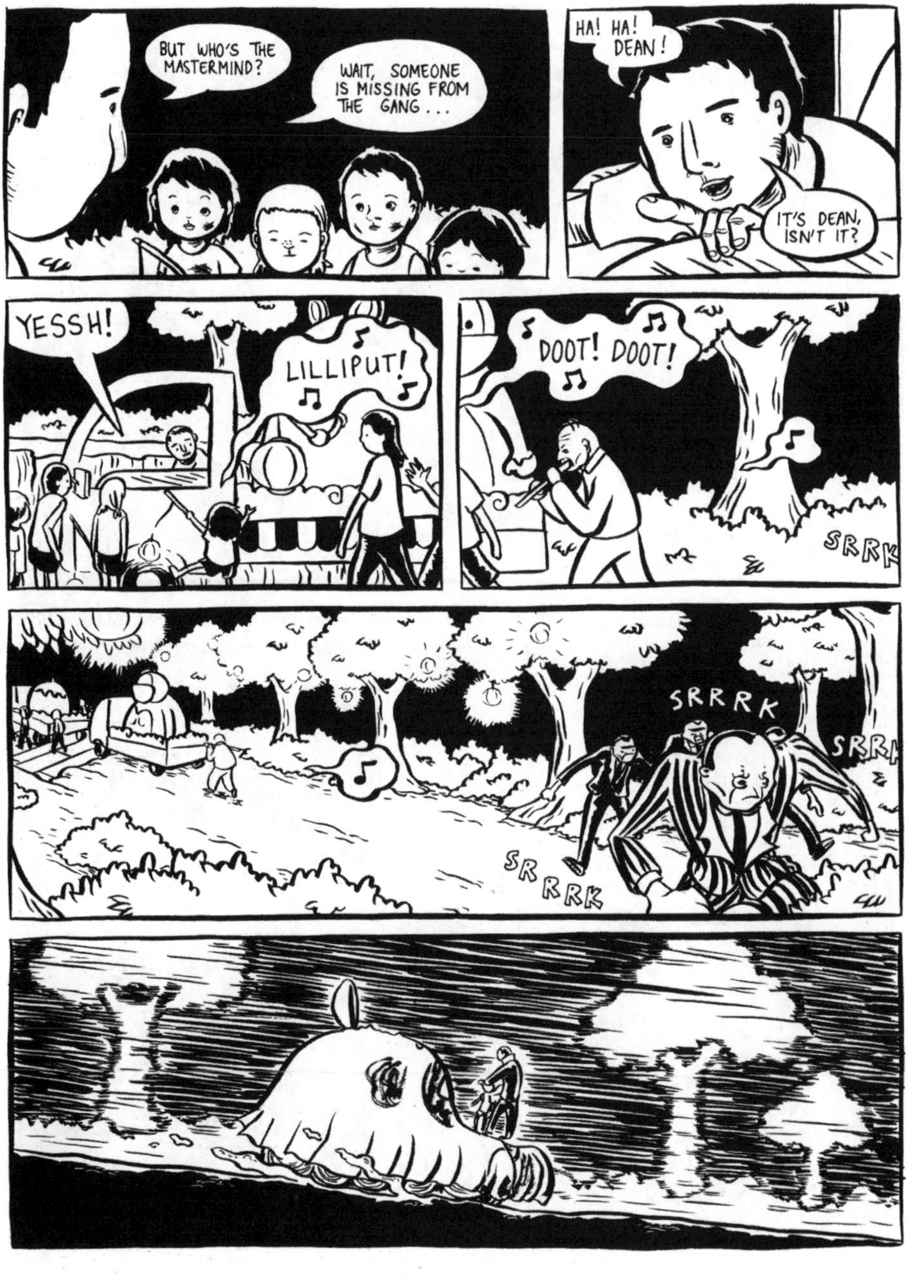
BUT WHO'S THE MASTERMIND?
WAIT, SOMEONE IS MISSING FROM THE GANG...
HA! HA! DEAN!
IT'S DEAN, ISN'T IT?
YESSH!
LILLIPUT!
DOOT! DOOT!
SRRK
SRRRK
SRRK
SRRRK

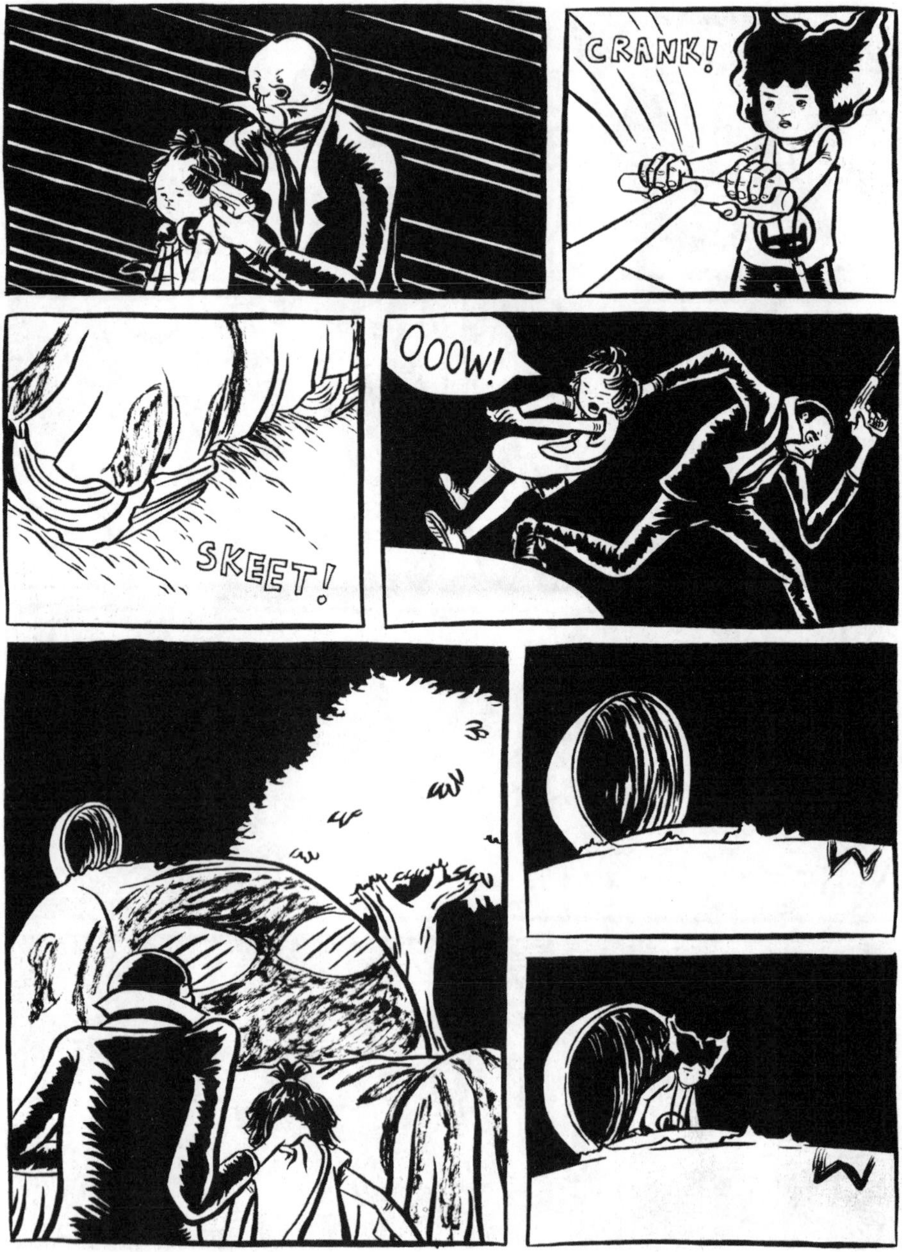
CRANK!
SKEET!
OOOW!

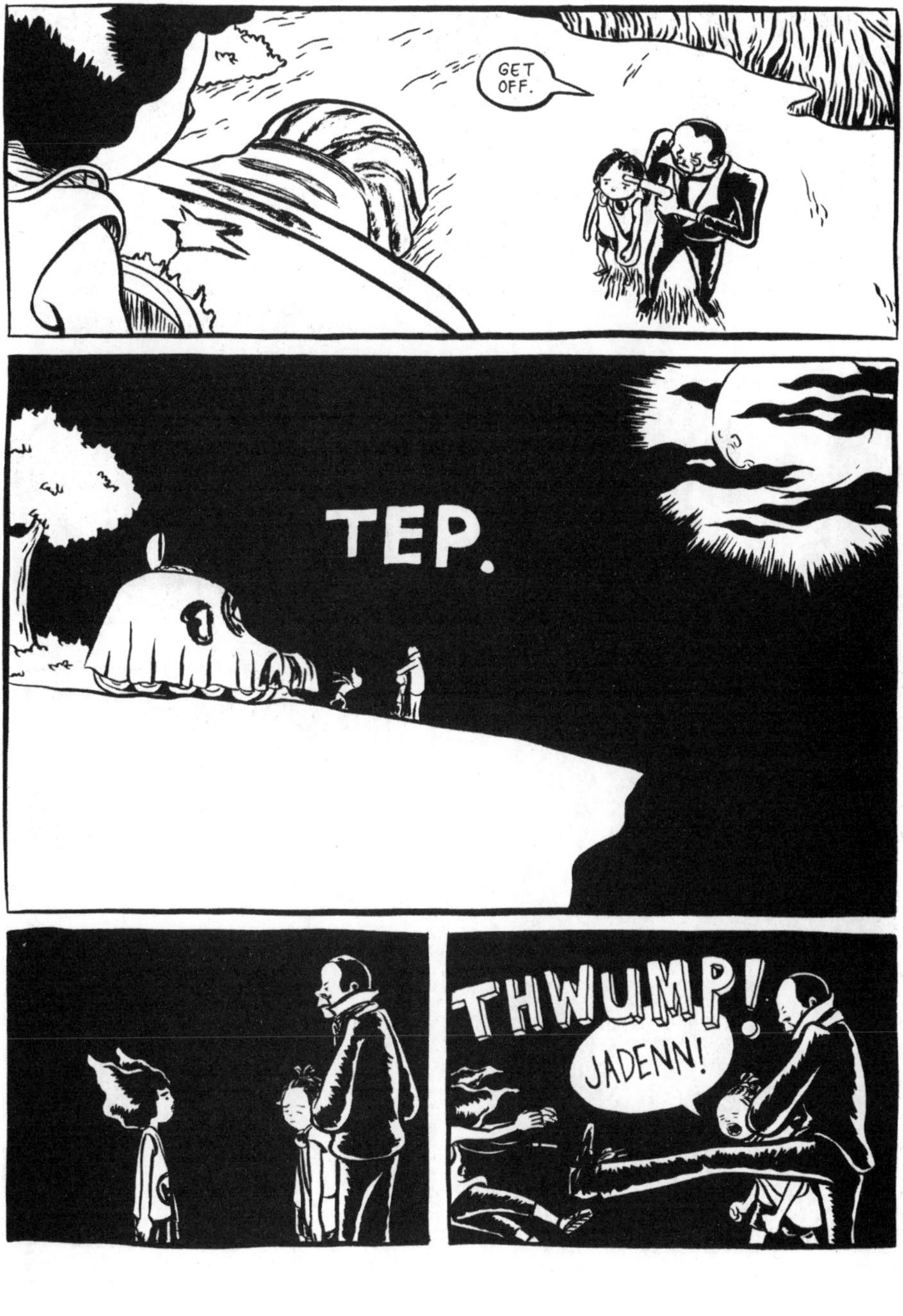
GET OFF.
TEP.
THWUMP!
JADENN!

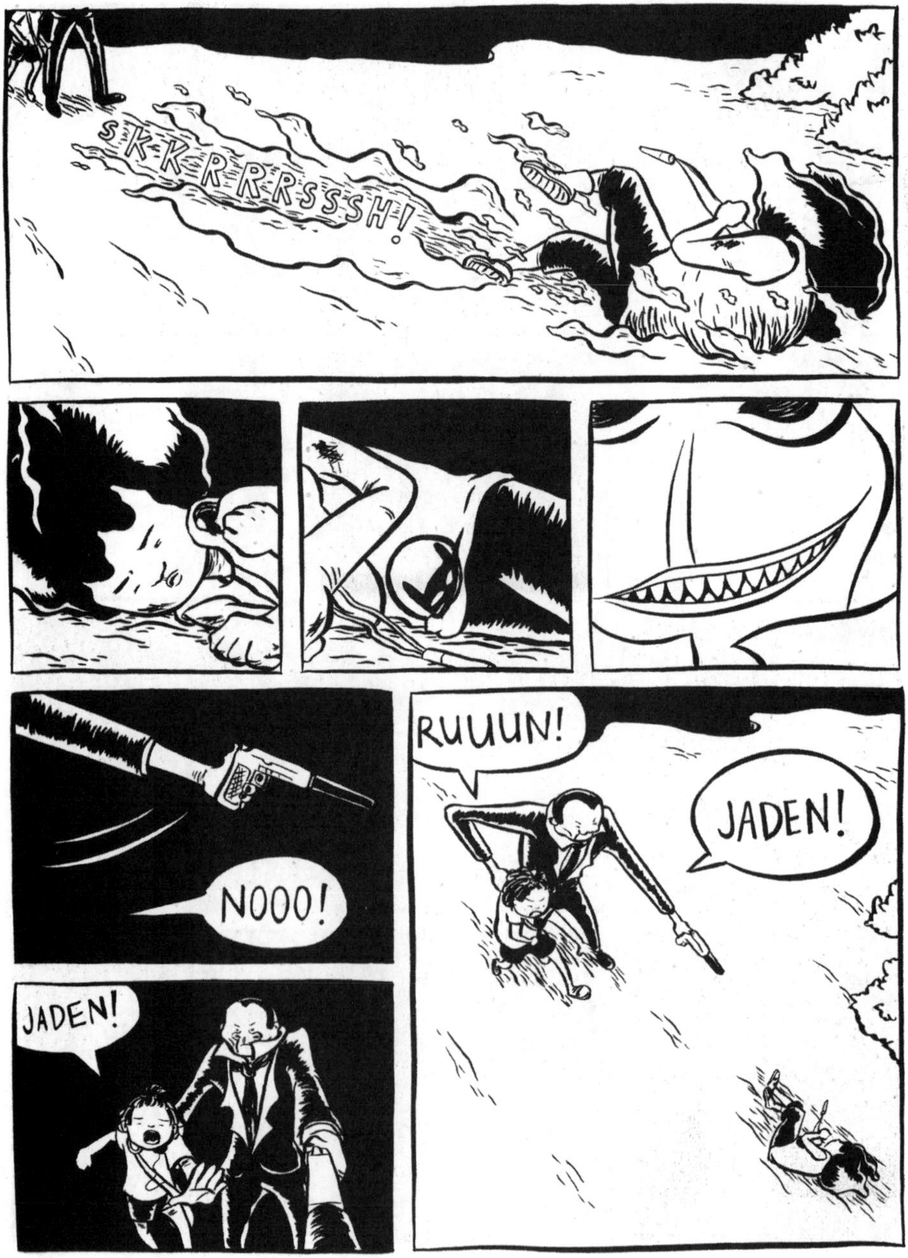
SKKRRRRSSSSH!
NOOO!
JADEN!
RUUUN!
JADEN!

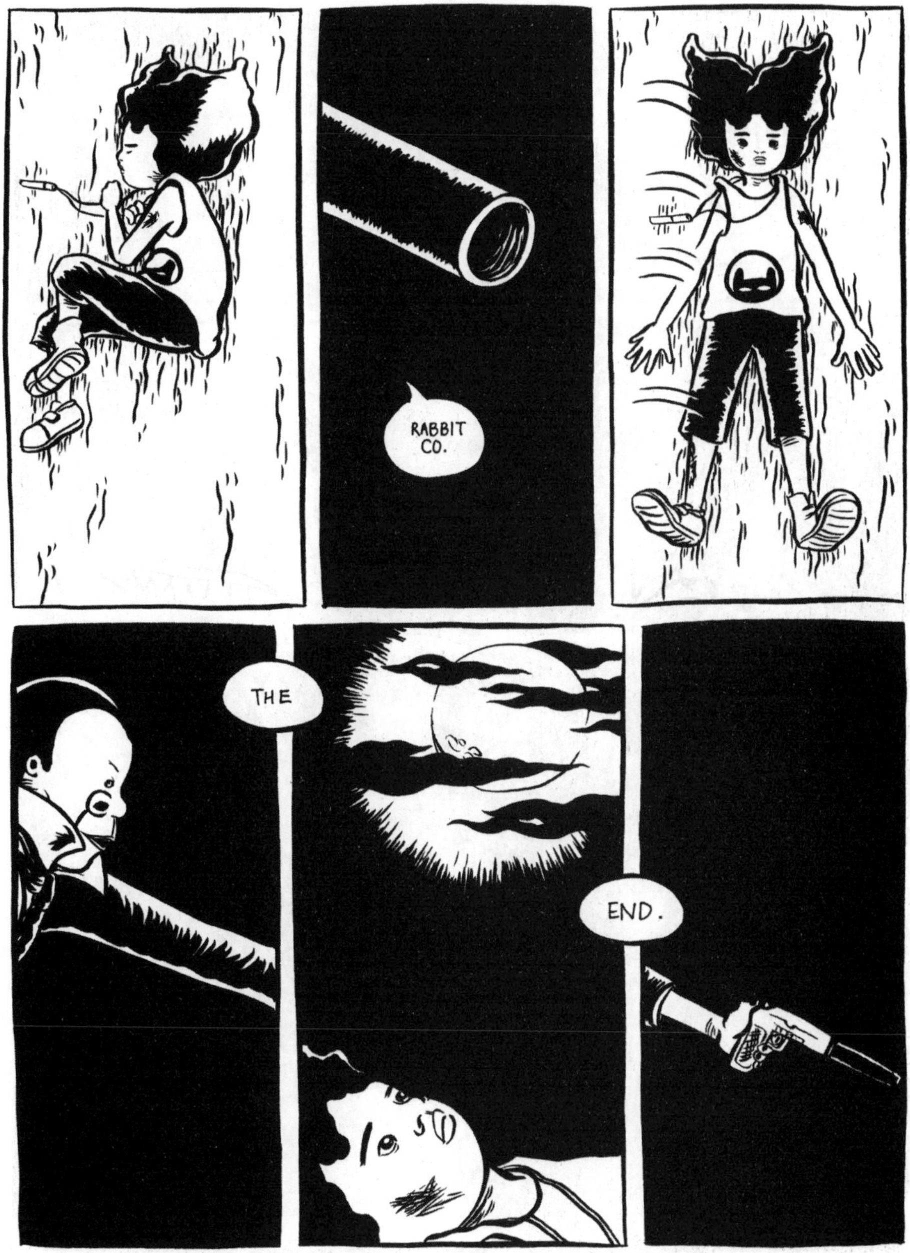
RABBIT CO.
THE
END.

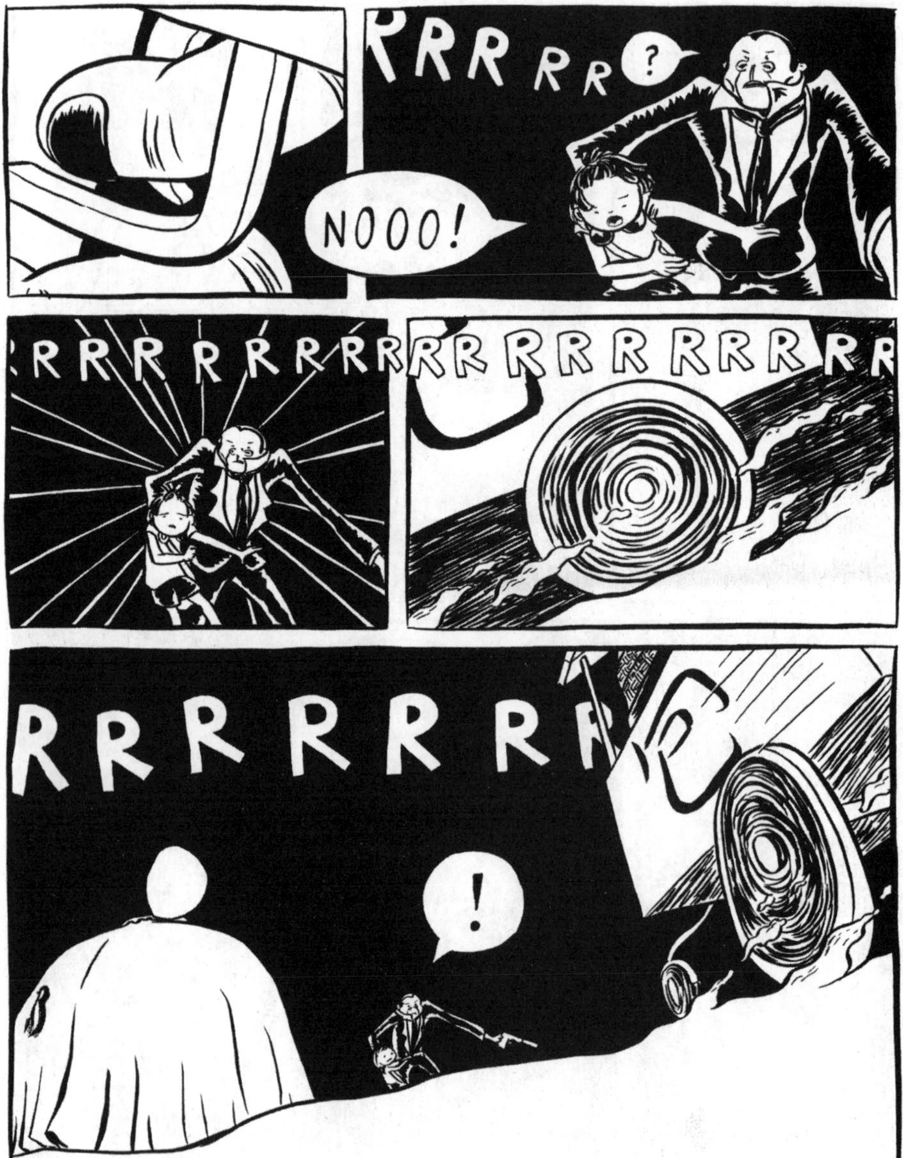
RRRRR
?
NOOO!
RRRRRRRRRRRRRRRRRRR
RRRRRRR
!

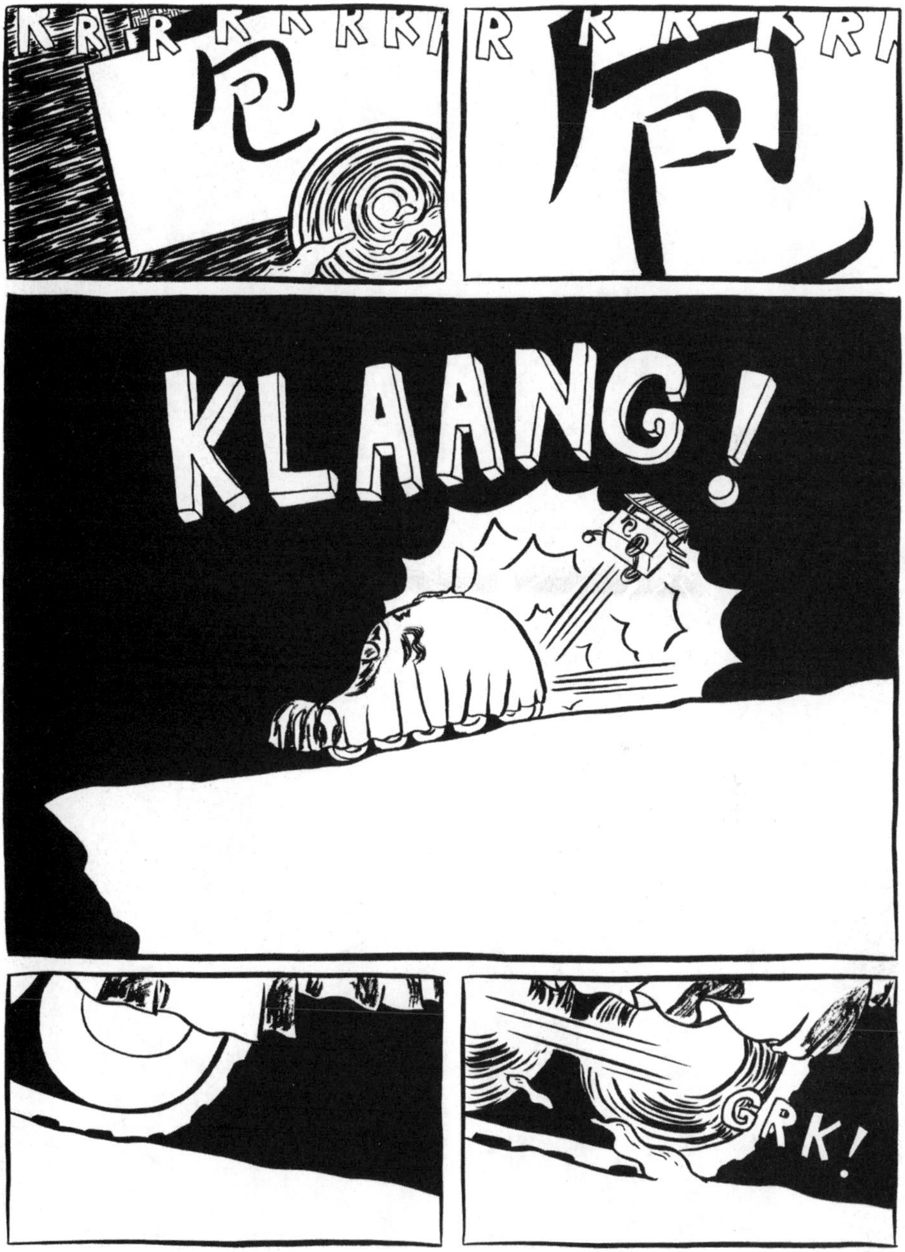
KLAANG!
GRK!

SKRRRRRRRR

RRRRR

!!!

GRRK...

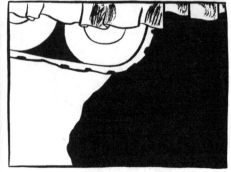

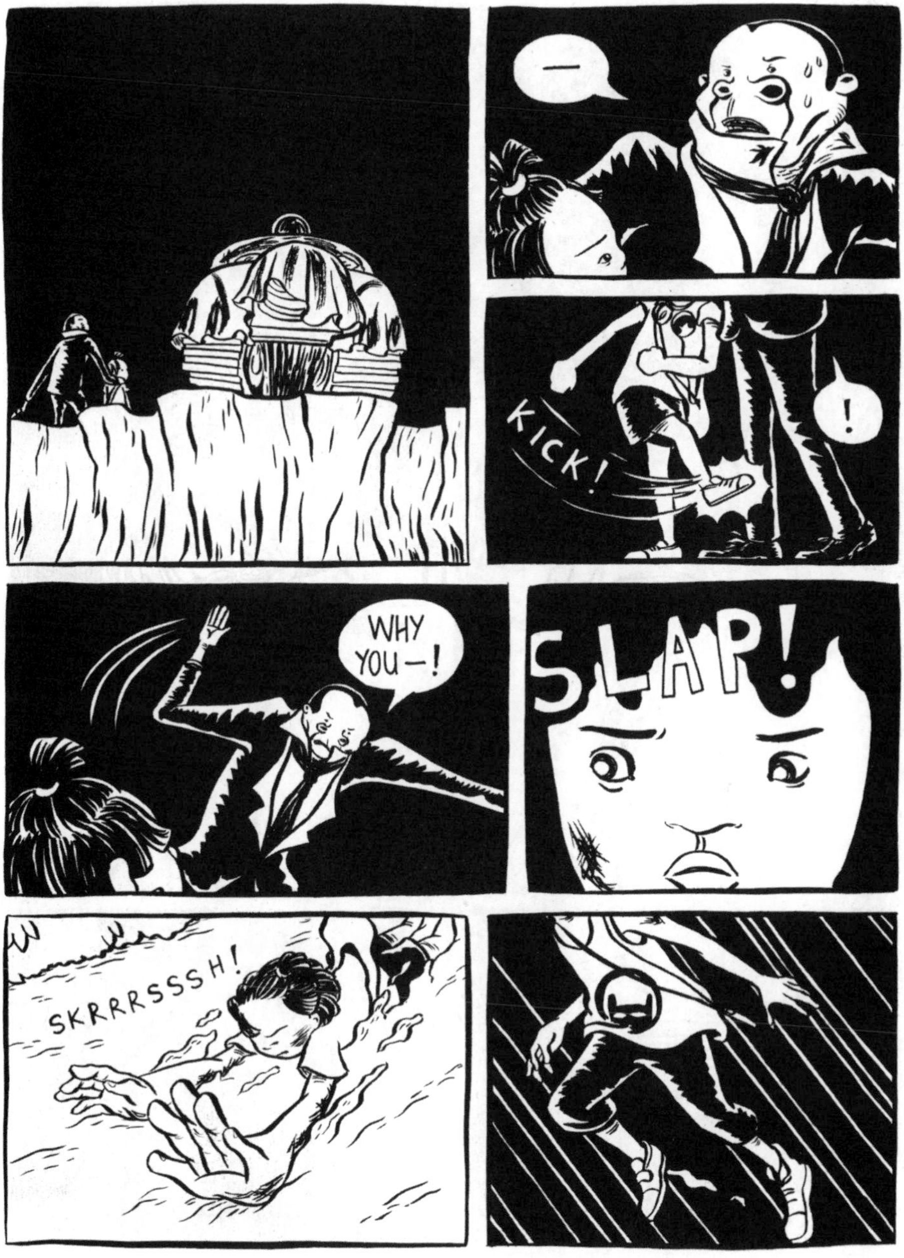
—
KICK!
!
WHY YOU—!
SLAP!
SKRRRSSSH!

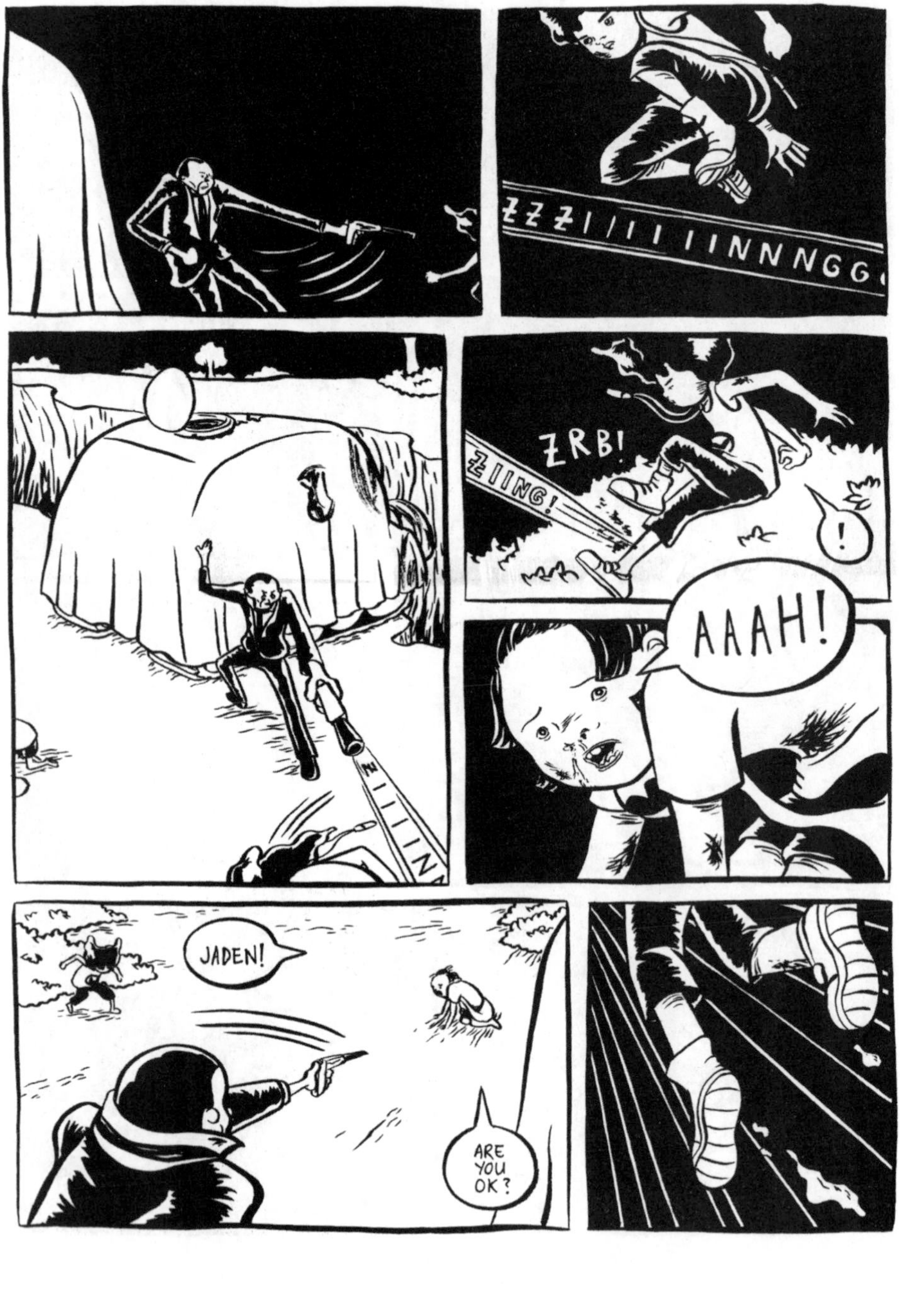
ZZZIIIIII IINNNGG
ZRB!
ZIING!
!
AAAH!
JADEN!
ARE YOU OK?

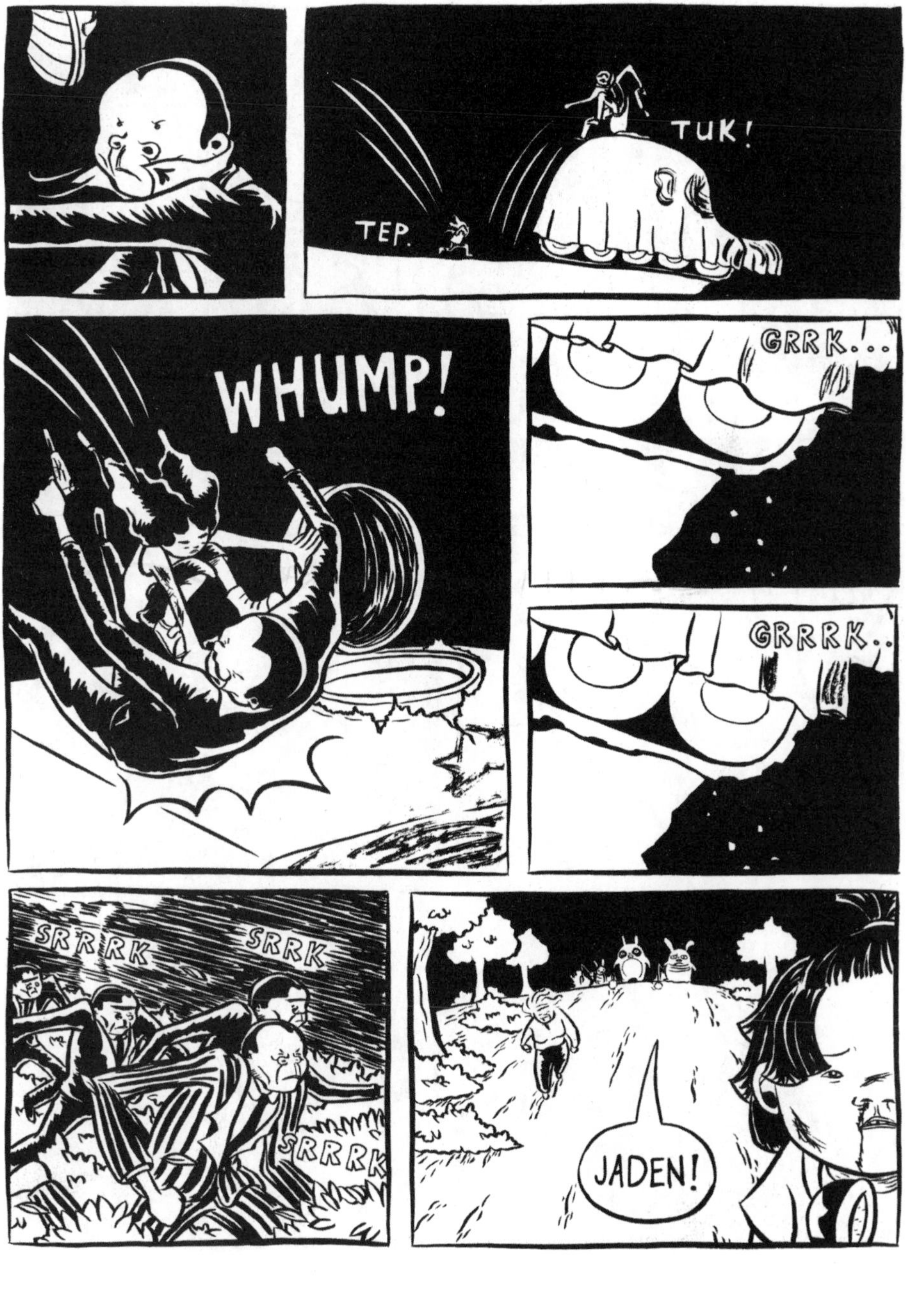
TUK!
TEP.
WHUMP!
GRRK...
GRRRK..
SRRRK
SRRK
SRRRK
JADEN!

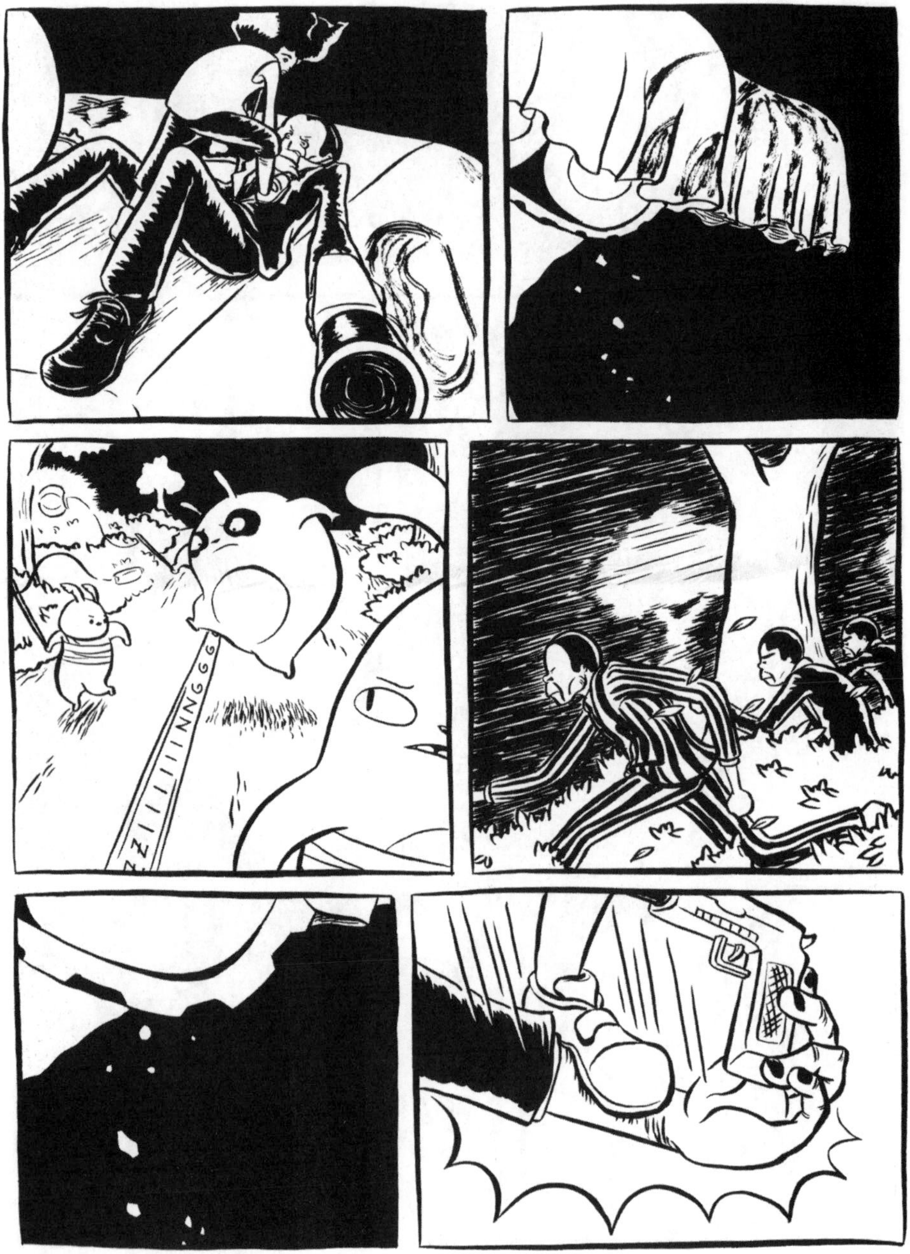
ZZIIIIIINNGGG

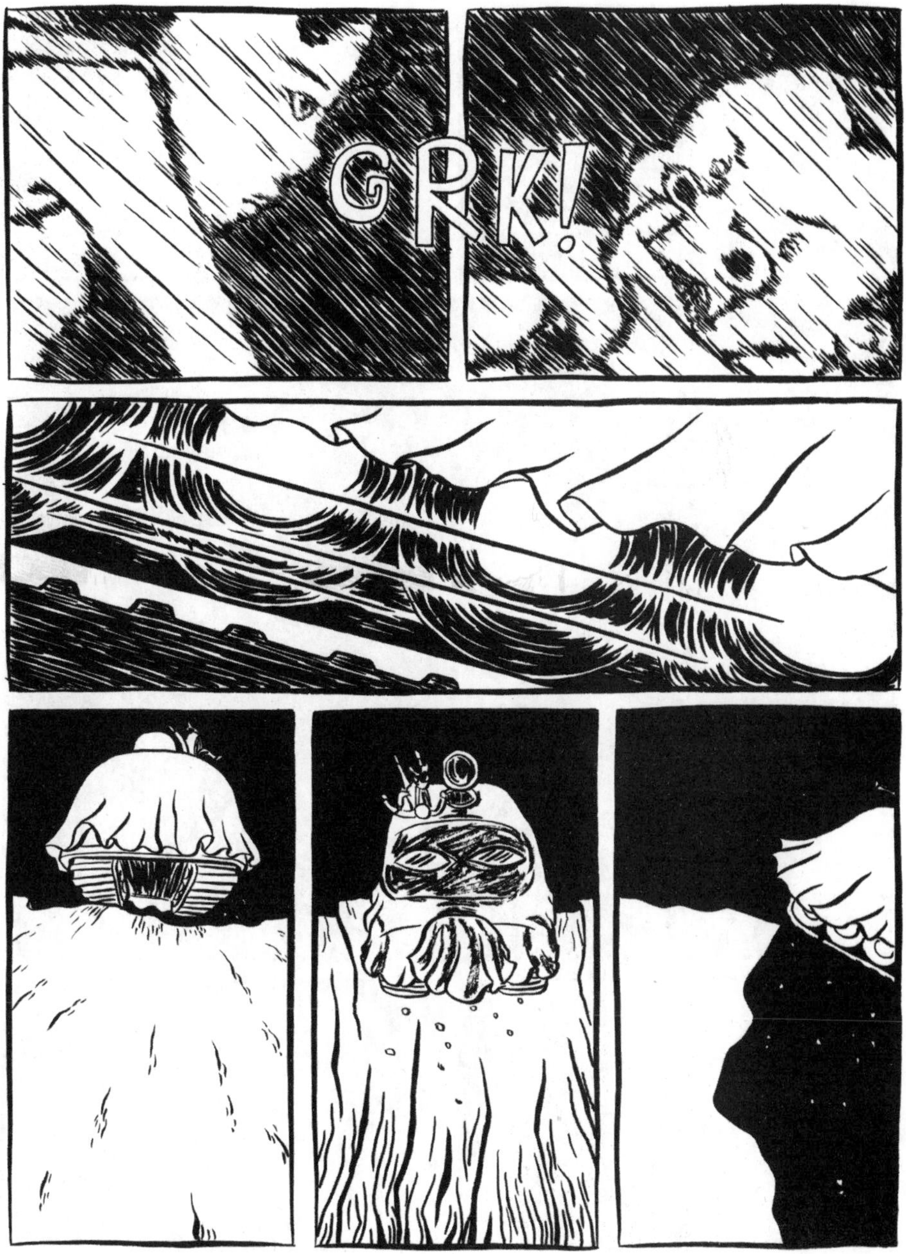
GRK!

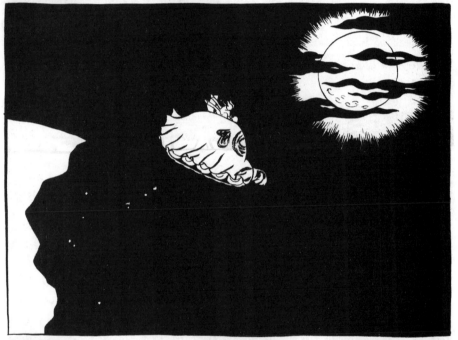

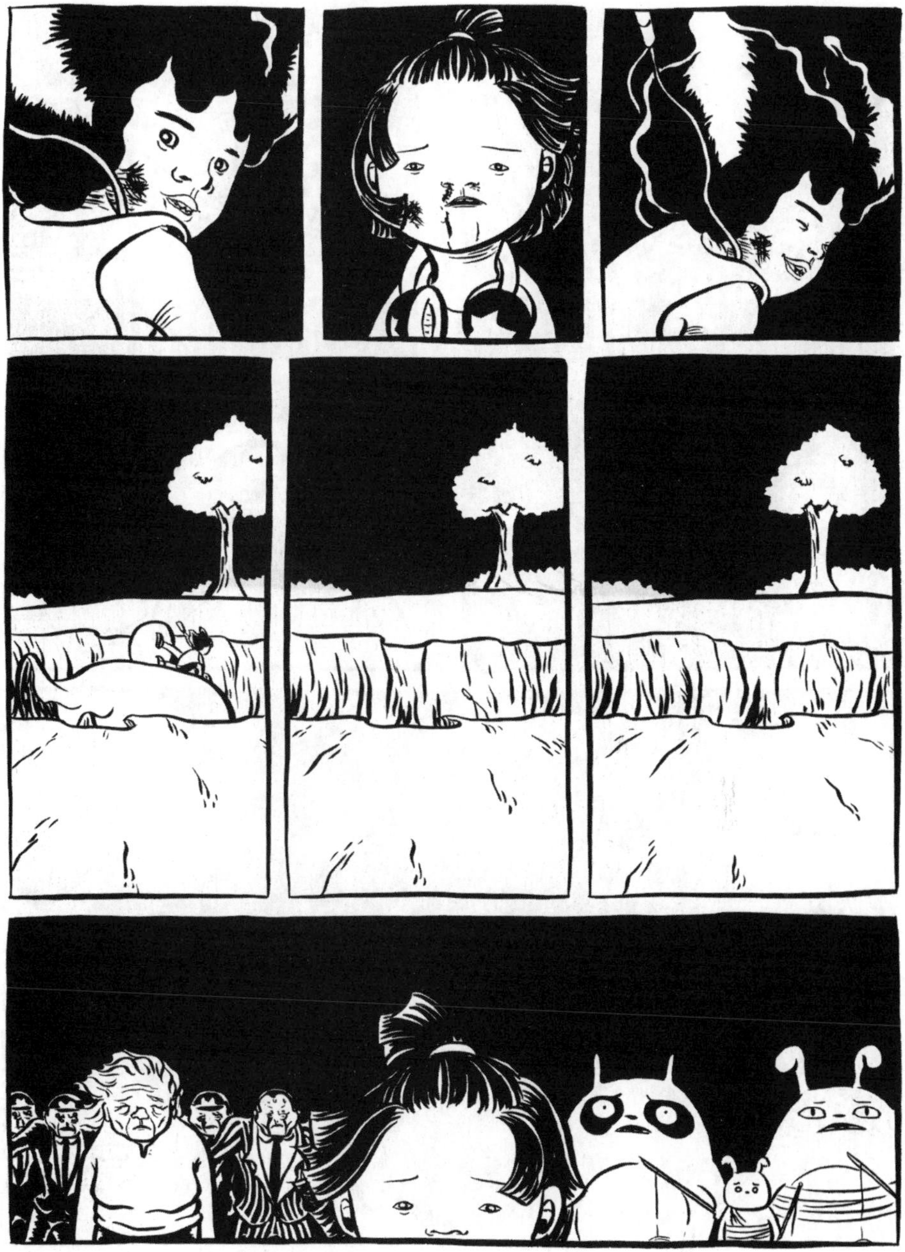

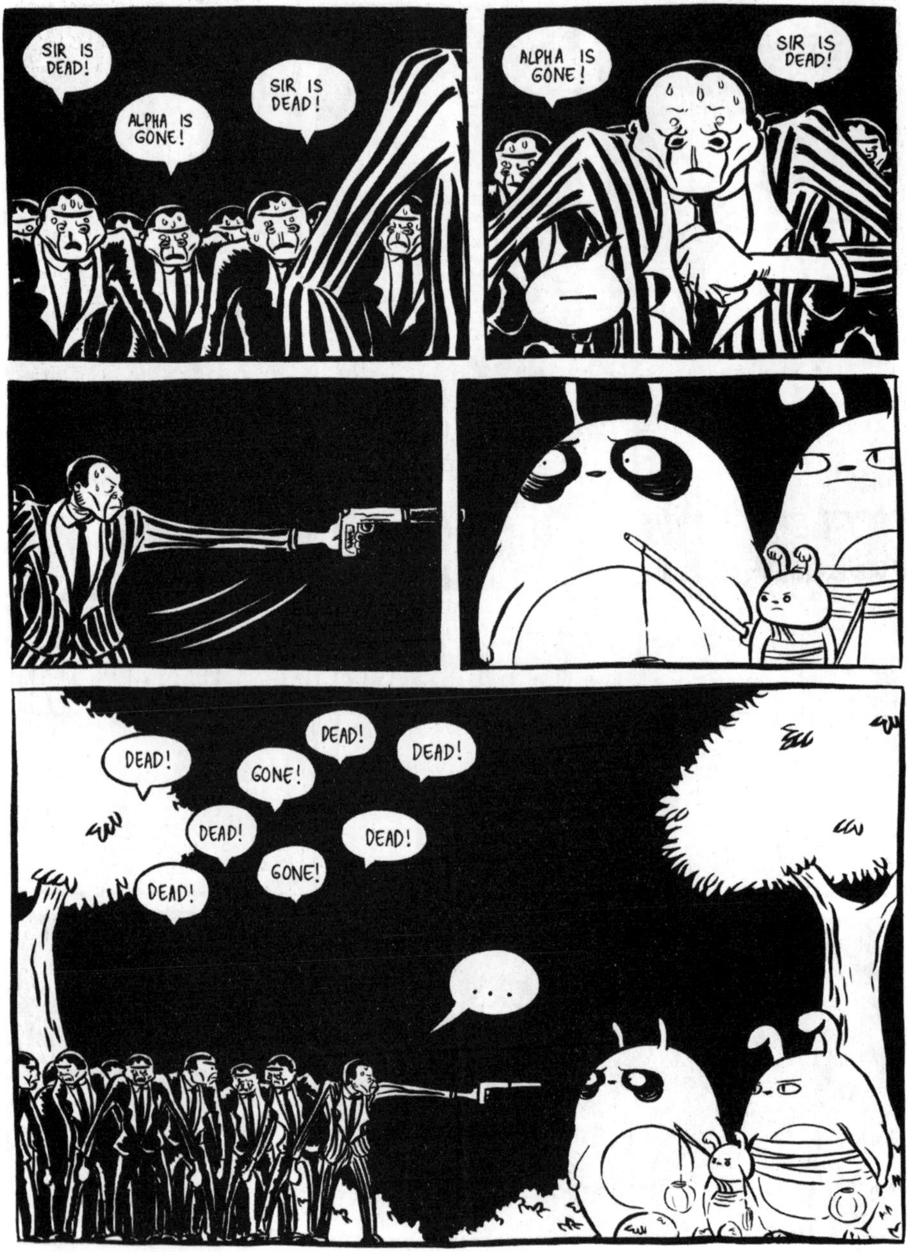
SIR IS DEAD!
ALPHA IS GONE!
SIR IS DEAD!
ALPHA IS GONE!
SIR IS DEAD!
DEAD!
GONE!
DEAD!
DEAD!
DEAD!
DEAD!
GONE!
DEAD!
...

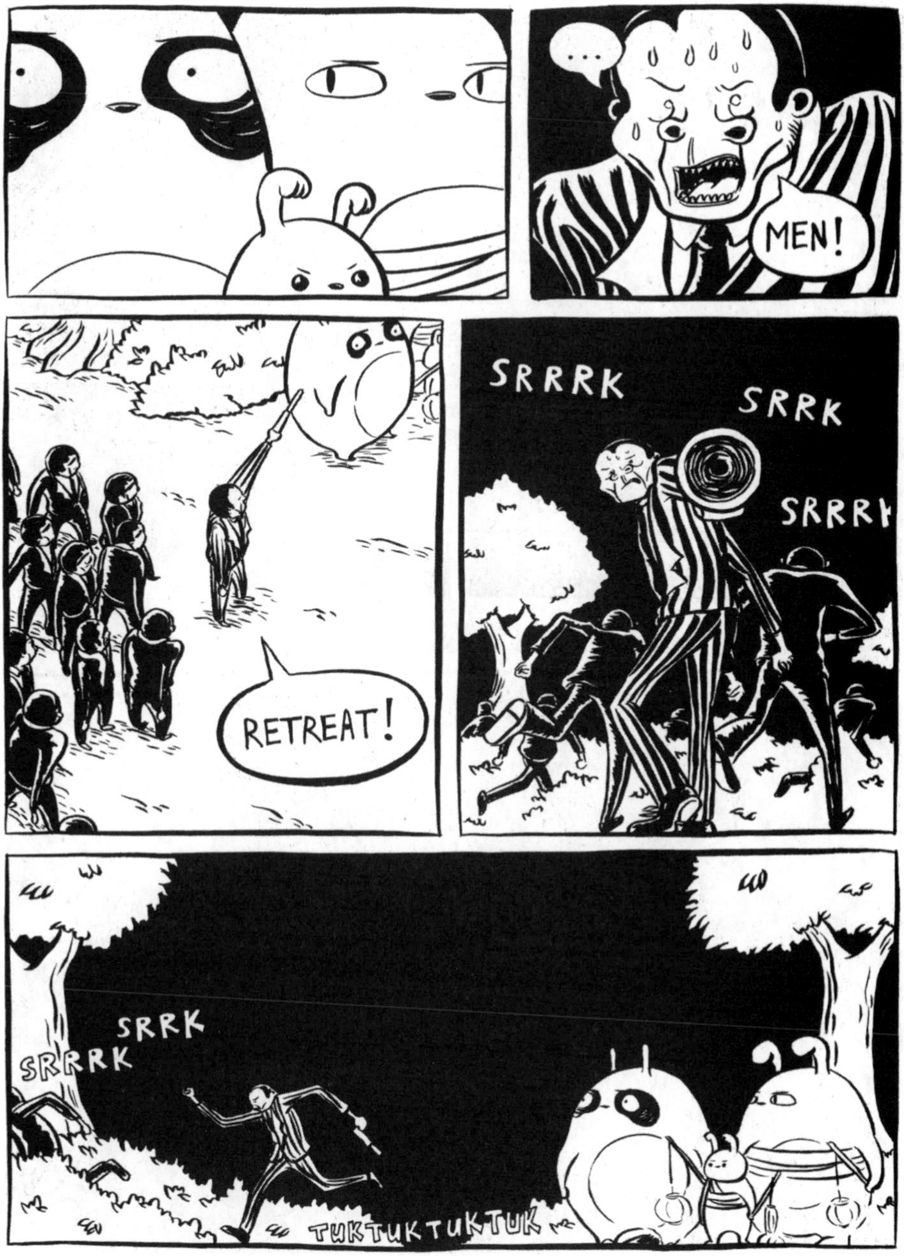
...
MEN!
RETREAT!
SRRRK
SRRK
SRRRK
SRRK
SRRRK
TUKTUKTUKTUK

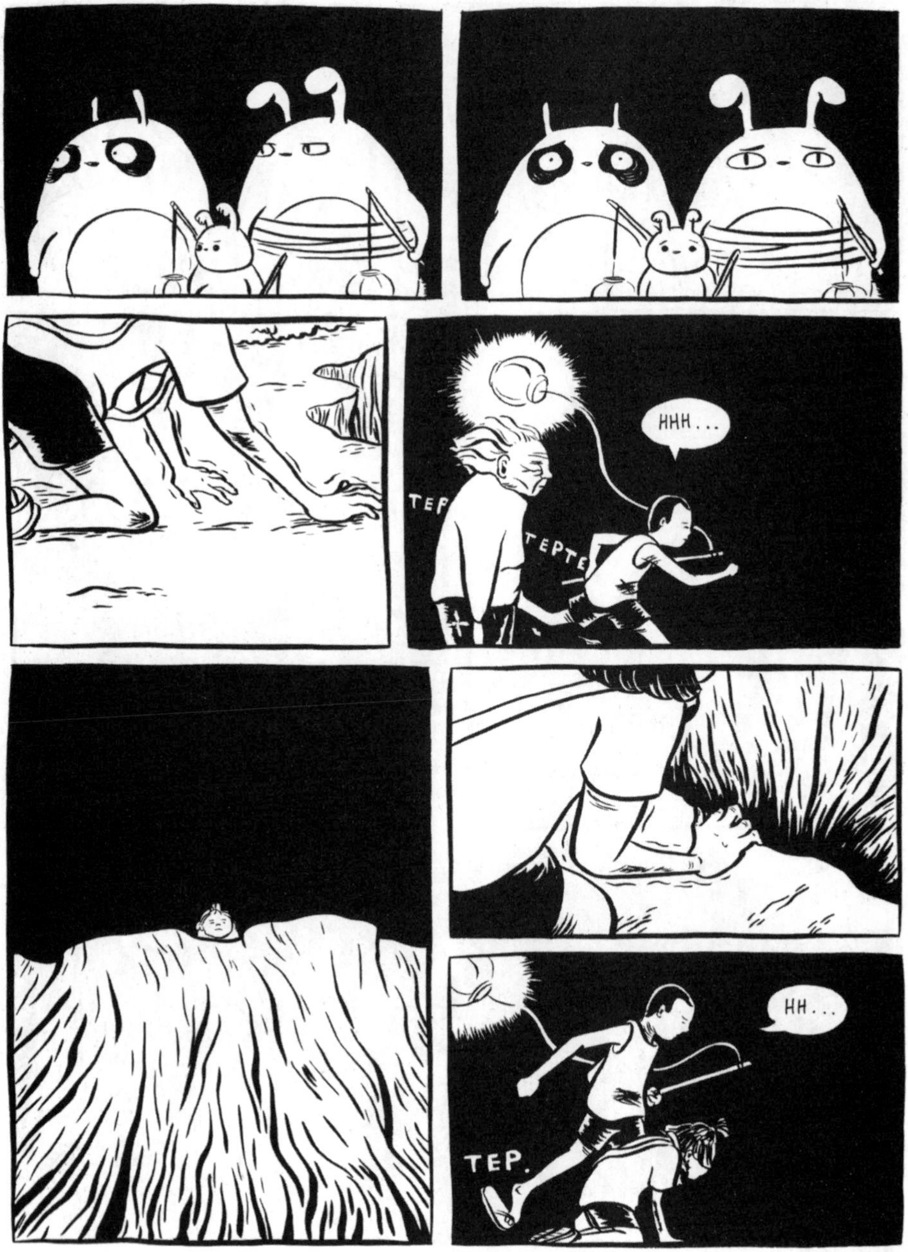
HHH...
TEP
TEPTE
HH...
TEP.

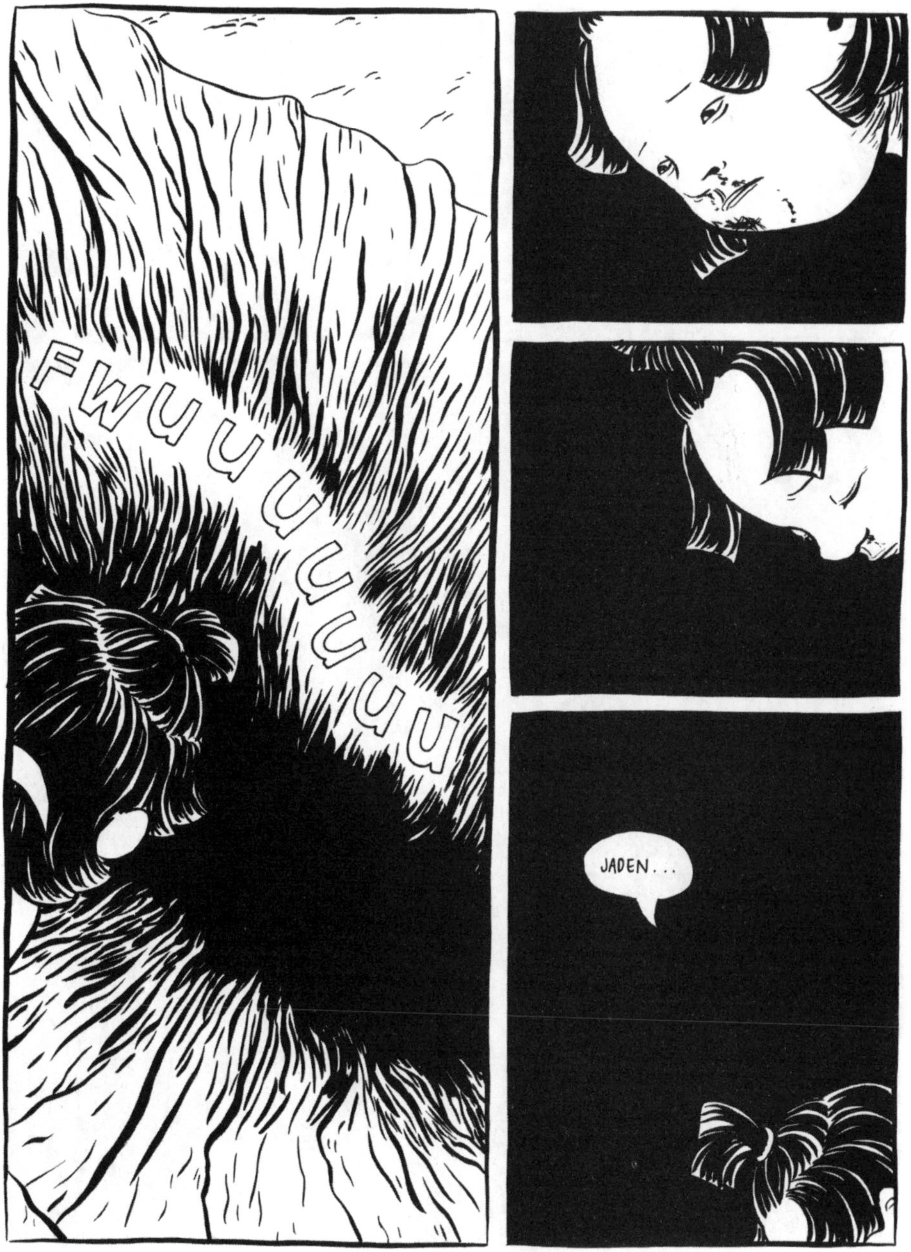
FWUUUUUUUUU
JADEN...

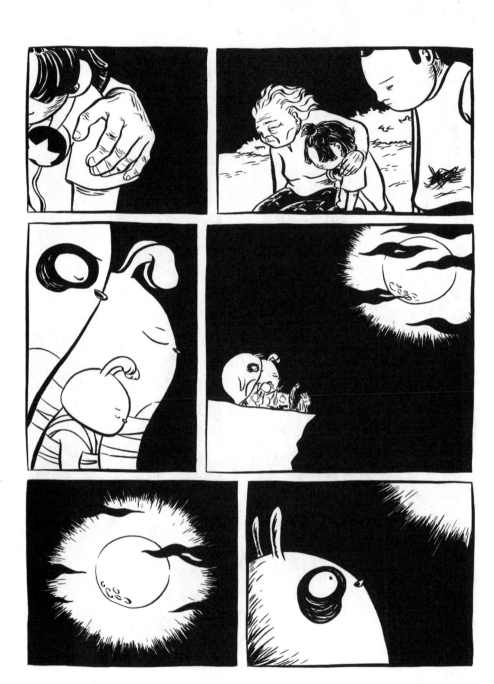

290

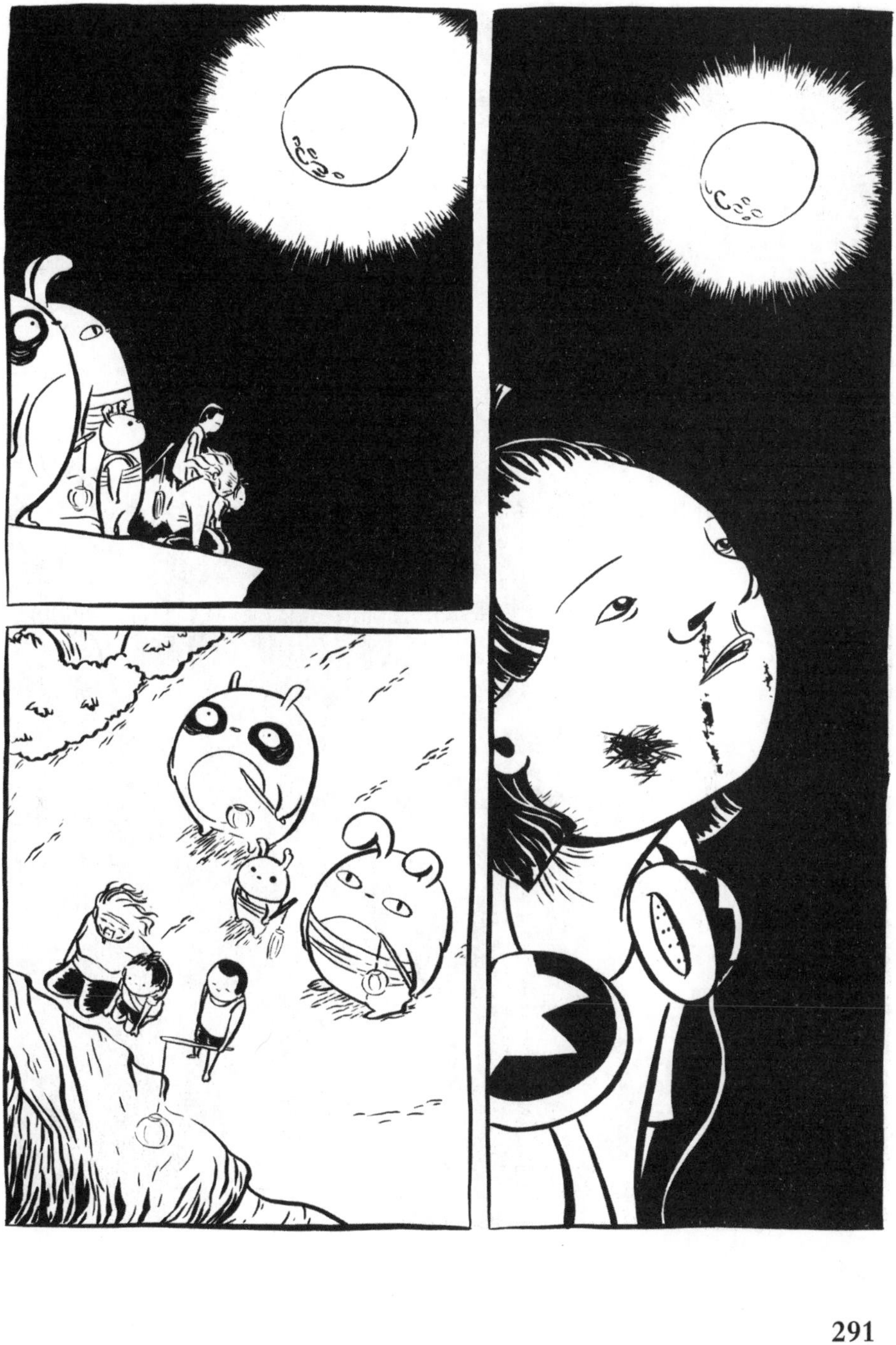

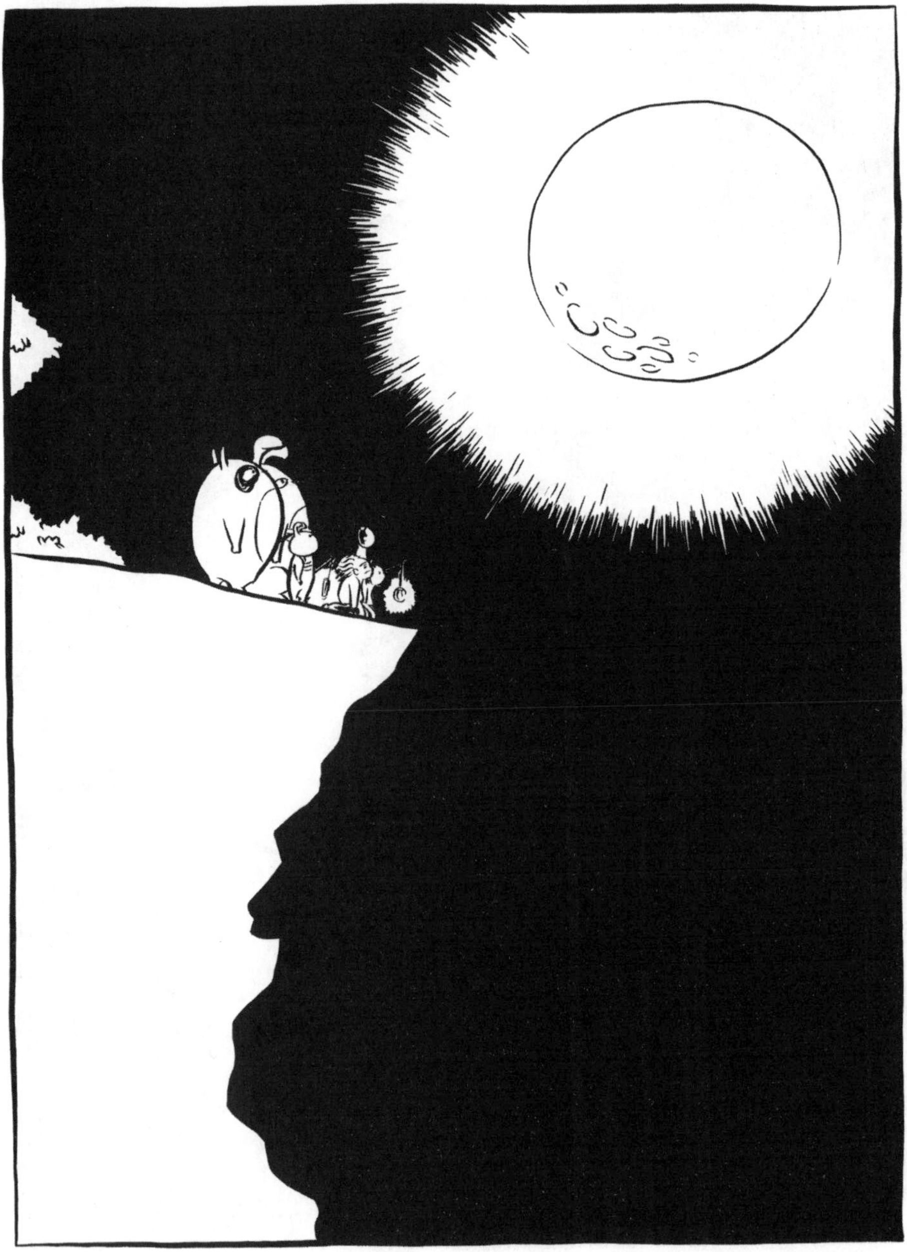

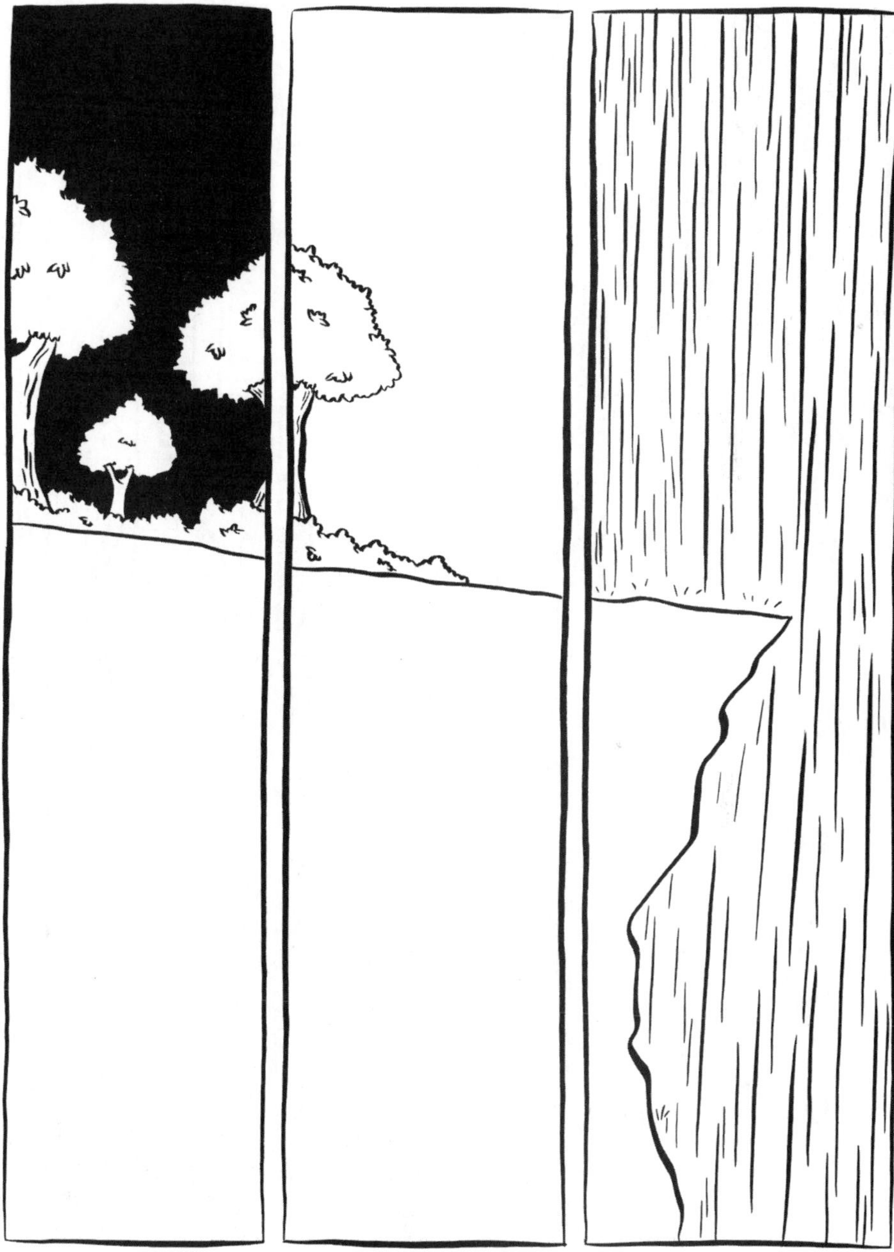

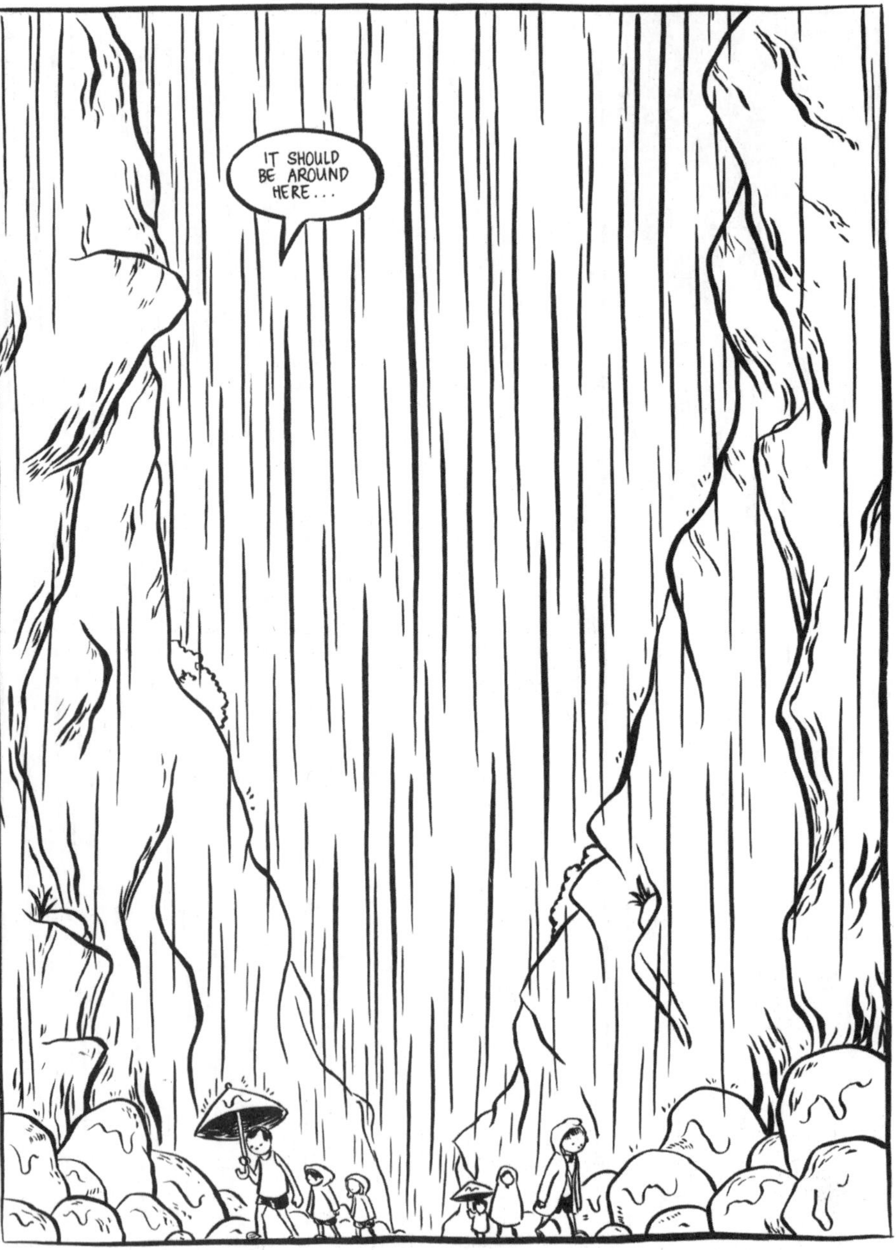
IT SHOULD BE AROUND HERE...

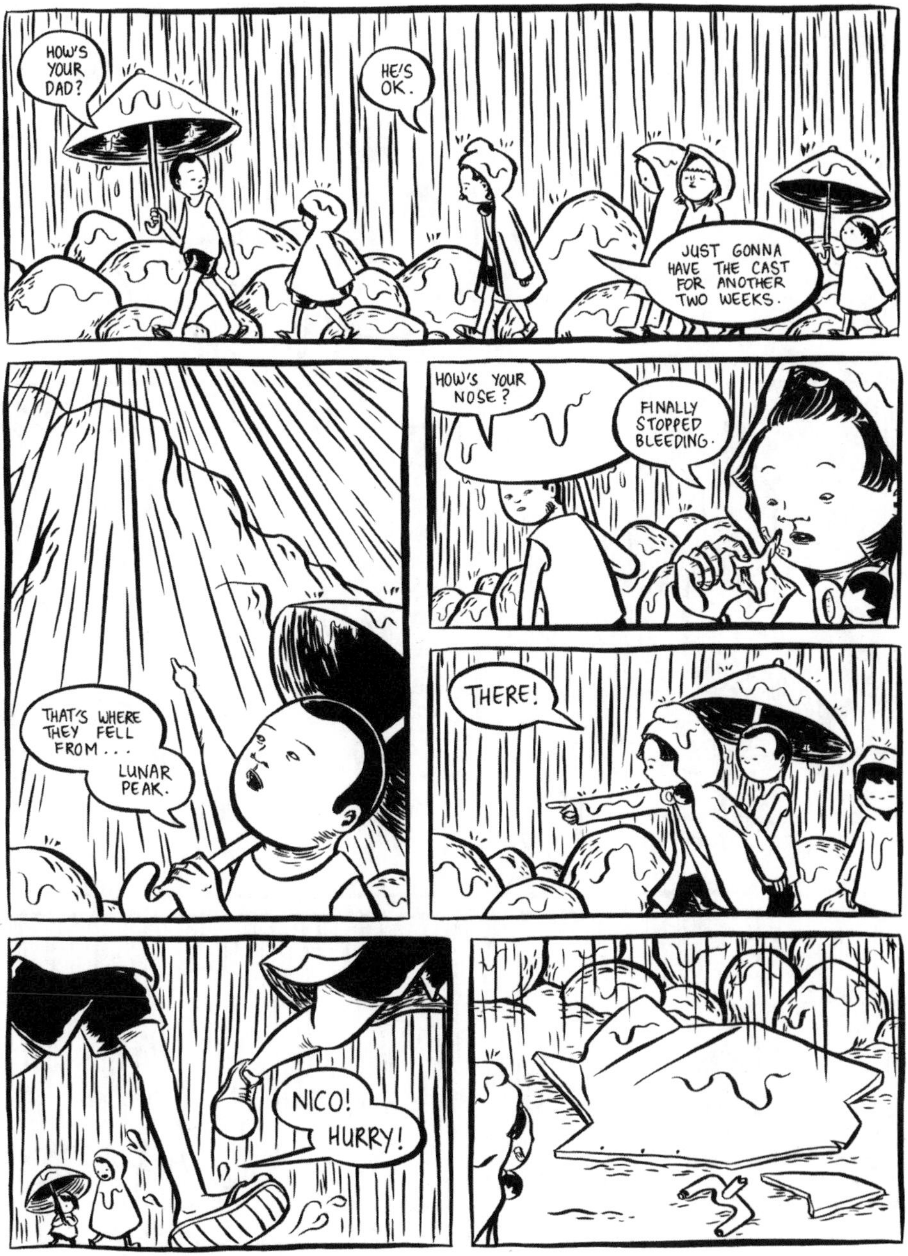
HOW'S YOUR DAD?
HE'S OK.
JUST GONNA HAVE THE CAST FOR ANOTHER TWO WEEKS.
THAT'S WHERE THEY FELL FROM...
LUNAR PEAK.
HOW'S YOUR NOSE?
FINALLY STOPPED BLEEDING.
THERE!
NICO! HURRY!

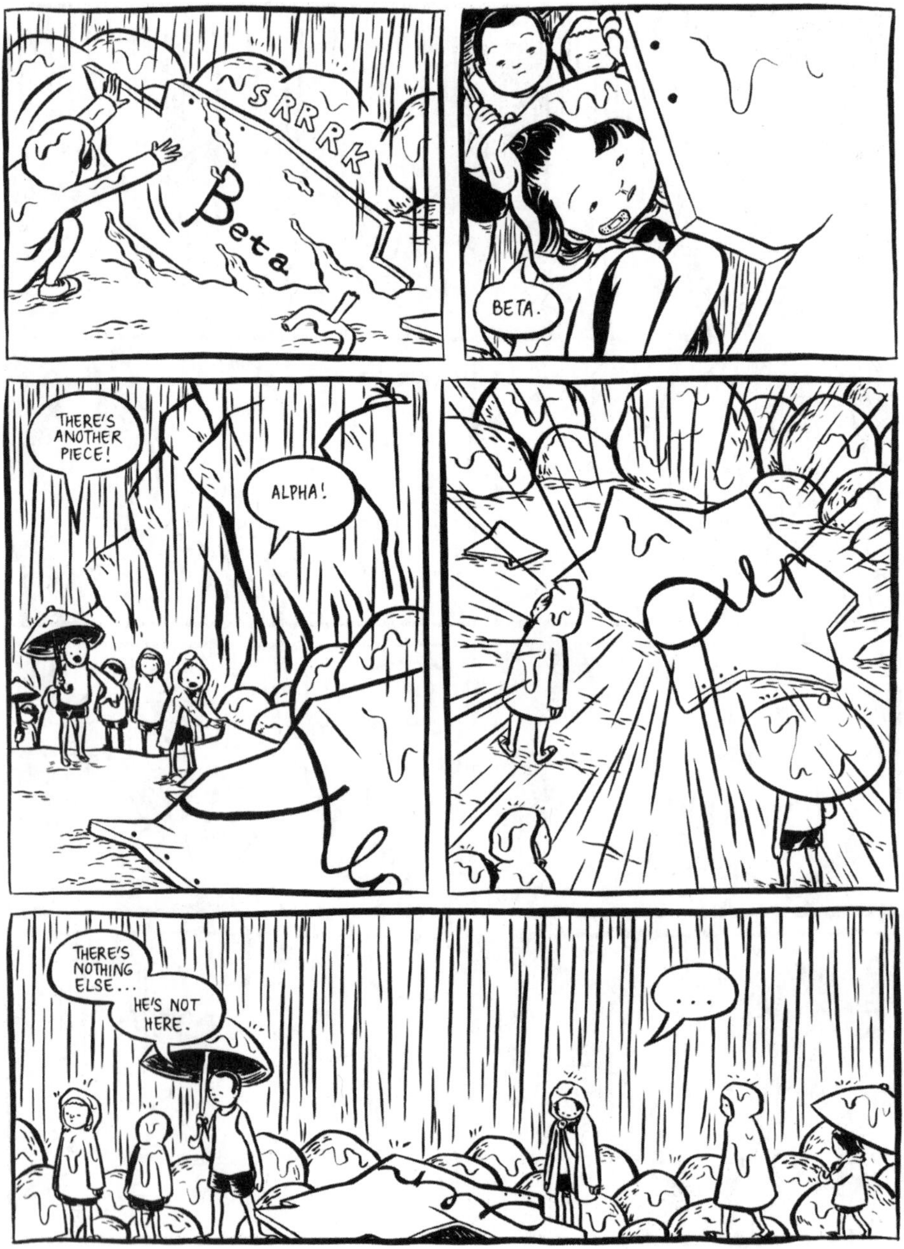
SRRRRK
Beta
BETA.
THERE'S ANOTHER PIECE!
ALPHA!
THERE'S NOTHING ELSE...
HE'S NOT HERE.
...

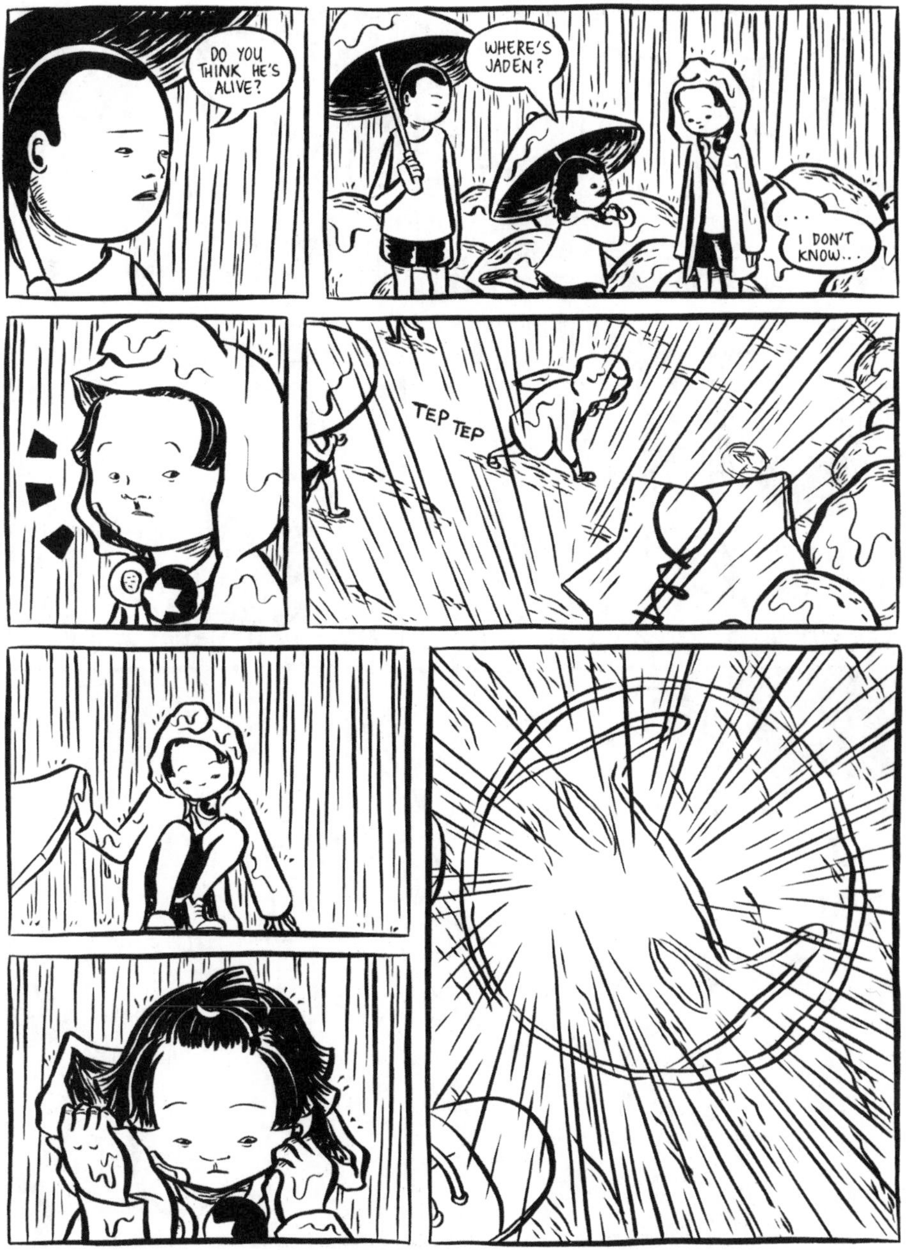
DO YOU THINK HE'S ALIVE?
WHERE'S JADEN?
... I DON'T KNOW...
TEP TEP

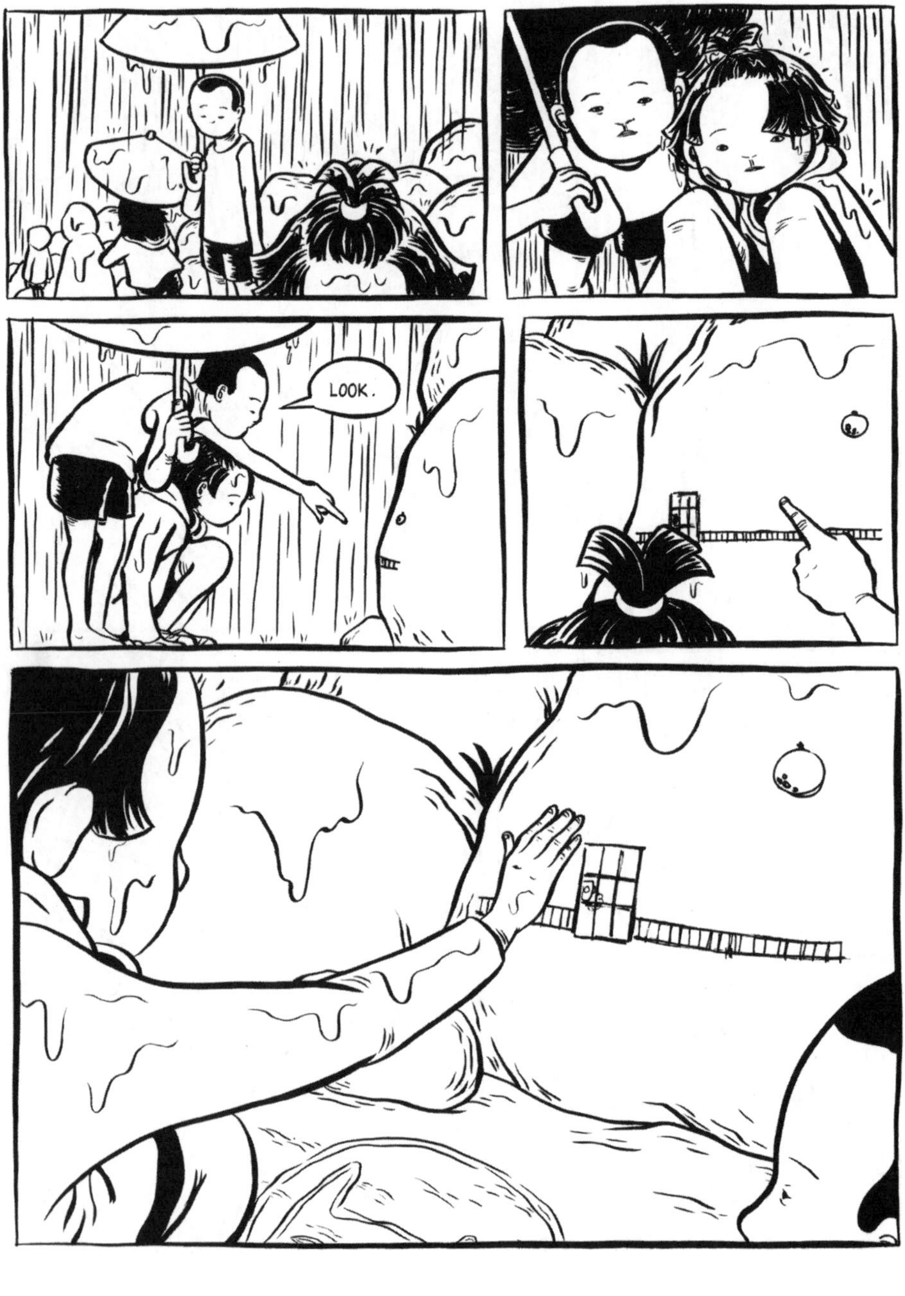
LOOK.

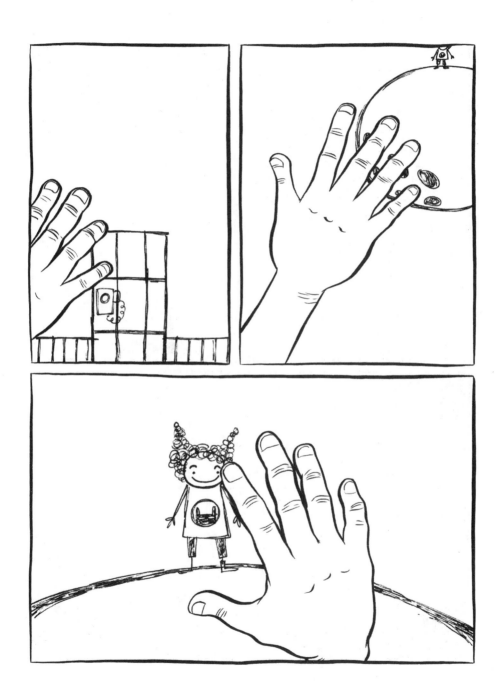

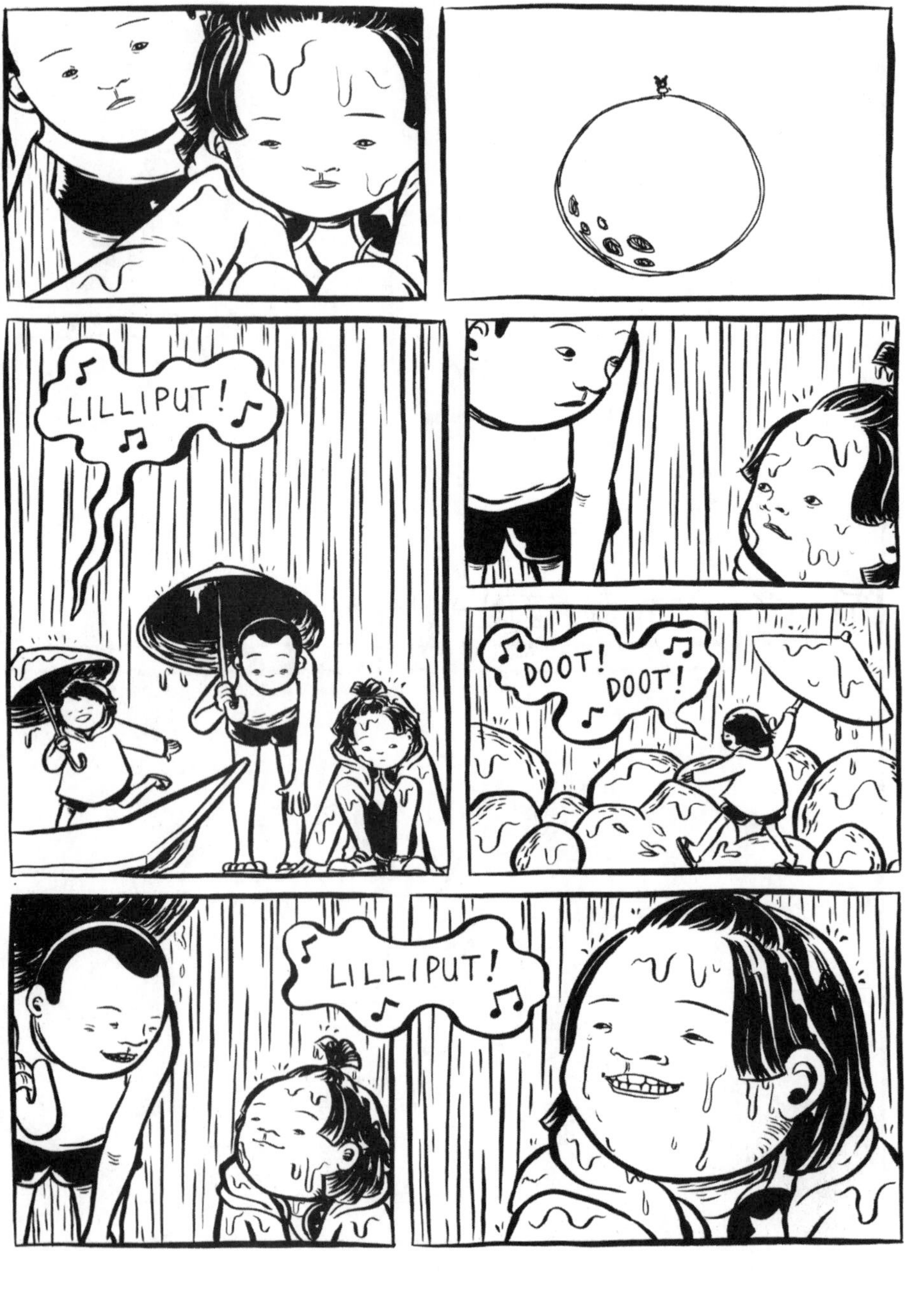
LILLIPUT!
DOOT! DOOT!
LILLIPUT!

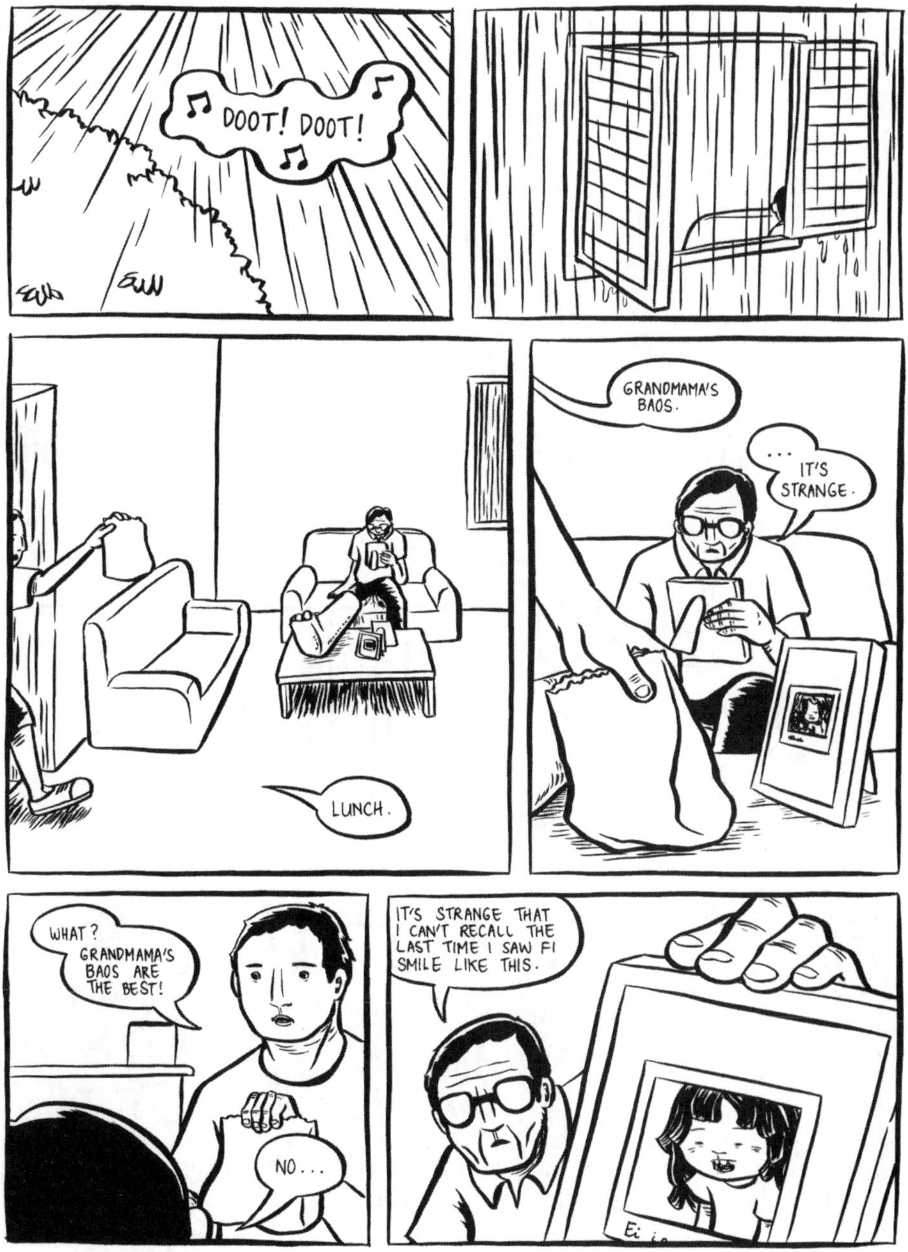
DOOT! DOOT!
LUNCH.
GRANDMAMA'S BAOS.
... IT'S STRANGE.
WHAT? GRANDMAMA'S BAOS ARE THE BEST!
NO...
IT'S STRANGE THAT I CAN'T RECALL THE LAST TIME I SAW FI SMILE LIKE THIS.

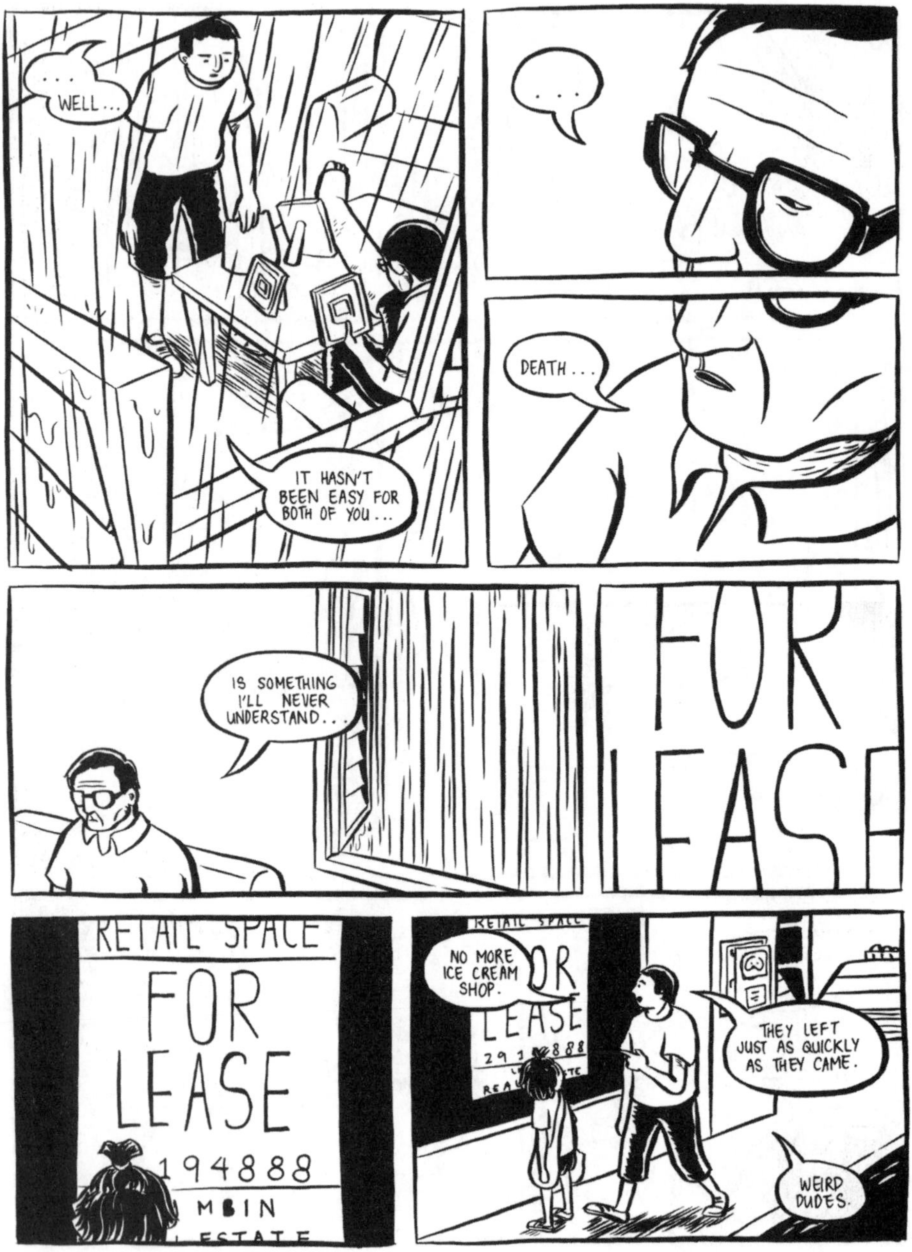
. . .
WELL . . .
IT HASN'T BEEN EASY FOR BOTH OF YOU . . .
. . .
DEATH . . .
IS SOMETHING I'LL NEVER UNDERSTAND . . .
FOR LEASE
RETAIL SPACE
FOR LEASE
194888
NO MORE ICE CREAM SHOP.
THEY LEFT JUST AS QUICKLY AS THEY CAME.
WEIRD DUDES.

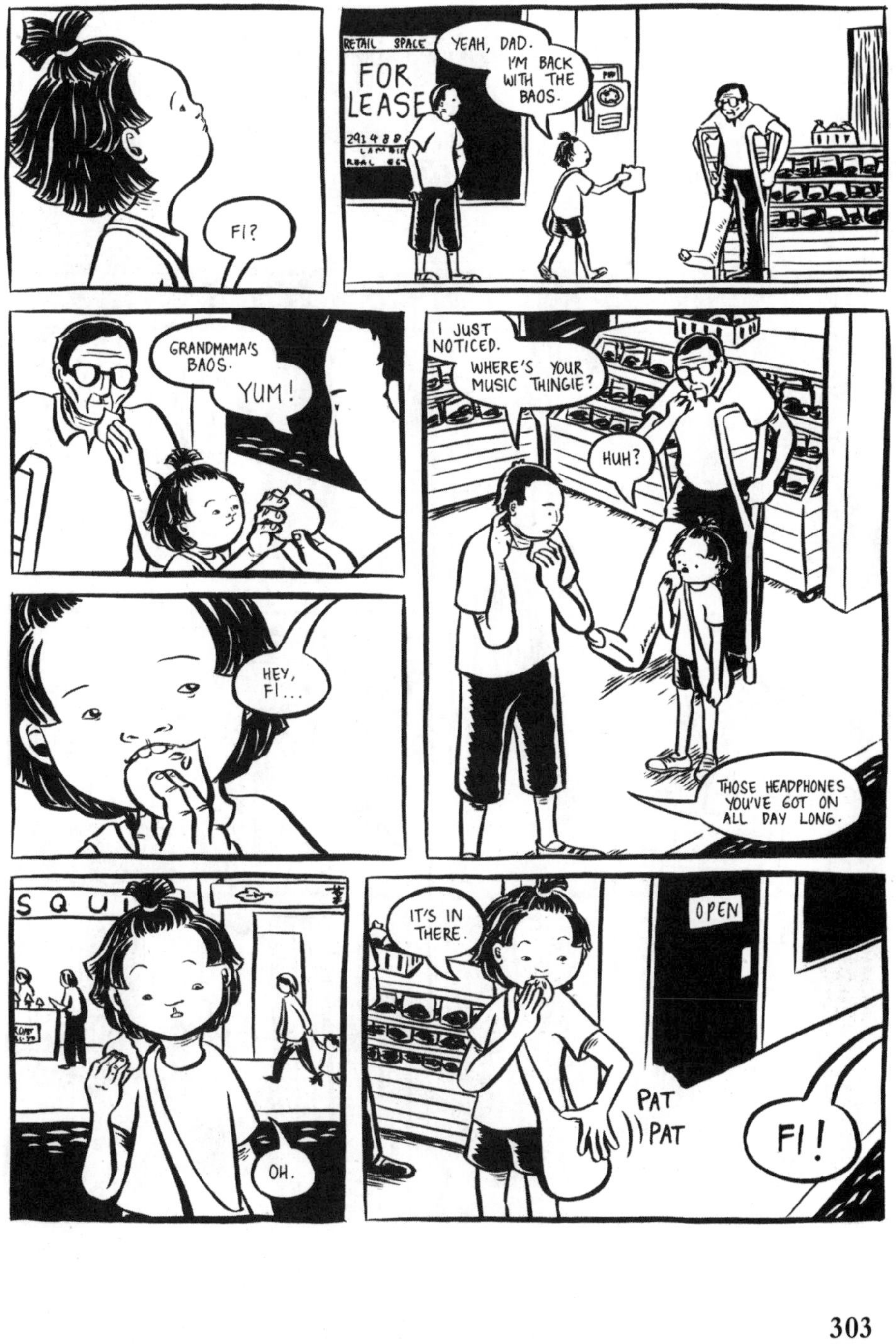
FI?
RETAIL SPACE
FOR LEASE
YEAH, DAD.
I'M BACK WITH THE BAOS.
GRANDMAMA'S BAOS.
YUM!
I JUST NOTICED.
WHERE'S YOUR MUSIC THINGIE?
HUH?
HEY, FI...
THOSE HEADPHONES YOU'VE GOT ON ALL DAY LONG.
SQU
OH.
IT'S IN THERE.
OPEN
PAT PAT
FI!

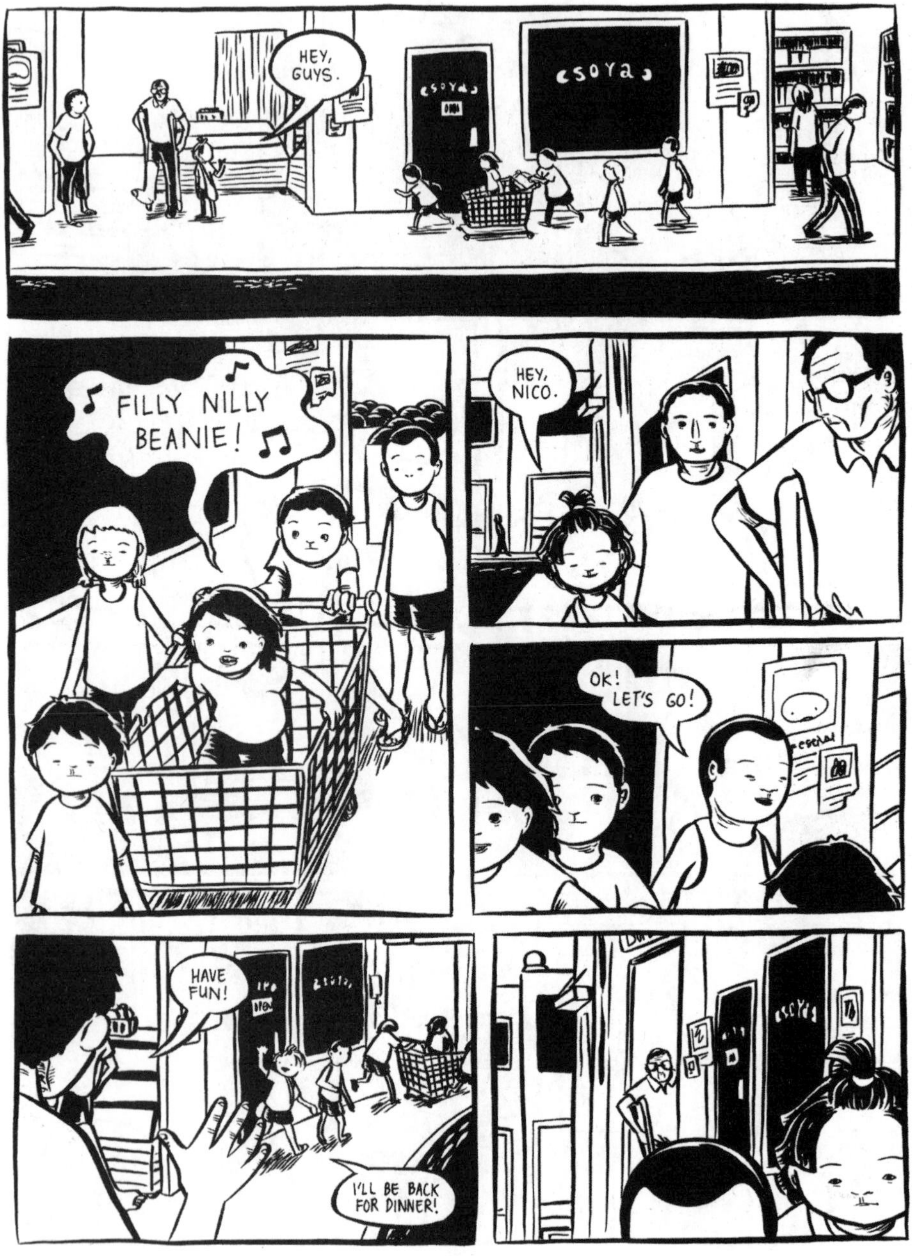
HEY, GUYS.
soya
FILLY NILLY BEANIE!
HEY, NICO.
OK! LET'S GO!
HAVE FUN!
I'LL BE BACK FOR DINNER!

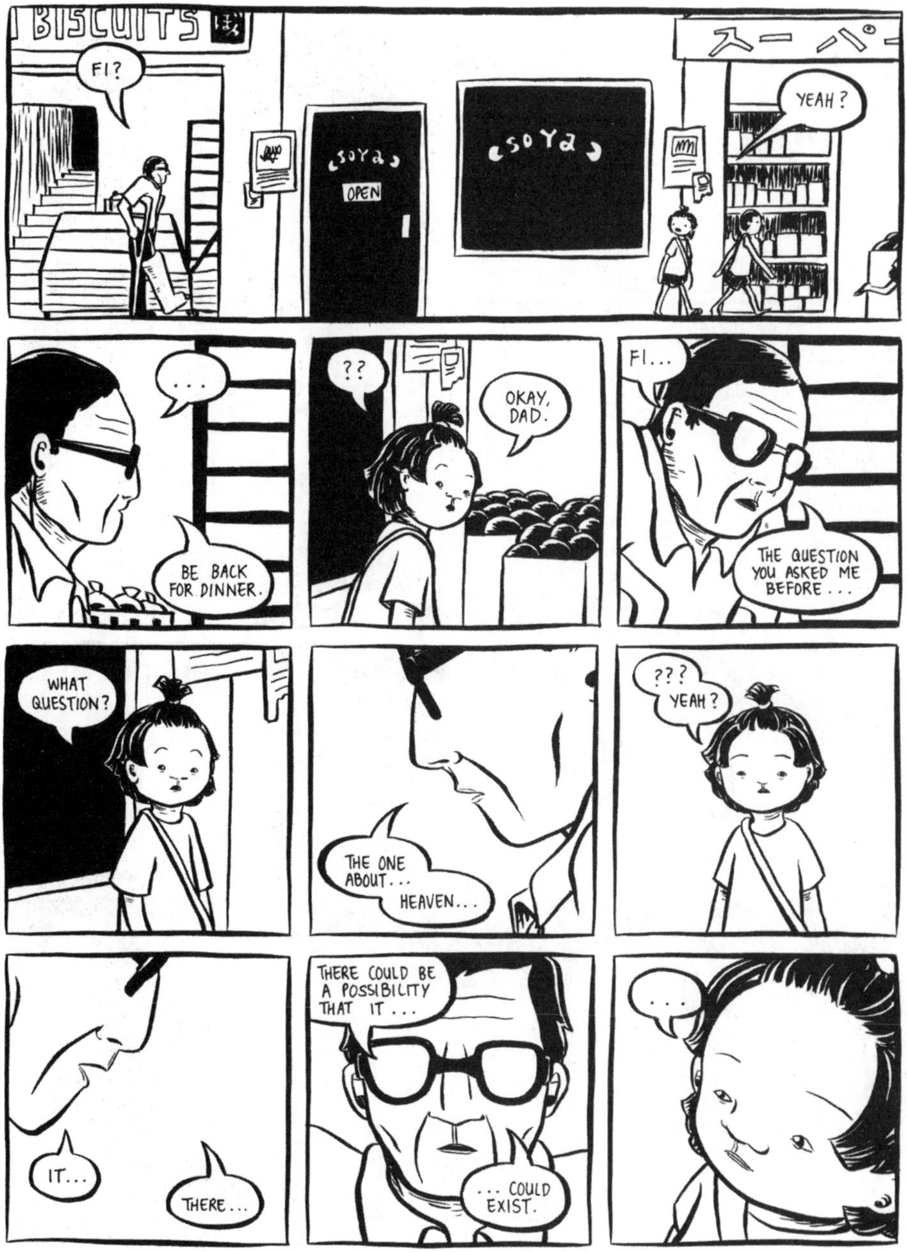
BISCUITS
スーパー
FI?
SOYA
OPEN
SOYA
YEAH?
...
BE BACK FOR DINNER.
??
OKAY, DAD.
FI...
THE QUESTION YOU ASKED ME BEFORE...
WHAT QUESTION?
THE ONE ABOUT... HEAVEN...
???
YEAH?
IT...
THERE...
THERE COULD BE A POSSIBILITY THAT IT...
... COULD EXIST.
...

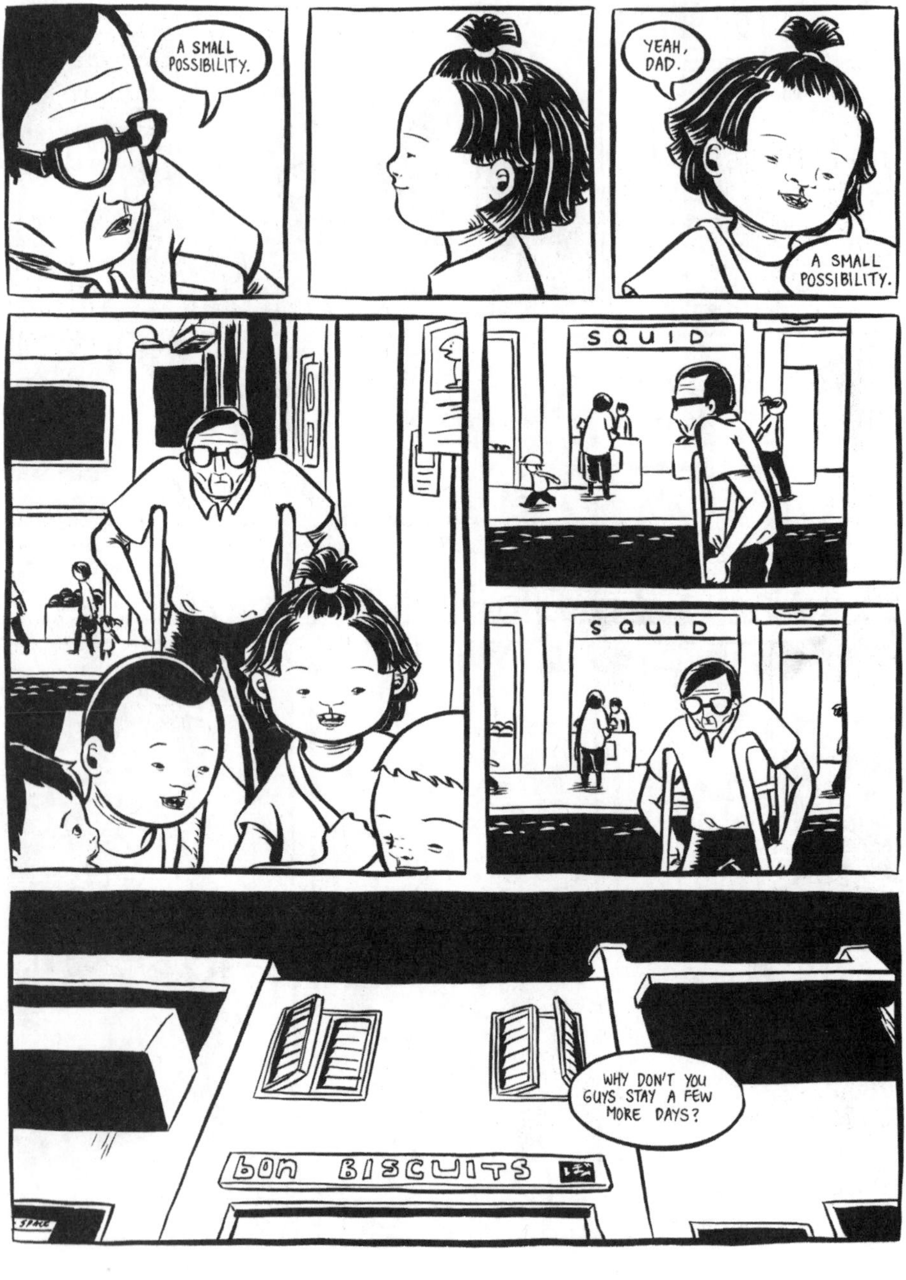
A SMALL POSSIBILITY.
YEAH, DAD.
A SMALL POSSIBILITY.
SQUID
SQUID
WHY DON'T YOU GUYS STAY A FEW MORE DAYS?
BON BISCUITS

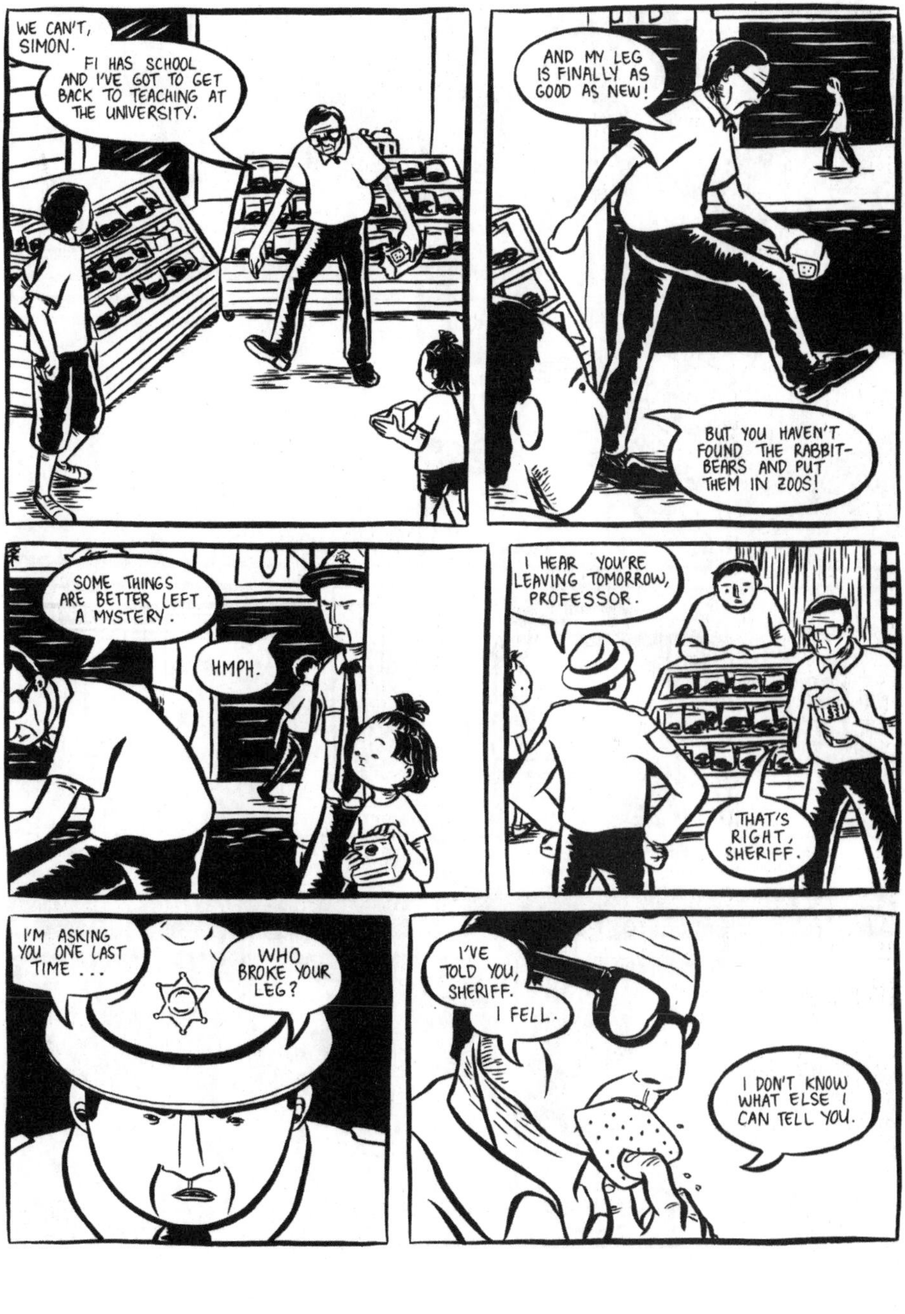
WE CAN'T, SIMON.
FI HAS SCHOOL AND I'VE GOT TO GET BACK TO TEACHING AT THE UNIVERSITY.
AND MY LEG IS FINALLY AS GOOD AS NEW!
BUT YOU HAVEN'T FOUND THE RABBIT-BEARS AND PUT THEM IN ZOOS!
SOME THINGS ARE BETTER LEFT A MYSTERY.
HMPH.
I HEAR YOU'RE LEAVING TOMORROW, PROFESSOR.
THAT'S RIGHT, SHERIFF.
I'M ASKING YOU ONE LAST TIME ...
WHO BROKE YOUR LEG?
I'VE TOLD YOU, SHERIFF.
I FELL.
I DON'T KNOW WHAT ELSE I CAN TELL YOU.

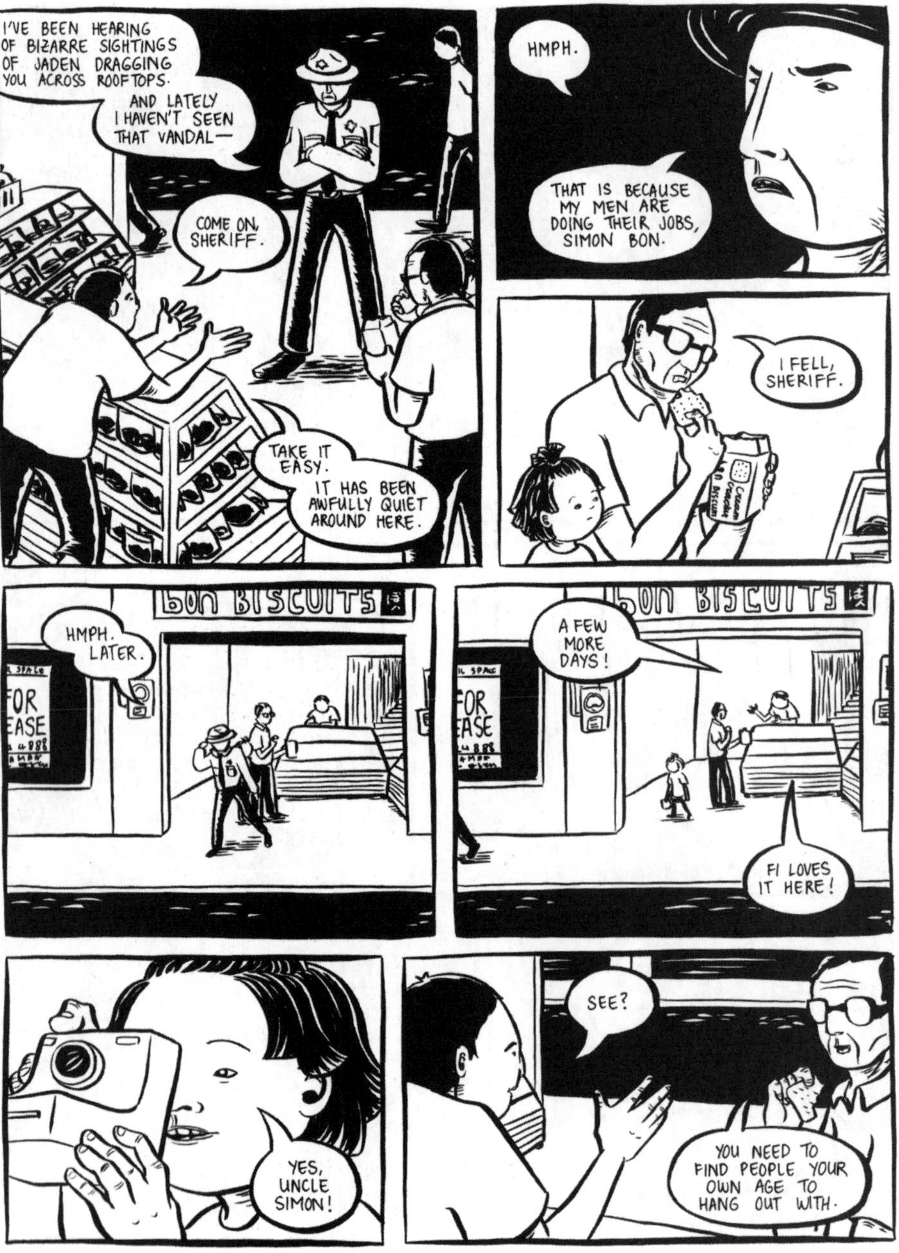

I'VE BEEN HEARING OF BIZARRE SIGHTINGS OF JADEN DRAGGING YOU ACROSS ROOFTOPS.
AND LATELY I HAVEN'T SEEN THAT VANDAL—
COME ON, SHERIFF.
TAKE IT EASY.
IT HAS BEEN AWFULLY QUIET AROUND HERE.
HMPH.
THAT IS BECAUSE MY MEN ARE DOING THEIR JOBS, SIMON BON.
I FELL, SHERIFF.
BON BISCUITS
HMPH. LATER.
FOR LEASE
BON BISCUITS
A FEW MORE DAYS!
FOR LEASE
FI LOVES IT HERE!
YES, UNCLE SIMON!
SEE?
YOU NEED TO FIND PEOPLE YOUR OWN AGE TO HANG OUT WITH.

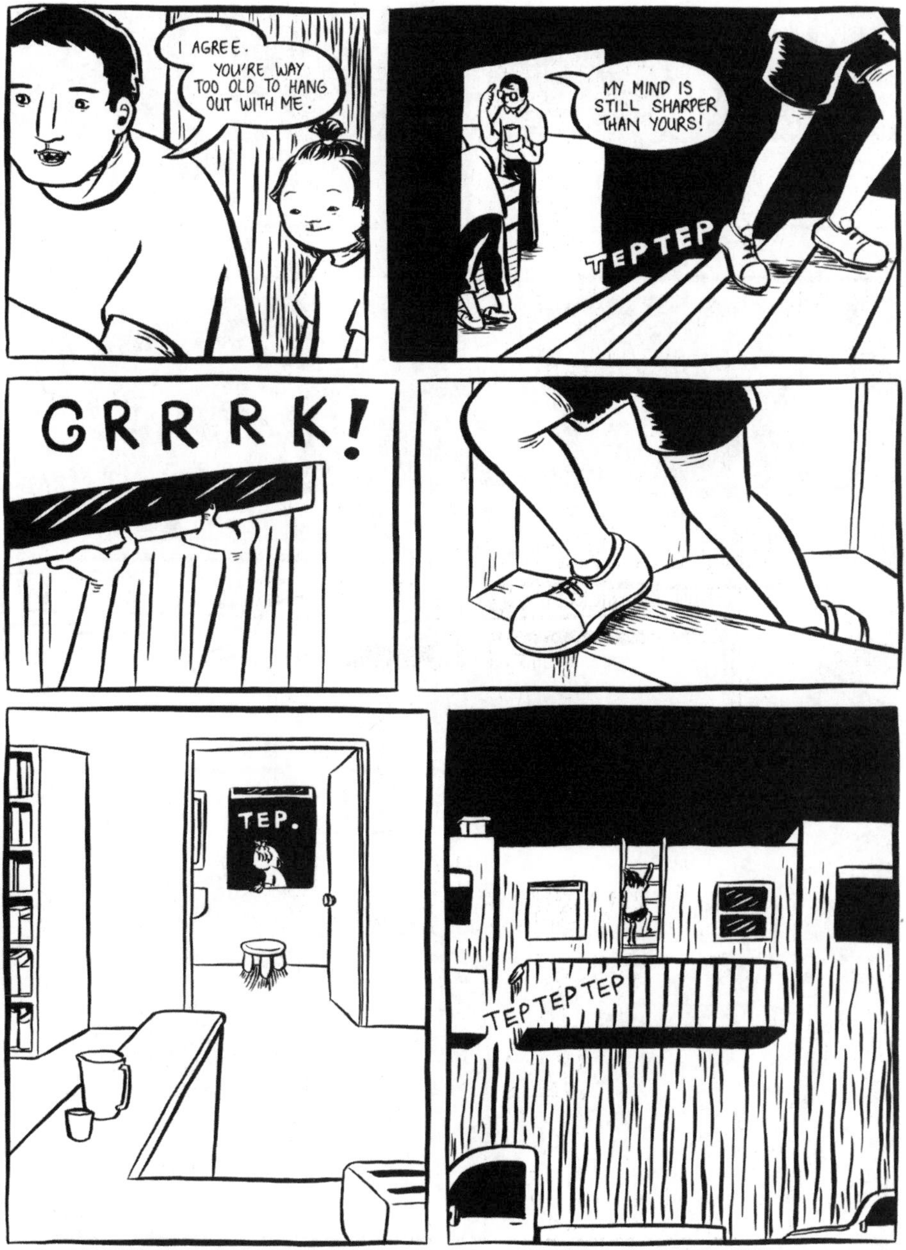
I AGREE. YOU'RE WAY TOO OLD TO HANG OUT WITH ME.
MY MIND IS STILL SHARPER THAN YOURS!
TEPTEP
GRRRK!
TEP.
TEPTEPTEP

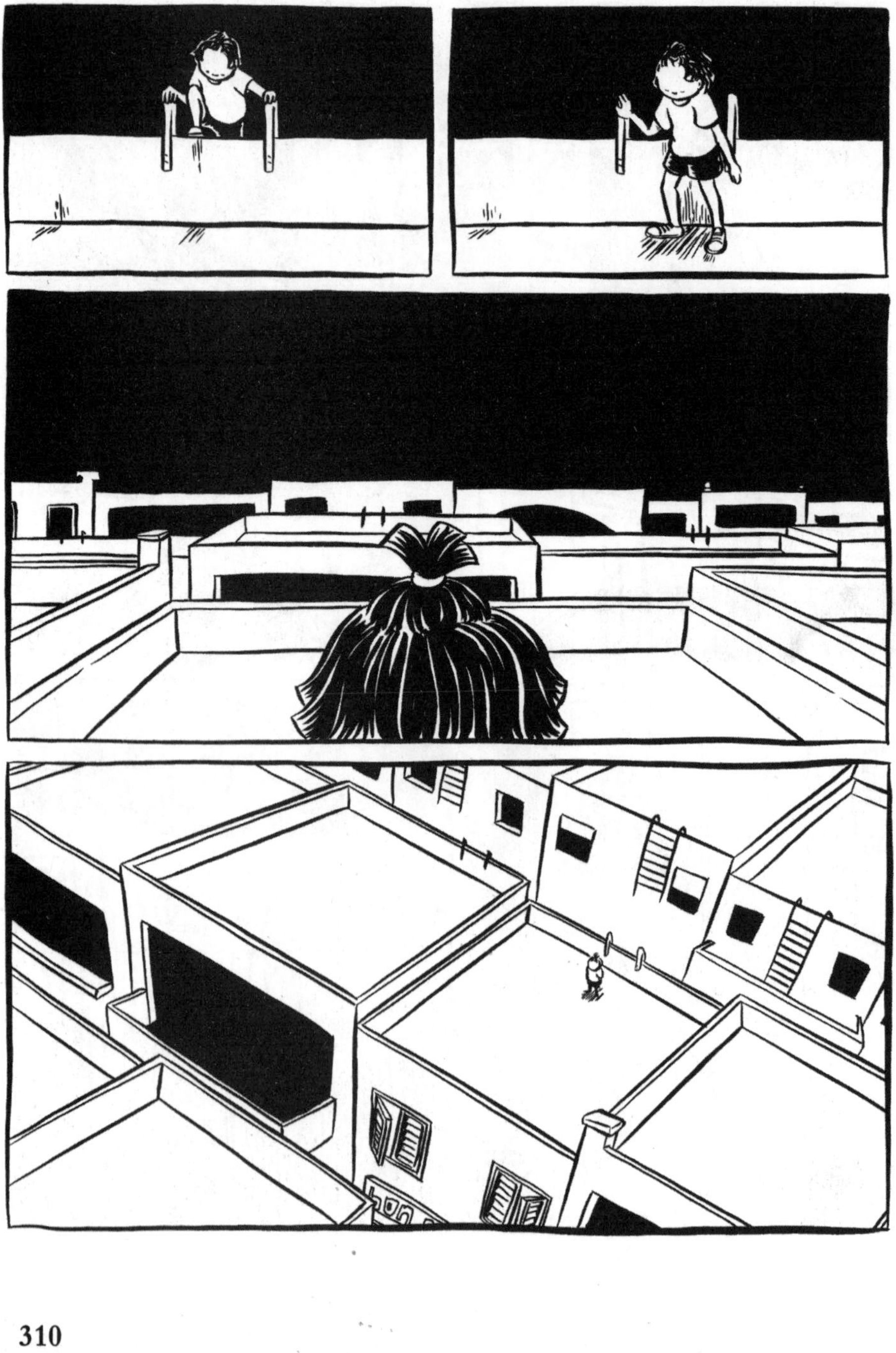

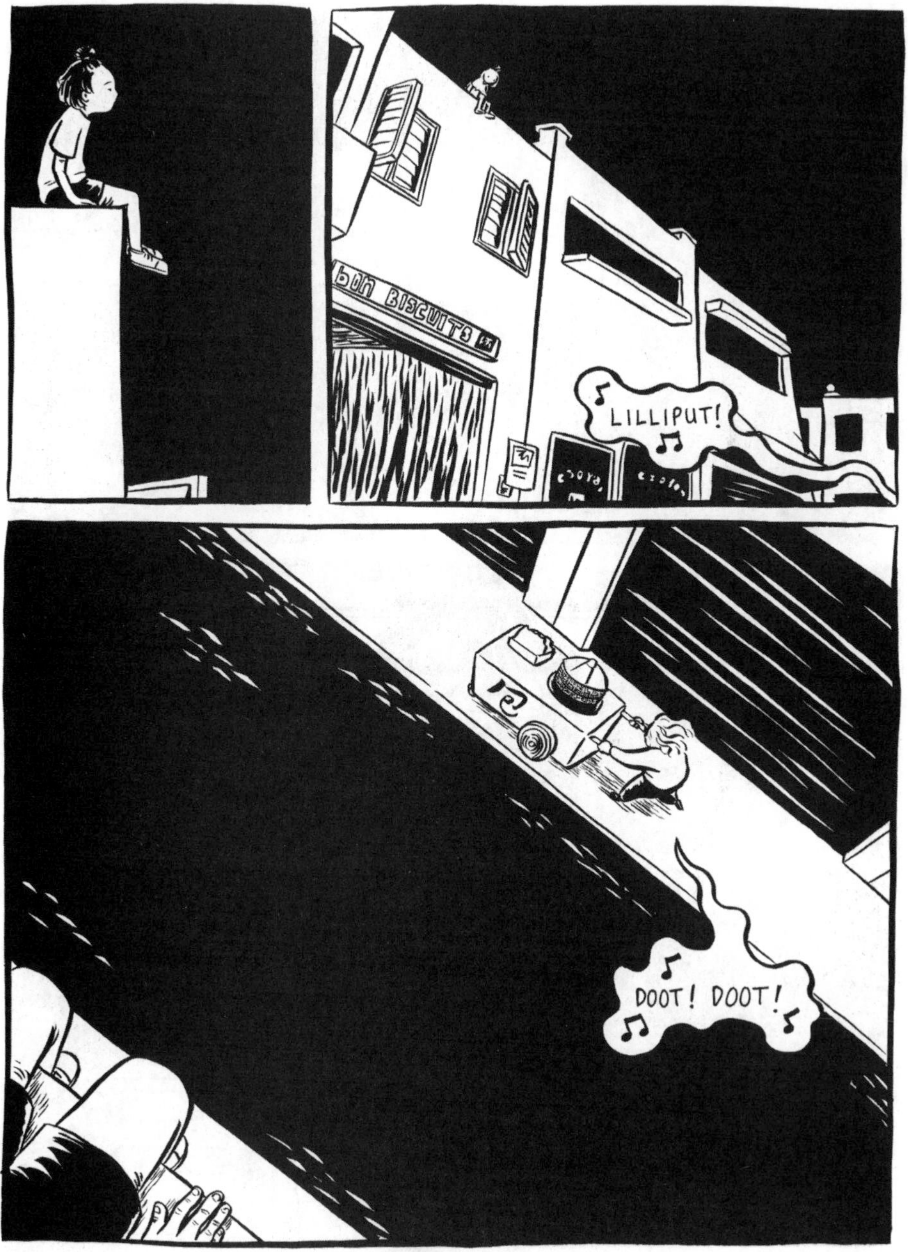
BISCUITS
LILLIPUT!
DOOT! DOOT!

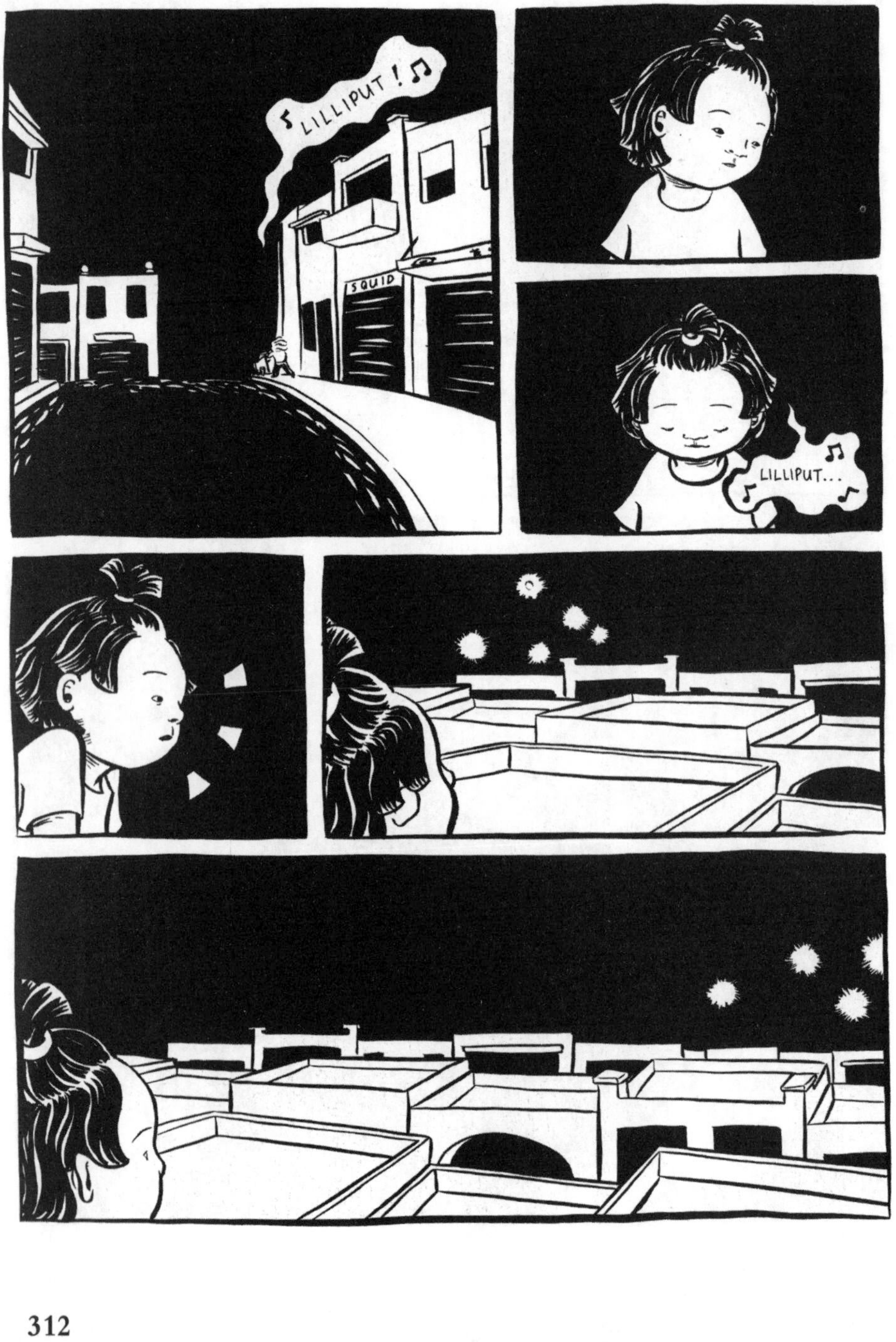
LILLIPUT!
SQUID
LILLIPUT...

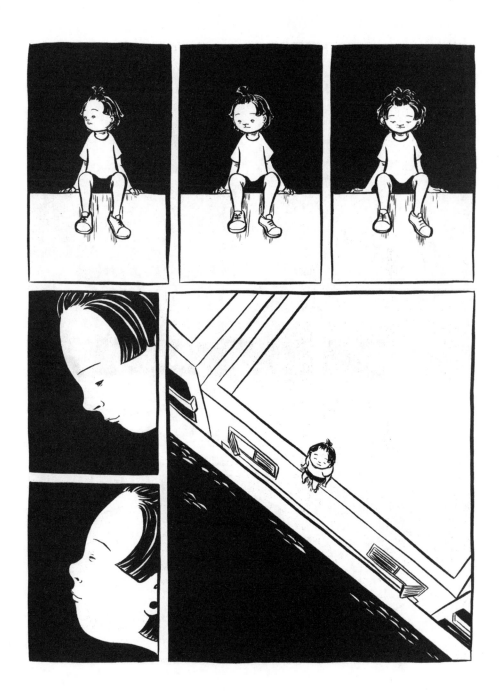

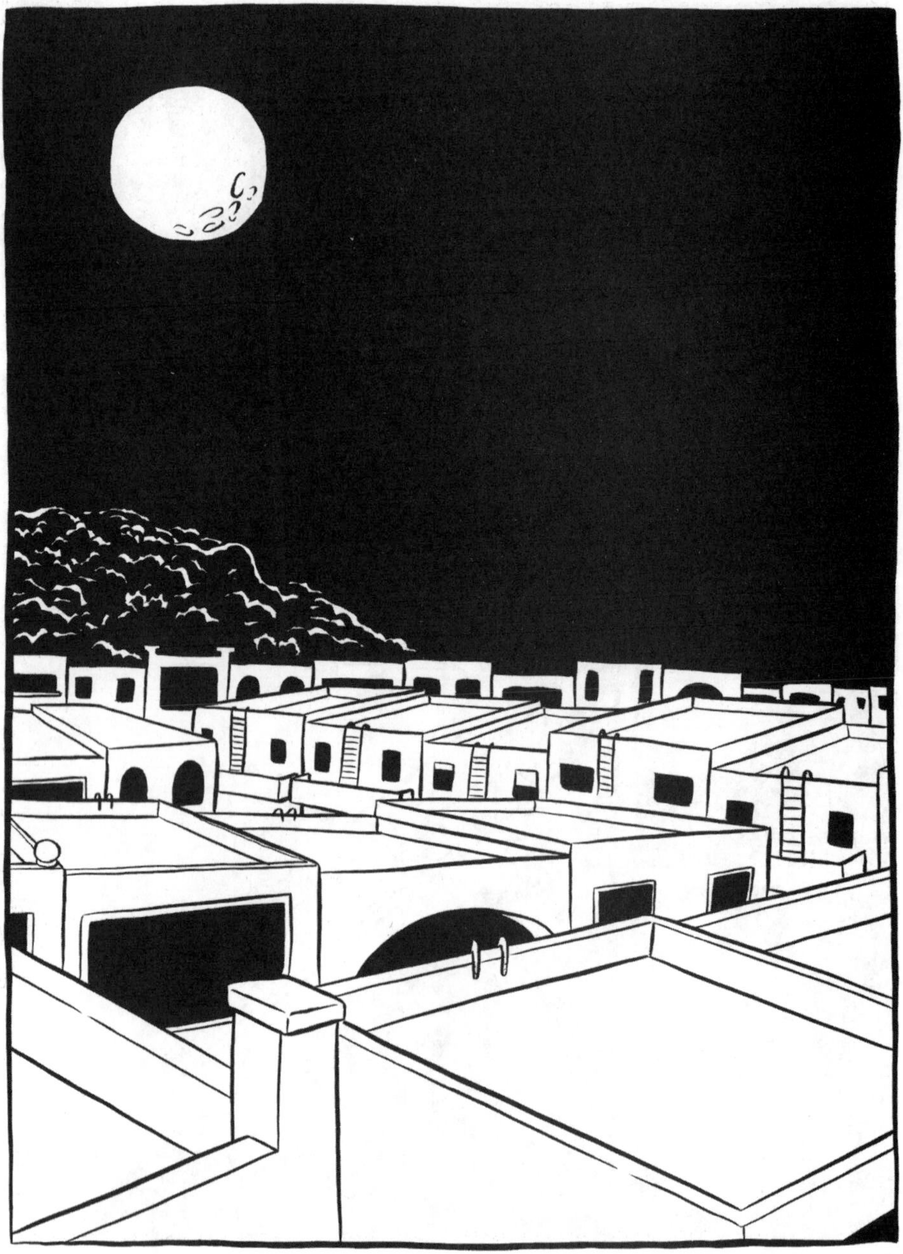

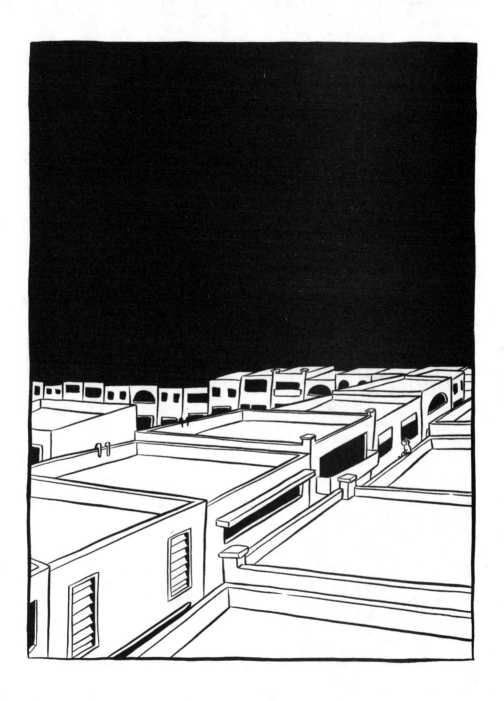

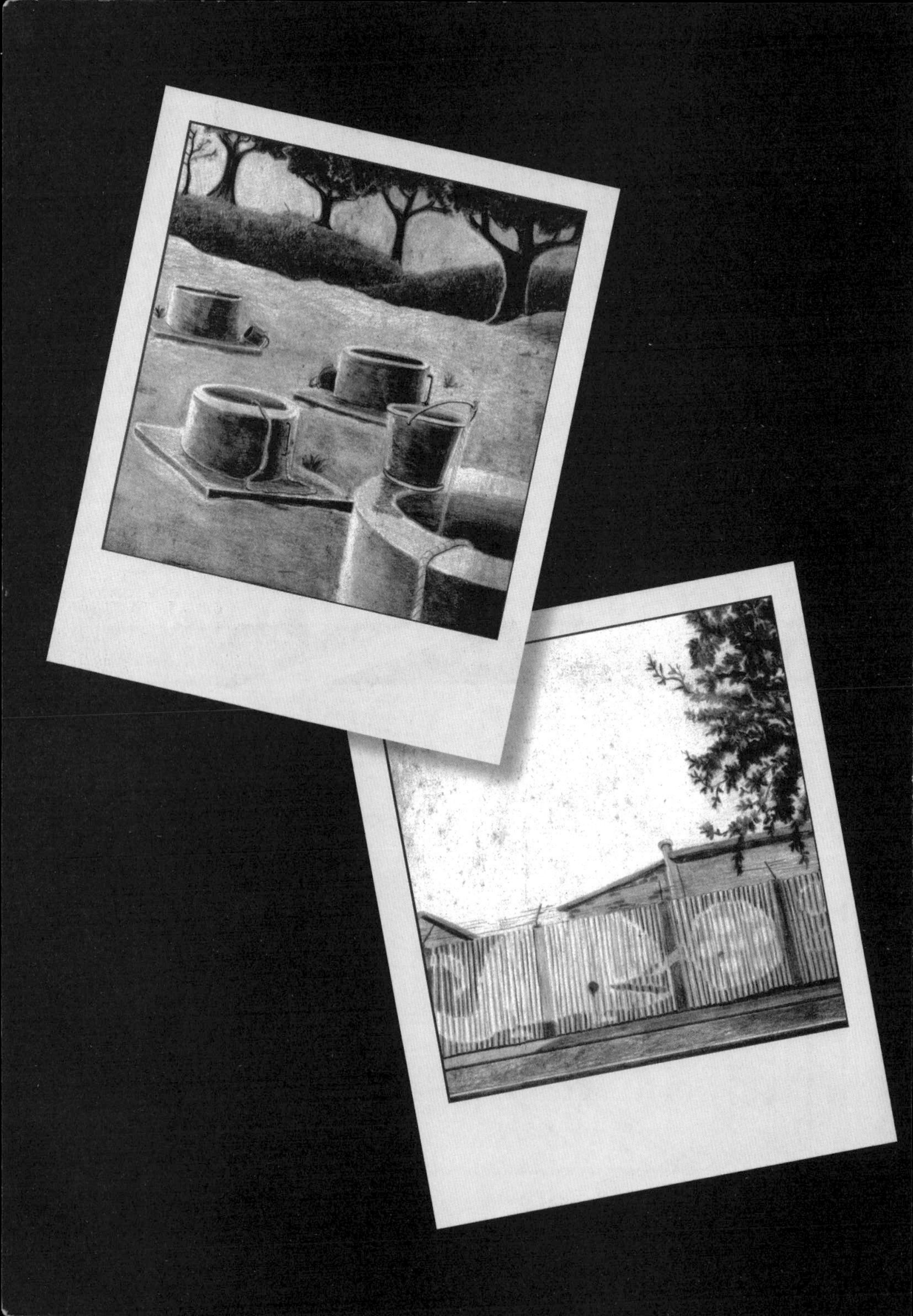

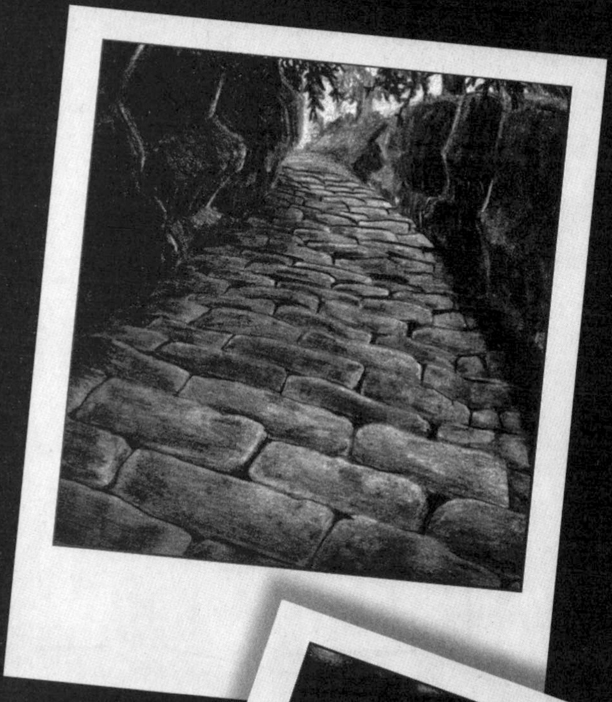

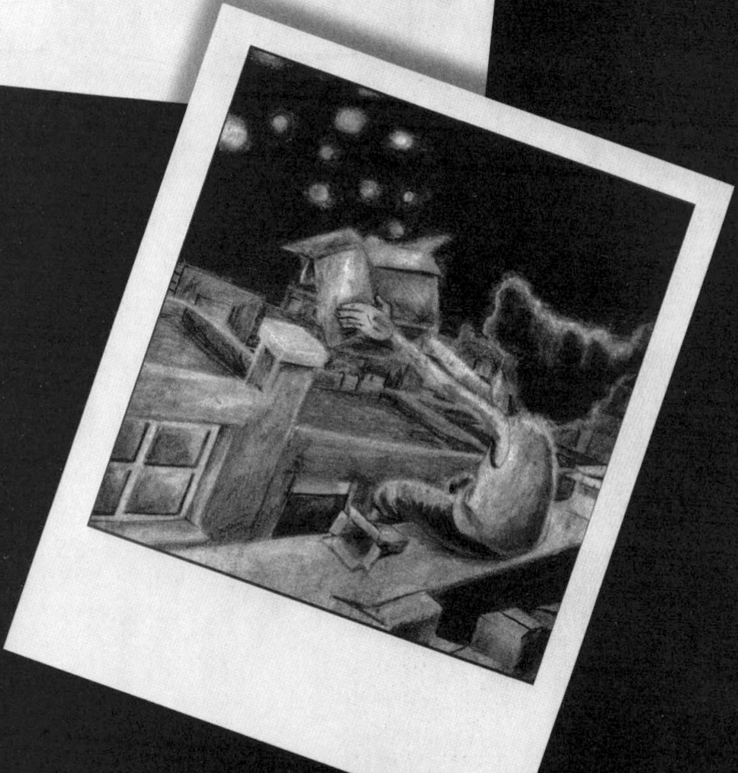

This book would not have been possible without Brett Warnock, Chris Staros and the awesome people of Top Shelf. And Studio Ghibli, for Totoro.

Huge thanks to my family, who lets me be me, in spite of their better judgement.

And to you, for picking up this book.

Diana Thung makes comics, in between daydreaming and exploring the wooded trails of Sydney with her scruffy dog, Pazu.